Communications in Computer and Information Science 1909

Rationale

The CCIS series is devoted to the publication of proceedings of computer science conferences. Its aim is to efficiently disseminate original research results in informatics in printed and electronic form. While the focus is on publication of peer-reviewed full papers presenting mature work, inclusion of reviewed short papers reporting on work in progress is welcome, too. Besides globally relevant meetings with internationally representative program committees guaranteeing a strict peer-reviewing and paper selection process, conferences run by societies or of high regional or national relevance are also considered for publication.

Topics

The topical scope of CCIS spans the entire spectrum of informatics ranging from foundational topics in the theory of computing to information and communications science and technology and a broad variety of interdisciplinary application fields.

Information for Volume Editors and Authors

Publication in CCIS is free of charge. No royalties are paid, however, we offer registered conference participants temporary free access to the online version of the conference proceedings on SpringerLink (http://link.springer.com) by means of an http referrer from the conference website and/or a number of complimentary printed copies, as specified in the official acceptance email of the event.

CCIS proceedings can be published in time for distribution at conferences or as post-proceedings, and delivered in the form of printed books and/or electronically as USBs and/or e-content licenses for accessing proceedings at SpringerLink. Furthermore, CCIS proceedings are included in the CCIS electronic book series hosted in the SpringerLink digital library at http://link.springer.com/bookseries/7899. Conferences publishing in CCIS are allowed to use Online Conference Service (OCS) for managing the whole proceedings lifecycle (from submission and reviewing to preparing for publication) free of charge.

Publication process

The language of publication is exclusively English. Authors publishing in CCIS have to sign the Springer CCIS copyright transfer form, however, they are free to use their material published in CCIS for substantially changed, more elaborate subsequent publications elsewhere. For the preparation of the camera-ready papers/files, authors have to strictly adhere to the Springer CCIS Authors' Instructions and are strongly encouraged to use the CCIS LaTeX style files or templates.

Abstracting/Indexing

CCIS is abstracted/indexed in DBLP, Google Scholar, EI-Compendex, Mathematical Reviews, SCImago, Scopus. CCIS volumes are also submitted for the inclusion in ISI Proceedings.

How to start

To start the evaluation of your proposal for inclusion in the CCIS series, please send an e-mail to ccis@springer.com.

Alla G. Kravets · Maxim V. Shcherbakov ·
Peter P. Groumpos
Editors

Creativity in Intelligent Technologies and Data Science

5th International Conference, CIT&DS 2023
Volgograd, Russia, September 11–15, 2023
Proceedings

 Springer

Editors
Alla G. Kravets (iD)
Volgograd State Technical University
Volgograd, Russia

Maxim V. Shcherbakov (iD)
Volgograd State Technical University
Volgograd, Russia

Peter P. Groumpos (iD)
University of Patras
Patras, Greece

ISSN 1865-0929 ISSN 1865-0937 (electronic)
Communications in Computer and Information Science
ISBN 978-3-031-44614-6 ISBN 978-3-031-44615-3 (eBook)
https://doi.org/10.1007/978-3-031-44615-3

This Springer imprint is published by the registered company Springer Nature Switzerland AG
The registered company address is: Gewerbestrasse 11, 6330 Cham, Switzerland

Paper in this product is recyclable.

Preface

Since 2015, the Conference on Creativity in Intelligent Technologies and Data Science has been a well-known worldwide place for open discussions on technical issues of Creativity in modern life. The conference puts together both theoretical and practical findings on how to create novel and more efficient solutions using cutting-edge digital technologies. Creativity itself is a process of building new and incomparable solutions. It is considered to be a property of human beings. Nowadays, Artificial Intelligence (AI) and other approaches bring possibilities to create counterintuitive but efficient artefacts such as images, texts, program code, and so on. The phenomenon of AI is the subject of research and study.

The main objective of CIT&DS 2023 was to bring together researchers and practitioners to share their ideas in using creativity for new intelligent and decision-making systems engineering. Readers will find here the results of creating new technologies based on state-of-the-art research.

This book contains 40 papers selected out of 148 submissions through a double-blind 3 reviews process by the international program committee. It begins with two keynote papers entitled "On the Problem of Cyber-Physical Systems Architectures Synthesis Using Generative Models" by Alla G. Kravets and "Explainable Machine Learning in Service Management of Transport Corporation" by Vladimir Tsyganov.

The papers are arranged into ten sections covering three topics. Topic 1 "Artificial Intelligence & Deep Learning Technologies for Creative Tasks" includes Section 1 "Knowledge Discovery in Patent and Open Sources", Section 2 "Open Science Semantic Technologies", and Section 3 "Computer Vision and Knowledge-Based Control".

Topic 2 "Cyber-Physical Systems & Big Data-Driven world" has the following sections: Section 4 "Pro-Active Modeling in Intelligent Decision Making Support", Section 5 "Industrial Creativity (CASE/CAI/CAD/PDM)", and Section 6 "Intelligent Internet of Services and Internet of Things".

Finally, Topic 3 "Intelligent Technologies in Social Engineering" consists of papers grouped in Section 7 "Data Science in Social Networks Analysis and Cyber Security", Section 8 "Creativity & Game-Based Learning", Section 9 "Intelligent Technologies in Medicine & Healthcare", and Section 10 "Intelligent Technologies in Urban Design & Computing".

We hope these proceedings will help to stimulate your creativity and bring new insights to you.

Sincerely yours,

August 2023

Alla G. Kravets
Maxim V. Shcherbakov
Peter P. Groumpos

Organization

Program Committee Chairs

Alla Kravets	Volgograd State Technical University, Russia
Peter Groumpos	University of Patras, Greece
Maxim Shcherbakov	Volgograd State Technical University, Russia

Program Committee Members

Abdel-Badeeh M. Salem	Ain Shams University, Egypt
Adriaan Brebels	i.LECO Ltd., Belgium
Alena Zakharova	Institute of Control Sciences of Russian Academy of Sciences, Russia
Alexander Bozhday	Penza State University, Russia
Alexandr Bolshakov	Peter the Great St. Petersburg Polytechnic University, Russia
Alexandr Davtian	Moscow Institute of Physics and Technology, Russia
Alexandr Sokolov	VNIKTI Rosneft, Russia
Alexey Finogeev	Penza State University, Russia
Alexey Kizim	Volgograd State Technical University, Russia
Alin Moldoveanu	University Politehnica of Bucharest, Romania
Amani Ahmad Sabbagh	University of Aleppo, Syria
Anatoly Karpenko	Bauman Moscow State Technical University, Russia
Andrey Andreev	Volgograd State Technical University, Russia
Anna Matokhina	Volgograd State Technical University, Russia
Anton Anikin	Volgograd State Technical University, Russia
Anton Ivaschenko	Samara State Medical University, Russia
Anton Tyukov	Volgograd State Technical University, Russia
Bal Krishna Bal	Kathmandu University, Nepal
Carla Oliveira	Lisbon University, Portugal
Christos Malliarakis	University of West Attica, Greece
Cuong Sai	Control Automation in Production and Improvement of Technology Institute, Vietnam
Dang Phuong	University of Science and Technology - The University of Danang, Vietnam

Contents

Keynotes

On The Problem of Cyber-Physical Systems Architectures Synthesis
Using Generative Models 3
  Alla G. Kravets

Explainable Machine Learning in Service Management of Transport
Corporation 19
  Vladimir Tsyganov

**Artificial Intelligence and Deep Learning Technologies for Creative
Tasks. Knowledge Discovery in Patent and Open Sources**

The New Method of Predicting the Importance of Patented Technologies 35
  *Alexander Rublev, Dmitriy Korobkin, Sergey Fomenkov,
  and Alexander Golovanchikov*

MPNN- Based Method for Identifying the Pharmacological Activity
of a Synthesized Chemical Compound 49
  *Alla G. Kravets, Dmitry Gorbatenko, Natalia Salnikova,
  Svyatoslav Birukov, and Elizaveta Smolova*

Hybrid Cyber-Physical System QUIK-LUA-Random Forest for Trading
on MoEx 64
  *Nikolay Lomakin, Olga Golodova, Maxim Maramygin,
  Tatyana Kuzmina, Oksana Minaeva, and Uranchimeg Tudevdagva*

**Artificial Intelligence and Deep Learning Technologies for Creative
Tasks. Open Science Semantic Technologies**

A CycleGAN-Based Method for Translating Recordings of Interjections 83
  Liubov Polianskaya and Liliya Volkova

On Capturing Functional Style of Texts with Part-of-speech Trigrams 98
  Liliya Volkova, Alexander Lanko, and Vyacheslav Romanov

Artificial Intelligence and Deep Learning Technologies for Creative Tasks. Computer Vision and Knowledge-Based Control

Visual Data Models in Scientific Search for Interpretation
of Multiparametric Signals 117
    Alena Zakharova, Aleksey Shklyar, and Evgeniya Vekhter

Inverse Kinematics for Multisection Continuum Robots with Variable
Section Length 131
    Olga M. Gerget and Dmitrii Yu. Kolpashchikov

The ThermoEMF as a Tool for Increasing the Autonomy of Technological
Machines 143
    Zhanna Tikhonova, Dmitriy Kraynev, Evgeniy Frolov,
    Alexander Bondarev, and Alla Kozhevnikova

Modeling the Movement of Vehicles with an Anti-lock Braking System
on Various Types of Road Surface Using the Principles of PID Control 155
    Grigory Boyko, Alexey Fedin, M. Petrenko, I. Leskovets, and Jozef Redl

Cyber-Physical Systems and Big Data-Driven World. Pro-Active Modeling in Intelligent Decision Making Support

Business Process Optimization of Technological Map in Farm
Management System 171
    Mohammed A. Al-Gunaid and Vladislav Trubitsin

Problem of Building High-Quality Predictive Model of River Hydrology:
The Combined Use of Hydrodynamic Simulations and Intelligent
Computing 191
    Anna Yu. Klikunova, Maxim V. Polyakov, Sergei S. Khrapov,
    and Alexander V. Khoperskov

Business Model Innovation: Considering Organization as a Form
of Reflection of Society 206
    Aleksandr Davtian, Olga Shabalina, Natalia Sadovnikova,
    Danila Parygin, and Olga Berestneva

Methodological Bases for Decision Support in the Management
of Services, Taking into Account the Personal Information of Customers 220
    Diana Bogdanova, Gyuzel Shakhmametova, and Albert Niiazgulov

Complex Dynamics Modeling Algorithm Application in Comparative
Study of Innovation Processes 232
    Alexey B. Simonov and Alexey F. Rogachev

Cyber-Physical Systems and Big Data-Driven World. Industrial Creativity (CASE/CAI/CAD/PDM)

Methods and Technologies for Improving the Efficiency
of Multi-assortment Production Optimal Planning 251
    Tamara B. Chistyakova, Olga E. Shashikhina, Ivan G. Kornienko,
    and Aleksandr A. Plekhanov

Intelligent Technologies for Designing Digital Information Models
of Chemical and Technological Objects 262
    Tamara B. Chistyakova, Dmitry N. Furaev, and Inna V. Novozhilova

Information Channel for Proactive Control of Machining Conditions:
A Cyber-Physical System on the Basis of a CNC Machine 274
    Julius Tchigirinsky, Alexey Zhdanov, Zhanna Tikhonova,
    Alexander Rogachev, and Nataly Chigirinskaya

New Algorithm for Determining the Shape of Particles and the Size
of Adulteration Areas in Meat for a Decision Support System 288
    Alexander Bolshakov, Renata Kallimulina, and Marina Nikitina

Improving the Quality of Dental Services Based on Metal Additive
Technologies: Unified Digital Workflow of Treatment 306
    Viktor P. Radchenko and Alexander V. Khoperskov

Cyber-Physical Systems and Big Data-Driven World. Intelligent Internet of Services and Internet of Things

Detecting Anomalies in Multidimensional Time Series Using Binary
Classification 323
    Mohammed. A. Al-Gunaid, Maxim. V. Shcherbakov,
    Vladimir O. Artyushin, Dmitry V. Shkolny, and Sergey V. Belov

Neural Network-Based Optimization of Traffic Light Regulation
of a Transport Hub with Data Fetched During Simulation in SUMO Package ... 337
    Dmitry Skorobogatchenko, Vladislav Zhokhov, Olga Astafurova,
    and Pavel Fantrov

Analysis of Numerical Simulation Results in a Symbolic Numerical
System for Some Strain Energy Potentials 351
    Yulia Andreeva, Natalia Asanova, and Boris Zhukov

Intelligent Technologies in Social Engineering. Data Science in Social Networks Analysis and Cyber Security

Digital Integrated Monitoring Platform for Intelligent Social Analysis 365
  Anton Ivaschenko, Irina Dubinina, Oleg Golovnin,
  Anastasia Golovnina, and Pavel Sitnikov

Model and Method of Decentralized Secure Storage of Students Digital
Portfolios in an Educational Environment Based on Distributed Ledger
Technology 377
  Mikhail Deev, Alexey Finogeev, Igor Kamardin,
  and Alexander Grushevsky

Optimal Management of Tourism Products Based on the Analysis of User
Preferences 390
  Leyla Gamidullaeva and Alexey Finogeev

Intelligent Technologies in Social Engineering. Creativity and Game-Based Learning

Lattice-Based Adaptation Model for Developing Adaptive Learning Games 405
  Olga Shabalina, Alexander Khairov, Alexander Kataev,
  and David C. Moffat

Can a Robot Companion Help Students Learn Chinese Tones? The Role
of Speech and Gesture Cues 420
  Anna Zinina, Artemiy Kotov, Nikita Arinkin, and Anna Gureyeva

Interaction with Virtual Objects in VR-Applications 433
  Alla G. Kravets, Ivan D. Pavlenko, Vitaly A. Egunov, and Evgeny Kravets

The Structure Oriented Evaluation of Five Courses Teach by the Single
Teacher 450
  Gantsetseg Sukhbaatar, Selenge Erdenechimeg,
  Bazarragchaa Sodnom, and Uranchimeg Tudevdagva

Intelligent Technologies in Social Engineering. Intelligent Technologies in Medicine and Healthcare

Two-Dimensional Walsh Spectral Transform in Problems of Automated
Analysis of Ultrasound Images 467
  Alexander Kuzmin, Hasan Chasib Al-Darraji, Artem Sukhomlinov,
  and Sergei Filist

A System for Management of Adaptable Mobile Applications for People
with Intellectual Disabilities 478
    Vladislav Guriev, Angelina Voronina, Alexander Kataev,
    and Tatyana Petrova

Models and Methods for Processing Heterogeneous Data for Assessing
the State of a Human 488
    Angelina Voronina, Vladislav Guriev, David C. Moffat,
    and Irina Molodtsova

Comprehensive Assessment of the Driver's Functional Readiness Before
the Trip 500
    Maksim Dyatlov, Rodion Kudrin, Aleksej Todorev,
    and Konstantin Katerinin

Exploring the Interaction Between Daytime and Situational Sleepiness:
A Pilot Study Analyzing Heart Rate Variability 513
    Valeriia Demareva, Nikolay Nazarov, Inna Isakova, Andrey Demarev,
    and Irina Zayceva

**Intelligent Technologies in Social Engineering. Intelligent technologies
in Urban Design and Computing**

The Concept of Complex Assessment System for Territories 527
    Aleksander Bershadsky, Pavel Gudkov, and Ekaterina Podmarkova

Balance Model of Interests of a Transport Company and Passengers
in Urban Transportation by Automatic Transport 538
    Vasily Shuts and Alena Shviatsova

Using Generative Design Technologies to Create Park Area Layouts
for Urban Improvement 549
    Nikolay Rashevskiy, Danila Parygin, Artem Shcherbakov,
    Nikita Shlyannikov, and Vasily Shlyannikov

Spatial Data Analysis for Decision Support in Urban Infrastructure
Development Planning 568
    Ivan Danilov, Alexey Shuklin, Ilya Zelenskiy, Alexander Gurtyakov,
    and Mikhail Kulikov

Author Index 579

Keynotes

On The Problem of Cyber-Physical Systems Architectures Synthesis Using Generative Models

Alla G. Kravets[1,2(✉)] [iD]

[1] Volgograd State Technical University, 28 Lenin Av., Volgograd 400005, Russia
allagkravets@yandex.ru
[2] Dubna State University, 19 Universitetskaya st., Dubna, Moscow Region 141982, Russia

Abstract. The paper dwells on the problem of holistic perception of heterogeneous information by a computing system - text, images, formulas, etc. that remains open. It is to the problem of holistic perception that the task of synthesizing the CPS architecture for implementing adaptive control mechanisms can be attributed. This paper discusses experiments on the synthesis of CPS architectures using open pre-trained generative models, on retraining of a neural network model Stable Diffusion, as well as a new model based on the generative-adversarial approach for the synthesis of CPS architectures.

Keywords: Cyber-Physical Systems · Architectures Synthesis · Holistic Perception · Generative Models · Neural Network · Stable Diffusion

1 Introduction

Cyber-Physical Systems (CPS) are a unique fusion of the virtual and physical worlds, where computer systems and physical processes interact and collaborate to achieve optimal results. These systems combine advanced information technology, networking, and physical objects to provide continuous data exchange and interaction between various system components, creating a new generation of intelligent systems capable of adapting to the environment and making autonomous decisions.

The key characteristics of cyber-physical systems are their ability to self-organize, flexibility, and autonomy. They are able to analyze data, predict events, make decisions, and act in real time. CPSs play an important role in improving the efficiency and safety of systems, optimizing resources, and improving people's lives. Moreover, each of the cyber-physical systems has its own architecture and purpose.

The development of modern technologies is steadily bringing us closer to a new era, where the virtual and physical worlds become inextricably linked. Cyber-physical systems are becoming the basis of this transformation that can change our lives in many areas.

Therefore, CPSs have a rather complex architecture, which depends, among other things, on platforms and technological implementation stacks.

A. G. Kravets et al. (Eds.): CIT&DS 2023, CCIS 1909, pp. 3–18, 2023.
https://doi.org/10.1007/978-3-031-44615-3_1

Along with the development of cyber-physical systems, neural networks are stepping in step, which literally cover more and more possibilities every day and their computing and generation powers can amaze the imagination. Explosive interest in generative models of neural networks is primarily due to the emerging technical feasibility of implementing previously developed and theoretically substantiated approaches.

At the same time, the question of a holistic perception of heterogeneous information by a computing system - text, images, formulas, etc. remains open. It is to the problem of holistic perception that the task of synthesizing the CPS architecture for implementing adaptive control mechanisms can be attributed. Designing the architecture of a complex system is a process of engineering creativity, which combines both a sufficiently high level of the designer's qualifications, his deep knowledge of standards, platforms and technology stacks, and today's fairly developed intelligent technologies for supporting design decisions.

This article discusses experiments on the synthesis of CPS architectures using open pre-trained generative models, on retraining of a neural network model Stable Diffusion, as well as a new model for the synthesis of CPS architectures.

2   Generation of CPS Architectures

The formal statement of the problem of architecture synthesis is based on the CLIP / unCLIP methods [1] and can be represented as

$$P(f\,|c) = P(f; m_i|c) = P(f|m_i;\ c)P(m_t|c), \tag{1}$$

where P is a probabilistic model; (f; c) - a pair of images f and their corresponding captions c; m_i CLIP image; m_t embedded text.

In this case, the embedded text is understood as the name of the figure or other descriptive text used when training models. In addition, special attention should be paid to the fact that, at the moment, researchers [1, 2] have not been able to obtain any "meaningful" text (including the clock's digits) embedded in the image (Fig. 1 and 2).

Fig. 1. Example of generated images [1]

Fig. 2. Samples from unCLIP for the prompt, "A sign that says deep learning." [1]

3 CPS Architectures Development

The architectures development of a complex system in general and cyber-physical systems, in particular, is a complex task and includes the following steps;

1.1.1. Analysis of functional and non-functional requirements for the system being designed.

$$RQ =< RQ_f, RQ_n >$$ (2)

2. Analysis of the technological environment Ts, including the possibilities of platforms for implementation.
3. Choice of implementation platform Pl based on system requirements and available resources.
4. Analysis of the available notations N for the chosen platform.
5. Synthesis of the architecture, taking into account the technological environment features and available notations.

$$A(RQ) => A(Ts, Pl, N)$$ (3)

When synthesizing architectures, not only graphic notation is of great importance, but the semantics of named entities, which depends on the CPS implementation platform (Fig. 2) (Fig. 3).

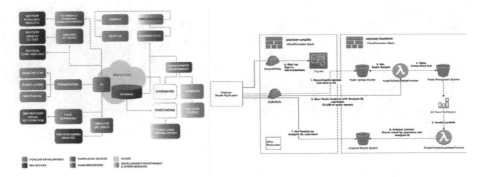

Fig. 3. Architecture of one CPS on the platforms IBM (left) and Amazon (right)

4 Representation of Neural Networks About Cyber-Physical Systems, Their Architecture, and Purpose

Most popular platforms include less than 1% queries about flowcharts, UML and other diagrams, systems' architecture, etc. For experiments the following platforms with pre-trained neural networks were used: Lexica, Fusion Brain, Problembo, Hugging Face, and Stable Diffusion.

All generation requests included the keywords "architecture", "cyber – physical" "system".

4.1 Lexica[1]

For the first experiment with Lexica, it's decided to use the most detailed query: "block diagram schema, architecture cyber-physical systems, English text, detailed text, hd, 4k, 8k".

The result is a black-and-white image with white characters, more precisely, images that look like characters (Fig. 4).

For the second experiment with the model, a more general query was used: "architecture of a cyber-physical system (diagram)". As a result, more diverse scheme architectures were obtained (Fig. 5). However, none of them reproduced any meaningful text.

---

[1] https://lexica.art/

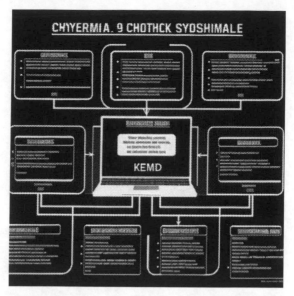

Fig. 4. Lexica's view of the CPS architecture. First experiment.

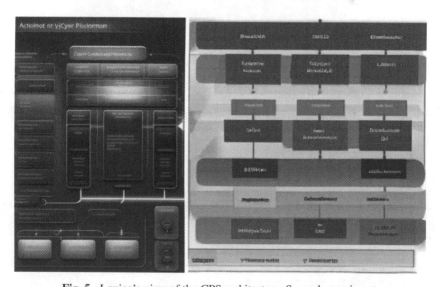

Fig. 5. Lexica's view of the CPS architecture. Second experiment.

4.2 Fusion Brain[2]

Fusion Brain is an open platform based on the Kandinsky model [3] for image generation and editing.

---

[2] https://fusionbrain.ai/

For the experiment with the model, the same query as with Lexica was used: "architecture of a cyber-physical system (diagram)".

Rather monotonous diagrams were obtained, made in different colors, with unreadable symbols (Fig. 6).

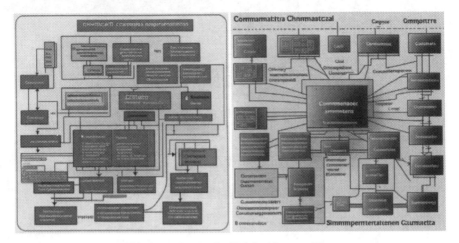

Fig. 6. Fusion Brain CPS Architecture View

4.3 Problembo[3]

Problembo platform proposes several models, including MidJourney[4], for images generation in various styles (Anime, Fantasy, etc.)

The language that should be used for a generation was detailed in the query: "architectural scheme of a cyber-physical system in English".

Despite the rather diverse images obtained with the models available on the platform, the number of characters belonging to the English alphabet is negligible (Fig. 7).

It should be noted that the use of different models makes it possible to obtain schemes with a set of various basic elements. This, hypothetically, will allow the use of various notations for the synthesis of CPS architectures.

---

[3] https://problembo.com/en/services/ai-image-generator.

[4] https://www.midjourney.com/

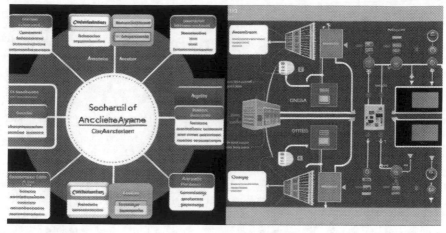

Fig. 7. Representation of the CPS architecture from Problembo with models: RealRender (left) PhotoStab (right)

4.4 Hugging Face[5]

Hugging Face is "the platform where the machine learning community collaborates on models, datasets, and applications" [4].

Since the term "cyber-physical systems" is quite new, it was decided to expand the search query and add "software and hardware complexes" there. The query: "architecture of software and hardware complexes, cyber-physical systems".

Analysis of the generation results showed that the Hugging Face models use new notation elements depicting databases compared to previous platforms (Fig. 8).

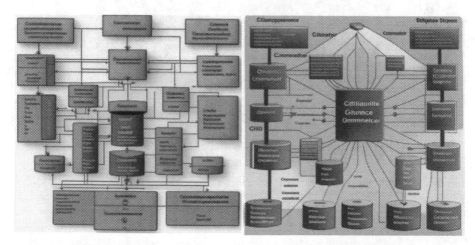

Fig. 8. Representation of the CPS architecture from Hugging Face

---

[5] https://huggingface.co/

4.5 Stable Diffusion[6]

"Stable Diffusion is a latent text-to-image diffusion model capable of generating photo-realistic images given any text input, cultivates autonomous freedom to produce incredible imagery, empowers billions of people to create stunning art within seconds" [5].

Based on previous platform Hugging Face results it was decided to keep the same search query: "architecture of software and hardware complexes, cyber-physical systems".

The results shown by the Stable Diffusion model allow us to conclude that the model most accurately reproduces the characters of the English alphabet and even character sequences similar to words (Fig. 9 and 10). Despite the variety of colors of the resulting schemes, the number of basic elements used is quite small, the diagrams are uniform. The Stable Diffusion model showed quite good results and, in addition, it allows retraining. In this regard, the Stable Diffusion model was chosen for further experiments.

Fig. 9. Representation of the CPS architecture from Stable Diffusion

5 Stable Diffusion Model Retraining

The next step of the experiments was retraining on a dataset collected from open sources with images of the CFS architectures of the neural network Stable Diffusion, which showed the best results in the first stage.

---

[6] https://stablediffusionweb.com/

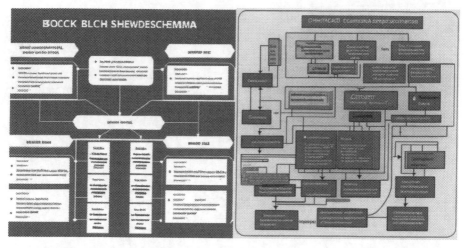

Fig. 10. Representations of the CPS architecture from Stable Diffusion

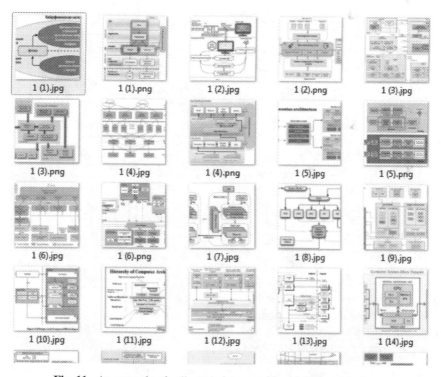

Fig. 11. An example of collected pictures with real CPS architectures

5.1 Image Dataset Preparation

This is a key step in neural network training. The result will depend directly on the quality of the selected images. On average, from 10 to 30 pictures are needed, but for higher quality, it's necessary to prepare up to 90 images. An increase in the number of examples does not always lead to an increase in quality, but the content is of particular importance.

To train the model, pictures with real architectures of cyber-physical systems from books [6–10] and journals [11–13] were collected (Fig. 11 and 12).

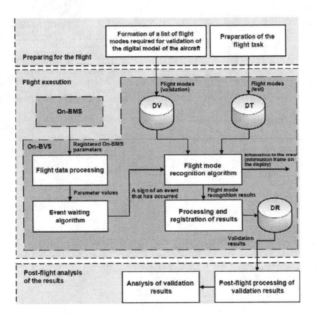

Fig. 12. An example of a real CPS architecture [14]

5.2 Neural Network Training

Neural network training Stable Diffusion runs (Fig. 13) on the Google platform Collab[7].

To start uploading the model to private Google Drive used the Model download function (Fig. 14). Model version 1.5 is used.

Next block Instance Images adds prepared images dataset. Smart_Crop parameter was turned off since the images were edited manually for resolution 512px.

In the Training block (Fig. 16) need several parameters were set:

- Unet_Training_Steps. For 10 pictures, the value is 650. For 20 pictures, indicate 1300. If you have 30 pictures, write 1950 and so on.

---

[7] https://colab.research.google.com/github/TheLastBen/fast-stable-diffusion/blob/main/fast-DreamBooth.ipynb#scrollTo=O3KHGKqyeJp9.

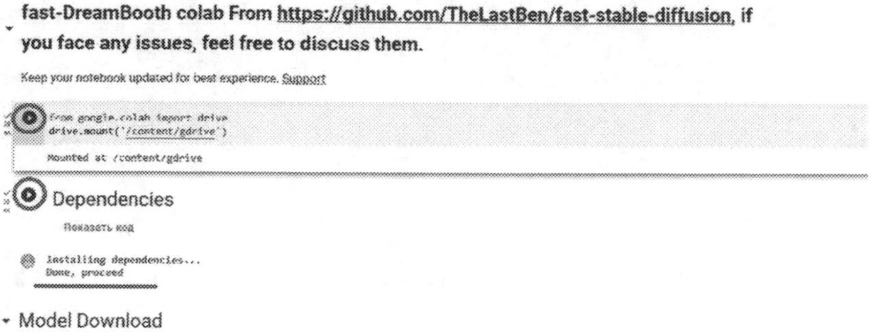

fast-DreamBooth colab From https://github.com/TheLastBen/fast-stable-diffusion, if you face any issues, feel free to discuss them.

Keep your notebook updated for best experience. Support

```
From google.colab import drive
drive.mount('/content/gdrive')

Mounted at /content/gdrive
```

⊙ Dependencies

Показать код

Installing dependencies...
Done, proceed

▾ Model Download

Fig. 13. Running the model in Stable Diffusion

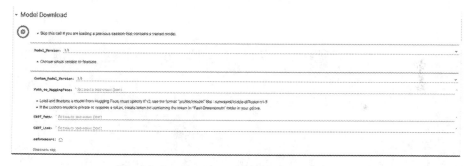

Fig. 14. Loading the model into Stable Diffusion

- Text_Encoder_Training_Steps. It is not recommended to exceed the value of 450.
- Resolution. Check that it is less than 512px since all the images were reduced to this parameter.

After the completion of model training, all results are in the private Google Drive (Fig. 15 and 16).

```
Training the text encoder...
'########;'########::::;'###::::'####:'##:::'##:'####:'##::;'##::'#####:::
... ##..::'##....'##:::'##'##::::.'##:;'##:;'##::'##:;'##::'##....'##::
::: ##::::'##:::;'##::;'##:.'##::;'##:'####:'##::'##::'####:'##:'##:::..::
::: ##::::'########::'##::::.'##::'##'##'##::'##::'##'##'##::'##::'####:
::: ##::::'##..'##::'#########::'##::.'##.'####::'##::.'####:'##:::'##::
::: ##::::'##:.'##::'##....'##::;'##::;'##:.'###::'##:.'###:'##:::'##::
::: ##::::'##::.'##:'##:::'##:'####:'##::;.'##:.'##:.'##:;'#####:::
:::..:::::..:::..:..:::..:..:::..::..::..:::..::.

Progress:█                    | 3% 15/450 [00:18<05:25, 1.34it/s, loss=0.148, lr=9.67e-7] arcstl
```

Fig. 15. Starting the model training process in Stable Diffusion

Fig. 16. Completion of model training in Stable Diffusion

5.3   Generation Results with Retrained Model

As a result, images were generated with Guidance Scale (CFG Scale, exact query match vs creativity) as a control parameter (Fig. 17).

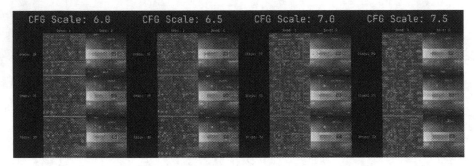

Fig. 17. Comparison of image detail on different CFG Scale

CFG Scale is responsible for how much artificial intelligence should approach the literal image of the request. The lower CFG Scale - the more creative the AI will be. The higher CFG Scale the more accurately the AI will try to represent the request.

Despite some improvement in the results (Fig. 18 and 19 low CFG) in terms of generating characters similar to the English alphabet, it was not possible to obtain architecture diagrams.

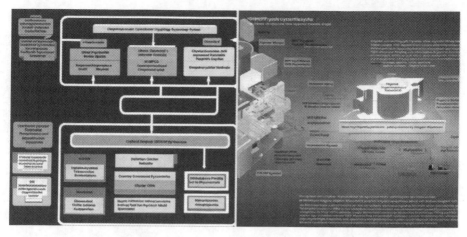

Fig. 18. Examples of generation with high CFG

6 Discussion

An analysis of more than 100 received images showed that, despite the variety of graphic patterns, the drawings do not contain not only semantically meaningful text but also syntactic constructions. In fact, generative models create some kind of symbols, often not corresponding to any alphabet.

Neural networks have certain limitations and weaknesses when it comes to generating images with embedded text. Some of the reasons why neural systems may not perform well at this task include:

1. *Data limitation*: To efficiently generate text on an image, a neural network must have access to a large amount of data containing images and corresponding text. But in reality, there is not always a sufficiently large and diverse data set, and this can lead to limitations in neural network training.
2. *Context Constraint*: A neural network can have difficulty understanding the context of an image, which can be important for generating relevant text. For example, multiple objects may be depicted in the same image, and the neural network may have difficulty in determining which object to focus on in order to generate the corresponding text.
3. *Ambiguity*: Some images may contain ambiguous elements that may be difficult for a neural network to interpret. For example, if the image shows a person holding a book, then the neural network may have difficulty deciding which text should be generated because the book may be an ambiguous entity.
4. *Difficulty in Image Processing*: Image processing can be a challenging task for neural networks. Images can contain a lot of detail that can be difficult for a neural network to interpret, and this can make it difficult to generate the corresponding text.
5. *Computer Vision*: The neural networks used to generate text on images rely on computer vision, which has its limitations and weaknesses. For example, a neural network may have difficulty in determining the color, shape, or size of objects in an image, which can make it difficult to generate appropriate text.

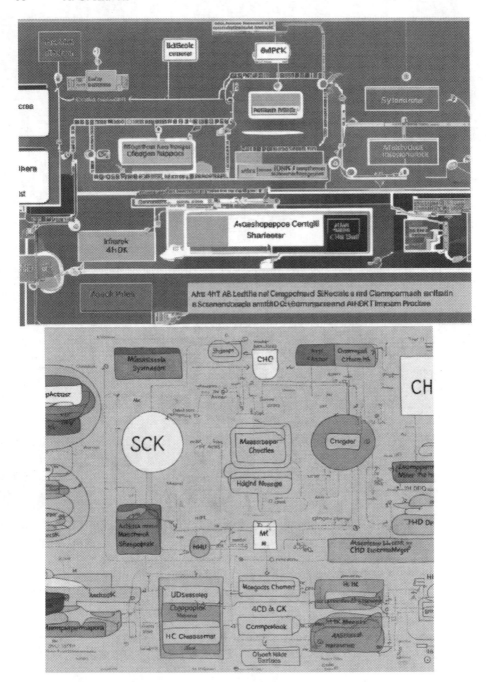

Fig. 19. Examples of generation with low CFG

As a result of the research, a new model for the synthesis of architectures based on (1)-(3) and a generative-adversarial approach has been proposed:

$$A(Ts, Pl) = \begin{cases} P(f|c) \\ P(c|t) \\ N(f'|t) \\ L(f\prime, x, y|t) \end{cases} \tag{4}$$

where Ts is a set of technological stack parameters, Pl is a set of CPS implementation platform parameters, P is a generative probabilistic model, $(f; c)$ is a pair of images f and their corresponding captions c; $(c; t)$ is a pair of labels c and the corresponding embedded text t; $(f'; t)$ - a pair of image fragments - graphic patterns f' of the notation N and the corresponding embedded text t; (x, y) are the coordinates of the location of the text t relative to the pattern f' as a result of adversarial recognition L of the resulting image f.

The problem from formula (3) has been widely discussed by researchers since the end of the last century [15]. To date, there are quite a few approaches that describe attempts to turn system requirements in natural language into various diagrams [16, 17], including those in the UML language [18].

7   Conclusion

So, need to sum up some results of this research. First of all, cyber-physical systems are systems that connect the IT world with the real, physical world. Each cyber-physical system has its own purpose of creation and application, as well as the nuances of use and structure.

As for neural networks, as well as retrained model, with the help of which were generated various images of the CPS architecture, the neural networks, and the model, due to some of their limitations and shortcomings, do not distinguish embedded text in pictures well, respectively, they can poorly reproduce text in any language when generating an image. Accordingly, for about some time, while neural networks have problems with reading and reproducing embedded text in a picture, humanity will not be able to generate the architecture of CPS, and other schemes, and architectures [19], where there should be text in one way or another, using artificial intelligence or neural systems.

The implementation of the proposed architecture synthesis model is possible on the basis of an ensemble approach that combines generative-adversarial methods, computer vision methods, and transformer models. It is also possible to use a perceptual hash [20] to determine analogies in the process of architecture synthesis.

Acknowledgement. I express my gratitude to the 3rd year undergraduate students N. Orlov, A. Kozyakin, I. Grigoriev, S. Novruzov, N. Samorokov, and R. Poleshko who during the research practice took part in preparing data and conducting experiments.

References

1. Ramesh, A., et al.: Hierarchical Text-Conditional Image Generation with CLIP Latents. arxiv Preprint arxiv: 2204.06125 (2022)
2. Saharia, C., Chan, W., et al.: Photorealistic Text-to-Image Diffusion Models with Deep Language Understanding. arxiv Preprint arxiv: 2205.11487 (2022)
3. Kandinsky 2. https://github.com/ai-forever/Kandinsky-2. Accessed 22 July 2023
4. Hugging Face https://huggingface.co/. Accessed 22 July 2023
5. Stable Diffusion Online https://stablediffusionweb.com/. Accessed 22 July 2023
6. Kravets, A.G., Bolshakov, A.A., Shcherbakov, M.V. (eds.): Cyber-Physical Systems Engineering and Control. Studies in Systems, Decision and Control, vol 477 (2023)
7. Kravets, A.G., Bolshakov, A.A., Shcherbakov, M.V. (eds.): Cyber-Physical Systems: Modelling and Industrial Application. Studies in Systems, Decision and Control, vol. 418 (2022)
8. Kravets, A.G., Bolshakov, A.A., Shcherbakov, M.V. (eds.): Cyber-Physical Systems: Design and Application for Industry 4.0. Studies in Systems, Decision and Control, vol. 342 (2021)
9. Kravets, A.G., Bolshakov, A.A., Shcherbakov, M.V. (eds.): Cyber-Physical Systems: Modelling and Intelligent Control Studies in Systems, Decision and Control, vol. 338 (2021)
10. Kravets, A.G., Bolshakov, A.A., Shcherbakov, M.V. (eds.): Cyber-Physical Systems: Industry 4.0 Challenges, Studies in Systems, Decision and Control, vol. 260 (2020)
11. ACM Transactions on Cyber-Physical Systems. ACM
12. Cyber-Physical Systems. Taylor & Francis
13. IET Cyber-Physical Systems: Theory & Applications. John Wiley & Sons Inc.
14. Bogomolov, A.V., Osipov, A.A., Soldatov, A.S.: Flight mode recognition algorithms that provide validation of the digital twin of an aircraft during flight tests. In: Kravets, A.G., Bolshakov, A.A., Shcherbakov, M.V. (eds.) Cyber-Physical Systems Engineering and Control. Studies in Systems, Decision and Control, vol 477. Springer, Cham (2023) https://doi.org/10.1007/978-3-031-33159-6_6
15. Mich, L.: NL-OOPS: from natural language to object oriented requirements using the natural language processing system LOLITA. Nat. Lang. Eng. 2(2), 161–187 (1996)
16. Zhou, N., et Zhou X.: Automatic Acquisition of Linguistic Patterns for Conceptual Modelin. INFO 629: Artificial Intelligence (2004)
17. Ambriola, V., et Gervasi, V.: On the Systematic Analysis of Natural Language Requirements with CIRCE. Automated Software Engineering 13(1), 107–167 (2006)
18. Dawood, O.S., Sahraoui, A.-El-K. From Requirements Engineering to UML using Natural Language Processing Survey Study. EJERS, European J. Eng. Res. Sci. 2(1), 44-50 (2017)
19. Kravets, A.G.: On approach for the development of patents analysis formal metrics. Commu. Comp. Info. Sci. 1083, 34–45 (2019)
20. Kravets, A.G., Kolesnikov, S., Salnikova, N., Lempert, M., Poplavskaya, O.: The study of neural networks effective architectures for patents images processing. Commu. Comp. Info. Sci. 1084, 27–41 (2019)

Explainable Machine Learning in Service Management of Transport Corporation

Vladimir Tsyganov[✉] [iD]

Institute of Control Sciences, 65 Profsoyuznaya, Moscow 117998, Russia
tsyganov_v_v@mail.ru

Abstract. An effective tool for the formation of intelligent transport systems is machine learning (ML). But applying increasingly sophisticated machine learning technologies is creative. This allows us to speak about the significant subjectivity of the conclusions of ML. Thus, a gap is formed with the theory and practice of management based on ML. Intelligent technologies for managing transport systems using understandable machine learning are called upon to fill this gap. The article discusses an approach to the development of such a technology for a three-level service management system in a corporation. At its top level is the Boss, at the middle level is the Curator, at the bottom level is the Manager. The Boss should increase the scope of services provided by the corporation. But the Curator knows his abilities better than the Boss. In turn, the Manager knows his potential better than the Curator. Thus, both the Curator and the Manager can manipulate the scope of services they provide in order to get more incentives. To avoid this, a service management system is proposed that includes two explainable ML procedures. Sufficient optimality conditions for this control system are found. In their implementation, both the Curator and the Manager are interested in maximizing the scope of services provided. Such a management system provides algorithmic accountability, responsibility, trust and recognition of ML in the corporate team. The proposed approach is illustrated by the example of service maintenance repair of rolling stock.

Keywords: Intelligent Transport System · Control · Machine Learning · Decision Support · Corporation

1 Introduction

The widespread introduction of cyber-physical systems has led to the emergence of a new reality - a world driven by big data. To navigate this rapidly changing world, artificial intelligence (AI) is increasingly being used. Of all the AI tools, machine learning (ML) has proved to be the most effective in solving many complex problems.

Over time, however, ML technologies (and, especially, deep learning) have become so complicated that it has become impossible to track causal relationships and, moreover, to identify patterns in the evolution of the control object. The conclusions obtained with their help are often not amenable to interpretation. Accordingly, it is not possible

© The Author(s), under exclusive license to Springer Nature Switzerland AG 2023
A. G. Kravets et al. (Eds.): CIT&DS 2023, CCIS 1909, pp. 19–32, 2023.
https://doi.org/10.1007/978-3-031-44615-3_2

to explain the findings and recommendations to decision makers (DMs) and other stake-holders. The explainability of the results of applying ML is not a purely technological problem. The reason is that explainable ML (XML) entails accountability, trust, fairness, and ethical decisions.

Moreover, the application of complex ML technologies in practice is increasingly creative. Big contribution to the final result of ML is made by the developer using a specific ML technology (package) for a managed object. This allows us to speak about the significant subjectivity of the conclusions of ML. It also motivates the creation of XML.

Thus, the objective complexity of ML technology, combined with the subjectivism of the developer, makes it very difficult for the DM to make recommendations and make responsible decisions. There is a break with the traditional management practice, in which DM is based on repeatedly tested knowledge and identified objective patterns of object evolution.

On the other hand, traditionally, such patterns are revealed with the help of formal (mathematical, simulation or proactive) modeling of the evolution of an object under changes. With its help, on the basis of control theory, control actions are developed, which are then recommended to DM. And since ML technology does not allow to identify the patterns of the evolution of an object with changes, it is not built into this kind of approach. Thus, there is a gap between ML technology and traditional technology and control theory.

The elimination of these gaps between technology and management practice, on the one hand, and AI&ML, on the other, can be achieved by creating a technology for intelligent decision support and management. This requires creativity in intelligent technologies & data science.

This article discusses a methodological approach to the development of technology for intelligent decision support and management and an example of its application based on two-level ML. This approach is aimed primarily at bridging the gap between ML and control theory.

1.1 Machine Learning and Control Theory

Traditionally, ML is a field associated with both control theory in a broad sense (including system identification, optimization, and other disciplines studied in the control community) and computer science [1]. ML is of great interest to both management scientists and professional managers. Thanks to advances in computer science (the advent of graphics processors, which led to a significant increase in computer performance and the development of special software that allows you to work with big data), ML is often associated with computer science.

However, historically, learning algorithms that provide convergence and a convergence rate sufficient for the learning process arose within the framework of control theory. The origin of ML in its modern sense is associated with the name of F. Rosenblatt. Based on ideas about the work of the human nervous system, he developed a machine for recognizing letters of the alphabet [2]. The machine, dubbed the "perceptron", used both analog and discrete signals and included a threshold element that converted the analog signals to discrete ones. The Perceptron became the prototype of modern artificial neural networks, and its learning model was close to animal and human learning models developed in psychology.

Based on the idea of the perceptron, a large number of learning and control algorithms have been developed. Summarizing them, Y. Tsypkin proposed a unified approach to learning and adaptation using the random approximation mechanism [3]. He developed the most systematic scheme based on the idea of maximizing the average risk. This idea arose earlier in operations research, and was developed by A. Feldbaum in the control of uncertain systems [4].

Tsypkin showed that the random approximation mechanism includes, as special cases, a large number of learning and control algorithms proposed by different authors. An appropriate choice of random approximation parameters ensures the maximum rate of convergence of the algorithm. Since Tsypkin's work, random approximation has become a plan tool in the study of adaptation and learning algorithms. An analysis of the history of machine learning and adaptation [1] shows that during the last four decades of the 20th century, the fields of adaptive control and learning theory were very close to each other, and the scientists working in them fruitfully collaborated with each other.

The turning point in the history of ML was the beginning of the 21st century. This is due to three synchronous trends, which together have produced a noticeable synergistic effect. The first trend is big data: the volume of data has become so large that new approaches have been implemented due to practical necessity, and not out of the curiosity of scientists [5]. The second trend is to increase the cost of parallel computing and memory. The third direction is the development of new deep ML algorithms, the inheritance and development of the idea of the perceptron.

ML researchers needed a means to compare the performance of their methods. But it has been difficult to find reliable mathematical tools to test the performance of the numerous proposed methods. Therefore, plan training and testing datasets were proposed that could be used to evaluate ML algorithms.

But the further development of ML at the beginning of the 21st century led to a certain discrepancy with control theory [6]. Management-related views have been published by Bristow et al. for narrower areas of iterative learning [7] and reinforcement learning [8]. For this reason, the possibility of a closer interaction between adaptive control and ML in the future is still unclear, although several papers co-written by both control and machine learning specialists have been published and well received [6]. What is a problem for control theorists is that there are very few rigorous mathematical proofs in the new deep learning tsunamis [1]. Therefore, this discrepancy is the subject of discussion in the management community on the topic "Control and learning - is there really a gap?" Among the issues currently being discussed are [6]:

- Will learning-based methods replace established control theory in industrial applications?
- What is missing for learning-based methods to be applicable in safety-critical applications?
- How can we use control theory to improve and robustify ML algorithms?

1.2 Human Factors in Machine Learning

In the era of AI and ML, there has been an increased interest in human-centric digital management. The main direction of increasing the efficiency of labor resources in conditions of uncertainty is associated with the disclosure of internal reserves and resources of organizations by activating their employees. To do this, it is necessary to consider the organization as a hierarchy, take into account the interests of its employees and related activities. It is also necessary to take into account the unawareness of managers [9].

For such consideration, hierarchical games with non-opposing interests were proposed [10]. To activate the human factor, the theory of organizational management was developed [11]. An important place in this theory is occupied by mathematical models of adaptive control and learning. This opens up broad prospects for the practical use of modern ML tools in solving large-scale monitoring and digital control problems.

To regulate the sustainable development of complex organizations, the concept of intelligent control mechanisms was proposed [12]. Based on this concept, intelligent control technologies are being developed under conditions of asymmetric awareness [13] using ML in three areas.

The first direction is related to the use of digital learning for adaptive identification and control (see, for example, [14]). The second direction is devoted to the direct application of digital self-learning procedures (unsupervised learning) in control problems (see, for example, [15]). In the works of the third direction, procedures of digital supervised learning (training with a teacher) with simultaneous control are used (see, for example, [16]).

Further prospects for the development of intelligent control technologies using ML are associated with systems engineering [17]. This approach makes it possible to integrate the procedures of adaptive identification, self-learning, and supervised learning with control procedures (see, for example, [18]).

1.3 Improvement of Transport Companies Services with Machine Learning

The concept of intelligent transport systems (ITS) [19] has created opportunities for using AI, ML and intelligent control mechanisms [12] in complex transport systems, in particular, to improve service in conditions of asymmetric awareness [13]. Particular attention was paid to service management in large-scale corporations.

For example, in [20], the organizational system of digital management service maintenance repair of passenger wagons was studied. Self-learning procedures were used in the mechanism for managing the repair of wagons [15]. Decision making and supervised learning in wagon-repairing was considered in [21]. In [22], service maintenance repair of rolling stock was modeled based on a multi-agent approach. In [23], the repair system in service maintenance management is considered as a multichannel system. Methods for control of overhaul of rolling stock with simultaneous digital learning with a teacher were developed in [16].

The application of systems engineering [17] makes it possible to combine mathematical models of organizational management theory and ML to build safe, flexible and autonomous service systems in transport companies. For example, integrated self-learning procedures have been used to manage rolling stock repairs in a large-scale carriage repair company [15]. A combination of adaptive identification and self-learning procedures was used in mechanisms for repair management at Russian Railways holding [18]. Comprehensive mechanism with adaptive identification, self-learning and supervised learning procedures are used for four-level energy cost control in the overhaul of wagons in the carriage repair company [24].

Practical applications of these and other theoretical results and applied developments help to understand the potential impact and fundamental limitations of service management systems using ML. These applications show how the human factor manifests itself in transport companies. To achieve their own goals, their employees can manipulate the scope of services to influence ML outcomes and stakeholder decisions in their favor. Accordingly, an important direction in the organization and management of services is associated with the disclosure of internal reserves and resources through the activation of employees. Below, we develop a comprehensive mathematical model for digital management of services scope with XML in a transportation corporation.

1.4   Three-Level Service Management Model in a Corporation

Let us consider three-level model of service management in a corporation. Its services are controlled by the Boss. Corporation has an affiliate headed by the Curator. To the affiliate is subordinated the subdivision, which directly provides services. This subdivision is headed by the Manager.

Scope of services is affected by random external influences. Therefore, the Boss does not have complete information about the scope of services provided by the affiliate. To increase this scope, the Boss uses information about affiliate services received from the Curator. In turn, the Curator, using advantage of the Boss's lack of knowledge, can downplay scope of services to achieve greater incentives. In other words, the Curator can manipulate services scope to influence the Boss decisions in order to increase own incentives. Therefore, the Boss needs to learn and simultaneously control the Curator to maximize services scope under random influences.

When making decisions, the Curator knows services scope at the affiliate level. But he does not know maximal scope of services which can be provided by the subdivision at random influences. From his side, the Manager knows this maximum services scope. Thus, the Manager can manipulate scope of subdivision services to influence the Curator's decisions about the Manager's incentives. To eliminate this uncertainty, the Curator also needs to learn and simultaneously motivate the Manager. For this, the Curator uses the conclusions of the Specialist.

2   Control of the Manager by the Curator

2.1   The Curator and the Specialist

Let denote t a discrete time period, $t = 0,1,\ldots$ Denote s_t the scope of services provided by the Manager in the period t. The Curator and the Specialist obtain information about s_t from the Manager. The maximum possible subdivision services scope is S_t, so $s_t \epsilon \Sigma_t = [0, S_t]$. We suppose that S_t is stationary random value, $S_t \epsilon \Sigma = [0, \beta]$. Value of S_t become known to the Manager in the beginning of period t. Both the Curator and the Specialist do not know S_t. Thus, the Manager can choose s_t, $s_t \in \Sigma_t$. To control the Manager, the Curator uses services scope index:

$$e_t = s_t/\beta, e_t \in \mathrm{E}_t = [0, E_t], E_t = S_t/\beta, E_t \in [0, 1], t = 0, 1, \ldots \quad (1)$$

Thus, the Curator should motivate the Manager to increase services scope index e_t to its maximum E_t. Assume that the Curator assigns the Manager category 0 for insufficient services scope. Otherwise, the Manager gets category 1, and rewarded. To do such assignment, the Curator uses supervisory learning [16]. The role of a supervisor plays a Specialist who knows services scope s_t and index e_t.

So, in period t the Curator uses the Specialist's conclusion $c_t(e_t)$ on whether services scope is sufficient. If the Specialist considers this scope to be sufficient, then $c_t(e_t) = 1$, otherwise $c_t(e_t) = 0$. Let's represent this conclusion in the form

$$c(e_t) = \begin{cases} 1, if\ e_t \geq \mu \\ 0, if\ e_t < \mu \end{cases}, \mu \geq 0, t = 0, 1, \ldots, \quad (2)$$

where μ is a parameter of the Specialist's decision rule.

The Specialist reports conclusion (2) to the Curator. After that, the Curator's job is to assign a category of the Manager. In case of incorrect assignment to the Manager of category 0 (although the Manager deserves category 1), losses of the Curator are i_{10}. In case of incorrect assignment of category 1, such losses are i_{01}.

If e_t is a stationary random value, then Curator assignment should minimize the average losses. In [16] it is shown that such assignment can be carried out on the basis of the decision rule

$$m_t = M(p_t, e_t) = \begin{cases} 1, if\ e_t \geq p_t \\ 0, if\ e_t < p_t \end{cases}, \quad (3)$$

where the decision rule parameter $(p_\tau, \tau = 0, 1, \ldots)$ is calculated with the aid of supervised learning algorithm [16]:

$$p_{t+1} = P(p_t, e_t) = p_t - \alpha_t[p_t - 0.5 - i_{01} + (i_{01} + i_{10})c_t(e_t)], \quad p_o = p^0, \quad (4)$$

where $0 < \alpha_{t+1} < \alpha_t, \sum_{\tau=0}^{\infty} \alpha_\tau < \infty, t = 0,1,\ldots$

Using (3), the Curator determines the Manager's category m_t. Therefore, $M(p_t, e_t)$ will be called Manager's categorization procedure. At the same time, p_τ makes sense the Manager's plan of services scope in period τ, $\tau = 0, 1, \ldots$ Therefore, $P(p_t, e_t)$ will be called the planning procedure. These two procedures (3) and (4) form control system by the Curator scope of services rendered in affiliate (briefly, the affiliate system) $A = (M, P)$.

2.2   The Manager's Decisions

In period t, at affiliate system A, the Manager's present value PVM_t increases with current and some future categories:

$$PVM_t = PVM[m_t, m_{t+1}, \ldots, m_{t+\phi}], PVM_\tau \uparrow m_\tau, \tau = \overline{t, t+\phi}, t = 0, 1, \ldots, \quad (5)$$

where $PVM[\bullet]$ is a non-decreasing function, ϕ is the Manager's vision. To increase (5), the Manager chooses in period t services scope s_t, which determines the index e_t (1).

Suppose, when eliminating a future uncertainty, the Manager is guided by the principle of maximum guaranteed result [11], and he knows only that $S_\tau \in \Sigma$ and $s_\tau \in \Sigma_\tau$, $\tau = \overline{t+1, t+\phi}$. Then the Manager is interested in maximization of own goal function $G_t(A, e_t)$ which is defined as the maximum guaranteed value of present value (5):

$$G_t(A, e_t) = \min_{\tau = \overline{t+1, t+\phi}} \ \min_{S_\tau \in \Sigma} \ \min_{s_\tau \in \Sigma_\tau} PVM_t \xrightarrow[e_t \in E_t]{} max \qquad (6)$$

Then the set of Manager's best decisions at affiliate system A is

$$B_t(A) = \{e_t^*, e_t^* \in E_t | G_t(A, e_t^*) \geq G_t(A, e_t), e_t \in E_t\}. \qquad (7)$$

The hypothesis of the Manager's benevolence towards the Curator is assumed: if $E_t \in B_t(A)$, then $e_t = E_t$, $t = 0,1,\ldots$

2.3   Affiliate System

Suppose the Curator interests to increase services scope s_t to its maximum S_t. By (3), the Manager's category m_t in period t increases when index e_t increases to plan p_t. On the other hand, in the practice of corporations, the future plan of services scope often increases when the actual scope increases to the current plan. Formally, the plan p_{t+1} in the next period (t + 1) increases when the scope index e_t increases to the current plan p_t. But, according to (3), the higher the plan p_t, the higher index e_{t+1} will be needed in order to increase the Manager's category in the period t + 1. Thus, visionary Manager may not be motivated in increasing scope index e_t above plan p_t. This is typical problem for planning from the achieved level [11].

Statement. The affiliate system $A = (M, P)$ is sufficient for the Manager's interest in increasing the scope of subdivision services in each period:$s_t = S_t$, $t = 0,1,\ldots$.

Proof. The affiliate system $A = (M, P)$ includes procedures (3) and (4). According to (5), the goal function of the Manager (6) increases with an increase in both the current and the future category m_τ, $\tau = \overline{t, t + \phi}$. According to (3), the current category $m_t = M(p_t, e_t)$ does not decrease with increasing of e_t.

Consider the dependence of the future category $m_\tau = M(p_\tau, e_\tau)$, $\tau = \overline{t + 1, t + \phi}$, on e_t. According to (2), $c_\tau(e_\tau)$ does not decrease with increasing e_t. According to (4), plan p_τ does not increase with increasing e_t. In addition, according to (3), Manager's category $m_\tau = M(p_\tau, e_\tau)$ does not increase with increasing p_τ. Consequently, the category $m_\tau = M(p_\tau, e_\tau)$ in the period τ does not decrease with e_t increasing,$\tau = \overline{t + 1, t + \phi}$.

Thus, from (5) and (6) it follows that the goal function $G_t(A, e_t)$ does not decrease with e_t increasing. Since $e_t \leq E_t$ according to (1), then $G_t(A, E_t) \geq G_t(A, e_t)$. So by (7), $E_t \in B_t(A)$, and by hypothesis of the Manager's benevolence towards the Curator, $e_t^* = E_t$. Then from (1) it follows that $s_t = S_t$, $t = 0, 1, \ldots$, Q.E.D.

Informally, this Statement means that in order to interest the Manager in increasing scope of subdivision services, the Curator is sufficient to use affiliate system $A = (M, P)$. Note that this system uses ML based on supervised learning algorithm (4). The use of such a transparent algorithm allows us to talk about the algorithmic accountability and explainability of ML used in the affiliate system $A = (M, P)$. The managerial and social consequences of the interpretability of the affiliate system $A = (M, P)$ using XML are responsibility, ethics, trust and, ultimately, the recognition of this system by the Manager and other employees of the subdivision.

3   Control of the Curator by the Boss

3.1   Interaction Between the Boss and the Curator

Suppose that in period t the Curator informs the Boss:

- Of assessment a_t of the subdivision's service scope s_t.
- Of assessment of additional services scope o_t provided by the affiliate through outsourcing.

There $a_t \in \Phi_t = [0, s_t]$, $o_t \in \Lambda_t = [0, O_t]$, where O_t is stationary random value: $O_t \in \Lambda$. But the Boss do not know services scope s_t, that the Manager told the Curator. In addition, the Boss do not know O_t - maximum of additional services scope provided by the affiliate through outsourcing.

On the other hand, the Curator become known values of s_t and O_t at the beginning of the period t. This allows the Curator to manipulate a_t and o_t to their advantage, $a_t \in \Phi_t$, $o_t \in \Lambda_t$. From his side, the Boss's needs to increase a_t and o_t.

Recall that maximum subdivision scope of services which the Manager can reported to the Curator, is S_t, so $s_t \leq S_t$, $t = 0,1,...$ Neither the Curator nor the Boss do not know maximum scope S_t.

The Boss needs to ensure $a_t = S_t$, $o_t = O_t$. Consider what tasks the Boss must solve in order to do this. The assessment a_t reported to the Boss by the Curator, according to (8), depend on the information that the Curator receives from the Manager (i.e., from s_t). Therefore, the Boss must ensure that the Curator does not understate the reported scope a_t (i.e., $a_t = s_t$).

Also, the Boss should ensure that the Curator encourages the Manager to maximize the scope reported (i.e. $s_t = S_t$). To do this, the Boss delegates to the Curator the right to set the system to control the Manager Ψ, $\Psi \in \Xi$, where Ξ is the set of permissible control systems. Also, the Boss must ensure that the Curator does not understate reported additional services o_t provided through outsourcing (i.e. $o_t = O_t$).

3.2   Reported Affiliate Scope of Services

Since the Curator reports to the Boss about the values of a_t and o_t, the Boss can calculate full affiliate scope of services $z_t = a_t + o_t$ in period t. Remember $a_t \leq s_t$, where service scope s_t is previously reported by the Manager to the Curator. Then maximum value of full affiliate scope, that the Curator to the Boss can report, is $Z_t = s_t + O_t$. The value of Z_t becomes known to the Curator in period t, before a_t and o_t are chosen, and z_t is calculated. From $s_t \leq S_t$ it follows $z_t \leq S_t + O_t$. Thus, $Z_t \in \Omega_t = [0, V_t]$, where $V_t = S_t + O_t$, $V_t \in H$. Essentially, V_t is the maximum of services scope provided by affiliate in the period t.

Of course, the Boss does not know V_t. So, the Curator can manipulate affiliate scope of services a_t and o_t to determine z_t in his favor, $z_t \leq Z_t$. Such manipulations often occur with hierarchical management and unawareness [9, 11, 13].

The Boss should motivate the Curator in reaching V_t: $z_t = V_t, t = 0, 1, \ldots$. To do this, the Boss ranks the Curator to maximize the scope of affiliate services z_t. Namely, the Boss gives the Curator a first rank if scope is rational, and second rank if it is inadequate. The Curator is rewarded only for first rank.

3.3   The Boss's Self-Learning

First suppose the Boss knows the maximum scope V_t. To determine Curator's rank in period t, the Boss needs to assign V_t to one of two disjoint subsets H_1 and H_2 which make up the set H, $H_1 \cup H_2 = H$. If V_t belongs to subset H_1, then the Curator gets first rank. Otherwise, the Curator gets second rank. The wrong ranking results in losses. The task is to determine the subsets H_1 and H_2, at which the expected losses are minimal.

Because of S_t and O_t are stationary random values, then V_t is also stationary random value. For this reason, the Boss can use the method of minimization of average losses using self-learning [15]. Namely, for each unknown set H_1 and H_2, the Boss considers losses functions:

- $h_1(d, V_t) = V_t - rd$ – losses in case if the Boss believes that $V_t \in H_1$ (and the Curator obtain the first rank), while in fact $V_t \in H_2, 0 < r < 1$.
- $h_2(d, V_t) = k(d - V_t)$ – losses in case if the Boss believes that $V_t \in H_2$ (so the Curator obtain the second rank), while in fact $V_t \in H_1, k > 0$.

Here d is unknown parameter, which estimation d_{t+1} in period $t + 1$ is determined by recursive algorithm of self-learning [15]:

$$d_{t+1} = D(d_t, V_t) = \begin{cases} d_t + \gamma_t r, & \text{if } V_t < f_t \\ d_t - \gamma_t k, & \text{if } V_t \geq f_t \end{cases}, d_o = d^o, \qquad (8)$$

where $f_t = d_t(k + r)/(k + 1)$, $0 < \gamma_{t+1} < \gamma_t$, $\sum_{\tau=0}^{\infty} \gamma_\tau < \infty$, $t = 0, 1, \ldots$

Assume now that the Boss knows only z_t. Then, to obtain estimation u_{t+1} of d_{t+1}, the Boss can use formula (8), in which unknown V_t is substituted for known z_t:

$$u_{t+1} = D(u_t, z_t) = \begin{cases} u_t + \gamma_t r, & \text{if } z_t < y_t \\ u_t - \gamma_t k, & \text{if } z_t \geq y_t \end{cases}, u_o = d^o, \qquad (9)$$

where $y_t = u_t(k + r)/(k + 1)$. Procedure (9) is called rationing procedure. Using y_t, the Boss determines the Curator's rank:

$$q_t = Q(u_t, z_t) = \begin{cases} 1 & \text{if } z_t \geq y_t \\ 2 & \text{if } z_t < y_t \end{cases} \qquad (10)$$

Procedure $Q(u_t, z_t)$ is called the ranking procedure. Essentially, y_t is the norm used by the Boss to determine a rank of the Curator: if the scope z_t is not smaller the norm y_t ($z_t \geq y_t$) then the Curator gets the first rank ($q_t = 1$) otherwise – the second rank ($q_t = 2$).

Rationing procedure (9) and ranking procedure (10) are combined into the control system by the Boss scope of services rendered in affiliate (briefly, the corporation system) $\Gamma = (D, Q)$.

The use of ML procedure based on the explainable algorithm (9) allows us to talk about algorithmic accountability and the presence of XML in corporation system $\Gamma = (D, Q)$. The managerial and social implications of the interpretability of XML-based corporation system $\Gamma = (D, Q)$ are responsibility, ethics, trust, and ultimately recognition among corporate employees.

3.4 The Curator's Decisions

The Curator strives to make decisions that provide him with higher current and future ranks. These decisions concern:

- Service scope a_t reported to the Boss, $a_t \in \Phi_t$.
- Outsourcing scope o_t reported to the Boss, $o_t \in \Lambda_t$.
- The system to control the Manager Ψ, $\Psi \in \Xi$, where Ξ is the set of control systems allowed by the Boss.

The Curator chooses a set of these decisions (Ψ, a_t, o_t) based on present value of current and future ranks:

$$PVR_t = PVR[q_t, q_{t+1}, ..., q_{t+\pi}], PVR_t \downarrow q_j, j = \overline{t, t + \pi}, \qquad (11)$$

where $PVR[\bullet]$ is a non-increasing function of ranks today and in the future, π is the Curator's vision.

To eliminate future uncertainties, the Curator is guided by the principle of the maximum guaranteed result [11]. Suppose that the Curator knows that $S_\tau \in \Sigma$, $s_\tau \in \Sigma_\tau$, $O_\tau \in \Lambda$, $o_\tau \in \Lambda_\tau$, $\tau = \overline{t + 1, t + \pi}$. Then the Curator's goal function $N_t(\Psi, a_t, o_t)$ is defined as the maximum guaranteed value of present value (11):

$$N_t(\Psi, a_t, o_t) = \min_{\tau = \overline{t+1, t+\pi}} \min_{O_\tau \in \Lambda} \min_{o_\tau \in \Lambda_\tau} \min_{S_\tau \in \Sigma} \min_{s_\tau \in \Sigma_\tau} G_t \to \underset{\Psi \in \Xi, a_t \in \Phi_t, o_t \in \Lambda_t}{\max} \qquad (12)$$

The Curator takes Ψ, a_t, o_t to maximize the goal function (12). Thus, the set of Curator's decisions is

$$\underset{\Psi \in \Xi, a_t \in \Phi_t, o_t \in \Lambda_t}{Arg \max} N_t(\Psi, a_t, o_t) = \{\Psi^*, a_t^*, o_t^* | N_t(\Psi^*, a_t^*, o_t^*) \geq N_t(\Psi, a_t, o_t),$$

$$\Psi \in \Xi, a_t \in \Phi_t, o_\tau \in \Lambda_\tau\}. \qquad (13)$$

Let us accept the hypothesis that the Curator supports the Boss: if $(A, S_t, O_t) \in \underset{\Psi \in \Xi, a_t \in \Phi_t, o_t \in \Lambda_t}{Argmax} N_t(\Psi, a_t, o_t)$ then the Curator chooses $\Psi^* = A$, $a_t = S_t$, $o = O_t$, $t = 0,1,...$

3.5 Services Scope Control with Explainable Machine Learning

Combining affiliate system $A = (M, P)$ and corporation system $\Gamma = (D, Q)$, we obtain control system of services scope $X = (A, \Gamma)$ (see Fig. 1). This control system is based on 4 explainable procedures (3), (4), (9), (10), including 2 ML procedures:

- Digital supervised learning procedure based on algorithm (4).
- Digital self-learning procedure based on algorithm (9).

The use of these two explainable ML procedures allows us to talk about the presence of XML in control system of services scope $X = (A, \Gamma)$. Therefore, in fact, $X = (A, \Gamma)$ is a control system of services scope with XML (see Fig. 1).

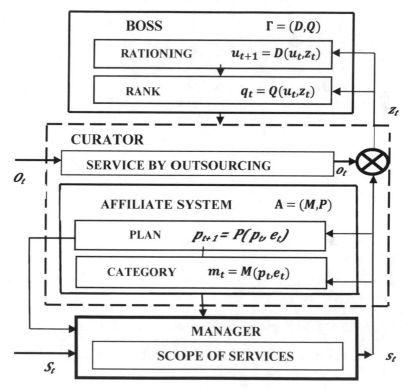

Fig. 1. Control system of services scope $X = (A, \Gamma)$ with explainable machine learning

Theorem. Assume the affiliate system $A = (M, P)$ belongs to the set Ξ of the allowed management systems of the Manager defined by the Boss: $A \in \Xi$. Then control system of services scope with XML $X = (A, \Gamma)$ is sufficient to maximize full scope of services in every period: $z_t = V_t, t = 0, 1, \ldots$.

Proof. $X = (A, \Gamma)$ includes subsystem $\Gamma = (D, Q)$ with procedures (9) and (10). On (10), as z_t grows, then $q_t = Q(u_t, z_t)$ does not increase. Further, it follows from (9) that u_τ does not increase with increasing z_t, $\tau = \overline{t+1, t+\pi}$. But, according to (10), q_τ does not decrease as u_τ increases. Thus, $q_\tau = Q(u_\tau, z_\tau)$ do not increase with increasing z_t. Therefore, according to (11), PVR_t does not decrease with increasing z_t for $S_\tau \in \Sigma, s_\tau \in \Sigma_\tau, O_\tau \in \Lambda, o_\tau \in \Lambda_\tau, \tau = \overline{t+1, t+\pi}$. Thus, according to (12), $N_t(\Psi, a_t, o_t)$ does not decrease with increasing z_t.

From $z_t = a_t + o_t$, it follows that $N_t(\Psi, a_t, o_t)$ does not decrease with increasing both a_t and o_t, for $S_\tau \in \Sigma, s_\tau \in \Sigma_\tau, O_\tau \in \Lambda, o_\tau \in \Lambda_\tau, \tau = \overline{t+1, t+\pi}$. Therefore, $N_t(\Psi, a_t, o_t)$ reaches a maximum at $a_t = s_t$ and $o_t = O_t$. So, by (13), $(\Psi, s_t, O_t) \in$ $\underset{a_t \in \Phi_t, O_t \in \Lambda_t}{Argmax} N_t(\Psi, a_t, o_t), z_t = s_t + O_t$, and $N_t(\Psi, a_t, o_t^*) = N_t(\Psi, a_t, O_t)$.

Consider the dependence of $N_t(\Psi, a_t, O_t)$ on s_t. On (10), as s_t grows, then $q_t = Q(u_t, z_t)$ does not increase. Further, it follows from (9) that u_τ does not increase with increasing $s_t, \tau = \overline{t+1, t+\pi}$. But, according to (10), q_τ does not decrease as u_τ increases. Thus, $q_\tau = Q(u_\tau, z_\tau)$ does not increase with increasing $s_t, \tau = \overline{t+1, t+\pi}$.

Therefore, according to (11), PVR_t does not decrease with increasing s_t for $S_\tau \in \Sigma, s_\tau \in \Sigma_\tau, O_\tau \in \Lambda, o_\tau \in \Lambda_\tau, \tau = \overline{t+1, t+\pi}$. Thus, according to (12), $N_t(\Psi, a_t, O_t)$ does not decrease with increasing s_t. Then, by (13), $(\Psi, S_t, O_t) \in$ $\underset{s_t \in \Sigma_t, o_t \in \Lambda_t}{Argmax} N_t(\Psi, a_t, o_t)$.

Thus, to achieve the maximum of $N_t(\Psi, a_t, O_t)$ in s_t, it is enough for the Curator to ensure equality $s_t = S_t, t = 0, 1, \ldots$. In turn, for this, according to Statement, the Curator it is enough to use the affiliate system $A = (M, P)$. Thus, $N_t(\Psi, a_t, O_t)$ reaches its maximum in s_t at $\Psi = A$. Therefore, $N_t(\Psi, a_t, o_t)$ reaches its maximum at $\Psi = A, s_t = S_t$, and $o_t = O_t$. According to (13), this means $(A, S_t, O_t) \in$ $\underset{\Psi \in \Xi, a_t \in \Phi_t, o_t \in \Lambda_t}{Argmax} N_t(\Psi, a_t, o_t)$.

But, by the conditon of Theorem, $X = (A, \Gamma)$ includes affiliate system $A \in \Xi$. Then, according to the hypothesis that the Curator supports the Boss, the Curator chooses $\Psi^* = A, s_t^* = S_t, o_t^* = O_t, t = 0, 1, \ldots$ In this case $z_t = a_t^* + o_t^* = S_t + O_t = V_t$, $t = 0, 1, \ldots$, QED.

Note that in order to increase full service scope, it is enough for the Boss to use corporation system $\Gamma = (D, Q)$, which is of interest to the Curator:

- Establish affiliate system $A = (M, P)$, which interests the Manager in increasing the scope of subdivision services: $s_t = S_t$.
- Do not underestimate the scope of subdivision services: $a_t = s_t$.
- Use the opportunity to increase the scope of outsourcing services: $o_t = O_t$.

4 Example: Control of Service Maintenance Repair of Passenger Wagons

Consider the example of an application of control system of services scope with XML $X = (A, \Gamma)$. Following the methodology developed in [20, 22, 23], we consider the control system of service maintenance repair of passenger wagons in a transport corporation (such as Russian Railways holding).

The structure of this control system includes the hierarchy with three managers (as agents) connected by direct and feedback channels. The corporation manager of this service is the prototype of the Boss. His subordinate head of the affiliate of service maintenance repair of passenger wagons can be considered as the prototype of the Curator. This affiliate includes subordinated subdivision provided this service, and headed by the Manager.

The Boss should learn himself and simultaneously rewarding the Curator to increase affiliate scope of service of passenger wagons. As follows from what was said in the end of paragraph 3.5, to interest the Curator to increase services scope, it is enough for the Boss to use corporation system $\Gamma = (D, Q)$. Thus, the Boss should monthly monitor full affiliate services scope. In this case, t is the number of the month, z_t is the full affiliate scope of service maintenance of passenger wagons in the month t, and $y_t = u_t(k + r)/(k + 1)$, where u_t is calculated by (9). Then by (10) the Boss determines a rank of the Curator $q_t = Q(u_t, z_t)$. In the event that the Curator takes first rank, he receives a bonus. This encourages the Curator to increase affiliate scope of services maintenance of passenger wagons.

This example illustrates the simplicity and transparency of control system with XML $X = (A, \Gamma)$ to the management of services scope. The managerial and social implications of the interpretability of such control system with XML are algorithmic accountability, ethics, trust, and ultimately recognition within the corporate team.

5 Conclusions

The concept of this study is to show how to combine in a coherent framework the results of modern research and development of explainable ML-based organizational management models for application in intelligent transport systems (ITS). In accordance with this concept, in this paper we pursue a threefold goal:

- To round up reference material for newcomers and researchers willing to join the dynamic area of hierarchical service control models with multilevel ML in XML, by introducing them to fundamental concepts and topics of organizational control theory.
- To provide interested and more experienced researchers with a timely holistic view of existing and potential methods and techniques for enabling and improving the interpretability of organizational control with ML in transportation systems.
- To discuss the ethical and social implications of ML explainability in the context of ITS. Such explainability is not a purely technological issue; it entails trust, fairness, and ethical considerations. The managerial and societal implications of the inter-pretability of the developed XML-based service scope management system include algorithmic reporting, accountability, and ultimately recognition among affiliate and corporate employees.

References

1. Fradkov, A.: Early history of machine learning. IFAC-PapersOnLine **53**(2), 1385–1390 (2020)
2. Rosenblatt, F.: Perceptron simulation experiments. Proc. Inst. Radio Engineers **18**, 301–309 (1960)
3. Tsypkin, Y.: Adaptation and learning in automated systems. Academic Press, NY (1971)
4. Feldbaum, A.: Dual control theory. Autom. Remote. Control. **21**, 874–880 (1961)
5. Wu, X., Zhu, X., Wu, G.: Data mining with big data. IEEE Trans. Knowl. Data Eng. **26**(1), 97–107 (2014)

6. Recht, B.: Reflections on the learning-to-control renaissance. IFAC-PapersOnLine **53**(1), 275–280 (2020)
7. Bristow, D., Tharayil, M., Alleyne, A.: A survey of iterative learning control. IEEE Control Syst. Mag. **26**(5), 96–114 (2006)
8. Bertsekas, D.: Reinforcement learning and optimal control. Athena Scientific, Massachusetts (2019)
9. Schipper, B.: Unawareness – a gentle introduction to both the literature and the special issue. Math. Soc. Sci. **70**, 1–9 (2014)
10. Ho, Y.-C., Luh, P., Muralidharan, R.: Information structure, Stackelberg games, incentive controllability. IEEE Trans. Automat. Control **26**(2), 454–460 (1981)
11. Burkov, V., Kondratiev, V., Korgin, N., Novikov, D.: Mechanism design and management. Mathematical methods for smart organizations. NOVA Publishers, New York (2013)
12. Tsyganov, V.: Regulation of decentralized active system development intelligent control mechanisms. IFAC-PapersOnline **9**, 94–98 (2010)
13. Auster, S.: Asymmetric awareness and moral hazard. Games Econom. Behav. **82**, 503–521 (2013)
14. Tsyganov, V.: Learning mechanisms in digital control of large-scale industrial systems. In: Proceedings of the Global Smart Industry Conf., pp. 32–39. IEEE, Chelyabinsk (2018)
15. Tsyganov, V.: Twin self-learning and holding intelligent control of fabrication. IFAC-PapersOnLine **55**(15), 186–191 (2022)
16. Tsyganov, V.: Training of quartering in digital control of overhaul. IOP Conf. Ser.: Mater. Sci. Eng. **919**, 042015 (2020)
17. Kossiakoff, A., Sweet, W., Seymour, S., Biemer, S.: Systems engineering. Principles and practice. John Wiley, New York (2011)
18. Tsyganov, V.: Mechanisms for learning and production management of a vertical concern. In: Silhavy, R. (ed.) 10th COMPUTER SCIENCE CONFERENCE, LNNS, 228, pp. 466–475. Springer, Cham (2021)
19. Leviäkangas, P.: Intelligent transport systems – technological, economic, system performance and market views. Internat. J. Technol. **4**(3), 288–298 (2013)
20. Bannikov, D., Sirina, N.: Service maintenance repair of passenger cars in the concept of Digital Enterprise. IOP Conf. Series: Materials Sci. Engineering **918**, 012168 (2020)
21. Tsyganov, V.: Decision making and learning in wagon-repairing. In: Proceedings of the 12th International Conference on Management of Large-Scale System Development, pp. 1–5. IEEE, Moscow (2019)
22. Alexandrov, A., Bannikov, D., Sirina, N.: Agent-based modeling of service maintenance repair of rolling stock. IOP Conf. Ser.: Earth Environmental Sci. **403**, 012193 (2019)
23. Bannikov, D., Sirina, N., Smolyaninov, A.: Model of the maintenance repair system in service maintenance management. Transport problems **13**(3), 5–14 (2018)
24. Tsyganov, V.: Comprehensive mechanism for four-level energy cost control. IFAC-PapersOnLine **55**(9), 366–371 (2022)

Artificial Intelligence and Deep Learning Technologies for Creative Tasks. Knowledge Discovery in Patent and Open Sources

The New Method of Predicting the Importance of Patented Technologies

Alexander Rublev, Dmitriy Korobkin$^{(\boxtimes)}$ ⓘ, Sergey Fomenkov ⓘ,
and Alexander Golovanchikov

Volgograd State Technical University, 28 Lenina Ave., Volgograd 400005, Russia
dkorobkin80@mail.ru

Abstract. Building of all spheres of life at a qualitatively new technological level and possession of one's own technological keys to the creation of goods and services of the next generations is necessary to ensure one of the key principles of the development of the state, namely the achievement of technological sovereignty. In modern realities, the development of enterprises cannot be carried out without coordination with partners from Russia, as well as China, India and other countries. The selection of potential partners can be carried out on the basis of the revealed significance of their patented technological solutions. Further ranking of potential partners can be carried out on the basis of the revealed significance of their patented technological solutions. At the same time, it is proposed to use three criteria: the mass nature of the subject of the patented invention in the current period, the predicted mass nature of the subject (technology) in the future period, the success of the patent in the information field. The novelty of the developed method of forecasting the significance of patented technologies is the use of the generated metrics of innovation potential (prospects) to analyze the global patent array according to the sphere of interests of key enterprises of the Volgograd region. The developed software module provides the following functions: a) parsing of patent documents is carried out from Yandex Patents and Google Patents; b) the formation of a list of IPC classes corresponding to the spheres of interests of enterprises of the Volgograd region, and the extraction of patents of these classes from Google Patents; c) the determination of the mass content of the subject of the invention in the current period is carried out by clustering the patent array based on the lists of keywords provided by Google Patents; d) the predicted mass content of the subject (technology) in the future the period is determined by the ARIMA method; e) success in the information area is determined based on the information provided by Google Patents about the citation of the patent.

Keywords: patent · parsing · forecast · clustering · enterprise · information · data · python

1 Introduction

In 2022–2023, various factors put pressure on the Russian economy, from the unfavorable situation on world markets to complications in the foreign policy situation. There was a decrease in the level of declarative patent activity compared to 2021 due to the outflow

A. G. Kravets et al. (Eds.): CIT&DS 2023, CCIS 1909, pp. 35–48, 2023.
https://doi.org/10.1007/978-3-031-44615-3_3

of foreign applicants [1]. At the same time, it is obvious that the patenting system itself contributes to technological development by stimulating the creation of new technologies and providing conditions for their industrial application [2]. As part of the support for domestic companies, it is necessary to assess the competitiveness of patented technical solutions created in Russia.

The development of enterprises cannot be carried out without coordination with partners from Russia, as well as China, India [3], and other countries, and their choice can be made on the basis of the similarity of the technological problems being solved. Further ranking of potential partners can be carried out on the basis of the revealed significance of patented technological solutions [4].

2 Analysis of the Research Domain and Existing Solutions

The current process of evaluating the significance of patented technologies is quite complex and time-consuming in terms of the amount of information needed for analysis and comparison. It is necessary to find patents in one of the search engines (Yandex.Patents, Google Patents, USPTO, FSIP Rospatent, etc. [5]), extract patent information, highlighting specific criteria of interest, find patents with a similar class of IPC, compare the similarity of technologies, as a result which, having collected all the necessary information, make a decision on the relevance and significance of the developed technology [6]. A diagram of the existing process is shown in Fig. 1.

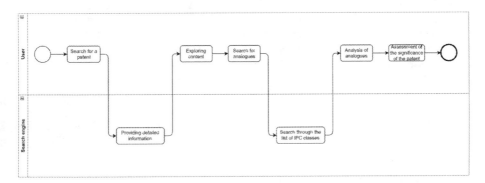

Fig. 1. AS-IS diagram

The projected process of assessing and predicting the significance of technologies is designed to accelerate the speed of identifying the assessment of the significance of patented technologies, as well as save the resources of the person interested in this. A diagram of the automated process is shown in Fig. 2.

A comparison was made of existing solutions to the problem of extracting patent data according to the following criteria: (a) citation of this patent; (b) key terms; (c) the IPC classification; (d) availability of information on patents from Russia [7].

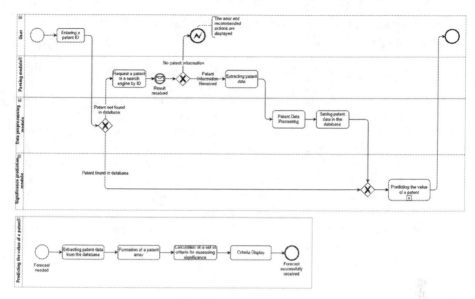

Fig. 2. TO-BE diagram

The results of the comparative analysis of existing solutions are presented in Table 1.

Table 1. Results of comparison of existing solutions.

Criterion\solution	Yandex Patents	Google Patents	FIPS	Patentscope WIPO	Espacenet EPO
Availability of patent citations	No	Yes	No	No	Yes
Availability of key terms	No	Yes	No	No	No
Availability of IPC classification	Always present	Possible absence	Always present	Possible absence	Always present
Availability of patents of Russian enterprises	Yes	Yes	Yes	Yes	Yes

Based on the results of the analysis, it is necessary to develop a software module for predicting the importance of patented technologies based on the analysis of the patent array. At the same time, it is proposed to use three criteria: the mass character of the subject matter of the invention in the current period, the predicted mass character of the subject matter (technology) in the future period, and success in the information field [8].

3 The Method of Forecasting the Significance of Patented Technologies

3.1 The Algorithm for Parsing a Patent Array

The patent parsing algorithm includes the choice of a database provider, the initialization of the parsers of the Yandex.Patents or Google Patents search engines, and the choice of a data source [9]. Among the data sources available are such options as industrial enterprises of the Volgograd region, search by entering the name of the organization or the name of the patent, as well as a generated local file containing more than 20,000 patents by class corresponding to the activities of the enterprises of the Volgograd region.

To parse a patent, you must first download it from a search engine. If the patent is not yet contained in the database, then data is retrieved from its html-representation. In the absence of an IPC classification, a search will be made in another search engine. After extraction, all data is stored in the database. The block diagram of the patent parsing algorithm is shown in Fig. 3.

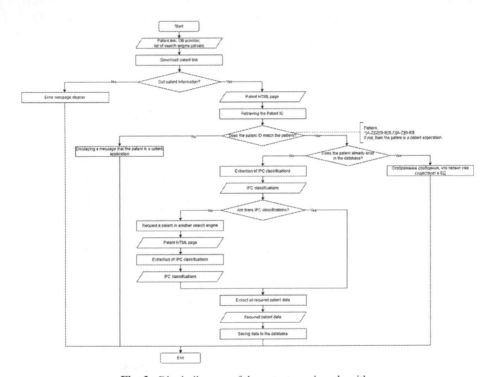

Fig. 3. Block diagram of the patent parsing algorithm

3.2 The Algorithm for Calculating the Mass Content of the Subject Matter of a Patented Invention in the Current Period

The process of calculating the mass character of the invention in the current period consists of loading a patent array from the database, calculating TF-IDF (TF - term frequency - word frequency, IDF - inverse document frequency - inverse document frequency) [10] based on the list of key terms of all patents of the patent array, distribution of the obtained term-frequency vectors over clusters using the K-Means method [11] with further calculation of the mass character and saving the results in the database.

To calculate the term-frequency vectors, it is necessary to transform the initial data on the number of use of terms in a document using the TF-IDF metric according to the following formula:

$$w_{x,y} = tf_{x,y} * \log(N/df_x), \tag{1}$$

where $tf_{x,y}$ = the ratio of the number of occurrences of word x in document y;

df_x = number of documents containing the word x;

N = total number of documents.

The block diagram of the algorithm for calculating term-frequency vectors is shown in Fig. 4.

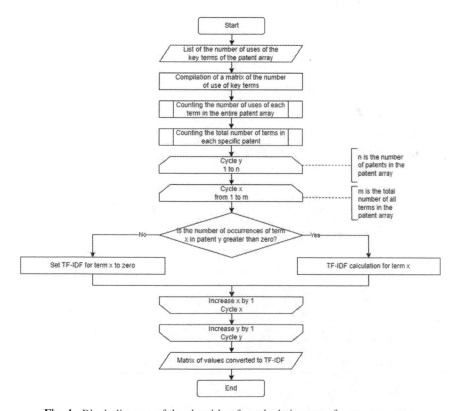

Fig. 4. Block diagram of the algorithm for calculating term-frequency vectors

Within the framework of the developed system, the calculation of term-frequency vectors is necessary for further clustering, which determines whether the patent belongs to the features of any subject [12]. It is possible to determine the optimal number of clusters by using the silhouette method, which calculates the average distance between points in its cluster and the average distance from the points to the next nearest cluster. The optimal number of clusters will be the maximum value of the silhouette coefficient [13].

Having received a list of labels that correlate patents with clusters, it is necessary to determine the number of patents in each cluster, as well as the cluster with the largest number of patents. The calculation of mass in the current period based on certain clusters is determined as follows:

$$f(x) = round\left(\frac{cd_x}{cd_{max}} * 10\right), \tag{2}$$

where x = patent document in question;

cd_x = the size of the cluster to which the evaluated patent document belongs;

cd_{max} = largest cluster size;

$round$ = rounding to the highest integer.

The mass character in the current period is rounded to a ten-point scale for ease of use. The block diagram of the algorithm for calculating the mass character in the current period is shown in Fig. 5.

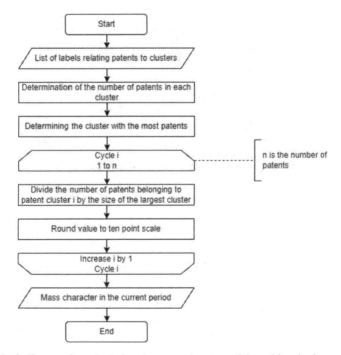

Fig. 5. Block diagram for calculating the mass character of the subject in the current period

3.3 The Algorithm for Predicting the Mass Content of Topics in the Future Period

To determine the mass character in the future period, its size is calculated within each cluster for each of the considered quarters from the date of publication of the first patent in this cluster. These values are used to determine the size of the thematic cluster for the next year. The criterion is defined as the size of the cluster related to the patent to the size of the largest cluster for the next period of time. To make a forecast for the next year, the ARIMA (Autoregressive integrated moving average) model [14] is used, the mathematical formula of which is as follows:

$$Y_t = \alpha + \beta_1 Y_{t-1} + \beta_2 Y_{t-2} + ... + \beta_p Y_{t-p}\epsilon_t + \varphi_1\epsilon_{t-1} + \varphi_2\epsilon_{t-2} + ... + \varphi_q\epsilon_{t-q}, \quad (3)$$

where t = current row number;

α = constant evaluated by the model;

β_p = lag coefficient p of the series;

$Y_{t-p} = t\text{-}p$ series lag;

φ_q = forecast delay error coefficient q series;

$\epsilon_{t-q} = t\text{-}q$ series forecast lag error.

The block diagram of the algorithm for predicting the mass character of topics in the future period is shown in Fig. 6.

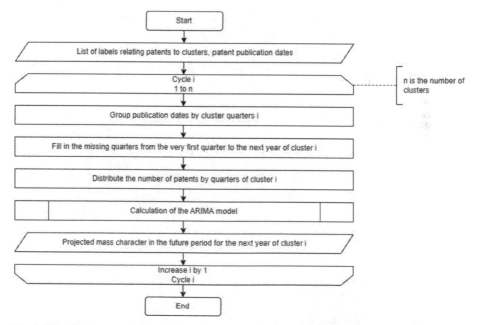

Fig. 6. Block diagram of the algorithm for predicting the mass character of the subject in the future period

3.4 The Algorithm for Determining the Success of a Patent in the Information Field

Success in the information field is determined based on the information provided by Google Patents on the citation of the patent.

The determination of the success of a patent in the information field is carried out by the following formula:

$$f(x) = \begin{cases} False, x \leq 5 \\ True, x > 5 \end{cases},$$

(4)

where x = number of patent citations.

$f(x)$ = success.

4 The Software for Predicting the Significance of Patented Technologies

The main components of the program are modules for parsing, data preprocessing, mass forecasting in the current and future periods, success and visualization of criteria. The parser, receiving a link to a patent from a certain list of available search engines, extracts data from the HTML page of the patent, then, after pre-processing, the information is stored in the database. A user wishing to obtain an assessment of the significance of a patented technology makes a request, which results in a database request for information about the patent. Then the data is sent for processing to each of the forecasting modules, as a result of which a list of calculated criteria is formed, which are returned back to the user along with the plotted graphs. The application architecture diagram is shown in Fig. 7.

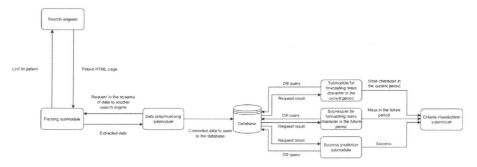

Fig. 7. Layout of the overall application architecture

To ensure the interchangeability of parsing algorithms from different search engines, the "Strategy" pattern is used [15]. The need for its implementation lies in the fact that if any information is not found in one search engine, then you can try to search in another at the stage of program execution. To work with different search engines, it is necessary to provide for the possibility of creating web drivers and patent loaders configured to work

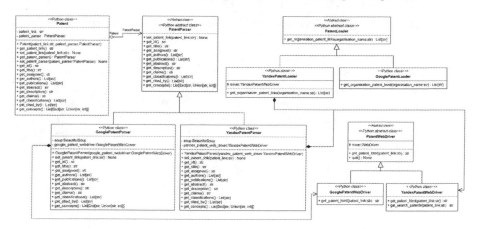

Fig. 8. Parser's Class diagram

with each particular system [16]. The class diagram diagram for the parser is shown in Fig. 8.

If it is necessary to ensure the choice of the database used, the "Strategy" pattern can be applied similarly. The class diagram for database providers is shown in Fig. 9.

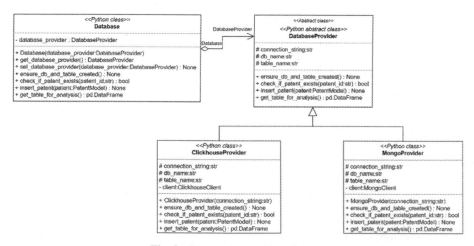

Fig. 9. DB providers' Class diagram

The application of the above pattern will make it possible to simply replace the database with another one, regardless of the data organization structure: SQL or NoSQL [17].

5   Checking the Effectiveness of the Developed Software

To calculate the significance of patented technologies, it is necessary first of all to form a table of the terms used in the patent array. Patents that do not have a term should have the value set to zero, which means that the term is not used in the current patent. To further calculate the mass character in the future period, the date of publication of the patent will be required, and for success, the number of citations. All of the above data must be entered into the database in advance, from where they will be retrieved.

Then it is necessary to form term-frequency vectors, which are determined using the TF-IDF metric. On the constructed term-frequency vectors for documents, clustering by topics is performed using the K-Means method. To determine the number of clusters, the silhouette method is used, which implies repeated cyclic execution of the algorithm with an increase in the number of selected clusters, as well as subsequent plotting of the clustering score on the graph. The maximum value on the graph is the optimal number of clusters. An estimate for determining the optimal number of clusters is shown in Fig. 10.

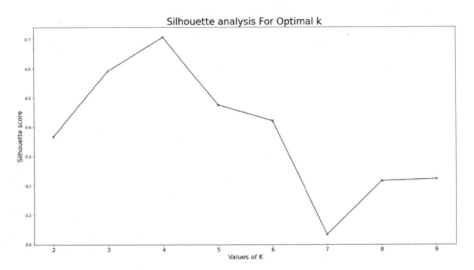

Fig. 10. Determination of the optimal number of clusters

Having determined the optimal number of clusters into which term-frequency vectors must be divided, the distribution of patents by clusters will be obtained. An example of distribution is shown in Fig. 11. Mass character in the current period is calculated as the ratio of the size of the cluster to which the evaluated patent document belongs to the size of the largest cluster, rounded to a ten-point scale.

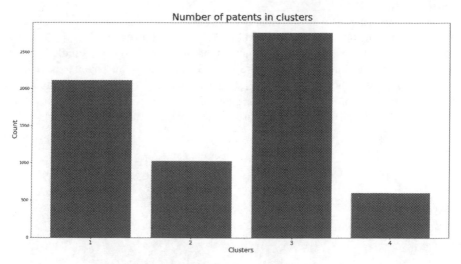

Fig. 11. Diagram of the distribution of patents by clusters

Mass character in the future period is determined on the basis of clustering data obtained at the stage of determining the first criterion. Within each cluster, its size is calculated for each of the quarters. The ARIMA model is used to make forecasts for the next year. The forecast value is shown in Fig. 12. The criterion is close to the mass character in the current period, it is defined similarly - as the size of the cluster related to the patent to the size of the largest cluster for the next period of time. The forecast accuracy formed on the training sample from historical data reaches an average result of 70%.

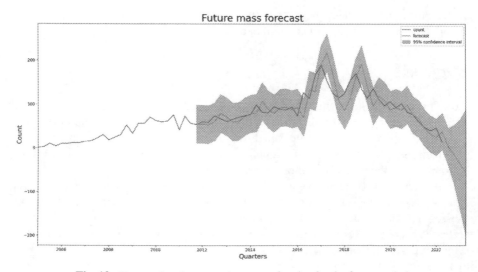

Fig. 12. Forecasting the mass character of topics for the future period

The success criterion in the information field only applies to patents that have existed for a relatively long time. It is determined by the number of patent citations [18]. Based on the analysis of the patent array, it is known that more than half of the studied patents have a citation rate of approximately five [19]. Based on this, all patents are divided into two classes of citation: high and low [20]. The first category includes patents whose citation is greater than five, and the second includes patents whose citation is less than or equal to five. The distribution of patent success is shown in Fig. 13.

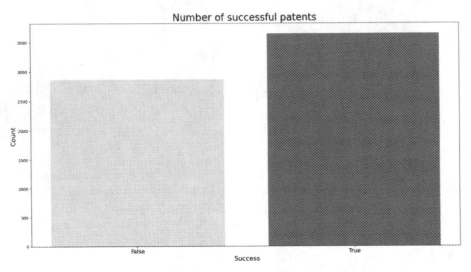

Fig. 13. Patent success chart

As shown in the image above, there were slightly more successful patents in the compiled patent array than unsuccessful ones.

6   Results

The software for predicting the significance of patented technologies based on the analysis of the patent array was designed and implemented. The scope of the developed module is complex software solutions in the field of analyzing information about industrial enterprises, as well as decision support in identifying potential partners based on the similarity of the technological problems being solved.

The main direction of improvement and further development of the developed system is to increase the number of both the set of criteria by which the significance will be assessed and the characteristics taken into account, and, as a result, the expansion of the list of characteristics extracted from the patents of industrial enterprises not only of the Volgograd region, but of the whole of Russia, as well as the development and improvement of algorithms for calculating evaluation criteria.

7 Conclusions

The novelty of the developed method for predicting the significance of patented technologies lies in the use of the formed metrics of innovative potential (prospects) for the analysis of the global patent array according to the area of interest of the key enterprises of the Volgograd region. In this case, three criteria are used: the mass character of the subject matter of the invention in the current period, the predicted mass character of the subject matter (technology) in the future period, and success in the information field. The mass content of topics in the current period is calculated as the ratio of the size of the cluster to which the patent belongs to the size of the largest cluster, which consist of compiled term-frequency vectors based on a list of keywords. The mass character in the future period is based on clustering data, is estimated similarly to the mass character of topics in the current period, and the size of each cluster for the next year is calculated, which is formed by making a forecast using the ARIMA model. The success of a patent in the information field is determined by the number of its citations.

Acknowledgments. The study was supported by the grant of the Russian Science Foundation No. 22-21-20125, https://rscf.ru/en/project/22-21-20125/ and the Administration of the Volgograd Region.

References

1. Rospatent facts & figures 2022 - https://rospatent.gov.ru/content/uploadfiles/annual-report-2022-short-version-en.pdf (2023). Accessed August 8
2. Ma, M.Y.: Fundamentals of Patenting and Licensing for Scientists and Engineers, 2nd edition (2015). https://doi.org/10.1142/9789814452540
3. Vanyushkin, A., Druzin, R., Prikhodko, I., Mirankov, D.: Prospective forms of innovative cooperation Russia with China and India. Sustainable and Innovative Development in the Global Digital Age, No. 003 (2022). https://doi.org/10.56199/dpcsebm.sdth6411
4. Bezruchenko, A., Korobkin, D., Fomenkov, S., Kolesnikov, S., Vasiliev, S.: The Software for Identifying Technological Complementarity Between Enterprises Based on Patent Databases. CIT&DS 2021. Communications in Computer and Information Science, vol 1448. Springer, Cham (2021) https://doi.org/10.1007/978-3-030-87034-8_4
5. Kashevarova, N.: Technological development modeling based on patent analysis: Review of the state-of-the-art. AIP Conf. Proc. **2383**, 070004 (2022). https://doi.org/10.1063/5.0074758
6. Borodin, N., Korobkin, D., Bezruchenko, A., Fomenkov, S.: The search for R&D partners based on patent data. Journal of Physics: Conference Series 2060 (2021). AIDTTS II-2021. https://doi.org/10.1088/1742-6596/2060/1/01202
7. Viet, N.T., Kravets, A., Duong Quoc Hoang, T.: Data Mining Methods for Analysis and Forecast of an Emerging Technology Trend: A Systematic Mapping Study from SCOPUS Papers. In: Kovalev, S.M., Kuznetsov, S.O., Panov, A.I. (eds.) Artificial Intelligence. RCAI 2021. Lecture Notes in Computer Science, Vol 12948. Springer, Cham (2021). https://doi.org/10.1007/978-3-030-86855-0_7
8. Korobkin, D.M., Fomenkov, S.A., Zlobin, A.R., Vereshchak, G.A., Golovanchikov, A.B.: The Formation of Metrics of Innovation Potential and Prospects. Cyber-Physical Systems Engineering and Control. Studies in Systems, Decision and Control, vol 477. Springer, Cham (2023). https://doi.org/10.1007/978-3-031-33159-6_2

9. Liu, J., Liu, M.: Patent Examination of Artificial Intelligence-related Inventions: An Overview of China An Overview of China. Artificial Intelligence and Intellectual Property (Oxford, 2021) (2021). https://doi.org/10.1093/oso/9780198870944.003.0012

10. Understanding TF-IDF (Term Frequency-Inverse Document Frequency) - https://www.geeksforgeeks.org/understanding-tf-idf-term-frequency-inverse-document-frequency/ (2023). Accessed August 8

11. Viet, N.T., Kravets, A.: A novel method for predicting technology trends based on processing multiple data sources. Adv. Sys. Sci. Appli. 23(1), 69–90 (2023). https://doi.org/10.3390/en15186613

12. Tiwari, A.K.: Artificial Intelligence in Patent Analytics. The IPR Gorilla, May, 2021 (2021)

13. Krasnov, F.: Comparative analysis of the accuracy of methods for visualizing the structure of a text collection. Int. J. Open Info. Technol. 9(4) (2021)

14. ARIMA Model – Complete Guide to Time Series Forecasting in Python - https://www.machinelearningplus.com/time-series/arima-model-time-series-forecasting-python/ (2023). Accessed August 8

15. Design Patterns - Strategy Pattern - https://www.tutorialspoint.com/design_pattern/strategy_pattern.htm (2023). Accessed August 8

16. Lamleh, D.: Utilizing AI in Test Automation to Perform Functional Testing on Web Application. Intelligent Computing, Proceedings of the 2022 Computing Conference, Vol. 2 (2022). https://doi.org/10.1007/978-3-031-10464-0_24

17. Khan, M.Z., Zaman, F.U., Adnan, M., Imroz, A., Rauf, M.A., Phul Z.: Comparative Case Study: An Evaluation of Performance Computation Between SQL And NoSQL Database. Sindh J. Headw. Softw. Eng. 01(02) (2023)

18. Somonov, V., Nikolaev, A., Murashova, S., Gordeeva, E.: Using patent analytics in additive manufacturing evaluation for monitoring and forecasting business niches. Networks and Systems in Cybernetics, 108–121 (2023). https://doi.org/10.1007/978-3-031-35317-8_11

19. Igami, M., Okazaki, T.: Current State of Nanotechnology: Patent Analysis. Foresight-Russia. 2, 32–43 (2008). https://doi.org/10.17323/1995-459X.2008.3.32.43

20. Feng, S.: Strategic Citations in Patents: Analysis Using Machine Learning. Qeios (2023). https://doi.org/10.32388/VUK7QO.2

MPNN- Based Method for Identifying the Pharmacological Activity of a Synthesized Chemical Compound

Alla G. Kravets[1,2]([⊠]) [iD], Dmitry Gorbatenko[1], Natalia Salnikova[3],
Svyatoslav Birukov[4], and Elizaveta Smolova[3]

[1] Volgograd State Technical University, 28 Lenin Av., Volgograd 400005, Russia
AllaGKravets@yandex.ru, gorbatenko-2000@bk.ru
[2] Dubna State University, 19 Universitetskaya St., Dubna, Moscow Region 141982, Russia
[3] Volgograd Institute of Management – branch of the Russian Presidential Academy of National
Economy and Public Administration, 8 Gagarin St., Volgograd 400131, Russia
ns3112@mail.ru, elizavetasmolova5@gmail.com
[4] Volgograd State University, 100 Universitetskiy Av., Volgograd 400062, Russia
bir.slav@yandex.ru

Abstract. The paper describes the stages of developing a deep learning model-based method for identifying the pharmacological activity of a synthesized chemical compound. The implemented software is designed to prepare data for training, and testing, using a deep-learning neural network MPNN, obtaining the results of the neural network in the form of a concentration coefficient of half-maximal inhibition. The approaches and technologies used to solve the problems of predicting the activity of a synthesized substance are disclosed.

Keywords: Artificial Intelligence · Data Mining · MPNN · Neural Networks · Neural Network Architecture · Neural Network Models · Machine Learning · Deep Learning Models · Personalized Medicine · Drugs · Chemical Compounds

1 Introduction

Neural networks help to automate a large number of tasks, in particular, the task of primary selection of molecules in the development of new drugs [1]. From a practical point of view, the use of neural networks can reduce the time of drug development and reduce the cost of the process. From a theoretical point of view, the application and development of new neural network models in the field of analyzing the properties of new drugs allow the development of related areas, for example, personalized medicine, the development of which will help prescribe more effective therapy for HIV-infected and oncological patients [2]. These facts speak to the importance of research and development in this area.

In this regard, the purpose of this work is to develop a new method and software for determining the potential activity of the synthesized chemical compound. To achieve this goal, it was necessary to solve the following tasks:

© The Author(s), under exclusive license to Springer Nature Switzerland AG 2023
A. G. Kravets et al. (Eds.): CIT&DS 2023, CCIS 1909, pp. 49–63, 2023.
https://doi.org/10.1007/978-3-031-44615-3_4

- to analyze the methods for the development of new drugs and existing software;
- study modern concepts in the field of machine learning, in particular, in training deep neural networks;
- design a model and train it;
- develop and test a new software for identifying the pharmacological activity of the synthesized substance.

2 Methods for the New Drugs Development

The development of drugs is a complex and time-consuming process that requires the involvement of highly qualified specialists. As a result, pharmaceutical companies spend large amounts of money on the development of new drugs. On average, the development of a new drug costs 100 million dollars and 5–15 years. For complex diseases, the creation of at least some effective remedy requires even more time [3]. Such a long process of studying substances did not always exist. Until the 70s of the last century, drugs went on sale on the market after a small amount of research [4]. Possible side effects have not been studied practically. This was a fatal mistake and the consequences of this approach are known in history under the name "Thalidomide tragedy". The fact is that the drug "Thalidomide" had fatal consequences when taken by women at an early stage of pregnancy, this led to the birth of children with pathologies of the limbs and the central nervous system. After litigation, the laws of many countries regarding the release of new drugs have been revised and tightened.

To create a prototype of a new drug, it is necessary to determine the molecule of the active substance. The active substance of the drug is the most important part, it is it that solves the main task assigned to the drug. Pharmaceutical companies have huge databases of biologically active molecules. So out of 10,000–1,000,000 candidate molecules, only one usually becomes a real drug. And for all of them, it is necessary to conduct a primary selection.

To conduct such a selection, 2 methods are usually used: computer methods and natural screenings in the laboratory. Laboratory methods allow hundreds of thousands of test substances to be added to the wells of panels with a specially prepared test system. A variety of detectors record signals about the interaction of the test substance in each well with the target protein of the test system. Laboratory assistants need to carry out the synthesis of molecules, check the results of screening, and observe many factors of a natural experiment. Firstly, it is long and, as a result, it is expensive due to the cost of man-hours, but the high cost of preclinical testing includes not only the time of biochemists but also intermediate costs for expensive consumables, depreciation costs of expensive installations, etc. To determine the approximate activity of a substance, and its chemical properties, neural networks can be used, their use allows you to very quickly process large volumes of molecules of a potential drug from the company's database and obtain an assessment of the activity of the substance or specific properties of the molecule. This approach allows you to quickly understand the "outsiders" and not waste time or money on them.

3 Designing a MPNN-Based Method for Identifying the Pharmacological Activity of a Synthesized Chemical Compound

3.1 Description of a Graph Neural Network

To solve the problem of extracting data about a molecule from a string of canonical SMILES (Simplified Molecular Input Line Entry System) notation [5], which makes it possible to uniquely describe the composition and structure of a molecule in the form of a character string, we used a pre-trained neural network model with MPNN architecture. MPNN (Molecular Property Prediction with Message Passing Neural Network) is a graph neural network that uses the message-passing algorithm [6].

Graph neural networks are used to solve problems on graphs. First, you need to describe what a graph is. In a mathematical sense, a graph is a collection of two sets: a set of vertices or nodes and a set of their edges or connections. G = (V, E), where V are nodes and E are edges. This abstraction allows you to represent a set of related entities in the form of a graph. In this paper, graphs and all things related to them are considered as an application to machine learning methods. Here is a list of just some of the data that can be represented in the form of a graph, these are images, texts, molecules, a list of friends in social networks, tree structures, file systems, tabs in the interface of nested lists of categories.

The image graph consists of pixels as nodes, the edges do not carry special information, although they can be discussed below. The images represent the complete graph. A complete graph is distinguished by the presence of connections with all nodes. Texts and sentences in them can be represented as a directed graph, where nodes are words, and directed links point to the next word. With molecules, too, everything is very clear, it is convenient to visualize the branched structures of organic chemistry in the form of a graph. Of course, this (classical) interpretation of graphs has disadvantages, for example, their spatial incompleteness. That is, even in a case with a description of molecules using a graph represented only by nodes and edges, one cannot take into account how the molecule looks in a three-dimensional representation, and this is a very important aspect. When solving machine learning problems, there is a need to have more information about the object represented by the graph. And there is a solution to this, but first, you need to see how the graphs can be represented in a form convenient for the machine. There are two common approaches - graph adjacency matrix and adjacency list, more commonly using a matrix. To represent a graph with N vertices, you need an NxN adjacency matrix. The adjacency matrix is a matrix of rows and columns which are the nodes of the graph, if two nodes have a common edge, then the cell of their intersection is filled with one, otherwise with zero [7].

It is also possible to expand the information represented by the graph, for example, in accordance with each node, indicate the vector of features that are needed. Such vectors are called embeddings. By analogy with nodes, embeddings can also be assigned to graph edges. With the help of such vectors, you can describe a lot of information, for example, describe a molecule. The vertices of the graph are heavy atoms (not hydrogen), and bonds are electron pairs. Vertices can be embedded with information about the atom in this node, the number of hydrogen atoms associated with the heavy atom of the vertex, spatial arrangement, and angles. For bonds, you can set their type, electron density, etc. With this approach, each individual graph element has information specific to it, but its embeddings have no information about its environment. There are several approaches to solving this problem: linear transformations of matrices and propagation algorithms [8].

Linear transformations of matrices perform well until the original graph needs to be restored. Propagation algorithms are much more interesting for this class of problems. One of these algorithms is message passing. Its main idea is that each element of the graph has its own state (vector representation) and the algorithm updates this state at each iteration based on neighboring elements. Elements can be both vertices and edges. For edges of neighbors, the vertices of the ends of the edge. For neighbor vertices, vertices have a common connection with the current vertex. There is a general formula that uses an aggregation function that collects information about neighbors and an update (combination) function that uses the current state of the element and the aggregated state of the neighbors. First, the data is aggregated using the aggregation function, and then the update function is applied to it. Of course, the number of iterations should not be too large or too small. It must be such that the final representation is complete. With too many iterations, the states will begin to "overwrite" each other, which will lead to the loss of some information about the graph. Insufficient data will be incomplete.

3.2   MPNN-Based Method Development

The main stages of developed method are following (Fig. 1). The method receives a string in SMILES notation as input. In order to extract the necessary data from this formula, it is required to represent the molecules in the form of a graph, the nodes and edges of which are feature vectors. After converting a string into a feature graph, it is required to process the graph so that all the necessary information is taken into account in the final vector representation. To solve these problems, the neural network model presented in the paper uses a pre-trained model with the MPNN architecture. Molecular property prediction with message passing neural network is a common graph neural network architecture used to predict the properties of molecules. The message-passing algorithm is based on the concept of message passing between graph nodes, where each node represents an atom or a bond in a molecule. In MPNN networks, nodes are processed with an activation function that takes input and generates output. Each node then sends a message to its neighboring nodes based on a certain message-passing function. This process is repeated several times until all nodes have been processed. After that, information from all nodes is aggregated to obtain a global representation of the molecule. MPNN networks make it possible to predict various properties of molecules, such as binding energy, solubility, protein activity, and others.

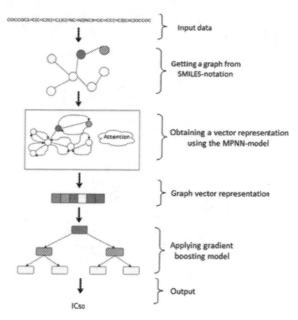

Fig. 1. Scheme of the designed MPNN-based method

In addition, the model uses the attention mechanism to calculate the most important properties of the molecule. The concept of the Transformer model is used to implement the attention mechanism.

The architecture of the Transformer model (Fig. 2) is a stack of encoders and decoders, each of which consists of several layers.

The encoder works as follows, the encoder receives embeddings as input, which are parsed inside its layers. Each encoder layer contains 2 sublayers: a self-attention sublayer, which allows the model to access different parts of the input sequence with different weights, given the context from all parts of the sequence, and a fully connected layer, which aggregates information.

In addition, a normalization layer is used to bring the dimensions of the output data to the required values.

The decoder, on the other hand, consists of sublayers similar to the encoder but differs from it by the addition of an attention sublayer, which is called the latent attention layer. It helps to process the sequence without the need to additionally analyze the elements before the section under consideration. Before embeddings are passed to the input of the encoder and decoder, they are converted into the trained embedding layers. Input embeddings are complemented by positional embeddings that reflect the position of each element in the sequence. During the inference process, the model applies self-attention to generate an output sequence using the context of the input sequence.

Thanks to the attention algorithm, each node in the graph is given weights according to its importance in predicting the target property. These weights are then used to aggregate information from all nodes using a pooling function.

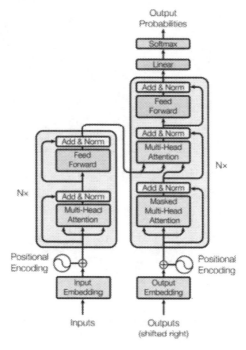

Fig. 2. Diagram of the Transformer model

The vector representation of the graph at the output of the MPNN subnet has a dimension of 128.

After obtaining the embedding of the molecule, it is passed to the gradient boosting model to predict the final value.

Gradient boosting builds a prediction on an ensemble of poorly trained models. This means that each individual model makes a small contribution to the predicted value and is not able to obtain the required accuracy. However, knowing the error of the previous model, the next model can learn to give an answer more accurately between the reference value and the value that the previous model produced. An important hyperparameter for training a gradient-boosting model is the depth of the tree. The depth of the tree is the number of models in the training ensemble. In addition, a large tree depth with a high complexity of the underlying algorithm can lead to retraining the final model. To prevent overfitting for gradient boosting, there is another hyperparameter – learning rate. At its core, the learning rate is a step of approximation of the predicted value, that is, the lower the learning rate, the less each model will contribute.

To assess the accuracy of the model, the following metrics were chosen: MAE (Mean Absolute Error), R2 (determination coefficient), and MSE (Mean Squared Error).

MAE and MSE will give an understanding of how the model's predictions differ from the real data. R2 allows you to evaluate how good the model is in principle, that is, for predicting data sets on which it was not trained.

3.3 Dataset Description

The dataset for training and testing the model was taken from the GDSC (genomic of drug sensitivity in cancer) database. The dataset itself, in addition to data on molecules and the IC50 coefficient, has data on gene expression inside, many drugs presented in this dataset have been tested on different cell lines, therefore they have different IC50 indicators since the model being developed does not use information about gene structures, it was necessary to clear the dataset of extraneous information. The final sample (Fig. 3) included 207 drugs.

Fig. 3. Data fragment for model training

4 Implementation of the Software for Identifying the Pharmacological Activity of the Synthesized Chemical Compound

4.1 Software Requirements

The developed software for identifying the pharmacological activity of the synthesized chemical compound should provide the ability to perform the following functions:

- input of string data into input fields;
- data entry in the form of a file from the input field;
- assessment of the activity of a chemical compound according to the chemical formula;
- creation of a graphical representation of a molecule of a chemical compound entered into the program through the input field;
- validation of user input based on SMILES notation rules;
- saving calculation results when entering data through the input field;
- deleting a settlement history record;
- saving the results of calculations in a CSV-file when entering through a file, the location of which the user can choose independently;
- saving molecules that have not passed validation to a CSV file, the location of which is determined by the user.

The input data is entered by the user through a graphical interface [9, 10].

The user can enter a string representation of the molecule in SMILES notation through the text entry field or specify the file from which to read data. For the correct operation of the program in the input data file in the CSV format, you must specify a column named "Drug", the column values must be strings in the SMILES notation. If this column is missing, a modal window will be displayed with an error.

4.2 Technologies Used in Software

The application is written entirely in Python. To implement the neural network, the DGL-Life and CatBoost libraries were used [11, 12]. DGL-Life is a library providing tools for graph-based machine learning in the domain of chemoinformatics [13]. It has a convenient interface for working with molecular graphs and provides functions for working with them, for example, to obtain information about atoms, bonds, and valency. In addition to utility functions for analysis, the library contains many deep learning models for solving various problems related to chemistry, such as predicting the properties of molecules, including the activity of biological molecules, predicting the properties of materials, etc. CatBoost provides a gradient boosting algorithm [14]. The main advantage of CatBoost is its ability to work with categorical features, which are often found in real-world machine-learning problems. This is achieved through the use of special methods for encoding categorical features and allows no using one-hot encoding. The library package has solutions that allow you to visualize the process of training a model, compare several parallel training models with visualization, and also save the best state of the model by discarding the part of the tree on which retraining occurred.

Numpy and Torch – these libraries inside the software are necessary for working with feature matrices and vector representations [15, 16].

RDKit is another library from the domain of chemoinformatics, RDKit is widely used in the pharmaceutical industry, academic research, and other areas where chemistry plays an important role [17]. In the project, it is necessary to obtain a molecule object from a string in SMILES notation, as well as to obtain an image of a molecule based on SMILES.

Tkinter is a framework for writing a graphical user interface for a software [18].

PyMongo is a library that allows you to work with the MongoDB DBMS [19].

MongoDB is a non-relational database management system needed to store the history of analyzed substances [20].

Table 1 provides a comparative description of technologies with advantages and disadvantages in the context of the project being developed.

Table 1. Assessment of technologies used

Technology	Advantage	Disadvantage
DGL-Life	Has models of suitable architecture, models trained on relevant data. Inside the library, there are utility functions necessary for solving the problem of obtaining the properties of atoms and their bonds. Using the library, you can fully solve the problem of obtaining embeddings without using other libraries, which has a positive effect on the number of dependencies and the final "weight" of the application	It would be better if the required model was trained on the GDCS dataset
Numpy	Allows you to simply solve the problem of transforming data arrays	Not detected
Torch	Solves the problem of working with tensors and is an industry standard	Not detected
RDKit	It has a complete set of necessary tools, which allows you to conveniently obtain images of the analyzed molecule. Also a popular choice	Can be challenging for novice users due to the amount of functionality and documentation
PyMongo	A very simple solution that allows you to completely solve the problem	The inability to create a model for the collection, imposes additional responsibility on the developer if the data in the documents is uniquely defined
MongoDB	In this project, there is no significant difference in the use of a DBMS or database type. Both relational and non-relational databases would do just as well	Not detected
Tkinter	A simple tool that makes it relatively easy to write very simple interfaces for applications running in the Python environment	Inability to pass data to the event handler. To write a large application or a small, one but with a low level of connectivity of components, you will have to write a large number of abstractions. There is no way to inspect the graphical interface, such as in a browser

4.3   The Architecture of the Software for Identifying the Pharmacological Activity of the Synthesized Chemical Compound

The software can be divided into several parts: a graphical representation, a neural network, services that describe the business logic of the application, and a database (Fig. 4).

At the initial stages of development, a model of interaction within the software was designed, reflected in the class diagram (Fig. 5).

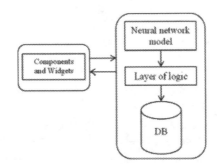

Fig. 4. General scheme of the software

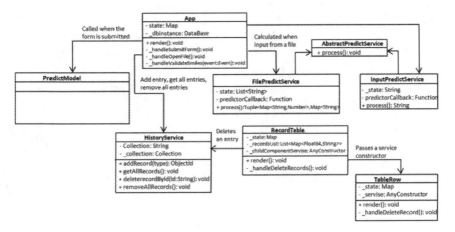

Fig. 5. Class diagram

For the most part, the project is written in the OOP style, but there are a number of utility functions that did not find any logical place, so it seemed superfluous to create a class for them.

The `PredictModel` class prepares data for the model and calculates the value of the IC50 coefficient.

In the constructor, the model is loaded, the reference to the class of which is placed in the `_mpnnModel` class field.

The class has a single public prediction method that calls the methods it needs.

The `_getDictFeatures` methods are needed to get a dictionary with embeddings received from the model. These vectors are obtained by a separate `_extractEmbedding` method.

To describe the operation of the `_extractEmbedding` method in Fig. 6 is a functional diagram.

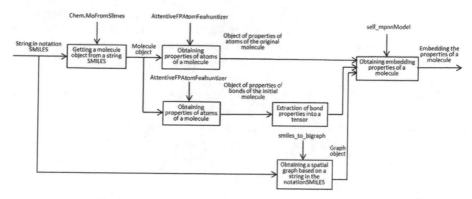

Fig. 6. Function diagram of the _extractEmbedding method

The diagram shows several previously undescribed entities – `AttentiveFPAtomFeaturizer` and `AttentiveFPBondFeaturizer`, these are classes from the `dgllife` package designed to extract specific characteristics of a molecule [21, 22].

An instance of the `AttentiveFPAtomFeaturizer` object contains one-hot encodings of the following parameters:

- information about the type of atom, all atoms of organic compounds are supported;
- number of degrees of freedom of an atom;
- formal charge of an atom;
- information about atom hybridization;
- whether the atom is aromatic;
- information about the number of hydrogen atoms;
- whether the atom is a chiral center of the molecule;
- information about the type of atom's chirality.

An instance of the `AttentiveFPBondFeaturizer` object contains one-hot encodings of the following parameters:

- information about the type of connection;
- communication configuration information;
- whether the connection is rung;
- information about the stereo link configuration.

Also, in the prediction method, to work with the gradient boosting model, it is necessary to convert the dictionary into a DataFrame object from the Pandas library. This task is handled by the `_dictToDataframe` method.

It was possible not to create a separate method, but immediately write embedding in the DataFrame, but the decision was made because the dictionary is a structure for data exchange within the project, as an alternative to JSON. If the functionality of the software is expanded in the future, then it is much more convenient to operate with the results of the embedding extraction operation in a dictionary than in a DataFrame, this is the contract of the project.

After the transformation, you need to pass the resulting DataFrame to the gradient boosting model and get the result.

Initialization of an instance of the CatBoostRegressor class and loading of the previously trained model occurs in the predict method of the PredictModel class. It is worth noting that an instance of the Pool object is passed to the CatBoostRegressor method. This is a special data type for CatBoost, it is preferred to use it, and it also offers more powerful tooling.

To obtain the optimal model, hyperparameters were selected for the depth of the gradient boosting model, the learning rate, and the loss function. The selection was made empirically, for this the code of the method for converting a dictionary into a DataFrame was written. The result of code execution is shown in Fig. 7.

index	Loss Function	Iterations	Learning Rate	MSE	MAE	R2
model_0	RMSE	100	0.02	5.648709836204983%5	2.8752373281053332	0.11855832790229703
model_1	RMSE	500	0.02	5.30552397810945%8	1.98817130774818%8	0.17182908232062396
model_2	RMSE	1000	0.02	5.30552397810945%8	1.9081713077481835	0.17182908232062396
model_3	RMSE	100	0.15	5.03759137888803%3	1.957467839749614%7	0.213653136290399873
model_4	RMSE	500	0.15	5.03759137888803%3	1.957467839749614%7	0.213653136290399873
model_5	RMSE	1000	0.15	5.03759137888803%3	1.957467839749614%7	0.213653136290399873
model_6	RMSE	100	0.2	5.02179988889996%79	1.87499904309357906	0.21615181215781634
model_7	RMSE	500	0.2	5.02179988889996%79	1.87499904309357906	0.21615181215781634
model_8	RMSE	1000	0.2	5.02179988889996%79	1.87499904309357906	0.21615181215781634
model_9	RMSE	100	0.25	5.17314829996689%76	3.826680916412335%16	0.1924911159698%781
index	Loss Function	Iterations	Learning Rate	MSE	MAE	R2
model_20	MAE	500	0.15	5.18222898543651885	1.83893740798855788	0.19103758628950703208
model_21	MAE	1000	0.15	5.18222898543651885	1.83893740798855788	0.19103758628950703208
model_22	MAE	1500	0.15	5.18222898543651885	1.83893740798855788	0.19103758628950703208
model_23	MAE	100	0.25	3.968623882957381	1.64792470773310877	0.380351447898303569
model_24	MAE	500	0.25	3.968623882957381	1.64792470773310877	0.380351447898303569
model_25	MAE	1000	0.25	3.968623882957381	1.64792470773310877	0.380351447898303569
model_26	MAE	1500	0.25	3.968623882957381	1.64792470773310877	0.380351447898303569
model_27	MAE	100	0.35	3.35281166430579%4	1.59780982740%9721	0.47866401761188887
model_28	MAE	500	0.35	3.35281166430579%4	1.59780982740%9721	0.47866401761188887
model_29	MAE	1000	0.35	3.35281166430579%4	1.59780982740%9721	0.47866401761188887
index	Loss Function	Iterations	Learning Rate	MSE	MAE	R2
model_30	MAE	1500	0.35	3.35281166430579%4	1.59780982740%9721	0.47866401761188887
model_31	MAE	100	0.45	3.3529422976490%757	1.589084906651450%97	0.47661978480247014
model_32	MAE	500	0.45	3.3529422976490%757	1.589084906651450%97	0.47661978480247014
model_33	MAE	1000	0.45	3.3529422976490%757	1.589084906651450%97	0.47661978480247014
model_34	MAE	1500	0.45	3.3529422976490%757	1.589084906651450%97	0.47661978480247014

Fig. 7. The result of the selection of model hyperparameters

According to the data presented in Fig. 7, it can be seen that model_30 was able to achieve the best accuracy. The result was influenced by the loss function of the mean absolute error (MAE), as well as depth hyperparameters equal to 1500 decision models and a learning rate equal to 0.35. The mean absolute error loss function allows you to penalize the model for large deviations, which is important in a specific regression problem.

5   Testing the Software for Identifying the Pharmacological Activity of the Synthesized Chemical Compound

5.1   Functional Testing

For functional testing, manual tests were carried out for compliance with the functions that the system should perform. All testing steps were sequentially completed: launching the application, entering data in the input field, entering data through a CSV file, selecting a file for entering data through a CSV file, calculating a target indicator when entering through an input field, calculating a target indicator when entering through a file, transition to viewing history, deleting an entry from history. Thus, all the required functions have been implemented and tested, as a result of which no errors or inconsistencies have been identified.

5.2   Fault Tolerance Testing

Fault tolerance testing consisted of reproducing edge cases of data entry.

In the process of testing fault tolerance, 3 tests were carried out. Their description is given below.

Test 1. Trying to enter a random string in the input field:

- when an invalid SMILES string is entered, the message "Invalid SMILES string" appears in the interface, and the calculation start button becomes inactive.

    Test 2. Transferring a CSV file without the necessary "Drug" column:

- when transferring a file without a "Drug" column, a warning window appears with the inscription "Drug column is missing".

    Test 3. There is an erroneous line in the data set or a line that is not correct for SMILES notation:

- when calculations are completed after processing the results of valid chemical compounds, a file system manager window appears to write erroneous data to a CSV file specified by the user.

6   Conclusion

As a result of the work, a software for predicting the activity of the synthesized chemical compound was developed, which is capable of working with molecules of antitumor drugs and predicting the IC50 index. A graphical interface was implemented for the software, in the form of a desktop application, which allows you to get IC50 predictions for a single molecule and get its structural formula in the form of a picture, as well as transfer molecules in the form of a CSV file and receive a CSV file with predicted values of the drug type – prediction.

The developed software is useful for rapid assessment of the suitability of molecules in further studies on the synthesis of new drug compounds.

There are two directions for improving the software. To improve the prediction accuracy of the model, it is necessary to implement a multitasking deep learning model that will work not only with the chemical properties of the molecule but also take into account genomic information. This will allow not only to improve the accuracy of the model prediction but also to use it within the framework of solving a class of personalized medicine problems, which is a promising and intensively developing direction. The second direction of improving the information system can be the method of delivering the model to the user, it is supposed to transfer the model and business logic of the application to a remote server. This will allow using the capabilities of the information system on various platforms. Transferring the main components of the application to a remote server will allow you to flexibly change the capabilities of the application due to the microservice architecture.

References

1. Al-Gunaid, M.A., et al.: Analysis of drug sales data based on machine learning methods. In: 2018 International Conference on System Modeling & Advancement in Research Trends (SMART), pp. 32–38. Moradabad, India (2018). https://doi.org/10.1109/SYSMART.2018. 8746968
2. Salnikova, N.A., Lempert, B.A., Lempert, M.B.: Integration of methods to quantify the quality of medical care in the automated processing systems of medical and economic information. In: Communications in Computer and Information Science (CIT&DS 2015), vol. 535, pp. 307–319 (2015)
3. Babaria, K., Ambegaokar, S., Das, S., Palivela, H.: Algorithms for ligand based virtual screening in drug discovery. In: 2015 International Conference on Applied and Theoretical Computing and Communication Technology (iCATccT), pp. 862–866 (Oct 2015). https://doi.org/10.1109/ICATCCT.2015.7457004
4. Kravets, A.G., et al.: J. Phys. Conf. Ser. **1015**, 032073 (2018)
5. SMILES strings explained for beginners. [Electronic resource]. Access mode: URL: https://archive.epa.gov/med/med_archive_03/web/html/smiles.html, Date of the application 25 May 2023
6. Message-passing neural network (MPNN) for molecular property prediction. [Electronic resource]. Access mode: URL: https://keras.io/examples/graph/mpnn-molecular-graphs/, Date of the application 25 May 2023
7. Loshmanov, V., Petraevskiy, V., Fantrov, P.: Methodology for preclinical laboratory research using machine learning. In: Kravets, A.G., Shcherbakov, M., Parygin, D., Groumpos, P.P. (eds.) Creativity in Intelligent Technologies and Data Science. CIT&DS 2021. Communications in Computer and Information Science, vol 1448. Springer, Cham (2021). https://doi.org/10.1007/978-3-030-87034-8_45
8. Andreev, A., Egunov, V.: Solving of eigenvalue and singular value problems via modified householder transformations on shared memory parallel computing systems. In: Supercomputing: 5th Russian Supercomputing Days, RuSCDays 2019, Moscow, Russia, September 23–24, 2019, Revised Selected Papers 5, pp. 131–151. Springer International Publishing (2019)
9. Kravets, A.G., Salnikova, N.A., Mikhnev, I.P., Orudjev, N.Y., Poplavskaya, O.V.: Web portal for project management in electronics design software development. In: International Seminar on Electron Devices Design and Production (SED 2019), Proceedings, p. 8798472 (2019)
10. Lempert, L.B., Kravets, A.G., Lempert, B.A., Poplavskaya, O.V., Salnikova, N.A.: Development of the intellectual decision-making support method for medical diagnostics in psychiatric practice. In: 2018 9th International Conference on Information, Intelligence, Systems and Applications (IISA), pp. 1–5. Zakynthos, Greece (2018). https://doi.org/10.1109/IISA. 2018.8633671

11. DGL-LifeSci: Bringing Graph Neural Networks to Chemistry and Biology. [Electronic resource]. Access mode: URL: https://lifesci.dgl.ai/, Date of the application 25 May 2023
12. Fast Gradient Boosting with CatBoost. [Electronic resource]. Access mode: URL: https://habr.com/ru/companies/otus/articles/527554/, Date of the application 25 May 2023
13. Chemoinformatics and molecular modeling. [Electronic resource]. Access mode: URL: https://kpfu.ru/chemistry/abiturientu/040401-mag-chemistry/profiles/hemoinformatika, Date of the application 25 May 2023
14. Solving Machine Learning Problems Using the Gradient Boosting Algorithm. [Electronic resource]. Access mode: URL: https://proglib.io/p/reshaem-zadachi-mashinnogo-obuche niya-s-pomoshchyu-algoritma-gradientnogo-bustinga-2021-11-25, Date of the application 25 May 2023
15. Numpy vs PyTorch for Linear Algebra. [Electronic resource]. Access mode: URL: https://ric kwierenga.com/blog/machine%20learning/numpy-vs-pytorch-linalg.html, Date of the application 25 May 2023
16. PyTorch and Fully Connected Neural Networks. [Electronic resource]. Access mode: URL: https://mipt-stats.gitlab.io/courses/ad_fivt/nn_simple_examples.html, Date of the application 25 May 2023
17. Getting Started with the RDKit in Python. [Electronic resource]/ Access mode: URL: https://rdkit.org/docs/GettingStartedInPython.html, Date of the application 25 May 2023
18. Tkinter – Python interface to Tcl/Tk. [Electronic resource]. Access mode: URL: https://docs.python.org/3/library/tkinter.html, Date of the application 25 May 2023
19. What is PyMongo? Getting Started with Python and MongoDB. [Electronic resource]. Access mode: URL: https://www.mongodb.com/languages/python/pymongo-tutorial, Date of the application 25 May 2023
20. MongoDB: what is this DBMS, pros, cons, pitfalls. [Electronic resource]. Access mode: URL: https://skillbox.ru/media/code/mongodb-chto-eto-za-subd-plyusy-minusy-pod vodnye-kamni/, Date of the application 25 May 2023
21. AttentiveFPAtomFeaturizer. [Electronic resource]. Access mode: URL: https://lifesci.dgl.ai/generated/dgllife.utils.AttentiveFPAtomFeaturizer.html, Date of the application 25 May 2023
22. AttentiveFPBondFeaturizer. [Electronic resource]/ Access mode: URL: https://giters.com/awslabs/dgl-lifesci/issues/123, Date of the application 25 May 2023

Hybrid Cyber-Physical System QUIK-LUA-Random Forest for Trading on MoEx

Nikolay Lomakin[1]([envelope]), Olga Golodova[2], Maxim Maramygin[3], Tatyana Kuzmina[4], Oksana Minaeva[1], and Uranchimeg Tudevdagva[5]

[1] Volgograd State Technical University, Volgograd, Russia
tel19033176642@yahoo.com
[2] Volgograd State University, Volgograd, Russia
[3] Ural State University of Economics, Ekaterinburg, Russia
[4] Russian Economic University. G.V. Plekhanov, Moscow, Russia
[5] Technische Universität Chemnitz, Chemnitz, Germany

Abstract. The article discusses the theoretical foundations of hybrid cyber-physical systems as complex systems in the context of the digitalization of the economy. The relevance of the study is due to the fact that there is a rapid increase in the use of intelligent technologies in all areas of both the real sector of the economy and in the financial sector. The scientific novelty lies in the fact that, in contrast to the previously used methods of algorithmic exchange trading, a new one has been proposed that is fundamentally different from those used previously. It combines both a system for sending orders, functioning on the basis of logical algorithms, and an intelligent system based on machine learning "Random Forest", which forms a forecast of the closing price of a financial instrument, the joint operation of which, in the process of responding to market changes, ensures a decision on buying/selling in automatic stand-alone mode, thus enabling efficient speculative "intraday" trading. The practical significance lies in the fact that the application of this development provides an increase in competitiveness in exchange trading due to highly profitable speculative operations on an hourly timeframe based on an accurate forecast. The implemented software has a Certificate of Rospatent for a computer program No. 2022662398 dated 06/22/2022.

Keywords: Hybrid cyber-physical system · Random Forest machine learning model · exchange trading · speculative operations · high profitability · digital economy

1 Introduction

The purpose of the work is to form a hybrid cyber-physical system that would consist of at least two systems of intellectual support for making a decision to buy / sell an exchange-traded asset on the Moscow Exchange (MoEx) using the Quick trading terminal. Firstly, which would be able, reacting to market changes based on the processing of the five-dimensional vector of the hourly candlestick of the SIS3 futures contract, to calculate

© The Author(s), under exclusive license to Springer Nature Switzerland AG 2023
A. G. Kravets et al. (Eds.): CIT&DS 2023, CCIS 1909, pp. 64–79, 2023.
https://doi.org/10.1007/978-3-031-44615-3_5

the predicted values of the futures closing price. Secondly, send the required order to the exchange to buy / sell a futures contract, using the function of placing stop orders, in order to minimize the risk of losses and increase the profitability of speculative trading.

To achieve this goal, the following tasks were set and solved:

– explore the theoretical foundations for the formation of hybrid cyber-physical systems, as well as trends in the development of Internet trading automation tools on the MoEx;
– to form an intelligent subsystem that, reacting to market changes based on the processing of the time series of hourly candles of the IS3 futures contract, could cyclically calculate the forecast of the futures closing price using the values of the five-dimensional vector (Ps, etc.) and return the forecast value of the required parameter the second subsystem;
– to create algorithms for the subsystem, which, taking from the first subsystem the changing forecast values of the closing price, comparing its value with the actual closing price, firstly, would return a buy / sell signal and send an order to the stock exchange to the Quick trading terminal, secondly, to minimize financial risk, it would make a decision and place stop orders for take profit and stop loss.
– to develop a controller module responsible for the success of the entire process from the timely automatic start / stop of the system, to control the operation and ensure uninterrupted operation, by restoring the Internet connection.
– to develop a module from the generated sensors-parsers responsible for controlling the number of traded securities, the balance of funds on the brokerage account;
– to develop a module (risk module) responsible for the security and safety of the login and password, as well as for performing other functions.

As known, financial risk is a risk that is associated with the probability of losing financial resources, for example, cash. With the development of digital money circulation, the problem of minimizing financial risks is of particular importance. Identification, calculation and minimization of financial risks are an important integral part of working with financial assets, especially in conditions of market uncertainty [1].

Market uncertainty can be expressed in the form of certain conditions in which the decision-making process takes place related to the use of financial assets, the price changes of which are difficult to predict and evaluate. Incomplete or lack of information is common, especially in the field of economics and finance. The nature of market uncertainty is such that it cannot be completely eliminated, but it can be reduced.

According to experts, the relevance of the issue of reducing the financial risk of trading in exchange-traded assets will only increase over time. It is very important to use neural network analysis to predict the closing price of an exchange-traded asset based on the processing of a time series of Japanese candlesticks and trading volume based on the use of the Random Forest Regressor deep learning model in order to provide support for making managerial decisions on buying / selling when conducting speculative operations.

In the course of the study, the relationship between factorial signs (purchase price, maximum, minimum, closing price, trading volume) was revealed, a hybrid cyber-physical system was formed, consisting of two subsystems of intellectual support for making a decision to buy/sell an exchange-traded asset on the MoEx using a trading terminal Quick. Hybrid FSC is capable of responding to market changes based on signals taken by sensor modules, and subsequent processing of the five-dimensional vector of the hourly candlestick of the futures contract SIU3, to return a highly accurate forecast of the value of the closing price of the futures based on the generated Random Forest Regressor machine learning model. Then the process continues in the "LUA-QUICK" subsystem, where, based on the developed logical algorithms, a decision is made to buy / sell an asset - placing an order "long" - to buy, or "short" - to sell. Moreover, in order to minimize the risk and increase the efficiency of trading, the "Risk-module" of the system places take-profit and stop-limit orders, which operate in a cycle within the hourly timeframe, each time they are placed again and again, if a sharp movement in the price of an asset on the exchange breaks stop order levels.

Studies show that modern artificial intelligence technologies are being used all over the world more and more widely. So, for example, Bataev A.V., Gorovoy A.A. and Denis Z. in the process of conducting a comparative analysis of the use of neural network technologies in the whole world and in Russia, found that the most important prerequisites for the widespread use of artificial intelligence are the growing processes of large-scale development of information and communication technologies, and a sharp increase in the volume of processed information, as well as the development of productive capacities computers in data processing centers and other factors [2].

Some authors Bril A. and others [3], Demidova S. with colleagues [4] and Ilin I. [5] note that there are features of the processes of segmentation and positioning in the neural network economy. Researchers come to the conclusion that the features of segmentation and positioning processes in the neural network economy are largely due to factors such as: applied computing, computers and business.

Practice shows that the use of artificial intelligence systems is interconnected with digitalization processes in all areas, including financial ones. One of the important aspects of digitalization, according to Goncharova N., is the development of methods for providing financial services to people with dementia in the context of digitalization: partnership between citizens and the state [6].

Considering the problems of further development of the financial sector, it should be noted the achievements in the use of blockchain technology for customer identification by financial institutions. For example, Bataev A., Plotnikova E., Lukin G. and Sviridenko M. evaluated the economic efficiency of the blockchain for identifying customers by financial institutions. Based on the study conducted by the authors, it was revealed that the financial sector is one of the drivers of the digitalization of the economy, which led to the emergence of fintech, an innovative industry based on the merger of modern digital and financial technologies [7].

During the collaboration of efforts, the authors Lomakin N., Lukyanov G. and others developed a neural network model that made it possible to predict profits at enterprises in the real sector of the economy in conditions of market uncertainty and risk. The analysis showed that the financial risk of receiving income of enterprises (sigma) in chronological sequence increased unsustainably from the level of 0.4 from the second quarter of 2015 to a maximum of 3.1 with subsequent consolidation up to 2.8 billion rubles, while its average value was 2.09 billion rubles [8].

Many scientists, such as Janusz Kacprzyk, note that the development of Industry 5.0 technologies covers almost all areas of cyber-physical systems, autonomous systems, sensor networks, control systems, energy systems, automotive systems, biological systems, vehicles, network and connected vehicles, aerospace systems, automation, manufacturing, smart grids, non-linear systems, power systems, robotics, social systems, systems in the economy and other systems [9].

The prototype of the developed hybrid cyber-physical system was the results of research presented in the work by a team of authors led by Lomakin N [10].

A group of authors headed by Klachek P. M. a promising approach is proposed, which is interdisciplinary in nature, since it is on the border of the following areas: hybrid intelligent systems, synergistic artificial intelligence, neuro- and psychophysiology, philosophy, cybernetics, economic and mathematical modeling, etc. [11] The authors, based on the study of the fundamentals of the structural organization of functional hybrid intelligent decision-making systems designed to solve hard-to-formalizable production and economic tasks, proposed a new cognitive approach in the development of integration and effective management of formalized and weakly formalized knowledge in decision-making systems.

In [12–14], the authors considered in detail the main features and formal foundations of complex weakly formalizable multicomponent economic systems (MES) and the corresponding difficult to formalize production and economic problems.

The main goal of the research is the development of effective methods and the search for applied tools for improving the efficiency of intelligent information processing and management systems, namely, computer decision support systems that are used when performing hard-to-formalize production and economic tasks based on functional hybrid intelligent decision-making systems (FHIDMS). Such systems, as practice has shown, are able to successfully solve complex hard-to-formalizable production and economic problems and develop solutions of appropriate quality in various subject areas.

Thus, it becomes possible to set the order on the cause-and-effect and time scales when solving the initial heterogeneous problem-system, which leads to the possibility of obtaining some new, system-forming property of the system, called emergence (emergence, appearance of a new one).

For an inhomogeneous task-system, with the variability of its composition and structure, the method-system for solving it is constructed over a certain interconnected set of niches - autonomous operators [13, 14], and leads to the creation of FHIDMS as systems that have an information exchange architecture and function in inhomogeneous space of states described by the vector $(m, x) \in M * \Re^n$.

The transition between the discrete states m_i and m_j is triggered when the continuous state x reaches the set j_{ij} in R^n. Let us define the hybrid trajectory of the system behavior based on the initial discrete state of the hybrid system, m_0, and the corresponding transition set J_{m0m1} (J_{01}). However, in the case. if $x \notin J_{m_0m_1}$, then the functioning of the system will be determined by vector f (m_0, x(t)), based on $\dot{x}(t) = f(m_0, x(t))$.

Thus, if the behavior of the system at time t_1, $x(t_1) \in J_{m_0 m_1}$ changes to m_1, then the hybrid trajectory of the system behavior will be determined based on $\dot{x}(t) = f(m_0.x(t))$, with the initial condition $x(t_1) = x_1$ and output signal $O_1 = \omega(m_1)$. It is customary to call such functioning a hybrid simulation process [13].

An example of the organization of a hybrid simulation process in FHIDMS in a polymorphic mode is shown below (Fig. 1).

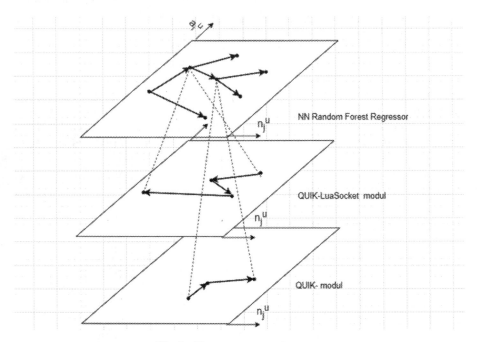

Fig. 1. Heterogeneous task-system

The general formal scheme of work of the GIM MES can be expressed by the following equation.

$$\dot{m}_{GVM}^a \big|^{Ga} = < M^u, M^h, T_{rc}, I^{GVI} >, \tag{1}$$

where, $M^u = \left\{ m_1^u, \ldots, m_{N_u}^u \right\}$ - is the set of basic model structures;

$M^h = \left\{ m_1^h, \ldots, m_{N_h}^h \right\}$ - many complementary model structures.

$(\forall_i^u \exists M^h = \left\{ m_1^h, \ldots, m_{N_h}^h \right\}, i = 1, \ldots, N_\Pi, \forall_i (N_h = vary), m_1^u \in M^u);$

T_{rc} - hybrid strategy table;

I^{GVI} - interpreter representing four processes:

$$I^{GVI} = < I^{G1}, I^{G2}, I^{G3}, I^{G4} >, \tag{2}$$

where, I^{G1} - the process of studying the hybrid correlation of basic and complementary model structures;

I^{G2}- selection process in accordance with Tg from the GVI hybrid computational intelligence method;

I^{G3}- development process in accordance with the GVI method of a hybrid computational model;

I^{G4}- the process of selecting or developing a hybrid computing scheme.

This approach allows for fast transition to the automated process of FHIDMS development based on multi-agent systems (MAS). On Fig. 2 shows the FHIDMS architecture based on MAS.

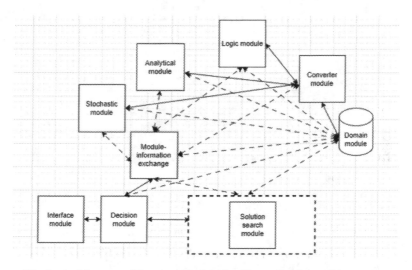

Fig. 2. Architecture of functional hybrid intelligent decision-making system

The architecture of the innovative FHIDMS with the technological process of trading in a futures contract on the MoEx is presented below (Fig. 3).

There are Intelligent monitoring system, Analysis Subsystem, Subsystem for storing, processing, extracting and presenting information, Decision Subsystem, Dual control subsystem, Optimal Control Subsystem and Complex of hybrid computing models in the architecture of the innovative FHIDMS.

The decision-making subsystem, which performs the functions of an exchange trading bot, is implemented software, since it has a Certificate of Rospatent [15].

Practice shows that among the main directions of development of exchange market technologies, one can single out the use of artificial intelligence both in separate autonomous models and as part of cyber-physical systems.

The conducted research makes it possible to obtain an increase in knowledge that allows to close the scientific gap regarding the influence of factors influencing the complex processes of forming the price of an exchange asset in modern conditions. At the same time, the scientific approach is based on the use of the capabilities underlying the functioning of hybrid cyber-physical systems, the optimization of the flow of the exchange trading process includes the use of both a multifactor correlation-regression

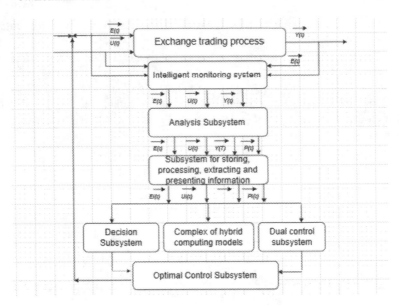

Fig. 3. The architecture of the innovative FHIDMS

model and the hyperparameter optimization method in the Random Forest deep learning model.

Trading was carried out using a combat brokerage account on the MoEx with a trading instrument futures contract SiU3 using the QUIK trading terminal (Fig. 4). QUIK terminal is widely used in exchange trading on the MoEx.

Fig. 4. Trading of futures contract SiU3 on the QUIK terminal

2 Materials and Methods

In the presented work, such research methods were used as: monographic, analytical, statistical, multivariate correlation-regression model, as well as the artificial intelligence system Random forest deep learning model, which, together with the LUA-QUICK socket, were included in the Hybrid Cyber-Physical System.

The dataset obtained from the five-dimensional vector through the LUA socket for training the deep learning neural network model "Random Forest Regressor" in order to obtain the predicted value of the closing price of the SIU3 futures is presented below (Table 1).

Table 1. The dataset obtained from the five-dimensional vector through the LUA socket

	OpenPrice	HighPrice	LowPrice	ClosePrice	Volume	target
0	88,952	89,005	88,819	88,859	28,520	88,859
1	88,237	89,097	88,160	88,959	178,429	88,959
2	88,679	88,790	88,098	88,234	120,404	88,234
3	88,679	88,679	88,679	88,679	109	88,679
...	...	...	...	...	...	...
2116	63,475	63,609	63,430	63,430	347	63,430
2117	63,537	63,656	63,433	63,470	460	63,470
2118	63,997	63,997	63,810	63,810	60	63,810

3 Results

Approbation of the proposed solutions was carried out on the example of the creation of the FHIDMS management, business processes of an exchange trading bot. As a result of the study, a hybrid cyber-physical system was formed. With its help, predicted values of the closing price of a futures contract on an hourly timeframe were obtained. Predictive values were obtained in two different ways:

1. based on a correlation-regression model followed by the formation of a multivariate regression equation;
2. deep learning neural model "Random forest regression".

3.1 Analysis Subsystem. Neural Network DL Model "Random Forest Regressor"

The analysis subsystem includes the neural network model of deep learning "Random Forest Regressor" (DL RF). The neural network graph is shown below (Fig. 5).

The following parameters of the SiU3 tool are included in the model: date – Date in the format "yy.mm.dd"; OpenPrice- Opening price, rub.; HighPrice - maximum price,

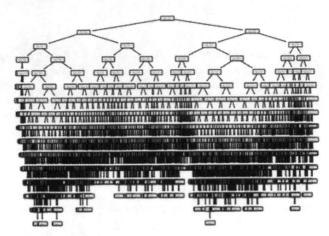

Fig. 5. One of the decision trees obtained from the ensemble of trees of the DL RF model

rub.; LowPrice - minimum price, rub.; ClosePrice - Close price, rub.; Volume - Trading volume, thousand rubles. The original dataset data was split into train and test sets using Scikit-Learn's model_selection library, which contains the train_test_split method, which we use to randomly split the data into train and test sets. For this, the following code is executed.

```
X = dataset.drop(['target'], axis=1)
y = dataset['target']
from sklearn.model_selection import train_test_split
X_train, X_test, y_train, y_test = train_test_split(X, y,
test_size=0.20)
from sklearn.tree import DecisionTreeRegressor
regressor = DecisionTreeRegressor()
regressor.fit(X_train, y_train)
import pandas as pd
import numpy as np
import matplotlib.pyplot as plt
```

4   Optimal Control Subsystem

The optimal control subsystem is responsible for the selection of certain parameters that ensure the effectiveness of the hybrid cyber-physical system as a whole. For example, in the Analytical subsystem (Random Forest), hyperparameters are set by random selection. To train the Random Forest model, combinations of hyperparameter settings in the GridSearchCV library were used.

```
# 1. Model
#2. Hyperparameter Grid
from sklearn.model_selection import GridSearchCV
model = RandomForestRegressor()
param_grid = {
    "n_estimators": [5, 10, 50],
    "criterion": ["squared_error", "absolute_error",
"poisson"],
    "max_depth" : [2, 5, 10],
}
gs = GridSearchCV(model, param_grid, scor-
ing='neg_median_absolute_error', cv=3)
gs.fit(X_train, y_train)
```

Thus, for training and subsequent assessment of the quality of forecasts of the DL RF model, the following hyperparameters were chosen:

1. Number of decision trees in the ensemble ("n_estimators"): 5, 10, 50.
2. Criteria for assessing the accuracy of the model ("criterion"): "squared_error", "absolute_error", "poisson".
3. Maximum depth of trees ("max_depth"): 2, 5, 10.

The total number of combinations used in the learning process was $27 = 3 \times 3 \times 3$.

Studying the documentation of the Scikit-learn 0.24.0 method revealed that the product developers have proposed a wide range of methods.

During operation, the RF model can generate an arbitrarily large number of DT models (decision trees) that differ in the composition of input parameters and the level of correlation between factors. Certain approaches that were laid down in an earlier study were used in the present model [6].

The results of assessing the quality of the model are presented below (Table 2).

Table 2. Results of assessing the quality of the model

	The share of the test sample in the dataset, 0.20	The share of the test sample in the dataset, 0,30
Model Quality Options	MAE = 48.0832222137942 MAX = 155.3113764362634 R2 = -0.25736547939940047	MAE = 49.014007518796994 MAX = 162.523 R2 = -0.33819286737869647

MAE is a metric that tells us the average absolute difference between the predicted values and the actual values in the dataset.

$$MAE = \frac{1}{n} * \sum |y_i - \hat{y}_i|, \qquad (3)$$

where: Σ is the symbol that means "sum";

y_i - observed value for the i-th observation;
$y\hat{}_i$ - predicted value for the i-th observation;
n -is the sample size.
The lower the MAE, the better the model fits the dataset.
Mean Squared Error is used when it is necessary to emphasize large errors and choose a model that gives less large errors. Large error values become more noticeable due to the quadratic dependence. MSE is calculated using the formula:

$$MSE = \frac{1}{n} * \sum_1^n \left(y_{i-}\hat{y}_i\right)^2, \tag{4}$$

where: n - the number of observations on which the model is built and the number of forecasts,
    y_i - the actual value of the dependent variable for the i-th observation,
    y^_i is the value of the dependent variable predicted by the model.
Standard deviation (RMSD) or standard error (RMSE) otherwise R2 is a commonly used measure of the difference between values (sample or population values) predicted by a model or estimator and observed values. RMSD is the square root of the second sampling point of differences between predicted values and observed values. Root Mean Squared Error is calculated simply as the square root of the MSE:

$$RMSE = \sqrt{\frac{1}{n} * \sum_1^n \left(y_{i-}\hat{y}_i\right)^2}, \tag{5}$$

Data analysis allows us to conclude that the forecast is highly accurate, since the level of the average absolute error of the model does not exceed the value of 49.01 rubles, and the level of the maximum absolute error does not exceed the value of 162.52 rubles, while MSE, or R2 is -0.25736547939940047 for the option in which the share of the test sample in the dataset was 0.20.

5   Correlation-Regression Model

The correlation matrix of paired correlation coefficients was calculated using the Pandas, Numpy, Seaborn, and Sklearn libraries. The matrix of paired correlation coefficients has the form. (Table 3).

The coefficient of determination R2 = 1.0 shows that 100% of the total change in the closing price due to the influence of factors included in the model. The estimation of the statistical significance of the regression parameters was examined using Student's t-statistics. We put forward the hypothesis H0 about the statistically insignificant difference of indicators from zero and determine the Student's criterion. In fact, the value of the t-statistic exceeds the tabular values, so the hypothesis H0 is rejected, i.e. the event is non-random, non-zero and statistically significant. Fisher's F-test evaluates the reliability of the regression equation as a whole, as well as the tightness of the links.

Table 3. Correlation matrix

	OpenPrice	HighPrice	LowPrice	ClosePrice	Volume
OpenPrice	1.000000	0.999593	0.999567	0.999339	0.042092
HighPrice	0.999593	1.000000	0.999284	0.999656	0.055629
LowPrice	0.999567	0.999284	1.000000	0.999633	0.025516
ClosePrice	0.999339	0.999656	0.999633	1.000000	0.040879
Volume	0.042092	0.055629	0.025516	0.040879	1.000000
target	0.999339	0.999656	0.999633	1.000000	0.040879

The actual value of Fisher's F-test, indicates an acceptable level of statistical significance of the regression equation.

By substituting the values of the factorial features obtained from the last candle of the year into the equation, the program returns the predictive value of the resulting feature for the next time frame (Fig. 6). Comparative prediction accuracy is presented in Table 4.

Fig. 6. Regression Equation Coefficients

Table 4. Comparative prediction accuracy

	Average Pc	DL RF-model		Correlation - Regression model	
		Error, rub	Error, %	Error, rub	Error, %
MAE	66,665.31	48.083	0.072126	4979.765	−7.4698
MAX	66,665.31	155.31	0.23297	4979.765	−7.4698
Average value	66,665.31	101.6965	0.15255	4979.765	−7.4698

The forecast error obtained using the correlation-regression model is an order of magnitude higher than the level of the forecast error obtained by the DL RF Model, the maximum error of which does not exceed 155.31 rubles, or 0.23%.

It is important to develop a decision-making subsystem based on the QUIK-LUA socket and the trading bot.

5.1   Decision Subsystem. QUIK-LUA Socket and Bot for Trading

QUIK-LUA Socket
QUIK-LUA socket plays an important role in the operation of a hybrid cyber-physical system. Lua Socket is a library of Lua extensions that consists of two parts:

1. C core that provides support for the TCP and UDP transport layers, and
2. set of Lua modules that provide support for functions needed in applications that work with the Internet. The most commonly used client protocols include SMTP (for sending e-mail), HTTP (for accessing the WWW), and FTP (for downloading and uploading files). They provide a very natural and generic interface to the functions defined by each protocol.

Bot for Trading
The developed trading robot is a practically autonomous algorithm that does not require outside intervention or any actions in the trading process. The main functions of a trading bot include the following:

- automatically monitors the set parameters;
- sends a transaction to the broker's server;
- waiting for a response that the transaction was accepted by the broker.

If the transaction is accepted by the broker, then further, the robot waits for a response from the exchange that the order has been placed in the trading system. After receiving a response from the exchange that the order has been placed, the robot writes the current position to the corresponding variable and then starts tracking the exit from the current position and the possibility of entering the opposite position.

The calculated efficiency of the Hybrid Cyber-Physical System turned out to be high. The most important parameter of the competitiveness of exchange trading bots, as studies show, is the criterion of profitability. In many cases, this is classified information. Calculations indicate that the developed algorithm of the Random Forest deep learning model, which was built into the Hybrid Cyber-Physical System, showed a high estimated profitability. The increase in the variation margin was positive and for the period under review of 126 days and amounted to 77,427.5 rubles, which is higher than the value of the deposit (GO-guarantee) at the beginning of trading 12,234 rubles, or about 6 times, increasing on average per day by 5.02%

6   Discussion

Correlating the results obtained with the questions that were presented in the introduction, we can say that for further research it is advisable to use the approaches used, for example, in more advanced Hybrid cyber-physical systems based on neural network models, not only Random Forest, but also Long-term-short-term time models. periods, as well as Convolutional Neural Networks. A Convolutional Neural Network is a deep learning algorithm that can take input parameters, assign importance (digestible weights and biases) to different areas/objects depending on the purpose of the study.

This study provides an increase in scientific knowledge that allows closing the scientific gap in terms of identifying and evaluating the influence of factors that determine the formation of a forecast for the price of an exchange asset on the MoEx in modern conditions.

In particular, the cognitive model of industry transformation "Industry 5.0" presented by the authors Fedorov A.A. and Lieberman I.V. is of practical importance. The structure of neuro-digital ecosystems for the implementation of the concept of "Industry 5.0", as well as a conceptual model of the digital ecosystem of production and economic systems of various types and purposes, created within the framework of the concept of "Industry 5.0" [16].

According to the authors A.V. Babkin, A.A. Fedorov, I.V. Lieberman, P.M. Klacek the use of collective intelligence and metasystem technologies in all areas life should become the basis for creating a fundamentally new socio-economic and cultural strategy for the development of society. A neuro-ecosystem model of the Industry 5.0 concept is presented, which will allow us to set the task of implementing systems of global metasystem strategic development of cognitive production and industry [17].

The authors have identified the main directions for the development of hybrid cyber-physical, cognitive-social systems in line with the development of technologies for a new technological redistribution Industry 5.0 [18].

Among the important areas that deserve attention for research in the future, the following topics should be noted. The study by Franklin A. regarding the pricing of trusted loans, especially unaffiliated loans, which include fundamental and informational risks, which predetermine the reaction of the stock market [19]. Also noteworthy is a study by Greg Buchak and colleagues on identifying the forces driving fintech adoption [20].

7   Conclusions

The result of this study was the development of approaches to the formation of a Hybrid Cyber-Physical System for conducting speculative operations on the derivatives market on the MoEx when trading a futures contract for the SIS3 dollar based on the predictive capabilities of the created Deep Learning Model "Random Forest Regressor".

As the study showed, the Hybrid Cyber-Physical System for conducting speculative transactions in the derivatives market showed a predictive value that has an absolute deviation from the actual value (MAE) ranging from 48.083 to 155.31 rubles.

This study provides an increase in scientific knowledge that allows closing the scientific gap in terms of identifying and evaluating the influence of factors that determine the formation of a forecast for the price of derivative financial instruments on the exchange market in modern conditions.

References

1. Overview of the banking sector of the Russian Federation (online version) analytical indicators, https://cbr.ru/Collection/Collection/File/14239/obs_196.pdf, last accessed 15 July 2023

2. Bataev, A.V., Gorovoy, A.A., Denis, Z.: Comparative analysis of the use of neural network technology in the world and Russia. In: Proceedings of the 33rd International Business Information Management Association Conference, IBIMA 2019: Education Excellence and Innovation Management through Vision 2020, Vol. 2, pp. 70–81 (2019)
3. Bril, A., Kalinina, O., Ilin, I.: Small innovative company's valuation within venture capital financing of projects in the construction industry. MATEC Web of Conferences 106, 08010 (2017)
4. Demidova, S., Gusarova, V., Kulachinskaya, A.: Features of segmentation and positioning processes when creating an educational brand in neural network economy. In: ACM International Conference Proceeding Series DEFIN 20: Proceedings of the III International Scientific and Practical Conference March 2020. Article No.: 28. pp. 1–5 (2020). https://doi.org/10.1145/3388984.3390634
5. Ilin, I., Lepekhin, A., Levina, A., Iliashenko, O.: Analysis of Factors, Defining Software Development Approach. Adva. Intell. Sys. Comp. **692**, 1306–1314 (2018). ISBN 978-3-031-32718-6
6. Goncharova, N.L.: Development of financial service methods for people with dementia during digitalization: a partnership between citizens and the russian state december. Int. J. Technol. **11**(8), 1547 (2020). https://doi.org/10.14716/ijtech.v11i8.4543
7. Bataev, A., Plotnikova, E., Lukin, G., Sviridenko, E.: Evaluation of the economic efficiency of Blockchain for customer identification by financial institutions. In: IOP Conference Series: Materials Science and Engineering **940** (2020). https://doi.org/10.1088/1757-899X/940/1/012038
8. Lomakin, N., Lukyanov, G., Vodopyanova, N., Gontar, A., Goncharova, E., Voblenko, E.: Neural network model of interaction between real economy sector entrepreneurship and financial field under risk. Advances in Economics. Business and Management Research, volume 83, 2nd International Scientific Conference on Competitive. Sustainable and Safe Development of the Regional Economy (CSSDRE 2019) (2019). http://creativecommons.org/licenses/by-nc/4.0/
9. Kacprzyk, J.: Lecture Notes in Networks and Systems. Systems Research Institute, Polish Academy of Sciences, Warsaw, Poland. Digital Transformation on Manufacturing, Infrastructure & Service: DTMIS 2022 Springer Link
10. Lomakin, N., Yurova, O., Terekhov, T.V., Shabanov, N.T.: Development of a robo-adviser based on artificial intelligence using the "Random Forest" method as a factor in increasing the investment activity of the population. p-Economy: Electron. Magazine **16**(3), 7–21 (2023). https://doi.org/10.18721/JE.16301
11. Klachek, P.M., Babkin, A.V., Liberman, I.V.: Functional hybrid intelligent decision-making system for hard-to-formalize production and economic tasks in the digital economy. Sci. Tech. Statem. SPbSPU. Eco. Sci. **12**(1), 21–32 (2019)
12. Gavrilov, A.V.: Hybrid intelligent systems. Publishing house of NSTU, Novosibirsk (2003)
13. Klachek, P.M., Polupan, K.L., Koryagin, S.I., Liberman, I.V.: Hybrid Computational Intelligence. Fundamentals of theory and technology for creating applied systems. Kaliningrad: Publishing house of BFU n.a. I. Kant (2018)
14. Kolesnikov, A.V.: Hybrid intelligent systems: Theory and development technology. Publishing house of St. Petersburg STU, St. Petersburg (2001)
15. Certificate of registration of the computer program EXCHANGE TRADING QUIK-BOT. Lomakin N.I. 2022662398, 07/04/2022. Application No. 2022661988 dated 22 June 2022
16. Fedorov, A.A., Lieberman, I.V., Koryagin, S.I., Klachek, P.M.: Technology for designing neuro-digital ecosystems to implement the concept of Industry 5.0 SPbSPU Scientific and Technical Bulletin. Economic Sciences **14**(3) (2021)
17. Babkin, A.V., Fedorov, A.A., Lieberman, I.V., Klacek, P.M.: Industry 5.0: concept, formation and development. Russian J. Indus. Econo. **14**(4), 375–395 (2021)

18. Viet, N.T., Kravets, A., Duong Quoc Hoang, T.: Data mining methods for analysis and forecast of an emerging technology trend: a systematic mapping study from SCOPUS papers. In: Kovalev, S.M., Kuznetsov, S.O., Panov, A.I. (eds.) Artificial Intelligence. RCAI 2021. Lecture Notes in Computer Science, Vol. 12948. Springer, Cham (2021). https://doi.org/10.1007/978-3-030-86855-0_7

19. Allen, F., Qian, Y., Tu, G., Yu, F.: Entrusted loans: A close look at China's shadow banking system. J. Fina. Econ. **133**(1), 18–41 (2019). https://doi.org/10.1016/j.jfineco.2019.01.006

20. Buchak, G., Matvos, G., Piskorsk, T., Seru, A.: Fintech, regulatory arbitrage, and the rise of shadow banks. J. Fin. Econ. **133**(1), 18–41 (2019). https://doi.org/10.1016/j.jfineco.2019.01.006

Artificial Intelligence and Deep Learning Technologies for Creative Tasks. Open Science Semantic Technologies

A CycleGAN-Based Method for Translating Recordings of Interjections

Liubov Polianskaya[1] and Liliya Volkova[1,2(✉)]

[1] Bauman Moscow State Technical University, 2-ya Baumanskaya ul. 5-1, 105005 Moscow, Russia
liliya@bmstu.ru
[2] Russian State University for the Humanities, Miusskaya pl., 6, 125993 Moscow, Russia

Abstract. This article is dedicated to a new method for translating audio recordings of interjections between two domains. The original speaker's voice is transformed to the target one within a given voice pair, and vice versa. Basing on an overview conducted, mel-frequency cepstral coefficients are selected as main features of signal. The introduced method is implemented and approbated on the grounds of a book-reading training dataset and sample interjections for a number of voice pairs, including human-robotic. Recommendations are given on the method applicability and on dataset recording. Obtained results testify that we found the solution to the problem of overcoming constraints of existing speech-synthesizing software, namely that of the limitedness of interjections forms and that of the poor intonations variety. The method is to be applied in order to fill reactions databases for dialogue systems designed for affective communication, such as the F-2 interlocutor robot. The introduced method will enable spoken reactions corpora developers to record interjections of interest and to translate them to the selected synthetic voice.

Keywords: Interjections · Speech Synthesis · CycleGAN · Affective Communication · Human-Machine Interaction · Dialogue systems

1 Introduction

The future of AI is in interacting fluidly with humans.
Paul Robertson

Providing more natural and effective communication means is one of key tasks in human-machine interaction (HMI), as the capacity of computers is not used in full [33]. In order to solve this global problem of HMI, dialogue systems adopted the multimodal communication approach, which facilitates communication [11]. For a number of dialogue systems the task is set as companionship: holding a conversation, recognizing human moods and intents, and responding to one's needs dynamically [5]. Beyond modules for text and speech analysis and synthesis, which are an essential part of existing solutions, methods for processing extratextual data on human behaviour and for synthesizing analogous behavioural reactions are of big importance [3, 20, 30, 36, 39].

A. G. Kravets et al. (Eds.): CIT&DS 2023, CCIS 1909, pp. 83–97, 2023.
https://doi.org/10.1007/978-3-031-44615-3_6

This article focuses on interjections — linguistic items that typically function as standalone utterances, namely those formed of vowels. As stated in [10], no class of words has better claims to universality than interjections, and no category has more variable content than this one. Campbell [7] shows that in natural communication 49% of utterances can be non-lexemic, namely interjections (basing on the Expressive Speech Processing project's corpus of conversational everyday speech [6], in particular a sample subcorpus of 150,000 utterances of one of volunteer speakers over a period of 4 years).

An interjections classification is three-fold [37].

1. Exclamations expressing the mood (emotive exclamations).
2. Imperative-communicative exclamations: when (a) addressing, and (b) greeting.
3. Onomatopoeic exclamations.

One more classification could be stated: (i) secondary interjections that originate from words ("goodness", "blast") and are used as interjections (e.g. as an analogue of the interjection "oh"), and (ii) primary ones which do not [4]. As to the latter, prototypical interjections can be described basing on two sufficient formal characteristics: monolexemicity and conventional utterancehood [10]. Some scientists point out semantic criteria linking interjections to the expression of feelings or mental states [14, 40, 41], but this approach excludes a class of one-word utterances less clearly aimed at expressing affect [10]. Nevertheless, interjections are commonly understood as public emissions of private emotions, not necessarily intentional, but often including a specific appeal-to-the-listener-function [13] from the communicative point of view at the dialogue conducted.

This work is concerned with primary interjections of the first type, namely those appears to be Sect. 5. They contain a limited set of sounds and are short — their maximum length constraint is implied by the outward breath duration. The monoleximicity implies no need for subdivision into lexemes during signal analyzing and synthesizing. Hence, on one hand, short interjections are a limitation of the developed method, but on the other hand, that simplifies the task: compared to multilexemic speech synthesis, the intonation is considered the most important signal feature due to the absence of lexeme-wise alignment. Thus the method discussed is enabled to focus on the very intonation in its mathematical model: it should preserve the individual intonation of an interjection utterance and change the voice parameters.

The difficulty is, it is most impossible to record a parallel corpus where two corresponding interjections for a voice pair do follow absolutely the same pattern: either one mismatches the intonation, or the timing varies, even when recording the voice of the same person. Hence, the following **requirement to the method for spoken interjections generation** is formulated: it must be trained on a non-parallel dataset of voice recordings, not on a parallel corpus.

The task of interjections synthesis is solved in general by existing speech synthesizing software, namely by Yandex SpeechKit [43], the key solution for Russian. The Yandex voice assistant Alice [42] uses it, as well as Yandex services and as research projects such as F-2 [39]. The SpeechKit has a basic mechanism for bringing in intonation, however, it utilizes a few preset intonations, limited in number, and researchers state that resulting sounded interjections sometimes appear "strange". This fact testifies that multimodal dialogue systems are in acute need of special methods for generating sounded interjections with a given intonation, as well as of enriching the intonations spectrum. This can be achieved by a method for importing specified voice traits into a voice record with a given intonation, a sort of translator which preserves the intonation pattern but changes the speaker's voice.

2 Signal Features Selection

Human voice is commonly understood as any sound coming out of human larynx. The voice is a set of sounds that are diverse in their characteristics, resulting from fluctuations in the elastic vocal folds. The sound of a voice is formed by vibrations of air particles propagating in the form of waves of condensation and irritation. All the infinite variety of sounds of the human voice is the result of changes of only three most important acoustic parameters of sound over time: (i) the frequency of vibrations, (ii) their amplitude and composition of a complex sound, (iii) its spectrum. These parameters are, respectively, pitch, strength and timbre of sound [38].

Intonation is a complex of super-segmental means: pauses, logical stress, intensity, melody, range pitch, timbre, tempo. Intonation performs two functions: syntactical and pragmatical. The latter is associated with the expression of the speaker's emotional attitude to the subject of speech, of one's emotional state at the time of speech. It depends on to whom it is addressed, for what purpose it is pronounced, etc. The syntactic function is associated with a certain subdivision of the speech stream into phrases, syntagmas, with expression of relations between parts of the utterance [18].

To represent the signal, we selected 4 spectral and frequency voice characteristics.

1. **The (voice) pitch frequency** is the frequency of repetition of the amplitude spectrum peaks. It accounts for the maximum signal power at spectrum frequencies that are multiples of the pitch frequency. For speech, the pitch frequency is in the range from 65 to 350 Hz [32]. The HARVEST algorithm is used for calculation [28].
2. **The envelope of the speech spectrum** describes the shape of the vocal tract. It connects each frequency formant in the speech spectrum with a smooth curve [12], to be obtained with the CheapTrick algorithm [27].
3. **The aperiodic parameter** is associated with the mixed arousal. It is based on the wave form, the pitch frequency and the speech spectrum envelope, as calculated according to the PLATINUM algorithm [26]. This feature is required, because the arousal source should use not only periodic signals in order to obtain natural sound.
4. **Mel-frequency cepstral coefficients (MFCC)** are designed to represent the most approximate data to that received by the auditory analyzer of human brain. MFCC take account of the psychoacoustic principles of speech perception, since they use the mel scale associated with critical hearing bands. People are much better at distinguishing small pitch changes at low frequencies than at high ones. The Mel scale matches the perceived frequency or pitch of the pure tone (mel) to the actual measured frequency (Hz). This dependence is described by the following formula for the frequency f and the mel M:

$$M(f) = 1127.01048 \cdot \ln(1 + f/700). \tag{1}$$

MFCC are used for speech recognition [17, 35] and speaker recognition [21] — the two somehow controversial tasks, the first one minimizing the speaker's variability, the second one maximizing it and at the same time minimizing the linguistic variability. Successful application of MFCC to both tasks proves these features are suitable for both tasks, regarding the complexity of separating one variability from another.

MFCC are obtained by sampling the signal into frames with a fixed offset, and by following transformations of each frame [9, 22]:

– pre-filtering to reduce negative effects of audio signal processing;
– discrete Fourier transform of a sequence of samples;
– obtaining logarithm of spectrum energy for a set of triangle mel-frequency filters;
– discrete cosine transform applied to obtained energy values for filters.

The latter two steps are intended for decorellation: energy of neighbour frequencies is preserved in each frame [2]. Figure 1 shows sample representations of 3 recordings of 2 voices via an MFCC map (frame-wise) and a spectrogram.

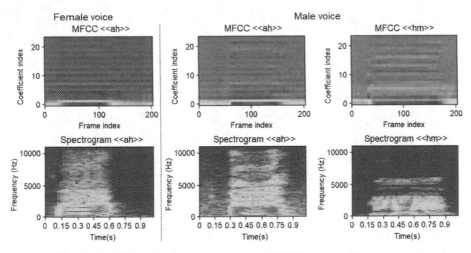

Fig. 1. Sample interjections representation: MFCC maps and spectrograms.

3   The GAN-Based Method for Interjections Translation

3.1   The Generative Artificial Network Selection

To transform a recording of an utterance with one voice in order to pronounce the same utterance with another voice, it is necessary to develop a converter that solves the translation problem. Machine learning methods can show better results in solving this problem than signal processing methods based on standard matrix filters of digital signal processing. The condition of the successful solution of the problem is as follows: it is necessary to provide such methods with input data on the cepstrum and other data (or meta-data) extracted from the signal. Then the method would be enabled to take into account a number of features of speech that cannot be easily characterized by basic digital signal processing methods. Last but not least, the method should preserve some general context of the original signal unchanged during the translation process.

Generative Concurrent Artificial Neural Networks (GANs) are designed for solving the imposed problem of transferring (a several subset of) features of some area of the signal. An analogy can be drawn between the task of translation and the task of changing some fragments of the image according to a template while preserving the original context, e.g. painting horses into zebras and vice versa. The pix2pix conditional GAN [19] requires a parallel dataset and thus doesn't meet the requirement imposed in Sect. 1, while the CycleGAN does.

CycleGAN is selected as the fundamental method for translating interjections recordings, presented as MFCC maps — images to process. This is a deep learning GAN comprising 2 convolutional neural network (CNN) types: generators and discriminators. Through a number of learning cycles a pair of CNNs plays a concurrent game, essaying at outwitting each other [1]. The generator CNN can use noise or existing images as seed for generating brand new data, which are actually generated, and not only remembered by the CNN. The goal of the generator is to process random input data and to create results plausible enough to the discriminator (to fit into its latent features space), while the opposite "player" learns not to be deceived [15]. The discriminator should teach the generator until the point of hardly distinguishing real data from fake. A CycleGAN contains 4 CNNs — 2 of each type, learning altogether, most often conducting binary classification.

CycleGANs provide an approach to learning how to translate an image from the source domain X to the target domain Y in the absence of paired examples. The purpose of a CycleGAN is to construct a mapping $G: X \rightarrow Y$ in such a way that the generated images $G(X)$ were indistinguishable from real images from the target data class Y (see Fig. 2 depicting the original model from [45]).

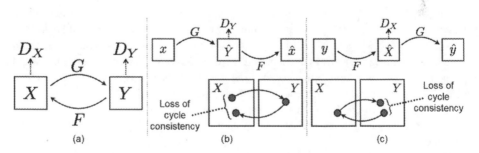

Fig. 2. A CycleGAN scheme: CNNs, mappings, domains.

Two areas X and Y are given with training datasets $\{x_i\}_{i=1}^N$, $x_i \in X$ and $\{y_i\}_{i=1}^N$, $y_i \in Y$. Let the data distribution be denoted as $x \sim pdata(x)$ and $y \sim pdata(y)$. A Cycle-GAN comprises two generators ($G: X \rightarrow Y$ and $F: Y \rightarrow X$) and two discriminators (D_X and D_Y), where D_X attempts at distinguishing images x and translated images $F(y)$, while D_Y attempts at distinguishing y and $G(x)$. In order to achieve these goals, following loss functions are utilized: (i) adversarial loss [15] to compare the distribution of generated images to the distribution of data in the target area, (ii) cycle consistency loss for preventing mappings G and F from conflicting each other, and (iii) identity-mapping loss.

Both CNNs are trained simultaneously until balance is reached. Since both compete with each other and try to improve themselves at each iteration, the losses will not necessarily be constantly decreasing, as in general classifiers. One of CycleGAN creators, Jun-Yan Zhu, when asked when to stop training, replied [44] that automatic evaluation of results is an open research problem for the research on GANs. In the CycleGAN case, it is possible to evaluate the results with some amount of verification data, if given several paired reliable samples. But for many creative applications, results are subjective and difficult to evaluate without involving human assessors. J.-Y. Zhu also notes [44] their adopted number of epochs value of 200 for generating competitive networks for medium-sized data sets (e.g. several hundred or a thousand of images); this implies an analysis of the loss function and does not imply the choice of the optimal number of epochs, but only of the sufficient value regarding some preferred accuracy value.

Mean-square error is selected as loss function for generators. Binary cross-entropy is chosen as the loss function for discriminators. It is designed for binary classification, which is the case: either the discriminator "believes" the generator, or not. It is the negative average of the log of corrected predicted probabilities:

$$I_p(q) = -N^{-1} \cdot \sum_{i=1}^{N} (y_i \cdot \log(p(y_i)) + (1 - y_i) \cdot \log(1 - p(y_i))), \qquad (2)$$

where $p(y_i)$ is the predicted probability of the assignment of the correct label (for all N points), y_i is the label, q is the estimation of the neural network algorithm.

3.2 The Neural Networks Architecture

The residual network (ResNet) architecture is selected as basic for the generator CNN in the CycleGAN: it solves the problem of fading gradients. The process of error backpropagation finds derivatives for the entire network, from the last layer to the first [16]. A chain rule for calculating derivatives is used, and the derivatives of each layer are multiplied by each other to obtain derivatives for the input layers. This repetitive multiplication can make derivatives infinitely small, which means that the weights and thresholds of input layers will not be efficiently updated in each training round. Since these input layers are critical for recognizing key elements of the input data, this can lead to inaccuracy of the entire neural network.

The residual CNN adds input data to the output so that the gradients wouldn't fade too fast. Figure 3 from [16] shows the difference unit (DU) of the residual CNN. This DU changes the purpose of the set of layers from training ideal weights and thresholds $F(x)$ to training the DU output $H(x) = F(x) + x$. Rearrangement of the terms of this equation gives $F(x) = H(x) - x$, which means that the DU is trying to train «input minus output» — in other words, the difference function $F(x)$. Each block now adjusts the output of the previous block, and it does not have to generate the desired output from scratch [16].

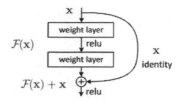

Fig. 3. The ResNet difference unit.

A modified approach in utilized in [8] for forming the concurrent CNN topology: basic convolutional layers with an activation function are used not solely, but in combination with gated linear units (GLU). The main principle is to enable a CycleGAN to control the amount of information passing through a given path, analogous to the logic gate principle. Given the input X of the layer h_l, the following output of h_l is formed by a GLU:

$$h_l(X) = (X \cdot W + b) \otimes \sigma(X \cdot V + c), \tag{3}$$

where W and V, b and c are weights and offsets correspondingly, σ is a sigmoid function, $\otimes$ stands for the element-wise matrices multiplication.

Two independent convolutions should be performed to obtain two outputs. Then, an additional sigmoid activation function is to be applied to one of the outputs, followed by the results element-wise multiplication.

In [8], a study was conducted which compared the convergence in condition of using the following alternatives: a GLU, a gated tangential unit (GTU) which forms the output of the h_l layer as $h_l(X) = tanh(X \cdot W + b) \otimes \sigma(X \cdot V + c)$, and of CNNs that use standard ReLU or Tanh activation functions. Models with GLU converge faster.

Figure 4 shows our CNNs architecture. A DU adds output data to input data to solve the problem of fading gradients. In generators, upsampling units (UU) are used before the GLU operation: the input matrix is converted into a new one, where each row of the input matrix is repeated twice to restore the original size of the MFCC map.

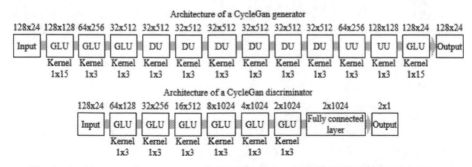

Fig. 4. Architecture of generators and discriminators of the CycleGAN for interjections.

3.3 Signal Features Transforming and Resulting Signal Synthesis

During signal conversion, the pitch frequency is transformed with a normalized conversion [23]:

$$P_t = (P_s - E_s) \cdot D_t/D_s + E_t, \tag{4}$$

where P_s is the pitch frequency for a given input recording with the source voice, E_s and D_s are mathematical expectation and dispersion of different recordings with the same source voice, E_t and D_t are mathematical expectation and dispersion of other recordings with the target voice, P_t is the pitch frequency for the source voice, transformed to the pitch of the target voice.

MFCC are transformed with a trained converter, and the speech spectrum envelope is reconstructed from the resulting MFCC.

The signal is restored from the transformed pitch frequency, the reconstructed spectrum envelope, and the original aperiodic parameter. The aperiodic parameter is not changed, since the study [31] showed that conversion of this parameter does not affect the quality of speech. The final speech synthesis requires convolution of the minimum phase spectrum with the arousal signal, performing backwards steps of the PLATINUM algorithm [25, 26, 29].

Figure 5 presents the developed method. Sample signal, its features and intermediate values are given for a female voice transformed into a male one.

4 Dataset Fulfilling and CycleGANs Training

A corpus of book-reading audios was recorded for 2 male voices (M1 and M2) and 2 female voices (F1 and F2), and additionally for one male voice (S1) synthesized by Yandex SpeechKit. Audios in ".wav" contain phrases from "Wonderful doctor" by A. I. Kuprin in Russian, read by native speakers with expression in voices — but not too dramatic, rather closer to colloquial speech. Each dataset of one reader's voice contains 2300–2500 frames. For voices M1, F1, S1 226 identical phrases were recorded, most of which are 4 to 6 s long. For voices M2 and F2 319 identical phrases were recorded, most of which are 1 to 3 s long. Each training dataset for a given pair of voices contains corresponding subcorpora of recorded speech, from which 2 MFCC map sets are obtained.

We formulated following recommendations for dataset fulfilling.

1. Phrases recordings duration should be from 0.7 to 6 s.
2. Phrases recordings should not contain pauses nor interfering sounds, including other voices. A person should talk during all of one's recording time.
3. Emotions expression must not be too dramatic: that would reduce the quality of audios generated by CycleGANs trained on this data.
4. Pre-processing of recordings should be executed before extracting features.
5. The recommended minimum number of frames for one person Nmin is 2300. Cycle-GANs trained on 600, 1000, 1500 frames generated signals with extraneous noise, the voices didn't sound naturally, artifacts appeared frequently.

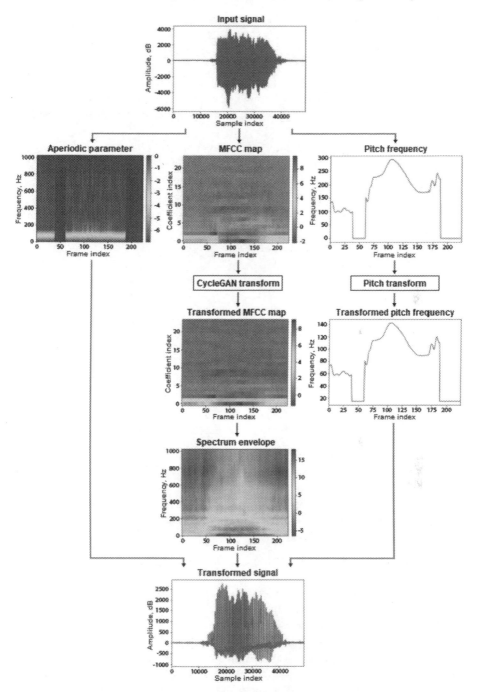

Fig. 5. The introduced method: signal transformation scheme.

The number of frames N for one recording is 0 in case $L < 640$ ms, otherwise

$$N = [(L - 640)/25] + 1, L \geq 640 \,\text{ms},\tag{5}$$

where L is the signal duration (ms) after cutting off silence (under 15 dB) at both ends of the audio, 640 ms is the length of each frame, 25 is the offset of one frame from another. These values enable to preserve the energy of neighbor frequencies; mel-frequency filters keep it in each frame [2].

Figure 6 shows the loss function (binary cross entropy) plots for discriminators of the CycleGan trained to convert records from male voice M1 to M2 and vice versa. The rest of the results are pretty much the same. The recommended number of epochs for training is 300, however, if necessary, it can be changed based on graphs of loss functions or poor quality of the converted signals.

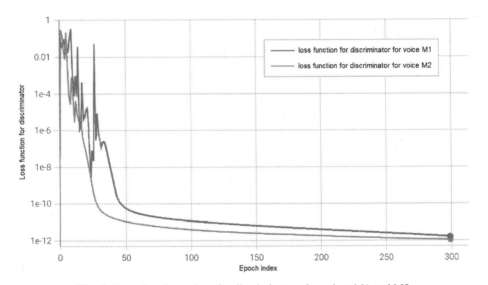

Fig. 6. Loss function values for discriminators for voices M1 and M2.

The training was carried out for 300 epochs, then the most suitable epoch was selected according to the loss functions, and the weights obtained at this stage were further used. It was necessary to (i) evaluate the loss functions of both discriminators of each trained CycleGAN, and then (ii) to evaluate the quality of signal generated for seed interjections by GANs trained for given voice pairs — the latter via subjective assessment based on listening and comparing. In such tasks human ear and brain are supreme judges: this is a test without any standard answer, and generated signals are intended to sound naturally to assessors.

Each CycleGAN was trained for a pair of voices on Nvidia Tesla V100 SXM3 32 GB GPU. One CycleGAN training takes circa 25 h for 2500 frames, and circa 5 h for 600 frames.

5 Discussion

Monophonemic interjections recordings served input to the trained CycleGANs, each not exceeding 2 s. For speech synthesis tasks, the most important criterion of quality estimation is human assessment. 20 respondents assessed every single generated interjection audio. The following 5-points scale is used for quality estimation:

5 — very good, the voice on the recording is similar to the target one, there is no noise on the recording or it is not noticeable, the voice sounds natural;

4 — good, the voice on the recording is similar to the target one, but with minor artifacts or noise, the voice sounds natural;

3 — medium, similar to the target voice, but with noticeable artifacts or noise, the voice sounds natural;

2 — bad, poorly similar to the target voice or artifacts make the result unsatisfactory, the voice does not sound natural;

1 — very bad, the voice does not sound like the target one, the sound is very noisy or does not sound natural.

Artifacts are understood as sound conversion effects that negatively affect the perception of the signal, for example, extraneous crackling.

In Table 1 average values of respondents' assessment are given for 7 Russian interjections (transcribed in English) and 6 voice pair types: "m" stands for male, "f" stands for female, "mr" stands for male robotic voice obtained with Yandex SpeechKit. The direction of transformation in a voice pair is marked with " →" (only for assessment). There were CycleGANs pre-trained for combinations of 4 voices: 2 male and 2 female voices.

Table 1. Average assessment values for translated interjections audios.

Interjection	Voice pair types					
	m → m	m → f	f → m	f → f	m → mr	f → mr
"ah"	3.9	4.4	4.6	4.3	4.2	4.1
"aha" / "aga"	4.1	4.2	4.3	4.2	4.3	3.9
"oh"	4.2	4.1	4.2	4.4	4.1	4.4
"oho" / "ogo"	4.3	4.5	4.4	4.5	4.2	4.5
"oohoo"	3.5	3.9	4.1	4.1	3.9	4.2
"hm"	4.5	4.8	4.5	4.6	4.5	4.4
"ekh"	4.4	4.5	4.1	4.4	4.2	4.3

Most of the estimations are positive. The average score for human-human voice pair types is 4.3, for human-robot the ranking is 4.2. Excluding the questionable "oohoo" interjection, the average estimation values arise to 4.35 and 4.3, correspondingly, which is a good result: the translated recordings sound natural and are perceived as similar to the target voice. The latter points out that the method is applicable in practice for Russian.

The "oohoo" interjection showed the lowest ratings for 5 voice pair types out of 6, which can be explained after listening attentively to corresponding audios. The sounds combination is abuzz in three input interjections of this class, which differs from regular speech from the training dataset: humming is a different kind of sound production. Such errors are due to the fact that speakers happened to pronounce the interjection literally, as people do when they only imagine a word in a book, but they have never heard it being sounded by a human. The following conclusion can be drawn: either an acceptable replacement should be selected (closer to how "mhm" sounds, though it is a relatively rare transcription in books — e.g. RusCorpora [34] doesn't find a single occurrence, except for three misspelled "khm"-s, while "aha" and the target "ugu" occur frequently), or the speaker should be well instructed how interjections should not sound while recording to avoid humming and entailed errors of the sound translation method, which is not adapted to that sort of sounds.

Particular attention must be paid to fullfillment of the robotic voice recordings dataset: we used basic text generated with Yandex SpeechKit, with present basic intonations, which are a constraint to our method. Forward enhancement of the available intonations set in the SpeechKit library would affect the variety of intonations in our training dataset and consequently the assessment of audios generated by a pre-trained CycleGAN.

The introduced method is also applicable to transforming audios from human voices to robotic, which enables developers of multimodal dialogue systems to enrich their reactions databases with interjections, recorded by humans with rich intonations and thereafter translated into a basic machine-synthesized voice associated with such a dialogue system. Interjections can implement reactions matched to different dialogue strategies: asking clarifying questions, expressing confirmation, agreement and disagreement, simulating surface emotional phenomena [39] and developing politeness strategies [24]. Hence, affective robots and voice assistants will be enabled to show more and more natural reactions. This would be one more step towards a full-fledged natural language interface for HMI, including those designed for artificial intelligence systems.

Acknowledgements. This research is supported by the grant of the Russian Science Foundation № 19-18-00547, https://rscf.ru/project/19-18-00547/.

We would like to thank our volunteer speakers who helped us recording a dataset, and our assessors whose opinions are priceless to our sort of projects, when it comes to crowdsourcing (only the final CycleGan results assessments are stated in this article; inbetween translations were estimated thoroughly as well). We also express gratitude to Edward Klyshinsky for his repeated affirmative "mhm", which led us to the answer to the puzzling "oohoo" question.

We would like to thank Alexey Yuryevich Popov from IU-6 department, BMSTU, for his kind permission to use his devices of high computational capability in order to train our CycleGANs, and Kirill Leonidovich Tassov from IU-7 department, BMSTU, for his priceless remarks, which helped us to improve our results.

References

1. Ahirwar, K.: Generative Adversarial Networks Projects. Packt Publishing, Birmingham (2019)

2. Antsiferova, V.I., Pesetskaya, T.V., Yuldoshev, I.I., Syanyan, L., Tsin, V., Lavlinskiy, V.V.: One of approaches towards determining relevant features for audiosignals: a sample research on interjections (in Russian). In: Zol'nikov, V.K. (ed.) Sovremennye aspekty modelirovaniya sistem i protsessov: Materialy Vserossiyskoy nauchno-prakticheskoy konferentsii, 2021, pp. 15–20. Voronezh State University of Forestry and Technologies named after G.F. Morozov, Voronezh (2021)

3. Becker, C.W., Kopp, S., Wachsmuth I.: Simulating the emotion dynamics of a multimodal conversational agent. In: Affective Dialogue Systems, Tutorial and Research Workshop, ADS 2004, LNCS 3068, pp. 154–165. Springer, Heidelberg (2004)

4. Bloomfield, L.: An introduction to the study of language. Holt, New York (1914)

5. Cai, Y.: Empathic Computing. In: Cai, Y., Abascal, J. (eds.) Ambient Intelligence in Everyday Life. LNCS (LNAI), vol. 3864, pp. 67–85. Springer, Heidelberg (2006). https://doi.org/10.1007/11825890_3

6. Campbell, N.: Recording techniques for capturing natural everyday speech. In: Proc. Language Resources and Evaluation Conference (LREC-02), pp. 2029–2032. European Language Resources Association, Paris (2002)

7. Campbell, N.: Extra-semantic protocols; input requirements for the synthesis of dialogue speech. In: Proc. Affective Dialogue Systems, Tutorial and Research Workshop, ADS 2004, LNCS 3068, pp. 221–228. Springer, Heidelberg (2004)

8. Dauphin, Y.N., Fan, A., Auli, M., Grangie, D.: Language modeling with gated convolutional networks. In: Precup, D., Teh, Y.W. (eds.) Proc. of the 34th International Conference on Machine Learning, PMLR 70. MLResearchPress (2017)

9. Davis, S.B., Mermelstein, P.: Comparison of parametric representations for monosyllabic word recognition in continuously spoken sentences. IEEE Trans. Acoust. Speech Signal Process. **28**(4), 357–366 (1980)

10. Dingemanse, M.: Interjections (preprint). In: van Lier, E. (ed.) The Oxford Handbook of Word Classes. Oxford University Press, Oxford (2021)

11. Drijvers, L., Holler, J.: The multimodal facilitation effect in human communication. Psychon. Bull. Rev. **30**(2), 792–801 (2022)

12. Efimov, A.P., Nikonov, A.V., Sapozhkov, M.A., Shorov, V.I.: Acoustics: Spravochnik (in Russian). In: Sapozhkov, M.A. (ed.) Radio i svyaz', Moskva (1989)

13. Elffers, E.: Interjections and the language functions debate. Asia Paci. J. Human Resou. **50**(1), 17–29 (2008)

14. Goffman, E.: Response cries. Language **54**(4), 787–815 (1978)

15. Goodfellow, I., et al.: Generative adversarial networks. Advances in Neural Information Processing Systems (NIPS 2014) **27**, 2672–2680 (2014)

16. He, K., Zhang, X., Ren, S., Sun, J.: Deep residual learning for image recognition. In: 2016 IEEE Conference on Computer Vision and Pattern Recognition (CVPR), pp. 770–778. IEEE, Piscataway (2016)

17. Huang, X., Acero, A., Hon, H.-W.: Spoken language processing: a guide to theory, algorithm, and system development. Prentice Hall PTR, New Jersey (2001)

18. Ippolitova, N.A.: Ritorics. Prospekt, Moscow (2013). (in Russian)

19. Isola, P., Zhu, J.-Y., Zhou, T., Efros, A.A.: Image-to-image translation with conditional adversarial networks. In: CVPR 2017, pp. 5967–5976. IEEE, Piscataway (2017)

20. Kollias, D., Zafeiriou, S.: Expression, affect, action unit recognition: Aff-wild2, multi-task learning and arcface. In: 30th British Machine Vision Conference, pp. 78.1–78.15. BMVA Press, Durham (2019)

21. Kozlov, A.V., Kudashev, O., Matveev, Y.: A system for dictors identification by voice for NIST SRE 2012 contest (in Russian). Trudy SPIIRAN **2**, 350–370 (2013)

22. Kudashev, O.Y.: A system for dictors separation based on probabilistic linear discriminant analysis. Ph.d. thesis (in Russian). ITMO, Saint-Petersburg (2014)

23. Liu, K., Zhang, J., Yan, Y.: High quality voice conversion through phoneme-based linear mapping functions with straight for mandarin. In: Fourth International Conference on Fuzzy Systems and Knowledge Discovery (FSKD 2007), vol. 4, pp. 410–414. IEEE, Piscataway (2007)

24. Malkina, M., Zinina, A., Arinkin, N., Kotov, A.: Multimodal hedges for companion robots: a politeness strategy or an emotional expression? In: Selegey, V.P., et al. (eds.) Computational Linguistics and Intellectual Technologies: Papers from the Annual International Conference "Dialogue", issue 22, pp. 319–326. RSUH, Moscow (2023)

25. Morise, M., Yokomori, F., Ozawa, K.: WORLD: a vocoder-based high-quality speech synthesis system for real-time applications. IEICE transactions on information and systems, E99-D(7), 1877–1884 (2016)

26. Morise, M.: Platinum: A method to extract excitation signals for voice synthesis system. Acoustic Science & Technology 33(2), 123–125 (2012)

27. Morise, M.: Cheaptrick, a spectral envelope estimator for high-quality speech synthesis. Speech Commun. 67, 1–7 (2015)

28. Morise, M.: Harvest: a high-performance fundamental frequency estimator from speech signals. In: Proc. INTERSPEECH 2017, pp. 2321–2325. ISCA, Baixas (2017)

29. Morise, M.: Implementation of sequential real-time waveform generator for high-quality vocoder. In: Proceedings of APSIPA Annual Summit and Conference, pp. 821–825. IEEE, Pictasaway (2020)

30. Niewiadomski, R., Bevacqua, E., Mancini, M, Pelachaud, C.: Greta: an interactive expressive ECA system. In: Proceedings of The 8th International Conference on Autonomous Agents and Multiagent Systems, vol. 2, pp. 1399–1400. International Foundation for Autonomous Agents and Multiagent Systems, Richland (2009)

31. Ohtani, Y., Toda, T., Saruwatari, H., Shikano, K.: Maximum likelihood voice conversion based on GMM with STRAIGHT mixed excitation. In: Proc. INTERSPEECH 2006, pp. 2266–2269. IEEE, Pictasaway (2007)

32. Plotnikov, V.N., Sukhanov, V.A., Zhigulevtsev, Y.: Spoken dialogue in control systems. Mashinostroeniye, Moscow (1988). (in Russian)

33. Ronzhin, A.L., Karpov, A.A., Lee, I.V.: Speech and multimodal interfaces. Nauka, Moscow (2006). (in Russian)

34. RusCorpora: the Russian National Corpus of texts, https://ruscorpora.ru/en/, last accessed 15 June 2023

35. Sahidullah, M., Saha, G.: Design, analysis and experimental evaluation of block based transformation in MFCC computation for speaker recognition. Speech Commun. 54(4), 543–565 (2012)

36. Shröder, M.: Towards a standards-based framework for building emotion-oriented systems. Advances in Human-Computer Interaction 2010, article ID 319406 (2010)

37. Stijovic, R., Lazic-Konjik, I., Spasojevic, M.: Interjections in the contemporary Serbian language: classification and lexicographic treatment (in Serbian). Juznoslovenski filolog 75, 37–61 (2019)

38. Volkova, L.S., Shakhovskaya, S.N. (eds.): Logopediya: Uchebnik dlya studentov defektologicheskikh fakul'tetov (Fakul'tetov korrektsionnoj pedagogiki) pedagogicheskikh universitetov i institutov, 3rd edn. Gumanit. izd. tsentr VLADOS, Moscow (1998). (in Russian)

39. Volkova, L., Ignatev, A., Kotov, N., Kotov, A.: New communicative strategies for the affective robot: F-2 going tactile and complimenting. In: Creativity in Intelligent Technologies and Data Science, CCIS 1448, pp. 163–176. Springer, Heidelberg (2021)

40. Wharton, T.: Pragmatics and non-verbal Communication. Cambridge University Press, Oxford (2009)

41. Wierzbicka, A.: The semantics of interjection. J. Pragmat. **18**(2–3), 159–192 (1992)
42. Yandex LLC: Yandex Alice, https://yandex.ru/dev/dialogs/alice/doc/nlu.html, last accessed 16 March 2023
43. Yandex LLC: Yandex SpeechKit, https://cloud.yandex.ru/services/speechkit, last accessed 16 March 2023
44. Zhu, J.-Y.: How to know the training should stop. CycleGAN and pix2pix in PyTorch/Jun-Yan Zhu github, https://github.com/junyanz/pytorch-CycleGAN-and-pix2pix/issues/166, last accessed 16 March 2023
45. Zhu, J.-Y., Park, T., Isola, P., Efros, A.A.: Unpaired image-to-image translation using cycle-consistent adversarial networks. In: 2017 IEEE International Conference on Computer Vision (ICCV), pp. 2242–2251. IEEE, Piscataway (2017)

On Capturing Functional Style of Texts with Part-of-speech Trigrams

Liliya Volkova[1,2(✉)], Alexander Lanko[1], and Vyacheslav Romanov[1]

[1] Bauman Moscow State Technical University, 2-ya Baumanskaya ul. 5-1, 105005 Moscow, Russia
liliya@bmstu.ru
[2] Russian State University for the Humanities, Miusskaya pl. 6, 125993 Moscow, Russia

Abstract. This article is dedicated to automatic detection of natural language texts functional style. Part-of-speech N-grams are selected as text features for capturing word order, which depends on functional style in Russian. The introduced approach was approbated within the task of texts classification by functional style and within a content-oriented book recommender system, which uses basic and modified probabilistic topic modeling and selects writings basing on their styles similarity to the input. Successful style-based books selection showed that an expectation gap for recommender systems can be filled, since it became possible to match books by style, successfully crossing the genre boundaries. The results are applicable for texts classification by functional style in libraries and publishers software, for personalized writings selection in recommender systems for news, scientific articles and fiction, as well as for further style modelling in dialogue systems and conversational communicative robots in order to select appropriate style depending on the interlocutor's one and on the polilogue pragmatics and participants' roles.

Keywords: Functional Style · Natural Language Processing · Word Order · Classification · Probabilistic Topic Modelling · Recommender Systems

1 Introduction

The research interest of this paper lies in the field of computational and structural linguistics, which consider language as a sign system with clearly distinguishable structural elements (units of language, their classes, etc.) and pursues a strict formal description of the language [68]. Pragmatics is a related area of scientific exploration within semiotics and linguistics which is concerned with the functioning of linguistic signs in speech [68]. Charles Bally underlines 3 functions of language, each affecting the speech form choice by the speaker: *informational*, *affective* and *social* [3]. The latter function takes into account *who* communicates, *and when, and how much, and with whom,* — to paraphrase Omar Khayyam.

Traditionally, functional styles of language are large classes of speech patterns and rhetorical devices, which seem to be formed as clusters in a natural way during centenaries of pragmatical use by native speakers under conventional circumstances. These

A. G. Kravets et al. (Eds.): CIT&DS 2023, CCIS 1909, pp. 98–113, 2023.
https://doi.org/10.1007/978-3-031-44615-3_7

functionally conditioned styles exist and are described in comparison to each other. In Russian and in most languages there are 2 functional super-classes (or registers [8]) of speech — literary (bookish) and colloquial, the latter sometimes borrowing particular traits from other styles, as to O.A. Lapteva. The literary functional style (FS) is subdivided as follows [35]: belletristic (literary, or high style), publicistic (journalistic, newspaper), scientific, official (administrative, legislative), and religious (cult-religious, which stands aside as an adaptation of an ancient Church Slavonic language to modern Russian). The list is given in ascending normativity order, except for the religious FS [5], which borrows publicistic invocatory traits; the least strict FS is the colloquial one.

Methods for FS detection and classification are applicable in following tasks and software based on natural language processing:

1. plagiarism detection (via comparative analysis of text areas);
2. linguistic expertise in cases of doubtful text authorship [57];
3. publisher utilities for checking and further adjusting stylistic homogeneiety of large texts — dissertations, monographs, novels [23, 42];
4. book recommender systems, in particular for libraries;
5. recommender systems and filters for social networks content personalization (for those operating with posts of medium and large size);
6. news and periodicals aggregators, namely for automatic metadata extraction from texts, as well as for texts classification and clusterization for further personalized filtration of papers for end-point users;
7. spam filters.

From the speech synthesis point of view, understanding linguistic means corresponding each FS would enable scientists developing dialogue systems (DS) to vary the manner of speech when synthesizing texts. In a conversational DS, be it virtual or embodied in a robot, FS selection would (a) allow adapting to the interlocutor's speech, and (b) reflect the conversation context defined by current conversation register, by interlocutors' roles, age difference, and mood (*high style* for solemn occasion).

Texts classification by FS will be further described along with typical language constructs. A class of features will be selected for texts comparison by FS, and 2 task solutions will be discussed which use these features as basis in their implementation.

2   Related Work: Functional Styles

In the beginning of the XX century Ferdinand de Saussure established the following idea: the process of using language involves choosing from a specifiable set of options. His idea of signs as terms in a system was elaborated in 1920s–1940s by the Prague linguistic circle, which considered the language as a functional system, i.e. as "a system of expression devices serving a specific purpose" [58]. Mathesius, the circle's first president, in 1929 states that "new" linguistics based on the functional principle "starts from the needs of expression and inquires what means serve to satisfy these communication needs in the languages being studied", and therefore "proceeds from function to form" [40]. S. Bally describes the concept of functional choice: numerous synonymous forms and their series are stated in the language. Among the latter a "neutral background" is compared to other backgrounds differentiating in additional tonality — namely stylistic. Bally understood this tonality mainly as expressive: colloquial or, on the contrary, "high", bookish-styled [68], as register.

Stylistics is a branch of linguistics that studies expressive devices and possibilities of language along with its patterns of use in various spheres of social activity and communication situations [35]. Its subject is style in all its meanings. In studies of Russian, style is "a socially induced and functionally conditioned, internally united set of techniques for the use, selection and combination of means of speech communication in the sphere of a national language, as compared to other similar ways of expression that serve for other purposes, perform other functions in the social speech practice of a given people" [63]. In the middle of the XX century style was accentuated as functional, and the focus was set on speech organization of text. FS is defined as a peculiar character of speech (of one of its socially defined varieties), corresponding to the sphere of communication and activity, correlated with a certain form of consciousness, this character beingwhich is created by the peculiarities of the functioning of linguistic means in this sphere and specific speech organization, speech system.

The conception of style traits has undergone significant changes: from contrasting them by polarity (e.g., unambiguousness, imagery, emotionality — and the contrary poles) to their field organization based on the principle of ratio of nuclear and peripheral features [35]. The regularities of the FS system are probabilistic and statistical in nature: they are created not so much at the expense of stylistically marked means existing in the language, as at the expense of different use frequency of certain linguistic units and their organization, of speech consistency formed under the influence of its dominant in each FS (otherwise: constructive principle; e.g. for official FS imperative in formulations is the dominant principle) [35]. Rosenthal treated FS as different variations of a language, characterized by a unique set of lexical, phraseological and syntactic means used entirely or predominantly in this variant. As to semantic templates, rhetoric devices aimed at appealing are common to religious [65] and publicistic FS [7, 31]: in order to invoke readers' emotional response which is sensitive to specific semantic markers, media can manipulate the nomination in text [11]. Although from a logical point of view the variation in labeling doesn't affect the truth value of the utterance, humans are quite sensitive to such semantic shifts, they can be manipulated and even enjoy journalistic articles, rich with rhetorical figures [31].

In [64] a classification of FS along with their typical linguistic devices (or constructs) in Russian prose is given in Table 1, where peculiarities of different FS at lexical and syntactic levels of language representation are described in detail. We limit our research with prose, while poetic texts function in a different way [4]. Beyond religious FS, the 5-fold classification is typical for most languages [13, 35, 59]. This would serve ground for classifying texts by functional style basing on the vector of style markers [10, 28, 29, 57]. Depending on the applied task, it is possible to consider styles blending or dissolving of one style into others [64].

To highlight the FS distinctive features, statistical analysis of morphology and vocabulary is to be performed [52, 54, 55, 69]. Morphological parameters (partial spectrum of the text) belong to the markers of FS and therefore can be used for automatic classification of texts by styles [13]. Hudlomer is an automatic classifier of the text FS based on

Table 1. Characteristics and typical linguistic devices of functional styles in Russian.

FS destination	Characteristics	Typical linguistic devices
Colloquial: personally addressed informal communication, often unrelated to professional activity, mostly the household sphere	Predominance of communicative and affective functions of language over the informative one; free expression of thoughts and feelings, minimal restrictions to the form of expression, often low style, barbarisms, slang	Emotional vocabulary, parcellation, dashes and ellipses, exclamations and interrupted sentences, predominance of uncomplicated sentences, widespread use of pronouns and particles, of simple prepositions
Belletristic: drawing pictures with words, expressing attitudes to the subject, influencing feelings and imagination	High imagery, a variety of shades and subtleties of speech	Epithets, descriptive constructions, synonyms antonyms;word combinations individuality, verbal repetition within a sentence, metonymic transfer of sense ("white smell"), subordinate clauses replacement with infinitive constructions with a short non-verbal adjective
Publicistic: impact on mass consciousness through socially significant information	Logical, imaginative, value-laden, invocatory character, a combination of expression and standard, often focus on the novelty of expression, possibility of slang words	Widespread use of epithets, exclamation sentences, rare use of participial and adverbial phrases
Scientific: delivering scientific information, explanation with presentation of appropriate arguments	Formality, logicality, objectivity, semantic accuracy, widespread use of stereotypes of special vocabulary, exclusion of emotional epithets	Rare personal pronouns, frequent use of participles, adverbs and corresponding clauses; complex sentences, impersonal and indefinite-personal sentences; nominativity — wider use of nouns (rather in Russian than in English [34])
Official: statement of status, state of affairs, prescriptions in the legislative, legal, administrative, commercial spheres	Precision that does not allow misinterpretation; imperativeness, standardization of speech, lack of emotion, avoidance of imagery, "unhealthy thoroughness of the language" (D.S. Likhachev)	Cancelarisms [17], complex sentences, imperatives and infinitives, the rarity of pronominal verb forms of 1st and 2nd person, words with collecting function, verbal nouns, passive voice, impersonal and indefinite-personal sentences
Religious: service of the sphere of church-religious social activity in accordance with the religious form of public consciousness	Clearly expressed communicative purpose; explicit character, which does not allow various interpretations of religious idiology; archaic stylistic tonality of speech; invocatory areas interspersed with publicistic style	Church Slavonic inclusions, theological terminology, means of enhancing expression, a modal frame of congratulations, appeals, instructions, praises of the activities of the Church institution

word length spectrum analysis; it is dependent on text length [18]. The richness of the used vocabulary is itself a marker of style [57]. A number of research papers discover quantitative approaches to distinguishing between different literary genres [21]. In statistical studies of quantitative parameters, "significant differences" of author styles are revealed, however, the question of selecting such differences is a difficulty of the statistical approach to establishing the style [20]. Whereas there is an established tendency to use the spectra of individual administrative words [41, 43], when processing large text corpora the results of such an approach should "fluctuate around the average number, obeying the general laws of language," which makes it difficult to distinguish the authors, according to Markov [39]. However, according to a study based on a corpus of works by writers of the XVIII–XX centuries, it is statistically proved that the proportion of all service words (service parts of speech) in long prose texts solely constitutes the so-called author invariant [20].

Syntactic analysis of sentences is useful for capturing phrase types most typical for a particular FS [34, 46, 66]. However, during a natural language sentence synthesis, namely when projecting a dependency tree to one and only dimension in order to form a sentence word-by-word, word order variations are possible. Interrupted and non-projective constructions occur quite often in languages with high probability of free word order, and analysis of projectivity violations along with depth of nesting [22] appears useful when distinguishing FS (e.g., a bigger value of nesting depth is more characteristic for the belletristic style). The drawback of syntactic analysis is induced by homonymy and variations of word order in texts: one sentence can result in several dependency trees; this ambiguity of parsing results is a factor affecting the FS determining quality. Despite non-gradient approaches to word order have been traditionally dominant in cross-linguistic studies, recent research based on big corpora proved that gradient approach to word order ought to be used: authors of [36] argue for the presumption of variability in word order research, stating that languages vary in degree but not kind when it comes to word order variability.

Text structure features are one substantially informative class of natural language text features, which result from and, vice versa, determine the FS. Within this class, **word order is in the focus of this research**. Combining these features of interest with other features is considered as a further research direction.

3   Detecting Text Style via Word Order: PoS Trigrams

In different languages degrees of word order variability can be measured the by using quantitative measures [36]. It is a typical situation in Russian wheh there is nothing pragmatically marked about putting a newsworthy object first in a phrase (except for Russian gesture language). Word order tends to differ in Russian from one FS to another, as to statistics. We introduced an approach to capturing word order via analyzing structures analogous to first derivatives of N-grams extracted out of texts [65].

An N-gram in the alphabet V is an arbitrary string of length N, for example, a sequence of N letters of the alphabet V of one word, one phrase, one text, or, in a more interesting case, a sequence of grammatically acceptable descriptions of N consecutive words. First we mine trigrams of consequent words out of each sentence, preserving word order and normalizing word forms via morphological analysis with the pymorphy2 library (see the list of 17 parts of speech at [45]). Then we convert these temporary trigrams of normalized word forms into part-of-speech trigrams (PoS trigrams) — ordered triads of parts of speech of initial N-grams of words. PoS trigrams are comparable to derivatives of initial N-grams, as they show the word order. We count the number of occurrences of each PoS trigram in the text, and their TF-IDF values for a set of texts. This sort of statistics is selected as text features, analogous to a spectrogram of chemical elements in a sample of substance subject to analysis.

Five trigrams are extracted from a sample sentence "All for one and one for all", where "one" has the meaning of pronoun: < all, for, one >, < for, one, and >, < one, and, one >, < and, one, for >, < one for all >. PoS trigrams follow: < pronoun, preposition, pronoun > — 2 occurrences, < preposition, pronoun, conjunction > — 1, < pronoun, conjunction, pronoun > — 1, < conjunction, pronoun, preposition > — 1.

Our hypothesis is as follows: classification of texts in Russian by FS can be carried out basing on results of morphological analysis, namely by PoS trigrams frequencies.

To prove this hypothesis, we conducted experiments: texts were clusterized with the k-means method, omitting existing FS labels, and clusters homogeneity was evaluated. To demonstrate the operability of the introduced approach, only three styles were selected: publicistic (news from SynTagRus [44]), scientific (articles from the journal «Science and life» and conference papers), belletristic (excerpts from A.S. Pushkin's classic novel «Dubrovsky»), and blended FS (excerpts from E.M. Remarque's «Three comrades» are a mixture of belletristic and publicistic FS, as Remarque was a journalist who came into big literature). Text sizes were similar for these experiments. Texts were morphologically annotated with the Solarix library, all the undetected cases were resolved manually. 93% correct attributions were observed for 28 texts from «Science and life», SynTagRus and Remarque. For 44 Pushkin, «Russian gazette» and «Science and life» texts 90% attributions were correct, and 10% errors assigning several belletristic texts to news. Including pure and blended styles in one dataset brings in errors: «Science and life» often tends to publish high style papers, and several Remarque texts are confusingly attributed to publicistic articles.

Clustering results prove the PoS trigrams approach applicability to FS detection.

4 From PoS Trigrams to a Space of Latent Features: A Recommender System Learnt to Compare Text Styles

Bookselling is a self-sustaining process, with loads of books written every week. By 2010, Google has counted books from over 150 libraries and stated 130 million original book titles. The most urgent problem of a reader is that of book choice. A person comes to a bookshop (be it physical or virtual) willing to pick up a book or two out of a huge variety presented. Books are commonly grouped by countries, genres, fiction/non-fiction type, and so on. Metadata seem to be insufficient for metasearch systems [46]. Book summary is supposed to be a key to the solution, but it "doesn't really *just* tell the reader what the main premise of the book is; it often gives them an idea of what genre the story is" [26]. Automatic recommender methods most often use flat ranking and collaborative filtration, both concerned only with averaged scoring and ignoring what is personal about reader advisory. Reviews by readers can be useful, as some book-lover forums do. Yet there's practically no automation in personal recommendation by books content, but by metadata, including genres.

There is an expectation gap here — that of contents analysis: existing book recommenders don't do book texts processing (e.g. LiveLib, Bookmix, ReadRate, Goodreads process book reviews and ratings). There is but one aspect still little explored in recommender systems: author/functional style of books. As we have proven our hypothesis of texts separability by typical word order and FS, we essayed at building a recommender system designated for filling the gap.

Beyond genre borders, there are subdivisions of functional style, which are familiar to experienced readers. This is partly observable via structure of dependency trees corresponding to sentences [46], but syntactic analysis doesn't catch word order, which is quite informative itself. All books differ, but some, by principle of agglomerative clusterization, are very much closer by FS than others (in the absence of a borderline term, in this section we generalize the groups of authors' styles under the aegis of FS), as to recognizable word order. It depends on many factors: on author's own favourite books, on one's mood, on the writers circle to which one belongs, on direct imitation or writing a text according to some manual, and on the translator who often puts his imprint on the translated text [17, 70].

4.1 Recommender Systems

Recommender system (RS) is the name of a subclass of information filtering methods aimed at providing suggestions for items that are most pertinent to a particular user [50]. Following strategies of RS take into account various aspects of user preferences.

Collaborative filtering groups users with similar preferences in presupposition that a user can be matched to an existing template of user preferences by one's choice. User profiles similarity is evaluated basing on aposteriori choice data, which is stored in profiles, often along with ratings assigned to objects of interest. Two clustering approaches exist: by users and by preferences [49]. The key disadvantage of this strategy is the cold start problem — that of recommending to new users with no data available on their preferences [48]. The second major issue is the white crow problem, or the maverick problem [19]: not all users can be attributed to existing groups by their preferences. Moreover, while mass users relatively rarely consume niche content, collaborative filtering deamplifies it [25]. The third issue: relying solely on correlation without considering the underlying causal mechanism may lead to various practical issues such as fairness, robustness, echo chamber, controllability and bias problems for the RS to face, accounting on ratings being part of the problem [16, 67].

The *case-based strategy* fights the problem of user preferences variability in time [14, 56]. Within the framework of this method, groups or types of users are distinguished (e.g., for book RS there would be connoisseurs of classical art, business enthusiasts, young parents) or scenarios to which the user's choice relates (for example, books to ease one's mind [9]). The age category of the user can also be taken into account here [56]. Books metadata are source for this strategy (genres, tags in electronic services), expert work is required to select reader types and corresponding appropriate books (what good librarians do). Experts subjectivity is a possible problem here [27]. The cold start problem isn't solved, nor is the maverick problem.

Content-based filtering uses a set of user preferences obtained via a questionnaire filled during registration or when forming a request to the RS. The key idea of this method is based on the following assumption: the user is interested in objects similar to those that interested him or her previously [15]. Moreover, objects similarity is determined by characteristics of the object itself, and not by a set of actions of a set of users, as in collaborative filtering. A similarity measure is required to compare objects; the cosine measure is widely used for objects represented in multidimensional space. In the recommendation process, clustering and ranking-based methods are applicable [37]. For varying recommendations generated by the RS, as well as for solving the problem of user preferences obsolescence, it would be enough for a user to specify new thematic categories and, possibly, a blacklist of categories. This strategy is selected as it solves the cold start problem and the maverick problem.

Hybrid methods can combine advantages of basic methods, leveling their disadvantages [1]. Hybridization is considered as further development of the RS of interest.

4.2   Feature Selection: Basic and Modified Probabilistic Topic Modelling

The introduced method implements a content-based RS strategy and accounts for users' preferences via estimating texts structural and thematic similarity. We cluster texts in two independent spaces, each constructed via PTM (probabilistic topic modelling); in each we select each input text neighborhood as a cluster containing it (except for input texts), then we get recommendations as a list of texts from both clusters ranged by decreasing cosine similarity of a given text to the input one (if a text belongs to both clusters, the sum of similarities is used instead).

We use basic PTM [24, 62] for constructing a latent space of features. Using the principle of factor analysis, the PTM method discovers latent mutual relationships between documents and words (terms, representing all forms of this word) and identifies factors (topics) characteristic for all documents and terms. PTM is based on the assumption that the appearance of each term in a document can be explained by some latent topic from a given finite set of topics. Probabilistic topic model describes observable term frequencies in each document by a probabilistic mixture of term distribution weighted by topic probabilities for documents [62]. The conditional independence hypothesis is considered to be fulfilled: each topic generates tokens regardless of the document [62]. Given documents d_i, $i \in [1, n]$, words w_k, $k \in [1, z]$, and topics t_j, $j \in [1, m]$, PTM defines probabilities $p(d_i$ is dedicated to the topic $t_j)$ via probabilities $p(w_k$ is dedicated to the topic $t_j)$, see Fig. 1 (A) from [12]. We form a matrix A terms-to-documents for a books dataset: cells store terms TF-IDF values. In order to reduce the matrix dimensions, the singular value decomposition (SVD) is used, for it allows preserving the structure of dependencies, while significantly reducing the amount of calculations and thereby reducing the time of a large corpus analysis. For any matrix A of order ($z \times n$) there exists a singular decomposition in the form of a product of three matrices: $A = \mathrm{U} \cdot \mathrm{S} \cdot \mathrm{V}^{\mathrm{T}} \approx \tilde{A}$, where S is a diagonal matrix where elements are ranged in descending order, and last small elements are excluded, resulting in the matrix $\tilde{A}$. Figure 1 (B) illustrates the SVD, excluded rows and columns are hatched. Basic PTM forms the 1st latent features space for identifying books similar in content.

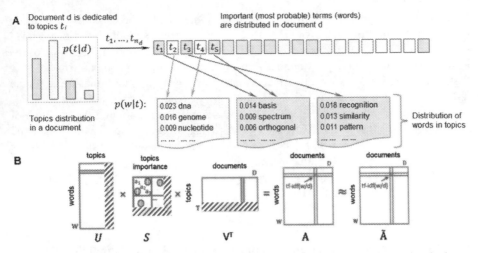

Fig. 1. Scheme of (A) PTM [12], annotated, and (B) SVD, reduced values are hatched.

Next, we construct a modified method which uses PoS trigrams TF-IDF instead of words TF-IDF. While the basic PTM extracts a set of latent topics from a collection of text documents, our modification is aimed at extracting topics as styles basing on word order usage frequencies. This second PTM is to identify books that are similar in structure, namely in word order, in the 2nd constructed latent features space.

For 453 texts of literary and publicistic styles, 4394 unique PoS trigrams were mined. Their number was reduced to 3716 via filtering by TF-IDF. Two 40-dimensional spaces of latent features are constructed. The cosine measure of proximity is selected for comparing texts in each multidimensional space. Text clustering is performed in each space, and a sorted list of texts is recommended for each seed text d_u from the input query, comprising texts from 2 clusters comprising d_u — one from the 1st latent space and another from the 2nd latent space — ordered in descending order by the sum of the cosine proximity values between the input and d_u (located in the same cluster). The result is a list of texts selected from each pair of clusters (for each d_u): first all 1st recommendations from each list, then all 2nd recommendations, etc. Top 10 results are shown, and plus 10 for consequent pressing the "More" button.

For a collection of texts we execute following stages of processing.

- Texts tokenization (all numerals replaced with corresponding words, all punctuation marks eliminated).
- Morphological analysis and words normalization via pymorphy2 library.
- Calculating terms TF-IDF, filtering = > LSA by terms TF-IDF = > texts clustering by thematic similarity in the 1st latent features space (k-means, cosine measure).
- Obtaining PoS trigrams from texts = > PoS trigrams TF-IDF calculation, filtering = > LSA by PoS trigrams TF-IDF = > texts clustering by structural similarity in the 2nd latent features space (k-means, cosine measure).
- Obtaining a sorted list of recommendations for each input text d basing on a union of 2 clusters containing this input text (1 cluster from each space).

– Forming a ranged list of recommendations r_{uv}, $u \in [1, q]$, q is the number of input documents, $v \in [1, w_u]$, w_u is the number of texts in the list of recommendations for the input document d_u: $< r_{11}, r_{21}, ..., r_{q1}, r_{12}, r_{22}, ..., r_{q2}, ..., r_{qv} >$ in the descending order of relevance for each u.

4.3 Discussion

Figure 2 shows a sample of 10 recommendations formed by our software for an input query consisting of two input books: memoirs and a thriller (Russian book titles are given in translation; genres and book quotes are depicted only for visualization). We intentionally ignore genre labels which are present in data, but we observe that genres are considered by our method by construction: memoirs are marked with green, juvenile literature — with yellow, thrillers — with purple, classic literature — with white. Predictably, books from one genre are recommended, but books from a different genre juvenile literature are recommended as well. We opened the books to compare the style, and there we found evidence to success: style matched in Henry Ford memoirs and in "Walking castle" by Diana Wynne Jones. Translators were different. This is also evidence to successful crossing genre boundaries.

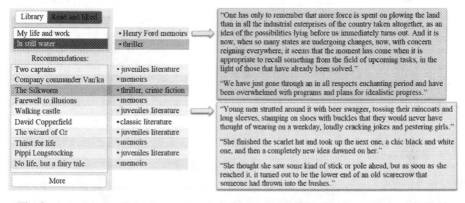

Fig. 2. An example: 10 books recommended for a query of 2 books (memoirs and thriller).

An important metric of quality of recommendations formed by the RS is evaluation aggregated from users. We invited 10 respondents, they submitted circa 140 opinions. There was a differentiation in reader experience: 2 beginners, 2 experienced readers, the rest of respondents submitted equal amounts of requests as beginners and as experienced readers in a particular genre. They were given three categories of opinions (positive, neutral and negative, indicated in Table 2 as ' +', ' ~' and '–') and three scenarios of selecting seed books for a query: (a) books of the same genre, (b) books of various genres, (c) books by the same author. Table 2 presents the results. We asked our respondents to press the "More" button and to evaluate extended results, and to rate the diversity of recommendations.

Table 2. Feedback submitted by respondents.

Queries scenario	Reader experience by genre	Submitted opinions category			Positive opinions after pressing the "More" button	Positive opinions on recommendations diversity
		+	~	−		
a	Beginner	88%	4.5%	7.5%	97% (+ 9%)	94%
a	Experienced	95.5%	4.5%	0%	98.5% (+ 3%)	96%
b	Beginner	91.5%	3%	5.5% *	93% (+ 1.5%)	100%
b	Experienced	94%	2%	4% *	94%	100%
c	Beginner	91%	6%	3%	97% (+ 6%)	96%
c	Experienced	90%	4%	6%	94% (+ 4%)	97%

An asterisk marks two cases where most negative opinions were due to the label "juvenile literature" displayed in the "Library" mode; in a number of cases readers marked stylistic similarity of texts positively and pointed out that genre classification should be detailed, e.g. introducing "adventure", "young adult", "for kids" labels.

Most of submitted feedback is positive, hence, our RS achieved its goal, according to the crowdsourced data. The developed content-oriented method of forming book recommendations basing on their structural similarity to books in the input query proved to be successfully solving its task. Automatic analysis of PoS trigrams enables RS users to get texts similar to seed ones by theme and by structure, namely by word order. Our approach to catching functional style (comprising groups of similar author styles) is verified and is recommended for book recommender systems.

5 Conclusion

This article introduced an approach to text style detecting by word order, in particular PoS trigrams TF-IDF are selected as text features. The introduced approach was verified observationally within two described tasks. An essay at texts classification by FS proved our approach applicability for styles; as to substyles, the designed book recommending system showed successful selection of writings basing on their word order similarity to the input. The introduced content-oriented recommender system enables readers to automate book choice out of a library with an inexhaustible publisher source, be it a paperback mine or an electronic endless stream of novels. The implemented RS solves the cold start problem and that of mavericks, also called the "white crow" problem: a user is supposed to pick one or several books of interest, and the RS engine selects books of similar style. The implemented RS successfully crosses genre boundaries, which is adequate according to the fact that one book genre generally embraces texts of different functional (sub)styles, while other works eliminate texts of ambiguous style [53]. The introduced approach to detecting FS via word order is applicable not only for Russian, but for other languages as well due to their word order variability, which is a continuous variable [36].

Pragmatics (in a narrow sense) of speech is such conditions of communication that include certain characteristics of the addresser, of the addressee and of the situation which affect the linguistic structure of communication. Allan Bell states: «Style is essentially speakers' response to their audience. In audience design, speakers accommodate primarily to their addressee. Third persons — auditors and overhearers — affect style to a lesser but regular degree. < ... > Nonaudience factors like topic and setting derive their effect by association with addressee types. These style shifts are mainly responsive caused by a situational change» [6]. FS selection is one of available means of "the function of differentiating meaning" (a term by Trubetzkoy, 1939 [60]): speakers can also use style as initiative, to redefine the existing situation [6]. As to synthesizing cues and texts in natural languages, our results could be further applicable for dialogue management in dialogue systems: communicative robots as the Russian F-2 project [61] and texts generating software [47]. Research [51] shows that in particular communication cases strict adherence to standard language may potentially evoke perceptions of inequality in interlocutors. In order to make communication more comfortable, hedges are used in multimodal human-machine interaction. Hedges help robots to appear nice to people, even in the quite common conflict case in task-oriented communication: both when the speaker loses his social face and when one has to attack the social face of the hearer [38]. The of applicable hedges could be adapted to the selected FS defined by conversation context which sets different linguistic limitations on possible lexics in general and hedges in particular. What humans select with the speed of experience (if they fail, most often interlocutors' reaction would be anger or deploring — sometimes with a hedge again), a dialogue system would select on the base of probabilistic rules (e.g. with Markov models, with special control whether the original message content was preserved unchanged [2]) or appropriate dictionaries and rule banks, grounded on thorough corpus-driven research, in particular following the investigation approach described in [30, 31, 33].

Acknowledgements. This research is partly supported by the grant of the Russian Science Foundation № 19-18-00547, https://rscf.ru/project/19-18-00547/.

References

1. Adomavicius, G., Tuzhilin, A.: Toward the next generation of recommender systems: a survey of the state-of-the-art and possible extensions. IEEE Trans. on Knowl. and Data Eng. **17**, 734–749 (2005)
2. Babakov, N., Dale, D., Gusev, I., Krotova, I., Panchenko, A.: Don't lose the message while paraphrasing: a study on content preserving style transfer. In: Métais, E., Meziane, F., Sugumaran, V., Manning, W., Reiff-Marganiec, S. (eds.) Natural Language Processing and Information Systems. NLDB 2023. LNCS, vol. 13913. Springer, Cham (2023)
3. Bally, C.: Traité de stylistique française (in French), vol. 1. Winter, Heidelberg (1951)
4. Barakhnin, V.B., Kozhemyakina, O.Y., Pastushkov, I.S.: Automated determination of the type of genre and stylistic coloring of Russian texts. ITM Web of Conferences, Vol. 10. Art. 02001 (2017). https://doi.org/10.1051/itmconf/20171002001
5. Bektoshev, O., Nishonova, S., Maxsudova, U., Hoshimova, D., Mahmudjonova, H.: Formation of religious style in linguistics. Journal of Positive School Psychology **6**(12), 118–124 (2022)

6. Bell, A.: Language style as audience design. Lang. Soc. **13**(2), 145–204 (1984). https://doi.org/10.1017/S004740450001037X
7. Bell, A.: Language and the Media. Annu. Rev. Appl. Linguist. **15**, 23–41 (1995)
8. Bell, A.: A review on In: Biber, D., Finegan, E. (eds.) Sociolinguistic perspectives on register. Oxford University press, Oxford & New York, 1994. pp. xi, 385. Language in Society **24**(2), 265–270 (1995)
9. Berthoud, E., Elderkin, S.: The novel cure: an A–Z of literary remedies. Cannongate, Edinburgh (2013)
10. Biber, D.: Dimensions of register variation: a cross-linguistic comparison. Cambridge University Press, Cambridge (1995)
11. Blakar, R.M.: Language as a means of social power. Pragmalinguistics, pp. 131–169. Mouton, The Hague (1979)
12. Bolshakova, E., Vorontsov, K., Efremova, N., Klyshinsky, E., Lukashevich, N., Sapin, A.: Automatic natural language texts processing and data analysis (in Russian), pp. 198–205. HSE, Moscow (2017)
13. Braslavsky, P.: A study in automatic classification of texts by styles (based on the material of documents from Internet) (in Russian). In: Russian language in the Internet, compilation of articles, pp. 6–15. Otechestvo, Kazan (2003)
14. Bridge, D., Goker, M., McGinty, L., Smyth, B.: Case–based recommender systems. Knowl. Eng. Rev. **20**(3), 315–320 (2006)
15. Candillier, L., Jack, K., Fessant, F., Meyer, F.: State-of-the-art recommender systems. In: Collaborative and Social Information Retrieval and Access — Techniques for Improved User Modeling, pp. 1–22. IGI Global, Hershey (2009)
16. Chen, J., Dong, H., Wang, X., Feng, F., Wang, M., He, X.: Bias and debias in recommender system: a survey and future directions. ACM Trans. Info. Sys. **41**(3), 1–39 (2023)
17. Chukovsky, K.: The art of translation. In: Leighton, L. (ed.). University of Tennessee Press, Knoxville (1984)
18. Delitsyn, L.: Hudlomer. Automatic classification of text style (in Russian), archived, https://web.archive.org/web/20180402152210/http://teneta.rinet.ru:80/hudlomer/article.html,   last accessed 15 June 2023
19. Ferraro, A., Ferreira, G., Diaz, F., Born, G.: Measuring commonality in recommendation in cultural content: recommender systems to enhance cultural citizenship. In: RecSys'22: Proceedings of the 16th ACM Conference on Recommender Systems, pp. 567–572. ACM, New York (2022). https://doi.org/10.1145/3523227.3551476
20. Fomenko, V.P., Fomenko, T.G.: Author's invariant of Russian literary texts (in Russian). In: Fomenko, A.T. (ed.) New Chronology of Greece: Antiquity in the Middle Ages, vol. 2, pp. 768–820. MSU, Moscow (1996)
21. Fucks, W.: Mathematical theory of word-formation. In: Cherry, C. (ed.) Information theory, pp. 154–170. Butterworths Scientific Publications, London (1955)
22. Gladkiy, A.V.: Syntactic structures of natural language, 2nd edn. LKI, Moscow (2007). (in Russian)
23. Grashchenko, L.A., Romanishin, G.V.: An essay at automated analysis of self-repetition in scientific texts (in Russian). In: New information technologies in automated systems: Proceedings of eighteenth scientific and practical seminar, pp. 582–590. Keldysh Institute of Applied Mathematics, Moscow (2015)
24. Hofmann, T.: Probabilistic latent semantic analysis. In: Proceedings of the Fifteenth conference on Uncertainty in artificial intelligence, pp. 289–296. Morgan Kaufmann Publishers Inc., Waltham (1999)
25. Horta Ribeiro, M., Veselovsky, V., West, R.: The amplification paradox in recommender systems. In: Lin, Y.-R., Cha, M., Quercia, D. (eds.) Proceedings of the International AAAI

Conference on Web and Social Media, 17(1), pp. 1138–1142. AAAI Press, Palo Alto (2023). https://doi.org/10.1609/icwsm.v17i1.22223

26. How book synopses set reader expectations and why that matters/Pages Unbound Book Reviews & Discussions, https://pagesunbound.wordpress.com/2021/07/20/how-book-syn opses-set-reader-expectations-and-why-that-matters/, last accessed 15 June 2023

27. Jin, D., et al.: A survey on fairness-aware recommender systems (preprint), https://ssrn.com/abstract=4469569 (2023). https://doi.org/10.2139/ssrn.4469569, last accessed 15 June 2023

28. Karlgren, J., Cutting, D.: Recognizing text genres with simple metrics using discriminant analysis. In: Proceedings of the 15th International Conference on Computational Linguistics (COLING '94), pp. 1.071–1.075 (1994)

29. Kessler, B., Nunberg, G., Schütze, H.: Automatic detection of text genre. In: Proceedings of 35th Annual Meeting. Association for Computational Linguistics, pp. 32–38. ACL, Stroudsburg (1997)

30. Kotov, A.: Application of D-Script Model to Emotional Dialogue Simulation. In: André, E., Dybkjær, L., Minker, W., Heisterkamp, P. (eds.) ADS 2004. LNCS (LNAI), vol. 3068, pp. 193–196. Springer, Heidelberg (2004). https://doi.org/10.1007/978-3-540-24842-2_19

31. Kotov, A.A.: Accounting for irony and emotional oscillation in computer architectures. In: Proc. of International Conference on Affective Computing and Intelligent Interaction ACII 2009, pp. 506–511. IEEE, Amsterdam (2009)

32. Kotov, A.A.: Mechanisms of the speech influence. RSUH, Moscow (2021). (in Russian)

33. Kotov, A., Budyanskaya, E.: The Russian emotional corpus: communication in natural emotional situations. In: Computational Linguistics and Intellectual Technologies, vol. 11(18), pp. 296–306. RSUH, Moscow (2012)

34. Kozerenko, E.B.: The problem of language structures equivalence within translation and semantic alignment of parallel texts. In: Iomdin, L.L., Laufer, N.I., Narinyani, A.S., Selegey, V.P. (eds.) Computational Linguistics and Intellectual Technologies: Papers from the Annual International Conference «Dialogue 2006» (Bekasovo, 31 May – 4 June 2006), pp. 252–258. RSUH, Moscow (2006)

35. Kozhina, M.N., Bazhenova, E.A., Kotyurova, M.P., Skovorodnikov, A.P. (eds.): Stylistic encyclopedic dictionary of Russian (in Russian). 2nd edn. Flinta, Nauka, Moscow (2006)

36. Levshina, N., et al.: Why we need a gradient approach to word order. Linguistics (2023). https://doi.org/10.1515/ling-2021-0098

37. Li, Y., Liu, K., Satapathy, R., Wang, S., Cambria, E.: Recent developments in recommender systems: a survey (preprint) (2023). https://doi.org/10.48550/arXiv.2306.12680

38. Malkina, M., Zinina, A., Arinkin, N., Kotov, A.: Multimodal hedges for companion robots: a politeness strategy or an emotional expression? In: Selegey, V.P., et al. (eds.) Computational Linguistics and Intellectual Technologies: Papers from the Annual International Conference "Dialogue", issue 22, pp. 319–326. RSUH, Moscow (2023)

39. Markov, A.A.: On one application of the statistical method (in Russian). Transactions of the Imperial Academy of Sciences., series. 6, vol. X(4). Publisher House of the Imperial Academy of Sciences, Petrograd (1916)

40. Mathesius, V.: Functional linguistics. In: Vachek, J., Dušková, L. (eds.) Praguiana: Some basic and less known aspects of the Prague Linguistic School, pp. 121–142. John Benjamins, Amsterdam and New York (1983)

41. Meier, H.: Deutsche Sprachstatistik (in German). Georg Olms Verlagsbuchhandlung, Hildesheim (1964)

42. Mizernov, I.Y., Grashchenko, L.A.: Analysis of methods for text complexity estimation (in Russian). In: New information technologies in automated systems: Proceedings of eighteenth scientific and practical seminar, pp. 572–581. Keldysh Institute of Applied Mathematics, Moscow (2015)

43. Morozov, N.A.: Linguistic spectra: A means of distinguishing plagiarism from the true works of a known author: A stylometric etude (in Russian). Transactions of the Department of Russian language and Philology of the Imperial Academy of Sciences XX(4), pp. 93–134 . Publisher House of the Imperial Academy of Sciences, Petrograd (1915)
44. Nivre, J., Boguslavsky, I.M., Iomdin, L.L.: Parsing the SynTagRus treebank of Russian. In: Proceedings of the 22nd International Conference on Computational Linguistics. COLING 2008, 18–22 August 2008, Manchester, pp. 641–648. ACL, Stroudsburg (2008)
45. Notation for grammemes (for Russian) — Morphological analyzer pymorphy2 (in Russian), https://pymorphy2.readthedocs.io/en/stable/user/grammemes.html, last accessed 15 June 2023
46. Perfiliev, A.A., Murzin, F.A., Shmanina, T.V.: Methods of syntactic analysis and comparison of constructions of a natural language oriented to use in search systems. Bull. Nov. Comp. Center, Comp. Science **31**, 91–109 (2010)
47. Petukhova, K., Smilga, V., Zharikova, D.: Abstract user goals in open-domain dialog systems. In: Selegey, V.P., et al. (eds.) Computational Linguistics and Intellectual Technologies: Papers from the Annual International Conference "Dialogue", issue 22, supplementary volume, pp. 1097–1107. RSUH, Moscow (2023)
48. Poirier, D., Fessant, F., Tellier, I.: Reducing the cold-start problem in content recommender through opinion classification. In: Proceedings of IEEE/WIC/ACM International Conference WI-IAT, pp. 204–207. IEEE Computer Society, Washington (2010)
49. Resnick, P., Varian, H.R.: Recommender systems. Commun. ACM **40**(3), 56–58 (1997)
50. Ricci, F., Rokach, L., Shapira, B.: Recommender systems: techniques, applications, and challenges. In: Ricci, F., Rokach, L., Shapira, B. (eds.) Recommender Systems Handbook. 3rd edn, pp. 1–35. Springer, New York (2022). https://doi.org/10.1007/978-1-0716-2197-4_1
51. Rombouts, E., Fieremans, M., Zenner, E.: Talking very properly creates such a distance': Exploring style-shifting in speech-language therapists. Int. J. Lang. Commun. Disord. (2023). https://doi.org/10.1111/1460-6984.12896
52. Salton, G., Buckley, C.: Term-weighting approaches in automatic text retrieval. Inf. Process. Manage. **24**(5), 513–523 (1988)
53. Savchenko, E., Lazebnik, T.: Computer aided functional style identification and correction in modern russian texts. J. Data Info. Manage. **4**(3), 1–8 (2022). https://doi.org/10.1007/s42488-021-00062-2
54. Sirotinina, O.B.: Modern colloquial speech and its peculiarities. Znanie, Moscow (1974). (in Russian)
55. Sirotinina, O.B. (ed.): Colloquial speech in the system of functional styles of the modern Russian language. Saratov University Publishing House, Saratov (1983). (in Russian)
56. Smyth, B.: Case-based recommender. In: Brusilovsky, P., Kobsa, A., Nejdl, W. (eds.) The Adaptive Web, LNCS 4321, pp. 342–376. Springer-Verlag, Heidelberg (2007)
57. Stamatatos, E.: A survey of modern authorship attribution methods. J. Am. Soc. Inform. Sci. Technol. **60**(3), 538–556 (2009)
58. Vachek, J., Dušková, L. (eds.) Praguiana: Some basic and less known aspects of the Prague Linguistic School, pp. 33–58. John Benjamins, Amsterdam and New York (1983)
59. Trosborg, A.: Text typology: register, genre and text type. In: Text typology and translation, pp. 3–23, John Benjamins Publishing Company, Amsterdam (1997)
60. Trubetzkoy, N.S.: Principles of phonology. University of California Press, Berkeley (1969)
61. Velichkovsky, B.M., Kotov, A., Arinkin, N., Zaidelman, L., Zinina, A., Kivva, K.: From social gaze to indirect speech constructions: how to induce the impression that your companion robot is a conscious creature. Appl. Sci. **11**(21), 10255 (2021)
62. Veselova, E., Vorontsov, K.: Topic balancing with additive regularization of topic models. In: Proceedings of the 58th Annual Meeting of the Association for Computational Linguistics: Student Research Workshop, pp. 59–65. ACL, Stroudsburg (2020)

63. Vinogradov, V.V.: Results of stylistics issues discussion (in Russian). Linguistic Issues **1**, 60–87 (1955)
64. Volkova, L.L.: Towards the problem of detecting functional style of a natural language document (in Russian). In: New information technologies in automated systems: Proceedings of eighteenth scientific and practical seminar, pp. 615–626. Keldysh Institute of Applied Mathematics, Moscow (2015)
65. Volkova, L.L., Lanko, A.A.: A method for selecting features of natural language texts for classification by functional style (in Russian). In: Tikhonov, A.N., Uvaysov, S.U., Ivanov, I.A. (eds.) Innovations on the base of information and communicative technologies: Proceedings of international scientific and practical conference, pp. 287–289. NRU HSE, Moscow (2015)
66. Wang, L., Zhang, K.: Space efficient algorithms for ordered tree comparison. Algorithmica **51**(3), 283–297 (2008)
67. Xu, S., Ji, J., Li, Y., Ge, Y., Tan, J., Zhang, Y.: Causal inference for recommendation: foundations, methods and applications (preprint) (2023). https://doi.org/10.48550/arXiv.2301.04016
68. Yartseva, V.N. (ed.): Linguistic encyclopedic dictionary. Sovetskaya entsiklopediya, Moscow (1990). (in Russian)
69. Zasorina, L.N. (ed.): Frequency dictionary of Russian. Russkiy Yazyk, Moscow (1977). (in Russian)
70. Zhao, D., Chen, Q.: Translation style: a systemic functional perspective. Int. J. Eng. Litera. **14**, 27–32 (2023). https://doi.org/10.5897/IJEL2023.1569

Artificial Intelligence and Deep Learning Technologies for Creative Tasks. Computer Vision and Knowledge-Based Control

Visual Data Models in Scientific Search for Interpretation of Multiparametric Signals

Alena Zakharova[1]([✉]) [iD], Aleksey Shklyar[2] [iD], and Evgeniya Vekhter[2] [iD]

[1] V. A. Trapeznikov Institute of Control Sciences of Russian Academy of Sciences, Moscow, Russia
zaawmail@gmail.com
[2] Tomsk Polytechnic University, Tomsk, Russia
{shklyarav,vehter}@tpu.ru

Abstract. Modern visualization methods are used to convey information about an object or process and as a tool for search and decision-making process. Data and signals, in analog and digital form, are only valuable if they are analyzed for a specific goal. In this work we etablish the classification of visualization tasks from the point of analyzing heterogeneous multidimensional data, including the case when at the initial stage it is required to formulate a research hypothesis. A classification of visualization metaphors is presented, which is necessary for a conscious choice of tools for visualization and data analysis. This is important for understanding and managing the interpretability of information, the formation of the correct meaning and operational understanding. We demonstrate examples of static and dynamic models of visualization. Based on the semantic model and proposed classification, the principles of visual metaphors formation for solving several applied tasks in various fields of knowledge (oil and gas production, biomedicine, materials science, education, management, etc.) are formulated.

Keywords: Visual metaphor · scientific visualization · heterogeneous data analysis

1 Advantages of Visualization

The main purpose of visualization is to increase the understanding of user data essence [1–4]. One of the priority issues in this field is the definition of the term "understanding" and the introduction of a quantitative measure necessary as a comparative characteristic [5]. The next task is to identify factors that can create obstacles in the process of user understanding. Some of them are indicated in [6] and referred to the problems of information visualization; however, they can be attributed to general issues. It should be noted that overcoming the negative role of many well-known factors currently remains an unresolved problem and, therefore, is important.

From the point of scientific and data visualization, one of the controversial factors is the influence of preliminary information awareness, i.e., the actual knowledge possessed by the user, on understanding of a visual image. "Preliminary information awareness"

A. G. Kravets et al. (Eds.): CIT&DS 2023, CCIS 1909, pp. 117–130, 2023.
https://doi.org/10.1007/978-3-031-44615-3_8

refers to both knowledge types: (i) knowledge accumulated by the observer and (ii) subjective experience of the observer. It is assumed that they largely determine features of thinking and, therefore, become the basis for interpreting visualized information. Thus, the factors affecting the use of visualization are not limited to technical issues of obtaining visual images.

Factors that characterize the uncontrolled influence of visualization on the viewer can be highlighted as a special category [7–9]. This refers to the influence of the aesthetics of perception on thinking. Mechanisms of such influence are poorly understood, however, at least two aspects are known in which aesthetics is significant: firstly, it has a psycho-emotional impact on the viewer, and secondly, it characterizes the data based on what kind a visually perceived object is obtained. Aesthetics of perception can act as a subjective, but quick criterion for evaluating visualization results when choosing a matching rule between the input data and visual image.

Choice of analytics tools can have a significant impact on the result when solving analysis problems related to studying data and making a decision. For example, when studying empirical data in the absence of an analytical model of the studied phenomenon, the choice of research methodology is part of the solution methodology and, at the initial stage, can predetermine results or their qualitative criteria [10–14]. The use of visualization as an independent analytical tool requires justification when the replacement or supplement of approaches to data analysis is considered.

Problems similar in content are considered in [15], where a comparative study of approaches of visual analytics and machine learning was carried out in the development of classification models. Theoretical and empirical data were presented, confirming the usefulness of visual analytics approaches for the indicated purposes and the specifics of the problem statement. This indicates the need to obtain generalizing conclusions that will justify the use of visualization as a method of solving applied problems.

An advantage of visualization as an analytical tool is the solution "transparency" i.e., high availability of intermediate stages of the decision making process for its evaluation by the researcher [16, 17]. The importance of this circumstance is associated with the need to control and correct the solution for most real problems, since this allows to reduce time for obtaining the final decision. Another important circumstance, which is a consequence of visualization, is its cognitive significance, which forms the observer's mental model of the phenomenon under study in the research process [18–21]. In many cases, this fact becomes the most important result, as it allows to increase the efficiency of solving similar problems.

2 Task Classification

Generalization of experience in solving data analysis problems with similar characteristics of the source data allows us to raise the question of visual analysis task classification. Classification of analysis tasks may allow to achieve the following results:

- Fast decision-making based on visual analytics tools.
- Experience accumulation in the use of visual analysis tools and its systematization, complementing the classification.

- Predictive analysis of the applicability of new visual analytics tools based on comparison with existing models and experience of their use.
- Evaluation of possible results of combining various visualization techniques and processing the data obtained in the developing of complex solutions.

The study of known models of visualization processes [16, 22] and the interpretation of their results leads to the identification of several task types that differ from each other both in internal features and potential results.

2.1 The Task of Visual Informing

In tasks of this type, the goal is only to choose one of the possible solutions based on the study of incoming data. The task of the visual data model is to inform the observer about a change in state or, more correctly, about the occurrence of an expected event. A visual image is used as a state indicator of the observed system, and the task is to inform the user of the model about the need to move to the other predefined actions.

2.2 The Task of Visual Learning

A variant of the data research problem in which the goal is to transfer a new mental model to the user as a result of change in awareness [10]. It is assumed that there is a known interpretation of the data under study, and a visual model is a tool that allows the user to establish a mental relationship between the data and proposed interpretation. Considering the definitions of direct and inverse processes [23]. This task can be formulated differently: informing the recipient of a visual message based on the transmission in the message of both the initial data and the hypothesis of their interpretation. Hypothesis verification uses only formal logic aimed at checking the correctness of constructing a visual message. In a simplified form, the task of visual learning is to convey to the observer the necessary amount of information, reliability of which is beyond doubt.

2.3 The Task of Making a Visual Decision

Visual data models are widely used in decision support systems. In this case, the task of analysis usually has the following features: (i) it is necessary to make a decision after studying all the available information, (ii) the decision time is of great importance and should be minimal, (iii) there are several possible answers, and (iv) the choice cannot be made on the basis of formal logic. The determining condition for these problems is the active use of the researcher's knowledge and experience for obtaining additional information that affects the further course of the decision-making process [9, 18, 24]. Evaluating this additional information and generating hypotheses based on it becomes part of the process and can be improved with visual models.

2.4 Analytical Visual Models

Each variant of the visual analysis tasks described above is based on the implicit assumption that the answer to the question can be obtained as a result of a single interaction between the researcher and the visual model. This is true only for a few tasks, formulation of which implies the possibility of posing a direct question and obtaining an answer to it as a necessary result. For many practical areas of research related to data analysis, achieving the goal is possible after sequential solving of several problems, including the situation when setting the next intermediate task is possible only after obtaining the solution of the previous one. An iterative procedure is being formed, its control becomes an independent problem for experts interested in the visualization theory.

An example of analysis problems with similar properties is the study of empirical data obtained during the solving practical tasks with a low level of subject area description formalization [25–27]. In this case, the purpose of the visual analysis is to obtain new knowledge based on the discovery of internal patterns in the data being examined and the study of their properties. On this basis, tasks requiring consistent study, possibly with the use of various analysis tools, are classified as analytical. Assuming that task properties can be associated with a certain type of visual models, such models can be considered as analytical visual models.

3 Examples of Applied Problems and Their Visual Solutions

3.1 Data Visualization with a Low Level of Formalization

A typical example of research characterized by the tendency to reduce the time spent is analysis of large amounts of unsorted information related to individual objects or events related to a selected area of interest. The purpose of analysis in such studies is to form a holistic view of the information available to the researcher and to obtain grounds for conclusions that correspond to the goals of the researcher. [28–32]. An obstacle to achieving this goal is the lack of a formal model of the knowledge area and the incompleteness or significant amount of data (Fig. 1).

As a practical task for studying the effectiveness of visual models, the problem of representing the total amount of knowledge in the subject area containing experimental information has been solved. The initial data are characterized by a large number of heterogeneous sources of information (publications containing a description of experimental studies in a given area) and the associated heterogeneity and inconsistency of the data. For practical verification of the method, empirical data on the current state of the study of silicon carbide obtaining processes by the electric arc method were selected [33]. The visual model simultaneously presents information about 260 experiments on the production of carbon ultrafine materials in the plasma of a direct current electric arc.

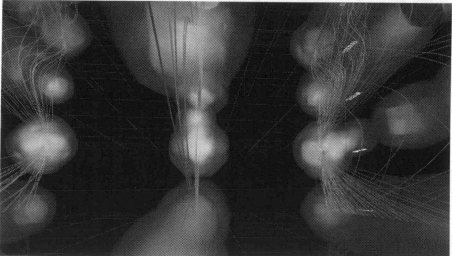

Fig. 1. An example of a visual data model designed to search for a formal model of the knowledge area. The model metaphor focuses on the possibility to interactively changing the space and parameters of the model in order to determine the basis for the hypothesis about the mutual influence of values in the data. Visual detection of image clusters of informative objects becomes the basis for determining parameter hierarchy in the formal model of the phenomenon.

The visual model proposed for solving the analysis problem is a complex spatial introduction of the parallel coordinates method used in visualization of multidimensional data. The advantage of the proposed visual model which implements the classification of visual analysis tasks and visual research tools, is the possibility of simultaneous representation in the perceived image of different data types, multidimensional ones, with missing values of some variables. An important practical advantage of this visual research is the possibility to determine the research hypothesis during the analysis. It allows the reuse of an already built data image to answer new questions. This possibility can be considered as a factor of increasing the efficiency of visual analysis.

3.2 Visualization of Experimental Data Volumes

The main feature of modern experimental approaches is simultaneous assessment of a large number of parameters characterizing one or another aspect of a biological object: genome, gene expression, protein composition, representation of symbiotic microbial communities, metabolic composition, etc. The number of measured factors in one object varies from hundreds to thousands, and the amount of raw information can be tens of gigabytes from one sample. At the same time, in order to reliably establish biological patterns within an experiment, it is necessary to study hundreds of samples. The presence of such a large amount of information requires new approaches to its analysis and interpretation [34–36]. An example of experimental multidimensional data analysis, the effectiveness of which can be improved using visual analytics tools, is the work with data obtained during examination of gut microbial communities (microbiota) of patients with Parkinson's disease in comparison with the microbiota of healthy donors and patients with other neurological disorders.

The visual model proposed for medical and biological data makes it possible to conduct an analytical study using the advantages of visual perception, which can significantly reduce the analysis time [37]. The advantage of the proposed solution is the possibility to simultaneously study a large amount of initial data, while the effectiveness of the analysis increases with its volume. The created metaphor for visual representation has shown high efficiency in the study of experimental data characterized by different levels of reliability. Efficiency evaluation is determined by a multiple reduction in the analysis time, formulation and verification of new hypotheses, as well as information exchange among the participants of the analysis process.

The visual model can help to solve the problem of interdisciplinary training of specialists involved in data analysis, since it creates conditions for the participation in solving problems of researchers qualified in the subject area which is the source of the data. During the pretesting of the developed model, visual solutions were built to perform preliminary and predictive analysis of experimental data. The visualized data contained multidimensional descriptions of 5 – 20 groups of experimental samples (~200). The model made it possible to quickly identify properties in the initial data that correlate with each other. This creates conditions for a fast transition to the building of analytical model.

4 Importance and Problems of Research-Oriented Tasks

In the case of using an analytical visual model [38–41], consistent approach to the solution of the problem leads to the need for constant and mandatory user participation in the analysis process (Fig. 2). The presence of interactive control of the visual image provides user's direct participation in image manipulation and is the basis for deep data analysis. A substantiated system of interactive control creates conditions for posing new research questions and obtaining quick answers, thus accelerating the achievement of the result. Therefore, by adding a control interface to a visual model, it is possible to make it an analytical solution tool for problems that do not have a formally justified logical solution.

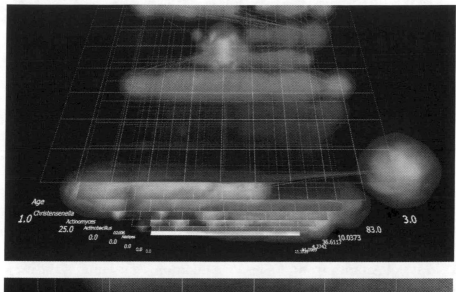

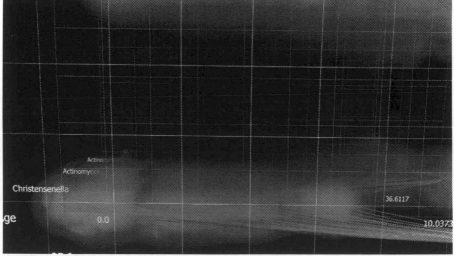

Fig. 2. An example of a data model with a high degree of uncertainty. The visualization metaphor provides interactive highlighting of the most likely relationships between individual values, making decisions about the reasons of the observed uncertainty. At the next step, the images of the initial data (point clouds) are replaced by visualization of relationships (relationship lines). As a result, a hypothetical model of the phenomenon is formed.

The main idea that provides an increase in both cognitive and overall efficiency of visual analysis is the directed application of user capabilities, organized and controlled by means of a visual model [37, 42, 43]. Promising directions in this case include involvement of the awareness and peculiarities of the user's thinking, both for the formation of a decision hypothesis and for making a decision about its reliability. In the case of studying data characterizing phenomena and objects which do not have a full-fledged formal description, the use of visual models not only becomes a way to discover new patterns, but also forms understanding of their meaning. For example, a visual model that, simultaneously presents to the observer an image of both the initial data and the patterns found, can be used as a formal visual model of a knowledge area. This can have a significant impact on the viewer's thinking, since the available amount of mental resources changes and the research process becomes not explorative but developing [5, 44].

Analysis of the logical structure of a visual model allows to answer questions related to increasing the efficiency of visual analysis and is the basis for determining rules for combining elementary solutions. The main criteria of the effectiveness of a visual model include two parameters: reliability of the obtained result, and time spent to achieve it. Therefore, the purpose of the preliminary study, which arises as a stage of the complex solution of the task, is to implement a methodological approach to organizing the rational use of available resources.

5   Ways of Adapting and Using Visualization Tools of an Arbitrary Type in Scientific Search Tasks (Cognitive Visualization)

The decision on acceptable ways of data visualization can be made based on information about a potential user of the tool, the type of task, as well as experience in solving similar problems. The resulting solution is a set of rules and recommendations that restrict subsequent technological solutions in order to reduce the time spent on creating a visual analysis tool. Existing methods of visual representation that do not correspond to the task of analysis and characteristics of the predefined type of a visual model are excluded from consideration. In addition, requirements and restrictions are formed for the searching new and unparalleled ways of visual representation.

5.1   Choice of Visual Representation Metaphor

Valid expressive means are combined into a single consistent system which represents a data visualization metaphor. Compatibility of individual visual techniques can be pre-estimated based on formal rules related to the possibilities of visual perception (Fig. 3). After defining the visualization metaphor, it becomes possible to obtain a data image, evaluate it, and make a decision on the correctness of the proposed metaphor [45].

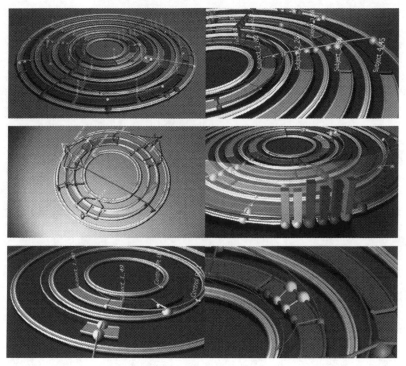

Fig. 3. States of an interactively managed data model. A visualization metaphor is presented, developed for the analysis and modification of parameters describing the state of a complex multi-level system (educational program). Metaphor is characterized by the ability to search for correct states, design errors and hidden reserves.

5.2   Defining the Degree of Acceptable Variability of the Visual Image

Within the chosen visualization metaphor, the data model can be changed in order to find the most beneficial representation of the data from the researcher's point of view. The degree of variability has to be determined based on the requirements of maintaining adequate interpretation of visual information and searching for a representation method that reduces time to build a data image. An additional condition affecting the variability of the visual representation is the need to use a changing representation in order to form hypotheses and responds to cognitive queries.

5.3   Creating Controls for Model Properties

The development of user tools for influencing the visual image is necessary for organizing functional interaction between the user and visual model [32]. Tasks of the controls, which form the system for managing model properties, are purposeful change in the visual representation within the allowable variability, implementation of data input and output operations, additional processing and filtering of initial data, transition to a new representation, phased coordination of research objectives and the visual data model state.

5.4 Creating Controls for Research Process

Supplementing the control system with the ability to transition to the state of visual model (which is important in search procedures) is aimed at verifying hypotheses. There are two requirements for technical solutions that provide such capabilities, (i) compliance with the previously obtained description of the potential user of the visual model, which is necessary to reduce the time of research, (ii) the possibility of their use when changing the expressive means that make up the visual representation metaphor [46].

5.5 Creating Ways of Attracting Additional Data

Visual research tool capabilities are expanded by creating conditions for including additional information in the visual image. The choice of additional information occurs at the user's initiative, therefore, the control system, if such an extension is necessary, must provide the possibility of a conflict-free representation of the required information and return to the initial state of the visual data model.

6 Classification of Visualization Metaphors

As follows from the analysis of the examples of visualization tasks and the experience of practical use of visual analytics tools, visualization metaphor does not limit its role to the formal mapping of data space into a user-perceived representation. Based on a visualization goal and possible ways to achieve it, the following classes of visualization metaphors can be defined:

- Statement. Formulation of the initial volume of factual data with the help of visually perceived images. Creating a new wording to ensure that the user understands its meaning through the application of familiar associative structures.
- Study. A visual description of concepts, phenomena or processes that do not yet have a complete definition, or are "empirically inaccessible". In this case, cognitive properties of visualization are manifested at the stage of comparing the concept and the image of an object that has well-perceived visual properties. Search for a visual concept that matches the features of the data under study.
- Generalization. A variant of a toolkit for systematizing a significant amount of information (including heterogeneous or unrelated), as a result of combining it in a single analyzed visual space. Visual metaphor becomes a source of new knowledge, being a much more capacious way of storing and transmitting information, supplemented by means of denoting dependencies.

In any case, a visual object, using natural mechanisms of metaphorical interpretation, becomes a stimulus for cognitive processes, for which the presence of restrictions on possible interpretation of the information basis of visualization is a significant factor.

7 Conclusion. Technology of Adaptive Visual Analytics and its Advantages in Hypothesizing

The possibility of changing properties of a model during its study provides conditions for conducting an experimental study of the initial object (process). Besides, the model, being an artificial analogy, is always subjective. This means the presence of an authorship factor, which manifests itself in influencing the way the real or imaginary object is presented as a result of modeling. Proper use of this circumstance can have a positive impact on the achievement of the intended modeling outcomes.

Let us define a visual data model as a visually perceived image associated with this data according to some rule. As a model, such an image must meet a number of requirements. For visual models, subjectivity of an image is the reason for its inaccurate interpretation. However, mental processing of the information received consists in recognition of the observed contradiction, formulation of the question associated with this contradiction, and the subsequent mental construction of the hypothesis. Interaction of the user with the visual model space becomes an experiment with the researcher's perception. Interactive control of a visual model is a bidirectional process that combines mental and visual image of the studied phenomenon.

Unlike a static visual object, a changeable image gives the viewer more reason to form a mental hypothesis that seeks to explain its meaning. Therefore, visual model controllers, which solve the problem of monitoring the compliance of the model with the requirements imposed on it, can be assigned the function of regulating and implementing dynamic changes in the visual model. Thus, the interactive capabilities of visual modeling environment can generally act as cognitive search tool.

In the case of a complex model, successive approaching to the solution of the problem leads to the user's continuous and mandatory presence in the process. The completeness of a logical scheme of visual model functioning cannot be achieved without including the fourth mandatory element in it – a particular user's capabilities that affect the result of the analysis throughout the entire sequence of images. A valid control system creates conditions for formulation of new research questions and quick answers, accelerating the achievement of the analysis goal. Thus, addition of a visual model with a control interface corresponds to the proposed structure of visual analysis and makes it an analytical tool for solving a wider range of problems [47].

The main idea that provides an increase in cognitive efficiency of visual analysis is the directed application of the user's capabilities, implemented due to the properties of the visual model. This creates a possibility of attracting additional resources to solving the analysis problem. In this case, the involvement of the awareness and peculiarities of user's thinking is a promising direction, both for formation of a hypothesis and for making a decision about its reliability.

Analytical potential of a visual model is determined by the choice of methods for visual modeling of the studied data, the maximum possible speed of constructing a visual image while maintaining all nuances of a visual representation that are necessary in terms of functionality. Perhaps the most significant element of the model is its interface, which is important for application of the informative and cognitive potential of the user.

References

1. Tufte, E.R.: The visual display of quantitative Information. The Visual Display of Quantitative Information, 1–191 (2008)
2. Ware, C.: Foundation for a Science of Data Visualization (2012)
3. Blascheck, T., John, M., Kurzhals, K., Koch, S., Ertl, T.: VA2: A Visual Analytics Approach for // Evaluating Visual Analytics Applications. IEEE Trans. Vis. Comput. Graph. **22**(1), 61–70 (2016)
4. Purchase, H.C., Andrienko, N., Jankun-Kelly, T.J., Ward, M.: Theoretical foundations of information visualization. Inf. Vis. **4950**(4950), 46–64 (2008)
5. Sacha, D., et al.: Human-centered machine learning through interactive visualization. In: 24th European Symposium on Artificial Neural Networks, Computational Intelligence and Machine Learning, pp. 27–29 (2016)
6. Chen, C.: Top 10 unsolved information visualization problems. IEEE Comput. Graph. Appl. **25**(4), 12–16 (2005)
7. Chen, M., Golan, A.: What may visualization processes optimize? IEEE Trans. Vis. Comput. Graph. **22**(12), 2619–2632 (2016)
8. John, R.: Cognitive Psychology and its Implications **53**(9) (2013)
9. Green, T.M., Ribarsky, W., Fisher, B.: Visual analytics for complex concepts using a human cognition model. In: 2008 IEEE Symposium on Visual Analytics Science and Technology, pp. 91–98 (2008)
10. Cui, Q., Ward, M.O., Rundensteiner, E.A., Yang, J.: Measuring data abstraction quality in multiresolution visualizations. IEEE Trans. Visual Comput. Graphics **12**(5), 709–716 (2006)
11. Ware, C.: Information Visualization: Perception for Design, 2nd Edition (2004)
12. Ward, M.O., Theroux, K.J.: Perceptual benchmarking for multivariate data visualization. Sci. Visualiz. Conf. Dagstuhl **1997**, 314–321 (1997)
13. Chen, C., Czeerwinski, M.P.: Empirical evaluation of information visualizations: An introduction. Int. J. Human Comp. Stud. **53**(5), 631–635 (2000)
14. Smith, K., Moriarty, S., Barbatsis, G., Kenney, K.: Handbook of visual communication: theory, methods, and media. Handbook of visual communication: Theory, methods, and media (2005)
15. Tam, G.K.L., Kothari, V., Chen, M.: An analysis of machine- and human-analytics in classification. IEEE Trans. Vis. Comput. Graph. **23**(1), 71–80 (2017)
16. Elmqvist, N., Yi, J.S.: Patterns for visualization evaluation. Inf. Vis. **14**(3), 250–269 (2015)
17. Lee, S., Kim, S.-H., Hung, Y.-H., Lam, H., Kang, Y., Yi, J.S.: How do people make sense of unfamiliar visualizations?: a grounded model of novice's information visualization sensemaking. IEEE Trans. Vis. Comput. Graph **22**(1), 499–508 (2016)
18. Groesser, S.N., Schaffernicht, M.: Mental models of dynamic systems: taking stock and looking ahead. Syst. Dyn. Rev. **28**(1), 46–68 (2012)
19. Grudin, J.: Three faces of human-computer interaction. IEEE Ann. Hist. Comput. **27**(4), 46–62 (2005)
20. Guo, H., Gomez, S.R., Ziemkiewicz, C., Laidlaw, D.H.: A case study using visualization interaction logs and insight metrics to understand how analysts arrive at insights. IEEE Trans. Vis. Comput. Graph **22**(1), 51–60 (2016)
21. Mahyar, N., Tory, M.: Supporting communication and coordination in collaborative sense-making. IEEE Trans. Vis. Comput. Graph **20**(12), 1633–42 (2014)
22. Pirolli, P.: Information foraging theory: adaptive interaction with information. Information Foraging Theory, 1–28 (2007)
23. Pirolli, P., Card, S.: The sensemaking process and leverage points for analyst technology as identified through cognitive task analysis. In: Proceedings of International Conference on Intelligence Analysis, vol. 2–4 (2005)

24. Green, T.M., Ribarsky, W., Fisher, B.: Building and applying a human cognition model for visual analytics. Inf. Vis. **8**(1), 1–13 (2009)
25. Endert, A., North, C., Chang, R., Zhou, M.: Toward usable interactive analytics: coupling cognition and computation. In: KDD 2014 Workshop on Interactive Data Exploration and Analytics (IDEA) (2014). Online: URL http://poloclub.gatech.edu/idea2014/papers/p52-endert.pdf, 30 January 2023
26. Gorg, C., Kang, Y.A., Liu, Z., Stasko, J.: Visual analytics support for intelligence analysis. Computer (Long Beach Calif) (2013)
27. Rowley, J.: The wisdom hierarchy: representations of the DIKW hierarchy. J. Inf. Sci. **33**(2), 163–180 (2007)
28. Carpendale, S., et al.: Ontologies in biological data visualization. IEEE Comput. Graph. Appl. **34**(2), 8–15 (2014)
29. Klein, G., Moon, B.: Making sense of sensemaking 2: A macrocognitive model. IEEE Intell. Syst. **21**(5), 88–92 (2006)
30. Klein, G., Moon, B.: Making sense of sensemaking 1: Alternative perspectives. IEEE Intell. Syst. **21**(4), 70–73 (2006)
31. Saraiya, P., North, C., Duca, K.: An insight-based methodology for evaluating bioinformatics visualizations. IEEE Trans. Visual Comput. Graphics **11**(4), 443–456 (2005)
32. Saket, B., Kim, H., Brown, E.T., Endert, A.: Visualization by demonstration: an interaction paradigm for visual data exploration. IEEE Trans. Vis. Comput. Graph. **23**(1), 331–340 (2017)
33. Shklyar, A., Zakharova, A., Vekhter, E., Pak, A.: Visual modeling in an analysis of multidimensional data. J. Phys: Conf. Ser. **5**(1), 125–128 (2018)
34. Klein, G., Phillips, J.K., Rall, E.L., Peluso, D.: A data-frame theory of sensemaking. Expertise Out of Context, 113–155 (2007)
35. Matsushita, M., Kato, T.: Interactive visualization method for exploratory data analysis. In: Proceedings Fifth International Conference on Information Visualisation, 671–676, (2001)
36. Dang, N., Yang, F., Xiao, B., Zhu, Y.: WebScope: a new tool for fusion data analysis and visualization. In: 2009 16th IEEE-NPSS Real Time Conference, pp. 141–143 (2009)
37. Shklyar, A., Zakharova, A., Zavyalov, D., Vekhter, E.: Visual detection of internal patterns in the empirical data. In: CIT&DS 2017: Creativity in intelligent technologies & Data science. 12–14 September, 2017, vol. 754, pp. 215–230. Volgograd, Russia (2017)
38. Shklyar, A., Zakharova, A.: Facilities of visual analysis while searching for regularities in dissimilar experimental data. In: Infografika i informacionnyj dizajn: vizualizacija dannyh v nauke materialy Mezhdunarodnoj nauchno-prakticheskoj konferencii. Omsk, pp. 61–67 (2017). Online: URL https://elibrary.ru/item.asp?id=32480792, 30 January 2023
39. Zakharova, A., Shklyar, A.: Visualization metaphors. Scientific Visualization **5**(2), 16–24 (2013)
40. Van Long, T.: A new metric on parallel coordinates and its application for high-dimensional data visualization. In: 2015 International Conference on Advanced Technologies for Communications (ATC), pp. 297–301 (2015)
41. North, C., Shneiderman, B.: Snap-together visualization: can users construct and operate coordinated visualizations? Int. J. Hum. Comput. Stud. **53**(5), 715–739 (2000)
42. Branchini, E., Savardi, U., Bianchi, I.: Productive thinking: Tlie role of perception and perceiving opposition. Gestalt Theory **37**(1), 7–24 (2015)
43. Sacha, D., Stoffel, A., Stoffel, F., Kwon, B., Ellis, G., Keim, D.: Knowledge generation model for visual analytics. Visuali. Comp. Graph. IEEE Trans. **20**(12), 1 (2014)
44. Isenberg, P., Isenberg, T., Hesselmann, T., Bongshin Lee, U., von Zadow, T.A.: Data Visualization on Interactive Surfaces: A Research Agenda. IEEE Comput. Graph. Appl. **33**(2), 16–24 (2013)
45. Shklyar, A.V., Zakharova, A.A., Vekhter, E.V.: The applicability of visualization tools in the meta-design of an educational environment. European J. Contemp. Edu. **8**(1), 43–51 (2019)

46. Batch, A., Elmqvist, N.: The interactive visualization gap in initial exploratory data analysis. IEEE Trans. Vis. Comput. Graph. **24**(1), 278–287 (2018)
47. Zakharova, A.A., Vekhter, E.V., Shklyar, A.V.: Methods of solving problems of data analysis using analytical visual models **9**(4), 78–88 (2018)

Inverse Kinematics for Multisection Continuum Robots with Variable Section Length

Olga M. Gerget[1]([✉]) [iD] and Dmitrii Yu. Kolpashchikov[2] [iD]

[1] V.A. Trapeznikov Institute of Control Sciences of Russian Academy of Sciences, Moscow, Russia
olgagerget@mail.ru
[2] Tomsk Polytechnic University, Tomsk 634050, Russia

Abstract. Continuum robots are robots with high flexibly and maneuverability, which allows use them in confined workspaces with many obstacles. Continuum robot's motion planning and control are depends on inverse kinematics. Existing inverse kinematics solvers have high computational cost and often fail to find a solution. Moreover inverse kinematics solutions for continuum robots with variable section length underrepresented as well as solutions for multisection robots with mixed sections. This paper presents a further development of FABRIK-based inverse kinematics algorithm that allows operating? with multisection continuum robots with variable length. The paper presents analytical solution single section with variable length as well. Our experiments show that proposed algorithm show have higher solution rate and lower solution time in comparison with Jacobian-based inverse kinematics.

Keywords: Kinematics · FABRIK · Continuum robot

1 Introduction

Continuum robot is an extreme case of hyper-redundant robot comprises an infinite number of rotate joints with links length between them tends to be zero [1]. Those features provide continuum robots with high flexibility and maneuverability, which in turn allow them to avoid unwanted collisions in a confined workspace, maneuver using collisions, or grasp objects using their body. In industry, they are used for machining [2], non-destructive testing and repairing inside complex devices [3, 4]. Continuum robots also used to access dangerous for human areas, such as outer space [5] and underwater [6]. In medicine, these robots are widely used as endoscopes and surgical instruments for minimally invasive surgery [7–9].

In general, multisection continuum robots consist of fixed-length bending sections. Extensible sections [10] or telescopic connection [11] can increase the workspace of the continuum robot by variable section length. However, this complicates their inverse kinematics.

Inverse kinematics used to define robot configuration (section length, bending angles, and rotation angles) that needed to reach specific position and/or orientation. Today, a number of approaches that solve the inverse kinematics problem of multisection continuum robots are known: data-driven [12–14], bioinspired [15], Jacobian-based or heuristic iterative methods.

Jacobian-based algorithms are widely used to solve the inverse kinematics problem. Those algorithms are successfully applied to various types of multisection continuum robots: described by constant curvature assumption [16], variable curvature assumption [17] and concentric tube robots [18]. They use the minimum-norm and minimax iterative algorithms to solve the inverse kinematics problem, e.g. Newton's method. The Jacobian-based methods are accurate and capable of working in real-time. However, they suffer from high computational complexity, badly scalable and sometimes unable to find a solution.

Recently, heuristic iterative inverse kinematics algorithms for multisection continuum robots based on the Forward And Backward Reaching Inverse Kinematics (FABRIK) algorithm have appeared. The modified FABRIK replace section of the robot by either two rigid links (tangents) [19] or one link (chord) [20] to solve inverse kinematics problem for 5 degree of freedom (DoF) case (roll not specified). Further development extended FABRIK by adding ability to solve 6-DoF cases [21], use variable curvature assumption [22], and speeding up solution [23].

All above mentioned inverse kinematics algorithms focused on fixed-length continuum robots. There are only a few solutions for continuum robots with extensible sections, e.g. a closed-form solution for inverse kinematics problems for continuum robots with extendible sections [24]. However, the authors note that this solution cannot be directly generalized to continuum robots made of fixed-length sections.

This paper presents a further development of FABRIK-based inverse kinematics algorithm for continuum robots. We present a fast and accurate algorithm that solves the inverse kinematics problem for continuum robots with different combinations of section types (fixed-length, extensible and telescopic). To do that, the paper also describes a closed-form solution to the inverse kinematics problem for a single section suitable for an extensible continuum section.

2   Forward Kinematics

This paper study kinematics of three continuum sections:

- Fixed-length section serially connected with previous (fixed-length section);
- Extensible section serially connected with previous [10] (extensible section);
- Fixed-length section telescopically connected with previous [11] (telescopic section).

All of those sections have similar forward kinematics that can be described based on a constant curvature assumption. This assumption claims that the optimally constructed section will bend with constant curvature.

The transformation matrix T_Q to describe the end-effector frame of Q-section continuum robot is defined as follows:

$$T_Q = T_0 \cdot \prod_{i=1}^{Q} (T_Z(\omega_i) \cdot T_Z(\varphi_i) \cdot T_B(\theta_i, S_i) \cdot T_Z(-\omega_i)) \tag{1}$$

$$T_B(\theta, S) = \begin{bmatrix} \cos(\theta) & 0 & \sin(\theta) & S \cdot (1 - \cos(\theta))/\theta \\ 0 & 1 & 0 & 0 \\ -\sin(\theta) & 0 & \cos(\theta) & S \cdot \sin(\theta)/\theta \\ 0 & 0 & 0 & 1 \end{bmatrix} \tag{2}$$

$$S = S_C + S'_\Delta \tag{3}$$

where Q – number of sections, T_0 – robot's base frame, T_Z – rotation around the Z axis by the rotation angle ω or φ, $T_B(\theta, S)$ – the transformation matrix describing a plane bend of a section with length S at bending angle θ, S'_Δ – the current length of the variable part of the section and S_C – the length of the constant part of the section. The bending scheme is shown in Fig. 1.

Rotation angles ω and φ describe two ways of spatial bending. Angle ω used when spatial bending performed by simultaneous bending in several planes. Angle φ used when a section can to rotate around axis Z of the section frame.

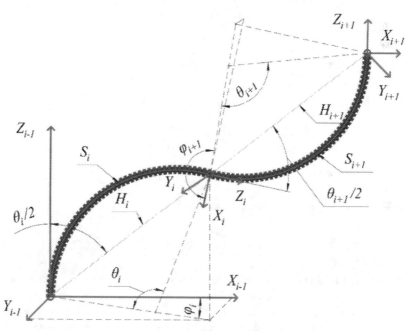

Fig. 1. Bending scheme of a multisection continuum robot (H – chord that connects the beginning and the end of the section).

Section length divided into two parts: constant part S_C, that remain fixed, and variable part S'_Δ which can take any value from the range $[0, \ldots, S_\Delta]$, where S_Δ is the maximum length of variable part.

Fixed-length sections are unable to change its length and rotate at its base, so such section have $S_\Delta = 0$, $S_C \neq 0$ and $\omega = 0$. Extensible sections can change its length, but total section length S can not be 0, since fully retracted section becomes a rigid link of length S_C. They also cannot rotate at its base. So extensible sections have $S_\Delta \neq 0, S_C \neq 0$ and $\omega = 0$. Sections, telescopically connected with previous, uses previous section as a steerable sheath. Such sections can fully retract into the sheath and telescopic connection allows rotate section around its base, so they have $S_\Delta \neq 0$, $S_C = 0$ and can use both rotation angles ω or φ.

3 Inverse Kinematics

3.1 Single-Section Inverse Kinematics

The single-section inverse kinematics algorithm finds a single possible robot configuration that satisfies end-effector position P_T given in the world coordinate system. The algorithm uses the following input data: target-point P_T, section lengths S_C and S_Δ, section base T_{i-1} (end-effector of previous section). The output data are configuration variables such as bending angle θ, rotation angle φ (for single section $\varphi = \omega$), and the length of the variable part of the section S'_Δ.

The rotation angle φ of the section is defined using P_X and P_Y components of the target point P_T in the T_i frame:

$$P_T = T_{i-1}^{-1} \cdot P_T \tag{4}$$

$$\varphi = \omega = \mathrm{atan2}(P_Y, P_X) \tag{5}$$

The angle between the Z_{i-1} axis and the chord that connects the beginning and the end of the section is the half of the bending angle θ, so it is defined as follows:

$$\theta = 2 \cdot \mathrm{acos}(Z_i \cdot P_T / |P_T|) \tag{6}$$

The length of the variable part S'_Δ is defined by:

$$S'_\Delta = \frac{|P| \cdot \theta}{2 \cdot \sin(\theta/2)} - S_C \tag{7}$$

Equation (7) is redundant for a fixed-length section.

Equations (4)–(7) are sufficient to define the inverse kinematics solution, if P_T lays within section workspace. In case when P_T lays outside the workspace, additional steps are needed. Target can be unreachable because of section length (sectors 1 and 3 in Fig. 2) and/or bending angle (sector 2 in Fig. 2). Sector 1 is the case when $S'_\Delta > S_\Delta$. Sector 3 is the case when $S'_\Delta < 0$. Sector 2 is the case when $\theta > \theta'_{max}$. θ'_{max} – the local maximum of the bending angle. It is the maximum bending angle for a certain S'_Δ. To define θ'_{max} we assume that the bending capabilities of the robot decrease with the length of the variable part:

$$\frac{S_\Delta}{S'_\Delta} = \frac{\theta_{max}}{\theta'_{max}} \tag{8}$$

Then θ'_{max} is defined as follows:

$$\theta'_{max} = \begin{cases} \theta_{max} \cdot S'_\Delta / S_D & if \ S_\Delta \neq 0 \\ \theta_{max} & otherwise \end{cases} \tag{9}$$

If $S'_\Delta > S_\Delta$ or $S'_\Delta < 0$, then S'_Δ should be redefined as follows:

$$S'_\Delta = \begin{cases} 0 & if \ S'_\Delta < 0 \\ S_\Delta & if \ S'_\Delta > S_\Delta \end{cases} \tag{10}$$

If $\theta > \theta'_{max}$ then bending angle should be redefined $\theta = \theta'_{max}$. However, if we redefine S'_Δ by (7) for new θ and then θ'_{max} by (9) for new S'_Δ we see that inequality $\theta > \theta'_{max}$ persists, but the difference between them decreases. Thus, to obtain solution we should redefine θ until $|\theta - \theta'_{max}| > \varepsilon$, where ε if an angular tolerance for single section.

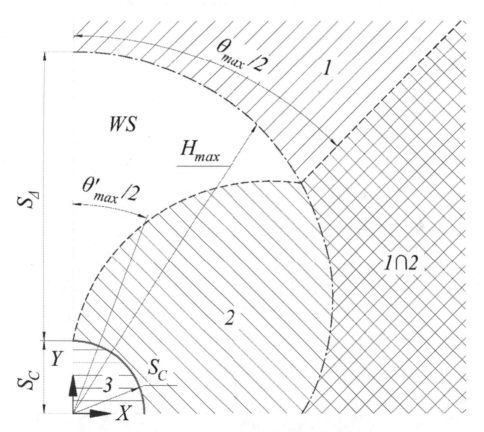

Fig. 2. Target point located outside workspace

The flowchart of the single-section inverse kinematics algorithm is presented in Fig. 3.

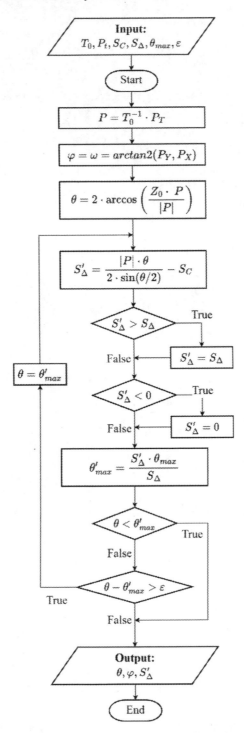

Fig. 3. Flowchart of the single-section inverse kinematics algorithm

3.2 Multisection Inverse Kinematics

The multisection inverse kinematics algorithm finds a robot configuration that satisfies end-effector position P_T and orientation Z_T. The algorithm uses the following input data: target-point P_T, orientation vector Z_T, sections lengths S_C and S_Δ, robot base T_0 and, optionally, initial robot configuration. The output data are configuration variables such as bending angle θ, rotation angles φ and/or ω, and the length of the variable part $S_{\Delta'}$ for each section.

To do that, each section of multisection continuum robot replaced by two links, which tangent to the beginning and the ending of the section. Thus, single section i is defined by three keypoints: the beginning of the section P_{2i-1}, the ending of the section P_{2i+1} and intersection point of section tangents P_{2i}. Whole robot defined by $2Q + 1$ keypoints: base of the robot P_1, the ending of each section P_{2i+1} and the intersection point for each section P_{2i}.

Initial Pose. If the initial configuration is not specified, then bending angles θ and rotation angles φ and ω set to zero. Variable parts are set to its maximum $S'_{\Delta_i} = S_{\Delta_i}$ and then scaled so that $\sum (S_{C_i} + S'_{\Delta_i}) = |P_T|$:

$$S'_{\Delta_i} = S'_{\Delta_i} \cdot \frac{|P_T| - \sum S_C}{\sum S_\Delta} \tag{11}$$

Keypoints P_{2i+1} of each section are calculated using forward kinematics. Intersection points P_{2i} are defined as follows:

$$L_i = S_i \cdot \tan(\theta_i/2)/\theta_i \tag{12}$$

$$P_{2i} = P_{2i-1} + Z_{2i-1} \cdot L_i = P_{2i-1} - Z_{2i+1} \cdot L_i \tag{13}$$

where L_i is tangent length of i section.

Forward Reaching. In the forward reaching stage, the algorithm processes the robot as if it consists of only rigid links L_i connected together by spherical joints under no restrictions on the bending angles.

In the first step, the endpoint P_{2Q+1} is set to the target point P_T and $Z_Q = -Z_T$.
Then all chain points are redefined starting from the point P_{2Q} according to formulas:

$$P_{2(Q-i)} = P_{2(Q-i)+1} + Z_{Q-i} \cdot L_{Q-i} \tag{14}$$

$$Z_{Q-i-1} = \begin{cases} \overrightarrow{-Z_0} & \text{if } i = Q - 1 \\ \overrightarrow{P_{2(Q-i)}P_{2(Q-i-1)}}/|\overrightarrow{P_{2(Q-i)}P_{2(Q-i-1)}}| & \text{otherwise} \end{cases} \tag{15}$$

$$P_{2(Q-i)-1} = P_{2(Q-i)} + Z_{Q-i-1} \cdot L_{Q-i} \tag{16}$$

where $i = [0, \ldots, Q - 1]$.

Backward Reaching. Forward reaching is followed by backward reaching. In this stage the algorithm is applied to the robot from its beginning to the end $i \in [1, ..., Q]$. During this stage the algorithm redefines configuration parameters $(\theta, \varphi, S'_\Delta)$ for each section using single-section inverse kinematics for the target position P_i. The base frame for each next section is defined by forward kinematics using current configuration parameters $(\theta_i, \varphi_i, S'_{\Delta_i})$.

After the backward reaching stage, the algorithm checks if position error E_{Lin} and orientation error E_{Or} fall within linear tolerance.

3.3 Jacobian-Based Inverse Kinematics

The Jacobian-based approach is the most common way to solve the inverse kinematics problem for both continuum and rigid robots. In this work, we use Newton's method to find the solution to the inverse kinematics problem:

$$x_{k+1} = x_k + \left[J(x_k)^T \cdot J(x_k) + W \right]^{-1} \cdot J(x_k)^T \cdot (G - F(x_k)) \qquad (17)$$

where x_k and x_{k+1} are current and next robot configuration parameters (bending angles, turning angles, length of the variable part), W is a positive definite diagonal matrix used to avoid singular configurations. G is a vector consisting of the coordinates of the target position and the desired difference between the target orientation vector Z_T and the current orientation vector of the robot Z_Q. G is defined as follows:

$$G = (P_T \ 0)^T \qquad (18)$$

where $F(x_k)$ is a vector consisting of the current tip position and its orientation error for the current parameters x_k. The current position $F(x_k)$ is defined by positional part P_Q of forward kinematics and the angle between the target and the current vector:

$$F(x_K) = \left(P_{2Q+1} \angle (Z_Q, Z_T) \right)^T \qquad (19)$$

where $J(x_k)$ is the Jacobian matrix for T_Q for the parameters x_k. The Jacobian matrix can be defined by the differentiation:

$$J = dF/dx \qquad (20)$$

4   Results

The algorithm was tested in numerical experiments for three-section continuum robots. The number of sections was limited by three since real-life robots of more sections are quite rare. Each section has at least two degrees of freedom – bending and turning. The combination of these movements allows sections bend omnidirectionally. Sections with a variable length also can have an additional degree of freedom – section length.

All 27 possible combinations of section types (fixed-length, telescopic, extensible) were studied. Experiments for each robot were performed with different maximum bending angles in the range from 9 to 180 degrees with the step of 9 degrees. This made the total of 20 cases for each section combination. For each case, 10^4 position and orientation samples were used as input for inverse kinematics algorithms. For this samples size, the sampling error is 1% for 95% confidence level. Each position and orientation sample was received from random input variables by the forward kinematics introduced in Sect. 2. The use of forward kinematics ensures that all samples have at least one inverse kinematics solution. In total 5 400 000 experiments were done.

The performance of the algorithm was evaluated by the percentage of solutions, mean solution time, and a mean number of iterations. It was assumed that the algorithm reached the target point and the target vector if the distance from the tip to the target point was less than 10 μm and the angle between the target vector and the tip orientation vector was less than 0.01 rad. The time limit for each experiment was 50 ms. The mean solution time and mean number of iterations showed the speed of the algorithm. The performance of the proposed algorithm was compared to the performance of Jacobian-based inverse kinematics.

Section parameters used for sample generation are presented in Table 1. $W = 0.1$ for the Jacobian-based algorithm. The Jacobian matrix was formed using the in-built MATLAB tools and converted into a function in order to reduce the calculation time.

Table 1. Sections' parameters

	Serial	Extensible	Telescopic
S_C	50	40	0
S_Δ	0	10	50

In this section, experiment results are presented. Experiments were carried out using MATLAB 2020a on Windows 10 with Intel Core i7-4790K 4.00 GHz CPU and 16.0 GB RAM. Results are presented Table 2.

Table 2. Results

Algorithm	Solution rate			Mean time, ms	Mean iterations
	Min	Mean	Max		
Jacobian	10.7	74.1	99.2	11.7	90.0
FABRIK	39.0	83.0	99.8	5.7	120.4

Sampling error for FABRIK with confidence level 99% is 0.33%. Sampling error for Jacobian with confidence level 99% is 0.63%.

Experiments show that the FABRIK-based algorithm generally copes better with inverse kinematics problems for different multi-section continuum robots than the

Jacobian-based inverse kinematics algorithm even with high accuracy requirements (linear tolerance 10 μm and orientation tolerance 0.01 radians). The FABRIK-based algorithm is on average two times faster than the Jacobian inverse kinematics algorithm.

The performance of the algorithms differs from one case to another. In some cases, the Jacobian-based algorithm overperforms the FABRIK-based algorithm by 40.3% max. In other cases, the FABRIK-based algorithm overperforms the Jacobian-based algorithm by 81.9% max. The minimal solution percentage for the FABRIK-based algorithm is 39.0% while it is 10.7% for the Jacobian-based inverse kinematics algorithm. Thus, the FABRIK-based algorithm can be used to solve the inverse kinematics problem for multi-section continuum robots regardless of section combination and their limits. However, it is worth choosing the algorithm after tests to ensure the best results in each specific case.

A combination of FABRIK-based main solutions with Jacobian-based main solutions increases the total solution percentage to 94.4%. Thus, both algorithms could be used simultaneously to ensure better results.

5   Conclusion

The article presents the inverse kinematics algorithm based on the FABRIK algorithm and used for a multi-section continuum robot. The algorithm suits to operate with various combinations of extensible and non-extensible continuum sections. To do this, single-section forward and inverse kinematics based on the constant curvature approach is applied.

The algorithm was compared to the Jacobian-based inverse kinematics algorithm. The experiments have shown that the FABRIK-based algorithm demonstrates better performance in terms of speed and ability to find solutions to inverse kinematics problems. The mean operating time of the proposed algorithm is 2–4 times less than that of the Jacobian-based inverse kinematics algorithm. At the same time, the proposed algorithm shows a better ability to solve inverse kinematics problems regardless of combination of sections and their restrictions. A combination of both algorithms could produce better results in terms of speed and ability to find a solution.

The algorithm is easy to deploy and modify and does not require complex calculations. It chains together single-section forward and inverse kinematics solutions to find solutions for a multi-section robot. This feature makes it possible to replace constant curvature kinematics with a more complex and accurate approach.

The algorithm could be used for motion planning and control of multi-section continuum robots in real-time applications. This improvement cloud increases the degree of autonomy of such robots.

References

1. Robinson, G., Davies, J.B.C.: Continuum robots – a state of the art. In: Proceedings 1999 IEEE International Conference on Robotics and Automation (Cat. No.99CH36288C), pp. 2849–2854. IEEE (2003)

2. Axinte, D., Dong, X., Palmer, D., et al.: MiRoR—miniaturized robotic systems for holistic *in-situ* repair and maintenance works in restrained and hazardous environments. IEEE/ASME Trans. Mechatron. **23**, 978–981 (2018). https://doi.org/10.1109/TMECH.2018.2800285
3. Dong, X., Wang, M., Mohammad, A., et al.: Continuum robots collaborate for safe manipulation of high-temperature flame to enable repairs in challenging environments. IEEE/ASME Trans. Mechatron. **27**, 4217–4220 (2022). https://doi.org/10.1109/TMECH.2021.3138222
4. Buckingham, R., Graham, A.: Nuclear snake-arm robots. Ind. Rob. **39**, 6–11 (2012). https://doi.org/10.1108/01439911211192448
5. Nahar, D., Yanik, P.M., Walker, I.D.: Robot tendrils: long, thin continuum robots for inspection in space operations. In: 2017 IEEE Aerospace Conference, pp. 1–8. IEEE (2017)
6. Liljeback, P., Mills, R.: Eelume: A flexible and subsea resident IMR vehicle. In: OCEANS 2017 – Aberdeen, pp. 1–4. IEEE (2017)
7. Burgner-Kahrs, J., Rucker, D.C., Choset, H.: Continuum robots for medical applications: a survey. IEEE Trans. Robot. **31**, 1261–1280 (2015). https://doi.org/10.1109/TRO.2015.2489500
8. Zhang, Y., Lu, M.: A review of recent advancements in soft and flexible robots for medical applications. Int. J. Med. Robot. Comput. Assist. Surg. **16**, e2096 (2020). https://doi.org/10.1002/rcs.2096
9. da Veiga, T., Chandler, J.H., Lloyd, P., et al.: Challenges of continuum robots in clinical context: a review. Prog. Biomed. Eng. **2**, 032003 (2020). https://doi.org/10.1088/2516-1091/ab9f41
10. Nguyen, T.-D., Burgner-Kahrs, J.: A tendon-driven continuum robot with extensible sections. In: 2015 IEEE/RSJ International Conference on Intelligent Robots and Systems (IROS), pp. 2130–2135. IEEE (2015)
11. Li, Z., Chiu, P.W.Y., Du, R.: Design and kinematic modeling of a concentric wire-driven mechanism targeted for minimally invasive surgery. In: 2016 IEEE/RSJ International Conference on Intelligent Robots and Systems (IROS), pp. 310–316. IEEE (2016)
12. Grassmann, R., Modes, V., Burgner-Kahrs, J.: Learning the forward and inverse kinematics of a 6-DOF concentric tube continuum robot in SE(3). In: 2018 IEEE/RSJ International Conference on Intelligent Robots and Systems, pp. 5125–5132 (IROS). IEEE (2018)
13. Lai, J., Huang, K., Chu, H.K.: A learning-based inverse kinematics solver for a multi-segment continuum robot in robot-independent mapping. In: 2019 IEEE International Conference on Robotics and Biomimetics (ROBIO), pp. 576–582. IEEE (2019)
14. Melingui, A., Merzouki, R., Mbede, J.B., et al.: Neural networks based approach for inverse kinematic modeling of a compact bionic handling assistant trunk. In: 2014 IEEE 23rd International Symposium on Industrial Electronics (ISIE), pp. 1239–1244. IEEE (2014)
15. Djeffal, S., Mahfoudi, C., Amouri, A.: Comparison of three meta-heuristic algorithms for solving inverse kinematics problems of variable curvature continuum robots. In: 2021 European Conference on Mobile Robots (ECMR), pp. 1–6. IEEE (2021)
16. Jones, B.A., Walker, I.D.: Kinematics for multisection continuum robots. IEEE Trans. Robot. **22**, 43–55 (2006). https://doi.org/10.1109/TRO.2005.861458
17. Mahl, T., Hildebrandt, A., Sawodny, O.: A variable curvature continuum kinematics for kinematic control of the bionic handling assistant. IEEE Trans. Robot. **30**, 935–949 (2014). https://doi.org/10.1109/TRO.2014.2314777
18. Sears, P., Dupont, P.E.: Inverse kinematics of concentric tube steerable needles. In: Proceedings 2007 IEEE International Conference on Robotics and Automation, pp. 1887–1892. IEEE (2007)
19. Zhang, W., Yang, Z., Dong, T., Xu, K.: FABRIKc: an efficient iterative inverse kinematics solver for continuum robots. In: 2018 IEEE/ASME International Conference on Advanced Intelligent Mechatronics (AIM), pp. 346–352. IEEE (2018)

20. Kolpashchikov, D., Laptev, N., Danilov, V., et al.: FABRIK-based inverse kinematics for multi-section continuum robots. In: Proceedings of the 2018 18th International Conference on Mechatronics (2018)
21. Liu, T., Yang, T., Xu, W., et al.: Efficient inverse kinematics and planning of a hybrid active and passive cable-driven segmented manipulator. IEEE Trans. Syst. Man Cybern. Syst. **52**, 4233–4246 (2022). https://doi.org/10.1109/TSMC.2021.3095152
22. Kolpashchikov, D., Gerget, O., Danilov, V.: FABRIKx: tackling the inverse kinematics problem of continuum robots with variable curvature. Robotics **11**, 128 (2022). https://doi.org/10.3390/robotics11060128
23. Wu, H., Yu, J., Pan, J., et al.: CRRIK: a fast heuristic algorithm for the inverse kinematics of continuum robot. J. Intell. Robot. Syst. **105**, 55 (2022). https://doi.org/10.1007/s10846-022-01672-7
24. Garriga-Casanovas, A., Rodriguez y Baena, F.: Kinematics of continuum robots with constant curvature bending and extension capabilities. J. Mech. Robot. **11**, 011010 (2019). https://doi.org/10.1115/1.4041739

The ThermoEMF as a Tool for Increasing the Autonomy of Technological Machines

Zhanna Tikhonova$^{(\boxtimes)}$ (iD), Dmitriy Kraynev(iD), Evgeniy Frolov(iD),
Alexander Bondarev(iD), and Alla Kozhevnikova

Volgograd State Technical University, Volgograd, Russia
tikhonovazhs@gmail.com

Abstract. The authors dwell on the problem of appointing rational cutting modes for machining steels and alloys with a coated carbide tool. To solve it due to operational information about properties of each "coated tool–workpiece" contact pair, the authors have proposed to use the thermoEMF signal value (mV) of a dynamic thermocouple recorded during a test run. To justify the practical relevance of the method proposed, the theoretical foundations and study results of the thermoEMF signal information capacity when evaluating physicomechanical properties of the "steel billet–coated carbide tool" contact pairs for setting rational cutting modes are presented.

Keywords: ThermoEMF · Rational Cutting Modes · Turning · Test Run · Cyberphysical System · Autonomy of the Technological Machine

1 Introduction

The integration of digital technologies into the manufacturing sector promises significant competitive advantages for various industrial sectors. Individual components of the Industry 4.0 concept already increase the transparency of individual processes and the efficiency of enterprise management, provide opportunities for analyzing significant amounts of information, and much more. But innovative introductions are also aimed at ensuring evolution at the level of production facilities. Any product is embodied through appropriate technological processes and operations, including machining processes and cutting processes in relation to mechanical engineering.

In this case, we are talking about the synergy of intellectual (digital) and material (physical) directions.

The demand for innovative technologies is particularly high in the production of expensive components and parts in such industries as the aerospace industry and the automotive industry, the development of which has led to the creation of a high-tech and highly qualified industry. And although Europe is the world's largest manufacturer of equipment and machine tools for these industries, the role of Asian manufacturers is also growing [1]. Therefore, machine tool builders strive to increase the competitiveness of products through the introduction of such achievements in the field of information

© The Author(s), under exclusive license to Springer Nature Switzerland AG 2023
A. G. Kravets et al. (Eds.): CIT&DS 2023, CCIS 1909, pp. 143–154, 2023.
https://doi.org/10.1007/978-3-031-44615-3_10

and communication technologies as cyber-physical systems (CPS) [2], the Internet of Things (IoT) [3] and cloud computing [4].

Thus, in paper [5], a new generation of machine tools is proposed, which, in addition to the CNC device, have monitoring and data collection systems, intelligent human-machine interfaces and a cyber-double of the machine. Digital twins significantly facilitate and accelerate the technological preparation of production, allowing you to work out the technological process, find and correct systematic errors of technology, but they cannot solve all pressing production issues.

Digital twins can significantly reduce the full range of technological preparation of production, but great prospects are assigned to cyber-physical systems. Therefore, in addition to digital twins, which can significantly reduce the full range of technological preparation of production, great hopes are pinned on cyber-physical systems. They combine systems of different nature in order to increase the efficiency of management and interaction with the physical process, as well as adaptation to new conditions in real time [6]. Such systems should combine physical, network and computing processes. That is, in addition to directly technological means, for example, a CNC machine that implements the physical process of shaping, diagnostic and monitoring tools are needed, as well as tools for analyzing and developing appropriate corrective control commands in order to maintain the specified process parameters and requirements for the result.

Of great interest in this context is the choice of sensors for the monitoring system. The selection of the sensors for data acquisition is dependent on the type of machine tool, mounting options, technological factors, signal amplitudes and process disturbances. As a rule, modern CNC machines are equipped with a set of internal sensors that track the position along the axes of the machine, control the effective power on the drives, and more. Their main purpose is to control the operation of the main components of the machine and prevent emergencies. They can be used to monitor the processing process, but have a number of functional limitations in terms of reliability of providing the required processing results [7, 8].

External sensors are used to obtain information about the processing process itself. A typical example of such sensors are accelerometers [9], cutting force sensors [10] and vibration sensors [11, 12]. They are usually installed in a tool mandrel, but can be used to effectively implement feedback in an adaptive control system.

Of course, the implementation of a cyber-physical system based on technological equipment requires solving a set of tasks, among which one can distinguish: collection, transmission and storage of operational information, analysis and signal processing, development of corrective control actions and much more. But one of the main tasks at this stage is the selection of informative signals for monitoring the processing process that are applicable in production conditions and do not require significant modernization of technological equipment, which determines the possibility of practical implementation.

Thus, the effective functioning of cyber-physical production systems requires the creation of tools, techniques and algorithms that endow technological equipment with not only a certain degree of adaptability, but also autonomy. One of such applied tasks that needs to be solved is the assignment of processing modes that ensure reliable performance of the corresponding operation, taking into account the actual characteristics of the raw materials (blanks and tools), as well as their variability.

2   Assignment of Rational Processing Modes

Until now, reference and normative literature does not have analytical models for calculating the permissible cutting speed when using coated carbide tools that take into account the increased, but variable cutting properties of the tool. Currently, firms that supply each group of coated tools recommend their own tabular method for setting the rational cutting speed; the method is based on the average value of the initial (tabular) cutting speed and correction factors that take into account the processing conditions. These are the mechanical properties of the steel grade being processed, the specified tool durability, the values of feed and depth of cut, and some cutters' geometric corrections. We use the term "rational speed" to mean its calculated value that together with the feed taken, the depth of cut and the selected processing conditions ensures the specified time of reliable tool operation (the number of parts processed). In order to ensure the reliability of the selected cutting speed for the specified tool durability, the foreign suppliers' techniques of setting the cutting speed give its initial (tabular) average statistical value, considering not only the chemical composition of the coating, but also the physical and mechanical properties of its carbide matrix at the upper carbon boundary within its two-phase field. For example, this is 6.53 weight percent for the VK10 alloy (Fig. 1).

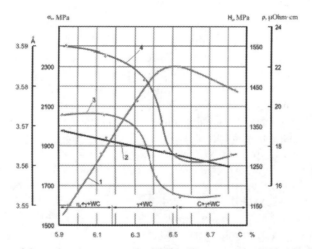

Fig. 1. Influence of the carbon content on the VK10 alloy properties [13]. 1 is the bend strength σ_b; 2 is the Vickers hardness H_V; 3 is the lattice pitch of the cobalt phase, Å; and 4 is the electrical resistance of the alloy ρ, μOhm·cm.

Alloys with a carbon content of less than 6.53 weight percent to the lower boundary of the two-phase field, i.e. up to a value of 6.22, will have improved properties, which is a reliability guarantee of the cutting speed selected according to the firms' techniques. This reliability margin is most often realized by machining an additional number of parts while maintaining the initial machining modes or by increasing the tool durability. If the manufacturers are focused on the properties of a two-phase field carbide matrix in choosing the initial (tabular) cutting speed for alloys with coatings, they recommend higher cutting speeds. If the techniques are focused on the use of a three-phase field carbide matrix (WC + γ + C), i.e. with graphite content, reduced cutting speeds are recommended.

Table 1 shows the results of cutting ShKh-15 steel (P Group) at permissible (recommended by the manufacturer) cutting speeds with coated carbide cutting tools from various suppliers according to their recommendations for similar processing conditions, namely, the feed of 0.12 mm/rev, the cutting depth of 1mm, without a coolant-cutting fluid. Accepted durability is 15 min.

Table 1. Results of machining ShKh-15 steel (P Group) at cutting speeds recommended by the manufacturer.

Coated carbide grade	BP20AM KZTS	SANDVIK MKTC	PRAMET
Cutting speed recommended by the manufacturer, m/min	100	150	190
Actual range of tool durability, min	13–16	15–18	15–20

There is a big difference in the values of the permissible speeds recommended by manufacturers that provide the specified tool durability. This directly indicates the different level of cutting capability of the tool. The cutting properties of a tool are understood as the function of a set of factors and include the properties of the tool material, including the chemical composition (material grade), structural condition, hardness, tensile strength, bending and compression strength, temperature resistance (red hardness) and wear resistance. Moreover, the authors conducted resistance tests and revealed a deviation of the actual durability of hard-alloy plates from the specified one, being increased or decreased (Table 1). To improve the accuracy of determining the cutting speed and rational use of the cutting capabilities of the tool, it is necessary to have operational information about the properties of each coated carbide tool in combination with the workpiece being processed. In this regard, when developing a technique for on-line diagnostics of the cutting properties of this class of tools, it is necessary to have information on the properties of the matrix and properties of coatings or integrally assess properties of the hard-alloy matrix and multilayer coating.

To obtain operational information about the properties of each "coated tool–workpiece" contact pair, the authors have proposed to use the magnitude of the thermoEMF signal (mV) of a dynamic thermocouple that always accompanies the cutting process. For this purpose, we propose to consider its physical foundations (Seebeck effect), as well as to study the information capacity of this technique when assessing properties of a coated carbide tool.

It follows from the Seebeck effect that a thermoelectromotive force E appears in a complete electrical circuit composed of a series-connected carbide tool and a steel part, with the temperature difference between the hot junction (a) and cold junction (b) being maintained (Fig. 2).

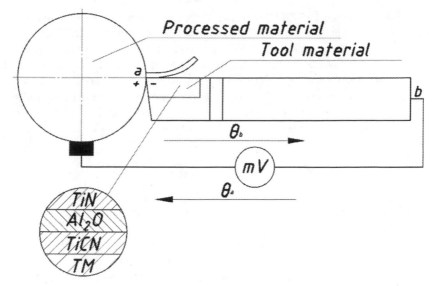

Fig. 2. Electrical circuit of a dynamic thermocouple.

Displayed equations are centered and set on a separate line. In a small range of temperature variation in the cutting zone, the thermoEMF (E) value is presented in the following form:

$$E = (\alpha_a - \alpha_b) \cdot (\theta_a - \theta_b) = \alpha_{1-2} \cdot (\theta_a - \theta_b), \tag{1}$$

where αa and αb are the specific values of the thermoEMF of two different thermoelement materials, mV; θ_a and θ_b are the temperature, °C at points a and b, respectively; and α_{1-2} is the specific or differential thermoEMF for a given pair, depending on the nature of the bodies in contact.

It should be borne in mind that the resulting value of the specific thermoEMF of a pair consists of three components, i.e. phonon, bulk and contact ones; and the contribution of each of them to the E value should be estimated:

$$\alpha_{1-2} = \alpha_{ph} + \alpha_b + \alpha_c, mV. \tag{2}$$

Near the end of the conductor with a higher temperature, the energy of atoms' thermal vibrations increases which leads to the propagation of vibrations towards the cold end. Phonons – energy quanta of lattice vibrations – collide with electrons, transfer part of their energy to them and, as it were, drag them along, creating a directed motion of current carriers from the warmer end of the conductor to the colder one. The phonon component α_{ph}, that is, the phonon drag effect, considerably influences the resulting value of the specific thermoEMF of a pair only in the low temperature range, when the cutting temperature is below the Debye temperature. For steels and steel alloys, the Debye temperature is $\approx$350–400 °C.

In the test run mode when processing metals with carbide tools, the temperature in the cutting zone is in the range of 500–550 °C, therefore, the effect of the phonon component α_{ph} can be ignored.

The volumetric thermoEMF component is determined by a directed motion of current carriers formed in a conductor in the presence of a temperature gradient. The differential thermoEMF that corresponds to this component, taking into account the operating temperatures of the cutting zone, will also be small and its influence can be neglected.

The contact component of the specific thermoEMF is due to the dependence of the contact potential difference on the temperature associated with the dependence of the chemical potential μ on the temperature. The condition of equalizing the electrochemical potentials of electrons in the contacting surfaces of metals implies that:

$$\alpha_K = \frac{\mu_1 - \mu_2}{e} = \frac{\chi_2 - \chi_1}{e}, \text{MB} \tag{3}$$

where μ_1 is the chemical potential of the part material; μ_2 is the chemical potential of the tool material; χ_2 is the electronic work function of the part; χ_1 is the electronic work function of the hard alloy; and e is the electron charge.

The analysis of expression (3) shows that under conditions of a test run at constant cutting conditions, the different thermoEMF value of the "coated carbide cutting tool – steel workpiece" pair is determined by the difference between the electronic work function of steel and hard alloy, that is the αc value and temperature difference between the hot and cold junctions of the dynamic thermocouple. When at least one element of a dynamic thermocouple is changed, the value of a new thermoEMF contact pair may turn out to be different due to the inevitable, but permissible according to the technical manufacturing conditions, range of scatter of the chemical material compositions of its branches and the probabilistic nature of the formation of contact pairs. So, it is possible to obtain information about the properties of each contact pair in the actual operating conditions of the lathe.

The application of the value of the electronic work function of a metal as a method of physicochemical analysis is shown in [14]. The work emphasized that the work function is sensitive to volumetric changes in alloys, with the composition and structure being changed and new phases being developed, and reflects the force of interatomic bonding, along with other properties of metals (density, melting point, elastic modulus, electrical conductivity and thermal conductivity).

Numerous publications [15–17] also indicated a close correlation between the thermoEMF magnitude of a dynamic thermocouple and the properties of its constituent branches, which makes it possible to apply the thermoelectric effect always accompanying the cutting process using the contact component of the specific thermoEMF of a test run to diagnose the properties of multicomponent contact pairs. In the technical literature there is no information about the thermoEMF value of contact pairs composed of coated carbide tools and steel blanks used to assess their properties. Given the ever-increasing volume of this type of tool applied, the development of methods for obtaining such information is an urgent task. In this case, it is important to reveal how the chemical composition of a single-layer or multi-layer coating affects the thermoEMF magnitude of a test run.

Understanding of the physical basis of the thermoEMF generation in conductors makes obvious three basic rules (laws) of handling thermoelectric circuits [18]. These are the "Rule of intermediate metals" (the law of additivity of material readings), "Magnus's rule" (the law of a homogeneous chain) and "The rule of successive temperatures" (the law of additivity of temperature readings). Of greatest interest is the "Rule of Intermediate Metals." Let us consider it in more detail. "The algebraic sum of thermoEMF in a circuit, consisting of any number of different conductors, is equal to zero if the entire circuit is at the same temperature":

$$Eac(\theta a, \theta b) = Eab(\theta a, \theta b) + Ebc(\theta a, \theta b) = 0. \tag{4}$$

An important practical property of thermocouples follows from the law, i.e. the introduction into a circuit, consisting of two dissimilar conductors a and b, whose junctions are at θ_a and θ_b temperatures, and the third conductor c that has a constant temperature along its entire length (for example, θ_1 or θ_2), does not change the thermoEMF Eab (θ_a, θ_b).

3   Theoretical or Experimental Research

In this work, the authors propose to study the application of the test technique for assessing the properties of contact pairs in relation to the conditions of cutting steels with a coated carbide cutting tool. The task was to reveal the influence of both single-layer and multi-layer coatings on the thermoEMF signal generation of a test run and the applicability of the additivity rule of a dynamic thermocouple thermoEMF to coated alloys.

For this purpose, it is proposed to consider the electrical circuit of a dynamic thermocouple (contact zone) made up of a machined steel part and a carbide tool with a multilayer coating shown in Fig. 2. For example, we consider a contact pair of 40X steel – TC20 RT hard alloy of the Kirovograd hard alloys plant (KZTS).

Note that in the electrical circuit (contact zone) there is a TTK hard-alloy plate (matrix) with a three-layer coating applied in Fig. 3. The chemical compositions of the matrix and each coating layer are shown in Fig. 2.

At first glance, according to the additivity rule, the coating layers shown schematically should not affect the readings of a measuring device or an oscilloscope.

Table 2 shows the thermoEMF values for turning Steel 45 in the test run mode with the same carbide plates with wear-resistant coatings and with coatings removed.

During the experiment, the thermoEMF signal of the coated plate was measured first. Then, the coating was removed from the cutting surfaces of the plate, and this plate was used to re-process in the test run mode, with the thermoEMF signal of the carbide plate being fixed without a coating.

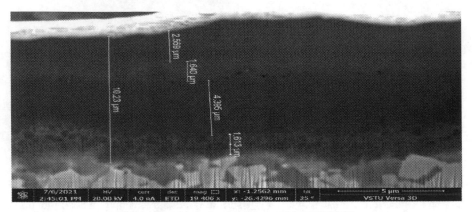

Fig. 3. Carbide indexable insert TC 20PT(KZTS).

Table 2. ThermoEMF values in turning Steel 45 in the test run mode with carbide plates with wear-resistant coatings and without coatings.

Indicators	Carbide grade				
	HS123 (MC111)	HS345 (MC131)	HG30 (MC241)	SANDVIK MKTC	TC 20PT(KZTS)
	Single-layer coating			Multi-layer coating	
	TiN	TiN	TiN		
E, mV	10.1	12.4	14.6	7.8	7.2
Without coating					
E, mV	11.2	13.6	15.3	9.2	9.0

4 Results and Discussion

Experiments on turning steels in the test run mode with coated and uncoated carbide tools showed that.

1. The additivity rule is not observed in relation to these conditions of metalworking, because the entire circuit (contact zone) does not have the same temperature, which is repeatedly shown by the measured isotherms on the front and back surfaces of the tool (Fig. 4).
2. The reduced thermoEMF values of the test run of carbide plates with a single-layer and multi-layer coatings are a consequence of the fact that the deposition of coatings caused a modified multicomponent layer formed on the cutting surfaces, contributed to a smooth transition between the layers of the coating and the matrix, with their chemical composition and physical and mechanical properties being changed, namely, the thermoEMF signal magnitude in this case acts as an integral characteristic, evaluating the properties of both the matrix and the coating, and can be introduced into the structure of known mathematical models for calculating the cutting speed [20].

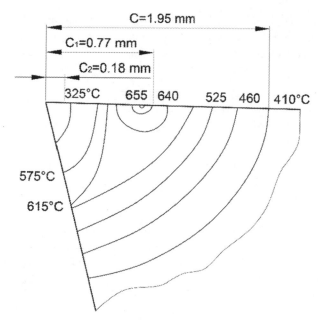

Fig. 4. Carbide indexable insert TC 20PT(KZTS) [19].

3. To calculate the cutting speed in semi-finishing turning, it is proposed to provide for a trial cutting operation [21, 22] i.e. pre-treat metal (steel billet) and measure thermoEMF in a "coated tool – billet" pair. Further, with respect to the thermoEMF magnitude of the pair and operating parameters of the technological process (feed s, depth of cut t and specified durability T), we determined the permissible cutting speed that provides the specified durability according to the following formula in general form (5):

$$V = \frac{C_v' \cdot E^{p_v}}{t^{x_v} \cdot s^{y_v} \cdot T^m},$$ (5)

where $C_v' = 559^{2.778}$; $p_v = -2.778$; $x_v = 0.83$; $y_v = 0.556$; $m = 2.778$; E is the thermoEMF of each "coated carbide cutting tool – steel billet" contact pair; T is the specified durability, min.; s is the feed, mm/rev; t is the depth of cut, mm; and V is the speed, m/min.

The method for obtaining the proposed dependencies is given in the article [23].

The difference between formula (5) and the one recommended by the reference and normative literature [20] is that the constant value of the speed dimensionless coefficient CV is determined promptly for each new contact pair directly on the machine before starting work and acquires physical meaning as a generalized amount of energy, characterizing the combination of physical and mechanical (thermophysical) properties of the contact pair.

Another difference between the corrected formula and the current ones is that it allows solving both the direct problem of choosing a reliable value of the cutting speed, and the reverse one. That is, the selected cutting speed, the adopted values of feed and cutting depth and the thermoEMF magnitude of the test run enable determining (predicting) the cutter's consistent performance time according to the dependence:

$$T = \frac{559 \cdot E^{-1}}{t^{0.3} \cdot s^{0.2} \cdot V^{0.4}},$$
(6)

where E is the thermoEMF of each "coated carbide cutting tool – steel billet" contact pair; T is the specified durability, min.; s is the feed, mm/rev; t is the depth of cut, mm; and V is the speed, m/min.

5 Conclusions

For processing steels with a coated carbide tool, a hypothesis on the applicability of the known technique for evaluating the properties of the "carbide cutting tool without coating – processed material" contact pair by the thermoEMF magnitude of the test run has been proposed and confirmed.

The authors investigated the peculiarity of the electric thermoEMF circuit of the test run formed when using coated hard alloys and found that the additivity rule about the non-influence of intermediate layers of coatings on the readings of the measuring device is not observed. The thermoEMF magnitude of the test run fixes the change in the chemical composition and the appearance of new phases. It also can be used for a preliminary assessment of the physical and mechanical properties of the "steel billet – coated carbide tool" contact pairs.

The thermoEMF value of the test run introduced into the structure of the mathematical model for calculating the cutting speed or calculating the model's durability period is used not as the value of the cutting temperature, but as an integral characteristic of the combination of properties of the contact pair "assembled" in a random way.

The proposed method of assigning cutting modes allows you to adjust the values according to the established processing tasks directly on the technological equipment, does not require its significant modernization and allows you to integrate the appropriate algorithm into the control system. Thus, the degree of autonomy of technological equipment.

References

1. Armendia, M., et al.: Machine tool: from the digital twin to the cyber-physical systems. In: Armendia, M., Ghassempouri, M., Ozturk, E., Peysson, F. (eds.) Twin-Control: A Digital Twin Approach to Improve Machine Tools Lifecycle, pp. 3–21. Springer International Publishing, Cham (2019). https://doi.org/10.1007/978-3-030-02203-7_1
2. Rajkumar, R., Lee, I., Sha, L., Stankovic, J.: Cyber-physical systems: the next computing revolution. In: 47th ACM/IEEE, Design Automation Conference (DAC). Anaheim, CA, USA (2010). https://doi.org/10.1145/1837274.1837461
3. Dervojeda, K., Rouwmaat, E., Probst, L., Frideres, L.: Internet of Things: Smart machines and tools. Report of the Business Innovation Observatory for the European Commission, p. 14. Brussels, Belgium (2015)

4. Kagermann, H., Wahlster, W.: Recommendations for Implementing the strategic initiative INDUSTRIE 4.0. Final Report of the Industrie 4.0 Working Group. https://en.acatech.de/wp-content/uploads/sites/6/2018/03/Final_report__Industrie_4.0_accessible.pdf. Accessed 20 July 2023

5. Liu, C., Xu, X.: (2017) Cyber-physical machine tool—the Era of Machine Tool 4.0. In: The 50th CIRP Conference on Manufacturing Systems. Taichung, Taiwan https://doi.org/10.1016/j.procir.2017.03.078

6. How to implement cyber physical systems? Nexus Integra. https://nexusintegra.io/implementing-cyberphysical-systems. Accessed 19 July 2023

7. Zheng, B., Xu, J., Li, H., Xing, J., Zhao, H., Liu, G.: Development of remotely monitoring and control system for Siemens 840D sl NC machine tool using Snap 7 codes. In: 2nd International Conference on Electrical, Automation and Mechanical Engineering (EAME 2017) (2017). https://doi.org/10.2991/eame-17.2017.26

8. Weck, M., Brecher, C.: Werkzeugmaschinen 3 – Mechatronische Systeme, Vorschubantriebe, Prozessdiagnose. Springer, Berlin (2006). https://doi.org/10.1007/978-3-540-32506-2

9. Chen, J.C., Chen, W.L.: A tool breakage detection system using an accelerometer sensor. J. Intell. Manuf. **10**(2), 187–197 (1999)

10. Reyes-Uquillas, D.A, Yeh, S.S.: Tool holder sensor design for measuring the cutting force in CNC turning machines. In: 2015 IEEE International Conference on Advanced Intelligent Mechatronics (AIM), pp. 1218–1223. Busan (2015). https://doi.org/10.1109/aim.2015.7222705

11. Kozochkin, M., Allenov, D., Andryushchenko, I.: Use of vibro-acoustic monitoring for stabilization stress–strain state of surface layer of workpiece during cutting. In: Radionov, A.A., Kravchenko, O.A., Guzeev, V.I., Rozhdestvenskiy, Y.V. (eds.) Proceedings of the 4th International Conference on Industrial Engineering: ICIE 2018, pp. 1355–1363. Springer International Publishing, Cham (2019). https://doi.org/10.1007/978-3-319-95630-5_143

12. Khusainov, R.M., Krestyaninov, P.N., Safin, D.D.: Experimental optimization of cutting modes for milling based on vibroacoustic analysis. In: Radionov, A.A., Kravchenko, O.A., Guzeev, V.I., Rozhdestvenskiy, Y.V. (eds.) Proceedings of the 4th International Conference on Industrial Engineering: ICIE 2018, pp. 1483–1489. Springer International Publishing, Cham (2019). https://doi.org/10.1007/978-3-319-95630-5_158

13. Tretyakov, V.I.: Fundamentals of Metal Science and Production Technology of Sintered Hard Alloys, p. 527. Metallurgy, Moscow (1976). (in Russian)

14. Sergeev, A.S. et al.: Method for measuring thermo-EMF of a «tool-workpiece» natural thermocouple in chip forming machining. In: MATEC Web of Conferences. https://www.matec-conferences.org/articles/matecconf/pdf/2017/43/matecconf_icmtmte2017_01044.pdf. (2017) Accessed 17 June 2023

15. Plotnikov, A.L., Krylov, E.G., Frolov, E.M.: Diagnostics of the state of a multicutter hard-alloy tool on the basis of thermoelectric phenomena in the cutting zone. Russ. Engin. Res. **30**, 161–165 (2010). https://doi.org/10.3103/S1068798X10020140

16. Plotnikov, A.L., Chigirinskii, Y.L., Frolov, E.M., et al.: Formulating CAD/CAM modules for calculating the cutting conditions in machining. Russ. Engin. Res. **29**, 512–517 (2009). https://doi.org/10.3103/S1068798X09050207

17. Tikhonova, Z., Kraynev, D., Frolov, E.: Thermo-emf as method for testing properties of replaceable contact Pairs. In: Radionov, A.A., Kravchenko, O.A., Guzeev, V.I., Rozhdestvenskiy, Y.V. (eds.) Proceedings of the 5th International Conference on Industrial Engineering (ICIE 2019): Volume II, pp. 1097–1105. Springer International Publishing, Cham (2020). https://doi.org/10.1007/978-3-030-22063-1_117

18. Lewis, K.: Thermocouple Laws. sciencing.com, https://sciencing.com/thermocouple-laws-5517216.html. Accessed 17 March 2023

19. N.V. Talantov Physical Foundations of Tool Cutting, Wear and Tear, p. 240. Mashinostroenie, Moscow (1992). (in Russian)
20. Dalsky, A.M., Kosilova, A.G., Meshcheryakova, R.K., Suslov, A.G. (eds.), Handbook of a Technologist and Mechanical Engineer, p. 912. Mashinostroenie, Moscow (2003). (in Russian)
21. Tikhonova, Z.S., Frolov, E.M., Krainev, D.V., Plotnikov, A.L.: Experimental research method when developing a mathematical model for calculating cutting speed in the course of turning steels with a coated tool. In: MATEC Web of Conferences: The Proceedings International Conference on Modern Trends in Manufacturing Technologies and Equipment: Mechanical Engineering and Materials Science (ICMTMTE 2019). https://doi.org/10.1051/matecconf/201929800134
22. Frolov, E., Krainev, D., Tikhonova, Z.: Cyber-physical machining systems based on commercial CNC equipment. In: 2018 International Russian Automation Conference(RusAutoCon), pp. 1–4. Sochi, Russia (2018). https://doi.org/10.1109/RUSAUTOCON.2018.8501684
23. Tchigirinsky, Y.L., Chigirinskaya, N.V., Tikhonova, Z.S.: Regression modeling of machining processes. In: Radionov, A.A., Gasiyarov, V.R. (eds.) Proceedings of the 6th International Conference on Industrial Engineering (ICIE 2020), vol. II, pp. 1101–1108. Springer International Publishing, Cham (2021). https://doi.org/10.1007/978-3-030-54817-9_128

Modeling the Movement of Vehicles with an Anti-lock Braking System on Various Types of Road Surface Using the Principles of PID Control

Grigory Boyko[1(✉)], Alexey Fedin[1], M. Petrenko[2], I. Leskovets[2], and Jozef Redl[3]

[1] Volgograd State Technical University, Lenin Ave. 28, Volgograd, Russian Federation
boyko@vstu.ru
[2] Belarusian-Russian University, Mira Ave. 43, Mogilev, Belarus
{tea,le}@bru.by
[3] Slovak University of Agriculture in Nitra, Nitra, Slovak Republic
jozef.redl@uniag.sk

Abstract. The relevance of the article is justified by the increase in the speed and intensity of traffic in Russia and in the world, and, as a result, a decrease in the distance between cars in the traffic flow, leading to an increase in the frequency of accidents. To reduce the number of such situations, modern cars are equipped with an anti-lock braking system, the effectiveness of which is determined by the algorithms implemented in it and its control system and interaction between the controller and actuators. The scientific novelty of the research lies in the combined approach to the study of the use of fuzzy logic elements in the electronic control unit of the braking system. The study of the possibility of using a fuzzy controller to calculate the braking parameters of an automobile wheel equipped with an anti-lock system for different types of road surface has been carried out.

Keywords: Wheeled vehicle · braking process · anti-lock braking system · simulation · control · optimization · fuzzy logic

1 Introduction

As is known, the task of the automatic control system of the anti-lock braking system is to maintain the value of the argument S, corresponding to the maximum value of the function $\varphi(S)$, by transferring the braking torque to the brake disc. Note that for different types of pavement, the maximum of the function $\varphi(S)$ is in the vicinity of the value of the argument 0.2, while the maximum values of the functions themselves differ significantly.

To determine the linear speed of the vehicle, there are different methods based on: processing the signals of the speed sensor of the output shaft of the gearbox (with a known radius of the wheel and the gear ratio of the axle drive gear) [1, 2]; simultaneous processing of signals from several sensors of the angular velocity of the vehicle wheels

[2]; processing of accelerometer data [3]; data processing of the GPS module [4], as well as various combinations of the indicated methods [4, 5].

For further data processing, methods using the PID controller can be applied.

One of the most fully satisfying the indicated requirements in relation to the adequacy of modeling the movement of an automobile wheel in the braking mode in real time is the method of applying fuzzy logic.

The generalized format of fuzzy rules is as follows:

If the condition (premise) of the rule, **then** the conclusion of the rule;

or:

If the condition (premise) of rule-i and the condition (premise) of rule-j, **then** the conclusion of rule-k.

The condition of the rule characterizes the current state of the object, and the conclusion – how this condition will affect the object. The general form of conditions and conclusions cannot be distinguished, since they are determined by a fuzzy logical conclusion. Each rule in the system has a weight – this parameter characterizes the significance of the rule in the model.

2   Materials and Methods

The simplest systems in terms of describing the mathematical model and the technical implementation of the solution, as a rule, have the worst adequacy in relation to real processes. Solutions with greater adequacy can be significantly more difficult in terms of mathematical modeling and require deep knowledge from developers in several different areas of several different scientific disciplines at once. Thus, designing an automatic control system for an anti-lock braking system with an abundance of existing solutions remains a non-trivial task [6–12].

Let's imagine a system of differential equations that describes the process of braking an automobile wheel [7, 13, 14].

$$\begin{cases} M = f(t), & (1) \\[2mm] \dot{\omega} = \dfrac{1}{j} \cdot \left[-M + \mu \cdot m \cdot g \cdot r \right], & (2) \\[2mm] \omega = \omega_0 + \displaystyle\int \dot{\omega} dt, & (3) \\[2mm] \dot{v} = -\mu \cdot g, & (4) \\[2mm] v = v_0 + \displaystyle\int \dot{v} \cdot dt, & (5) \\[2mm] \lambda = 1 - \dfrac{\omega \cdot r}{v}, & (6) \\[2mm] \mu = \dfrac{f_0 \cdot \lambda}{a \cdot \lambda^2 + b \cdot \lambda + c}. & (7) \end{cases}$$

where is t- current time value;

M - braking torque applied to the wheel;

ω_0, v_0- initial values of angular and linear speed;

$\dot{\omega}$, ω- angular acceleration and rotational speed;

$\dot{v}$, v- linear acceleration and wheel speed;

j, m- wheel moment of inertia and mass per wheel;

g- gravity factor;

r- dynamic radius of the wheel;

μ- coefficient of the longitudinal traction of a wheel with a road surface;

λ- coefficient of the longitudinal slipping;

a, b, c- empirical coefficients (descriptors of the road surface);

f_0- tire-to-surface friction coefficient on full-lock skidding

This is following next physical phenomena:

1. the dependence of the braking torque on time;
2. change in the angular acceleration of the wheel;
3. change in the rotational speed of the wheel;
4. change in the deceleration of the translational motion of the mass concentrated in the center of the wheel and creating a normal load in the contact patch;
5. change in the linear speed of the wheel;
6. the ratio between the translational speed and the circumferential speed of the tread in the center of the contact spot is the coefficient of relative slippage;
7. dependence of the tire-to-surface friction coefficient in the longitudinal direction on the coefficient of relative slippage and road surface.

In the calculation part, we will determine the braking parameters of an automobile wheel both using a numerical method and a deliberately small integration step (to ensure high accuracy of the results obtained) and using a fuzzy controller with the same initial data.

Next, it will be necessary to compare the results obtained and draw the appropriate conclusions. In this article, a more complete analysis will be carried out, which will consider the process of braking an automobile wheel on an ice-type road surface (Table 1).

Table 1. The initial data and the constant values adopted for the solution of the system

Name	Designation	Value
Linear speed value at the initial moment of time	v_0	60 km/h
Linear and angular acceleration at the initial moment of time	$\dot{\omega}_0, \dot{v}_0$	0
Wheel moment of inertia	j	$0,9\,m \cdot s^2$
Mass per wheel	m	350 kg
Gravity factor	g	$9,8\,m \cdot s^2$
Dynamic radius of the wheel	r	0,3 m
Empirical coefficients characterizing the road surface - dry surface:	$a; b; c; f_0$	0,342; 0,612; 0,046; 0,7
- wet surface:	$a; b; c; f_0$	0,4; 0,584; 0,016; 0,4
- ice-type:	$a; b; c; f_0$	0,057; 0,398; 0,032; 0,1
Braking torque applied to the wheel at the initial moment of time	M_0	0
Angular speed value at the initial moment of time	$\omega_0 = \frac{v_0}{r}$	
The law of braking torque variation	1000 t	

3   Results

A detailed calculation scheme is presented in the sources [13] and [14]. The calculation results are presented in Figs. 1, 2 and 3 . Figures 1 and 2 show the dependence of the braking parameter on the process time, moreover, the blue line corresponds to the numerical solution, and the red line corresponds to the solution using a fuzzy controller for surfaces such as "dry surface" and "ice surface". Figure 3 shows the differences between the obtained solutions for surfaces of the "dry surface" and "ice surface", and the exact solution is the solution obtained using the numerical method, the difference is expressed as a percentage.

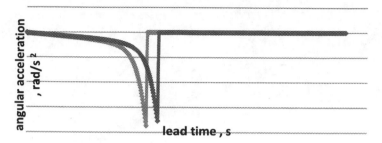

a) angular acceleration of a car wheel

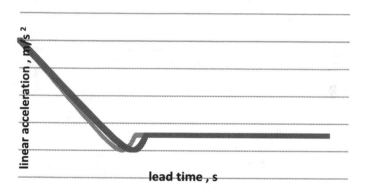

b) linear acceleration of a car wheel

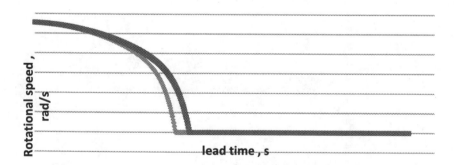

c) the angular velocity of the car wheel

Fig. 1. Braking parameters of an automobile wheel on the surface of "dry surface " (blue line - numerical solution, red line - solution obtained using a fuzzy controller)

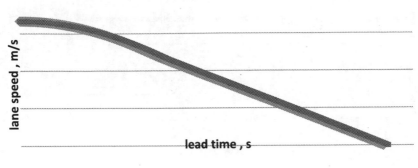

d) linear speed of a car wheel

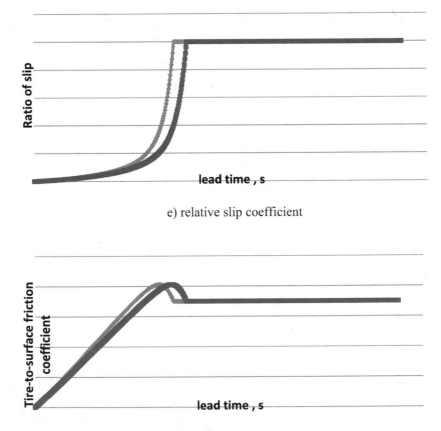

e) relative slip coefficient

f) coefficient of adhesion of the wheel to the road

Fig. 1. (*continued*)

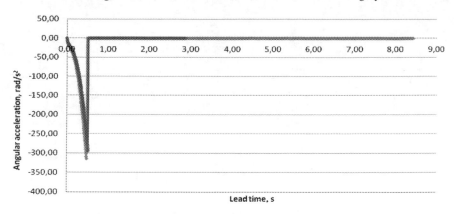

a) angular acceleration of a car wheel

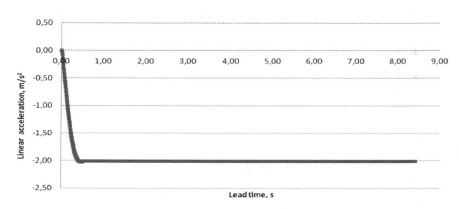

b) linear acceleration of a car wheel

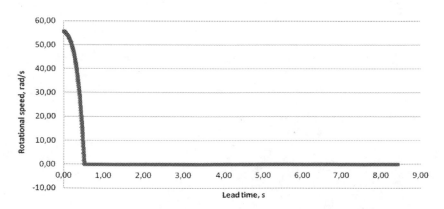

c) the angular velocity of the car wheel

Fig. 2. Braking parameters of a car wheel on the "ice" surface (blue line - numerical solution, red line - solution obtained using a fuzzy controller)

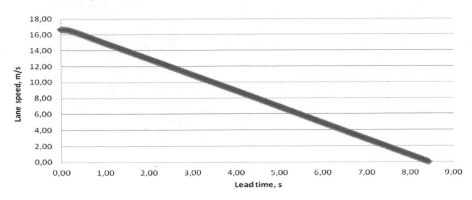

d) linear speed of a car wheel

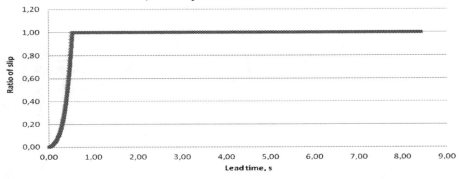

e) relative slip coefficient

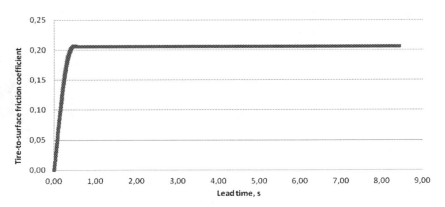

e) coefficient of adhesion of the wheel to the road

Fig. 2. (*continued*)

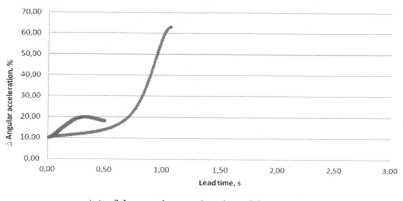

a) Δ of the angular acceleration of the car wheel

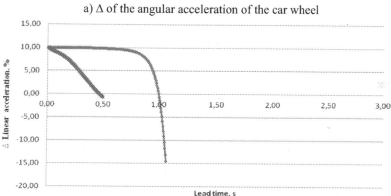

b) Δ linear acceleration of a car wheel

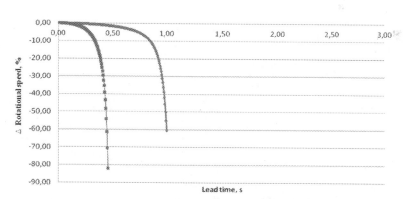

c) Δ of the angular velocity of the car wheel

Fig. 3. Differences between the braking parameters of an automobile wheel calculated in different ways (blue line - for the "dry" surface, red line - for the "ice" surface)

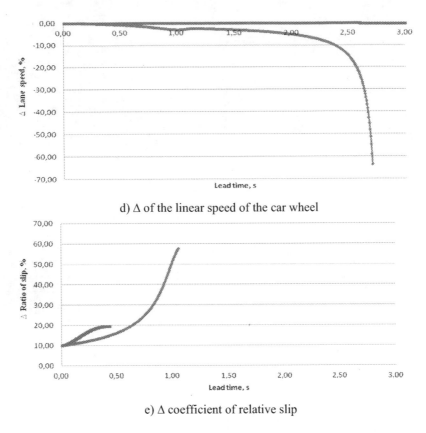

d) Δ of the linear speed of the car wheel

e) Δ coefficient of relative slip

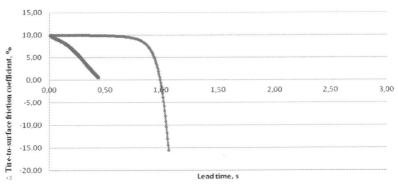

f) Δ coefficient of adhesion of the wheel to the road

Fig. 3. (*continued*)

Further, in Tables 2 and 3, we present an analysis of the discrepancy between the values of the braking parameters of an automobile wheel, calculated using a numerical method and using a fuzzy controller. We will compare the closeness of values by two parameters: the maximum value of the difference in percent modulo and the tendency for this difference to change as the process under study proceeds.

Table 2. The maximum value of the difference between the values of the braking parameters of an automobile wheel

Maximum value of braking parameter difference						
Parameter	$\dot{\omega}$	$\dot{v}$	ω	v	λ	μ
Surface "dry asphalt"	63%	−15%	-60%	−65%	57%	−15%
Ice surface	20%	10%	−85%	−3%	20%	10%

Table 3. Trend of change in the magnitude of the difference between the values of the braking parameters of an automobile wheel over time of the process under study

Maximum value of braking parameter difference						
Parameter	$\dot{\omega}$	$\dot{v}$	ω	v	λ	μ
Surface "dry asphalt"	↑	↑	↑	↑	↑	↑
Ice surface	↓	↓	↑	↓	↓	↓

From the data presented in Table 2, we can conclude that the maximum value of the difference in braking parameters does not exceed 65% in absolute value when braking on a road surface of the "dry asphalt concrete" type and 85% when braking on a road surface of the "ice" type. It can also be seen from this table that the difference values are significantly smaller for the braking parameters of an automobile wheel on an ice-type road surface (with the exception of the angular velocity of an automobile wheel). As shown in [13, 14], such error values when calculating the braking parameters of an automobile wheel are acceptable in engineering calculations when modeling the process under consideration.

From the data presented in Table 3, we can conclude that the studied difference between the calculated values of the braking parameters of an automobile wheel tends to increase for all parameters when braking on a "dry asphalt concrete" type surface. On the road surface of the "ice" type, on the contrary, the studied difference tends to decrease for all calculated parameters, except for the angular acceleration of the wheel.

Thus, it can be concluded that, over the entire range of the braking process of an automobile wheel, a fuzzy PID-like controller provides a satisfactory correspondence to the exact values of the braking parameters on different types of road surface.

4 Conclusion

With regard to the process of computer simulation of the movement of an automobile wheel in braking mode in real time, it is currently possible to recommend the following:

1. A preliminary analysis of the system and the choice of the type of controller are necessary, since, despite the seeming simplicity and obviousness, fuzzy controllers in some cases are not well predictable and are not always able to provide the required control accuracy. Where it is possible and a satisfactory quality of regulation is ensured, it is preferable to use classical PID controllers. In the considered examples, in relation to the ABS of a car, the use of an adaptive fuzzy controller is justified and adequate.

2. When developing a fuzzy controller, the introduction of an additional input parameter in addition to the deviation value improves the quality of the model. In the proposed simplified model, the value of the vehicle speed is used. However, it is preferable to use the first or second derivative of either vehicle speed, wheel speed, or deviation change. The use of numerical values (through the values of derivatives, or according to the accelerometer data) and signs of accelerations in the fuzzy model makes it possible to take into account the prediction of the system's behavior.

3. To improve the adequacy of the model, one should take into account the time delay, taking into account the action of the hydraulic brake system and data processing by the processor. It is necessary to predict in real time the value of the slip coefficient at the next point in time and use it to control the error. To do this, in the model, at the output of the slip coefficient signal, the subsystem should be switched on, taking into account the time delay.

4. The calculation of the braking parameters of an automobile wheel equipped with an anti-lock braking system using a fuzzy controller method allows obtaining a satisfactory correspondence with the exact values of the braking parameters on different types of road surface over the entire range of the process under study on different road surfaces.

5. Further research is required on the possibility of using a fuzzy controller to calculate the braking parameters of an automobile wheel equipped with an anti-lock braking system in different modes: road surfaces, braking intensity, initial values of wheel speed and vertical load.

References

1. Genta, G., Genta, A.: Road Vehicle Dynamics: Fundamentals of Modeling and Simulation, p. 996. World Scientific, Series On Advances In Mathematics For Applied Sciences (2016)
2. Rill, G., Arrieta Castro, A.: Road Vehicle Dynamics: Fundamentals and Modeling with MATLAB (2nd ed.). CRC Press (2020). https://doi.org/10.1201/9780429244476
3. Takahashi, H., et al.: Antiskid Brake Control System Bazed on Fuzzy Inference. United States Patent 4 842342 (1989)
4. Venkatesh, K.A., Mathivanan, N.: CAN network based longitudinal velocity measurement using accelerometer and GPS receiver for automobiles. Measur. Sci. Rev. 13(3), 115–121 (2013)
5. Venkatesh, K.A., Mathivanan, N.: Design of MEMS accelerometer based acceleration measurement system for automobiles. Measur. Sci. Rev. 12(5), 189–194 (2012)
6. Balakina, E.V., Zotov, N.M., Zotov, V.M., Platonov, I.A., Fedin, A.P., Bakhmutov, S.V.: Problems of modeling dynamic's processes in real time (on example of vehicle's brake dynamics). Monograph, Moscow, p. 299 (2013). (in Russian)

7. Balakina, E.V., Zotov, N.M., Fedin, A.P.: Modeling of the motion of automobile elastic wheel in real-time for creation of wheeled vehicles motion control electronic systems. In: IOP Conference Series: Materials Science and Engineering, vol. 315, no. 1, p. 012004 (2018)

8. Dygalo, V., Lyaschenko, M., Boyko, G., Dygalo, L.: Application of virtual physical modeling technology for the development of elements of the autonomous (unmanned) vehicles' systems. In: IOP Conference Series: Materials Science and Engineering, vol. 315, no. (1), p. 012007 (2018)

9. Balkwill, J.: Performance Vehicle Dynamics. Engineering and Applications. Department of Mechanical Engineering and Mathematical Sciences, Oxford Brookes University, Elsevier Inc., p. 360 (2018)

10. Arnold, M., Burgermeister, B., Führer, C., Hippmann, G., Rill, G.: Numerical methods in vehicle system dynamics: State of the art and current developments. Veh. Syst. Dyn. **49**(7), 1159–1207 (2011)

11. Tujrin, S., Boyko, G., Revin, A., Fedotov, V.: Research to longevity brake lines on the exploitations. Transp. Prob. **10**(2), 75–81 (2015)

12. Chung, E., Dumont, A.-G.: Transport simulation: Beyond traditional approaches (2019).https://doi.org/10.1201/9780429093258

13. Fedin, A., Kalinin, Y., Marchuk, E.: ANN in car antilock braking systems modeling. In: 2019 3rd School on Dynamics of Complex Networks and their Application in Intellectual Robotics, DCNAIR 2019, p. 49, 8875513 (2019)

14. Fedin, A.P., Kalinin, Y.V., Marchuk, E.A.: Antilock braking system fuzzy controller optimization with a genetic algorithm in a form of cellular automaton. Conference Proceedings - 4th Scientific School on Dynamics of Complex Networks and their Application in Intellectual Robotics, DCNAIR 2020, pp. 78–81, 9216912 (2020)

Cyber-Physical Systems and Big Data-Driven World. Pro-Active Modeling in Intelligent Decision Making Support

Business Process Optimization of Technological Map in Farm Management System

Mohammed A. Al-Gunaid[1,2(✉)] and Vladislav Trubitsin[1,2]

[1] Volgograd State Technical University, Lenin Avenue, 28, Volgograd 400005, Russian Federation
mohammadalgunaid@gmail.com, v.trubitsin@bilaboratory.com
[2] LLC Business Intelligence Laboratory "BILAB", Lenin Avenue, 28A, Volgograd 400005, Russian Federation

Abstract. Technological maps are the primary planning document and economic analysis in an agricultural enterprise and its divisions, serve as the basis for the development and adoption of specific management decisions in the crop production industry, financial and long-term plans of the enterprise. Technological map planning is currently carried out by compilation using various tools or in paper form, and can take up to several working weeks, depending on the land bank of the enterprise and the depth of planning. This paper describes the developed method for analyzing the costs of performing the stage of field work within the framework of the technological map of cultivation of an agricultural crop, based on the processing of statistical data on the results of the actual performance of field work. The developed method has been tested at an enterprise with an average field area in Russia (6,500 hectares). After the introduction of a management system at the enterprise with a planning tool for technological maps of growing crops, the time spent on planning was reduced by 50%. When using the proposed method, this indicator improved by another 20%.

Keywords: Forecasting · Machine Learning · Data Processing · Agroindustrial Complex · Technological Map · Planning

1 Introduction

Internal business processes automation of an agricultural enterprise is still an urgent task. The process of planning the cultivation of an agricultural crop is expressed in the form of a technological map of the agricultural crop cultivation. At the moment, there are only tools that make it possible to facilitate the process of drawing up a technological map by storing in digital form and automating calculations for labor costs and material resources.

The technological map in crop production is a plan of agrotechnical, organizational and economic measures for the cultivation of one or a group of crops that are homogeneous in technology, with the cost calculation of the final crop production.

© The Author(s), under exclusive license to Springer Nature Switzerland AG 2023
A. G. Kravets et al. (Eds.): CIT&DS 2023, CCIS 1909, pp. 171–190, 2023.
https://doi.org/10.1007/978-3-031-44615-3_12

Technological maps are the primary planning document and economic analysis in an agricultural enterprise and its divisions, serve as the basis for the development and adoption of specific management decisions in the crop production industry, financial and long-term plans of the enterprise.

This process is currently carried out by compilation using various tools or in paper form, and can take up to several working weeks, depending on the land bank of the enterprise and the depth of planning. However, in case of an unsatisfactory result, the process must be repeated, which leads to additional time costs. The purpose of this work is to improve the efficiency of the technological maps planning process, which means reducing time costs.

2 Challenge

In the agro-industrial complex, business processes for consumer purposes are classified into external and internal [1]. Internal processes include those processes in which an enterprise acts as a consumer [2].

In this case, only the main processes that are aimed at growing will be considered, namely:

- purchases;
- storage and distribution of products;
- production;
- planning.

The above processes are more or less subject of automation. To automate procurement, there are a number of tools to automate the process of paperwork [3–5].

To automate the storage and distribution of products, there are software solutions for warehouse management with specialization in a specific area of agro-industrial production [3, 4].

The production process itself is also subject to automation through the introduction of precision farming systems [6, 7], GPS tracking systems to control the efficiency and quality of work.

The planning process for the cultivation of crops is to develop a technological map. And as automation at the moment, solutions are offered to increase the efficiency of drawing up a technological map.

This paper describes the developed method for analyzing the costs of performing the stage of field work within the framework of the technological map of cultivation of an agricultural crop, based on the processing of statistical data on the results of the actual performance of field work.

Within the framework of the methodology, a model has been developed for forecasting the costs of performing the technological map's field work stage.

3 Related Works

There are many ready-made spreadsheet templates available for filling out a technological map. However, although this approach significantly speeds up the process relative to the paper version of maintenance, it requires manually filling in a large amount of information. This inevitably leads to a high investment of time.

The web platform "ExactFarming" [3] provides a convenient tool for templates of work, which allows to create a technological map of the agricultural crops cultivation with preset stages and estimated duration. However, the system does not allow editing the work list and does not make forecast values for the resources expended, which leads to the fact that in the event of an error, the planning process will need to be repeated.

"Program 1C: Enterprise 8. ERP Agro-industrial complex" [4] also provides functionality for drawing up technological maps of agricultural crops cultivation, but, like previous solutions, does not offer opportunities to increase the efficiency of drawing up a plan.

The listed analogs must be compared according to the criteria that affect the planning process. The following criteria are proposed:

- availability of initial data (reference books with the names of drugs, models of equipment, types of work, etc. are loaded into the system);
- the presence of templates for technological maps (the system has a tool for duplicating data by default);
- crop rotation (information about predecessors, to increase the efficiency of the choice of crops, fertilizers);
- cost forecasting of the work stage (automatic calculation based on the data of the execution statistics).

The scale for comparing these indicators is based on the principle of ranking these systems according to the selected criterion. If the system does not have this functionality, then the value is 0. If the compared systems have approximately the same indicator according to the criterion, then they are set to the same position. Figure 1 shows a diagram showing the result of comparing the developed system and implemented as a result of this study with the described analogs.

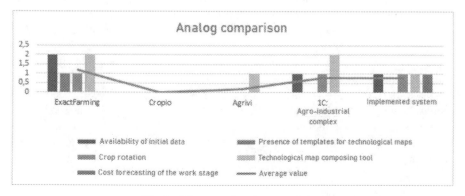

Fig. 1. Diagram of analog comparison

Mentioned systems allows to manage the enterprise efficiently, tracking the performance of work and the use of various resources. In this direction, many modern technologies are used, such as IoT [8, 31] and various web technologies [37], which allow the introduction and use of elements of artificial intelligence in agriculture.

Existing research uses smart algorithms to predict crop yields, product sales, identify pests, and more. In their work [9], the authors compare the machine learning methods described in various studies in relation to forecasting weather conditions for different purposes. As a result of the reviews, among the most accurate methods, the authors indicate a neural network, decision trees, a random forest and methods of fuzzy modeling.

Similar methods are used in [10, 22] to predict sales and prices of finished crop products, allowing for more efficient planning of the process of harvesting and storing grain crops.

Barley is one of the strategic agricultural products available in the world, and yield prediction is important for ensuring food security. The findings of the study [32] provide a powerful potential tool for the yield prediction of barley using multi-source data and machine learning.

In work [36], a model has been proposed which helps cultivators predict the yield of the crop even before cultivating directly onto the agricultural lands. The yield prediction based on location, acreage and fertilizer data for several regions in the United States has been experimented using various algorithms. The yield prediction results have shown that the gradient boosting regressor proved to be the best performer, returning a standalone accuracy score of 90.73% and 80.72% on being validated using the fivefold cross validation method.

To predict yield, in addition to regression methods, fuzzy modeling methods are used, such as fuzzy cognitive maps [11]. This technology is used in [12] to improve the efficiency of decision-making related to the cultivation of crops in conditions of uncertainty and allows you to track the patterns of influence of control actions on the final level of crop yield.

Modern agriculture is based on control and optimization, where monitoring is essential. But yield monitoring limited to spatial mapping of biomass is unsatisfactory for uniformity optimization. Authors of [25] propose a method for developing yield monitoring systems that can estimate physical dimensions of crops directly on-line.

In [13], data analysis methods are used to predict the climate by seasons, and the forecast results are aggregated with data on the cultivated crop and applied cultivation technologies, allowing to support decision-making on field work, calculating the duration of various phases of crop development.

The study [24] aimed to determine sugarcane production environments using a reduced number of low-cost variables through the machine learning technique. The descriptive statistics was performed to understand the behavior of the data, followed by the stepwise regression to determine which variables would be useful to the model. The stepwise regression was efficient in selecting the variables, while the decision tree was effective in determining the environments, with a satisfactory accuracy of 75% and the generation of more continuous management environments in the cultivation area.

To predict NDVI (Normalized difference vegetation index) indicators, linear and quadratic regression methods, as well as a neural network [14–16, 39], are used. The resulting prediction values track changes in landscape and vegetation over time, allowing for more efficient planting planning.

Fast and accurate plant disease detection is critical to increasing agricultural productivity in a sustainable way. Paper [27] outlines the latest advances in imaging technology for the automatic recognition of leaf pests and diseases. Recent efforts have focused on using deep learning instead of training surface classifiers using hand-crafted functions. Researchers have reported high recognition accuracies on particular datasets but in many cases, the performance of those systems deteriorated significantly when tested on different datasets or in field conditions.

Articles [17, 18, 23, 28, 30] presents some variants of using neural networks and deep learning methods to identify harmful objects in the field of agriculture. This work [17] describes a method for identifying defects on plant leaves and determining the presence of pests of various kinds by analyzing images. The use of the described system makes it possible to reduce labor intensity and reduce the time for examining crops, as well as improve the quality of work of agronomic services.

Paper [38] elucidates the diverse automation approaches for crop yield detection techniques with virtual analysis and classifier approaches. This research works are available as products for applications such as robot harvesting, weed detection and pest infestation. The methods which made use of conventional deep learning techniques have provided an average accuracy of 92.51%

In work [33], the authors investigate the capabilities of modern (SoA) object detection models based on convolutional neural networks (CNN) for the problem of detecting beetle-like pests in heterogeneous outdoor images from various sources. The results show the suitability of the current SoA models for this application, highlighting that the FasterRCNN with the MobileNetV3 backbone is a particularly good starting point for inference accuracy and latency. This combination provided an average accuracy score of 92.66%, which can be considered qualitatively no less good than the score obtained by other authors who adopted more specific models.

Very recently, a series of studies have demonstrated that the deep learning method of Convolutional Neural Networks (CNN) is very effective to represent spatial patterns enabling to extract a wide array of vegetation properties from remote sensing imagery. This [29] review introduces the principles of CNN and distils why they are particularly suitable for vegetation remote sensing.

Within the methodology considered in the problem statement section, the planning process can take a significant amount of time (depending on the sown area) and require calculations for a large number of parameters that may change during actual implementation.

Based on the analysis of the current state of research in this area, it can be concluded that the implemented system can compete with existing solutions, but its advantage lies in the possibility of improving and adding missing functionality.

4   Methodology

4.1   Data Collection and Preparation

To implement an automated system for planning a technological map, it is necessary to present functional requirements. Parameters that are passed to the subsystem input:

- sowing area;
- type of crop;
- type of seeds;
- type of field work stage;
- field work statistics data.
- The subsystem should return the following data as output:
- fuel costs;
- fuel volume;
- seed costs;
- payroll fund;
- total material costs.

The general algorithm of the system operation is shown in Fig. 2. In the initial state, it is assumed that the system must contain data. The first step is to select the planned crop, sowing area and type of seed and then download the relevant data regarding the selection. Further, a training sample is formed from the data by means of aggregations. The process of forming a training sample is given below, as well as the accompanying data transformation processes are described.

Algorithm 1: General algorithm of the system

---

1 function Estimate ();
    Input   : sowing area, type of crop, type of seeds, type of field work
            stage, field work statistics data.
    Output: fuel costs, fuel volume, seed costs, payroll fund, total material
            costs.
2 Data collection;
3 Sampling the collected data;
4 Formation of field work stages;
5 **for** *every field work stage in field work stages* **do**
6 | Forecast work stage's cost;
7 **end**
8 return work stages sample;

Fig. 2. General algorithm of the system

The first step in determining the costs of the field work stage is to calculate the number of standard shifts. This parameter is not predicted, but calculated because it directly depends on the area of work. Accordingly, in order to obtain the number of norm-shifts, it is necessary to find in the loaded norms the one that corresponds to the type of work and divide the sown area by the area specified in the norm.

The resulting value of the standard shifts also determines the performer's salary. The next step will be to determine the amount of consumed fuel. This parameter is logically related to two factors: the technique used by the driver and the area being worked. Since the technique is unknown at this stage, the only way out is to replace this factor by averaging the use over the entire technique. However, for example, when transporting and harvesting crops, a different type of equipment is used: a truck and a harvester, respectively. These types of equipment are very different in cost, but with the same type of work, they will be the same. Therefore, the average fuel consumption per hectare of work must be calculated for each type of work separately.

For the "Sowing" work type, you need to get the seed cost value. This parameter requires a separate allocation for this type of work, because for certain types the value of this parameter can differ by an order of magnitude and provide up to 90% of the costs at this stage. As well as with fuel costs, average values are calculated by converting the unit of measurement to the seed unit and linking to the rate change.

All previous values were obtained using explicit conversions and direct dependencies between parameters. However, the costs for the rest of the materials are of a more complex dependency nature and a forecasting model is used for it.

The algorithm for forming the recommended stages consists of three blocks: adding mandatory stages of work, adding the most probable ones, and removing duplicates. Work is mandatory if the growing process directly depends on this stage of work. For example, for cultivation, these actions are "sowing" and "harvesting", and for fallow, this is the product of soil cultivation.

Work shift performance data is information about the performer and how much of the actual work he performed. This takes into account what technique was used and how much material of various types was spent. Actual data can be calculated in different units of measurement (hectares, working hours, etc.). Accordingly, it is necessary, when unloading, to bring them to a universal measure of the amount of work performed. The norm change acts as such a measure. Agricultural enterprises calculate this indicator to convert the volume of work into a monetary equivalent, which is a wage bill.

Seeds of sowing crops must be divided into two types: "elite" and "self-reproductive seeds". This solution allows you to separate seed data, which can differ significantly in price and seeding rate. The fact of using seeds is data on the area on which a certain amount of material (seeds) was used. Seeds can be used in different units of measure (pieces, sowing unit, kilograms, tons). For the translation, a universal value has been selected - the sowing unit. When brought from other units, it was taken as a kilogram/hectare, piece/hectare. These indicators are comparable only within the same agricultural crop and type of seed, since the seeding rates for them are very different.

When collecting data on fuel use, it is also necessary to convert to liters. The weights indicated in units of measurement must be converted using the reference values for the density of the diesel fuel. Data on the fact of completing a stage of work is aggregated data on all actual performances of work shifts within this stage, as well as the materials used in this case.

The data collected and processed in this way can be used for analysis and further forecasting of costs for the stages of work.

4.2 Used Methods Description

Some of the most popular and effective machine learning methods used for this purpose include linear regression [34], random forest [35], support vector machines [26], and gradient boosting [36].

Linear regression is a model of the dependence of the variable x on one or more other variables (factors, regressors, independent variables) with a linear dependence function. Linear regression refers to the task of determining the "line of best fit" across a set of data points. The goal of linear regression is to find the line that best fits these points.

According to formula 1, the function f depends linearly on the parameters w. In this case, a linear dependence on the free variable x is not assumed,

$$y = f(w, x) + v \tag{1}$$

In this case linear regression is represented as following (2)

$$y = \sum_{j=1}^{W} w_j g_j(x) + v = (w, x) + v \tag{2}$$

The parameter values are found using the least squares method.

Random forest is a machine learning algorithm proposed by Leo Breiman and Adele Cutler, which uses a committee (ensemble) of decision trees. The algorithm combines two main ideas: the Breiman bagging method, and the random subspace method proposed by Tin Kam Ho.

Bagging is a simple technique in which we build independent models and combine them using some kind of averaging model (for example, weighted average, majority vote, or normal average). The algorithm is used for classification, regression and clustering problems. The main idea is to use a large ensemble of decision trees, each of which by itself gives a very low quality of classification, but due to their large number, the result is good.

Suppose there is some not the most accurate algorithm, for example, a decision tree. If you create a set of decision trees and average the result of their predictions (in the case of solving the regression problem) or make a decision by voting (in the case of classification), then the final result will be much more informative. This is how the ensemble training is arranged. An important point here is the element of randomness in the creation of each tree. Obviously, if you create many identical trees, then the result of their averaging will have the accuracy of one tree.

The main structural element of a random forest is a decision tree, on the construction of which the quality of work and the stability of the final model depend.

Support vector machine is an intelligent forecasting method based on statistical learning theory and the principle of minimizing structural risks. In the case of a classification problem into two disjoint classes, in which objects are described by n-dimensional real vectors: $X = R_n$, $Y = \{-1, 1\}$, the linear classifier is described as follows 3:

$$a(x) = sign\left(\sum_{j=1}^{n} w_j x_j - w_0\right) = sign(\langle w, x \rangle - w_0) \tag{3}$$

where $x = (x_1, x_2, \ldots, x_n)$ is an attribute description of the object x; the vector $w = (w_1, w_2, \ldots, w_n) \in R_n$ and the scalar threshold $x_0 R$ are parameters of the algorithm.

The equation $<w, x> = w_0$ describes a hyperplane separating classes in the space R_n.

Gradient boosting is a machine learning technique for classification and regression problems that builds a prediction model in the form of an ensemble of weak predictive models, usually decision trees [19].

Boosting is an ensemble-building technique in which predictors are not built independently, but sequentially.

The goal of any supervised learning algorithm is to determine the loss function and minimize it. For example, the root-mean-square error can be used as a loss function 4:

$$MSE = \frac{1}{n} \sum_{i=1}^{n} (F_i - R_i)^2 * 100\% \tag{4}$$

where n is the number of records in the test sample, Ri is the actual data, and Fi is the predicted value.

By using gradient descent and updating the predictions based on learning rate, you can get the values at which the MSE is minimal [20]. For this, formulas 5, 6, 7 are used.

$$R_i = R_i + \alpha * \delta L(F_i, R_i)/\delta R_i \tag{5}$$

$$R_i = R_i + \alpha * \delta^X (F_i - R_i)^2/\delta R_i \tag{6}$$

$$R_i = R_i - \alpha * 2 *^X (F_i - R_i) \tag{7}$$

where $L(F_i, R_i)$ is the loss function specified in formula 5, α is the learning rate coefficient, Ri is the actual data, and Fi is the predicted value. The predicted values are updated in such a way that the sum of the deviations tends to zero and the predicted values are closer to the real ones.

4.3 Software

As part of the study, an automated system for planning a technological map of cultivation of agricultural crops was developed, consisting of the subsystems presented at Fig. 3.

To access the functionality of the subsystems, a client application has been developed that provides a user interface.

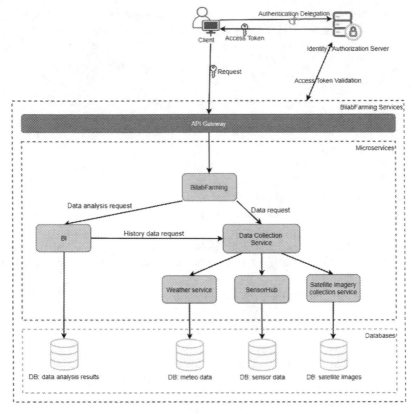

Fig. 3. Architecture of automated system

5 Experiment

Table 1 shows a fragment of the training sample for the "sowing" stage of work. The training sample consists of records containing data on the result of the actual work performed. Each record contains information about the amount of fuel used, the cost of seeds, and the total cost of materials. There is also information about the employee's salary for the performance of this work and its equivalent value in the number of shift rates and the volume of the processed area. The column "Seed cost" is added only in the "sowing" stage of work, since in other cases the value of this field is equal to zero.

Correlation analysis [40] is used to assess the degree of linear dependence between pairs of factors 8.

$$r = r(x, y) = \frac{\overline{xy} - \overline{x} * \overline{y}}{\sigma_x \sigma_y} \tag{8}$$

$$\overline{x} = \frac{1}{n} \sum x_i, \overline{y} = \frac{1}{n} \sum y_i, \overline{xy} = \frac{1}{n} \sum x_i y_i$$

Table 1. An example of records in the training set.

Area, ha	Material cost, RUB	Salary, RUB	Seeds, RUB	Fuel, RUB	Norms
30	75 300,00	1 206,90	75 300,00	–	0,9
312	712 019,00	13 693,20	607 000,00	105 019,00	9,7
60	124 169,60	3 249,20	114 000,00	10 169,60	2,3
197	571 270,00	8 045,70	502 900,00	68 370,00	5,7
94	223 060,00	3 781,50	205 000,00	18 060,00	2,7
45	108 330,00	1 810,30	95 000,00	13 330,00	1,3
204	690 319,80	10 838,30	672 000,00	18 319,80	7,7
140	611 967,20	9 269,50	601 181,80	10 785,40	6,6
240	787 276,40	–	765 093,70	22 182,70	5,3
173	888 080,10	5 221,30	834 000,20	54 079,90	3,7

It is performed with the aim of selecting and preprocessing input fields for use in training on these models. For example, the presence of a correlation between the input factors has an extremely negative effect when constructing a linear regression.

The modulus of the coefficient indicates the degree of dependence: the closer its value is to 0, the weaker the linear dependence. The closer the correlation coefficient is to 1, the stronger the direct linear dependence, the closer to −1, the stronger the inverse linear dependence. In practice, it is believed that if the modulus of the correlation coefficient is greater than 0.6, then the linear dependence is strong, and if it is less than 0.3, then it is almost absent.

Figure 4 shows the result of performing a correlation analysis on a training sample for the "Sowing" type of work. Since the modulus of the correlation coefficient for all parameters is greater than 0.3, then all factors (the area of the cultivated area, the wages fund (salary), the cost of seeds, the cost of fuel, the number of norms) affect the cost of materials.

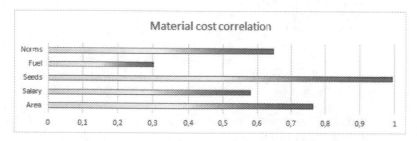

Fig. 4. Correlation in the stages of work like "Sowing"

The strongest linear dependence is formed by the cost of seeds - 0.995. This fact arises because in works such as "Seeding" the cost of seeds can be up to 90% of the cost of the entire stage of work. Figure 5 shows the results of the correlation analysis on a sample of works other than sowing. The smallest dependence appears with the factor "Fuel costs", only 0.301.

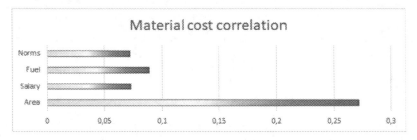

Fig. 5. Correlation in the stages of work other than the type of work "Sowing"

This figure shows that if the training sample is formed according to the data of all works, then the correlation coefficient will be low. Therefore, a logical action would be to extract data from the training sample for each separate type of work. However, this statement is true only for works in which the number of records in the sample is large. Such an example would be "Cultivation". Figure 6 shows the results of the correlation analysis for the type of work "Cultivation".

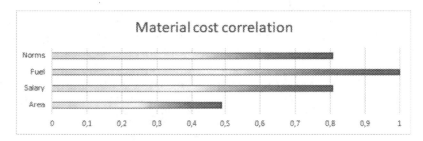

Fig. 6. Correlation in the stages of work like "Cultivation"

The Fig. 6 shows that the fuel in this case gives the maximum coefficient of dependence. This is due to the fact that other types of materials are not used in works such as "Cultivation".

To select a suitable forecasting method and model, an experiment was carried out to train mathematical models using linear regression, support vectors, random forests, and gradient boosting.

The sample of data for the experiment contains 171 records about the fact of the execution of work on the stage "Cultivation". To assess the forecast accuracy, the total sample was divided into training (85%) and tested (15%). Comparison results for methods using MAE, RMSE and MAPE scores are presented in Table 2 and Figs. 7, 8, 9 and 10.

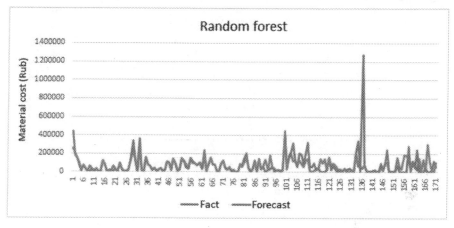

Fig. 7. The result of training using the "random forest" method

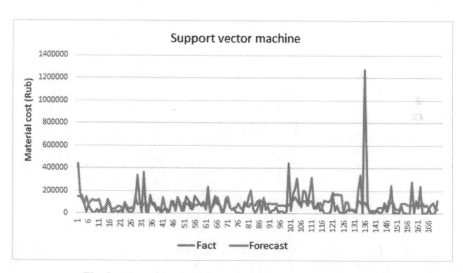

Fig. 8. The result of training using the support vector machine

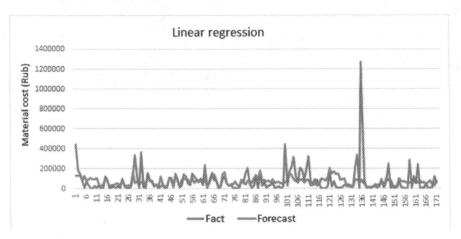

Fig. 9. The result of training using the "linear regression" method

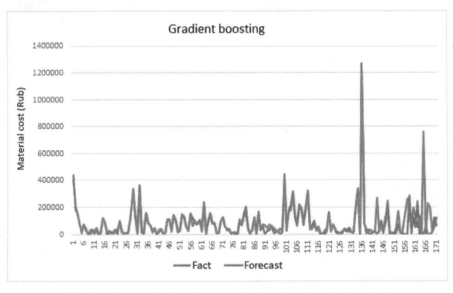

Fig. 10. The result of training using the "gradient boosting" method

As a result of comparing the trained forecasting models, the gradient boosting method turned out to be the most effective (the error probability was about 80%). The rest of the methods proved to be much worse. Therefore, in further experiments, it is advisable to use the gradient boosting method.

Table 2. Assessment of the accuracy of forecasting models

Method	MAE	RMSE	MAPE
Random forest	18 631.4	52 723.8	139.37
Linear regression	62 838.9	126 079.2	383.5
SVM	65 907.9	139 447	200.4
Gradient boosting	11 498.5	18 153.5	80.4

To identify the dependence of the accuracy of the constructed forecasting models on the size of the training sample, an experiment should be carried out to train the forecasting model on samples of different sizes and check their accuracy based on various evaluation criteria. The results of this experiment are shown in Table 3.

Table 3. Results of the experiment on training the forecasting model on samples of different sizes

Experiment number	Sample size, records	MAPE, %	RMSE
1	100	110	24 959
2	128	101	22 917
3	150	92	20 875
4	171	80.4	18 153

As you can see, with an increase in the volume of the training sample, the accuracy of the model increases (the probability of error decreases, the standard deviation decreases).

The experimental results show that the accuracy of the constructed forecasting model depends on the size of the training sample, despite the large number of influencing factors that the model takes into account.

The next experiment is to identify the number of influencing factors required to obtain the best forecast accuracy. This experiment involves training a forecasting model on samples with a different number of influencing factors and checking their accuracy based on various criteria for assessing accuracy. It is assumed that adding seed value data for a planting job has a positive effect on model accuracy. The results of the experiment are shown in Table 4.

Table 4. Results of the experiment to identify the number of influencing factors.

Experiment number	Number of factors	MAPE, %	RMSE
1	4	124,21	23 635
2	5	15	2 859

The results of the experiment show that when the factor of costs for seeds was added, the maximum error in the predicted value of costs for materials was about 2800 rubles. When using four factors, the maximum error in the predicted value of material costs turned out to be an order of magnitude higher, in the region of 23,600 rubles.

As a demonstration of the operation of the described forecasting model, it is necessary to use the developed automated system for planning the technological map of the cultivation of agricultural crops. The result of forecasting is shown in Table 5.

Table 5. Results of the experiment to identify the number of influencing factors

Stage Norms	Fuel, L	Fuel, RUB	Salary, RUB	Seeds, RUB	Material, RUB	MAE	MSE	MAPE %
Harvesting 22,73	3250,3	130 225	32 003	–	127 656	11 498	329 552	80,4
Sowing 8,33	1349,4	54 065	11 729	833 088	887 934	80	9 795	0,1
Cultivation 5,21	1870,3	74 936	7 336	–	59 734	11 499	329 552	80,4
Chemical 2,53	156,8	6 285	3 562	–	20 782	11 499	329 552	80,4

6 Discussion of Results

As part of testing the effectiveness of planning a technological map, an enterprise with an average field area in Russia (6,500 hectares) was interviewed. According to the company, planning on paper can take an average of 1 month (160 working hours of several employees and the head of the company). After the introduction of a management system at the enterprise with a planning tool for technological maps of agricultural crops cultivation, the value of this indicator improved by 50%, up to 80 h on average.

When using the proposed method, this indicator was improved by another 20%, up to 64 working hours, which is shown in Fig. 11.

The decrease by 20% is due to the fact that only the calculated part of drawing up a technological map is affected, namely:

- frequent stages are formed;
- the amount of fuel required;
- fuel costs;
- seed costs;
- wage fund;
- the duration of the stage in normal changes;
- total material costs.

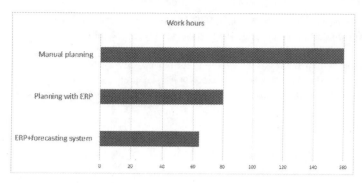

Fig. 11. Results of testing the creation of a technological map

The generated technological map contains only an assumption about the composition of the stages based on performance statistics. Therefore, this list requires clarification, which reduces the possible effectiveness of the method. A possible modification of this approach consists not in the selection of the most frequent stage of work, but in the recommendation of the most optimal crop in terms of profitability. But this approach requires more data on crop cultivation.

7   Conclusion and Final Remarks

Forecasting the costs of field work allows you to get values without filling in a large number of parameters, but does not guarantee high accuracy, however, it significantly reduces the time spent on planning.

At the same time, this estimate is tied to the actual actions and values during the field work of previous seasons, which allows you to make an analysis adjusted for a specific farm and its processes. But this approach is applicable only after the accumulation of a certain amount of data, for the formation of statistics of use, prices for materials, entering the reference values on the tariffs for the performance of work.

The prospect for the development of this work is the task of finding the most optimal list of parameters to achieve the greatest profit. This presupposes a greater variety of data (characteristics of the cultivated area, classified species of drugs) and the inclusion of cultivation results. This will allow you to determine the optimal combination of cost parameters and the resulting yield. This task is in line with the Efficient Hectare project launched by the Ministry of Agriculture of the Russian Federation to improve the efficiency of agricultural land use.

References

1. Krasilnikova, L.E.: Theoretical aspects of building business processes of management decisions for the effective development of the domestic agro-industrial complex. Perm Agrarian Bull. (1), 131–135 (2017)
2. Magomedova, N.G.: Classification of business processes in agro-industrial enterprises. Struct. Econ. (1), 41–45 (2012)

3. Online service for farm management. ExactFarming. https://www.exactfarming.com/ru/
4. ERP Agro-industrial complex 2. 1C: Enterprise 8. https://solutions.1c.ru/catalog/erpapk/fea tures
5. Technological map of the cultivation of agricultural crops. AgroSite. http://agrosite.org/index/ tekhnologicheskajakartavozdelyvanijaselskokhoz-jajstvennykhkultur/0-13
6. Equipment and solutions for precision farming AMS farming. John Deere. https://www.dee re.ru
7. Precision farming systems. StavTrack. https://www.stavtrack.ru/apk/tochnoe-zemledelie. html
8. Chen, K., Li, Z., Ma, L., Tang, Y.: Intelligent agriculture - agricultural monitoring and control management system. In: Xu, Z., Parizi, R.M., Hammoudeh, M., Loyola-González, O. (eds.) CSIA 2020. AISC, vol. 1146, pp. 317–325. Springer, Cham (2020). https://doi.org/10.1007/ 978-3-030-43306-2_45
9. Kumar, R.S., Ramesh, C.: A study on prediction of rainfall using datamining technique. Satyabama University, Chennai (2016)
10. Al-Gunaid, M.A., Shcherbakov, M.V., Trubitsin, V.V., Shumkin, A.M.: Time series analysis sales of sowing crops based on machine learning methods. Volgograd State Technical University (2018)
11. Kosko, B.: Fuzzy cognitive maps. Int. J. Man Mach. Stud. **24**(1), 65–75 (1986)
12. Al-Gunaid, M.A., Salygina, I.I., Shcherbakov, M.V., Trubitsin, V.N., Groumpos, P.P.: Forecasting potential yields under uncertainty using fuzzy cognitive maps. Agric. Food Secur. **10**, 32 (2021). https://doi.org/10.1186/s40066-021-00314-9
13. Han, E., Ines, A.V.M., Baethgen, W.E.: Climate-agriculture-modeling and decision tool: a software framework for climate risk management in agriculture. Environ Model Softw. **95**, 102–114 (2017)
14. Bolton, D.K., Friedl, M.A.: Forecasting crop yield using remotely sensed vegetation indices and crop phenology metrics. Agric. For. Meteorol. **173**, 74–84 (2013)
15. Fan, X., Liu, Y.: A comparison of NDVI intercalibration methods. Int. J. Remote Sens. **38**(19), 5273–5290 (2017)
16. Mkhabela, M.S., Bullock, P., Raj, S., Wang, S., Yang, Y.: Crop yield forecasting on the Canadian Prairies using MODIS NDVI data. Agric. For. Meteorol. **151**(3), 385–393 (2011)
17. Al-Gunaid, M.A., Shcherbakov, M.V., Tishchenko, V.V., Trubitsin, V.N.: The system of intelligent identification of harmful objects in the field of agriculture. In: Kravets, A.G., Shcherbakov, M., Parygin, D., Groumpos, P.P. (eds.) CIT&DS 2021. CCIS, vol. 1448, pp. 177–189. Springer, Cham (2021). https://doi.org/10.1007/978-3-030-87034-8_14
18. Bock, C.H., Poole, G.H., Parker, P.E., Gottwald, T.R.: Plant disease severity estimated visually, by digital photography and image analysis, and by hyperspectral imaging. Crit. Rev. Plant Sci. **29**(2), 59–107 (2010)
19. Gradientboosting simplified. Kaggle. https://www.kaggle.com/grroverpr/gradient-boosting-simplified/
20. Shcherbakov, M.V., Brebel's, A., Shcherbakova, N.L., Tyukov, A.P., Yanovskiy, T.A., Kamaev, V.A.: A survey of forecast error measures. World Appl. Sci. J. (WASJ) **24**(spec. issue 24), 171–176 (2013)
21. Correlation analysis. BaseGroup Labs. https://basegroup.ru/deductor/function/algorithm/cor relation-analysis
22. Cerna, R., Tirado, E., Bayona-Oré, S.: Price prediction of agricultural products: machine learning. In: Yang, X.-S., Sherratt, S., Dey, N., Joshi, A. (eds.) ICICT 2021. LNNS, vol. 2017, pp. 879–887. Springer, Singapore (2022). https://doi.org/10.1007/978-981-16-2102-4_78

23. Abayomi-Alli, O.O., Damaˇseviˇcius, R., Misra, S., Maskeliu¯nas, R.: Cassava disease recognition from low-quality images using enhanced data augmentation model and deep learning. Expert. Syst. **38**(7), e12746 (2021). https://doi.org/10.1111/exsy.12746

24. de Almeida, G.M., Pereira, G.T., de Souza Bahia, A.S.R., Fernandes, K., Júnior, J.M.: Machine learning in the prediction of sugarcane production environments. Comput. Electron. Agric. **190**, 106452 (2021). ISSN: 0168-1699. https://doi.org/10.1016/j.compag.2021.106452

25. Dolata, P., Wróblewski, P., Mrzygłód, M., Reiner, J.: Instance segmentation of root crops and simulation-based learning to estimate their physical dimensions for on-line machine vision yield monitoring. Comput. Electron. Agric. **190**, 106451 (2021). ISSN: 0168-1699. https://doi.org/10.1016/j.compag.2021.106451

26. Kok, Z.H., Shariff, A.R.M., Alfatni, M.S.M., Khairunniza-Bejo, S.: Support vector machine in precision agriculture: a review. Comput. Electron. Agric. **191**, 106546 (2021). ISSN: 0168-1699. https://doi.org/10.1016/j.compag.2021.106546

27. Ngugi, L.C., Abelwahab, M., Abo-Zahhad, M.: Recent advances in image processing techniques for automated leaf pest and disease recognition – a review. Inf. Process. Agric. **8**(1), 27–51 (2021). ISSN: 2214-3173. https://doi.org/10.1016/j.inpa.2020.04.004

28. Sambasivam, G., Opiyo, G.D.: A predictive machine learning application in agriculture: cassava disease detection and classification with imbalanced dataset using convolutional neural networks. Egypt. Inf. J. **22**(1), 27–34 (2021). ISSN: 1110-8665. https://doi.org/10.1016/j.eij.2020.02.007

29. Kattenborn, T., Leitloff, J., Schiefer, F., Hinz, S.: Review on convolutional neural networks (CNN) in vegetation remote sensing. ISPRS J. Photogram. Remote Sens. **173**, 24–49 (2021). ISSN: 0924-2716. https://doi.org/10.1016/j.isprsjprs.2020.12.010

30. Yu, Z., Amin, S.U., Alhussein, M., Lv, Z.: Research on disease prediction based on improved DeepFM and IoMT. IEEE Access **9**, 39043–39054 (2021). https://doi.org/10.1109/ACCESS.2021.3062687

31. Kashyap, P.K., Kumar, S., Jaiswal, A., Prasad, M., Gandomi, A.H.: Towards precision agriculture: IoT-enabled intelligent irrigation systems using deep learning neural network. IEEE Sens. J. **21**(16), 17479–17491 (2021). https://doi.org/10.1109/JSEN.2021.3069266

32. Sharifi, A.: Yield prediction with machine learning algorithms and satellite images. J. Sci. Food Agric. **101**, 891–896 (2021). https://doi.org/10.1002/jsfa.10696

33. Butera, L., Ferrante, A., Jermini, M., Prevostini, M., Alippi, C.: Precise agriculture: effective deep learning strategies to detect pest insects. IEEE/CAA J. Autom. Sin. **9**(2), 246–258 (2022). https://doi.org/10.1109/JAS.2021.1004317

34. Weisberg, S.: Applied Linear Regression, 3rd edn., pp. 1–310 (2005). https://doi.org/10.1002/0471704091

35. Breiman, L.: Random forests. Mach. Learn. **45**(1), 5–32 (2001). https://doi.org/10.1023/A:1010933404324

36. Sagar, B.M., Cauvery, N.K., Abbi, P., Vismita, N., Pranava, B., Bhat, P.A.: Analysis and prediction of cotton yield with fertilizer recommendation using gradient boost algorithm. In: Joshi, A., Mahmud, M., Ragel, R.G., Thakur, N.V. (eds.) Information and Communication Technology for Competitive Strategies (ICTCS 2020). LNNS, vol. 191, pp. 1143–1152. Springer, Singapore (2022). https://doi.org/10.1007/978-981-16-0739-4_105

37. Dhabal, G., Lachure, J., Doriya, R.: Crop recommendation system with cloud computing. In: 2021 Third International Conference on Inventive Research in Computing Applications (ICIRCA), pp. 1404–1411 (2021). https://doi.org/10.1109/ICIRCA51532.2021.9544524

38. Darwin, B., Dharmaraj, P., Prince, S., Popescu, D.E., Hemanth, D.J.: Recognition of bloom/yield in crop images using deep learning models for smart agriculture: a review. Agronomy **11**, 646 (2021). https://doi.org/10.3390/agronomy11040646

39. Tedesco, D., de Almeida Moreira, B.R., Júnior, M.R.B., Papa, J.P., da Silva, R.P.: Predicting on multi-target regression for the yield of sweet potato by the market class of its roots upon vegetation indices. Computer. Electron. Agric. **191**, 106544 (2021). ISSN: 0168-1699. https://doi.org/10.1016/j.compag.2021.106544
40. Hardoon, D.R., Szedmak, S., Shawe-Taylor, J.: Canonical correlation analysis: an overview with application to learning methods. Neural Comput. **16**(12), 2639–2664 (2004). https://doi.org/10.1162/0899766042321814

Problem of Building High-Quality Predictive Model of River Hydrology: The Combined Use of Hydrodynamic Simulations and Intelligent Computing

Anna Yu. Klikunova$^{(\boxtimes)}$ (ID), Maxim V. Polyakov (ID), Sergei S. Khrapov (ID), and Alexander V. Khoperskov (ID)

Volgograd State University, 100 Prospect Universitetsky, Volgograd 400062, Russia
{klikunova,m.v.polyakov,khrapov,khoperskov}@volsu.ru

Abstract. A high-precision forecast of the hydrological regime of a large river system is limited by poor knowledge of the dependence of the hydraulic resistance force on the flow parameters. Our research is aimed at developing a method for constructing a hydraulic resistance model based on the integration of direct hydrodynamic simulations and intelligent computing. The force of hydraulic resistance to flow is the sum of the impact of roughness, traditionally given by the Manning coefficient, and the force of turbulent friction. There are four free parameters in our hydrodynamic model, which are calculated by fitting the results of computational experiments with data from real measurements at gauging stations. Our analysis focuses on the hydrological regime of the Volga River in its lower reaches. We apply the Long Short-Term Memory neural network to determine these free parameters of the numerical hydrodynamic model, requiring the best agreement between the measured and model time series of water levels at three gauging stations during 2022. The dependences of water levels on the water discharge (hydrograph) in the channel show the presence of memory in the system, when the value of the water level depends on the behavior of the hydrograph over the previous few days. This leads to the appearance of a hysteresis-type dependence in the hydrological data for all three gauging stations. We define the structure of our training subsets, which allows us to determine the duration of such hydrological memory in the conditions of the Lower Volga. The best agreement between the time series of measured and model water levels is achieved for time interval of 4–6 days. The constructed solutions make it possible to qualitatively reproduce the ambiguous loop-like functions of the water level on the hydrograph of the hydroelectric dam.

This research was funded by the Russian Science Foundation (grant no. 23-71-00016 https://rscf.ru/en/project/23-71-00016/) by using the equipment of the shared research facilities of HPC computing resources at Lomonosov Moscow State University.

Keywords: Hybrid Models · Hydrological Resistance · River Flow ·
LSTM Neural Network · Hydrodynamic Simulations · Hydrological
Time Series · Hysteresis

1   Introduction

Direct hydrodynamic modeling of river systems makes it possible to investigate
various problems of land hydrology [1–3]. There are successes in the analysis
of the consequences of various disasters, including accidents on dams and other
hydraulic structures leading to the destruction of infrastructure [4,5]. Such calculations are a necessary element of the engineering design [6–8], allowing to
significantly improve the quality of such projects. Natural flooding of large areas
is a traditional problem, and high-quality forecast models can save lives and ease
the impact for a large number of people [9]. The task of building a digital river
based on the combination of Computer Aided Design and CFD technologies is
considered in a number of papers [10].

The numerical hydrodynamic model should give an adequate forecast of the
hydrological regime of the territory. The key problem in using such models is
our poor knowledge of hydraulic resistance. It is determined by a large number of mutually influencing factors, so the most widespread is the phenomenological approach based on the estimation of the integral roughness coefficient
(or the Manning coefficient n_M) [11]. The Manning coefficient is a fundamental parameter in the calculation of flow parameters in natural river channels
and various engineering channels. The estimates of n_M are based, as a rule, on
one-dimensional shallow water models, which allow one to consider sufficiently
extended systems [11,12]. The problem of specifying hydrological resistance for
2D flows is relevant for large lowland rivers [13,14] and especially for wide floodplain areas [2,13,15].

New opportunities are associated with the rapid development of intelligent
computing in hydrology [16,17]. This helps to build surrogate or hybrid models
with low prediction accuracy and low computational costs [18,19]. These most
simple conceptual models are very fast because they use engineering hydraulic
formulas. The quality of their prediction is low. Therefore, hybrid models are of
the greatest interest, in which advanced neural networks use the results of modeling based on valuable, physically-based equations of fluid dynamics. Intelligent
computing makes it possible to improve direct hydrodynamic models using real
measurement data.

Hydrodynamic models contain a number of phenomenological parameters that can only be determined using certain sets of measured time series
$\mathcal{B}^{(obs)}(t_n) = \left\langle B_n^{(1)}, B_n^{(2)}, \dots B_n^{(K)} \right\rangle$. The duration of such time series must be
at least one year with a frequency of one day or more often (for example,
$n = 1, 2, \dots, 365$). The most important series are the water charge through the
channel cross-section $B_n^{(1)} = Q_n$ (also called the hydrograph), the water levels
at the gauging stations $B_n^{(k)} = \eta_n^{(k)}$ (k is the gauging station number), water
flow velocity profiles in cross-sections ($\boldsymbol{u}(s)$), sediment flux, water turbidity, etc.

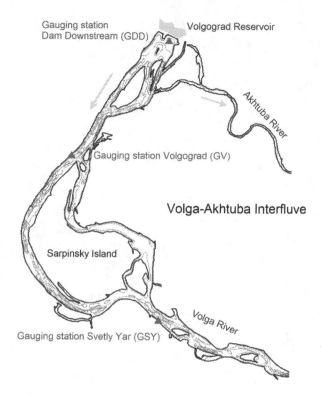

Fig. 1. The coastlines and isolines of the bottom topography of the Volga River system from the dam of the Volga hydroelectric power station for about 100 km along the riverbed are shown. The red line marks the river fairways.

The corresponding hydrodynamic model can give similar time series $\mathcal{B}^{(mod)}(t_n)$, which must be fitted with the data $\mathcal{B}^{(obs)}(t_n)$. This allows you to determine the free parameters of the hydrological resistance model.

The very high computational cost for solving the inverse problem is a limitation for calculating hydrological resistance characteristics and other free parameters based on large series of direct computational experiments. This requires new approaches to fit between $\mathcal{B}^{(mod)}(t_n)$ and $\mathcal{B}^{(obs)}(t_n)$ using different machine learning algorithms [17,24,25]. Application of the gene expression programming (GEP) method makes it possible to generate simplified prediction equations, significantly saving computational resources [24].

The aim of this work is to study the hydrological regime of the Volga River downstream of the dam of the Volga Hydroelectric Power Plant (Fig. 1) based on a symbiosis of direct hydrodynamic models and intelligent computing methods to determine unknown hydrological resistance parameters. Our efforts are aimed at analyzing the influence of the internal structure of the training dataset of the Long Short-Term Memory (LSTM) neural network on the results of reconstructing the hydrological resistance parameters.

2   Models and Methods

The shallow water model is based on the following system of equations [2,5,7, 15,20]:

$$\frac{\partial \boldsymbol{R}}{\partial t} + \frac{\partial \boldsymbol{G}_x}{\partial x} + \frac{\partial \boldsymbol{G}_y}{\partial y} = \boldsymbol{S}, \tag{1}$$

where

$$\boldsymbol{R} = \begin{pmatrix} H \\ Hu_x \\ Hu_y \end{pmatrix}, \qquad \boldsymbol{G}_x = \begin{pmatrix} Hu_x \\ Hu_x^2 + \dfrac{gH^2}{2} \\ Hu_x u_y \end{pmatrix}, \tag{2}$$

$$\boldsymbol{G}_y = \begin{pmatrix} Hu_y \\ Hu_x u_y \\ Hu_y^2 + \dfrac{gH^2}{2} \end{pmatrix}, \qquad \boldsymbol{S} = \begin{pmatrix} q \\ -gH\dfrac{\partial b}{\partial x} + f_x^{(hr)} \\ -gH\dfrac{\partial b}{\partial y} + f_y^{(hr)} \end{pmatrix}, \tag{3}$$

H is the water depth, $\boldsymbol{u} = \{u_x, u_y\}$ is the flow velocity, $b(x,y)$ is the bottom topography, $\eta = b + H$ is the water level, $\boldsymbol{f}^{(hr)} = \left\{ f_x^{(hr)}, f_y^{(hr)} \right\}$ is the hydraulic resistance force, $g = 9.8\,\mathrm{m\,sec}^{-2}$, q is the balance of water sources and sinks ($[q] = \mathrm{m/sec}$). The natural conditions of the lower reaches of the Volga River make it possible to limit ourselves to only one source of water through the hydroelectric dam. The integral power of the source or water charge Q is also called a hydrograph [2,20].

The Eq. (1) are vertically averaged equations of incompressible fluid dynamics. The characteristic propagation velocity of perturbations in such a model is equal to $c_s = \sqrt{gH}$, which is analogous to the sound speed. We compensate for our ignorance of the solution below the computational domain with the free parameter Θ_b, which has a simple physical meaning. It is equal to the tangent of the water level slope and needs to be calculated in our model.

Figure 2 shows the general structure of the approach used to determine the hydraulic resistance parameters and the relationship of the software modules used. There is data exchange between the numerical hydrodynamic model and the Long Short-Term Memory neural network.

We use an updated digital elevation model (DEM) for the Volga and adjacent areas which was created to analyze the dynamics of channel processes in 2022 [7]. The DEM is built as a result of combining three vector datasets, including the contour of the slope of the Volga River coastline, depth marks based on echolocation measurements, and depth profiles. The base DEM defines the topography of the computational domain with element size of 25 m [21]. It should be emphasized that when the water level rises, water begins to flow into the floodplain. Such outflow from the Volga channel occurs both through the Akhtuba branch and other smaller channels on the left bank of the Volga. The total capacity of

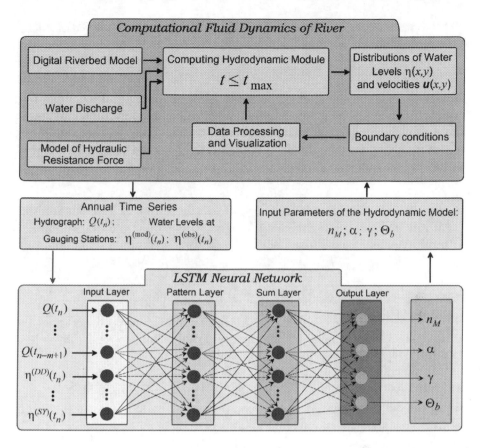

Fig. 2. Computational approach for determining the parameters of hydraulic resistance.

such water losses reaches approximately 10–15%. Therefore, modeling is carried out on the entire northern part of the territory of the Volga-Akhtuba interfluve.

The hydrological regime of the studied area of the river system is determined by the flow of water through the dam $Q(t)$ from the Volgograd reservoir (See Fig. 1). The positions of the three gauging stations are marked with triangles in this figure. The Akhtuba branch exits the Volga at a distance of 6 km below the dam on the left bank.

The Computing Hydrodynamic Module is based on the Combined Smoothed Particle Hydrodynamics—Total Variation Diminishin (CSPH-TVD) numerical algorithm and is described in detail in [20]. Here, we neglect the sediment dynamics, limiting ourselves to surface waters only. High performance computing is done on GPUs using NVIDIA CUDA. Features of parallel implementation are described in [22].

The outflow of water from the computational domain at the lower boundary of the channel is given by the condition

$$\nabla \mathcal{P}(x, y, t)_{|\Gamma} = \Phi,$$

where $\mathcal{P} = \{\eta, \boldsymbol{u}\}$ and $\Phi = \{\Phi_\eta, \Phi_u\}$ define conditions for water level and flow velocity, respectively. We restrict ourselves to $\Phi_u = 0$ and $\Phi_\eta = \Theta_b = \text{const}$ during the computation. The free parameter Θ_b is one of the four values, the definition of which should provide the best agreement between the model and the real data of measurements of water levels at gauging stations.

The hydraulic resistance force is given by the bottom roughness within the framework of the Gauckler-Manning-Strickler and other models [23]. We take into account an additional factor due to the fluid turbulence, which together leads to hydraulic resistance force

$$\boldsymbol{f}^{(hr)}(H, \boldsymbol{u}; n_M, \hat{\alpha}, \gamma) = g \frac{n_M^2 |\boldsymbol{u}|}{H^{4/3}} \boldsymbol{u} + \frac{\alpha}{\lambda} \left(\frac{g}{\lambda^3} \right)^{\gamma/2} |\boldsymbol{u}|^{1-\gamma} H^\gamma \boldsymbol{u}, \tag{4}$$

which is determined by the following three free parameters.

1) The Manning coefficient characterizes both the small-scale structure of the bottom surface and large-scale inhomogeneities of the riverbed. The unit of measure is: $[n_M] = \text{sec}/\text{m}^{1/3}$. This value can be in the range of $0.005 - 0.1$ for different river systems [3,11,14,24].

2) The parameter $\hat{\alpha}$ is proportional to the intensity of turbulent viscosity α:

$$\hat{\alpha} = \frac{\alpha}{\lambda} \left(\frac{g}{\lambda^3} \right)^{\gamma/2},$$

where λ is the spatial length characterizing the scale of turbulent fluctuations. Our estimates give the order of magnitude $\hat{\alpha} = 0.0001$ in International System of Units.

3) The exponent γ provides the dependence on H in the second term in the formula for the hydraulic resistance force (4). A natural constraint on γ is the condition $\gamma > 0$, which gives an increase in turbulent viscosity with increasing depth.

The first term in (4) is the traditional hydraulic resistance based on the Manning model for wide open channels. The second term describes the internal friction due to the turbulent viscosity ν_t under the assumption that

$$\nu_t \propto H u (H/\lambda)^{\beta_1} (u/c_s)^{\beta_2}.$$

Agreement with (4) is achieved at $\beta_1 = 1 + \gamma/2$, $\beta_2 = -\gamma$.

The resistance force (4) depends on the velocity and depth of the water in a complicated way. The contribution of two terms to (4) is determined by the phenomenological coefficients n_M and α, which must be calculated based on experimental data. The estimates of the parameters n_M, $\hat{\alpha}$, γ, Θ_b are based on the use of the LSTM neural network.

The architecture of the Long Short-Term Memory neural network is of the Recurrent Neural Networks (RNN) type, which allows both to contain feedback, passing information from one network step to another, and to save data [26,27]. The calculation process consists in successive transitions to the next LSTM layer (See Fig. 2).

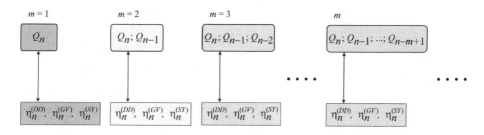

Fig. 3. Structure of the training data subset.

The result of numerical modeling of the hydrological regime for one year is three time series of water levels $\eta(t)$ at three gauging stations (See Fig. 1). Similar data of real measurements form a set of input data as:

$$\hat{A}_n^{(m)} = \hat{A}^{(m)}(t_n) = \left\{ A_n^{(m)}, A_{n-1}^{(m)}, \ldots, A_{n-m+1}^{(m)} \right\}, \tag{5}$$

where the number m characterizes the length of memory in the system, n is the number of the day from the total dataset ($n = 1, 2, \ldots, 365$), $\hat{A} = \langle \eta_k^{(obs)}, \eta_k^{(mod)}, Q \rangle$ is the tuple of input time series of the water levels at 3 gauging stations ($k = 1, 2, 3$) and the hydrograph Q, respectively.

The structure of the training data includes the formation of subsets of different lengths in order to set links between instantaneous data $\eta_n^{(DD)}, \eta_n^{(GV)}, \eta_n^{(SY)}$ in n-th day ($t = t_n$) and water discharge for the last m days (Fig. 3). The total length of the training time series decreases with an increase in the number m and is equal to $N = 366 - m$. Lack of memory ($m = 1$) or very long memory ($1 \ll m \sim 365$) cannot provide good solutions, which require choosing the optimal value of m. Each subset with length m (See Fig. 3) gives its own solution $\mathcal{D} = \langle n_M, \hat{\alpha}, \gamma, \Theta_b \rangle$ for which hydrodynamic simulations are performed and the water levels $\eta^{(mod)}$ in the model are fitted to the real measurements $\eta^{(obs)}$. This procedure allows us to calculate the optimal length of the training subset m.

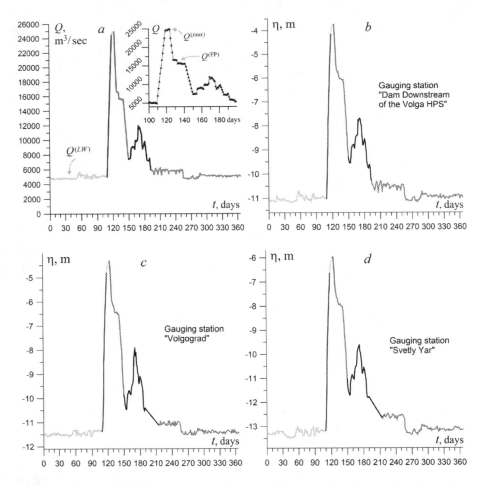

Fig. 4. Hydrograph $Q(t)$ for the dam (a) and dependencies of water levels at three gauging stations $\eta(Q)$ (b, c, d) for 2022. The inset on panel a represents the stage of seasonal flooding in more detail. The triangles on this panel show daily data.

3   Optimal Solutions and Hydrological Regime Verification

Our test numerical experiments show that without turbulent viscosity it is not possible to satisfactorily describe the annual dynamics of water levels at gauging stations.

Figure 4 shows the time series of the tuple (6) related to gauging stations data. Low water discharge values $Q^{(LW)} \simeq 5000 \, \mathrm{m^3 \, sec^{-1}}$ give different values of water levels η at gauging stations GDD, GV, GSY: $\eta^{(GDD)} \simeq -11 \, \mathrm{m}$, $\eta^{(GV)} \simeq -11.5 \, \mathrm{m}$, $\eta^{(GSY)} \simeq -13.3 \, \mathrm{m}$, which is related to the general slope of the river channel. It is important to emphasize the absence of an unambiguous relationship between the instantaneous values of $Q(t_n)$ and $\eta(t_n)$, which depend on the hydrological regime of the dam for several days before the day t_n. Analysis of the data in Fig. 4 gives a rule-of-thumb that $dQ/dt < 0$ results in larger η than $dQ/dt > 0$ for the same Q.

The input data for our study are the following time series (Fig. 4).

1) Discharge of water $Q(t)$ for 2022 (See Fig. 1, the dam fully regulates the hydrology of the river system). The different colors of the lines in Fig. 4a show the characteristic stages of the hydrological regime for that year. Low water levels lie within $Q^{(LW)} \simeq 5000{-}6000\,\mathrm{m}^3\,\mathrm{sec}^{-1}$ (green color is low water level before flood, orange line is low water in the second half of the year). The period of spring and early summer is characterized by a strong increase in Q, which is due to seasonal floods (See interval $t = (110 - 190)$ days in Fig. 4a). We highlight the rapid growth of Q to a maximum ($Q^{(\max)} = 25\,000\,\mathrm{m}^3\,\mathrm{sec}^{-1}$, dark blue line), approximately plateau for 8 days (cyan line), decrease stage (red line) to $Q^{(FP)} \simeq 16\,000\,\mathrm{m}^3\,\mathrm{sec}^{-1}$ (dark green, $t = (129{-}140)$ days). Then the magenta line shows a further decrease in Q. The local peak in late spring and early summer (black line) is an atypical behavior of the hydrograph and is due to some excess of the standard water supply in the Volgograd reservoir in 2022. The orange line shows the low water of the Volga River until the end of the year, as there is no autumn flooding due to the management of the water flow at the large Kuibyshev reservoir.

2) The water level in the immediate vicinity of the dam $\eta^{(DD)}(t)$ is the result of measurements at Gauging stations "Dam Downstream" (Fig. 4b). The colors of the lines correspond to the colors in Fig. 4a. Each feature of the function $Q(t)$ gives a corresponding peculiarity in the behavior of the water level, as shown in Fig. 4.

3) The function $\eta^{(GV)}(t)$ gives the water level at the location of Gauging stations "Volgograd" about 16 km below the dam near the right bank of the Volga River (Fig. 4c).

4) Figure 4d shows the water level $\eta^{(SY)}(t)$ at the gauging station "Svetly Yar", located 65 km from dams. The stream slope at such distances leads to a systematic decrease in the absolute water level by about 2.5 m.

Thus, the input tuple $\mathcal{H}$ is defined by four time series

$$\mathcal{H} = \langle Q(t_n), \eta^{(DD)}(t_n), \eta^{(GV)}(t_n), \eta^{(SY)}(t_n) \rangle \quad (n = 1, 2, \ldots, 365). \qquad (6)$$

Such a data set is available for each year, for example, the case of 2022 is shown in Fig. 4. The data of real measurements at gauging stations form the tuple of time series $\mathcal{H}^{(obs)}$. Numerical hydrodynamic simulations also give a similar tuple $\mathcal{H}^{(mod)}$ for given set of parameters $\mathcal{D} = \langle n_M, \hat{\alpha}, \gamma, \Theta_b \rangle$.

The training sample is built according to hydrodynamic modeling data. We model the time series $\mathcal{H}^{(mod)}$ for $N_E = 16$ different inputs $\mathcal{D}$. The result of these 16 hydrodynamic simulations is the formation of a training sample.

We built series of LSTM-NN forecasts for various m giving sets of input parameters $\mathcal{D} = \langle n_M, \hat{\alpha}, \gamma, \Theta_b \rangle$ from the results of the neural network (Table 1). The memory effect is absent for $m = 1$. The water level $\eta^k(t_n)$ in the model with

Table 1. Solutions for input parameters $\mathcal{D}$ as a result of LSTM-NN training with different memory lengths m based on 2022 data.

m	$n_M^{(opt)}$, sec·m$^{-1/3}$	$\hat{\alpha}^{(opt)}$, m^{-1}·sec$^{-\gamma}$	$\gamma^{(opt)}$	$\Theta_b^{(opt)}$
1	0.01398	$1.716 \cdot 10^{-4}$	0.6192	$0.584 \cdot 10^{-5}$
2	0.01436	$1.681 \cdot 10^{-4}$	0.6042	$0.660 \cdot 10^{-5}$
3	0.01518	$1.600 \cdot 10^{-4}$	0.5841	$0.642 \cdot 10^{-5}$
4	0.01522	$1.574 \cdot 10^{-4}$	0.5355	$0.628 \cdot 10^{-5}$
5	0.01531	$1.535 \cdot 10^{-4}$	0.5245	$0.623 \cdot 10^{-5}$
6	0.01548	$1.337 \cdot 10^{-4}$	0.5756	$0.671 \cdot 10^{-5}$
7	0.01778	$1.697 \cdot 10^{-4}$	0.5628	$0.596 \cdot 10^{-5}$
8	0.01883	$1.750 \cdot 10^{-4}$	0.6292	$0.521 \cdot 10^{-5}$

$m > 1$ depends on the hydrological regime in the river for the previous $m - 1$ days. Figure 5 shows the differences between the water levels $\eta_n^{(obs)}$ at gauging stations and simulation results $\eta_n^{(mod)}$ using solutions from Table 1. The degree of proximity of the time series $\eta_n^{(obs)}$ and $\eta_n^{(mod)}$ to each other is a quantitative measure of the quality of the input parameters $\mathcal{D}$ for the hydrodynamic model.

There are several physical mechanisms responsible for such memory. The fastest processes are associated with the time of establishment of a stationary flow in the channel. The characteristic velocity is the value $c_s \sim 7\,\text{km}\,\text{sec}^{-1}$, which gives time of about a day in the study area of the river about 100 km long. The water renewal time is determined by the velocity field in the flow. Since the maximum water velocity is approximately $1\,\text{km}\,\text{sec}^{-1}$ and there are zones with low velocity, the corresponding time is several days. There are slower processes associated with a change in hydraulic resistance due to the rearrangement of bottom shapes.

Figure 7 shows the difference between the water levels in the numerical model $\eta^{(mod)}$ and those measured at three gauging stations for different m from the Table 1. The value $\Delta\eta$ characterizes the quality of solutions. Models with $m = 1$ and $m = 8$ give higher deviations compared to the cases $m = 4 - 6$. Moreover, these deviations have the same sign ($\Delta\eta < 0$).

Table 2. Standard deviation σ calculated for models with different m

m	1	2	3	4	5	6	7	8
$\sigma^{(DD)}$, m	0.509	0.310	0.211	0.104	0.129	0.144	0.381	0.908
$\sigma^{(GV)}$, m	0.517	0.322	0.249	0.162	0.172	0.185	0.419	0.925
$\sigma^{(SY)}$, m	0.647	0.354	0.286	0.200	0.217	0.259	0.490	1.138

We calculated the standard deviations σ for the difference $\Delta\eta$, which are collected in the Table 2 for the three gauging stations under consideration. More distant measurements from the dam give a higher error.

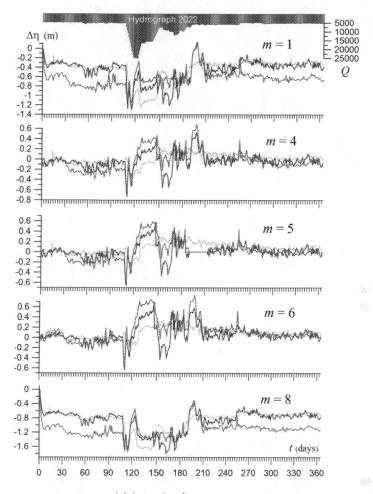

Fig. 5. Time series $\Delta\eta_n = \eta_n^{(obs)} - \eta_n^{(mod)}$ for 2022, constructed from the results of $N_E = 16$ numerical experiments for various m (green lines are measurements at gauging station "DD", blue lines—GS "V", red lines—GS "SY"). (Color figure online)

Clear evidence of the presence of nonlinear memory in the hydrological system of the Volga riverbed is the dependence $\eta(Q)$, which demonstrates a characteristic hysteresis character (Fig. 6). The hysteresis loop is bypassed counterclockwise. It is important to note the presence of small loops inside the main one (See black lines in Fig. 6, which correspond to the black line on the hydrograph in Fig. 4). The characteristic form of the dependence $\eta(Q)$ in the form of hysteresis is preserved along the river channel for at least 100 km of the computational domain. The shape of the functions $\eta(Q)$ at the gauging stations "GDD" and "GV" is very similar, although the distance between them is about 65 km.

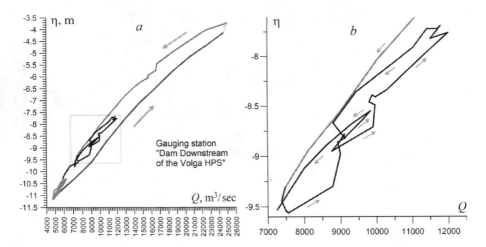

Fig. 6. Example of hysteresis for water level vs. discharge from measurements at GDD in 2022. The yellow box in panel *a* highlights the part of the curve that is shown in the right panel (*b*). The arrows indicate the direction of change over time. The line colors correspond to the colors of the hydrograph plots in Fig. 4*a*.

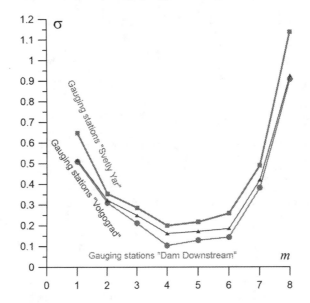

Fig. 7. Standard deviations σ ($[\sigma]$ = m) vs. memory duration m for three gauging stations in 2022.

Figure 7 shows the dependencies of the standard deviations between the measured and model series on the parameter m. The value of an error is nonmonotonic for all three gauging stations. The best result of LSTM-NN training is given by datasets with $m = 4 - 6$, for which there is a minimum of σ. These results allow us to choose the optimal memory length of 5 days.

4   Discussion and Conclusions

Our efforts are aimed at creating a high-quality hydrodynamic model of the Lower Volga River. This section of the river is the key for the entire unique region of the Volga-Akhtuba Floodplain. The main problem is the impossibility of setting the force of hydraulic resistance within the framework of only a theoretical analysis of physical processes.

We propose a two-factor hydraulic resistance force that includes the action of internal friction due to turbulence. Our approach contains three free parameters that determine the deceleration of the water flow. The fourth free parameter characterizes the boundary conditions in the zone of water outflow from the computational domain. The variation of these values in computational fluid dynamics experiments became the basis of the training dataset for the Long Short-Term Memory networks. There is a free parameter of LSTM that determines the duration of the memory in the hydrological system. The duration of the time interval of m days means that the measured water level at gauging stations depends on the behavior of the water discharge during the previous m days.

Neural network calculations made it possible to find the values of the above free hydraulic resistance parameters in the conditions of the Lower Volga in 2022. Additionally, it was possible to calculate the duration of the hydrological memory, which lies within $m = 4 - 6$ days. As a result, the standard deviations between time series of water levels at gauging stations and in numerical models does not exceed 0.1–0.2 m during the year.

Possible development of our approach for problems of hydrological forecasting are the following directions. Transition to LSTM using attention can improve results [16]. Various laboratory studies indicate more complex dependences of the Manning coefficient on channel geometry, Froude number, Reynolds number, small-scale bottom roughness [24]. Therefore, the next step may be the transition to neural network models, in which the Manning coefficient depends on time and/or coordinates.

Acknowledgement. The authors are grateful to A.N. Maltseva and E.O. Agafonnikova for their help with this work.

References

1. Belikov, V.V., Borisova, N.M., Rumyantsev, A.B.: Assessing inundation risks and protection of residential territories in river floodplains. Water Resour. **50**(1), 34–47 (2023). https://doi.org/10.1134/S0097807823010049
2. Isaeva, I.I., Voronin, A.A., Khoperskov, A.V., Kharitonov, M.A.: Modeling the territorial structure dynamics of the northern part of the Volga-Akhtuba floodplain. Computation **10**(4), 62 (2022). https://doi.org/10.3390/computation10040062
3. García-Navarro, P., Murillo, J., Fernández-Pato, J., Echeverribar, I., Morales-Hernández, M.: The shallow water equations and their application to realistic cases. Environ. Fluid Mech. **19**(1–2), 1235–1252 (2019). https://doi.org/10.1007/s10652-018-09657-7

4. Goeury, C., Bacchi, V., Zaoui, F., Bacchi, S., Pavan, S., El kadi Abderrezzak, K.: Uncertainty assessment of flood hazard due to levee breaching. Water **14**(23), 3815 (2022).https://doi.org/10.3390/w14233815

5. Voronin, A.A., Vasilchenko, A.A., Klikunova, A.Yu., Vatyukova, O.Yu., Khoperskov, A.V.: The problem of safe evacuation of large floodplains population during flooding. Adv. Syst. Sci. Appl. **22**(4), 65–78 (2022). https://doi.org/10.25728/assa.2022.22.4.1310

6. Tang, H., Yuan, S., Cao, H.: Theory and practice of hydrodynamic reconstruction in plain river networks. Engineering (2022). https://doi.org/10.1016/j.eng.2022.01.015

7. Khrapov, S.S.: Numerical modeling of self-consistent dynamics of shallow waters, traction and suspended sediments: II. Study of the transverse deformations of the channel and the redistribution of water discharges along the branches of the Volga River during industrial sand mining. Math. Phys. Comput. Simul. **25**(4), 52–65 (2022). https://doi.org/10.15688/mpcm.jvolsu.2022.4.5

8. Belikov, V.V., Aleksyuk, A.I., Borisova, N.M., Glotko, A.V., Rumyantsev, A.B.: Estimation of the level of floodplain inundation in the lower don under the effect of economic activity. Retrospective hydrodynamic modeling. Water Resour. **49**(6), 941–949 (2022). https://doi.org/10.1134/S0097807822060021

9. Abbaszadeh, P., Muñoz, D. F., Moftakhari, H., Jafarzadegan, K., Moradkhani, H.: Perspective on uncertainty quantification and reduction in compound flood modeling and forecasting. iScience **25**(10), 105201 (2022). https://doi.org/10.1016/j.isci.2022.105201

10. Brown, R.A., Pasternack, G.B.: How to build a digital river. Earth Sci. Rev. **194**, 283–305 (2019). https://doi.org/10.1016/j.earscirev.2019.04.028

11. Yang, F., et al.: Improved method for identifying Manning's roughness coefficients in plain looped river network area. Eng. Appl. Comput. Fluid Mech. **15**(1), 94–110 (2021). https://doi.org/10.1080/19942060.2020.1858967

12. Hauer, C., Schober, B., Habersack, H.: Impact analysis of river morphology and roughness variability on hydropeaking based on numerical modelling. Hydrol. Process. **27**(15), 2209–2224 (2013). https://doi.org/10.1002/hyp.9519

13. De Paiva, R.C.D., et al.: Large-scale hydrologic and hydrodynamic modeling of the Amazon River basin. Water Resour. Res. **49**(3), 1226–1243 (2013). https://doi.org/10.1002/wrcr.20067

14. Hostache, R., Lai, X., Monnier, J., Puech, C.: Assimilation of spatially distributed water levels into a shallow-water flood model. Part II: use of a remote sensing image of Mosel River. J. Hydrol. **390**(3–4), 257–268 (2010). https://doi.org/10.1016/j.jhydrol.2010.07.003

15. Arkhipov, B., Rychkov, S., Shatrov, A.: High-performance calculations for river floodplain model and its implementations. Commun. Comput. Inf. Sci. **1063**, 211–224 (2019)

16. Xu, K., et al.: Show, attend and tell: Neural image caption generation with visual attention. In: International Conference on Machine Learning, pp. 2048–2057. PMLR (2015)

17. Carreau, J., Guinot, V.: A PCA spatial pattern based artificial neural network downscaling model for urban flood hazard assessment. Adv. Water Resour. **147**, 103821 (2021). https://doi.org/10.1016/j.advwatres.2020.103821

18. Fraehr, N., Wang, Q.J., Wu, W., Nathan, R.: Development of a fast and accurate hybrid model for floodplain inundation simulations. Water Resour. Res. **59**(6), e2022WR033836 (2023). https://doi.org/10.1029/2022WR033836

19. Razavi, S., Tolson, B.A., Burn, D.H.: Review of surrogate modeling in water resources. Water Resour. Res. **48**(7), W07401 (2012). https://doi.org/10.1029/2011WR011527

20. Khrapov, S.S., Khoperskov, A.V.: Application of graphics processing units for self-consistent modelling of shallow water dynamics and sediment transport. Lobachevskii J. Math. **41**(8), 1475–1484 (2020). https://doi.org/10.1134/S1995080220080089

21. Khrapov, S.S., et al.: Numerical modeling of self-consistent dynamics of shallow waters, traction and suspended sediments: I. Influence of commercial sand mining on the safety of navigation in the channel of the Volga River. Math. Phys. Comput. Simul. **25**(3), 31–57 (2022). https://doi.org/10.15688/mpcm.jvolsu.2022.3.3

22. Dyakonova, T., Khoperskov, A., Khrapov, S.: Numerical model of shallow water: the use of NVIDIA CUDA graphics processors. Commun. Comput. Inf. Sci. **687**, 132–145 (2016). https://doi.org/10.1007/978-3-319-55669-7_11

23. Akhmedova, N.R., Naumov, V.A.: Calculation of the roughness of the Sheshupe riverbed according to hydrological yearbooks. IOP Conf. Ser. Earth Environ. Sci. **1112**, 012127 (2022). https://doi.org/10.1088/1755-1315/1112/1/012127

24. Azamathulla, H.Md., Ahmad, Z., Ghani, A.Ab.: An expert system for predicting Manning's roughness coefficient in open channels by using gene expression programming. Neural Comput. Appl. **23**, 1343–1349 (2013). https://doi.org/10.1007/s00521-012-1078-z

25. Harun, M.A., Ab. Ghani, A., Eslamian, S., Chang, C.K.: Handbook of Hydroinformatics Volume III: Water Data Management Best Practices/Sediment transport with soft computing application for tropical rivers, pp. 379–394 (2023)

26. Hochreiter, S., Schmidhuber, J.: Long short-term memory. Neural Comput. **9**(8), 1735–1780 (1997). https://doi.org/10.1162/neco.1997.9.8.1735

27. Lees, T., et al.: Hydrological concept formation inside long short-term memory (LSTM) networks. Hydrol. Earth Syst. Sci. **26**(12), 3079–3101 (2022). https://doi.org/10.5194/hess-2021-566

Business Model Innovation: Considering Organization as a Form of Reflection of Society

Aleksandr Davtian[1]([✉]), Olga Shabalina[2], Natalia Sadovnikova[2], Danila Parygin[2], and Olga Berestneva[3]

[1] Moscow Institute of Physics and Technology, Dolgoprudny, Russia
agvs@mail.ru
[2] Volgograd State Technical University, Volgograd, Russia
[3] Tomsk Polytechnic University, Tomsk, Russia

Abstract. Within the framework of the new concept of strategic management and entrepreneurship, it has become customary to represent an organization in the form of a business model reflecting core aspects of the organization in economic, social, cultural or other contexts. The article is devoted to the development of a concept of constructing business models, reflecting new ways of existence and functioning of organizations in conditions of continuous interaction with the information environment. A model of an organization as a fragment of an information network formed by a set of open interacting organizations has been built. The state of the system in terms of the finite network is modeled as the result of its interaction with the environment, determined by the input and output information flows. Changes of the input and output flows leads to changes in the system state. A topological model of a digital information space is built, which is represented by interconnections between organizations through input and output information streams. It is shown that in the space there always exist contours formed by chains of information flows, connecting organizations with each other. A method has been developed for finding the contours that determine the mission of each organization in society. The following concepts are proposed as characteristics of the contour that determine the current state of the organization: the length of the contour, the strength of the connectivity of the contour, the potential of the contour. The principle of building business models are based on considering the of managing the organization is formulated as the task of ensuring that the system belongs to the contours formed by the chains of information flows that ensure the inclusion of the system in the information space, predicting the emergence of new needs and inclusion in new contours to meet these needs. This approach allows us to correlate local goals and goals of society and organize management in organizations from the point of view of cooperation of goals. As part of further research, it is planned to develop a management support system (MSS) for supporting planning and decision making in organizations based on the proposed models and methods.

Keywords: organization · society · organization model · business model · information flow · network · digital information space · information contour · management in organizations

1 Introduction

Organizations arise and function to fulfill a certain mission assigned to them by society. The effectiveness of functioning of any organization created by society directly determines the well-being of society itself.

A necessary condition for the organization existence and functioning in society is managing its activities, ensuring successful fulfillment of its mission. Within the framework of the new concept of strategic management and entrepreneurship, it has become customary to represent an organization in the form of a business model reflecting core aspects of the organization in economic, social, cultural or other contexts.

The technical explosion, followed by the information explosion that took place in the society, created a global information space. Comprehensive changes in the society, caused by the influence of the information space, in which every organization inevitably immersed, have led to a qualitative change in the role of information in the management process of the organization. In the conditions of the natural evolution of organizations immersed in the information space, it is necessary to rethink the principles of business modeling and develop new business models in accordance with the new conditions for the functioning of organizations. The article is devoted to the development of a concept of constructing business models, reflecting new ways of existence and functioning of organizations in conditions of continuous interaction with the information environment.

2 Organization and Business Model: Concepts and Understandings

The concept of business model in relation to modeling organization behavior has evolved over the past twenty years, starting with the early studies of Osterwalder [1], who proposed general principles for business model construction. By now the business model concept has reached global impact, both for organization's competitive success and in management science [2, 3]. But despite its growing popularity, the term "business model" has not been uniquely defined so far [4, 5], and the academic literature on this topic «is fragmented and confounded by inconsistent definitions and construct boundaries» [6].

In most studies the business model is considered as an organization's core strategy for profitably doing business, as decisions enforced by the authority of the firm [7]. Business models generally include information like products or services the business plans to sell, target markets, and any anticipated expenses.

Currently, there are two directions of research in the domain of business modeling. The first direction considers business model as a technology for making a profit based on successful business decisions of individual companies that "guessed" the trends in the development of society and, thus, became participants in this development (such as so called "Starbucks Business Model", "Business model of Zara", "Business Model of Instagram", etc.). Researchers developing the second direction believe that business models should emphasize more systematic holistic approach to explaining how firms "do business" [8]. Moreover, some researchers [2] suggest to understand by a business model not just a description of what an organization currently is, but to complement it with a strategy and capabilities in order to face upcoming changes, i.e. consider the business model in the dynamics of its development. In some late studies the business model is considered in terms of IoT-oriented marketing management [9].

However, in general, regardless of the level of consideration, business models are based on the understanding of the organization as an independent and self-sufficient structure, while the environment is considered as an external resource for the organization itself. However, in modern conditions, the success of a business model depends not only on the strategy of the organization itself, but also on the extent to which the business model takes into account the interests of the environment. The principles of constructing business models, based on the primacy of the organization in relation to its environment, replace the essence of the existence of the organization, as a system created by the environment to fulfill the mission determined by the environment.

3 Organization and Society

In modern conditions, any organization exists in interaction with the continuously changing socio-economic environment. The interaction of the organization with the environment occurs through information flows that are constantly accumulating and continuously changing over time [2, 10]. To fulfill the mission entrusted to the organization by its environment, the organization must be open to these flows, must adequately perceive them, and be able to form its own information flows. Thus, openness, as an immanent property of any organization, is a form of its existence, providing the possibility of functioning in interaction with the environment [11, 12].

Within traditional models, internal flows that determine the functioning of the organization itself are considered as observable information flows, regardless of the method and degree of formalization, and external flows that form the interaction of the organization with the environment are modeled as factors affecting internal flows. Thus, the organization environment is considered as an external resource for the organization itself. But in fact exactly external information flows that determine what the organization is for the environment, and what the environment is for the organization. It is the external information flows that determine what the organization is for the environment, and what the environment is for the organization. Therefore, it is the external input and output flows that determine the interaction of the organization with the external environment that form the state and functioning of the organization as the fulfillment of its mission in the life of society.

However, openness as an immanent property of the organization is only a form of its existence. To ensure its existence in the future, the organization should continuously "study" itself in its continuously changing non-deterministic environment, i.e. be capable of learning.

Organization's learnability is realized through management, since it is management that allows organization to "adjust" 'itself to the continuous changes in the environment and develop the ability to fulfill its mission. Changes in the environment are perceived by the organization 'through input streams that carry information necessary for the formation of management goals.

Management in organizations is always associated with collecting and processing of data on the current state of the organization and its environment. In the pre-information age, there was a trade-off between the amount of data on paper and the ability of humans to process this data to make managerial decisions. The rapid development of modern information technologies has led to a multiple increase in the amount of data available to humans. Today, the intensity of information flows significantly exceeds the ability of humans to select and analyze the data from the information noise surrounding him, which are necessary to ensure the sustainable development of the organization.

Successful management in such conditions is possible only with the availability of computing resources and technologies that allow the continuous collection, processing and analysis of big data necessary to understand the system processes in the organization. At the same time, computing resources should be integrated with the organization on the principles of cybernetics, which determine the methods of managing information resources in the organization, and the management of information flows should be subordinate to the goals of the organization itself. An organization with a cybernetic "insert" into its structure can be defined as a cyber-social system (CSS) in which a continuous increase in spontaneous flows of information leads to the gradual replacement of the real system with its virtual representation in cyberspace [13]. And the management in the organization is replaced by the management of its information image based on the principles of cybernetics.

Understanding of an organization as an open learnable cyber-social system that functions in continuous interaction with the information environment determines the following principles that should be taken into consideration while constructing business model [14]:

- openness and learnability are the key properties of the organization, ensuring the possibility of its functioning in interaction with the environment;
- interaction of the organization and the environment is symmetrical, the actions of the organization generate the actions of the environment, and vice versa;
- functioning of the organization is determined by external (input and output) information flows that form its state;
- the input information flow forms the resources that the environment transfers to the organization to fulfill its mission, the output flow is formed as a transfer of the results of the organization activities demanded by the environment;
- the state of the organization is determined by the "balance" of input and output information flows;
- the dynamics of input and output information flows leads to a change in the state of the organization';
- the input and output flows are interconnected and interdependent by the fulfillment of the mission of the organization, which determines the very existence of the organization;
- management of information flows in organizations is implemented on the principles of cybernetics and is subordinated to the goals of the organization itself.

Thus, organization as an open learnable cyber-physical system created by the environment to fulfill the mission determined by the environment is considered as a form of interaction between the environment and itself, i.e. its reflection, which ensures its very existence, and the principles of modeling information flows reflect the dualism of the relationship between the organization and the environment.

4 Pseudo-mathematical Model of Organization

The proposed principles were implemented in modeling organization as open learnable cyber-physical systems. The state of the system as the ability to carry out a mission assigned by the environment is considered as the result of its interaction of the organization with the environment defined by the input and output streams:

$$SES_{State} = F(InputStream, OutputStream), \tag{1}$$

where SES_{State}– the state of the system;

   $InputStream$ – input stream (the influence of the environment on the system);

   $OutputStream$ – output stream (the influence of the system on the environment);

   F – a method of correlating input and output information flows that form the state of the system.

The resources that the environment transfers to the system to fulfill the mission (objects of material and intangible nature) act as input streams. Output streams are formed as a transfer of the results of the system's activities that are in demand by the environment (these can also be objects of a material and intangible nature).

A system itself is not a material object, it is an artifact generated by the activities of people, which provides the conditions for their very existence. In the context of the categorization of artifacts, the organization is an information phenomenon, since the state of the organization, the movement of input and output flows in the organization', is always identified with information flows. The concept of flow is associated with time, respectively each state of the system is associated with a specific moment in the life of the system.

Let:

   t – is a parameter of a linearly ordered set related to a specific lifetime of the system;

   $SES_{State\,t}$ – the state of the system, determined by the totality of resources at the current time t;

   $InputStream_t$, $OutputStream_t$ – input and output information flows (volumes of information) that form the state of the system at the time t.

Then the openness of the system, as a property to interact with the environment at time t, can be represented as:

$$SES_{State\,t} = F\left(InputStream_t, OutputStream_t\right). \tag{2}$$

Any change in input and output flows during time t leads to a change in the state of the system. To model the behavior of a system that can be described quantitatively, the theory of continuous and discrete dynamical systems is usually used. However, for organizational systems, as systems with objects of non-numerical nature, such theory is not applicable. Therefore, to model the dynamics of the state of organizational systems, it is necessary to add to the equation of state of the system (1) the equation of relations that specify the effect of changing the output flows on each other over a time interval Δt sufficient to establish this effect:

$$SES_{State\,t+\Delta t} = F\left(InputStream_{t+\Delta t}, OutputStream_{t+\Delta t}\right). \tag{3}$$

System learnability implies the influence of the state of the system and the change in the output stream on the change in the input stream relative to the given state. The learning process consists in the formation of a new input stream, leading to an acceptable state that ensures the existence of the system, i.e.:

$$InputStream_{t+\Delta t} = \Phi\left(SES_{State\,t}, OutputStream_{t+\Delta t}\right), \tag{4}$$

where Φ symbolizes a way of correlating the influence of the state of the system and the output stream formed by it on the reaction of the environment in the form of an input stream.

It is the generated input stream that ensures the existence of the system, i.e. the system learns during its functioning. The influence of output flows on the formation of input flows of the system in the classical control theory is called feedback. However, in the context of organization modeling, the representation of such an influence as a functional dependence is not possible due to the uncertainty of the environment's reaction to the system. Thus learnability can be interpreted as the "ability" to reduce the degree of this uncertainty. Correlation methods, indicated in formulas (3) and (4) as F and Φ, respectively, are chosen by a person, and, due to the non-numerical nature of thinking, are not reducible to functional dependencies. Therefore, in the general case, F and Φ symbolize the "mental" functions inherent in man. In most known behavioral models of organization, F and F are still represented as functional dependencies that define the system and its environment. But, in such models there is always some uncertainty in the form of parameters of the system and environment models that need to be selected in some way. The selection of these parameters, in fact, is learning, i.e. even in such models, the learnability property of the organization is implicitly reflected.

Organization learnability is realized through management, i.e. management allows the organization to "adapt" to the continuous changes in the environment and maintain the ability to fulfill its mission. Changes in the environment are perceived by the organization through input streams, which serve as the basis for the formation of management goals in the organization.

The formation of a new output stream is carried out as a result of actions performed by the organization in the form of a change in the output stream, determined by the input stream:

$$OutputStream_{t+\Delta t} = \Psi(InputStream_t) \oplus (\Delta OutputStream). \tag{5}$$

where «$\oplus$» is a pseudo-mathematical operation that reflects the way the new output stream is generated.

Thus, the system of equations:

$$
\begin{aligned}
SES_{State_t} &= F(InputStream_t, OutputStream_t), \\
SES_{State_{t+\Delta t}} &= F(InputStream_{t+\Delta t}, OutputStream_{t+\Delta t}), \\
InputStream_{t+\Delta t} &= \Phi\left(SES_{State_t}, OutputStream_{t+\Delta t}\right), \\
OutputStream_{t+\Delta t} &= \Psi(InputStream_t) \oplus (\Delta OutputStream).
\end{aligned}
\tag{6}
$$

is a pseudo-mathematical representation of an open learning cyber-physical system, reflecting the dynamics of the system existence and the fulfillment of its mission. At the same time, the "solvability" of the system of Eqs. (6) does not guarantee the eternal existence of the system. Moreover, all organizations are inherently finite, at least within the framework of the mission for which the system was formed.

In this context, management in the organization ultimately comes down to managing information flows, and the mental functions, denoted in (6) as F, Φ and Ψ, are a form of representing the results of accepted and implemented management decisions that cannot be modeled within the formal logic. Such an understanding of management recognizes a person's priority right to make managerial decisions based on narrative practice, i.e. as a subjective representation of a person in the present about the future, which determines not so much the future state of the system but the very existence of the system in the future [15]. At the same time management decision making and the responsibility for these decisions lie on the participants of managerial process, i.e. competencies of a person as a decision maker are not modeled.

5 Organization as a Fragment of Networked Information Space

The proposed approach to modeling organizations allows us to consider organizations as fragments of an information network formed by a plurality of open interacting (organizations, the number of which, by definition, is finite):

$$SES = \{ses_1, ses_2, \ldots, ses_i, \ldots, ses_n,\}, \tag{7}$$

where ses_i – i-th organization as an element of the information network;
  n – the number of network elements.

Then the state of the i-th organization, determined by the system of Eqs. (6), in terms of the finite network can be represented as following:

$$
\begin{aligned}
SES_{State_{it}} &= F(InputStream_{it}, OutputStream_{it}), \\
SES_{State_{i(t+\Delta t)}} &= F\big(InputStream_{i(t+\Delta t)}, OutputStream_{i(t+\Delta t)}\big), \\
InputStream_{i(t+\Delta t)} &= \Phi\big(SES_{State_{it}}, OutputStream_{i(t+\Delta t)}\big), \\
OutputStream_{i(t+\Delta t)} &= \Psi(InputStream_{it})(\Delta OutputStream_{it}).
\end{aligned}
\tag{8}
$$

The input and output information flows connecting the organizations with each other are interpreted in terms of the network as binary relations:

$$\rho \subset SES \times SES. \tag{9}$$

The formation of these relations is carried out by the environment of each organization, thus providing the conditions for its functioning.

From the point of view of the life of society, all organizations are directly or indirectly interconnected. Accordingly, the input and output flows of any organization include a set of flows connecting this organization with the others.

The division of flows into input and output ones determines the dual nature of the relationship between the organization and the environment. Any organization exists if and only if there is an input flow that determines the needs of the environment in the organization, and an output flow that determines the results of the activities of the organization that satisfy these needs. The absence of an input flow means that the environment has ceased to need this organization, i.e. in the results of its activities. The absence of an output flow indicates that the organization, for one reason or another cannot justify its existence to the environment, i.e. meet the needs of the environment.

The presence of input and input flows for each organization as an element of the network means the absence of the network boundary elements, i.e. the finite network formed by the set of organizations is connected. The existence of contours in the network, formed by chains of information flows, connecting organizations in the network, ensures the cyclical nature of the life of society. Any network element is included in at least one contour, which means that the network is closed. Each contour determines the presence of a particular need in society, and the functioning of each organization included in this contour determines the place of the organization in meeting this need.

6 Topological Model of Networked Information Space

Organizations as a set represent a simple named enumeration of them, and representation of connections between systems only by binary relations does not reflect the complexity and long-range influences of organizations on each other and dependencies between the flows themselves. The inclusion of the organization in the network determines its properties that are not associated with its name in the set, but with the functions that this organization is endowed with by the network. The properties that each organization as an element of the network is endowed with in relation to other elements of the network define such a network as space.

The stream $stream(i, j)$ associated with the pair $(i, j) \in \rho$ is an output stream relative to j for the i-th organization, i.e. $stream(i, j) = OutputStream_{ij}$ and for the j-th organization it is an input stream with respect to i, i.e. $stream(i, j) = InputStream_{ji}$, while $(\forall i)((i, i) \notin \rho)$.

The direct relationship between a pair of i-th and j-th organization means that there is such a j-th organization for which:

$$InputStream_{ij} = OutputStream_{ji}. \tag{10}$$

Then:

$$InputStream_i = \cup_j OutputStream_{ji},$$
$$OutputStream_i = \cup_j InputStream_{ij}. \tag{11}$$

where $InputStream_{ij}$ и $OutputStream_{ij}$ – input and output streams of the i-th organization, directly connected with the j-th organization.

Direct relationships that determine the nearest environment of i-th organization, define its neighborhood:

$$Neighborhood_i = \{j \epsilon SES : (i, j) \epsilon \rho \text{ or } (j, i) \epsilon \rho. \tag{12}$$

Each neighborhood of the i-th organization consists of two semi-neighborhoods - left and right, formed respectively by organizations connected with this organization through its input and output and flows:

$$Neighborhood_i^- = \{j \epsilon SES : (j, i) \epsilon \rho\} \text{ and } Neighborhood_i^+ = \{j \epsilon SES : (i, j) \epsilon \rho\}. \tag{13}$$

In this way:

$$Neighborhood_i = Neighborhood_i^- \cup Neighborhood_i^+, \qquad (14)$$

where $Neighborhood_i^-$ – left semi-neighborhood;
$Neighborhood_i^+$ – right semi-neighborhood.

If for two organizations:

$$Neighborhood_i \cap Neighborhood_j \neq \varnothing, \qquad (15)$$

then there exists a neighborhood of this pair, defined as:

$$Neighborhood_{ij}^+ = Neighborhood_i^+ \cup Neighborhood_j^+ \qquad (16)$$

and

$$Neighborhood_{ij}^- = Neighborhood_i^- \cup Neighborhood_j^-, \qquad (17)$$

and connections that determine their interaction through their environment:

$$Interaction(i,j) = (Neighborhood_i^+ \cap Neighborhood_j^-) \cup (Neighborhood_i^- \cap Neighborhood_j^+).Neighborhood_j^+). \qquad (18)$$

Organizations $i, j \in SES$ are connected if there are $i_1, \ldots i_k, i_1 = i, i_k = j, i_1, \ldots i_k, i_1 = i, i_k = j$, such that each pair $(i_m, i_{m+1}) \in \rho$ defines a stream $stream(i_m, i_{m+1})$, connecting these organizations.

The organizations defined in this way form an ordered connection:

$$Connection(i,j) = \{i_1, \ldots i_k, i_1 = i, i_k = j\} \qquad (19)$$

and the neighborhood of this connection:

$$Neighborhood_{Connection(i,j)} = \left(\bigcup_{j=1}^k U_{ij}^+ \right) \cup \left(\bigcup_{j=1}^k U_{ij}^- \right), \qquad (20)$$

as a set of organizations that influence this connection and depend on it.

The constructed system of neighborhoods defines the topology in the space of organizations, which determines both internal connections and interaction with the environment.

For any subset of systems $K \sqsubset SES$ there exists a right semineighborhood

The system of neighborhoods built in this way defines the topology in the space of organizations, which determines both internal connections and interaction with the environment.

For any subset of organizations $K \sqsubset SES$ there exists a right semineighborhood:

$$Neighborhood^+(K) = \bigcup_{j \in K} Neighborhood_j^+; Neighborhood^+(K) \subset SES, \qquad (21)$$

with the border:

$$\partial Neighborhood^+(K) = Neighborhood^+(K) \setminus K. \qquad (22)$$

Then for any ses_i there exists a system $Neighborhood_i^{+(n)}$ of right semineighborhoods:

$$Neighborhood_i^+(1) = Neighborhood_i^+;$$

...

$$Neighborhood_i^+(k) = Neighborhood^+\left(Neighborhood_i^+(k-1)\right); \tag{23}$$

$Neighborhood_i^+(k-1) \subset Neighborhood_i^+(k),$
where k – a level of the right semineighborhood for ses_i.
Similarly, there is a system of left semi-neighbourhoods of the element ses_i:

$$Neighborhood_i^-(1) = Neighborhood_i^-;$$

...

$$Neighborhood_i^-(l) = Neighborhood^-\left(Neighborhood_i^-(l-1)\right); \tag{24}$$

$Neighborhood_i^-(l-1) \subset Neighborhood_i^-(l),$
where l – level of the left semineighborhood for ses_i.

Thus, each subsequent neighborhood is a neighborhood of the previous one (neighborhood of a neighborhood).

Since the set SES is finite, for any ses_i there is at least one pair (k, l), such that:

$$Neighborhood_i^+(k) \cap Neighborhood_i^-(l) \neq \varnothing. \tag{25}$$

It follows that each ses_i is included in at least one chain that forms a contour in which the information flow circulates, ensuring the functioning of each organization as an element of this contour:

$$Contour = \{i_1, i_2, \ldots, i_r\}, \tag{26}$$

where $i_1 = i_r = i$, $(i_k, i_{k+1}) \in \rho$;
$k = 1 \div (r-1)$;
r – the number of organizations in a contour.

At the same time, the contours, as subsets, have neighborhoods that determine the interaction of the contour with its environment.

It follows that the network is closed and has the property of network connectivity. The properties that each element of the network is endowed with in relation to other elements of the network define such a network as a space. The presence of a contour in which the information flow circulates means that the organization satisfies any continuous needs of society. The task of management in the organization is formulated as the task of determining and maintaining the organization of its place in these contours, i.e. its importance in meeting the corresponding needs of society, anticipating the emergence of new needs and inclusion in new contours to meet these needs.

Management in the organization in the context of the network connectivity of the information space consists in finding the contours that include this organization and making management decisions based on an analysis of their characteristics. The following concepts are proposed as characteristics of the contour that determine the current state of the system: the length of the contour, the strength of the connectivity of the contour, the potential of the contour.

The length of the contour is determined by the number of interconnected and interdependent organizations in this contour, participating in the circulation of information and interested in the existence of modeling organization and the results of its functioning:

$$ContourLength = |Contour|. \tag{27}$$

The length of the contour is a temporal characteristic, meaning the "long-range action" of the organization, which can be interpreted as deferred obligations of the participants in the circulation of information in this contour. A long contour means that the reaction of the organization environment is delayed, and the organization does not know immediately, how the environment will react to certain management decisions.

Each flow $stream(i, j)$ in the network, connecting the i-th organization with the j-th organization, for the i-th organization is characterized by its activities, such as, for example, the main activity (production output); ancillary activities aimed at maintaining the main activity (financial activity) and other activities that do not significantly affect the main activity. In the general case, there are a finite number p of such activities.

To assess the connectivity strength of a pair (i, j) of network elements, each type of activity is compared with a weight coefficient $\alpha_i > 0, i = 1, 2, \ldots, p$. The weight coefficients rank activities according to their importance $\alpha_1 < \alpha_2 < \ldots < \alpha_p$. The connectivity strength of a contour is determined by the connectivity strength of pairs of elements of this contour:

$$Connection(Contour) = \frac{\sum_{k=1}^{r} Connection(i_k, i_{k+1})}{r}, \tag{28}$$

where $i_{r+1} = i_1$;

$Connection(i, j) = Connection(stream(i, j)) \epsilon Connection\_Values$ is Connectivity strength of a couple (ses_i, ses_j);

$Connection\_Values = \{\alpha_i > 0, i = 1, 2, \ldots, p\}$ – a set of values of connectivity strengths;

r - the number of organizations in the contour.

The strength of a pair's connectivity determines the readiness of the systems that form this pair to support the information flows that link them. The strength of a couple's connectivity can be determined by the long-term contracts of the parties, the reputation of the systems, informal commitments, and so on. The strength of the connection of the pair is determined by the ratio of the number of weak connections to the total number of pairs of nodes of the contour.

The potential of a contour for an organization is defined as the ratio of the connectivity strength of this contour containing this organization to the average connectivity strength of all contours containing this organization:

$$Potential_j^i = \frac{m * Connection(Contour_j^i)}{\sum_{j=1}^{m} Connection(Contour_j^i)}, \tag{29}$$

where i – organization identifier;

j – contour identifier;

m – the number of contours containing the i-th organization.

The potential of the contour is a comparative characteristic that shows the place of this contour among other contours in which the organization is included. The high potential of the loop means that most of the activities carried out by the organizations included in this loop belong to the main types, which is a sign of the sustainable existence of the organization in the network.

The contours of the organization are temporary formations that appear and disappear in the information space and ensure the inclusion of the organization in the environment. Therefore, the number of contours, as a characteristic of the organization itself, determines a wide range of interest of the environment in the results of the functioning of the organization and thus determines the stability of the existence of the organization.

Each organization, from which the modeling organization receives an input stream, is a Supplier for this organization. Each organization that receives the output stream from the simulated organization is a Customer for this organization. A Supplier is any organization that transmits information that allows this organization to fulfill its obligations. A Customer is any organization that receives information from the fulfillment of the organization's obligations to this organization. Closing the chains of Suppliers and Customers into a loop leads to the fact that each element of the loop is both a Customer and a Supplier, depending on the sequence of consideration of the organization in the contour (reference system).

The search for the contours in which the organization is included in the information space is associated with extracting information about Suppliers and Customers from open sources, mainly on the Internet. In general, information available in open sources may not be enough to close the contour. In this case, the chains of Suppliers and Customers are connected into a contour forcibly, i.e. the contour is factorized and the characteristics of the factorized contours are determined on a compulsorily limited set of organizations.

An analysis of the contours found for the organization allows the management that manages this organization to assess its current state in the context of its inclusion in the network of socio-economic systems.

The set of values of the characteristics of the contours as a measure of the inclusion of the organization in the network determines the stability of the existence of the organization in its environment. If the state of the organization is assessed by management as sustainable, then management decisions should be aimed at maintaining the measure of involvement that ensures this stability, i.e. to preserve the environment of the organization, through which this organization is included in the network. If the analysis of the state of the organization shows its weak inclusion in the network, then this means that there are risks of breaking the contours, and this can lead to a loss of stability of the organization in the network, and hence to the cessation of the existence of the system as such. In this case, in order to maintain the existence of the organization, management decisions should be aimed at reforming the environment of the organization (to search for new Suppliers and Customers), which will increase the degree of inclusion of the organization in the network and thus ensure its sustainability.

Thus, the proposed approach to constructing business models is based on the representation of the organization as a fragment of a network formed by this organization, analysis of the measure of the organization's involvement in the network, which ensures the organization's functioning in time, and the adoption of measures that ensure the most favorable existence of the organization in the network.

7   Conclusion

The implementation of the proposed concept of the organization leads to the inevitable evolution of the paradigm of a business model. The representation of a network formed by many interacting organizations as a topological space allows us to find for each organization such contours that determine the purpose of the organization in society. The presence of a contour in which the information flow circulates means the satisfaction of the organization with any continuous need of society. The continuous satisfaction of human needs is ensured by the cyclicity and isolation of information flows that arise and spread in the information space. Narrativity as an approach to management, removes the problem of finalizing the chosen management strategy, but ensures the need for the existence of the organization through its integrability into the process of social development.

Such an understanding of the organization's mission allows us to formulate the task of building a business model in the context of determining and maintaining the organization's place in these contours, i.e. its importance in meeting the corresponding needs of society, anticipating the emergence of new needs and inclusion in new contours to meet these needs.

The very emergence of contours in the network means the consistency of the goals of the organization and the goals of society and thus ensuring the needs of society. Thus, the proposed paradigm of building a business model makes it possible to move from the competition of organizations to their cooperation in the conditions of a total information space.

As part of further research, it is planned to develop a management support system (MSS) for planning and decision making in organizations based on the proposed models and methods.

Acknowledgments. The study has been supported by the grant from the Russian Science Foundation (RSF) and the Administration of the Volgograd Oblast (Russia) No. 22–11-20024, https://rscf.ru/en/project/22-11-20024/.

References

1. Osterwalder, A., Pigneur, Y.: An ontology for e-business models. In: Currie, W. (eds.) Value Creation from E-Business Models. Butterworth-Heinemann (2004). https://doi.org/10.1016/B978-075066140-9/50006-0
2. Wirtz, B.W., Pistoia, A., Ullrich, S., Göttel, V.: Business models: origin, development and future research perspectives. Long Range Plan. **49**(1), 36–54 (2016). https://doi.org/10.1016/j.lrp.2015.04.001
3. Spieth, P., Schneckenberg, D., Ricart, J.: Business model innovation – state of the art and future challenges for the field. R&D Manage. **44**(3), 237–247 (2014). https://doi.org/10.1111/radm.12071

4. Dasilva, C., Trkman, P.: Business Model: What it is and What it is Not. Long Range Plan. **47**(6), 379–389 (2013). https://doi.org/10.1016/j.lrp.2013.08.004
5. Zott, C., Amit, R., Massa, L.: The business model: recent developments and future research. J. Manag. **37**(4), 1019–1042 (2011). https://doi.org/10.1177/0149206311406265
6. George, G., Bock, A.: The business model in practice and its implications for entrepreneurship research. Entrep. Theory Pract. **35**(1), 83–111 (2011). https://doi.org/10.1111/j.1540-6520.2010.00424.x
7. Casadesus-Masanell, R., Heilbron J.: The Business Model: Nature and Benefits. Harvard Business School. Working Paper, No. 15–089 (2015)
8. Peric, M., Durkin, J., Vitezic, V.: The constructs of a business model redefined: a half-century journey. SAGE Open (2017). https://doi.org/10.1177/2158244017733516
9. Luo, J., Yu, D., Jiang, L.: Information flow – sustainability and performance implications. J. Oper. Res. Soc. **70**(8), 1253–1274 (2019)
10. Westrum, R.: The study of information flow: a personal journey. Saf. Sci. **67**, 58–63 (2014)
11. Pick, J.B., Azari, R.: A global model of technological utilization based on governmental, business investment, social, and economic factors. J. Manag. Inf. Syst. **28**(1), 49–83 (2011)
12. Brada, J.C., Frensch, R., Gundlach, E.: Introduction: openness, institutions, and long-run socio-economic development. Econ. Syst. **40**(2), 195–197 (2016). https://doi.org/10.1016/j.ecosys.2016.05.002
13. Davtian, A., Shabalina, O., Sadovnikova, N., Parygin, D.: Cyber-social system as a model of narrative management. In: Kravets, A.G., Bolshakov, A.A., Shcherbakov, M. (eds.) Society 5.0: Cyberspace for Advanced Human-Centered Society. SSDC, vol. 333, pp. 3–14. Springer, Cham (2021). https://doi.org/10.1007/978-3-030-63563-3_1
14. Davtian, A., Shabalina, O., Sadovnikova, N., Berestneva, O., Parygin, D.: Principles for modeling information flows in open socio-economic systems. In: Kravets, A.G., Bolshakov, A.A., Shcherbakov, M. (eds.) Society 5.0: Human-Centered Society Challenges and Solutions. SSDC, vol. 416, pp. 167–173. Springer, Cham (2022). https://doi.org/10.1007/978-3-030-95112-2_14
15. Shabalina, O., Davtian, A., Sadovnikova, N., Parygin, D., Erkin. D.: Narrative-based management in socio-economic In Piet Kommers (ed) Proceedings of the International Conference ICT, Society and Human Beings 2017: part of the Multi Conference on Computer Science and Information Systems 2017. IADIS (International Association for Development of the Information Society), pp. 73–79 (2017)

Methodological Bases for Decision Support in the Management of Services, Taking into Account the Personal Information of Customers

Diana Bogdanova[✉], Gyuzel Shakhmametova, and Albert Niiazgulov

Ufa University of Science and Technology, K. Marx 12, 450008 Ufa, Russia
dianochka7bog@mail.ru

Abstract. In this article, the methodological basis of decision support for controlling the process of providing services is designed. This framework includes new management mechanisms based on incorporating the analysis of personal and emotional information into the decision support process. This allows us to solve problems with poorly formalized subjective information, create models that reflect the properties of real objects, and increase customer satisfaction. The models and decision support methods developed formed the basis of a prototype decision support system (DSS).

Keywords: Service process management · Decision support · Emotionally colored information · Decision Support Intelligent System · Customer satisfaction

1 Introduction

The significant expansion of the services market has led to its extensive modernization and computerization, which has necessitated a radical overhaul of the organization and management principles to increase efficiency and save resources through the use of new technologies. In a market's environment over-saturation condition, it became necessary to use the client-oriented approach's advantages. This means that the role of factors such as considering individual client preferences, meeting individual client needs, and considering emotional states (and emotionally colored information overall) has increased.

The level of satisfaction in the service sphere, especially in the non-material service sphere, is directly dependent on the emotions that clients feel during the process of the service being provided to them. The emotions' role in controlling the service-providing process depends on strategic management tasks. For example, if an organization in the service sphere has the task of testing new services or surviving in the current market situation, the most valuable emotions are negative-colored ones, as they reveal errors in the service-providing process. If the organization has a task to reach a new level of interaction with certain clients and the things it can get from them, or a task to attract

A. G. Kravets et al. (Eds.): CIT&DS 2023, CCIS 1909, pp. 220–231, 2023.
https://doi.org/10.1007/978-3-031-44615-3_15

new customers, then positive emotions start to play a more important role: in this case, situations, when clients feel negative emotions during the service providing process, must be excluded.

In the first part of the article, the results of the analysis of the existing approaches to the control of the service-providing process are presented. In the second part, the approach to control the service-providing process considering the personal information of the client (clients' emotional state in particular) is proposed. In the third part, the designed scheme of control over the process of providing services considering the personal information of the client is presented and the structure of the decision support system is considered.

2 Existing Approaches to Control the Service Providing Process Analysis

Many scientists are doing research in the field of increasing the effectiveness of management in the service sphere.

Author [1] proposes a methodological basis for a systematic approach to identifying objectives when building a strategic management mechanism, based on the construction of a hierarchy of strategic objectives for cultural institutions.

Authors [2] use service management. An effective management mechanism has been developed that consists of establishing strategic benchmarks in the service organization. The practical application of service management makes it possible to identify and minimize management risks. An algorithm for the creation of a logistics management site for service processes has been developed.

Article [3] analyses the work on governance in the services' sector and proposes an economic model for building a business in the services' sector, through business process-based management, internal and external risk management, innovation, and management of resources, funds, and processes.

The article [4] describes the implementation of a Customer Service System (CSS) to improve management efficiency. Drawing on effective use theory, the authors investigate how digital representations of customer preferences support service providers in the process of personalizing services. The model developed suggests that the identification of customer preferences is a prerequisite for the effective use of CSS to provide customer value.

The paper [5] examines how home care management can be made more efficient through the introduction of an online information platform. Advances in information technology with a person-oriented approach have the potential to improve health and social care services in the home. The platform consists of four components: a comprehensive health and social needs assessment system, personalized home care planning, needs-based health and social services, and the involvement of health care organizations. The study analyzed data from 164 users. Comparing scores before and after using the platform, participants' reported quality of life increased significantly across all domains, with significant improvements in shared decision-making about health and social care services.

The paper [6] investigates the impact of digital technology on consumer decision making in the retail sector through information technology. The authors extend the

AISAS (awareness, interest, search, action and sharing) model to show that with digital technologies, the consumer decision-making process is no longer sequential. This suggests an increased role of the emotional component in customer decision making. The study involved respondents from two age groups. The authors found no significant difference in these effects between older and younger consumers.

The need to implement automated decision making systems in the public service sector is becoming increasingly urgent. The aim of the research in [7] is to investigate how the use of AI in the public sector can enhance existing management efficiency. To this end, legal and policy instruments related to the use of AI to strengthen the process management system are investigated. The paper identifies the need to develop a common framework for assessing the potential impact of the use of AI in the public sector. The paper discusses the specific impact of automated decision support systems on public services.

When managing healthcare facilities, managers have to analyze a large amount of information. The use of CRM system with artificial intelligence allows to quickly and accurately analyze patient data to make accurate and automated decisions. The article [8] discusses the organizational and human factors contributing to the implementation of CRM in hospitals. For this purpose, the maintenance of an integrated framework including the dimensions of human resources, technology, organization, environment and cost (HTOEC) is proposed. A fuzzy decision making trial and evaluation laboratory (DEMATEL) method is applied to determine the interdependence between implementation dimensions and variables. The maximum mean de-entropy algorithm (MMDE) is used to select the optimal threshold value in the DEMATEL method. Fuzzy analytic network process (ANP) is used to prioritize the implementation parameters.

One of the main changes associated with Industrial Revolution 4.0 is the complete automation and digitization of processes and the use of electronics and information technology. A significant increase in interest in e-services can be observed, which is not only due to the digitization of society but also due to the constraints of the Covid-19 pandemic. The service sector is dominated by small and medium-sized enterprises (SMEs), for whom the digitization process is often more challenging, mainly due to small financial resources. The article [9] discusses the assessment of the readiness of enterprises in the SME sector to digitize the service delivery process. The survey of enterprise managers showed what their knowledge about digitization of service delivery process is, what types of digitization solutions have been implemented in their enterprises and what is the status of their implementation. The results show the benefits of digitizing the service delivery process.

The paper [10] focuses on the concept of metaheuristic algorithm using data mining techniques to provide decision mechanism in health sector. This paper defines the problem of data analytics in health sector. It discusses various emerging technologies used in healthcare and allied sectors. The focus is on the importance of metaheuristic algorithms, artificial intelligence and implementation methodologies.

It is important to have a system for analyzing customer claims to manage an insurance service provider. The article [11] identifies significant factors to distinguish between fraudulent and genuine claims. In addition, claims analysis can also be used to understand the customer layers much better and further implement the results at the stage of insurance policy issuance and policy acceptance/rejection. The study utilizes exploratory data analysis (EDA) and feature selection techniques. In addition, machine learning algorithms are applied to the datasets and evaluated using performance metrics.

The paper [12] proposes to improve the management efficiency of SMEs in the service industry by adopting cloud technology. This study focuses on the organizational factors that influence an organization's decision to adopt cloud computing. The data was collected through a questionnaire survey of enterprise managers in Malaysia. The results show that of the three factors hypothesized to influence cloud computing adoption, only information technology (IT) resources were found to be significant. However, there is insufficient evidence to support the importance of top management support and employee knowledge on cloud computing adoption.

The paper [13] discusses the results of improving the efficiency of health care delivery process management in a Greek public hospital in Thessaloniki by taking into account the degree of customer satisfaction with the electronic appointment system. MUSA (Multi-criteria Satisfaction Analysis) method was applied to evaluate the satisfaction of the users of the electronic appointment system. This method provided useful data to administrators who could make more informed decisions and identify which service characteristics need improvement.

In [14], the integration of the following quality tools was applied to improve the service delivery process: the Kano model, SERVQUAL and quality function deployment (QFD). The effective integration of these tools requires proper management of their variables, which contains imprecisions and uncertainties because they are based on customer perceptions. Fuzzy approaches are possible alternatives to overcome these limitations and integrate these tools. Nevertheless, sophisticated fuzzy methods can better deal with these limitations. This paper proposes an integrative framework including SERVQUAL, Analytical Kano (A-Kano) and QFD using fuzzy approaches (fuzzy inference system and fuzzy linguistic representation from two tuples). The framework includes four main steps concerning: 1) identification of quality attributes and service processes using A-Kano and SERVQUAL; 2) integration of these two quality tools using Fuzzy Inference System (FIS); 3) integration between the results of A-Kano and SERVQUAL and the QFD matrix using a fuzzy linguistic representation of the two tuples; and 4) identification of improvement projects to exploit the opportunities identified in the previous steps. The proposed integrative framework was implemented in an education service provider company. A new method was developed to assess the perception of customer service quality, classify these perceptions according to their impact on customer satisfaction, prioritize improvements and identify technical requirements for the service delivery process.

The main research focus is on strategic management, taking into account the personalization of services. Figure 1 shows the dependence of cash flow on clients in a service organization at different phases of the client life cycle [15]. The figure shows that in the first and last phases, there is little return from the client and any manager will seek to shorten these phases by focusing on client retention and development. Shifting the life cycle curve towards higher financial returns from the clients is possible by increasing clients' loyalty. Considering emotionally colored information from the client will lead

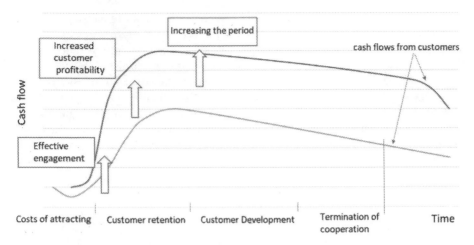

Fig. 1. Client life cycle and marketing tasks

to a higher level of satisfaction, which will ultimately help to retain the client, develop a long-term relationship with them and attract new ones through "word of mouth".

To increase the effectiveness of service delivery process management, it is necessary to increase the level of customer satisfaction at all phases of this process.

3 Suggested Approach to Controlling the Process of Providing Services Considering the Personal Information of the Client

The service industry solves the problem of decision support for managing the process of providing services based on emotionally colored information (ECI) in the sphere of information management of the organizational system. The process of information management includes [16]:

– Identifying information needs;
– Collecting and generating information;
– Analyzing and interpreting information;
– Accessing and disseminating information;
– Use of information.

In this article decision support is implemented for different phases of service providing process life cycle, such as collecting, generating, organizing, disseminating, and using information. On each phase of service providing process life cycle, the decision support is implemented through such problems as (see Fig. 2):

– Formation of complex service considering the emotional preferences of the client on provided services.
– Formation of the schedule of service providing considering the individual emotional strategy of service consumption.
– Operational management of service-consuming process with elements of individual emotional support of clients and finding the right type of service providing.

– Analysis of customer feedback in the form of ratings and emotional reactions to various service aspects.
– Evaluating the effectiveness of service providing, considering parameters reflecting the customer's emotions at the end of the service consumption process.

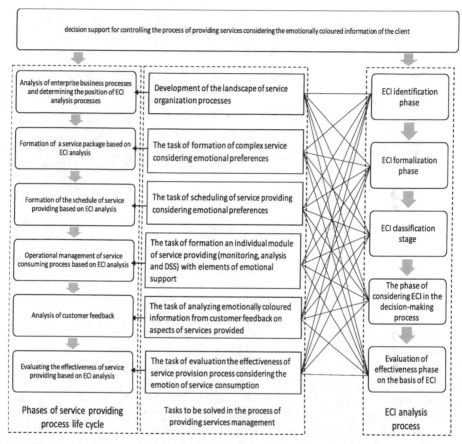

Fig. 2. Decision support for the service delivery process at different phases of the life cycle

To solve these problems, new management mechanisms based on the specific type of information reflecting the emotions of customers are designed. The use of appropriate management mechanisms in the organizational system ensures the implementation of management functions. Management mechanisms are used in different phases of management:

• Planning;
• Organizing;
• Stimulating;
• Controlling.

Professor D. Novikov in his book "Theory of organizational systems management" [17] provides his scheme of management mechanisms complex. In this scheme, the new management mechanisms are designed considering emotionally colored information, which is implemented at various stages of the life cycle of the service-providing process (see Fig. 3).

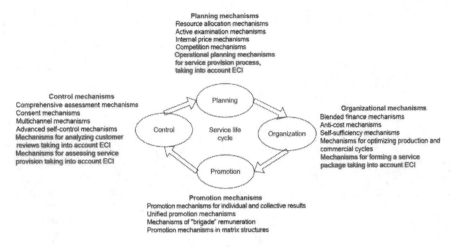

Fig. 3. Management mechanisms complex.

In the planning phase, operational planning mechanisms of service delivery processes were designed considering emotionally colored information [18].

In the organizing phase, the mechanisms of forming a service package considering emotionally colored information were designed.

In an organizational phase, the mechanisms for creating a service package were designed, considering emotionally colored information.

The control object in this organizational system is a service-providing process. The life cycle of this process is examined in detail in Fig. 2. The peculiarity of the proposed approach to the control of the organizational system in the service sphere is the design of new management mechanisms based on emotionally colored information in each phase of this life cycle.

At each stage of the service delivery life cycle, to consider customers' emotions when managing and implementing the proposed management mechanisms, an analysis of emotionally colored information is carried out. It consists of the following phases:

- ECI identification;
- ECI formalization;
- ECI classification;
- Considering ECIs in the decision-making process;
- Effectiveness assessment considering ECIs.

Following the methods of system analysis, the principles of service-providing management in the organization belonging to the service sphere are developed, which allows the designing of the decision-making methodology based on these principles for the management of the process of service-providing, considering emotionally colored information.

To build the Decision Support System (DSS for managing service providing process based on emotionally colored information, considering the requirements, basic system analysis principles were used, which can be interpreted as follows:

- Implementation of the principle of observability consists in the fact that at the moment of designing DSS based on ECI, it was ensured that in the system there are no elements and subsystems which can't be controlled by its higher level. This allowed it to reach the necessary level of reliability of functioning of the system and to reduce the probability of occurrence of errors in its operation.

- According to the feasibility principle all subsystems and elements of a complex system must be implemented by using available technologies; for this purpose, necessary resources must be allocated. For DSS based on ECI, such a resource is a database containing information from the ontological model and knowledge about precedents gained from experts.

- The principle of counter-intuitive design for DSS based on ECI means that in the design of this system, modules and subsystems based only on experts' intuition and experience were excluded. All elements of the DSS were designed considering generally accepted standards based on an approved problem statement.

- The principle of manageability means that DSS based on ECI doesn't contain modules, elements, or subsystems that can't be controlled because DSS is a complex system. All of them are affected by the purposeful controlling influence of the main system or higher-level elements.

- The principle of integration means that all elements and subsystems (in DSS based on ECI - these are modules, database, and the user interface) must be united into one system according to certain rules, and system-wide goals, objectives, and functions must be further developed.

- The principle of "good fit" means that all elements or subsystems at the same level must have the same functions, characteristics, and structure in all respects. For DSS based on ECI, this principle is fulfilled by the allocation of functions between elements in all phases of the system's work (e.g., between modules for working with data, calculating values, and making recommendations).

- The principle of coherence means that all elements of the system must be coherent with each other to achieve the required resulting system effectiveness. During the design of the DSS based on the ECI, tests were conducted to assess the mutual coherence of the work of the system elements.

- The principle of "system, goal and environment" is fulfilled in DSS based on ECI as follows: when designing the system, the basic parameters of the environment in which it should operate (e.g., health and beauty, education, financial and travel services) were taken into account and, depending on the type of organization, the DSS and its goals were adapted.

The resulting methodology is shown in Fig. 4.

The methodology of decision support for controlling the process of providing services considering emotionally colored information includes the following phases:

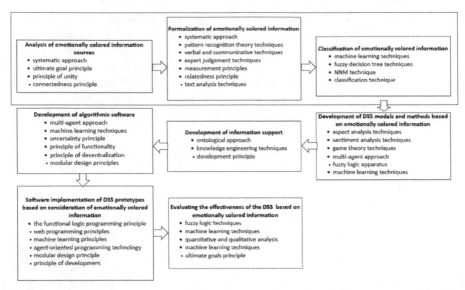

Fig. 4. Decision support methodology for controlling the service delivery process, taking into account emotionally colored information.

- – Analysis of ECI sources;
- – Formalization of ECI;
- – Classification of ECI;
- – Design of models and decision support methods based on ECI;
- – Design of informational and algorithmic provision;
- – Software implementation of DSS prototypes based on consideration of ECI;
- – Evaluation of effectiveness based on consideration of ECI.

Each of these phases is based on highlighted principles, approaches, and methods.

4   Scheme of Control over the Process of Providing Services, Considering the Personal Information of the Client

Figure 5 shows the control system for the service delivery process in the form of a structure diagram. Let's consider it in detail (emotionally colored information is highlighted in red).

The life cycle of the service provision process can be seen in the scheme of the designed control process. The planning process (planning block) includes such phases as the formation of the idea about the service, formation of the technological process, formation of the customer profile (here we get the formalized, emotionally colored information, marked with red color), formation of the service package, formation of the service delivery schedule. After that, the complete plan is sent to the service consumption process, in which the emotional support of the customer is carried out and the appropriate form of service provision is chosen, considering his emotional state.

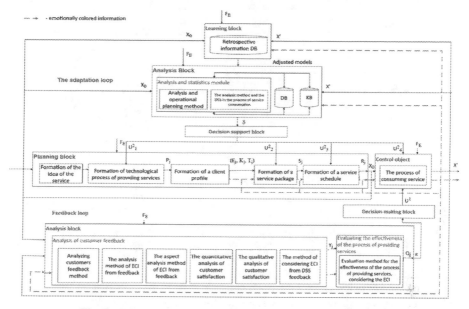

Fig. 5. Scheme of the service-providing process control system.

After the service is completed, customer feedback is analyzed in the form of ratings and formalized emotions about the service received. In a feedback assessment phase, the level of customer satisfaction and the integral effectiveness indicator is getting evaluated. This information is then sent to decision-makers and the feedback loop is closed.

An adaptation Loop contains models and ECI analysis methods designed to automate the decision-making process during the planning phase and operational management of the service consumption phase. The learning level contains the historical information database that allows the correction of the models used.

Let's consider in detail the decision support process model that uses our proposed decision support system (see Fig. 6).

To increase the effectiveness of the service-providing process, selected decisions are fed into the system as input from the decision maker (DM), and the result of the process execution comes out as output and is sent to the decision support system (DSS). During the service-providing process, the client has different feelings. The client's ECI is considered in the DSS. DSS includes a user interface, recommendation forming module, indicator assessment module, data processing module, data database, and knowledge base. DMs formulate their queries using the user interface and receive recommendations on how to improve the service delivery process. The DM's queries are sent from the user interface to recommendation forming, indicator assessment, and data processing modules.

After receiving the data from the query, recommendation forming, indicator assessment and data processing modules find the required information in the database and knowledge base and write the resulting information from the service-providing process into them. The knowledge base is filled with information from the ontological model

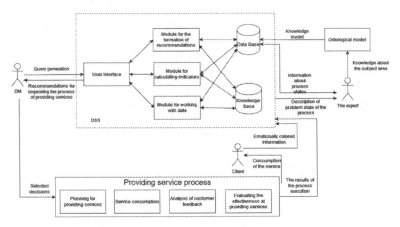

Fig. 6. Decision support process scheme.

and with information about the state of the system from the expert. The expert also fills up the ontological model with knowledge about the subject area. They also receive information from DSS about issues during the service delivery process.

5 Conclusion

Even if the service sphere is less capital-intensive it is still playing an important role in modern economics. A service sphere organization can gain a competitive advantage by increasing customer satisfaction by considering the individual characteristics and emotional states of customers during the service delivery process. In this paper, the approach to increase the effectiveness of control over the service-providing process through automated accounting clients' emotionally colored information and their traits with a decision support system on every phase of the life cycle of this process is proposed.

The new mechanisms of managing the organizational system in the service sphere based on considering the specific type of information that reflects clients' emotions were designed. The application of adequate management mechanisms in the organizational system ensures that management functions are fulfilled.

The life cycle of the service delivery process is considered. Decision support tasks at each phase of the process are formalized considering emotionally colored clients' information.

Based on the analysis of the proposed management principles, a methodology for decision support in the service-providing process management has been developed considering clients' ECI. The structural scheme of the service-providing process management system, including three control loops: feedback, adaptation, and learning has been developed. The model of the decision support process using the proposed decision support system, showing the interaction of DSS modules in solving the problems of management of the organizational system of the sphere of services has been developed.

Acknowledgments. The reported study was funded by the Russian Science Foundation according to the research project № 22–19-00471.

References

1. Fokina, M.L.: Determination of objectives of cultural institutions in forming strategic management system for service delivery. In: Proceedings of Russian State Pedagogical University named after A. I. Herzen (2010). issue 120
2. Dokukina, I.A., Makarova, J.L.: Management of service processes on the basis of service management. Srednerussky Vestnik of Social Sciences (2017). issue 1
3. Shaitura, S.V., Ordov, K.V., Zharov, V.G., Malitskaya, Y.O., Kolomeitsev, A.V., Madyarov, A.A.: Management issues in service sectors. Bulletin of Kursk State Agricultural Academy (2021). issue 3
4. Bonaretti, D., Bartosiak, M., Lui, T.W., Piccoli, G., Marchesani, D.: What can I(S) do for you?: How technology enables service providers to elicit customers' preferences and deliver personalized service. Inf. Manage. 57(6), 103346 (2020)
5. Park, M., et al.: ICT-based person-centered community care platform (IPC3P) to enhance shared decision-making for integrated health and social care services. Int. J. Med. Informatics 156, 104590 (2021)
6. Sharma, P., Ueno, A., Dennis, Ch., Turan, C.P.: Emerging digital technologies and consumer decision-making in retail sector: Towards an integrative conceptual framework. Comput. Hum. Behav. 148, 107913 (2023)
7. Kuziemski, M., Misuraca, G.: AI governance in the public sector: three tales from the frontiers of automated decision-making in democratic settings. Telecommun. Policy 44(6), 101976 (2020)
8. Dastjerdi, M., Keramati, A., Keramati, N.: A novel framework for investigating organizational adoption of AI-integrated CRM systems in the healthcare sector; using a hybrid fuzzy decision-making approach. Telematics Inform. Rep. 11, 100078 (2023)
9. Ingaldi, M., Klimecka-Tatar, D.: Digitization of the service provision process - requirements and readiness of the small and medium-sized enterprise sector. Procedia Comput. Sci. 200, 237–246 (2022)
10. Rahul, K., Banyal, R.K.: Metaheuristics approach to improve data analysis process for the healthcare sector. Procedia Comput. Sci. 215, 98–103 (2022)
11. Rawat, S., Rawat, A., Kumar, D., Sabitha, A.S.: Application of machine learning and data visualization techniques for decision support in the insurance sector. Int. J. Inf. Manage. Data Insights 1(2), 100012 (2021)
12. Hassan, H.: Organisational factors affecting cloud computing adoption in small and medium enterprises (SMEs) in service sector. Procedia Comput. Sci. 121, 976–981 (2017)
13. Kitsios, F., Stefanakakis, S., Kamariotou, M., Dermentzoglou, L.: E-service evaluation: user satisfaction measurement and implications in health sector. Comput. Stan. Interfaces 63, 16–26 (2019)
14. Lizarelli, F.L., Osiro, L., Ganga, G., Mendes, G., Paz, G.R.: Integration of SERVQUAL, analytical kano, and QFD using fuzzy approaches to support improvement decisions in an entrepreneurial education service. Appl. Soft Comput. 112, 107786 (2021)
15. Oyner, O.K.: Marketing Performance Management. Yurite, p. 343 (2012)
16. Information Management. Key Concepts in Information and Knowledge Management. https://www.tlu.ee/~sirvir/Information%20and%20Knowledge%20Management/Key_Concepts_of_IKM/information_management.html
17. Novikov, D.A.: Theory of organisational systems management. MPSI, p. 584 (2005)
18. Bogdanova, D.R.: Decision support system for the operational planning of the activity of a sanatorium resort organization. Materials of roundtable "Information technology and mathematical research methods in economics" of the Bashkir-Saxon Forum, USATU, pp. 11–24 (2007)

Complex Dynamics Modeling Algorithm Application in Comparative Study of Innovation Processes

Alexey B. Simonov$^{(\boxtimes)}$ (iD) and Alexey F. Rogachev (iD)

Volgograd State Technical University, Volgograd, Russian Federation
absimonov@gmail.com

Abstract. The analysis of the dynamics of economic processes and, in particular, innovation processes, has a great significance. However, the study of dynamics in economics is complicated by frequent qualitative changes in the time series. The problem is also complicated by a small amount of data, as they are often generated on the basis of annual reports. In this paper we propose to use an algorithm developed by the authors as an instrument of analysis and modeling of the socio-economic processes dynamics. This algorithm is effective taking into account the features of these processes. Our algorithm consists of preliminary decomposition of the time series into components by the SSA method, modeling of these components and selecting the best model basing on fuzzy rules. In this paper, the algorithm is used to study the dynamics of the revenue from new (innovative) products and services in some regions. As a result of the study, dynamics models were obtained that give a reasonable fit to real data and also give realistic forecasts. It has been shown that our model can be used for analytical purposes. The results of the work may be used in the innovation activity analysis in the regions and should be taken into account when making decisions in the management in the socio-economic sphere. The created algorithm proved to be effective for analyzing and forecasting of the innovation processes dynamics. The peculiarity of the algorithm is that it greatly simplifies the comparative analysis of the dynamics series.

Keywords: innovations · singular spectrum analysis · fuzzy logic · innovative activity · time series · economic development

1 Introduction

The task of the economic processes dynamics modeling and forecasting is of a great importance. A wide range of tools are used in the solving the problems of time series modeling in economics. These tools include statistical methods, methods of data mining. Benefits and drawbacks of them are reflected, in particular, in the work [1]. Special methods of dynamics analysis have been developed to solve individual problems. For example, methods of fundamental and technical analysis are used in the stock market. However, the available tools often can't give the expected result. In particular, statistical methods often do not take into account the whole variety of complex interrelated factors

A. G. Kravets et al. (Eds.): CIT&DS 2023, CCIS 1909, pp. 232–247, 2023.
https://doi.org/10.1007/978-3-031-44615-3_16

in the economy. As a result, a large number of unaccounted factors leads to the fact that the random error component has a strong influence on the simulation results. Moreover, unaccounted factors can lead to a sharp change in the trend. This will make forecasting based on the created model uninformative. Such bifurcations are very important. Therefore, special methods of change detection are rapidly developing.

On the other hand, frequent trend changes and a small amount of data on many indicators (information about which may be taken from annual or quarterly reports) significantly complicate the use of artificial intelligence methods. All these problems become even more acute when modeling the dynamics of innovation processes, which are characterized by a much higher level of uncertainty than the other economic processes.

One of the ways to solve these problems is to work not with statistical data, but with models of real objects. For example, in [2], the possibilities of using simulation modeling methods in innovation dynamics prediction are studied. However, the issue of ensuring the adequacy of the constructed model to real phenomena and processes is always acute when using such methods.

That's why it is relevant to search for algorithms that allow increasing the quality of modeling and forecasting of time series. The combination of various approaches is one of the directions of such an algorithms constructing. In particular, varieties of the singular spectrum analysis method (SSA, "caterpillar") are widely used to isolate individual components of a time series, followed by their processing by various methods. Thus, in [3] it is proposed to use Fourier series to model the components we obtained by decomposition with SSA method. This approach has proved to be quite effective in the absence of trend dynamics and significant autocorrelation in the studied series. In their paper [4] S. Vyalkova, O. Kornykova, I. Nadtoka proposed to decompose time series into components using Multivariate SSA (MSSA) method and then process the results using fuzzy neural network. This method was efficiently used to predict electricity consumption in Moscow. In [5], when studying road traffic, the SSA method was used to pre-process a time series before using recurrent neural networks (RNN). A year earlier, in the paper [6] SSA was used for preprocessing data on the load of the power grid in Greece. The results of decomposition were processed by one of the RNN varieties– Long short-term memory (LSTM) network, as well as MLP. According to the results «decomposition step reduces the prediction error for both MLPs and LSTMs».

In [7], a more complex combination of FCM-SSA-ARIMA was used to predict streamflow. Fuzzy C-means clustering (FCM) method was used in this issue before the SSA method. This made it possible to increase the accuracy of forecasting results when solving a problem that is important for decision-making in the field of economics, agriculture and environmental protection.

Thus, the use of time series preprocessing using SSA method before using other analysis methods has shown its effectiveness in solving many problems. In our work [8], we proposed an algorithm that develops this logic and has shown high results in solving practical problems. The main advantages of this algorithm are the capability to configure the rules and models used in time series forecasting, as well as the possibility of partial automation of the results of the calculations carried out.

In this paper, we study the possibility of using a modification of the created algorithm for forecasting and conducting a comparative analysis of the dynamics of revenue from new (innovative) products and services in the Russian Federation. The first task of the paper is to study the effectiveness of the modified algorithm proposed in [8] for solving practical problems. The second task of the work is to assess the features of the innovation processes dynamics in the regions of the Russian Federation, to draw conclusions about the features of these processes dynamics in different regions.

2   Methods and Materials

We propose to use a dynamics modeling algorithm developed by the authors to model the dynamics of the revenue from new (innovative) products and services. It consists of three stages (see Fig. 1). At the first stage, the SSA method is used for time series decomposition at components. At the second stage, it is proposed to compile a set of alternative models for each component. At the third stage the best models for each component are selected based on the application of the fuzzy rule base. The final model is also built in this step. It is determined as the sum of the modeled values by components. Since the application of fuzzy inference rules does not guarantee the selection of one best model for each component, it is possible to create several final models with expert selection of the best one. This final models can also be considered as alternative development options that should be taken into account. The resulting mathematical model can be further used to solve interpolation and extrapolation problems, to solve forecasting and planning problems when making decisions.

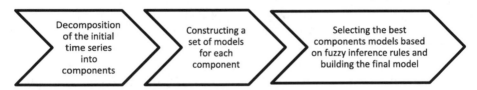

Fig. 1. The developed algorithm for the dynamics of processes modeling.

It should be noted that this algorithm is based on the algorithm proposed in [8]. But in this study, the stages of modeling and model selection are reversed. The advantage of this approach is that we can take into account not only the data of the preliminary analysis, but also the actual results of modeling when choosing a best model. The disadvantage of this approach is a significant increase in the running time of the algorithm. This is caused by the need to build a large number of unused intermediate models. One of the ways to optimize the running time of the algorithm is to use preliminary assessment of the component model quality immediately after its construction. If the quality of model is very high, then the less priority ones were not built.

Let's look at the stages of the algorithm in more detail.

At the first stage, the SSA method is used to decompose a time series into components. Let's consider this method in more detail.

This method is used for studying the original time series $F = (f1, f2, ..., fN)$ of length N. We also must choose window's length L [9], that is main parameter of SSA method. If we will take too large values of L, then we will have too little number of observations to make qualitative reconstruction. If we will take too small values of L, we will not be able to reconstruct long period oscillations. Therefore, L usually takes a value from quarter to half the time series length (N/4 … N/2) [10]. Another approach is to use the median value [11] as the optimal L value.

The SSA method consists of two phases, decomposition and reconstruction [12].

The first stage of decomposition phase is embedding. The original time series F is transformed into a trajectory matrix X that has dimension L × K. We can consider X as a set of K lagged vectors, each of which has a length L. The number of vectors can be calculated as:

$$K = N - L + 1 \tag{1}$$

Each column of matrix X is rolling window of length L, so the first column has elements $f_1 \dots f_L$, the second column has elements from $f_2 \dots f_{L+1}$, and so on.

$$X = \begin{pmatrix} f_1 & \cdots & f_{N-L+1} \\ \vdots & \ddots & \vdots \\ f_L & \cdots & f_N \end{pmatrix} \tag{2}$$

X is matrix with equal elements on all diagonals. If $L = N - L + 1$ it may be considered as a Hankel matrix.

The second stage of the decomposition phase is singular value decomposition (SVD) of trajectory matrix X. During this phase trajectory matrix X is decomposed into elementary parts X_i. These parts are matrixes the sum of which is equal to X. The singular value decomposition for X is

$$X = \sum X_i \tag{3}$$

Let us denote the eigenvalues of the matrix $S = X \times X^T$ as $\lambda_1, \lambda_2, \dots, \lambda_L$. They are non-decreasing ordered, and d is number of $\lambda_i > 0$. Let us also denote the eigenvectors of the matrix S as $U_1, U_2, \dots, U_L$, corresponding to the ordered eigenvalues λ_i [13]. After we calculate U and λi we can calculate elementary vectors Vi as

$$V_i = X^T \frac{U_i}{\sqrt{\lambda_i}} \tag{4}$$

Then the elementary matrices Xi are calculated by the formula:

$$X_i = \sqrt{\lambda_i} U_i V_i^T \tag{5}$$

After the calculation of X_i we can proceed to reconstruction phase. To reconstruct time series, we use diagonal averaging. Each matrix X_i is translated into a series of length N. Let us denote L^* as min (L, K), and K^* as max (L, K). For each element x of matrix X_i, let us also denote $x^*_{ab} = x_{ab}$, if $L < K$, and $x^*_{ab} = x_{ba}$, if $L > K$. So we will have matrixes Xi* that have dimension L × K with number of column K^* and number of rows L*, where L* > K*. Diagonal averaging [12] transforms each resulting matrix $\tilde{X}i^*$ into a series $\tilde{F}_i$ according to the formula for each element $\tilde{f}_{ik}$ as:

$$
\tilde{f}_{ik} = \begin{cases} \frac{1}{k+1}\sum_{n=1}^{k+1} x_{n,k-n+2}^*, \forall 0 \le k < L^* - 1 \\ \frac{1}{L^*}\sum_{n=1}^{L^*} x_{n,k-n+2}^*, \forall L^* - 1 \le k < K^* \\ \frac{1}{N-k}\sum_{n=k-K^*+2}^{N-K^*+1} x_{n,k-n+2}^*, \forall L^* - 1 \le k < K^* \end{cases} \tag{6}
$$

Series $\tilde{F}_i = (\tilde{f}_{i1}, \tilde{f}_{i2} \cdots \tilde{f}_{iN})$ can be considered as additive components of the time series F that was under study. Components $\tilde{F}_i$ can be also considered as a trend, cycle, or noise components of time series F [11], and can be used to analyze properties of F.

At the second stage of the algorithm, several models are built for each significant component obtained $\tilde{F}_i$. It is suggested that the significant component explains at least 1% of the initial time series variance. This allows you to discard some components and reduce the amount of calculations. The specificity of the proposed method is we are limited only by general knowledge about the types of models used in the subject area that when we choose models. Therefore, we can easily supplement and change the list of applied models and the way parameters of those models are estimated. In our case, the parameters of the model were mainly estimated by methods of multidimensional optimization, in particular, using evolutionary algorithms.

The models we used are represented below:

1. linear model: $\tilde{y}(t) = a_0 + a_1 t$

2. linear model with a change in a parameters: $\tilde{y}(t) = \begin{cases} a_0 + a_1 t \forall t < T \\ a_2 + a_3 t \forall t \ge T \end{cases}$

   the condition of continuity at the point of trend change was additionally set for this model

3. simplified oscillation model: $\tilde{y}(t) = a_0 + a_1 \sin(a_2 t + a_3)$

4. oscillation model with linearly varying amplitude:

$$\tilde{y}(t) = a_0 + (a_1 + a_2 t)\sin(a_3 t + a_4)$$

5. oscillation model with a quadratic varying amplitude:

$$\tilde{y}(t) = a_0 + (a_1 + a_2 t + a_3 t^2)\sin(a_4 t + a_5)$$

6. autocorrelation model with lag T: $\tilde{y}(t) = a_0 \cdot \tilde{y}(t - T)$

The study of existing systems for analyzing the states of the world prior art shows that all existing systems, in one way or another, use either the statistical or morphological properties of the states of the WPA. Existing systems may differ in performance, functionality, the number of connected databases, the availability and amount of processed information. Existing systems may even differ significantly from each other in architecture.

In all models, time-related parameters are denoted as T. These parameters are trend change step in Model 2, lag in Model 6. The remaining parameters are denoted as $a_0, a_1 \ldots$

The parameters were selected by the least squares method for the linear model, and by numerical analysis methods for the rest of models.

The order of the models in the list corresponds to their priority when choosing a model at the third stage of the algorithm. That is, if the linear model describes some component VERY WELL, then it will be chosen regardless of the quality of the other models. From the other hand if a linear model describes the component SATISFACTORILY, and a linear model with a change in a parameters describes the component WELL, then we can choose some model only at the third stage. This choice will be based on based on the fuzzy rules, which will be described below.

At the third stage of the algorithm, fuzzy rules were applied to select the best model for each of the components. One or more models of dynamics were built afterwards.

Initially the fuzzifier converts parameters of the components (that was extracted by SSA), and the measures of the models quality (for models obtained at the second stage) into fuzzy linguistic variables belonging to fuzzy sets A_j (individual for each indicator). In particular, we can use such measures as R^2, the results of the Cox-Stuart test and so on. We use a membership function (μ), to convert these parameters for fuzzy sets. Most often we used the triangular membership functions:

$$\mu_A(s) = \begin{cases} 1 - \frac{|s-c|}{d} \forall s \in [c-d, c+d] \\ 0 \forall s \notin [c-d, c+d] \end{cases} \tag{7}$$

where c is the center point of the triangle; d is the half of the triangle's width.

Using such a function we can construct fuzzy sets for any criteria.

At the next step, we use a set of fuzzy rules to choose the most relevant model for each component. These rules integrates the experience and knowledge of expert, and can be augmented and modified to improve the algorithm effectiveness and giving it high flexibility. Each rule can connect information of multiple variables through fuzzy set operations using t-norms and t-conorms:

$$\text{if S1 is A11 and S2 is A21, then Z is B,} \tag{8}$$

where S1 is a fuzzy value for one indicator, S2 for another indicator, and so on; Z is a fuzzy value for the resulting component type.

For example, "if R^2 for linear model is HIGH and L value obtained by Foster-Stewart method is HIGH, then the possibility of using a linear model is VERY HIGH".

Or "if the possibility of using a linear model is not VERY HIGH and the possibility of using a linear model with trend change is VERY HIGH then the linear model with trend change is VERY RELEVANT".

We have also developed rules for anomaly (noise) detecting. We are considering anomalies as the events that deviate from the normal progress of the process and that most likely will not to happen again. To detect these anomalies we use Sigma Rule and CUSUM anomaly detection (same as it described at [14]).

We also explored the possibility of oscillation models with variable amplitude usage for anomaly detection. We considered component model as an anomaly if such a model has a high significance for a particular component, while the amplitude changes sign during the period under study. We use such anomaly models for interpolation. But when extrapolating, we model this component as a constant (usually as 0, less often as offset

a_0). If the amplitude changes sign outside of the period under study, then we can consider this component as a potential outlier. In this case, we use either a model with constant amplitude, or model the component as a constant after changing the sign of the amplitude.

When we get the set of linguistic variables to choose the most relevant models, we can choose one or few most relevant models for each component. Researcher can choose one model for each component to make a set of models. He also can decide to include a number of models for some components to explore different scenarios of dynamics. This set of models can be used in the sequel to create the number of integrated models as the sum of components models.

A set of models created in automatic mode can be used for extrapolation. It also can be used to analyze the features of the studied processes dynamics. It is particularly effective to use a set of models for the comparative dynamics of a large number of processes to identify common points and differences.

3 Results

The developed algorithm is used in this paper to analyze the dynamics of the volume of innovative goods and services produced in the region. The Volgograd Region was chosen as the main object of study. It was compared with Moscow, St. Petersburg and Tatarstan. These regions traditionally occupy the first places in the ratings of innovative development of the regions of the Russian Federation. It is possible to find out common aspects in the dynamics of regions, as well as how the dynamics in different regions differ from each other as a result of our analysis. All data are taken from open sources – from the website of the Federal State Statistics Service of the Russian Federation [15]. The time series were obtained by combining information from the composite book "Regions of Russia. Socio-economic indicators" for different years.

The dynamics of the revenue from new (innovative) products and services in the Volgograd region (in millions of rubles, in 2020 prices) for 2003–2021 is considered. This was all the information at [15] available at the time of writing. It should be noted that to account for inflation, the indicators for each year were adjusted taking into account the GDP deflator index.

Dynamics of the revenue from new (innovative) products and services in the Volgograd region (see Fig. 2) has a significant anomaly in 2008–2011. In our opinion, this anomaly is associated with the activation of innovation policy in this period. However, we cannot say whether there was a real increase of innovations in this period or the anomaly is due to the imperfection of statistical tools in this period – this issue requires separate study. This anomaly significantly complicates the study of this time series anyway. We can also note a significant anomaly in 2014–2017. Probably, it is connected with the mounting of international tension during this period and the active policy of import substitution. At the same time, it is not possible to identify the trend and cyclical components in this time series without the use of mathematical tools.

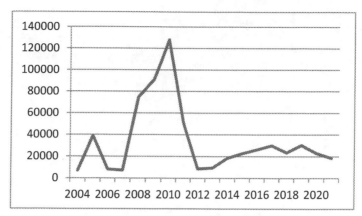

Fig. 2. Dynamics of the revenue from new (innovative) products and services in the Volgograd region in 2003–2021 (mln. rubles).

As a result of using the SSA method, eight components of the time series were identified. They are shown in Fig. 3.

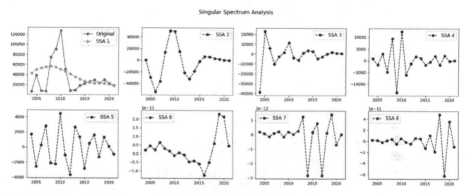

Fig. 3. Components of the revenue from new (innovative) products and services dynamics, identified by the SSA method (mln. rubles).

The last three components were discarded as insignificant. Next, models were built for each of the components 1–5. We show most interesting results obtained for components 1, 2, 5 in Figs. 4–6.

The first component (shown in Fig. 4) is most accurately modeled as an oscillation with a long period (which is longer than the studied period). However, according to the fuzzy rules, there was chosen a model with a change in parameters. The value of R^2 for this model is 0.936. Thus, a model with a change in parameters accurately describes the studied component.

The second component (shown in Fig. 5) was recognized as a model of anomaly. The oscillation model with a period of about three years and with a constant amplitude also describe the component well ($R^2 = 0,623$). But the oscillation model with variable

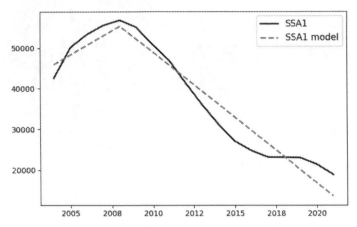

Fig. 4. The model of the 1st component identified by the SSA method

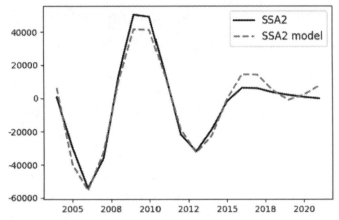

Fig. 5. The model of the 2nd component identified by the SSA method

amplitude describe it much better ($R^2 = 0{,}956$). At the same time, the second model indicates a sharp drop in amplitude to negative values in the last two steps. Sigma rule is also detects anomaly. Therefore, in the final model, the value of this component will be conditionally considered equal to zero for the purposes of extrapolation and calculated using a model with variable amplitude for the needs of interpolation.

Based on the rules of fuzzy, the fifth component (shown in Fig. 6) can be classified as one of two models with near degrees of membership. It can be considered both as modeling anomaly, and as fluctuations with a period of about three years.

In this case, two final models were constructed, from which the second one was chosen by the expert (using a model of oscillations with constant amplitude and a period of three years).

At the third stage of the algorithm application, models for the components were selected by the fuzzy rules use and two variants of the final model were constructed. From

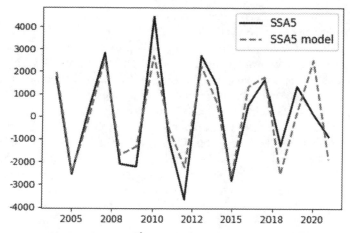

Fig. 6. The model of the 5th component identified by the SSA method

these options, an expert method was used to select a model in which the first component is modeled by a linear model with a changes in parameter values; the second, third and fourth components are classified as anomaly, and the fifth is modeled by oscillations with a three years period.

From an economist's point of view, it is important that fluctuations with a period close to 10 were recognized as an anomaly. Such fluctuations are traditionally associated with the replacement of fixed assets at enterprises. This may indicate the growing problems with the effective renewal of capital funds of Volgograd region enterprises. The simulation results based on the constructed model are shown in the Fig. 7a. For comparison, Fig. 7b shows us the results of the most accurate from the statistical methods used – ARIMA (0,0,2).

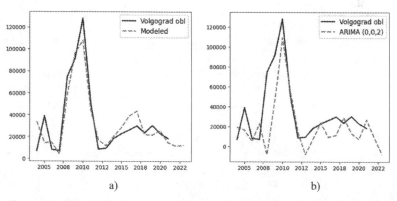

a)   b)

Fig. 7. The results of modeling the revenue from new (innovative) products and services dynamics in the Volgograd region, identified by the SSA method (a – model based on the proposed algorithm, b – values calculated on the basis of ARIMA (0,0,2)).

The created model is much more accurate compared to ARIMA(0,0,2)), which is confirmed by the value of R^2. $R^2 = 0,854$ for an algorithm-based model, and $R^2 = 0,346$ for ARIMA(0,0,2). The forecast compiled according to the author's model predicts a decrease in the output of innovations in 2022 and a slight increase in 2023. The simulation results can be used to analyze innovation activity in the Volgograd region and to support decision-making in the socio-economic sphere management of the region.

Similarly, the dynamics of the output of innovative goods and services in the most innovative regions of the Russian Federation was modeled. These regions are cities of Moscow, St. Petersburg and the Republic of Tatarstan. The results obtained for each of the regions are shown in Fig. 8. The solid line in this figure shows the real dynamics of the revenue from new (innovative) products and services (in 2020 prices), and the dotted line shows the forecast of dynamics according to the model.

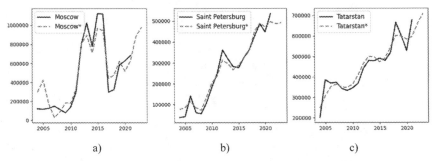

Fig. 8. Results of the revenue from new (innovative) products and services modeling in the most innovative regions of the Russian Federation (a – Moscow, b – St. Petersburg, c – Republic of Tatarstan).

As we can see, these regions are characterized by a significant increase in the innovation output (unlike the Volgograd region). In Moscow, the increase in the volume of innovative goods began in 2009 and turned into anomaly rapid growth in 2012–2016. Unlike the Volgograd region, after the end of the anomaly period the pronounced growth continued.

There were no such strong anomalies in St. Petersburg and Tatarstan, although there were significant deviations in some years. In St. Petersburg as a whole, growth was close to linear or exponential. The volume of innovative goods and services increased sharply in 2006 and 2012 in this region. In 2020, during the COVID-19 pandemic, there was a sharp decrease in innovative production in St. Petersburg. In Tatarstan, as in Moscow, there was a rapid growth in the innovative goods and services revenue after 2009. Starting in 2018, sharp fluctuations began. They achieve the maximum values in 2018 and 2019, and the minimum value in 2020 during the COVID-19 pandemic.

The modeling of dynamics was carried out for each region using the algorithm discussed above. In each case, the model described the available data more accurately compared to the best statistical methods. The results are shown in Table 1.

Table 1. Comparative results of the revenue from new (innovative) products and services modeling in some regions of the Russian Federation.

	Volgograd region	Moscow	St Petersburg	Tatarstan
Trend	linear with change	linear with change	linear	linear
The year of the trend change	2008	2016	-	-
Short-term (Kitchin) cycle	1* cycle model is included in the final model	2 cycle models are included in the final model, 1* cycle can be considered as an anomaly	2 cycle models are included in the final model, there is also a non-interpreted cycle with a period of 6 years	2* cycle models are included in the final model, there is also a non-interpreted cycle with a period of 6 years
Juglar cycle	yes*	yes	yes	yes
Number of components modeled as anomaly	2	-	-	-
The number of components that was specified as non-significant	3 (of 8)	3 (of 8)	3 (of 8)	3 (of 8)
R^2 for the final model	$R^2 = 0,854$	$R^2 = 0,877$	$R^2 = 0,972$	$R^2 = 0,895$
The best statistical model of the time series	ARIMA (0,0,2)	ARIMA (0,1,2)	linear	linear
R^2 for the best statistical model	$R^2 = 0,346$	$R^2 = 0,673$	$R^2 = 0,908$	$R^2 = 0,817$

Note: * means that the component can be interpreted as anomaly

As we can see from Table 1, the results of the model constructing with the proposed algorithm are quite accurate. A trend was funded in all time series. We can notice that the growing trend changed to a decline in the Volgograd region and in Moscow during period under study.

Short- and medium-period cycles were allocated in all regions. However medium-term cycles can be considered as having an anomalous form in the Volgograd Region (we can see only one cycle period). This may indicate problems with the renewal of fixed assets, which are traditionally associated with Juglar cycles.

Abnormal cycles with a period of about five years were also identified in St. Petersburg and Tatarstan. These are cycles that have no clear economic explanation. They may be associated with an important role in the innovation of these regions of certain types of fixed assets that have rapid physical or moral depreciation.

The constructed model allows us to highlight the features of the revenue from new (innovative) products and services dynamics in the Volgograd region in comparison with the most innovative regions of the Russian Federation. There is a large amount of anomaly in a time series, which may indicate a much lower robustness of the regional innovation system. In particular, there may be less resistance to manipulation of statistical data in the region. In addition, only the Volgograd region has no obvious growth of the innovation output in the period under study. This may indicate the presence of systemic mechanisms that increase the gap of the Volgograd region from the most innovative regions. It is also possible to note the abnormal behavior of the Juglar cycle in the Volgograd region dynamics, which may indicate difficulties with capital renewal. The identified features should be taken into account when making decisions on the management at the level of the Volgograd region and at the federal level.

4 Discussion

In this study, the algorithm proposed by the authors proved to be quite effective for forecasting and comparative analysis of time series in economics, in particular, in the field of innovation activity study. The efficiency of the algorithm in this study turned out to be significantly higher than the efficiency of traditional statistical methods. Additionally, the time series under study do not allow for effective training of the neural network due to the insignificant amount of data. That means that most modern methods of data mining will be ineffective for solving such problems. The development of this algorithm and its optimization can significantly improve the quality of solving problems in the economy for the purposes of decision support.

The algorithm can also be used for change detection. It should be noted that the SSA method used at the first stage of the algorithm itself is quite effective as a non-parametric method of change detection. As it shown in [16], significant differences between the components obtained by the analysis of the parts of the initial time series show possible qualitative changes in dynamics. In [17], a fairly detailed overview of the papers that are devoted to this issue is given. Paper studies the matters of methods for detecting changes in cyclic components, determining noise, and so on.

SSA application for a change detection can be used in the future to develop rules for detecting changes in time series trends in automatic mode. This will increase the analytical value of the algorithm. It will also provide an opportunity to track changes in components more effectively. It can be used for forecasting and planning purposes, allowing creating more accurate models of the process dynamics in economics.

Further development of the created algorithm may be associated with the identification of relationship in complex economic systems. A similar approach was proposed in [18] and proved to be quite effective in identifying relationship in complex mechanical systems. Thus, it seems possible to use the developed algorithm in the complex economic models creation. In particular, this will allow us to take a fresh look at the diagnosis of cause-and-effect relationships, the prediction of catastrophic changes in the economy, and so on.

An important way of the algorithm improvement is the development of the fuzzy rule base for choosing the best component model. The rules currently applied are imperfect and sometimes require the involvement of an expert to select the most reasonable model.

5 Conclusion

In this paper authors investigate the problem of modeling, forecasting and comparative analysis of the revenue from new (innovative) products and services dynamics in the regions of the Russian Federation. The possibilities of applying the dynamics modeling algorithm developed by the authors is examined. The developed algorithm consists of a preliminary analysis by the SSA method, component modeling and selection of the best models based on fuzzy rules. It has proven to be more effective compared to the tools commonly used in this field. The mathematical model obtained on the basis of the algorithm allows to interpolate and to extrapolate with high accuracy. Moreover, this model allows us to draw economically valid conclusions about the reasons that cause certain features of the innovation processes dynamics in different regions. This allows us to conclude that the created algorithm can be also used to solve other problems in close areas.

The models that were constructed show us that the gap between the values of the revenue from new (innovative) products and services in the Volgograd region and in the most innovative regions of the Russian Federation has increased in recent years. Moreover, it was shown that the dynamics of innovation activity in the Volgograd region is less stable; and the innovation activity itself may have problems with providing fixed assets.

On the other hand, the most innovative regions have similar dynamics of the revenue from new (innovative) products and services (with the exception of anomaly high values of this indicator in Moscow in 2012–2016).This may indicate a high integration of innovative systems of these regions, as well as the fact that the functioning of these systems is more stable and, possibly, more efficient. This should be taken into account when making management decisions at the regional level.

In general, the proposed algorithm seems to be a fairly good alternative to traditional statistical methods of dynamics analysis and data mining methods when studying the dynamics of processes with a frequently changing trend, the presence of anomaly and small data.

References

1. Nguyen, T.V., Kravets, A.: A novel method for predicting technology trends based on processing multiple data sources. Adv. Syst. Sci. Appl. **23**(1), 69–90 (2023). https://doi.org/10.25728/assa.2023.23.01.1251
2. Viet, N.T., Kravets, A., Duong Quoc Hoang, T.: Data mining methods for analysis and forecast of an emerging technology trend: a systematic mapping study from Scopus papers. In: Kovalev, S.M., Kuznetsov, S.O., Panov, A.I. (eds.) RCAI 2021. LNCS (LNAI), vol. 12948, pp. 81–101. Springer, Cham (2021). https://doi.org/10.1007/978-3-030-86855-0_7

3. Alexandrov, P.I.: Development of software for automatic allocation and prediction of additive components of time series in the framework of the Caterpillar-SSA./ Alexandrov, P.I. – Candidate of Physical Mathematics Sciences: 05.13.18. Ph.D. Thesis, St. Petersburg University, St. Petersburg, Russia, p. 152 (2006). (in Russian)
4. Vyalkova, S.A., Kornykova, O., Nadtoka, I.: Development of mathematical models for the short-term forecasting of daily consumption schedules of active power by Moscow. Ion: 5th International Scientific and Technical Conference on Mechanical Science and Technology Update, MSTU Omsk, 2021. J. Phys. Conf. Ser. 2021, 1901, 012082. [Electronic resource] (2021). Accessed 19 July 2023. https://iopscience.iop.org/article/10.1088/1742-6596/1901/1/012082/pdf
5. Xu, C., Zhang, A., Xu, C., Chen, Y.: Traffic speed prediction: Spatiotemporal convolution network based on long-term, short-term and spatial features. Appl. Intell. **52**(2), 2224–2242 (2022). https://doi.org/10.1007/s10489-021-02461-9
6. Stratigakos, A., Bachoumis, A., Vita, V., Zafiropoulos, E.: Short-term net load forecasting with singular spectrum analysis and LSTM neural networks. Energies **14**, 4107 (2021). https://doi.org/10.3390/en14144107
7. Nasir, N., Samsudin, R., Shabri, A.: Pre-processing Streamflow data through singular spectrum analysis with fuzzy c-means clustering. In: Proceedings of the 2nd Joint Conference on Green Engineering Technology and Applied Computing 2020, Bangkok, Thailand, 4–5 February 2020, vol. 864 (2020). Accessed 17 July 2023. https://iopscience.iop.org/article/10.1088/1757-899X/864/1/012085/pdf
8. Rogachev, A.F., Simonov, A.B., Ketko, N.V., Skiter, N.N.: Fuzzy algorithmic modeling of economics and innovation process dynamics based on preliminary component allocation by singular spectrum analysis method. Algorithms. **16**(1), 39 (2023). https://doi.org/10.3390/a16010039. https://www.mdpi.com/1999-4893/16/1/39. Accessed 19 July 2023.
9. Hassani, H., Mahmoudvand, R., Zokaei, M.: Separability and window length in singular spectrum analysis. Comptes Rendus Math. **349**, 987–990 (2011). https://doi.org/10.1016/j.crma.2011.07.012
10. Golyandina, N., Nekrutkin, V., Zhigljavsky, A.: Analysis of Time Series Structure: SSA and Related Techniques, p. 320. Chapman & Hall/CRC, London (2001)
11. Hassani, H., Mahmoudvand, R., Zokaei, M., Ghodsi, M.: On the separability between signal and noise in singular spectrum analysis. Fluctuation Noise Lett. **11**(02), 1250014 (2012). https://doi.org/10.1142/S0219477512500149. https://www.researchgate.net/publication/270725189_On_the_separability_between_signal_and_noise_in_singular_spectrum_analysis. Accessed 19 July 2023
12. de Carvalho, M., Rua, A.: Real-time nowcasting the US output gap: Singular spectrum analysis at work. Int. J. Forecasting, **33**, 185–198 (2017). https://www.researchgate.net/publication/292950827_Real-time_nowcasting_the_US_output_gap_Singular_spectrum_analysis_at_work. Accessed 17 July 2023
13. Vokhmyanin, S.V.: Testing the algorithm of the method «caterpillar-ssa» for reestablishing of time series (Ispytaniye algoritma metoda "Gusenitsa-SSA" dlya vosstanovleniya vremennogo ryada). Vestn. SibGAU, №2, pp. 59–62 (2010). www.elibrary.ru/download/elibrary_16347880_55371835.pdf. Accessed 17 Jul 2023
14. Krayushkin, E.S., Shcherbakov, M.V., Kazakov, I.D., Kolesnikova, V.O.: Detection of anomalies in multidimensional time series using an R package. Model. Optim. Inf. Technol. 9, № 3(34), 10 p – (2021). https://doi.org/10.26102/2310-6018/2021.34.3.001. https://moitvivt.ru/ru/journal/pdf?id=948. Accessed 17 July 2023. (in Russian)
15. Federal State Statistics Service. [Electronic resource]: Official Site. - Access mode: https://rosstat.gov.ru/. Accessed 17 Jul 2023

16. Moskvina, V., Zhigljavsky, A.: An algorithm based on singular spectrum analysis for change-point detection. Commun. Stat. Simul. Comput. **32**(2), 319–352 (2003). https://doi.org/10.1081/SAC-120017494

17. Mohammad, Y., Nishida, T.: On comparing SSA-based change point discovery algorithms. In: IEEE/SICE International Symposium on System Integration (SII), Kyoto, Japan, pp. 938–945 (2011). https://doi.org/10.1109/SII.2011.6147575

18. Mohammad, Y., Nishidam, T.: Discovering causal change relationships between processes in complex systems. In: 2011 IEEE/SICE International Symposium on System Integration (SII), Kyoto, Japan, pp. 12–17 (2011). https://doi.org/10.1109/SII.2011.6147411

Cyber-Physical Systems and Big Data-Driven World. Industrial Creativity (CASE/CAI/CAD/PDM)

Methods and Technologies for Improving the Efficiency of Multi-assortment Production Optimal Planning

Tamara B. Chistyakova$^{(\boxtimes)}$ (iD), Olga E. Shashikhina, Ivan G. Kornienko, and Aleksandr A. Plekhanov

St. Petersburg State Technological Institute (Technical University), Saint Petersburg, Russia
nov@technolog.edu.ru

Abstract. The article describes the development of methods and technologies of production planning as part of a scheduling for large-capacity multi-assortment production. The article presents a systematic analysis of this class of production characteristics and also proposes a formalized generalized statement of the mathematical problem of a production planning. The proposed methods and technologies can significantly reduce the production planning time for large-scale production planning tasks, as well as speed up the possibility of its rapid adjustment. The proposed software package allows reducing the time of production and simplify the process of making managerial decisions in the implementation of production planning.

Keywords: production planning · software package · optimization task · genetic algorithm

1 Introduction

The most important task in the planning of any production is the formation of the optimal sequence for placing and fulfilling orders on equipment.

This article is devoted to the development of a flexible and customizable problem-oriented software package for solving the problem of production planning using various optimization methods.

The result of software use is an optimized production schedule and its visualization created with different development technologies.

The computer system described in this article makes it possible to effectively solve the problem of scheduling in an acceptable time of computer calculations, allows, if necessary, to carry out operational rescheduling and can be used in making managerial decisions about the production schedule and equipment operation, taking into account all necessary features and limitations of each specific production.

A. G. Kravets et al. (Eds.): CIT&DS 2023, CCIS 1909, pp. 251–261, 2023.
https://doi.org/10.1007/978-3-031-44615-3_17

2 Class of Optimized Productions and their Characteristics

The planning problem is solved for continuous-discrete productions. Production equipment is reconfigured to manufacture various types of products, characterized by geometric characteristics, such as the thickness and width of the material, various raw material recipes, colors and requirements for consumer characteristics [1–3]. Examples of such industries are the production of polymer films and packaging, the production of paper, linoleum and rolled metal.

The class of considered continuous-discrete productions is characterized by three main properties:

1. The productions under consideration are multi-assortment, i.e. produce a wide range of products (up to 500 types of goods in various categories). To switch from fulfilling one order and manufacturing one type of product to another, many equipment reconfigurations are required. This entails the need for a special approach to planning and the use of models and methods that can take into account the specifics of this task.
2. Production can be carried out on a different number of production units of equipment: production lines, units, work centers (from 1 to 15) [4].
3. The production equipment is reconfigurable, the production lines are characterized by multifunctionality and multivariate work on raw materials, products and productivity (average number of reconfiguration options: 5–20). Thanks to technological adjustment, it is possible to produce a different range of products on the same equipment.

The optimal solution of the problem depends on the sequence of orders execution, optimization of which allows reducing the time of reconfiguration from one order to another and which directly affects the total time and the cost of production.

The number of schedule options (number of options for distributing N orders on M production lines) is found based on the distribution formula:

$$C_{N+M-1}^{N} = \frac{(N+M-1)!}{N!(M-1)!}.$$

The number of possible sequences of orders on each production line is N!. The total number of possible variants of distribution and fulfillment of orders can be calculated using formula:

$$C_{var} = \frac{(N+M-1)!}{N!(M-1)!} * N! = \frac{(N+M-1)!}{(M-1)!}.$$

Since the number of possible production plans increases exponentially with an increase of the orders number, this scheduling problem belongs to the class of NP problems of large dimensions, which requires taking into account a multiple range of products and a variety of configurations of various production lines when solving it, optimization of the production scheduling process requires significant computational costs and the use of modern methods for finding optimal values [5–9].

3 Description of the Optimal Planning Process for the Considered Class of Productions

3.1 Formation of Objective Functions of the Optimization Problem

The most commonly used optimization criterion for a similar class of problems is the total production time [10].

Therefore, when solving the optimization problem, the main objective function is the total time for fulfilling orders and setting up equipment (production line, unit, work center) to perform the required types of products for each j-th piece of equipment.

$$F_j(Q) = \sum_{k=1}^{L_j-1} \omega^{Ch}{}_{O_{j,k},O_{j,k+1}} * \tau^{ch}(O_{j,k}, O_{j,k+1}) + \sum_{k=1}^{L_j} \omega^O{}_k * \tau^O{}_{j,k},$$

where $j - s$ the number of the line on which orders are executed; $k = \overline{1, L_j}$, sequence number of the i-th order on the j-th line; $L_j -$ is the number of orders executed on the j-th line, $L_j \subset N$; $\tau^{ch}(O_{j,k}, O_{j,k+1}) -$ is the equipment setup time from the execution of order k to the next order number $k + 1$, $\tau^O{}_k$ is the execution time of the k-th order, $\omega^{Ch}{}_{O_{j,k},O_{j,k+1}} -$ weight coefficient that determines the priority setting from the production of the k-th order to the next order $k + 1$, $\omega^O{}_k -$ is a weight coefficient that determines the priority of manufacturing the k-th order, $R^{|Q|} -$ is the search space, $D -$ is the set of admissible values of the vector Q.

Expert information is the basis for the formation of a base of equipment reconfiguration rules. Equipment settings rules are presented as a production model.

Equipment setup time $\tau^{ch}(O_{j,k}, O_{j,k+1})$ is calculated on the basis of formalized expert information and technological regulations for equipment operation.

Order manufacturing time $\tau^O{}_{j,k}$ is based on the given quantity of products and equipment productivity:

$$\tau^O_{j,k} = \frac{Q^m{}_k}{V_j(O_k)},$$

where $Q^m{}_j -$ is the quantity of material in the i-th order; $V_j(O_k) -$ is the performance of the j-th line (unit, work center) when performing the k-th order.

The algorithm for solving the optimization problem also provides the formation of an objective function if there is information about the cost indicators of production. Then the optimization criterion will be the minimum cost of fulfilling the production plan:

$$F^P{}_j(Q) = \sum_{k=1}^{L_j-1} \omega^P{}_{O_{j,k},O_{j,k+1}} * \tau^{ch}(O_{j,k}, O_{j,k+1}) + \sum_{k=1}^{L_j} \omega^P{}_k * \tau^O{}_{j,k},$$

where $\omega^P{}_{O_{j,k},O_{j,k+1}} -$ is the cost of reconfiguring equipment from order k to the next order number $k + 1$, $\omega^P{}_k -$ is the cost of equipment operation when the plan is fulfilled.

3.2   General Statement of the Production Optimization Mathematical Problem

It is required to find such a value of the vector of variable parameters $Q^{opt} = \{Q_i: Q = (j, k, \tau oi, \tau i)\, j = \overline{1, Me},\, k = \overline{1, L_j},\, L_j \subset N,\, i = \overline{1, N}\}$, i.e. placement and order of execution of N orders on Me production lines (aggregates, work centers), in the search space for feasible solutions and within the planning period [$\tau b, \tau e$], which will provide the optimal value of objective functions.

In the case of solving the problem for one production line (unit, work center), minimization of the total time for fulfilling orders and setting up equipment is:

$$F_j\left(Q^{opt}\right) = \min_{Q \in D \subset R^{|Q|}} \left(\sum_{k=1}^{L_j-1} \omega^{Ch}{}_{O_{j,k},O_{j,k+1}} * \tau^{ch}\left(O_{j,k}, O_{j,k+1}\right) + \sum_{k=1}^{L_j} \omega^O{}_k * \tau^O{}_{j,k} \right),$$

To ensure a minimum production cycle for manufacturing orders on several production lines (aggregates, work centers) the time for manufacturing orders on the production line (unit, work center) for which it is maximum is minimized:

$$F_C\left(Q^{opt}\right) = \min_{Q \in D \subset R^{|Q|}} \max_{j=\overline{1,Me}} \left(F_j(Q)\right),$$

where $\tau^{ch}(O_{j,k}, O_{j,k+1})$ – is the equipment setup time from the execution of order k to the next order number k + 1, $\tau^O{}_k$ – is the execution time of the k-th order,, ω_k – is the weight coefficient of the k-th order, $k = \overline{1, L_j}$, he sequence number of the i-th order on the j-th line in the current schedule Q; j – is the number of the line on which orders are executed;; L_j – is the number of orders executed on the j-th line in schedule Q, $R^{|Q|}$ – is the search space, D – is the set of admissible values of the vector Q.

The solution to the optimization problem is such a vector of distribution of orders on production lines (aggregates, work centers) within the planning interval $Q^{opt} = \{Q_i: Q = (j, k, \tau oi, \tau i)\, j = \overline{1, Me},\, k = \overline{1, L_j},\, L_j \subset N,\, i = \overline{1, N}\}$, for which the objective function value for each production line (unit, work center) $F_j\left(Q^{opt}\right)$ and the total production cycle time $F_C\left(Q^{opt}\right)$ will be optimal.

Each order must be executed within the specified planning interval $\tau^b{}_i \leq \tau_i \leq \tau^e{}_i$, τ_i – is the execution time of the i-th order;

Figure 1 provides an informative description of the production planning process.

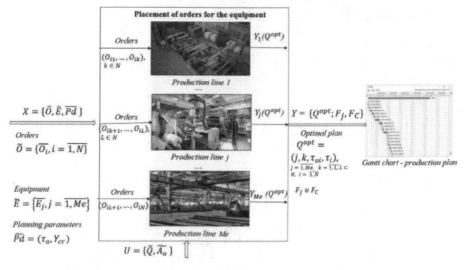

Fig. 1. Informative description of the production planning process.

3.3 Methods for Solving the Stated Optimization Problem

While solving the problem of optimal production planning with an increase in the number of orders, pieces of equipment and the number of its possible reconfigurations, the number of plan options (the range of acceptable values) grows exponentially. Therefore, to solve problems of different dimensions various methods are used in the software package. These methods are able to efficiently find a plan that provides the optimal value of the objective functions.

Methods for solving discrete optimization and scheduling problems can be divided into three groups: exact methods, heuristic and metaheuristic. Exact optimization methods make it possible to find the extremum of the objective function for sure, however the use of these methods for solving problems of large dimensions can take a long computer time, which will be unacceptable in real industrial production. In the software package it was decided to develop a software implementation of the exhaustive search method which allows finding the optimal solution for planning problems of small dimension.

The choice of the optimal planning method is based on the number of options. If the admissible dimension of the problem is exceeded, the planning problem is solved not by the exhaustive enumeration method, but by a more complex optimization method.

Heuristic and metaheuristic algorithms make it possible to find solutions that are close to optimal with acceptable computational complexity, and the use of such methods can significantly reduce the computer search time. However, they do not guarantee reaching the global extremum [11–14].

The genetic evolutionary optimization algorithm has a number of advantages that determined its use in the software package. Therefore, the formation of schedules for problems of larger dimensions in the software package implements a problem-oriented genetic algorithm.

To apply the genetic algorithm in the software package, a software module has been developed that converts the input parameters of the optimal planning problem into algorithm elements: gene, chromosome, single-point mutation operator, single-point crossover operator, fitness function, selection. When comparing two schedules, the values of the fitness function are compared (depending on the optimization criterion) and the components of the objective function are calculated - the time of order production and equipment reconfiguration times. After fulfilling the conditions of the breakpoint the algorithm ends its work and the user gets the resulting production plan with the best value of the fitness function in the last population.

3.4 Software Package Development

Since a large amount of internal production data is used to solve the problem of production planning, the software package is implemented as a desktop application, which also meets the functional requirements of the production management personnel of enterprises whose industrial data was used to test the software package.

The process of optimal production planning using the software package consists of several main stages:

1. Formalized description of the planning object with the formation of the type of objective function.
2. A system analysis. It is carried out for each specific production in order to determine the main characteristics of production orders and equipment for further formalization of the information received and its inclusion in the mathematical model of the planning problem to form the type of objective functions and to effectively develop a database.
3. Development of information support for the software package: a supplemented and updated database with information about the range of products, characteristics of production lines and orders.
4. Expert setup of the system: formation of a base of rules for reconfiguring equipment and knowledge base about the compliance and the possibility of manufacturing different assortment products on production equipment. Expert settings are carried out using forms that allow taking into account the specifics of technological and production processes when solving an optimization problem.
5. Solving the scheduling problem. For this, mathematical models, algorithms and software implementations of optimization methods for problems of different dimensions are developed.
6. Visualization of planning results. The result of the work is a production schedule that meets the technological requirements and deadlines, visualized in the form of a Gantt chart. At the end of the process of searching for a solution, the user is also offered a decision tree of the optimization problem with the possibility of demonstrating the progress of the solution.

The development of the software package was carried out using the object-oriented programming language C# in the Microsoft Visual Studio on the APS.NET 2.0 platform. The database was developed using the SQLite relational database management system.

Interaction with users in the software package is supported by ergonomic graphical interfaces: interface of the production director; database administrator interface; knowledge engineer interface.

The open architecture of the system provides possibilities for the expansion of the functionality of the software package by adjusting to a new type of production and its characteristics and also allows the inclusion of new optimization methods in the system and the addition of additional software modules [15].

Figure 2 shows an example of a Gantt chart obtained using the software package.

The numbers to the left of the chart are the numbers of production orders, the dates are indicated below the graph. The bar opposite the order number reflects the time of its execution, and the distance between the beginnings of the order bars within one production line reflects the time of reconfiguring the production line.

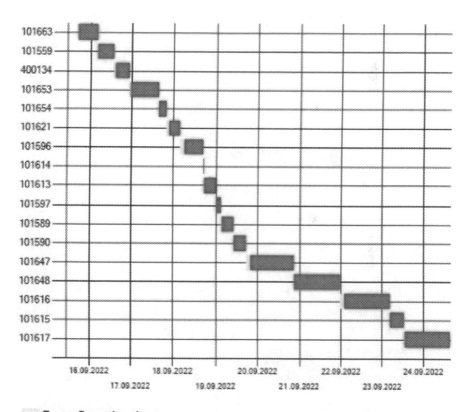

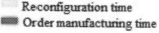
Reconfiguration time
Order manufacturing time

Fig. 2. Example of a Gantt chart obtained using the software package

4   Software Testing Results

Testing of the software package was carried out on the set of real industrial data of modern continuous-discrete production of polymer films in Russia and Germany (Klöckner Pentaplast Rus and Maria Soell Films).

Here is an example of one of the test cases. The schedule of the manufacturer of multilayer polymer films used for testing the software package included 58 orders manufactured on an extrusion production line, planning was carried out for 45 days. The number of different combinations of product parameters was more than 300, the number of rules for setting up equipment for the manufacture of orders of different assortments was more than 100.

For the effective use of the software package, an information description of the planning object was made.

Figure 3 shows mind maps of knowledge about the characteristics of polymer production.

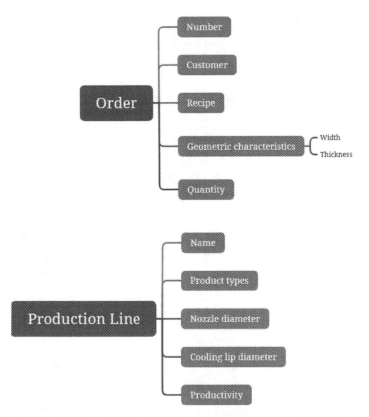

Fig. 3. Mind maps of knowledge about the characteristics of polymer production

The changeover time from one type of product to another was calculated according to the changeover rules based on expert knowledge of changeovers of extrusion production lines in a polymer film manufacturing plant.

$\tau^{ch}(O_k, O_{k+1})$ – equipment reconfiguration time from the previous order to the current one:

$$\tau^{Ch} = T^{Th}_{j,k} + T^{Wd}_{j,k} + T^{Rf}_{j,k}\left(F_{f_{k-1}}, F_{tk}\right) + T^{Nz}_{j,k}(Nz_k) + T^{Cb}_{j,k}(Cb_k) + T^{Cl}_{j,k}(Cl_k),$$

where $T^{Th}_{j,k}$ – is the time for readjustment along the thickness of the material; $T^{Wd}_{j,k}$ – is the time to reconfigure in width; $T^{Rf}_{j,k}\left(F_{f_{k-1}}, F_{tk}\right)$ – changeover time according to the film recipe; $T^{Nz}_{j,k}(Nz_k)$ – nozzle diameter retuning time; $T^{Cb}_{j,k}(Cb_k)$ – is the time for reconfiguring the diameter of the calibrating (forming) gap of the co-extrusion head; $T^{Cl}_{j,k}(Cl_k)$ – cooling ring diameter reset time.

To test the functionality of the software package real production data and schedules generated in production were used. For the same batch of orders and planning period, the production schedule was calculated using the software package. The plans were compared with each other in terms of improvement/deterioration in the value of the objective function, and a decision was made on the advisability of introducing the software package.

The test results are presented in table 1.

Table 1. Results of testing on the data of the production of polymer films

	Company Plan	Software package plan
Total production time	69610 min (44 days 14 h 33 min)	65725 min (42 days 01 h 33 min)
Order processing time	63175 min (40 days 02 h 48 min)	63175 min (40 days 02 h 48 min)
Changeover time	6435 min (4 days 11 h 45 min)	2505 min (1 day 22 h 45 min)

As far as we can see from Table 1 the described planning methods and technologies a sequence close to optimal was found and the total manufacturing time was reduced by 6% [16].

Testing showed the effectiveness and expediency of using a software package to automate the process of solving the problem of forming an optimal production plan. The implementation of the developed models, methods and software package in real production can improve the economic efficiency of the planning process, increase productivity and equipment utilization, improve sticking to deadlines and also simplify the process of managerial decision-making in various situations of production planning.

5 Conclusions

This article described the development of scheduling methods and technologies for planning and scheduling various large-capacity multi-assortment industries. The core of the software package is a library of optimization methods that allow to effectively solve planning problems of various dimensions. The setting subsystem of software package is based on the formalization of expert information about the planning object, its features and characteristics and allows expanding the variability of using the software complex in various industries.

The systematic approach to the development and adjustment of software package has been successfully tested on the data of various modern high-tech industrial productions. The use of the proposed software package makes it possible to obtain a production plan that reduces the time and cost of production. At the same time labor intensity and production time are reduced. As a result the planning efficiency significantly increases the productivity and competitiveness of the enterprise.

References

1. Parente, M., Figueira, G., Amorim, P., Marques, A.: Production scheduling in the context of industry 4.0: review and trends. Int. J. Prod. Res. **58**(17), 5401–5431 (2020)
2. Baldea, M., Harjunkoski, I.: Integrated production scheduling and process control: a systematic review. Comput. Chem. Eng. **71**, 377–390 (2014)
3. Diaz, J.L., Ocampo-Martinez, C.: Optimal production planning for flexible manufacturing systems an energy-based. IFAC PapersOnLine **53**(2), 10461–10467 (2020)
4. Shashikhina, O.E., Chistyakova, T.B., Kohlert, C.: Software package and mathematical models for optimal planning of multi-assortment polymer films industrial production. In: 2nd International Conference on Control Systems, Mathematical Modelling, Automation and Energy Efficiency, SUMMA 2020, pp. 561–565 (2020)
5. Georgiadis, G.P., Elekidis, A.P., Georgiadis, M.C. Optimal production planning and scheduling in breweries. Food Bioproducts Process. **51** (2020)
6. Sadok, T., Zied, H., Nidhal, R. Optimal production planning for a manufacturing system: an approach based on PA. In: 7th IFAC Conference on Manufacturing Modelling, Management and Control, pp. 513–518 (2013)
7. Sarker, B.R., Diponegoro, A.: Optimal production plans and shipment schedules in a supply-chain system with multiple suppliers and multiple buyers. Eur. J. Oper. Res. **194**, 753–773 (2009)
8. Vankova, L., Krejza, Z., Kocourkova, G., Laciga, J.: Geoinformation system usage options in facility. Procedia Comput. Sci. **196**, 708–716 (2022)
9. Barba, I., Valle, C.D.: A job-shop scheduling model of software development planning for constraint-based local search. Int. J. Softw. Eng. Appl. **4**(4), 1–16 (2010)
10. Ribas, I., Companys, R., Tort-Martorell, X.: The flowshop scheduling problem with blocking. Manage. Sci. **39**(3), 293–301 (2011)
11. Khormali, A., Mirzazadeh, A.: Faez F The openshop batch processing problem with non-identical processing times, using simulated annealing and genetic algorithms approaches. Int. J. Adv. Manuf. Technol. **59**(9–12), 1157–1165 (2012)
12. Oddi, A., Rasconi, R., Cesta, A., Smith, S.F.: Iterative improvement algorithms for the blocking job shop. In: Twenty-Second International Conference on Automated Planning and Scheduling (2012)

13. Essafi, I., Mati, Y., Dauzère-Pérès, S.: A genetic local search algorithm for minimizing total weighted tardiness in the job-shop scheduling problem. Comput. Oper. Res. **35**(8), 2599–2616 (2008)
14. Tasic, T., Buchmeister, B., Acko, B.: The development of advanced methods for scheduling production processes. J. Mech. Eng. **53**(12), 844–857 (2007)
15. Chistyakova, T.B., Razygrayev, A.S., Makaruk, R.V., Kohlert, C.: Decision support system for optimal production planning polymeric materials using genetic algorithms. In: Proceedings of the 19th International Conference on Soft Computing and Measurements, pp. 257–259 (2016) https://doi.org/10.1109/SCM.2016.7519746
16. Chistyakova, T.B., Shashikhinam O.E., Kornienkom I.G., Plekhanov, A.A.: Optimal planning software package for use in the control system of flexible extrusion production of polymer materials. In: IEEE IV International Conference on Control in Technical Systems, pp. 188–191 (2021)

Intelligent Technologies for Designing Digital Information Models of Chemical and Technological Objects

Tamara B. Chistyakova$^{(\boxtimes)}$, Dmitry N. Furaev , and Inna V. Novozhilova

St. Petersburg State Institute of Technology, St. Peterburg, Russia
{nov,novozhilova}@technolog.edu.ru, d.furaev@pmpspb.ru

Abstract. The intellectual technologies of computer expert systems are presented, which allow designing various chemical and technological facilities, including with the help of digital information models. The information support of these systems is described, including updated and supplemented knowledge bases developed on the basis of intelligence maps that allow graphically structuring information about the main characteristics of a production facility. Examples of the functional structure of intelligent systems for the processes of secondary oil refining and processing of industrial waste are given, increasing the efficiency of design and planning.

Keywords: digital information model · intelligent system · design · intelligence maps · expert knowledge

1 Introduction

In the process of development, an industrial facility goes through several successive stages of its life cycle: design, construction, operation, modernization (reconstruction), demolition and disposal.

The main catalytic processes of secondary oil refining include: reforming, cracking, hydrocracking, hydrotreating, isomerization, which account for about 80% of the world volume of catalysts. All these processes are large-tonnage, the total global capacity of these processes is more than 3,500 million. m^3/year, the difficulty of designing and controlling these processes is due to complex chemical reactions and numerous technological connections, expensive catalysts whose activity decreases during operation, a variety of industrial equipment and its layout options.

Design and construction are always associated with a large volume of various information: characteristics of an industrial facility, data on technological equipment, composition and parameters of technological pipelines, building structures, design and operational documentation (specifications of equipment, products and materials, isometric and installation drawings, estimates, passports for equipment and pipelines, all kinds of accounting documentation, plans and calendar schedules).

A. G. Kravets et al. (Eds.): CIT&DS 2023, CCIS 1909, pp. 262–273, 2023.
https://doi.org/10.1007/978-3-031-44615-3_18

And now there is a tendency to collect and store all information on an industrial facility at its various stages of its life cycle in a single information environment, in particular, a digital information model that would represent a single data source for all project participants [1, 2]. Intelligent technologies of information modeling of complex industrial facilities are being actively introduced and developed in order to improve the design efficiency [3]. Currently, a fairly large number of various computer-aided design systems are presented, but issues related to their information, mathematical and software are still relevant.

2   A Set of Intelligent Computer System Tools

Any intelligent computer system consists of a set of tools - the totality of all components of an automated system: information, mathematical, software, linguistic, technical, methodological support, presented in Fig. 1.

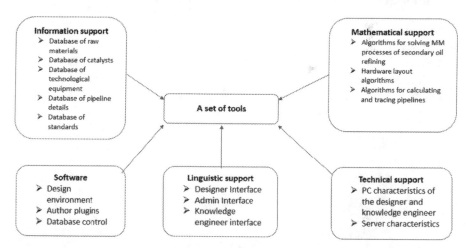

Fig. 1. Complex of intelligent computer system tools

The information support of the computer system consists of a database of technological equipment, pipeline parts and fittings, a database of characteristics of raw materials and catalysts from various manufacturers, regulatory documents and design rules.

The mathematical support includes mathematical models of technological processes of secondary oil refining (catalytic cracking, hydrocracking, catalytic reforming, isomerization), mathematical models for evaluating product quality, productivity, various algorithms of the software package: an algorithm for the layout of technological equipment, an algorithm for the formation of a design solution for automation systems.

The system software is integrated and includes various application software environments that implement various design stages – selection and layout of technological equipment, piping, as well as implementing the formation of a design solution that includes a digital information model and project documentation. The choice of software environments is influenced by the ability to correctly solve problems for this class of objects and the possibility of expanding the basic functionality.

Linguistic support is a set of tools and rules for creating a design language used when communicating a design specialist with a computer-aided design system, which allows you to set the elements of the system and obtain a design solution. In this case, this is the designer's interface, which allows him to set a design task and analyze the design solution at different stages of design: at the stage of technological design – compliance with the rules of layout and placement of equipment, verification calculation, at the stage of pipeline tracing – the ability to select from the database of pipeline parts, verification calculation of pipeline characteristics, the interface of an expert or engineer by knowledge, which allows you to form design rules for various stages of design.

Technical support represents the minimum characteristics of a computer for a design engineer and a knowledge engineer, as well as the server part.

3   Information Support and Knowledge Bases

The basis of any expert system, computer-aided design system is information support consisting of databases or knowledge bases of the subject area.

To visually reflect the hierarchical relationships between various characteristics of production, equipment, intelligence maps were developed as a form of representation of knowledge about the object. Figure 2 shows a fragment of the "Waste" intelligence map with an indication of the main classification features.

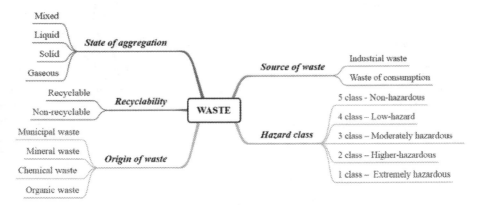

Fig. 2. Intelligence map of waste

Figure 3 shows a fragment of the intelligence map "Technological pipelines" with an indication of the main characteristics [4–6].

The information and reference system for industrial waste processing processes includes a relational database of technological regulations for the production of useful technical products. Table 1 describes the structure of the database of the information and reference system.

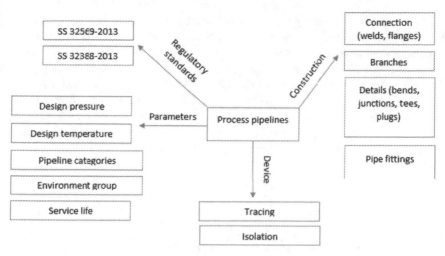

Fig. 3. Intelligence map of technological pipelines

Table 1. Description of the system database structure

Table name	Description
FkkWastes	Waste classification
Feed-stocks	List of raw materials
Products	List of useful technical products
Recycling Methods	Processing methods
Stages	Stages of processing
Equipments	Equipment
Parameters	Quality indicators of technical products
S_Object	Raw materials, products, processing stage
S_Aggregation	Aggregate state of waste
S_Education	Types of waste origin
S_Source	Sources of waste generation
S_Class	Waste hazard classes
FeedstocksMethods	Information about the relationship of raw materials with processing methods
ProductsMethods	Information about the relationship between the processing method and useful products
StagesEquipments	Information and connections of processing stages and equipment
ParametersObject	Values of quality parameters indicating the type of object

The information support of the system is adjusted to various characteristics of industrial waste recycling processes by changing the ranges of the corresponding parameters. This makes it possible to adapt the system for various industries, including recycling.

The information support of a computer system for designing oil recycling processes using a digital information model includes databases of typical technological equipment, pipeline parts and fittings, databases of raw material characteristics of various suppliers, regulatory documents for the design and operation of oil recycling facilities, existing technological design solutions. The Microsoft SQL Server database control system was used to develop information support for both of these systems (Fig. 4).

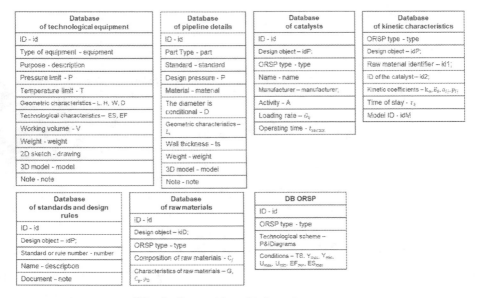

Fig. 4. Composition of information support

The database of technological equipment is one of the main ones and contains more than 500 pieces of equipment of the following types:

1. heat exchange equipment: heat exchangers, riboilers, evaporators, condensers;
2. capacitive equipment: horizontal and vertical tanks;
3. column equipment: distillation, vacuum, atmospheric, packing columns, absorbers, adsorbers, stabilizers, evaporators;
4. reactor equipment: cracking, reforming, hydrotreating, hydrocracking, isomerization reactors;
5. regenerators: tubular vertical and horizontal regenerators, block-sectional regenerators;
6. pumping equipment: horizontal and vertical centrifugal pumps, axial and diagonal pumps, electric pumps;
7. tubular furnaces, air cooling devices, dust collectors, receivers, separators. Examples of 3D models of technological equipment in the design environment are shown in Fig. 5.

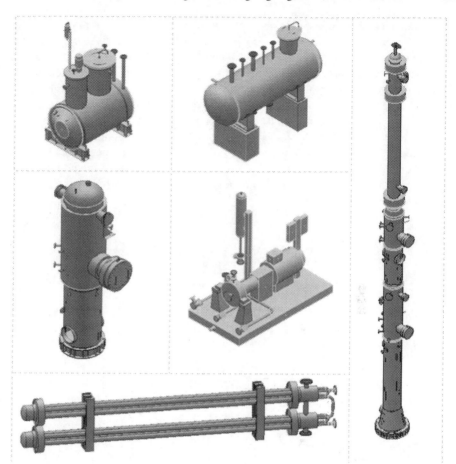

Fig. 5. Examples of three-dimensional models of equipment

In general, digital information models are a set of information-rich elements, the presence of which in the form of ready-made library components significantly upsets its development. It would be great to implement a unified information support for all CAD systems used in the design of complex industrial facilities. Manufacturers of technological equipment, fittings and elements of engineering systems could be interested in filling the existing information support, which would significantly accelerate the design stage.

4   Intelligent Design Algorithms

The mathematical support of software complexes consists of models for carrying out verification calculations and algorithms for the operation of individual modules of a computer system. Thus, the basis of mathematical support is the basic mathematical model of oil recycling processes, which is characterized by input parameters, control actions and output parameters.

Artificial intelligence technologies are used in the development of rules for the formation of control actions depending on the regeneration of the catalyst, which are production models depending on a given type of catalyst, the composition of raw materials. The main control actions for the processes of secondary oil refining are the temperature and consumption of raw materials, the values of which vary over the operating time, in DIM-1 ranges of control actions and requirements for automatic control systems are formed for the entire period of operation of the catalyst before regeneration (accuracy of variable stabilization). In DIM-2, the final requirements for automatic control systems are formed, taking into account the location of pipelines (requirements for actuators). DIM-3 generates complete documentation for automation systems, including primary devices, control systems, actuators. Figure 6 shows the algorithm for forming a design solution for automation systems.

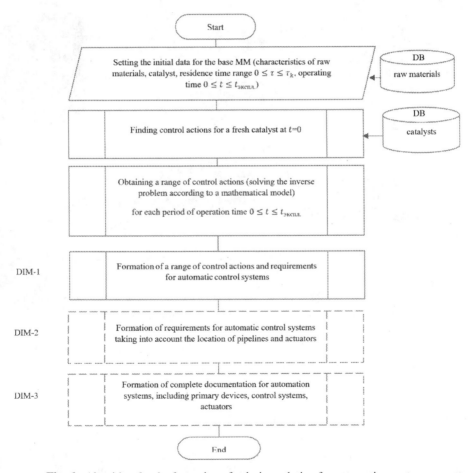

Fig. 6. Algorithm for the formation of a design solution for automation systems.

The main disturbing effect is a decrease in the activity of an expensive catalyst, which is compensated by a change in temperature and consumption of raw materials, therefore, the design solution includes program recommendations for changing the temperature and consumption of raw materials for the entire period of operation of the catalyst before regeneration.

Intelligent technologies are used not only at the stage of forming the terms of reference, but also at the final stage of design – during the formation of project documentation. Currently, the main product of project activity is project documentation [7], therefore, a method of automated formation of multilingual project documentation from a digital information model of the design object is proposed, using a production model of knowledge of the correspondence of design terms in various foreign languages and a knowledge representation model for the formation of documentation. The algorithm for the formation of multilingual project documentation from the digital information model of the design object is shown in Fig. 7.

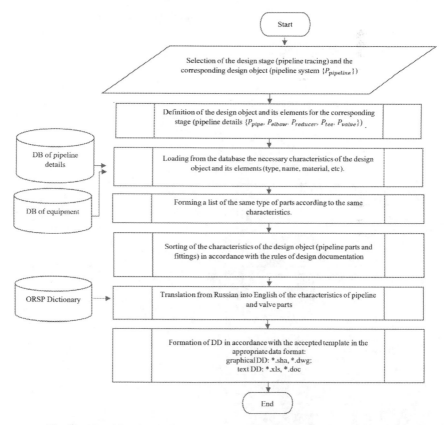

Fig. 7. Algorithm for the formation of multilingual project documentation.

From the digital information model, specifications of equipment, products and materials, a list of pipelines, as well as installation and isometric drawings are formed. The received documentation fully complies with the quality indicators regulated by international and Russian regulatory standards for the design and reconstruction of complex industrial facilities [8–12]. The project documentation obtained as a result of the use of the above algorithm has passed the state examination and has been used in the construction of design facilities.

5   Examples of Functional Structure

To solve the problem of forming a technological map of the processes of processing industrial waste into useful products, a functional structure of the information and reference system has been developed, shown in Fig. 8.

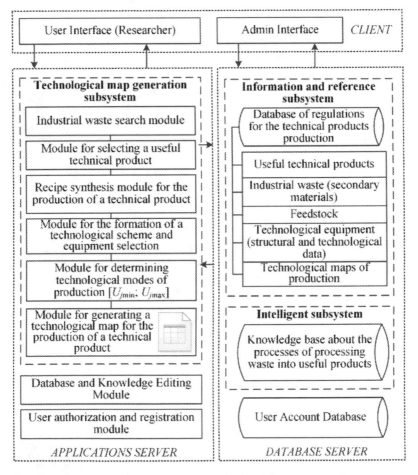

Fig. 8. Information and reference system of industrial waste processing processes

The system structure is based on a three-level client-server model. The client subsystem includes user interfaces (researcher and administrator), and the application server – the main modules of the system: a subsystem for searching for waste and analyzing its properties; a module for selecting a useful product for production based on the technology of processing the selected type of waste; a module for synthesizing recipes; a module for forming a technological scheme of production and equipment selection; a module for determining production modes; a module for formation of the technological map of production; the database and knowledge editing module, as well as the user authorization and registration module. The database server provides storage and control of information and reference and intelligent subsystems that make up the information model of a computer system [13, 14].

Based on the analysis of the stages of designing the processes of secondary oil refining, a functional structure of a computer system for designing the processes of secondary oil refining based on a digital information model, which is shown in Fig. 9, has been developed.

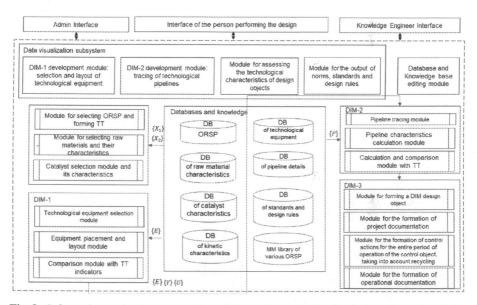

Fig. 9. Information and reference system of the environment for the design of an oil refining facility

The proposed structure includes: databases of raw material characteristics, characteristics of catalysts, process equipment, pipeline parts, norms and standards for design; a library of mathematical models of oil recycling processes (kinetics of chemical reactions, heat exchange processes, hydrodynamics), configurable for different periods of operation and activity of the catalyst, process equipment layout, pipeline tracing; engineer interfaces according to the knowledge of the designer, trainee, administrator; modules for developing a digital information model at various stages of design, specifying raw materials and their characteristics, selecting a catalyst and its characteristics, selecting technological equipment and its placement and layout, tracing pipelines and calculating its characteristics, deriving norms and standards for design, calculating and comparing indicators with the terms of reference, forming project documentation and operational regulations. The proposed structure is applicable for all types of oil recycling processes.

The modular principle of architecture construction allows you to build flexible and reconfigurable information and mathematical support.

6   Conclusion

Testing of the system of waste processing processes was carried out on the basis of the training center "Polymer Ecology" SPbSIT according to LLC "Komsomolskaya Pravda Plastics Processing Plant" on the example of the production of technical containers from recycled polymer raw materials. The use of the system makes it possible to increase the efficiency of the production of technical products from secondary raw materials (waste) by reducing the time spent on solving the problem of reconfiguring production to a new type of product, taking into account environmental requirements for production, as well as improving the characteristics of products.

The proposed computer system, which allows solving the problem of designing oil recycling facilities from the formation of a technical specification to the formation of a design solution – a digital information model with appropriate requirements for productivity, resource consumption, energy efficiency and subsequent release of design documentation, has been tested for catalytic cracking plants with a capacity of 2500 thousand tons/year and a power consumption of 23 thousand kW; isomerization of productivity 608 thousand tons/year and 44 thousand kW of power consumption, according to which the construction of these facilities was carried out, which confirmed the efficiency and operability of the presented system.

Acknowledgements. The study was carried out at the expense of a grant from the Russian Science Foundation (project No. 21-79-30029 Development of a complex of technologies for processing waste of hazard classes 3–5 with the production of useful products).

References

1. Dozortsev, V., Agafonov, D., Nazin, V., Novichkov, A., Frolov, A.: Computerized operator training: continued importance, new opportunities, and the human factor. Autom. Remote. Control. **81**, 935–954 (2020). https://doi.org/10.1134/S0005117920050124
2. Chistyakova, T.B., Reinig, G., Novozhilova, I.V.: Use of computer trainers for teaching management manufacturing. Personnel of chemical industries. Stud. Syst. Decis. Control **342**, 371–382 (2021)
3. Kureichik, V.M., Kureichik, V.V., Taratukhin, V.V., et al.: Continuous acquisition and life-cycle support (CALS) simulation models on the basis of the ERP and CAD technologies integration. In: Becker, J., Kozyrev, O., Babkin, E., Taratukhin, V., Aseeva, N. (eds.) Emerging Trends in Information Systems. Progress in IS, vol. 1, pp. 11–19. Springer, Cham (2016). https://doi.org/10.1007/978-3-319-23929-3_2

4. Chistyakova, T., Novozhilova, I., Kozlov, V., Shevchik, A.: Resource and energy saving control of the steelmaking converter process, taking account waste recycling. Energies **16**, 1302 (2023). https://doi.org/10.3390/en16031302

5. Meshalkin, V., et al.: State of the art and research development prospects of energy and resource-efficient environmentally safe chemical process systems engineering. Mendeleev Commun. **31**(5), 593–604 (2021). https://doi.org/10.1016/j.mencom.2021.09.00

6. Bosenko, V.N., Kravets, A.G., Kamaev, V.A.: Development of an automated system to improve the efficiency of the oil pipeline construction management. World Appl. Sci. J. **24**(24), 24–30 (2013)

7. Kapustin, V.M., Chernysheva, E.A.: Sovremennaia rossiiskaia neftepererabotka itogi i perspektivy. Energeticheskaia Polit. **1**, 46–53 (2019)

8. ISO/TS 12911:2012. Framework for building information modelling (BIM) guidance, Organization for Standardization. https://www.iso.org/standard/52155.html

9. ISO 6707-1:2020. Buildings and civil engineering works – Vocabulary – Part 1: General terms, Organization for Standardization. https://www.iso.org/standard/77077.html

10. ISO 15926-2:2003. Industrial automation systems and integration – Integration of life-cycle data for process plants including oil and gas production facilities – Part 2: Data model, Organization for Standardization. https://www.iso.org/standard/29557.html

11. Gradostroitel'nyj kodeks Rossijskoj Federacii. Redakciya [Urban Planning Code of the Russian Federation (2022)

12. SP 333.1325800.2020. Informacionnoe modelirovanie v stroitel'stve. Pravila formirovaniya informacionnoj modeli ob'ektov na razlichnyh stadiyah zhiznennogo cikla [Information modeling in construction. Rules for the formation of an information model of objects at various stages of the life cycle] (2020)

13. Chistyakova, T.B., Furaev, D.N.: Methods and technologies for designing digital information models of oil recycling processes. In: 2022 International Conference on Quality Management, Transport and Information Security, Information Technologies (IT&QM&IS), pp. 27–30 (2022). https://doi.org/10.1109/ITQMIS56172.2022.9976562

14. Chistyakova, T., Furaev, D.: Computer system for resource-saving design of industrial processes of secondary oil refining. In: Kravets, A.G., Bolshakov, A.A., Shcherbakov, M. (eds.) Cyber-Physical Systems: Modelling and Industrial Application. Studies in Systems, Decision and Control, vol. 418, pp. 15–24. Springer, Cham (2022). https://doi.org/10.1007/978-3-030-95120-7_2

Information Channel for Proactive Control of Machining Conditions: A Cyber-Physical System on the Basis of a CNC Machine

Julius Tchigirinsky[✉] [ID], Alexey Zhdanov[ID], Zhanna Tikhonova[ID],
Alexander Rogachev[ID], and Nataly Chigirinskaya[ID]

Volgograd State Technical University, Lenin av., 28, Volgograd 400005, Russia
julio-tchigirinsky@yandex.ru

Abstract. This paper presents findings of the research proving that the known method for automated assignment of rational cutting modes, in unmanned technology, to modern CNC lathe machines, which are essentially cyber-physical systems, can be applied to processing with the use of lubricating and cooling technological fluids. This requires both conducting a certain number of experiments and building appropriate regression mathematical models. These studies are aimed at teaching cyber-physical systems in mechanical engineering to make independent decisions in assigning machining modes based on preliminary or operational information on the thermo-physical properties of contact pairs "tool-work piece" and other measuring signals from the cutting zone without operator participation.

Keywords: Cutting Conditions · Technological Lubricants · Adaptive Systems

1 Introduction

In modern machining, the fleet of machine tools with program control is becoming wider, and a modern CNC lathe machine, which is, in fact, a full-fledged cyber-physical system, can perform a part processing cycle without operator intervention. The cyber-physical system is the more perfect, the more tasks it is able to solve without human manual. In metalworking, such systems should be able to work out emergency situations. For example, chipping of the cutting insert, increased wear of the insert, uneven allowance, uneven mechanical properties of the work piece surface, etc. – all this can affect the quality of processing. When working on versatile machines, the machine operator can adjust certain settings of the machine, relying on his experience, thus minimizing the error signals that he observes; i.e., a change in the type of chip, a change in sound and in vibration, etc. The assignment of rational processing modes and their adjustment in real time is one of the tasks that modern metal-cutting machines must be able to solve.

2 The Concept of an Intelligent Automated System for Assigning Rational Cutting Conditions to CNC Lathe Machines and its Area of Application

2.1 The Problem of Choosing Rational Machining Modes and Ensuring a Given Quality of the Surface of Steel Parts During Longitudinal Turning with Carbide Cutters on CNC Lathe Machines

The key problem in assigning machining modes is a wide range of recommended cutting speeds and calculated values of cutting forces, depending either on the selected source of literature (reference guide) or on the recommendations of the manufacturer of carbide inserts [1, 2]. Table 1 illustrates the comparison of the calculated values of cutting speed and cutting forces when calculating due to various engineering reference guides [3–7]. The calculation was carried out for the following conditions: steel 20, a cutter equipped with a T5K10 carbide insert with an entering angle $\varphi = 45^0$ at a feed rate of S = 0.33 mm/rev and at a cutting depth t = 2 mm.

Table 1. Comparison of the values of cutting speed and cutting forces during longitudinal turning when calculating due to various engineering reference guides

Reference guide	Cutting speed v, m/min		Cutting forces components, H					
			P_z		P_y		P_x	
	Наличие СОТС							
	–	+	–	+	–	+	–	+
[3]	375	N/D	635	N/D	205	N/D	231	N/D
[4]	220	N/D	1060	N/D	N/D	N/D	N/D	N/D
[5]	273	N/D	830	N/D	N/D	N/D	N/D	N/D
[6]	126	168	N/D	N/D	373	N/D	357	N/D
[7]	193	241	N/D	N/D	N/D	N/D	N/D	N/D
Range R	250	73	424	N/D	167	N/D	126	N/D
R/min, %	198%	44%	67%	N/D	81%	N/D	54%	N/D

According to Table 1, in some cases, the relative spread reaches 100 percent or more. Some guides [6, 7] don't provide instructions for determining the components of cutting forces. All of the guides have no information about the effect of the use of lubricating and cooling technological agents (LCTA) on cutting forces. The effect of lubricants and coolers on the cutting speed (tool life) is estimated only by introducing correction factors of 0.75–0.85.

There is a method [1, 2], which allows to reduce the error in the assignment of processing modes and technological restrictions to an acceptable value of ± 10% in relation to the experimentally measured parameters. The method is aimed at measuring the value of thermo EMF induced in the assembled electric circuit between the tool and the work piece and, on the basis of the derived regression mathematical models, at making the actual choice of cutting modes. In this case, the value of thermo EMF acts as an indicator, which reflects a set of properties for a particular contact pair "tool-work piece" - i.e., thermo-physical properties, cutting tool geometry, etc.

Today, this method can be applied in the turning of steel parts with a carbide tool without the use of lubricating and cooling technological fluids (LCTA). However, this method is promising for training cyber-physical systems (CNC lathe machines), where in the overwhelming majority of case, the presence of LCTA is necessary not only for the actual cooling, but also for chip removal from the cutting zone. After all, the CNC lathe machine has no operator who will remove the chips from the working bodies of the machine with a scraper. This process is automated for modern machine tools: LCTAs take the chips into the pallet, from which it is conveyed into the chip trays. Thus, expanding the application area of this technique, including LCTA-aided processing, is an urgent scientific and technological task.

2.2 Automation of the Process of Correcting Cutting Conditions in CNC Lathe Machines

To automate the process of thermo EMF measuring and the adjustment of cutting modes, a device prototype has been developed (Fig. 1, 2) [8–13]. The device comprises the following components (Fig. 2): an Arduino Nano microcontroller (hereinafter – the MC), an expansion board, an analog/digital converter (ADC), an UART ⟷ RS232 signal converter board, a power supply unit, and a DB9 ⟷ DB-25 interface cable.

The microcontroller is coupled to the expansion board, which is connected to the ADC module that forms a circuit for measuring the cutting EMF, as well as to the UART⟷RS232 signal converter module based on the MAX3232 microchip for converting UART signals in the range (0... + 5V), tolerated by the MC, into RS232 signals in the range (−18... + 18V), processed by the CNC device of the machine. The interface cable DB9(F) ⟷ DB-25(M) is used to connect the CNC lathe machine and the device.

Figure 3 shows the finished prototype of the device for automated assignment of cutting modes and measurement of thermo EMF in the assembled condition, in a plastic case, in the working position.

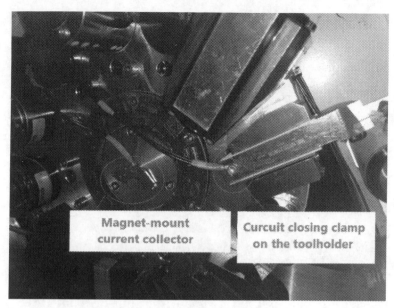

Fig. 1. Current collector mounted with a magnetic anchor on the capstan turret of a GENOS OKUMA – L300M CNC lathe machine

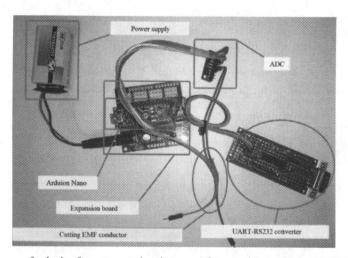

Fig. 2. Scheme of a device for automated assignment of processing modes in a GENOS OKUMA - L300M CNC lathe machine

Fig. 3. Prototype of the device for automated assignment of processing modes in a CNC lathe machine GENOS OKUMA - L300M, assembled in a plastic case in the working position

3 Research on the Possibilities of Predicting the Tool Life and Surface Roughness of the Work Piece During LCTA-Aided Turning

3.1 Experimental Setup and Research Methodology

To study the possibility of utilizing the known method for automated assignment of cutting modes in CNC lathe machines for LCTA-aided processing, an experimental setup based on a GENOS OKUMA - L300M CNC turret lathe machine was used (Fig. 4). The machine is equipped with a prototype device for automated assignment of processing modes (Fig. 1–3).

Description of the Calibration Procedure for Carbide Inserts. For each series of experiments, the plates were calibrated according to the following algorithm:

1. Numbering of plates and faces of each plate.
2. Measurement of the thermo EMF value for each face of each plate at the same cutting conditions (V = 100 m/min, S = 0.1 mm/rev, t = 1 mm) and saving the measured signals in the form of txt-files (the prototype of the device for automated assignment of processing modes is capable of measuring the thermo EMF value, saving the measurement results to a file and sending them to a smart-phone, see Fig. 5).
3. Processing of the measurement results (detection of the value of a stable thermo EMF signal for each face of each plate, determination of the spread of thermo EMF values between the faces and plates, sorting of the plates according to the thermo EMF value).
4. Selection of plates (faces) for research at the extreme points of the thermo EMF range (minimum, maximum, middle of the range).

Fig. 4. GENOS OKUMA - L300M CNC turret lathe machine

After the calibration procedure, only the inserts with the serial number of the faces and plates are transferred to further studies. Operators involved in further experiments have no idea about the matching of the number of the plate (face) with its specific thermo EMF range. Thus, "blinding" is achieved during the study.

Methodology of Wear Resistance Tests. The purpose of the study is to test the possibility of applying the known method for predicting the life of a cutting tool in the case of LCTA-aided processing.

The research algorithm is as follows:

1) Calibration of plates. When carrying out wear resistance tests, replaceable multi-faceted carbide inserts of the TC20PT brand produced by OAO Kirovogradskiy Zavod Tverdykh Splavov (Kirovograd Hard Alloy Plant, JSC) were used as a tool material. Base type - TTK alloy (WC + Co + TiC + (TaC, NbC)); wear-resistant coating application method - CVD; application area according to ISO - finishing and semi-finishing; coating type - multi-layer CVD coating, including TiN/MT-TiCN/Al2O3/TiN layers, with additional surface treatment to reduce internal stresses in the coating.

For the reliability of wear resistance tests, a calibrated selection of replaceable multi-faceted carbide inserts of the TC20PT alloy (trihedral double-sided insert) was sorted into 3 groups of 10 inserts each. In each group, the significance of differences in the average values in terms of thermo EMF was evaluated using the proven statistical Student and Fisher criteria.

Fig. 5. Screenshot of the working windows of the mobile application for the prototype of the device for automated assignment of cutting modes and thermo EMF measurement

In the batch of triangular plates, 3 plates were selected, corresponding to the minimum, average and maximum in the range of thermo EMF values, from the sample under consideration; i.e., No. 4 E = 19.02 mV; No. 9 E = 18.51 mV; No. 7 E = 18.19 mV.

2) Determination of the amount of wear of each plate every 5 min until it reaches 0.5 mm when processing a work piece made of U8 steel in the following modes: feed S = 0.1 mm/rev; cutting depth t = 1 mm; cutting speed v = 100 m/min; - in two modes - with and without LCTA. A large instrumental microscope BMI-1 was used to measure wear. Figure 6 illustrates the wear pattern in the BMI-1 microscope.

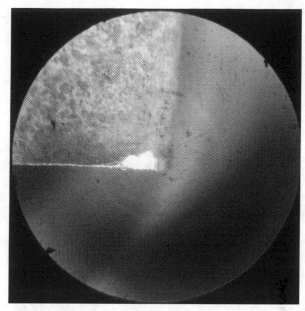

Fig. 6. Photo through the eyepiece of the microscope BMI-1 when measuring the wear of the cutting plate

The final wear value was additionally rechecked using a NORGAU NVM5040-D microscope equipped with the INSPEC CAD system software to make it possible to construct auxiliary geometry and to do computer-aided measuring in real time. Figure 7 shows a screenshot of the measurement scheme from the CAD editor environment of the NORGAU NVM5040-D microscope when measuring cutter wear.

3) Processing and analysis of experimental data.

Methodology for Studying the Effect of LCTA on the Parameters of Surface Roughness. The purpose of the study is to test the possibility of applying the known method for predicting the surface roughness parameters (Ra, Rz) in the case of LCTA-aided processing.

The research algorithm is as follows:

1) Calibration of plates. When carrying out roughness tests, rhombic carbide inserts with the VNMG160404-SF-AH630 surface produced in Japan were used as a tool material. The processed material - steel 40X. The plates were calibrated according to the thermo EMF value; groups of plates were distinguished according to the extreme points of the range of measured thermo EMF values.
2) Machining was carried out in the fine turning mode, while enumeration of the selected factors (cutting speed, feed, thermo EMF) was carried out to obtain 27 points for building regression models for machining with and without lubricants and coolant fluids. The experiment was repeated three times according to Student's criterion. The experimental matrix is shown in Table 2.

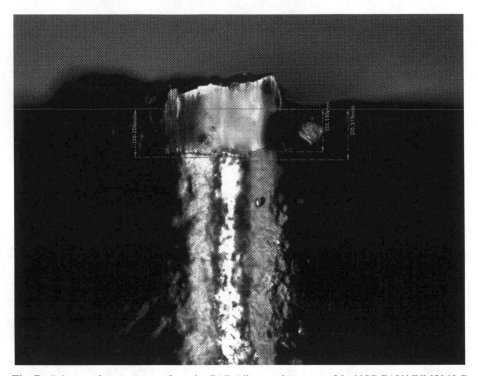

Fig. 7. Scheme of measurement from the CAD editor environment of the NORGAU NVM5040-D microscope when measuring cutter wear

Table 2. Matrix of experiments for building regression models of the dependence of roughness parameters both on the selected factors and on the presence of coolant fluids and lubricants in fine longitudinal turning of steel 40X with a VNMG160404-SF-AH630 cutter

#	Factors			Measured parameters	
	v, m/min	S, mm/rev	E, mV	Ra, μm	Rz, μm
1	150	0.05	12.98	–	–
2	175	0.09	12.65	–	–
3	200	0.14	12.3	–	–

The Ra and Rz parameters were recorded using a Mitutoyo Surftest SJ-210 profilometer. An example of a profilogram is shown in Fig. 8.

3) Processing and analysis of the results of the experiment.

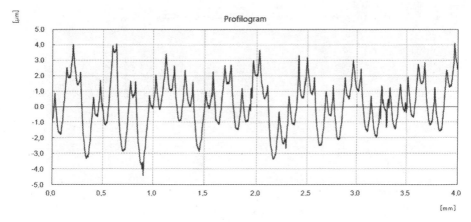

Fig. 8. Profilogram obtained using a Mitutoyo Surftest SJ-210 profilometer

3.2 Research Results

The Results of the Wear Resistance Tests. As a result of the tests, graphs of the dependence of cutter wear on time were obtained (Fig. 9, 10). Wear resistance tests have shown that we can talk about a certain coefficient of proportionality between the tool life when turning without LCTA and with LCTA (1.5… 1.75 within the obtained sample). The thermo EMF parameter can be used to build regression mathematical models to predict the tool life and assign adequate cutting speeds when turning with the use of LCTA; however, this requires separate series of experiments. It is necessary to separately analyze the effect of various types of LCTA on the resistance parameter, as well as to conduct similar studies on other groups of steels.

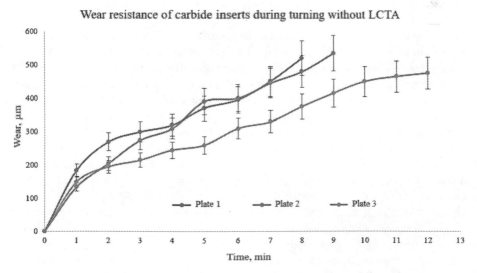

Fig. 9. Graph of insert wear during turning without LCTA

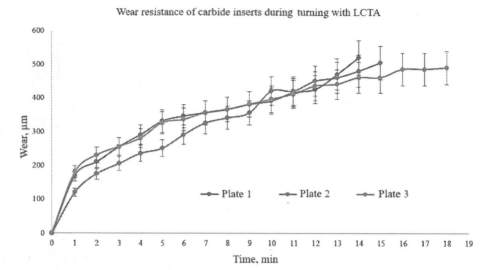

Fig. 10. Graph of insert wear during LCTA-aided turning

Results of Experimental Studies of the Influence of LCTA on the Ra and Rz Parameters of Surface Roughness. When studying the effect of the presence of LCTA on the Ra and Rz roughness parameters, graphs were obtained (Fig. 11, 12), and a multivariate regression analysis was performed for the cases of processing without LCTA and with LCTA (Table 3).

In Table 2, F0 is a statistical coefficient reflecting the cumulative influence of constant and unaccounted factors. Table 2 shows that cutting speed, for example, is the least significant factor that can be ignored for an exponential model. The geometric parameters that form the roughness are composed of two components. The first component is feed (S, mm/rev). The second component is the geometry of the cutting tool, in particular, the cutting edge angles and the radius of the cutting edge. This component is assessed in terms of the thermo EMF value, which acts as some complex indicator that takes into account both the thermo-physical and geometric properties of the tool. The influence of the thermo EMF parameter is very significant and is decisive in these models. This is also evidenced by the shape of the curves on the graphs (Fig. 11, 12, 13).

Thus, the data obtained allow saying that the known method of automated assignment of rational cutting modes in unmanned technology in modern CNC lathe machines, which are essentially cyber-physical systems, can be applied to processing with the use of lubricating and cooling technological agents, which requires carrying out a certain number of experiments and building the corresponding regression mathematical models. As the so-called information channel for proactive control of LCTA-aided processing conditions on CNC lathe machines, it is possible to use a well-proven complex indicator of the properties of contact pairs "tool-work piece", i.e., a thermo-power signal measured in the trial run mode. These studies are aimed at training cyber-physical systems in engineering to make independent decisions in the field of assigning processing modes based on preliminary or operational information about the thermo-physical properties

Table 3. Analysis of factor significance in the construction of regression models - linear, power, exponential - for the case of LCTA-aided processing

Model		Formula	Factor significance (normal regression)			
			F0	$E_{пр}$, mV	V, m/min	S, mm/rev
1	Linear, all factors	$R = C_0 + \sum_{i=1}^{N} F_i \cdot C_i$	−0.309	2.149	0.047	0.438
2	Linear, significant factors		−0.309	2.149	0.047	0.438
3	Power, all factors	$R = C_0 \cdot \prod_{i=1}^{N} F_i^{C_i}$	−0.100	1.842	−0.045	0.357
4	Power, significant factors		−0.100	1.842	−0.045	0.357
5	Exponential, all factors	$R = C_0 \cdot \prod_{i=1}^{N} C_i^{F_i}$	−0.100	2.131	−0.002	0.393
6	Exponential, significant factors		−0.100	2.131	–	0.393

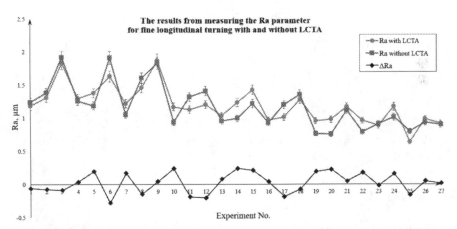

Fig. 11. Comparing experimental data on the measurement of the Ra parameter for fine longitudinal turning with and without LCTA

of the "tool-work piece" contact pairs and other measuring signals from the cutting zone without operator participation. Further study and scaling up of research is needed.

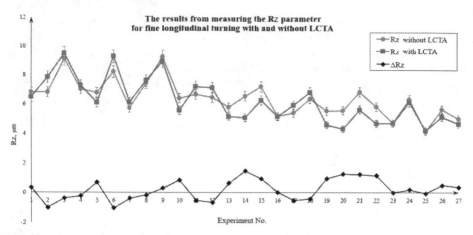

Fig. 12. Comparing experimental data on the measurement of the Rz parameter for fine longitudinal turning with and without LCTA

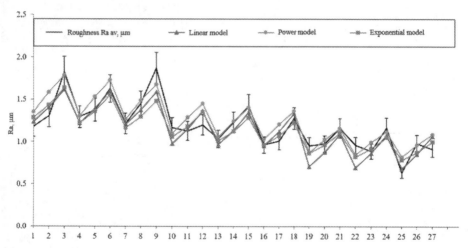

Fig. 13. Comparing the obtained regression models - linear, power, exponential - for the case of LCTA-aided processing

References

1. Plotnikov, A.L., Chigirinskii, Y., Frolov, E.M., Krylov, E.G.: Formulating CAD/CAM modules for calculating the cutting conditions in machining. Russ. Eng. Res. **5**(29), 512–517 (2009). https://doi.org/10.3103/S1068798X09050207
2. Plotnikov, A.L., Krylov, E.G., Frolov, E.M.: Diagnostics of the state of a multicutter hard-alloy tool on the basis of thermoelectric phenomena in the cutting zone. Russ. Eng. Res. **2**(30), 161–165 (2010). https://doi.org/10.3103/S1068798X10020140
3. Machinery technologist's handbook, In: Suslov, A.G. (eds.) Innovative Mechanical Engineering Pub. Moscow, Russia (2019)

4. Metal cutting data handbook. In: Baranovskiy, Y.V. (eds.), 3rd edn. Mechanical Engineering Pub. Moscow, Russia (1972)
5. Turner's Handbook. In: Shemetov, M.G., Bezyazychniy, V.F. (eds.), 2nd edn. Mechanical Engineering Pub. Moscow, Russia (2007)
6. Handbook of cutting data for metal cutting CNC machines. In: Guzeev, V.I. (eds.). Mechanical Engineering Pub. Moscow, Russia (2005)
7. Cutting tool constructor's handbook. In: Baranchikov, V.I. (eds.). Mechanical Engineering Pub. Moscow, Russia (1994)
8. Kraynev, D., Bondarev, A., Tikhonova, Z.: Mathematical apparatus for predicting cutting tool life in turning process after prior plastic deformation. In: Radionov, A.A., Kravchenko, O.A., Guzeev, V.I., Rozhdestvenskiy, Y.V. (eds.) ICIE 2019. LNME, pp. 1107–1114. Springer, Cham (2020). https://doi.org/10.1007/978-3-030-22063-1_118
9. Tikhonova, Z., Kraynev, D., Frolov, E.: Thermo-Emf as method for testing properties of replaceable contact pairs. In: Radionov, A.A., Kravchenko, O.A., Guzeev, V.I., Rozhdestvenskiy, Y.V. (eds.) ICIE 2019. LNME, pp. 1097–1105. Springer, Cham (2020). https://doi.org/10.1007/978-3-030-22063-1_117
10. Frolov, E.M., Rogachev, A.V.: Intellectual device for automated assignment of turning modes (Intellectualnoye ustroystvo avtomaticheskogo naznacheniya rezhimov tocheniya). In: Zverovshchikov, A.E. et al. (eds.). Actual Problems of Machine Building–2023 (Aktualnye problem stankostroyeniya), pp. 411–415. Penza State University, OO "StaknoMashStroy" et al., Penza (2023)
11. Frolov, E.M., Krainev, D.V., Tikhonova, Z.S.: Cyber-physical machining systems based on commercial CNC Equipment. In: 2018 International Russian Automation Conference (RusAutoCon). IEEE (2018) https://doi.org/10.1109/RUSAUTOCON.2018.8501684
12. Kraynev, D.V., Bondarev, A.A., Tchigirinsky, Y.: On-line monitoring and parameter control of a surface microprofile. Procedia Eng. **206**, 1285–1291 (2017). https://doi.org/10.1016/j.proeng.2017.10.632
13. Frolov, E.M., Rogachev, A.V.: The cutting data optimization for CNC machines. App. No. 2022614344. Bull. of Computer Programs, Databases, TIC. Moscow, Russia (2022)

New Algorithm for Determining the Shape of Particles and the Size of Adulteration Areas in Meat for a Decision Support System

Alexander Bolshakov[1] (✉) ⑩, Renata Kallimulina[1], and Marina Nikitina[2] ⑩

[1] Peter the Great St. Petersburg Polytechnic University,
29, Politekhnicheskaya Street, St. Petersburg 195251, Russia
aabolshakov57@gmail.com
[2] FSBIU "Federal Scientific Center for Food Systems named after V.M. Gorbatov" RAS,
26, st. Talalikhina, Moscow 109316, Russia

Abstract. The subject of the research is the approaches and methods of digital processing of images of slices of meat products related to the determination of the contour of the selected fragment, its shape, area and colour. The goal is to develop an algorithm for the automated detection of falsification in meat products based on the processing of digital images of histological sections. As a result of the study, a comprehensive analysis of the process of detecting falsification in meat products was carried out, and specific tasks requiring automation were formulated. The following tasks have been completed: determining the contours of the counterfeit image, determining the area of the regions and the shape of the particles, determining the colour of the counterfeit particles. To develop the developed algorithm of four modules, the Spark Streaming interface and the Python programming language were used. The architecture of a hybrid expert system, previously proposed by the authors, was used to support decision-making when determining the presence of a falsification. The developed software system was tested. After executing the four Spark Streaming modules and displaying the results, the user enters data into the decision support system: particle size (area), shape, draw a conclusion on a hypothetical topological invariant, select a colour from the drop-down list. The system automatically formulates a conclusion and gives the name of the counterfeit. If there is no falsification on the image, the object detection module does not allow it to be further processed by the system. The area of application of the results of the work is the production enterprises of the food industry with automation of the processes of quality control of meat products and the detection of falsification; regulatory organizations and supervisory bodies to improve the effectiveness of quality control; laboratories and scientific research centres for automatic analysis and image processing.

Keywords: falsification of meat products · decision support system · b-spline approximation · Monte Carlo method · polygonal approximation method · approximated lake method · topological data analysis · particle colour identification

A. G. Kravets et al. (Eds.): CIT&DS 2023, CCIS 1909, pp. 288–305, 2023.
https://doi.org/10.1007/978-3-031-44615-3_20

1 Introduction

There is a direct relationship between the quality of food and the occurrence of various diseases. Nutritional quality can be a contributing factor to obesity, cardiovascular disease, diabetes, cancer, and other diseases. This relationship can be described as a geometric progression over time. However, such approaches raise doubts about the quality of products. In addition, the breakdown of drugs can adversely affect the safety and quality of food products [1–3].

Previously, in the production of meat products, defective meat and offal were often used instead of high-quality meat raw materials. However, modern technologies and consumer requirements pose new challenges for manufacturers. Today, an important aspect is the use of herbal supplements with carbohydrate and protein structures instead of animal components [4, 5].

Modern methods to produce sausages and semi-finished products provide for the separation of components into plant and animal components, which may differ in their chemical and physical properties. Vegetable additives, such as phosphates, carrageenans and confectionery proteins, as well as other meat simulants, are used to create certain texture, structure and flavour characteristics of products [6–8]. They serve as substitutes or imitators of meat, providing similar properties and a visual effect [9, 10].

The conditions and duration of freezing, the degree of biochemical changes that occurred before freezing, and the speed of the freezing process itself affect the deterioration of the quality of meat products. The duration of storage of frozen meat depends on the initial quality of the meat, the type of livestock or poultry, their nutritional value, as well as storage technology parameters such as temperature, packaging, container sizes, and other factors [11, 12].

Determining the quality of meat products is an important aspect. Accuracy and speed of control of the characteristics of meat products play a significant role in ensuring the high quality of products offered to the consumer. However, the existing methods for quality control of raw meat remain laborious and require the use of expensive equipment [13–18].

The distribution of counterfeit products in the consumer market is a serious problem. One of the urgent tasks is the determination and identification of the components used in the production of meat raw materials and meat products, as well as the isolation of the corresponding components, which can be of animal or vegetable origin [19].

Considering these factors, the purpose of this work is to develop an automated method for identifying various types of falsification in meat raw materials and meat products. Currently, the identification process is carried out manually by technologists, which is time-consuming and prone to errors. Therefore, it is advisable to reduce the human impact by automating the analysis of meat products and determining the presence of falsification. It is proposed to create a method that analyses images of slices of meat products to detect falsification, based on their characteristics, such as geometric shape, colour properties and size.

Note that earlier the authors proposed the architecture of a decision support system for automating the detection of falsification in sections of meat products based on the histological method [19] in accordance with the accepted standard [20].

2 Development and Software Implementation of an Algorithm for Solving the Problem of Determining the Colour of Counterfeit Particles in Meat

2.1 Solving the Problems of Determining the Contours of a Counterfeit Image

The task of determining image contours is very important in the process of data processing in computer vision systems, as it represents the initial and fundamental stage of detection, identification, and segmentation of graphic objects. The selection of contours is necessary to solve the problem of establishing a one-to-one correspondence between the semantic description of an object and its graphical representation, determining the shape, imposing and combining different layers, and even segmenting. When segmenting the area of the graphical representation of an object [21], the features are identified and then combined according to the specified criteria.

Segmentation methods fall into two categories:

- region-oriented.
- edge-oriented.

The choice of segmentation method is determined both by the context of the task and the goal of the closed image processing process. In this work, the obtained images containing areas with a selected contour have several features:

- images are cleared of digital noise, areas are clearly traced;
- selected areas received incl. RGB analysis with customizable parameters, i.e., a variable range of each such area is available;
- a slightly pronounced robustness of the selected area is allowed due to a certain degree of similarity of the counterfeit between different areas of meat products.

As a result of the above, a combination of the following methods for approximating the selected contours was chosen:

- modified Hough transform (HFT);
- approximation by B-splines.

The algorithm for approximating the contours of the areas highlighted in the image takes as input a graphical representation of the object with the outline of the selected area, the hyperparameter N characterizing the minimum expected area of the counterfeit meat products area, and the output is the maximized area highlighted by the approximated contour obtained as follows way.

1. Initialization of the vector of parameters of mathematical models of the implemented methods for approximating the selected contours, bringing the input data into the required format.
2. Simultaneous launch of models.
3. Calculation of the total area S of the region highlighted by the approximate contour.
4. If S is not less than the given N, then the desired result is obtained, otherwise it is necessary to return to step 1 with the corrected vector of parameters.

The algorithm for calculating the area in step 3 is described in the next paragraph of the work.

The basis of PX is to map the points of the initial space of the graphical representation of an object into a given space of parameters. In the process of selecting straight contours based on HRP, it is preferable to use the normal equation of a straight line:

$$x\cos(\theta) + y\sin(\theta) = \rho,$$

where θ is the angle between the normal to the line and the abscissa axis, ρ is the distance of the line from the origin.

The implementation of PH is simplified by organizing the parametric space in the structural format of a cumulative array. A cell of such an array stores data on the number of lines passing through it. The value of the cell is equal to the power of the set of points belonging to the line in the initial space of the image.

The modification of the classic HRP consists in the following aspects:

- replacement of a single accumulative value AV with a weight one when working with a cumulative array, when calculating the next distance ρ_i and given θ_j, the value of the array cell $H(\rho_i, \theta_j)$ is incremented by the value AV, which is directly proportional to the probability that the points belong to straight lines, the initialization of AV is empirical and is compiled experimentally with a given set of graphical representations of the object.
- applying the rules when choosing the parameter θ, while specifying the directions of the straight lines with maximizing the probability using local image analysis by the window algorithm.

The above aspects reduce the computational complexity of the HRP with a large dimension of the feature space and eliminate the difficulties of approximating the contours of false areas.

The use of HRP with modifications for approximation ensures the formation of a set of features in the format of straight-line segments, where each feature is characterized by three elements: $\rho, \theta, H(\rho_i, \theta_j)$. However, the exact position of the segment cannot be unambiguously determined by these parameters, because target result of PH-set directly with the location of the segment.

In addition to the approximation using the modified HRP, the approximation by B-splines is also carried out. Traditional approximation methods, such as Lagrange methods, differ from B-spline methods. First, traditional methods use the polynomial y = p(x) where no two data points can have the same x coordinates; however, B-splines use a parametric shape. Secondly, in traditional methods, the degree of the polynomial is a function of the number of data points, and the degree of the B-spline uses the parametric shape of the points, which allows the use of lower degree curves/surfaces: 2 or 3. Thirdly, the input data for traditional methods is the set points (x_i, y_i), where x_i is the parameter value corresponding to y_i, while the B-spline method only requires a set of points. Fourth, traditional methods are global, because changing one data point affects the entire curve. However, the local B-spline approximation [22] limits the influence only to the neighbourhood of this point.

The B-spline approximation requires a set of $m + 1$ data points $D_k (0 \le k \le m)$ and a power p. Next, the curve $C(u)$ of the B-spline is searched for, which passes through all points in the given order. Parameters are not input, so you need to find the parameter set:

$$t_0 = 0 < t_1 < \ldots < t_m = 1,$$

so that the fitting curve of the B-spline can be "fixed" at these values, i.e., Dk = C(tk) for all k.

Usually, 4 methods are used to find parameters: equidistant, centripetal, chordal and universal. Each method has its own advantages and disadvantages, the resulting B-spline can be very different. In this work, we used the universal method, because it is easy to implement, works well when there are no better alternatives. This method calculates the value of the tk parameter:

$$t_k = d_k/d_m, \text{где } d_k = \textstyle\sum_{i=1}^{k} |D_i - D_{i-1}|.$$

Then a node vector is generated from the selected parameters using a simple moving average.

In many applications, the requirement that a curve/surface contain all data points may be too restrictive, and a curve/surface that can exactly follow the shape of the data points may be sufficient. This leads to a search for a global approximation. A B-spline curve given by data points and a given degree also approximates and follows the shape of the data points; however, this is not the best solution.

Given a set of $m+1$ data points D_k and degree p, find a B-spline curve $C(u)$ of degree p that fits the data points by the least squares method. Let this B-spline curve be $C = \sum_{i=0}^{m} N_{i,p}(u)P_i$, where n is a user-selectable value and P_i is the $n + 1$ unknown control points. For each parameter t_k, $|C(t_k) - D_k|$ is the distance between the "calculated" and real points. A good approximation method should minimize the sum of squares of the "error" distance:

$$f(P_0, \ldots, P_n) = \sum_{k=0}^{m} |C(t_k) - D_k|^2.$$

The P_i values that minimize $f(*)$ are the target breakpoints. To provide a unique solution, you must set $D_0 = P_0$ and $D_m = P_n$ to "clamp" the curve at both ends. Then equate the values of partial derivatives to 0, thus obtaining a system of linear equations, the solution of which is the target result. The surface case is similar. Given a set of $(m + 1) \times (n + 1)$ data points $D_{k, l} (0 \le k \le m$ and $0 \le l \le n)$ and degree (p, q), find a B-spline whose surface is $S(u, v)$ approximates the points $D_{k,l}$ for the least squares method. Thus, it is necessary to find control points $P_{i,j}(0 \le i \le e$ и $0 \le j \le f)$ such that the following function is minimized:

$$f(P_{i,j}\text{'s}) = \sum_{k=0}^{m} \sum_{l=0}^{n} |S(s_k, t_l) - D_{k,l}|^2$$

where e and f are user selectable values and s_k's and t_l's are parameters.

Curve fitting is applied to each column l of $D_{k,1}$ $(0 \leq k \leq m)$ to obtain a set of $(e+1) \times (n+1)$ "intermediate" control points $R_{i,l}$ $(0 \leq i \leq e)$. Then the curve fitting is again applied to each row i of $R_{i,1}$ to obtain the end control points $P_{i,j}$ $(0 \leq j \leq f)$. Thus, the surface approximating the B-spline is constructed with $(n+1) + (m+1)$ approximation curves. Although the resulting surface may not be optimal, it is simple enough to implement and tune the parameters.

The resulting surface does not contain all points and looks «smoother» than surfaces built using traditional approximation methods.

2.2 Solving the Problem of Determining the Area of Areas of Falsification

At the third step of the algorithm for approximating the contours of the areas selected in the image, it is necessary to calculate the area S of the area highlighted by the approximated contour. For this, an algorithm has been developed that implements the 3 most appropriate methods, the models of which work in parallel:

- Monte Carlo method (MMC);
- method of polygonal approximation (MPA) [23];
- approximated lake method (AOM) [24].

At the end of the work of the three models, different values of the area S_1, S_2, S_3, are obtained, from which it is necessary to choose the desired one as follows:

- the maximum value of S_{max};
- minimum value of S_{min};
- weighted average value of S_{opt}.

In the future, the choice of calculation option is made by the user.

Note that MCM is one of the numerical stochastic approximate methods that involve the generative mechanisms of pseudorandom variables. The area of an arbitrary figure according to MMK is calculated as follows:

$$S = \frac{n}{N},$$

where n is the number of points in the region of an arbitrary figure, and N is the total number of points, $N > 100$.

The efficiency of MMC is directly proportional to the number of experiments performed. The graphical representation of the counterfeit meat products is divided into an arbitrary number of circles of arbitrary size, the composition of which forms the desired arbitrary figure. Next, MCM is applied for each circle with a gradual increase in pixel density. The calculation of the total area S occurs when the local maximum number of pixels for a given number of circles and their size is reached.

The basis of the MPA is the approximation by polygons of the most difficult to calculate the area of sections of an arbitrary figure. The graphical representation of the falsification is processed from left to right and from right to left to identify the areas' most subject to approximation. The reference lines are equidistant parallel lines designed to define the boundaries of the areas being approximated.

For each identified area, a vector of polygons is calculated. Closedness and convexity of the search space is implied, otherwise the MPA convergence is not guaranteed. For the subject area of the present work, the condition for the convergence of the MPA is fulfilled automatically.

The resulting vectors of polygons undergo mathematical transformations to form the actual polygons. If the resulting polygon consists of more than half of the pixels that do not belong to the counterfeit particles, then it is discarded. The belonging of the particles to the counterfeit is determined unambiguously using the algorithms described in the following sections of this qualification work.

After approximating the polygons, the required area S is calculated as the internal area of the region of the set of polygons.

Further, the approximate lake method is based on the MCM, but does not involve partitioning the area into circles with a given number and size. Moreover, AOM was created as a method for calculating the area of the lake. In the context of the work, the graphical representation of the object of counterfeit meat products is like a similar representation of a lake in the following ways:

– arbitrary nature of the contour of the selected area;
– uneven distribution of particles in the image;
– the shape of the region is irregular and not robust to changes and noise.

In this case, the coloured area A is surrounded by a white rectangle R. The idea is to randomly release N particles into a square with a known area ($H \times W$), where H is the height of the image, $W = b - a$ is the width of the image. Let K represent the number of particles entering the lake. It is assumed in the work that one particle is sent to each pixel, so the formula for calculating the area is as follows:

$$A = \frac{K}{N}R,$$

where K is the number of colour pixels, N is the total number of image pixels, R is the image size.

Image segmentation is the first step in the most important tasks in image analysis. It is used either to separate objects from the background, or to separate the image into related areas. The efficiency of colour segmentation can significantly affect the quality of the image comprehension system. The most common features used in image segmentation include texture, shape and irregular shape, grayscale intensity, and colour.

Predicting the area of a scanned image can be tricky if you don't pay attention to a scan parameter called PPI (dots or pixels per inch), often referred to as scanner resolution. This option determines the amount of detail in the original image that is retained in the scanned digital image. The higher the PPI value, the larger and more detailed the scanned image.

The work assumes the presence of an image preprocessing mechanism that maximizes the value of the PPI value. Therefore, in the presence of noise, image inaccuracies, and other defects, stable operation of the original approximation algorithm described above is not guaranteed.

2.3 Solving the Problem of Determining the Shape of Counterfeit Particles

After approximating the contours of the selected area and calculating its area, the stage of determining the shape of the particles of the graphical representation of the counterfeit meat products follows. It is based on the adaptation of the method for determining the shape of a physical particle [25] with the characteristics of a solid body. The shape of the particles has a significant impact on the simulation of the solid phase using the Euler-Lagrange method to calculate the discrete phase model (DPM). Real particles are non-spherical, so the DPM shape factor is needed to calculate the drag coefficient.

Typically, the shape of a particle is judged by how close the geometry of the particle or 2D projection is to an ideal sphere or circle, respectively. Thus, the shape factor as the ratio of the surface area of a sphere with the same volume as the particle S_{sp} to the actual surface area of the particle S_p:

$$\psi = \frac{S_{sp}}{S_p}.$$

This equation is used to determine the drag coefficient in the DFM. Adaptation of such a method for solving the problem is possible based on developing a relationship between a two-dimensional measure of particle geometry using an image analysis program and a three-dimensional determination of the shape factor, as well as setting up image processing, under which the condition of the Cauchy theorem (TK) is satisfied for randomly oriented convex particles.

Image analysis does not allow direct calculation of the values of the shape factor parameters. Therefore, to determine the actual particle surface area S_p, TC is adopted. Here TK means that the average projective area A_p of randomly oriented convex particles is one quarter of the average surface area of these particles:

$$A_p = \frac{S_p}{4}.$$

Image transformation is done by ImageJ tools. The cases of ordered and disordered arrangements of particles are considered separately, since the density and degree of influence on the mutual arrangement of particles differ, which requires a separate adjustment of the instrumentation.

When calculating the shape factor by its implementation using the Python language, a hypothesis was formulated about the dependence of the particle shape on its relative position with other particles. To confirm it, the methodology of topological data analysis was used.

The image of the falsification is represented as a topological space X. It is necessary to determine the homology groups in the given space X, i.e., topological invariants from X, where its homology groups are represented:

$$H_0(X), H_1(X), H_2(X), \ldots,$$

where the homology group describes the number of K-dimensional holes in X.

To construct homology groups, it is necessary to assume about the shape of the particles. Let each particle have a shape factor as close as possible to a sphere, then the following is true:

$$H_k\left(S^2\right) = \begin{cases} \mathbb{Z}, \ k = 0,2 \\ \{0\} \end{cases}.$$

Next, simplicial complexes are constructed from given homology groups.

Since a simplicial complex is a topological space represented as a union of sets homoeomorphic to a simplex, to test the hypothesis, it is necessary to establish the number of holes on the topological surface where particles do not enter into complexes, i.e., violate the homeomorphism rule. Thus, the number of particles that differ in topological characteristics and, therefore, are not included in homology groups is directly proportional to the number of such holes. For the available sets of images of counterfeit meat products, the hypothesis is confirmed: the particles included in the homology groups have similar values of the shape factor with a given order for each group.

To correctly determine the shape, it is necessary to set the parametric value D, which determines the threshold number of holes. If the calculated amount exceeds D, then the algorithm does one of two things:

- in the case of an orderly arrangement of particles, the image is transferred to the stage of approximation of the contour of the selected area, since it is found that the shape does not depend on the location, the hypothesis is rejected, which is not allowed;
- in case of disordered arrangement of particles, the image is subjected to additional processing by cropping along the contour of the identified holes in the topological space; if this is not possible, then the image is removed from the processing stream with a mark of unsuitability and / or the need to remove noise, errors.

3   Development and Software Implementation of an Algorithm for Solving the Problem of Determining the Colour of Counterfeit Particles in Meat

Determining the colour of the particles of counterfeit meat products is reduced to the general task of identifying the colour of the particle and then concatenating the result for the particles based on the similarity of the obtained colour map of the three primary colours.

The three primary colours, red, green, and blue, are tracked using basic computer vision. After successful compilation, when the code is executed, the detector window is redirected to the image, the path to which is specified as an argument.

In addition, the name of the colour of the pixel is set, as well as the composition of 3 different colours: red, blue and green. This is necessary for mutually independent colour initialization for balanced particle colour detection [26]. The following is a description of the software implementation of the solution of the above-described problem using OpenCV tools.

The first step is to get a high-resolution image. Cv2.imread() is used to load an image from a file. The image of meat products must be in the working directory or the full path to the image must be specified: Img = cv2.imread(img path).

Next, you need to extract the RGB colour map. At this stage, three-layer colours are extracted from the input image. Digitally coloured images are created by a combination of red, green, and blue light. The analogy format is not considered in the context of this task.

Each primary colour has an intense value from 0 (lowest) to 255 (highest). When mixing three primary colours with different intensities, different colours are obtained. For example, if the intensity of the primary colours is 0, then this linear combination corresponds to black. If the intensity of the primary colours is 1, this linear combination corresponds to white:

$$Index=[\text{"colour"}, \text{" colour \_name"}, \text{"hex"}, \text{"R"}, \text{"G"}, \text{"B"}].$$

The next step is to calculate the minimum distance from the coordinates. The minimum distance is calculated by considering the movement to the origin of all colours to obtain the most suitable colour. The panda's library is a utility for performing various operations on data, for example, loading graphical representations of meat particles that have passed through the above software components to perform the following operations:

– approximation of the contours of the selected area;
– determination of the area of the counterfeit area;
– determination of the shape of counterfeit particles.

The minimum distance is obtained as follows:

```
D = abs(R-int(csv.loc[i ,"R"])) + abs (G-int (csv.loc[i
,"G"])) + abs (B-int (csv.loc [ i ,"B"])).
```

Next, the image is displayed with colour tints. The sliding rectangular window algorithm is used to display an image with colour tints. After double-clicking, the RGB values and the colour name are updated. The Cv2.imshow() method is used to display an image. Using the cv2.rectangle() and cv2.putText() functions, you can get the name of the colour and its intensity level:

```
text=getColourName(r,g,b) + 'R='+str(r) + 'G='+str(g)
+'B=' +str(b).
```

The architecture used includes a well-defined sequence diagram that is abstracted from the source code. The architecture is based on up-to-date and open technologies, such as the OpenCv library in Python.

As stated above, red, green, and blue are primary colours that can be mixed to create different colours. This colour detection software component takes an image path as an argument, and the result is the composition of three different colours in the given image.

The proposed implementation determines the required colour field from the RGB image. The various steps are implemented based on the OpenCv platform. However, it is also possible to use proprietary software such as Colour RecSys while maintaining the concept of the architecture.

The main positive point of the method used is its colour differentiation of monocolour. Thus, when setting weight coefficients for the original colour map, it is possible to isolate a specific colour or its shade, for example, to detect anomalies on seismic maps. In the context of this work, a fundamental emphasis on red is allowed, which, on the one hand, simplifies software implementation and speeds up, in fact, the process of determining the colour, on the other hand, reduces the generality of application. Therefore, it is necessary to provide for the operating conditions of all 4 software components combined into a platform based on Spark Streaming data processing for possible optimization of the operation of both the entire system as a whole and each individual component.

The proposed solution lacks an accurate representation of colours with hue accuracy. Computer vision data sets are used, and according to them, the number of shades that can be identified using 865 colour names along with their RGB and 16 values. The proposed system uses OpenCv. OpenCV is also used to sort primary colours.

4 Approbation of the Image Processing Algorithm to Determine the Presence of Falsification of Meat. Testing and Analysis of Results

Below is the output of each module described above. A platform based on stream data processing Spark Streaming has been implemented, which is used to detect counterfeit meat. Moreover, Spark Streaming is a component of the Apache Spark framework and provides scalable, high-performance, and fault-tolerant data processing in real time.

Using Spark Streaming, it is possible to receive and process continuous streams of data coming from various sources, such as Kafka, Kinesis or TCP sockets. In this case, the data stream contains information about meat products, which must be analysed for the presence of falsification. It is supposed to use the developed product in laboratories where it is possible to continuously send images of histological sections and receive high-quality information about the falsification if it is present on the original section.

4.1 Statement of the Problem of Determining the Presence of Falsification of Meat

To detect a counterfeit in a meat product, it is necessary to determine the corresponding area on the image of its slice. In this area, identify the particle shape, area and colour.

It doesn't matter what image format of the histological preparation is input to the system for further processing, since the formats are converted one into another using standard tools in the Python language. In this implementation, the converter is not used since the available images for testing are in one format – JPEG.

For the input image, its quality is important, which is determined in the PPI (pixels per inch) parameter. It refers to the resolution of digital images and indicates the number of pixels that are on one inch of a screen or printed surface. The higher the value of the parameter, the denser the resolution of the image, which usually results in a sharper and more detailed display. Thus, PPI must be at least $90 \div 100$. The study assumes the use of an image pre-processing mechanism, which is aimed at maximizing the value of the pixel density (PPI).

Soy protein products and pea flour are stained with a solution of haematoxylin and eosin according to the National Standards for Determining the Presence of Counterfeit. Signs of falsification of meat products are:

- rounded pink particles;
- cylindrical or round particles in shades of red;
- red or lilac fibber bundles;
- uncoloured particles.

To solve the problem of identifying falsification, a system is being developed that includes four main modules:

1. Determining the contours of the image.
2. Determining the area of the selected fragment.
3. Determining the shape of particles.
4. Colour definition.

Before running the implemented algorithm, the object detection module on OpenCV is used, which determines the presence or absence of a falsification in the image by the uniformity of the image. Figures 1 and 2 show longitudinal and transverse sections of meat, where a uniform structure is observed. Also, in Figs. 3 and 4, isolated round areas in the form of a "donut" or a colour uncharacteristic of meat are clearly visible.

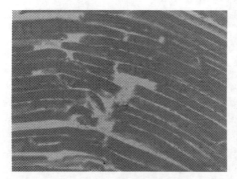 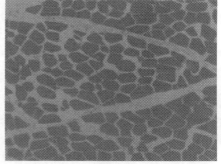

Fig. 1. Longitudinal section of a histological section of meat tissue stained with hematoxylin and eosin (20-fold increase)

Fig. 2. Cross section of a histological section of meat tissue stained with hematoxylin and eosin (20x magnification)

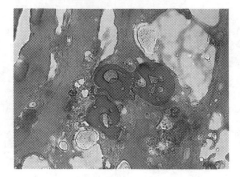 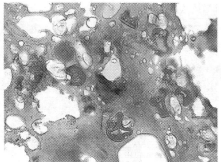

Fig. 3. Histological section of ham with isolated soy protein stained with hematoxylin and eosin (20x magnification)

Fig. 4. Histological section of boiled sausage supplemented with soy isolated protein after staining with hematoxylin and eosin (20x magnification)

Input data:

- Image of a histological specimen as a JPEG image.

Output:

- a JPEG format image with a highlighted falsified area (Fig. 2);
- a real number that determines the area of the alleged counterfeit in the appropriate units of measurement (micrometer^2);
- image of JPEG format with selected colour of counterfeit (Fig. 4);
- JPEG image of the topological invariant for the hypothetical particle shape.

The target output is an image with the fake area highlighted, an area value, and an image with the fake colour highlighted in the original image. The image of the topological invariant about the hypothetical shape of the particle is a side output value in the implemented algorithm since the quality of the original images used is low and the algorithm does not always work correctly.

When a falsification is detected in the input image, the user receives at the output the necessary qualitative characteristics of the histological section, which he introduces into the developed DSS, i.e., is called a falsification.

4.2   First Module. Determining the Contours of an Image

The implemented algorithm for determining the image contour is described above. Applying the Hough transform and the B-spline function, the falsification boundaries are approximated on the image. Figure 5 shows the control polygon built by the object detection module when entering the Spark Streaming unified information processing stream, and the approximate falsification boundaries.

During testing, the results of the Hough transform were incorrect for the given parameter values. Therefore, it was concluded that the hypothesis was not confirmed.

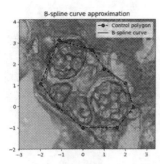

Fig. 5. Test 1. B-spline-approximated falsification boundaries

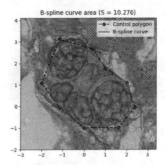

Fig. 6. Test 2. Calculating the area of the fake

4.3 Second Module. Determining the Area of the Counterfeit

The algorithm described above for determining the area of the counterfeit shows the result shown in Fig. 6. The green area is the desired fragment, the area of which is 10.276 mm^2.

It was supposed to implement the algorithm with three output values of the area, calculated by three different methods:

- the maximum value of S_{max};
- minimum value of S_{min};
- weighted average value of S_{opt}.

When testing, it was decided not to display 3 area values, since the difference is in the 5th decimal place. The output is the arithmetic mean of the area.

Below are the test results:

$$S_{max} = 10.276234;$$
$$S_{min} = 10.276238;$$
$$S_{opt} = 10.276231.$$

4.4 Third Module. Determination of the Form of Counterfeit

Figures 7 and 8 show control points and triangulation for further topological data analysis. The algorithm of the third module is described above, which performs triangulations and calculates a hypothetical topological invariant of the shape of meat adulteration particles.

The figure shows the first stage of filling the isolated falsification fragment with topological particles. Further, the entire topological space is randomly covered with topological particles, triangulation is performed and the maximum coverage of counterfeit particles is revealed.

To demonstrate testing, these stages were chosen, since the further stuffing of reference points looks unreadable. It is also concluded that the quality of the original images is important.

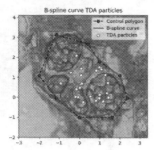
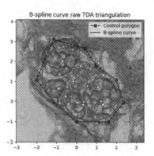

Fig. 7. Test 3. Calculation of the shape of the counterfeit. Topological particles

Fig. 8. Test 3. Calculation of the shape of the counterfeit. Triangulation

4.5 Fourth Module. Determining the Colour of Counterfeit

The algorithm for recognizing the colour of a fake is described above. Using the OpenCV library, it searches for a weighted average colour within a fragment of an image with a falsification. The found colour prevails on the selected area. Next, a filter mask of this colour is applied for a visually readable version of the image output to the user.

The decision was made: the result of the module is the output value of the entire developed algorithm for detecting counterfeit, since qualitative information from morphological tables may differ from the resulting colour by a small shade, while the selected counterfeit may have a different origin (Fig. 9).

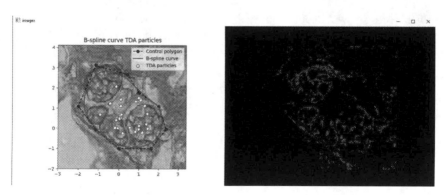

Fig. 9. Test 4. Calculating the colour of the counterfeit

To enter the qualitative characteristics of a counterfeit in the DSS, the participation of the user is required.

4.6 Conclusion of the Result of Determining the Presence of Counterfeit Meat

After executing the four Spark Streaming modules and displaying the results, the user enters data into the DSS. It is required to enter the size (area), the shape of the particles, making a conclusion based on a hypothetical topological invariant, and select a colour from the drop-down list. The system will automatically draw a conclusion and give the name of the counterfeit. If there is no falsification on the image, the object detection module will not allow it to be further processed by the system.

5 Conclusions

The article is devoted to the automation of the process of detecting falsification in meat products based on the histological analysis of the cut to improve the efficiency of the process of detecting falsification in meat based on the introduction of automated methods. Automation helps to reduce the "human factor" and time costs in the process of analysis and decision-making [21–29] about the presence of falsification in meat products.

As part of the study, a universal algorithm has been developed that allows you to determine the presence of counterfeit based on the analysis of images of sections of meat products samples.

In the course of the work, the following four tasks were solved:

- approximation of the boundaries of the areas selected on the image;
- determination of the area of regions;
- definition of the form of areas;
- defining the colour of areas.

The architecture of the decision support system has been developed, which is designed to automate the determination of the presence of falsification in meat products. As part of this work, two main subsystems have been created: an expert system and a decision support system. To make decisions about the presence of a counterfeit, production rules were used, which were formulated based on information contained in morphological tables that correspond to GOST standards. Prolog, which is the language of artificial intelligence, was chosen as the programming language for developing the expert system prototype. The proposed method is based on the methodology of building expert systems and is designed to create a system that can automatically detect the presence of falsification in meat products [20].

To solve the tasks set, the Spark Streaming framework was chosen, designed for processing and analysing continuous data in real time, and the Python programming language. A service has been implemented with four modules, each of which solves a specific task. The sequence of blocks is unambiguous: determining the contours of the image, determining the area of the regions, determining the shape of the particles and determining the colour of the particles.

During testing of the service, it was decided not to use a previously developed program in the C++ programming language to solve the problem of optimizing a polychrome image. The results of identifying the counterfeit were unsatisfactory. It was decided to use the original slice images.

Also, one of the conclusions of testing is the addition of a mechanism to the pre-processing module aimed at maximizing the value of the pixel density (PPI).

References

1. Mayer-Scholl, A., Gayda, J., Thaben, N., Bahn, P., Nöckler, K., Pozio, E.: Magnetic stirrer method for the detection of trichinella larvae in muscle samples. J. Vis. Exp. **121**, e55354 (2017)
2. Okulakrishnan, P., Kumar, R.R., Sharma, B.D., Mendiratta, S.K., Malav, O., Sharma, D.: Determination of sex origin of meat and meat products on the DNA basis: a review. Crit. Rev. Food Sci. Nutr. **55**(10), 1303–1314 (2015)
3. Tian, Y., Zhang, J., Chen, Y., Li, X., Cheng, H.: Applications of mass spectrometry-based proteomics in food authentication and quality identification. Se pu **36**(7), 588–598 (2018)
4. Duan, X.-Y., Feng, X.-S., Zhang, Y., Yan, J.-Q., Zhou, Y., Li, G.-H.: Progress in pretreatment and analysis of cephalosporins: an update since 2005. Crit. Rev. Anal. Chem. 51(1), 1–32 (2019). https://doi.org/10.1080/10408347.2019.1676194
5. Chernukha, I.M., Vostrikova, N.L., Khvostov, D.V., Zvereva, E.A., Taranova, N.A., Zherdev, A.V.: Methods of identification of muscle tissue in meat products. Prerequisites for creating a multi-level control system. Theory Pract. Meat Process. **4**(3), 32–40 (2019)
6. Tedtova, V.V., Temiraev, R.B., Kononenko, S.I., Tukfatulin, G.S., Kozyrev, A., Gazzaeva, M.S.: Effect of different doses of non-genetically modified soybean on biological and productive properties of pigs and consumer characteristics of pork. J. Pharm. Sci. Res. **9**(12), 2405–2409 (2017)
7. Surkov, I.V., Kantere, V.M., Motovilov, K.Y., Renzyaeva, T.V.: The development of an integrated management system to ensure the quality stability and food safety. Foods Raw Mater. **3**(1), 111–119 (2015)
8. Xu, C., Tang, X., Shao, H., Wang, H.: Salinity tolerance mechanism of economic halophytes from physiological to molecular hierarchy for improving food quality. Curr. Genomics **17**(3), 207–214 (2016)
9. Tseng, S.-Y., Li, S.-Y., Yi, S.-Y., Sun, A.Y., Gao, D.-Y., Wan, D.: Food quality monitor: paper-based plasmonic sensors prepared through reversal nanoimprinting for rapid detection of biogenic amine odorants. ACS Appl. Mater. Interfaces **9**(20), 17306–17316 (2017)
10. Kanareykina, S.G., et al.: The structure development of yogurt with vegetable ingredients. Int. J. Recent Technol. Eng. **8**(2), 1587–1592 (2019)
11. Gupta, A.J., Wierenga, P.A., Gruppen, H., Boots, J.-W.: Influence of protein and carbohydrate contents of soy protein hydrolysates on cell density and igg production in animal cell cultures. Biotechnol. Prog. **31**(5), 1396–1405 (2015)
12. Wang, Q., Zhang, J.: Research status, opportunities and challenges of high moisture extrusion technology. J. Chin. Inst. Food Sci. Technol. **18**(7), 1–9 (2018)
13. Pateiro, M., et al.: Essential oils as natural additives to prevent oxidation reactions in meat and meat products: a review. Food Res. Int. **113**, 156–166 (2018)
14. Hao, J., Liang, G., Li, A., Man, Y., Jin, X., Pan, L.: Review on sensing detection progress of "lean meat agent" based on functional nanomaterials. Nongye Gongcheng Xuebao **35**(18), 255–266 (2019)
15. Kancheva, V.D., Angelova, S.E.: Synergistic effects of antioxidant compositions during inhibited lipid autoxidation. Lipid Peroxidation: Inhibition, Effects and Mechanisms (2016)
16. Loutfi, A., Coradeschi, S., Mani, G.K., Shankar, P., Rayappan, J.B.B.: Electronic noses for food quality: a review. J. Food Eng. **144**, 103–111 (2015)
17. Faridnia, F., Bremer, P.J., Oey, I., Ma, Q.L., Hamid, N., Burritt, D.J.: Effect of freezing as pre-treatment prior to pulsed electric field processing on quality traits of beef muscles. Innov. Food Sci. Emerg. Technol. **29**, 31–40 (2015)
18. Shenoy, P., Ahrné, L., Fitzpatrick, J., Viau, M., Tammel, K., Innings, F.: Effect of powder densities, particle size and shape on mixture quality of binary food powder mixtures. Powder Technol. **272**, 165–172 (2015)

19. Nikitina, M.A., Chernukha, I.M., Pchelkina, V.A.: Artificial neural network technologies as a tool to histological preparation analysis. In: IOP Conference Series: Earth and Environmental Science 60. "60th International Meat Industry Conference, MEATCON 2019", p. 012087 (2019)
20. Bolshakov, A.A., Nikitina, M.A., Kalimullina, R.R.: Intelligent system for determining the presence of falsification in meat products based on histological methods. In: Kravets, A.G., Bolshakov, A.A., Shcherbakov, M. (eds.) Society 5.0: Cyberspace for Advanced Human-Centered Society. SSDC, vol. 333, pp. 179–201. Springer, Cham (2021). ISSN 2198-4182. https://doi.org/10.1007/978-3-030-63563-3_12
21. Keustermans, J., Seghers, D., Mollemans, W., Vandermeulen D., Suetens, P.: International Workshop on Graph-Based Representations in Pattern Recognition. In: GbRPR 2009: Graph-Based Representations in Pattern Recognition, vol. 5534, pp. 353–365 (2009)
22. Shaini, B., Rexhepi, S., Rufati, E.: Specific numerical properties of b-spline in function approximations. UDC: 517.518.8. (2022). https://www.researchgate.net/publication/365069944
23. Ramaiah, M., Prasad, D.K.: Polygonal Approximation of Digital Planar Curve Using Novel Significant Measure. Submitted In: November 26th, 2019 Reviewed: March 16th, 2020 Published: April 28th, 2020. (2020). https://doi.org/10.5772/intechopen.92145
24. Robert, L.F., Nie, H.: How to approximate the volume of a lake. Coll. Math. J. **47**(3), 162–170 (2016). https://doi.org/10.4169/college.math.j.47.3.162
25. Dukov, I., Taneva, D.: Determination of the particle shape factor using Cauchy's theorem and image analysis. In: Proceedings of the XXI Scientific Conference FPEPM, vol. 2, pp. 60–63 (2016)
26. Raguraman, P., Meghana. A., Navya, Y., Karishma, S.K., Iswarya, S.: Color detection of RGB images using python and OpenCv. Int. J. Sci. Res. Comput. Sci. Eng. Inf. Technol. **7**(1), 109–112 (2021). https://doi.org/10.32628/CSEIT217119
27. Chistyakova, T., Furaev, D.: Computer system for resource-saving design of industrial processes of secondary oil refining. In: Kravets, A.G., Bolshakov, A.A., Shcherbakov, M. (eds.) Cyber-Physical Systems: Modelling and Industrial Application. SSDC, vol. 418, pp. 14–24. Springer, Cham (2022). https://doi.org/10.1007/978-3-030-95120-7_2
28. Bolshakov A., Slobodyanyuk L., Shashikhina O., Kovalchuk Y.: A combined method for solving the problem of optimizing the production schedule of metal structure processing for use in a cyber-physical control system of a metallurgical enterprise. In: Kravets, A.G., Bolshakov, A.A., Shcherbakov, M. (eds.) Cyber-Physical Systems: Modelling and Industrial Application. SSDC, vol. 418, pp. 243–259. Springer, Cham (2022). ISSN 2198–4182. https://doi.org/10.1007/978-3-030-95120-7_21
29. Kravets, A.G.: On approach for the development of patents analysis formal metrics. Commun. Comput. Inf. Sci. **1083**, 34–45 (2019)

Improving the Quality of Dental Services Based on Metal Additive Technologies: Unified Digital Workflow of Treatment

Viktor P. Radchenko[✉][iD] and Alexander V. Khoperskov[iD]

Volgograd State University, Volgograd, Russia
{viktor.radchenko,khoperskov}@volsu.ru

Abstract. The research is aimed at building a digital workflow (DW) that implements an iterative procedure to create high-quality dental products for individual patient needs based on cobalt-chromium metal 3D printing techniques. The introduction of an additive technology for selective laser alloying of metal powder provides a reliable solution to this problem without expensive auxiliary operations. An important component of our digital workflow is the numerical simulation of temperature dynamics during the manufacture of dental metal structures, which affects the strength properties of products. Strong heating and cooling during metal 3D printing cause mechanical deformation due to spatial temperature inhomogeneity. The results of numerical simulations make it possible to mitigate this negative factor by adding complementary temporary support structures directly at the 3D printing stage.

Keywords: additive dentistry · digital workflow · numerical simulation · selective laser melting · treatment quality

1 Introduction

Additive technologies are still not very effective for mass production, but the highest ability to personalize final products underlies the widespread use of these approaches in dental medicine, where 3D printing is actively replacing traditionally used methods based on subtractive manufacturing (milling, casting), allowing you to achieve perfect accuracy when creating various prostheses, scaffolds and other dental products [1–3]. The combination of new technological methods based on a digital platform can significantly facilitate the work of dentists and the process of treating patients [4–7]. An important subsystem of the digital platform is a set of software for treatment planning and communication [5], which can be supplemented with tools for simulating the physical processes of 3D printing [8–10] and this is the purpose of our research.

This research was funded by the Russian Science Foundation (grant no. 23-71-00016 https://rscf.ru/en/project/23-71-00016/) by using the equipment of the shared research facilities of HPC computing resources at Lomonosov Moscow State University.

The aim of this work is to develop an interdisciplinary method for creating dental structures using a unified digital workflow, combining 3D modeling, 3D metal printing, numerical simulations of physical processes occurring both during product creation and its use by a patient. We restrict ourselves here to thermal processes and mechanical stresses that arise during the printing process. The next natural extension of our approach can be the consideration of mechanical effects during chewing, taking into account the individual characteristics of the patient, which will provide an even higher quality of dental services.

2 Structure of Digital Workflow

2.1 General Process Structure

Let's discuss the general structure of the workflow, including steps to improve the quality of dental products through numerical modeling of thermal processes and internal mechanical stresses. The biomechanical behavior of 3D printed dentures should comply with clinical protocols [9,11–13]. Special requirements for biomechanical analysis are imposed on full-arch fixed dental prostheses. A separate area of research is the analysis of spatial distributions of internal stresses in a 3D print sample for a more efficient placement of supporting structures (cylindrical columns that attach the dental product to the working platform during 3D printing). The selection of the heat treatment mode for the metal frame should ensure the quality of the dental product. Since, the improvement of the strength characteristics of implants ensures the long-term quality of life of the patient. Additional research is required on aging periods and long-term changes in mechanical characteristics of prostheses under real conditions of their use. Combining the possibilities of communication medicine with methods of processing medical images, including computed tomography, conducting stress studies of the quality of implants at all stages of manufacturing and treatment, is becoming the standard in dentistry and oral surgery [14–19].

Data flows and material transfers should cover spatially distributed medical and technical departments, such as dental offices, 3D printing technical centers, large consulting clinics, legal offices, etc. Digital integration of intraoral scans, 3D modeling of both the oral cavity and the implant, 3D printing, Cone Beam Computed Tomography (CBCT), virtual cross-mounting, facial scans leads to a unified digital workflow (DW) of the treatment process [2,3,6,7,11,20]. CBCT-based imaging is an important source of initial data, both for a doctor at the diagnostic stage and for building a 3D model of the musculoskeletal system [14]. The digital 3D model and standard manipulations with it according to proven algorithms in specialized CAD/CAM dentistry replace the traditional manual wax and plaster modeling, which requires a lot of experience and creative work for the technician. The quality of dental treatment is primarily determined by the individual characteristics and requirements of patients, which are most naturally solved by combining digital and additive technologies [12,15].

The digital workflow includes many software products such as CAD software, tools for creating a digital 3D model using intraoral scan or computed tomography data, 3D printing cutting software, G-codes for computer numerical control, data visualization system [2,6,12]. The development of full-color three-dimensional imaging seems to be an essential component of improving the quality of dental treatment both for the traditional approach to implantation and to a greater extent for the development of additive methods for medicine [2,14,16,21]. The digital workflow must be able to transfer digital models over the Internet to large specialized metal 3D printing centers, which results higher quality final dental products compared to using 3D printers in a medical office.

Figures 1 and 2 show our process of creating dental products from the initial examination of the patient to <<wide smile of 32 teeth>>. High-quality digital workflow should allow the transition to a linear additive manufacturing algorithm in medicine without branches and cycles. Reducing repetitive operations reduces the time and cost of treatment, improving the quality of services. In addition, reducing the amount of physical contact between the patient, doctors and technical staff is an additional reward, which is important in the context of viral epidemics. The authors of highlight the development of online services system in the healthcare system as an important area of digitalization of medical services based on industrial and manufacturing engineering. The ongoing digitalization of dentistry corresponds to the global processes of transition to a digital economy in the context of the global deterioration of the epidemiological situation due to COVID-19 [22]. The Digital Dentistry block in Fig. 2 is part of an overall workflow that brings together digital and computing technologies.

The first step in digital dentistry is the process of 3D scanning a plaster cast of teeth or an intraoral 3D scan. The resulting 3D model is the basis for the production of the metal frame. Virtual interocclusal recording and 3D modeling provide a more accurate relief of the occlusal surface, allowing you to form the necessary tilt angles for the cusps of the teeth on a computer, correlate the lateral sliding paths1 of the chewing group of teeth, canines and incisors, and thus create a harmonious occlusion of the dentition for the patient. Then we build a physical 3D model of the object with a volumetric distribution of mechanical and thermodynamic characteristics for numerical simulations of thermal and mechanical processes that occur during 3D printing. The smoothed particle method allows one to construct such a physical three-dimensional model with complex geometry [23]. The results of numerical modeling underlie the choice of the optimal geometry of dental structures during their manufacture. The 3D models are positioned on the 3D printer platform with their inner parts up to ensure the best fit on the stumps. The placement of the supporting structures is determined based on the results analysis of modeling the thermal processes and the emerging internal stresses.

Below, we consider the features of printing using the example of Concept Laser Mlab 3D printer. We use certified cobalt-chromium powder with a fraction of 10–63 μ, setting the oxygen level in the working chamber to 0–0.8% and 300% for the DOS-factor (the proportion of powder poured in one layer), which determines the container lifting coefficient with powder for applying a new layer of 3D printing. Typical printing occurs at 200% and the powder container is

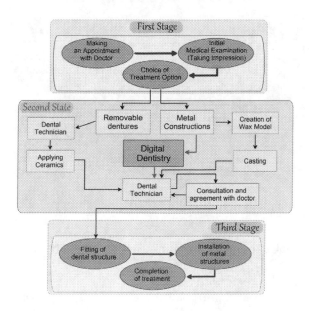

Fig. 1. A workflow diagram of the design and construction of a metal dental product using the underlying technologies. The central block << *DigitalDentistry* >> of the Second Stage is based on various digital technologies, including 3D modeling, 3D printing, numerical modeling of physical production processes (See details in Fig. 2).

raised 0.025 mm for a given 0.025 mm layer thickness. A value of 300% provides a container lift of 0.038 mm, which is necessary for uniform powder application on the first 5 layers of printing. After that the print mode can run at 200%. If the platform is filled with products as tightly as possible, then this parameter can be raised to 280–300% for the first 5 layers and 265–270% for subsequent layers. After 3D printing, finished metal structures undergo additional heat treatment according to a specific mode aimed at relieving mechanical stress.

Models are removed from the platform and examined for surface quality in the final steps of <<Digital Dentistry>> (see Fig. 2). The dental product is then handed over to the dental technician for cleaning and resurfacing (see Fig. 2). Below we will discuss some of the features of the stages in more detail.

2.2 Features of 3D Scanning and Printing for Dentistry

The input basis for 3D printing of a component of the patient's dental system is a digital 3D model for the construction of which various methods are used. High-tech approaches based on magnetic resonance imaging or computed tomography, however, give poor quality due to noise that is difficult to eliminate. Therefore, hand-held scanning devices provide an acceptable result. Intraoral scanning of a large cavity (more than 5 teeth) can also give a noticeable total error (see Fig. 2). Therefore, significant efforts are aimed at reducing errors, improving

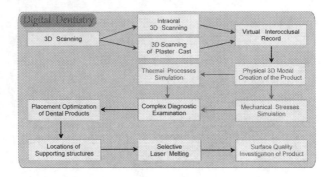

Fig. 2. Block structure <<Digital Dentistry>> as part of DW (See Fig. 1)

digital workflow when using an intraoral scanner under different edentulous conditions.

Dental prosthetics begin with a plaster cast. The old classical technology was based on making such an impression from wax and then casting from cobalt-chromium alloys. Plaster cast is also one of the main stages of additive manufacturing already to create a digital model. Figure 3 shows the Medit Identica T300 3D Scanner as an example of standard equipment for fast 3D model building in automatic mode with high accuracy. The size of the scanning working area ($90 \times 72 \times 60$ mm) allows you to examine the entire dental arch at once, which simplifies and speeds up the scanning process. Medit Identica T300 uses a blue backlight, which makes it independent of the lighting in the laboratory. The use of professional 3D scanners increases the productivity of the dental laboratory and reduces costs. Thus, the purpose of this stage is a digital impression model, which is the basis for 3D modeling of dental products of varying complexity, from simple crowns to clasp structures.

The 3D modeling process for a full 16-tooth arch is one of the more complex examples. The plaster cast forms the basis of the digital model of the implant (Fig. 4). There is a significant amount of software (e.g. ExoCad) that helps build digital models based on various tooth model templates. An important step in the modification of the template is the selection of the correct bite for a particular patient when creating caps for each tooth. The final stage of modeling involves the combination of all elements of the dental system into one arc.

The "Stereolithography" (STL) format is the standard for storing and using 3D models in CAM/CAD and is generally accepted in dentistry. This approach allows you to send stl-files from medical offices to specialized centers of additive technologies for metal printing. This separation of processes corresponds to the common practice of preparing 3D data and printing biological tissues and organs [13, 24–26].

Fig. 3. Device for 3D scanning of a plaster sample.

3 Optimization of Metal 3D Printing of Dental Products Using Computer Simulation Methods

Layer by layer 3D printing of metal products has negative consequences due to high temperature drops during the melting and solidification of the material. Large temperature gradients cause mechanical deformations that can greatly reduce the quality of finished products [27]. High temperature can cause unwanted phase transformations, which is especially critical for printing porous materials, for example, porous titanium nickel alloy, porous titanium alloy Ti-6Al-4V, etc. The mechanical requirements for dental products (implants, abutments, crowns, suprastructures) are very stringent and include wear resistance, high Vickers hardness, flexural strength, crack resistance, anti-corrosion properties of the surface. The dental full arch is a special case because it consists of a large number of components and this complex design is fundamentally different in mechanical properties, placing additional demands on the quality of the manufacturing process.

We can reduce temperature gradients and residual stresses in the 3D printing stage by using additional support structures (thin cylindrical legs and reinforcing tapered supports) equalize temperatures and reduce mechanical distortion. The influence of these auxiliary support structures on the thermal and mechanical characteristics of the product can be investigated based on the numerical solution of the equation of non-stationary heat transfer within the entire structure during the printing process.

The correct positioning of the 3D model on the working platform is the most important prerequisite for creating a quality product. This initial step includes setting the required height for removing the printed product, installing supporting structures, including reinforcing conical supports (Fig. 5). These additional structures enhance mechanical strength, preventing detachment of layers and changes in shape. We point out another significant factor that allows you to

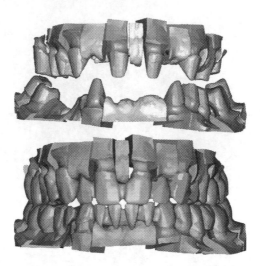

Fig. 4. Examples of digital models of dental systems.

control the distribution of temperature. The reduction of temperature gradients prevents the product from detaching from the working platform and its deformation. The high temperature gradient is due to the essence of 3D printing due to the layer-by-layer fusion of metal powder. The temperature of the new upper layers is significantly higher than the lower layers. High temperature gradients create internal stresses in the metal, which can lead to deformations. The creation of a 3D model should include setting the geometry of the supporting structures on the working platform in order to achieve the most uniform temperature at each time of 3D printing, which requires preliminary numerical simulations of thermal processes. The print material significantly affects the temperature fields, which requires special calculations. Printing with cobalt-chromium alloy heats the product up to $1100\,°C$ and then cools down to $\sim20\,°C$ in the working chamber for some time.

Thus, the optimal placement of supporting structures is aimed at reducing internal stresses by controlling the process of heat removal from the product.

3.1   Mathematical and Numerical Models

Temperature inhomogeneity $T(\boldsymbol{r})$ cause an additional connection between the stress tensor $\hat{\sigma} = \sigma_{ij}$ and the strain tensor $\hat{\varepsilon} = \varepsilon_{ij}$ [28]. The mathematical model of thermoelasticity is based on the equations of such a relationship in the linear approximation We use tensor thermoelasticity equations in a linear approximation to calculate the relationship between the stress tensor and the strain tensor in the following form [28]:

$$\sigma_{ij} - 2\mu\varepsilon_{ij} - \delta_{ij}\left(\lambda\varepsilon_{kk} - 3K\alpha_T\left(T(\boldsymbol{r}) - T_0\right)\right) = 0\,, \tag{1}$$

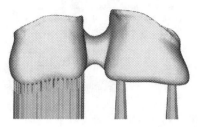

Fig. 5. Images of a system of thin supporting structures (left) and tapered supports (right).

where $\hat{\sigma} = \sigma_{ij}$ is the stress tensor, $\hat{\varepsilon} = \varepsilon_{ij}$ is the strain tensor, $T(r)$ is the temperature in the point r, T_0 is the temperature of the undeformed sample, α_T is the coefficient of thermal expansion, K is the bulk modulus, λ is the first Lame coefficient describes the transverse normal stresses, μ is the second Lame coefficient that determines the shear deformation, $\delta_{ij} = 1$ is the unit tensor. The strain tensor in Eq. (1)

$$\varepsilon_{ij} = \frac{\partial u_i}{\partial x_j} + \frac{\partial u_j}{\partial x_i} + \sum_{m=1}^{3} \frac{\partial u_m}{\partial x_i} \frac{\partial u_m}{\partial x_j} \tag{2}$$

is defined through the displacement vector of a point inside the body $\{u_1, u_2, u_3\}$.

Heat balance equation

$$c_\varepsilon \varrho \frac{\partial T}{\partial t} = \mathbf{\nabla}(k_T \mathbf{\nabla} T) + Q(r,t) - 3\alpha_T KT \sum_{m=1}^{3} \frac{\partial \varepsilon_{mm}}{\partial t}, \tag{3}$$

includes the influence of the dynamics of the tensor ε_{mm}, k_T is the coefficient of thermal conductivity, ϱ is the mass density, c_ε is the heat capacity at constant strain, density of heat sources and sinks in metal Q is determined by printing processes, $\mathbf{\nabla}$ is the differential operator nabla. The closing equation for the displacement in the linear approximation of the modulus of $\nabla \mathbf{u}$ is

$$\varrho \frac{\partial^2 \mathbf{u}}{\partial t^2} = -\alpha_T \left(1 + 2\mu/3\right) \nabla T + (\lambda + \mu) \nabla(\nabla \mathbf{u}) + \mu \, \Delta \mathbf{u}, \tag{4}$$

where Δ is the Laplace operator.

The numerical solution of the Eqs. (1), (3) is based on the finite element method, which is due to two factors. First, the computational domain is geometrically complex and the three-dimensional surface has small-scale irregularities. Secondly, the initial 3D model is built using CAD tools, where the construction of a triangulation grid is a natural result of geometric modeling. The platform size for the Concept Laser Mlab cusing R is $90\,\text{mm} \times 90\,\text{mm} \times 12\,\text{mm}$ (see Fig. 11). The maximum size of the finite element determines the quality of the numerical simulation. If a grid with a cell size of approximately $2\,\text{mm} \times 2\,\text{mm} \times 2\,\text{mm}$ is sufficient for the platform, then it is necessary to reduce the typical element size to 0.1 mm × 0.1 mm × 0.1 mm for a dental product. For rough and fast modeling, you can use a larger cell. The main input parameters of mathematical modeling of layer-by-layer fusion of metal powder are laser power, laser scanning speed, waiting time for applying a new layer of powder, temperatures of the inner chamber and platform before printing.

3.2   Optimizing the 3D Model and 3D Metal Printing

The goal of optimization is to prepare models of metal products for additive manufacturing, including the following:

- Checking the quality of the 3D model (the absence of unconnected edges, open faces, etc.).
- The optimal arrangement of elements on the working platform, ensuring the efficiency of the printing process related to productivity, powder consumption, printing time.
- Improving the quality of final products, characterized by strength mechanical characteristics, which are due to the influence of a non-uniform temperature distribution on internal stresses during cooling. This is determined by the location and geometric characteristics of the supporting structures and tapered supports.

The results of the numerical solution of the equations system (1)–(4) allow choosing a more optimal solution from a set of different variants (Fig. 6, 7). Numerical cell size scale should be limited to a print layer thickness of approximately 25 μ, which is equal to the average value of the metal powder fraction.

Fig. 6. Temperature distribution at the printing stage. The last printed layers are hot (shown in shades of red). Blue indicates the lower temperature of the first layers and support structures that are printed at the beginning. (Color figure online)

Calculations of internal stresses are based on modeling in a computer-aided design system. The input data of the model are, first of all, the 3D model of the product with the physical characteristics included in the mathematical model (1)–(4). The solution also depends on the powder, the thickness of the printed

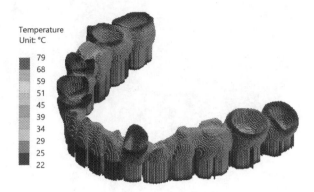

Fig. 7. The result of the temperature calculation for full dental arch model 5 min after the completion of printing.

layer, the operating mode of the laser, the conditions in the working chamber. Modeling is end-to-end and includes a model of the dental system, supporting structures and working platform. We calculate areas that need to be reinforced with support structures to reduce temperature gradients (Fig. 6). Special software allows you to analyze the spatio-temporal dynamics of temperature $T(x, y, z, t)$ both on the surface and inside the product and also calculate temperature gradients ∇T (see Figs. 6, 7, 8) defining the displacements and the corresponding strain tensor.

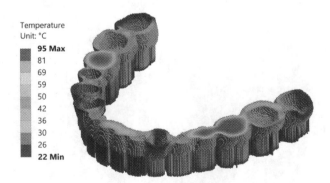

Fig. 8. The temperature distribution is as in the Fig. 6, but the upper part of the product has been cut off. The higher internal temperature of the metal is clearly visible.

Thus, any 3D model includes a dental system and supporting structures, as shown in the Fig. 9. The latter are needed as a support for printing and to improve the efficiency of heat transfer. The Fig. 10 shows the displacement distribution over the surface after 3D printing. Additional tapered supports can

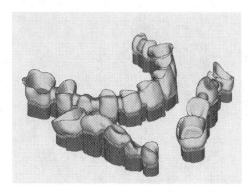

Fig. 9. The supporting structures are shown in blue at the bottom in the Materialize Magics software. Yellow highlights dental implants. (Color figure online)

reduce the appearance of defects due to uneven cooling. The 3D geometric model in CAD tools format must be specified as a discrete grid for numerical integration of differential equations. We use special software to build a system of numerical grid nodes in the Lagrangian approach in the form of SPH particles [23, 29]. The use of the SPH method makes it possible to effectively parallelize the computational code for computing systems with graphical processes. In conclusion, we note the possibilities for the development of such modeling associated with the chewing process, when the implant is subjected not to a single impact, but to a cyclic one, since when chewing food, the human lower jaw performs vertical, horizontal and transversal movements and mechanically interacts with the teeth of the upper jaw.

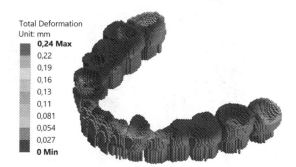

Fig. 10. Deformations of the dental full arches and supporting structures.

Our research is aimed at introducing methods of mathematical modeling of physical processes into the practice of 3D printing of dental structures. The initial setup of Concept Laser Mlab cusing R equipment (LaserCUSING) requires setting parameters for the most efficient operation, which can be limited by simulation results. Correct fusion of the first layer and the metal powder to the platform depends on the zero level calibration. It is necessary to reduce the oxygen content in the working chamber to a certain value by pumping in an inert gas (nitrogen), which affects both product quality and work safety.

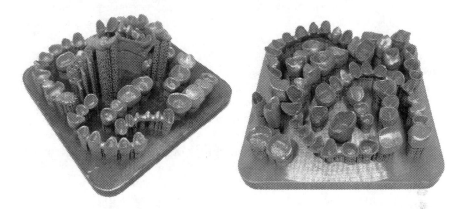

Fig. 11. Various distributions of dental products on a working platform for metal 3D printing: a – the method of positioning a clasp prosthesis along the Z axis, surrounded by metal crowns and bridges; b – ways to position the clasp prosthesis in the X, Y plane with other metal products around. More dense packing of units (crowns, bridges and clasps) is a more cost-effective solution with the technological ability to quickly remove objects without damage.

Figure 11 demonstrates two examples of metal 3D printing. Each work platform contains a large number of dental objects of various types from simple crowns to large dental arches and special fixtures. More dense packing of the arrangement of objects reduces the printing time and, in part, the powder consumption. However, the geometry of the entire structure affects the temperature dynamics. Such parallel printing of many metal dental products at once requires preliminary selection and distribution of them on the working surface while minimizing material and time resources depending on the workload of the dental clinic or 3D printing center (see the <<Selective laser fusion>> step in the Fig. 2).

Finished products cannot be immediately removed from the platform due to the presence of internal stresses that can change the geometry of the dental arch, which creates irreparable problems. Therefore, we place the platform with dental structures in a furnace for heat treatment, and only then can the finished metal frames be separated from the platform. Internal stresses in the printed product are an integral part of the technological process. Therefore, an attempt to separate such a complex dental structure from the working platform, as a rule, leads to a change in the geometry of the sample. A necessary stage of work is additional heat treatment in the special furnace, the mode of which should relieve the metal frame from internal stresses.

4 Discussion and Conclusions

The use of casting techniques in the creation of complex dental products requires significant additional refinements and medical procedures for the patient. Additive manufacturing can significantly improve manufacturing accuracy and speed up the treatment process. However, methods of laser melting of metal powder require modification of the technological process in order to reduce possible deformations due to large temperature gradients in the metal. Economic efficiency dictates its limitations associated with the simultaneous 3D printing of the maximum possible number of dental products on one working platform (see Fig. 11) in one technological cycle. This significantly reduces the cost of production, but may degrade the quality, since the temperature regime depends on the configuration of the location of various dental objects and the parameters of the supporting structures.

We propose to use mathematical modeling methods to control thermal processes during 3D printing by varying the parameters of supporting structures. The conducted numerical experiments show such a possibility. The combination of both thin supporting structures and powerful tapered supports is effective. This makes it possible to reduce temperature gradients and corresponding internal mechanical stresses. Our experience in creating dental products on the Concept Laser Mlab 3D printer based on cobalt-chromium powder points out the possibility of achieving an error of about 20 μ, which does not require additional manipulations for the patient.

Such modeling requires the 3D model construction of the jaw system of a particular patient, but these difficulties are compensated by the quality of prosthetics. The discussed approach combines metal 3D printing and mathematical modeling of physical processes in a product, significantly improving the quality of additive technology in various fields. For example, 3D printing of concrete structures with mechanical constraints analysis allows significantly improved mechanical characteristics at the printing stag. The development of sophisticated digital tools and software significantly expand the possibilities of additive technologies in dental surgery. A fully digital workflow for the aesthetic reconstruction of complex cases of maxillary and mandibular full-arches requires 3D modeling of a sequence of provisional and final restorations in CAD/CAM software prior to clinical treatment [7]. Improving the strength characteristics of the implantable system ensures a long-term quality of life for the patient.

References

1. Alauddin, M.S., Baharuddin, A.S., Mohd Ghazali, M.I.: The modern and digital transformation of oral health care: a mini review. Healthcare **9**(2), 118 (2021). https://doi.org/10.3390/healthcare9020118
2. Oberoi, G., Nitsch, S., Edelmayer, M., Janjic, K., Muller, A.S., Agis, H.: 3D printing-encompassing the facets of dentistry. Front. Bioeng. Biotechnol. **6**, 172 (2018). https://doi.org/10.3389/fbioe.2018.00172

3. Kessler, A., Hickel, R., Reymus, M.: 3D printing in dentistry-state of the art. Oper. Dent. **45**(1), 30–40 (2020). https://doi.org/10.2341/18-229-1

4. Ostapenko, G.F.: Creating a platform based business model in dental industry. Int. J. Prof. Bus. Rev. **24**(4), 1–11 (2019). https://doi.org/10.14295/bds.2021.v24i4. 2789

5. Coachman, C., Blatz, M.B., Bohner, L., Sesma, N.: Dental software classification and dento-facial interdisciplinary planning platform. J. Esthet. Restor. Dent. **33**(1), 99–106 (2021). https://doi.org/10.1111/jerd.12713

6. Revilla-Leon, M., Besne-Torre, A., Sanchez-Rubio, J.L., Fabrega, J.J., Ozcan, M.: Digital tools and 3D printing technologies integrated into the workflow of restorative treatment: a clinical report. J. Prosthet. Dent. **121**(1), 3–8 (2019). https:// doi.org/10.1016/j.prosdent.2018.02.020

7. Roberts, M., Shull, F., Schiner, B.: Maxillary full-arch reconstruction using a sequenced digital workflow. J. Esthet. Restor. Dent. **32**(4), 336–356 (2020). https://doi.org/10.1111/jerd.12582

8. Khoperskov, A.V., Radchenko, V.P.: Additive technologies in implant dentistry: 3D printing in metal and simulation of strength characteristics. AIP Conf. Proc. **2410**, 020009 (2021). https://doi.org/10.1063/5.0067877

9. Barbin, T., et al.: 3D metal printing in dentistry: an in vitro biomechanical comparative study of two additive manufacturing technologies for full-arch implant-supported prostheses. J. Mech. Behav. Biomed. Mater. **108**, 103821 (2020). https://doi.org/10.1016/j.jmbbm.2020.103821

10. Colosimo, B.M., Grasso, M., Garghetti, F., Rossi, B.: Complex geometries in additive manufacturing: a new solution for lattice structure modeling and monitoring. J. Qual. Technol. **54**(4), 392–414 (2022). https://doi.org/10.1080/00224065.2021. 1926377

11. Lepidi, L., Galli, M., Grammatica, A.C., Joda, T., Wang, H.-L., Li, J.: Indirect digital workflow for virtual cross-mounting of fixed implant-supported prostheses to create a 3D virtual patient. J. Prosthodont. **30**(2), 177–182 (2021). https://doi. org/10.1111/jopr.13247

12. Cicciu, M., et al.: 3D digital impression systems compared with traditional techniques in dentistry: a recent data systematic review. Materials **13**(8), 1982 (2020). https://doi.org/10.3390/ma13081982

13. Sacchi, M., Bansal, R., Rouwkema, J.: Bioengineered 3D models to recapitulate tissue fibrosis. Trends Biotechnol. **38**, 623–636 (2020). https://doi.org/10.1016/j. tibtech.2019.12.010

14. Goodacre, B.J., Swamidass, R.S., Lozada, L., Al-Ardah, A., Sahl, E.: A 3D-printed guide for lateral approach sinus grafting: a dental technique. Dent. Tech. **119**(6), 897–901 (2018). https://doi.org/10.1016/j.prosdent.2017.07.014

15. Haleem, A., Javaid, M.: Polyether ether ketone (PEEK) and its manufacturing of customised 3D printed dentistry parts using additive manufacturing. Clin. Epidemiol. Global Health **7**, 654–660 (2019). https://doi.org/10.1016/j.cegh.2019.03. 001

16. Khoperskov, A.V., et al.: Software for full-color 3D reconstruction of the biological tissues internal structure. In: Siuly, S., et al. (eds.) HIS 2017. LNCS, vol. 10594, pp. 1–10. Springer, Cham (2017). https://doi.org/10.1007/978-3-319-69182-4_1

17. Barazanchi, A., Li, K.C., Al-Amleh, B., Lyons, K., Waddell, J.N.: Additive technology: update on current materials and applications in dentistry. J. Prosthodont. **26**(2), 156–163 (2017). https://doi.org/10.1111/jopr.12510

18. Solis, D.M., Czekanski, A.: 3D and 4D additive manufacturing techniques for vascular-like structures - a review. Bioprinting **25**, e00182 (2022). https://doi.org/10.1016/j.bprint.2021.e00182
19. Adamov, A.A., Gndoyan, I.A., Dyatchina, A.I., Khramov, V.N.: Development of a classifier of photo images of pathologies for an ultra-small data set. Math. Phys. Comput. Simul. **26**(1), 33–48 (2023). https://doi.org/10.15688/mpcm.jvolsu.2023.1.3
20. Lee, Y.-C., et al.: Influence of edentulous conditions on intraoral scanning accuracy of virtual interocclusal record in quadrant scan. Appl. Sci. **11**, 1489 (2021). https://doi.org/10.3390/app11041489
21. Shin, S.-H., Doh, R.-M., Lim, J.-H., Kwon, J.-S., Shim, J.-S., Kim, J.-E.: Evaluation of dimensional changes according to aging period and postcuring time of 3D-printed denture base prostheses: an in vitro study. Materials **14**(20), 6185 (2021). https://doi.org/10.3390/ma14206185
22. Baumgart, D.C.: Digital advantage in the COVID-19 response: perspective from Canada's largest integrated digitalized healthcare system. NPJ Digit. Med. **3**(1), 114 (2020). https://doi.org/10.1038/s41746-020-00326-y
23. Titov, A., Khrapov, S., Radchenko, V., Khoperskov, A.: Aerodynamic models of complicated constructions using parallel smoothed particle hydrodynamics. Commun. Comput. Inf. Sci. **965**, 173–184 (2019). https://doi.org/10.1007/978-3-030-05807-4_15
24. Daly, A.C., Davidson, M.D., Burdick, J.A.: 3D bioprinting of high cell-density heterogeneous tissue models through spheroid fusion within self-healing hydrogels. Nat. Commun. **12**, 753 (2021). https://doi.org/10.1038/s41467-021-21029-2
25. Hodásová, L., et al.: Polymer infiltrated ceramic networks with biocompatible adhesive and 3D-printed highly porous scaffolds. Addit. Manuf. **39**, 101850 (2021). https://doi.org/10.1016/j.addma.2021.101850
26. Wang, H., Su, K., Su, L., Liang, P., Ji, P., Wang, C.: Comparison of 3D-printed porous tantalum and titanium scaffolds on osteointegration and osteogenesis. Mater. Sci. Eng. C **104**, 109908 (2019). https://doi.org/10.1016/j.msec.2019.109908
27. Moridi, A., et al.: Solid-state additive manufacturing of porous Ti-6Al-4V by supersonic impact. Appl. Mater. Today **21**, 100865 (2020). https://doi.org/10.1016/j.apmt.2020.100865
28. Landau, L.D., Lifshitz, E.M.: Theory of Elasticity, 2 edn, vol. 07, 544 p. Pergamon (1980)
29. Levshinskii, V., Polyakov, M., Losev, A., Khoperskov, A.: Verification and validation of computer models for diagnosing breast cancer based on machine learning for medical data analysis. Commun. Comput. Inf. Sci. **1084**, 447–460 (2019). https://doi.org/10.1007/978-3-030-29750-3_35

Cyber-Physical Systems and Big Data-Driven World. Intelligent Internet of Services and Internet of Things

Detecting Anomalies in Multidimensional Time Series Using Binary Classification

Mohammed. A. Al-Gunaid[2,3]([✉]), Maxim.V. Shcherbakov[2,3],
Vladimir O. Artyushin[2,3], Dmitry V. Shkolny[1], and Sergey V. Belov[1]

[1] RT-Infrastructure JSC, Petrovsko-Razumovskaya alley 10 Building 1, Moscow 127083, Russian Federation
{info,belov}@rt-in.ru

[2] LLC "Laboratory of Business Intelligence "Bilab", Lenin Avenue 28A, Volgograd 400051, Russian Federation
{info,maxim.shcherbakov}@bilaboratory.com

[3] Volgograd State Technical University, Lenin Avenue 28A, Volgograd 400051, Russian Federation

Abstract. The purpose of this work is to improve the efficiency of monitoring the composition of wastewater by developing a method for detecting anomalies in time series. The paper describes the concept of the system for collecting data from the pH/ORP sensor of the hardware-software complex for automated control of the composition of wastewater (PAK), the proposed approach for the automatic detection of discharges in wastewater using binary classification, as well as the method of automating the process of sampling and retraining the model based on the results of identification, taking into account the expert opinions of specialists. The result of the work is developing a more efficient method for finding anomalies in a time series using binary classification.

Keywords: anomaly · outlier · time series · binary classification

1 Introduction

Over the past few decades, growing awareness of the detrimental consequences of chemical discharges, waste, and other substances on water quality, along with advancements in environmental technologies, has led to stricter regulations and guidelines for wastewater treatment [6, 7]. Consequently, the effective monitoring of wastewater treatment plants has become a crucial responsibility for water utilities worldwide, carrying substantial environmental and cost-saving implications. Key to this endeavor is the measurement and monitoring of wastewater quality, which presents various challenges due to the harsh operating conditions, intricate microbial growth processes, and significant measurement delays [7, 8]. Parameters like BOD5 (biochemical oxygen demand for 5 days), COD (chemical oxygen demand), and TN (total nitrogen) pose particular difficulty.

A. G. Kravets et al. (Eds.): CIT&DS 2023, CCIS 1909, pp. 323–336, 2023.
https://doi.org/10.1007/978-3-031-44615-3_22

To describe the intricate physical, chemical, and biological reactions occurring in wastewater, a multitude of differential equations is typically required, making the construction of a process model cumbersome. Consequently, data-driven soft sensor technology has emerged as the favored method for measuring variables related to the quality of biological treatment processes in wastewater treatment [9]. This technology involves building specific mathematical models to establish relationships between input and output variables, enabling predictions of hard-to-measure variables without relying on an exact mechanism model.

The significance of easy access to high-quality water for public health, living conditions, economic development, and national security is widely acknowledged. With the substantial data generated by water utilities and the profound impact of the water industry on people's lives, there is an increasing need to explore improved methods for monitoring and predicting water quality. Innovative approaches, such as machine learning and data mining techniques, hold promise for addressing these challenges [10, 11].

Two prevalent data analysis problems faced in this context are unbalanced class distribution (ICD) and missing values (MV). These issues are indicative of data quality challenges [12–14] and continue to persist across various real-world tasks and applications [15, 16], including water quality anomaly detection. Conventional predictive machine learning algorithms often struggle to handle such problems as they assume data completeness and balanced class distribution [17, 18]. Consequently, if not appropriately addressed, these algorithms yield suboptimal results, leading to systematic errors, inaccuracies, and low-quality predictive capabilities of classifiers [16, 17, 19].

Of particular interest are water quality anomalies, rare events that can have significant implications in real-life scenarios. However, predicting these rare events using traditional machine learning approaches presents considerable challenges for researchers, primarily due to the inherent difficulties in handling imbalanced scenarios [20]. Traditional classifiers often encounter issues such as noise, overlapping minority and majority classes, performance metric biases favoring the majority class, and disjuncts in unbalanced data, which typically involves a small sample size with high feature dimensionality [21].

2 Analysis of Existing Solutions

Currently, there exists a range of methods that employ binary classification to detect anomalies in time series data. Numerous related studies have been conducted in this area. One such study [1] delves into the problem of detecting anomalies in binary unbalanced water quality data with missing values. The researchers evaluate various classifiers through stratified 5-fold cross-validation, using accuracy, ROC-AUC, and F1-measure as performance evaluation metrics. Additionally, they conduct experiments with different homogeneous and heterogeneous ensemble methods, incorporating resampling and missing values strategies during training, along with two optimized deep neural network models. The results demonstrate enhanced classifier performance, especially in addressing class imbalance and incomplete data issues. The neural network models exhibit superior capabilities in tackling both problems.

In the domain of spoofing protection [2], traditional approaches treat it as a binary classification problem, but such classifiers often fail to generalize well to unknown databases due to diverse face-swapping attacks, environmental factors, and limited sample sizes. Anomaly detection, an alternative approach, is gaining popularity. This work explores using images from non-specialized face databases and images in the wild to train classifiers for face spoofing protection. A convolutional autoencoder is employed to classify face images as clients or impostors based on the reconstruction error compared to a threshold value. Incorporating images in the wild in the training set significantly improves the classifier's ability to distinguish the unseen database, as evident by an increased area under the curve. The challenge lies in finding an appropriate operating point in the unseen database.

In another research [3], a scalable method for detecting anomalies in multimodal images for patency classification is introduced. The approach involves a feature extractor and normalization of the flow with RGB, depth, and surface normals inputs. This method achieves over 95% area under the ROC curve and is robust against samples out of distribution.

Anomaly detection is also explored in [4], where an ensemble of unsupervised anomaly detectors feeds features into a second-stage binary classifier. The study compares the predictive performance of this semi-supervised approach against standalone classification-based methods using multiple semesters of college data.

For multiclass anomaly detection in the GI domain, a novel multiclass classification algorithm is proposed in [5]. This algorithm can handle any number of classes and addresses the imbalance problem. It utilizes autoencoders, each trained on one class to extract features with high discrimination from other classes. The loss function of autoencoders is designed based on reconstruction, compactness, distance from other classes, and KL divergence. The extracted features are then classified using an ensemble of support vector data descriptors. Ablation studies are conducted to investigate the impact of each step of the algorithm, and the results are compared with existing work, showing the competitiveness of this approach.

Furthermore, [22] discusses various machine learning and deep learning approaches for detecting water quality anomalies based on time series data. [23] proposes a multi-objective machine learning method for feature selection and ensemble generation to detect online drinking water quality anomalies. Two imbalance boosting ensemble models, SMOTEBoost and RUSBoost, are introduced in [24], using oversampling and undersampling methods to balance training data, along with multipurpose pruning of base models for ensembles to optimize prediction and generalization efficiency. [25] presents two models—a BP neural network with adaptive learning rate and two-stage isolation, and a random forest—for water quality prediction in urban water supply scenarios, considering both physical and biological indicators.

While much work has focused on missing values and class imbalance in this area, it is essential to consider evaluating classifiers on unseen, unbalanced test sets with or without missing values, as this presents a distinct challenge.

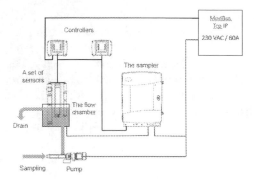

Fig. 1. Technological scheme PAK

3 Methodology

This section describes the concept of the subsystem for collecting data from the pH/ORP sensor of the software and hardware complex for automated control of the composition of wastewater (PAK), the proposed approach for automatically detecting discharges in wastewater, as well as automating the sampling process and retraining the model based on the results of identification with taking into account the expert opinions of specialists.

The technological scheme of the PAK is shown in Fig. 1. The order of operation is presented below.

The PAK is equipped with an inlet heated pipeline, the intake end of which is immersed in the controlled liquid flow.

At the command of the PAK controller, the screw self-priming pump ensures the renewal of the controlled liquid in the flow chamber, where it is analyzed by a set of signal sensors and measuring analyzers.

The liquid is drained from the flow chamber through the outlet heated pipeline, the outlet valve of which is located in the controlled liquid flow, downstream of the intake point (Fig. 4).

The pump operation time is determined by the frequency settings for measuring the controlled liquid. The operation of the pump ensures that the volume of the flow chamber and the inlet pipeline is completely updated immediately before readings from sensors and analyzers.

Readings coming from a set of sensors and analyzers are processed by the controller of the digital sensors module and the validation module, stored in the built-in, nonvolatile memory and transmitted via TCP / IP protocol to the application server for further processing.

In case of detecting a change in the chemical composition of the liquid (volley discharge) according to the controlled parameters, the PAK controller gives a command to the sampler to take a sample and store it in the built-in refrigeration chamber at t = 4 °C (Fig. 4).

Data on the detection of a salvo discharge and (or) the fact of sampling is transmitted to the application server for further processing and notifying the operator. The application server ensures that the received data is stored.

Additionally, the PAK is equipped with process sensors designed to monitor the equipment's performance, the absence of leaks and flooding, control the internal climate control system, monitor the integrity of the equipment (breaking the cabinet, registering shock loads, opening doors), and a GPS / GLONASS sensor.

3.1 Conceptual Diagram of an Intelligent Data Processing System for pH/ORP Sensors

Figure 2 shows a conceptual diagram of an intelligent system for processing data from pH/ORP sensors, which makes it possible to increase the efficiency of wastewater monitoring by:

- automating the process of monitoring, planning and registration of sampling results;
- creating the database (DB) on the locations of pH/ORP (MU) sensors, facts of anomalies, tasks for sampling and results of chemical analysis of the composition of samples;
- minimizing the response time to wastewater discharges based on the analysis of data obtained from pH/ORP sensors;
- identifying the types of discharges.

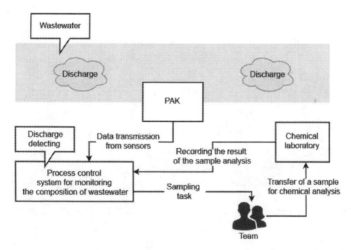

Fig. 2. Conceptual diagram of an intelligent data processing system for pH/ORP sensors.

3.2 Data Processing

To test the operation of the algorithm, data were taken from the intelligent wastewater monitoring process control system (Fig. 3), which collects data from pH/ORP sensors of the hardware and software complex for automated control of wastewater composition (PAK). To store data, ClickHouse is used - a columnar database management system (DBMS). The sensor has 8 channels. For training, a data sample was taken from one sensor for 2020.11.30–2021.11.23 (Fig. 3), a data fragment is presented in Table 1.. The sample size is 468,822. Water. Figure 4 show the software and hardware complex for automated control of the composition of wastewater.

The graphs (Fig. 5) clearly show anomalous values for each time series. Figure 6 shows time series graphs for 2021.05.01–2021.08.01.

Table 1. Data Fragment

Date	ch0	ch1	ch2	ch3	ch4	ch5	ch6	temp
30.11.2020 3:00	−16.710	−94.096	6.997	0.960	22.606	−101.56	7.707	16.90
30.11.2020 3:01	−16.646	−94.087	7.003	0.961	22.684	−101.54	7.707	16.91
30.11.2020 3:02	−16.609	−94.100	6.983	0.961	22.724	−101.53	7.680	16.92
30.11.2020 3:03	−16.569	−94.113	6.977	0.972	22.780	−101.52	7.664	16.93
30.11.2020 3:04	−16.508	−94.106	6.979	0.965	22.849	−101.50	7.657	16.94
30.11.2020 3:05	−16.458	−94.097	6.985	0.970	22.908	−101.49	7.652	16.94
30.11.2020 3:06	−16.426	−94.100	6.976	0.956	22.958	−101.50	7.626	16.95
30.11.2020 3:07	−16.387	−94.086	6.971	0.945	23.003	−101.50	7.603	16.96
30.11.2020 3:08	−16.356	−94.070	6.980	0.946	23.079	−101.501	7.585	16.96

Fig. 3. Intelligent control system for the process of monitoring wastewater

3.3 Mathematical Statement of the Problem

In the general case, binary classification is used to predict the probability of an event occurring by the values of a set of features. For this, the so-called dependent variable (event outcome) is introduced, which takes only one of two values (0 or 1), and a set of independent variables (also called features, predictors or regressors).

3.4 Binary Classification

We now mathematically describe the binary classification model we propose as follows. The distance values classified by chemical analysis and observation in the data set,

(a)   (b)

Fig. 4. Hardware and software complex for automated control of wastewater composition

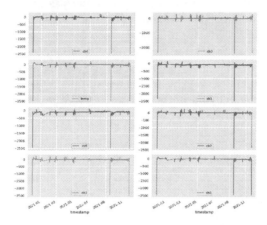

Fig. 5. Time series of sensor channels for 2020.11.30–2021.11.23

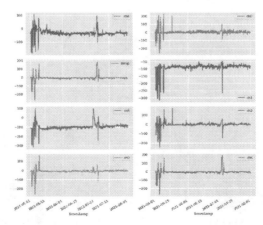

Fig. 6. Time series of sensor channels for 2021.05.01–2021.08.01

which implies similarity or dissimilarity between them, can be expressed in the following equation:

$$d_{ki} = \sum_{j} \left(\frac{w_j}{\sum_j w_j} \right) |X_{kj} - X_{ij}| \tag{1}$$

where d_{ki} are values classified by chemical analysis k and observation i (i = 1,2,...N); X_{kj}, between values classified by chemical analysis k value of the j-th variable (j = 1,2,...M); X_{ij} observation of the i-th value of the j-th variable; w_j, weight of j-th variable.

In Eq. 1, for each observation i, d_{ki} is calculated as much as the number of values classified by chemical analysis. Then the observation can be recognized as an anomalous value or not anomalous according to the value classified by chemical analysis, having a minimum value of $d_k i$'s (let's denote it as d_{k*i}). If, the classified value is an anomaly, then observation i is classified as an anomaly. Otherwise, the observation is classified as non-anomalous.

If all observations in the data set are classified in the manner described above, the hit ratio, the percentage of correct prediction, can be calculated. In this article, we use a genetic algorithm to find the weights and values of value classification variables from chemical analysis in order to maximize the hit ratio. This process can be expressed in the following equation:

Maximum

$$H = \frac{1}{N} \sum_{i=1}^{N} C_i$$

On condition

$$C_i = 1$$

if

$$B(i) = B(k*) \forall i \in \{1, 2, ..., N\} \tag{2}$$

$$C_i = 0$$

if

$$d_{k*i} = \min(d'_{ki}s)$$

where H is the hit ratio (the number of correct predictions relative to the number of all predictions for N observations); N, the number of observations in the data set; C_i either the prediction for observation i is correct ($C_i = 1$) or not ($C_i = 0$) (i = 1,2,...,N); B(i), any observation i is anomalous (B(i) = 1) or not (B(i) = 0); B(k*), or the value from chemical analysis is abnormal (B(k*) = 1) or not (B(k*) = 0); k*, value from chemical analysis, corresponding to d_{k*i}; d_{k*i} is the minimum distance between the value from chemical analysis k and observation i.

3.5 Mathematical Metrics for Model Identification

In the case when the fact of the presence of a discord is known, the following binary classification criteria are used: accuracy, completeness, F1 measure.

3.5.1 Accuracy (Precision, Positive Predictive Value)

The accuracy presented in formula 3 reflects what percentage of positive objects are correctly classified:

$$PPV = \frac{TP}{TP + FP} \tag{3}$$

where, TP is the number of correctly classified positive examples, FP is the number of incorrectly classified positive examples, is a type I error. Classifier errors are divided into two groups: the first and second kind. When the accuracy is 100% the mismatch matrix is diagonal and the errors cause the difference of two off-diagonal elements to be non-zero:

Type I Error occurs when an object is erroneously assigned a positive class ($=$ FP/m).

Type II Error occurs when an object is erroneously assigned a negative class ($=$ FN/m).

3.5.2 Completeness (Recall, Sensitivity, True Positive Rate, Hit Rate)

The completeness presented in formula 4 reflects the percentage of objects of the positive class that we correctly classified:

$$TPR = \frac{TP}{FN + TP} \tag{4}$$

3.5.3 F1-measure (F1-score)

The F1-measure (F1-score) (F1-score), presented in formula 5 is the harmonic mean of accuracy and recall, maximizing this functional leads to the simultaneous maximization of these two "orthogonal criteria":

$$F1 = \frac{2TP}{FN + 2TP + FP} \tag{5}$$

Accuracy and completeness can be informally referred to as "orthogonal quality criteria". It is easy to construct an algorithm with 100% completeness: it assigns all objects to class 1, but the accuracy can be very low. It is not difficult to construct an algorithm with close to 100% accuracy: it assigns to class 1 only those objects in which it is sure, while recall can be low.

In the case when the derangement time is determined, MAE, RMSE, bath-function errors are found.

The classification problem is divided into two classes (with labels 0 and 1) and the following notation is introduced: y_i is the label of the i-th object, a_i is the answer on this object of our algorithm, m is the number of objects in the sample.

Average deviation modulus shown in formula 6, Mean Absolute Error (MAE)

$$MAE = \frac{1}{m} \sum_{i=1}^{m} |a_i - y_i| \tag{6}$$

Mean square deviation reflected in formula 7, Mean Squared Error (MAE)

$$MSE = \frac{1}{m} \sum_{i=1}^{m} |a_i - y_i|^2 \tag{7}$$

or the root of this error, represented in formula 8: RMSE (Root Mean Squared Error) or RMSD (Root Mean Square Deviation)

$$RMSE = \sqrt{MSE} = \sqrt{\frac{1}{m} \sum_{i=1}^{m} |a_i - y_i|^2} \tag{8}$$

4   The Experimental Part

This section describes the results of evaluation metrics of the proposed binary classification algorithm methods. For the experiments, a data set was taken from the pH/ORP sensor of the hardware-software complex for automated control of the composition of wastewater (PAK).

4.1   Binary Classification Method Trained on Full Data Set

To search for anomalies using the binary classification of time series, the entire data set was taken. Figures 7–8 show the results for the "ch0" sensor channel in full data, and the time span for all sensor channels. Table 2. presents the metrics data for this method. Based on these results, we can conclude that this approach finds most of the anomalies.

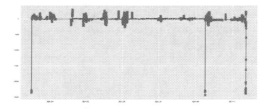

Fig. 7. Anomalies in the time series of the "ch0" sensor channel for 2020.11.30–2021.11.23.

4.2   Binary Classification Method Trained on Classified Values

For this approach, time series data that do not contain anomalies (Fig. 9) were selected and called the test sample. The period from 2021.06.01 to 2021.06.15 was chosen as such a site. It should be noted here that no anomalies were noted in the work, and the data considered are normal (paragraph 3.2).

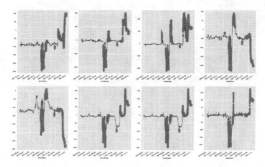

Fig. 8. Anomalies in the time series of the sensor for 2021.02.20–2021.03.01

Table 2. Binary classification in full

Accuracy	Completeness	F1-score
0.88	0.25	0.60

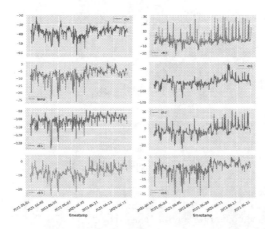

Fig. 9. Time series of sensor channels for 2021.06.01–2021.06.15

Figures 10–11 show the results of searching for anomalies using binary classification on the example of the "ch0" sensor channel on the full amount of data, and the time interval for all sensor channels. Table 3 presents the metrics data for this method. Based on these results, we can conclude that this anomaly approach is completely random, and is not suitable for use.

5 Results and Discussion

To evaluate the effectiveness of the proposed methods, a number of experiments were implemented, (Table 4).

Table 3. Binary classification of classified values

Accuracy	Completeness	F1-score
0.24	0.07	0.39

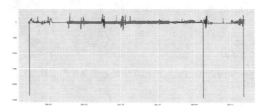

Fig. 10. Anomalies in the time series of the sensor channel "ch0" for 2020.11.30 2021.11.23

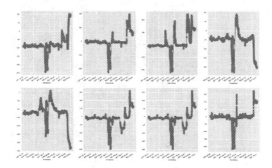

Fig. 11. Anomalies in the time series of the sensor for 2021.02.20–2021.03.01

Table 4. Evaluation of methods

Method	Accuracy	Completeness	F1-measure
Binary classification method trained on full data set	0.82	0.25	0.61
Binary classification method trained on classified values	0.46	0.11	0.43

Based on the experimental results, it can be concluded that the proposed binary classification method trained on the full data sample (paragraph 3.2) outperforms the binary classification method trained on classified values for six metrics. The more data involved in training this method, the more accurate the forecast will be.

6 Conclusion

In this paper, we propose a method for detecting anomalous values using binary classification. The comparison was carried out on a data set of a hardware-software complex for automated control of the composition of wastewater using an isolated forest. The quality of the binary classification result was assessed by 3 evaluation metrics. An important feature of the proposed approach is that it improves the accuracy of anomaly detection based on binary classification. It can be concluded that the proposed approach is becoming more efficient as the size of the analyzed data set increases. Future research will focus on the development and application of ensembles of algorithms for anomaly detection.

References

1. Dogo, E.M., Nwulu, N.I., Twala, B., Aigbavboa, C.O.: Empirical comparison of approaches for mitigating effects of class imbalances in water quality anomaly detection. IEEE Access **8**, 218015–218036 (2020)
2. Abduh, L., Ivrissimtzis, I.P.: Use of in-the-wild images for anomaly detection in face anti-spoofing. ArXiv, abs/2006.10626 (2020)
3. Sankar, S., et al.: Classification of SD-OCT volumes for DME detection: an anomaly detection approach. In: SPIE Medical Imaging (2016)
4. Lauría, E.J.: Framing early alert of struggling students as an anomaly detection problem: an exploration. In: CSEDU (2021)
5. Mohebbian, M.R., Wahid, K.A., Babyn, P.S.: Stack of discriminative autoencoders for multiclass anomaly detection in endoscopy images (2021)
6. Cheng, H., Wu, J., Huang, D., Liu, Y., Wang, Q.: Robust adaptive boosted canonical correlation analysis for quality-relevant process monitoring of wastewater treatment. ISA Trans. **117**, 210–220 (2021)
7. Kadlec, P., Gabrys, B., Strandt, S.: Data-driven soft sensors in the process industry. Comput. Chem. Eng. **33**, 795–814 (2009)
8. Li, D., Liu, Y., Huang, D.: Development of semi-supervised multiple-output soft-sensors with co-training and tri-training MPLS and MRVM. Chemom. Intell. Lab. Syst. **199**, 103970 (2020)
9. Daoping, H., Yiqi, L., Yan, L.: Soft sensor research and its application in wastewater treatment. CIESC J. **62**, 7–15 (2011)
10. Rehbach, F., Moritz, S., Chandrasekaran, S., Rebolledo, M., Friese, M., Bartz-Beielstein, T.: GECCO 2018 industrial challenge: monitoring of drinking-water quality. (2018). http://www.spotseven.de/wpcontent/uploads/2018/03/rulesGeccoIc2018.pdf. Accessed 19 Feb 2019
11. Dogo, E. M., Nwulu, N. I., Twala, B., Aigbavboa, C.: A survey of machine learning methods applied to anomaly detection on drinking-water quality data. Urban Water J. **16**(3), 235–248 (2019). https://doi.org/10.1080/1573062X.2019.1637002
12. He, H., Garcia, E.A.: Learning from Imbalanced Data. Tkde **21**(9), 1263–1284 (2009). https://doi.org/10.1109/TKDE.2008.239
13. Schafer, J.L., Graham, J.W.: Missing data: our view of the state of the art. Psychol. Meth. **7**(2), 147–177 (2002). https://doi.org/10.1037//1082-989X.7.2.147
14. Ilyas, I.F., Xu, C.: Data Cleaning. Morgan & Claypool, San Rafael (2019)
15. Lemaitre, G., Nogueira, F., Aridas, C.: Imbalanced-learn: a python toolbox to tackle the curse of imbalanced datasets in machine learning. J. Mach. Learn. Res. **18**, 1–5 (2017)

16. García-Laencina, P.J., Sancho-Gómez, J.L., Figueiras-Vidal, A.R.: Pattern classification with missing data: a review. Neural Comput. Applic. **19**(2), 263–282 (2010). https://doi.org/10.1007/s00521-009-0295-6

17. Prati, R.C., Batista, G.E., Silva, D.F.: Class imbalance revisited: a new experimental setup to assess the performance of treatment methods. Knowl. Inf. Syst. **45**(1), 247–270 (2014). https://doi.org/10.1007/s10115-014-0794-3

18. Khan, S.S., Ahmad, A., Mihailidis, A.: Bootstrapping and multiple imputation ensemble approaches for classification problems. J. Intell. Fuzzy Syst. **37**(6), 7769–7783 (2019). https://doi.org/10.3233/JIFS-182656

19. Krawczyk, B.: Learning from imbalanced data: open challenges and future directions. Prog. Artif. Intell. **5**(4), 221–232 (2016). https://doi.org/10.1007/s13748-016-0094-0

20. Roy, A., Cruz, R.M., Sabourin, R., Cavalcanti, G.D.: A study on combining dynamic selection and data preprocessing for imbalance learning. Neurocomputing **286**, 179–192 (2018). https://doi.org/10.1016/j.neucom.2018.01.060

21. Haixiang, G., Yijing, L., Shang, J., Mingyun, G., Yuanyue, H., Bing, G.: Learning from class-imbalanced data: review of methods and applications. Expert Syst. Appl. **73**, 220–239 (2017). https://doi.org/10.1016/j.eswa.2016.12.035

22. Muharemi, F., Logofătu, D., Leon, F.: Machine learning approaches for anomaly detection of water quality on a real-world data set. J. Inf. Telecommun. **3**, 1–14 (2019). https://doi.org/10.1080/24751839.2019.1565653

23. Ribeiro, V., Reynoso-Meza, G.: Online anomaly detection for drinking water quality using a multi-objective machine learning approach. In: Proceedings of the Genetic and Evolutionary Computation Conference (2018). https://doi.org/10.1145/3205651.3208202

24. Ribeiro, V., Reynoso-Meza, G.: Monitoring of drinking-water quality by means of a multi-objective ensemble learning approach. In: Proceedings of the Genetic and Evolutionary Computation Conference, pp. 1–2 (2018)

25. Wu, D., Wang, H., Seidu, R.: Smart data driven quality prediction for urban water source management. Futur. Gener. Comput. Syst. **107**, 418–432 (2020). https://doi.org/10.1016/j.future.2020.02.022

26. Al-Gunaid, M.A., Shcherbakov, M.V., Trubitsin, V.N., Shumkin, A.M., Dereguzov, K.Y.: Analysis a short-term time series of crop sales based on machine learning methods. In: Kravets, A.G., Groumpos, P.P., Shcherbakov, M., Kultsova, M. (eds.) CIT&DS 2019. CCIS, vol. 1083, pp. 189–200. Springer, Cham (2019). https://doi.org/10.1007/978-3-030-29743-5_15

Neural Network-Based Optimization of Traffic Light Regulation of a Transport Hub with Data Fetched During Simulation in SUMO Package

Dmitry Skorobogatchenko[1]([✉]) [iD], Vladislav Zhokhov[1] [iD], Olga Astafurova[2] [iD], and Pavel Fantrov[3] [iD]

[1] Volgograd State Technical University, 28 Lenin Av., Volgograd 400005, Russia
dmitryskor2004@gmail.com
[2] Volgograd Institute of Management – Branch of the Russian Presidential Academy of National Economy and Public Administration, 8 Gagarin Street, Volgograd 400131, Russia
[3] Volgograd State University, 100 Universitetskiy Av., Volgograd 400062, Russia

Abstract. The paper proves the necessity to optimize the time of a traffic light signal as the fastest and most cost-effective way to improve the efficiency of the urban street and road network in a continuously growing number of vehicles. The main traffic management strategies are analyzed and the conclusion is made that in some cases it is advisable to have effective software that switches the operation modes of traffic lights during peak load periods. The aim of the study is to develop a method of traffic management based on the application of a fixed time control method, taking into account the uneven traffic intensity and structure of the traffic flow during the day. The authors chose a segment of the road network in the city of Volgograd as an example of its use. The authors suggest a method for software calculation for traffic light objects in a section of the road network, minimizing the loss of time for vehicles in the morning and evening periods of peak traffic. The technique is based on a neural network with an error back propagation algorithm that uses data on adaptive traffic light cycles from SUMO package for neural network training. In the conclusion, a comparison is made about the efficiency of traffic organization on the urban street and road network under analysis with the existing traffic organization and with the developed plan for switching signals of traffic lights.

Keywords: Road network · Traffic management · Software for traffic light objects · Traffic light cycle · Neural networks · Road conditions

1 Introduction

The growth of urban population and the increase in household income contribute to a continuous growth in the level of motorization of urban agglomerations [1]. Despite the relatively small specific number of vehicles in Russia in comparison with the EU or the USA, in absolute terms, the number of vehicles in the territory of the Russian Federation has almost tripled in 20 years [2].

A. G. Kravets et al. (Eds.): CIT&DS 2023, CCIS 1909, pp. 337–350, 2023.
https://doi.org/10.1007/978-3-031-44615-3_23

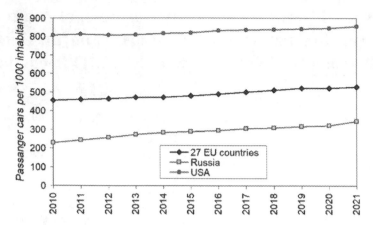

Fig. 1. Analysis of change in the number of vehicles per 1 thousand inhabitants over 2010–2021

The growth in the level of motorization requires the corresponding development of infrastructure in the form of the required density of road network, expansion of parking space, and improvement of traffic control facilities (see Fig. 1). However, as practice shows, that the pace of development of transport infrastructure lags behind the pace of motorization, which is especially important for the urban road network, extensive development of which is significantly limited [3]. The consequence of this is the fact that modern urban agglomerations are on the verge of road width depletion.

Thus, today we can state the existence of a problematic situation, which consists in the discrepancy between the capacity of urban road network and annually growing traffic needs caused by the growth in the total number of vehicles. This circumstance, in turn, leads to a number of serious social, technical, economic and environmental consequences. Thus, an increase in the traffic flow density leads to a drop in the average traffic speed in cities, relatively to the size of urban agglomerations [4].

Traffic congestion decreases the level of serviceability (LOS) of road networks. A decrease in LOS results in direct and indirect costs to society. Extensive studies have been carried out to estimate the impacts of congestion on the economy and society as a whole [5]. The first-hand impact of traffic congestion is the lost working hours. The detrimental impacts of congestion skyrocket when the value of time, as a commodity, increases drastically during emergencies. High congestion levels can result in aggressive behaviour by drivers [6]. High levels of congestion also result in higher greenhouse gas emissions [7].

To meet the ever-increasing demand for traffic, the urban transport system needs efficient solutions. However, changes in the infrastructure of the urban road network are capital-intensive, time-consuming, and sometimes it is impossible to change it technically. For this reason, traffic light time (TST) optimization is one of the fastest and most cost-effective ways to reduce road traffic congestion at intersections and improve the efficiency of the city's road network. Therefore, at present, issues related to the optimization of traffic signal control systems which minimize the average delays of vehicles taking into account the heterogeneous structure of the traffic flow, are of particular relevance [8].

2 Critical Analysis

When analyzing modern approaches to management of traffic light objects (tls-objects), it should be noted that currently there are fixed, activated and adaptive traffic control methods [9]. A detailed analysis of the main management strategies can be found in the following paper [10].

The fixed time control method establishes optimal signal plans for fixed sequences of signal phases with fixed time duration for each phase. The introduction of a fixedtime control method assumes relatively uniform traffic, generalized over a certain period. The activated control method collects real-time data from infrastructure detectors and determines whether the green light should be extended or the phase completed. The adaptive control method is a proactive activated strategy when conditions are predicted for the near future [11]. The control method strategy has been implemented using various algorithms, resulting in the development of several adaptive signal control systems ACS-Lite, SCATS, SCOOT, OPAC, MOTION, UTOPIA and RHODES.

There exist several traffic control methods which are used in practice: fixed time, actu-ated, or adaptive control methods, whether the state-of-the-art methods or the methods deployed in the real-world, such as SCATS, SCOOT, and TUC [12]. When employing the techniques mentioned above the Reinforcement Learning is generally used to improve the traffic signal control because traffic phenomena are very dynamic and Reinforce-ment Learning is helpful in adjustment to changing traffic conditions [13]. There also exist various method which solve research methods in this area. They are conventional methods (traffic theory) and heuristic methods [14].

Currently, the main attention of researchers is devoted to the development of acti-vated and adaptive control methods as the most promising ones. However, most modern adaptive control systems use detector-based vehicle passage data. Therefore, for their practical implementation, as a rule, it is necessary to install complex sensors, such as cameras, radars, or induction loops, which is not technically feasible and economically justified everywhere [15]. In some cases, it is advisable to have effective software that switches the operating modes of traffic light objects over time.

Another promising direction is the calculation of the length of traffic light cycles based on neural networks. Here another problem arises. Traffic modeling requires obtain-ing large amounts of data for network training with various options for organization of traffic light regulation. The solution to this problem is modern software packages of simulation modeling.

Thus, the aim of the paper is to optimize the traffic light control cycles of the transport hub using the training of neural network model according to simulation data in the SUMO environment (Simulation of Urban Mobility).

One of the key features of the SUMO package is its high ability to integrate with open platforms [16]. SUMO integrates with other microscopic and macroscopic simulators such as VISUM, Vissim, OpenDRIVE and MATsim; and with information systems, including Open Street Maps (OSM). In addition, this product is free, which is an essential parameter in our situation.

3 Experiment Description

The study was carried out on the example of Raboche-Krestyanskaya street starting from the tunnel after Kazakhskaya street and finishing in Volgograd by the area of the plant "Pivovar" (see Fig. 2).

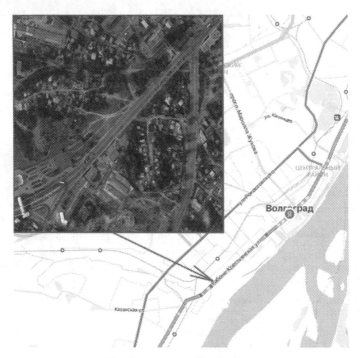

Fig. 2. Location of study object

The choice of road segment is not accidental. This section of the 1st Longitudinal Highway of Volgograd is one of the two most important transport corridor connecting the southern part of the city with the city center.

It should also be noted that on the territories directly adjacent from the south, the dormitory districts of the city with a significant number of people are mainly located. The center of the city as well as the areas adjacent to it from the north is characterized by both public and administrative places, and industrial and commercial areas. This circumstance determines the typical direction in the distribution of traffic during peak periods (see Fig. 3). In particular, in the morning the main flow is directed towards the center of the city, in the evening the reverse situation is observed. At the same time, the highway operates in overload mode that is why kilometer-long traffic jams regularly appear in the morning and evening hours.

The road segment under consideration includes three intersections with traffic lights, two of which are significant ones and, being on the 1st Longitudinal Highway, will be the subject of further study. Let's look at them in more detail.

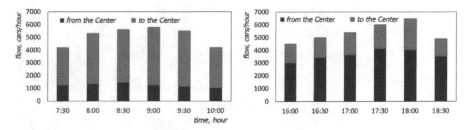

Fig. 3. Parameters of traffic intensity along the 1st Longitudinal Highway of Volgograd within the boundaries of the segment under analysis

Crossroads of the streets Raboche-Krestyanskaya and L. Tolstogo (see Fig. 4) is a T-junction with classic three-phase regulation.

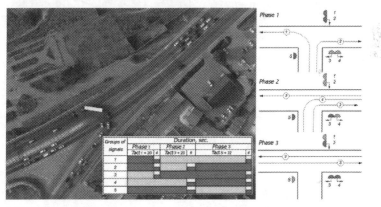

Fig. 4. Parameters of traffic light regulation of the intersection of the streets Raboche-Krestyanskaya and L. Tolstogo

A feature of this intersection is the prohibition of the right turn when moving from the south of Volgograd to the city center. A special lane for the right turn exists a little earlier, at the exit from the tunnel. Another feature of this intersection is the absence of pedestrian crossings, which significantly expands the possibilities for regulation of the duration of traffic light phases for the passage of vehicles. The duration and phase patterns of the junction work well outside of peak periods of intensity (see Fig. 4).

The intersection of the streets Raboche-Krestyanskaya and Bazisnaya (See Fig. 5) is also a T-shaped intersection with traffic lights equipped with additional sections for left and right turns. It is important to note that the intersection has lanes for left turns only.

To obtain data for neural network training, the area under consideration was simulated by SUMO package. When doing this, the osmWebWizard.py script and the netedit software were used to process the imported map.

For simulation modeling, the intensity of traffic and the structure of traffic flow in the morning and evening peak periods were set. At this stage, the duarouter software

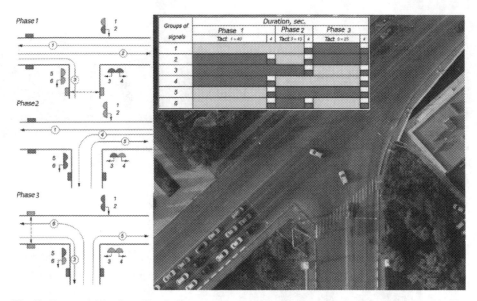

Fig. 5. Parameters of traffic light regulation at the intersection of the streets Raboche-Krestyanskaya and Bazisnaya

was used with the data of field observations entered in the morning and evening hours of weekdays during the warm seasons.

Simulation environment provides integration of micro and macro models using the SUMO simulation server and connection of external simulation environments via network connections. In the simulation, detectors are installed that record the passage of vehicles through them. The generation of vehicles is carried out in accordance with real data obtained by measurements directly on the roads. All results are written to CSV files or sent via the external socket to the external model that records the real time of computer simulation.

A gravitational model was used to construct the correspondence matrix. This is connected with the fact that this model accurately describes the transport flows of the city [17].

The gravity model connectes the intensity of the flow T_{ij} between the total number of departures from the i-th region Q_i and the arrival in the j-th region D_j and the cost of movement between regions i and j with c_{ij}:

$$T_{ij} = \frac{Q_i + D_j}{c_{ij}^2} \quad i = 1 \ldots N \quad j = 1 \ldots M \tag{1}$$

where N - total number of departure areas, M - total number of arrival areas. In this model, the distance between regions is considered as the distance between the centers of these regions.

In the simulation, a modified Krauss motion model, discrete in time and continuous in space, was used [18]. The model is based on the calculation of the distance between the vehicle and the leader necessary for a safe stop:

$$v_{safe}(t) = -\tau \cdot b + \sqrt{(\tau \cdot b)^2 + v_{leader}(t-1)^2 + 2 \cdot b \cdot g_{leader}(t-1)} \qquad (2)$$

where $v_{safe}(t)$ – safe speed at time t, m/s; τ is the reaction time of the driver, c; b – maximum deceleration, m/s^2; $v_{leader}(t)$ – leader speed during t, m/s; $g_{leader}(t)$ – distance between the front of the vehicle and the rear bumper of the leading car during t, m.

With restrictions on the values of the desired speed the formula looks as follows:

$$v_{des}(t) = \min\{v_{safe}(t), v(t-1) + a, v_{max}\} \qquad (3)$$

where vdes(t) – desired velocity, m/s; v(t) – current velocity, m/s; a – maximum acceleration, m/sec2; vmax – maximum speed, m/s.

One of the main features of the Krauss model is the assumption that the driver does not have to develop the desired velocity, which adds important features to the behavior of drivers.

For example, a random difference between the speeds of cars and the desired velocities leads to the spontaneous appearance of congestion and the slow start of cars at traffic lights, which is typical for real conditions. This feature of driver behavior is taken into account by including stochastic deceleration in the model:

$$v(t) = \max\{0, v_{des}(t) - r \cdot a \cdot \varepsilon\} \qquad (4)$$

where r – random number between 0 and 1; ε – degree of specificity (imperfection) of car driver, which assumes a value between 0 and 1; v(t) – final speed of the car at a time t, m/s.

The authors carried out a series of simulations, as a result of which data arrays were formed by the sensors of tls-objects, characterizing the length of the main cycles of the three phases of adaptive traffic light cycles, minimizing the loss of time for vehicles along the studied segment of Volgograd road network. The duration of the phases of adaptive tls-object varies from simulation to simulation. In addition, within an hour, the data may differ significantly.

The phase extension in SUMO package is caused by the lost of time by vehicles. The detectorRange parameter defines the detection distance from the stop line. In the paper, we determined the distance of 100 m. The loss of time for a vehicle accumulates as soon as it enters the detector's coverage area. If its accumulated time loss exceeds the time value specified in minTimeLoss parameter, an extension of the corresponding green phase is needed, if it is active. The instantaneous loss of time by a vehicle is defined as follows: $1 - v/vmax$, where v - its current speed and vmax permitted maximum speed [19]. To implement an adaptive traffic light, we will use the library TraCI (Traffic Control Interface) providing access to a running traffic simulation scenario. This allows us getting the values of the simulated objects and managing their behavior in real time. TraCI uses a client/server architecture based on the TCP protocol to provide access to SUMO package. The TraCI programming interface is available in different languages such as Python, Java, C++, .Net, Matlab. We will use the Python language to write a traffic ligt controller.

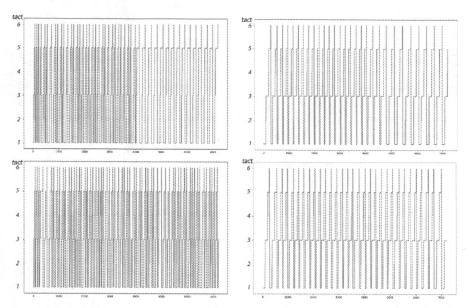

Fig. 6. The duration of cycles of intersections in the morning and evening rush hours with adaptive control: a) length of all cycles of traffic light regulation at the intersection of the streets Raboche-Krestyanskaya and Bazisnaya; b) the same parameter in the evening peak hours; c) duration of all cycles of traffic lights at the intersection of the streets Raboche-Krestyanskaya and L. Tolstogo; d) the same parameter during the evening peak hours.

As an example, we present the results of simulation duration of all cycles of two intersections in the morning and evening rush hours (see Fig. 6).

Further, the authors suggest software for control the traffic lights of section of the road network under analysis with a fixed hourly change in the length of cycles in the morning and evening heavy traffic. A multilevel neural network was used as a tool for each intersection (Fig. 7).

An artificial neuron is a function as shown:

$$y_i = \varphi \left(\sum_{j=0}^{m} w_{ij} x_{ij} \right) \tag{5}$$

where x_{ij} is the j-th feature (dimension) of the i-th m-dimensional data point in the dataset; wj (called weights) is the coefficient which is tuned during the training process of the neural network; φ - is a nonlinear activation function; y_i - is the output of the function on input x_i. Commonly used activation functions are: sigmoid.

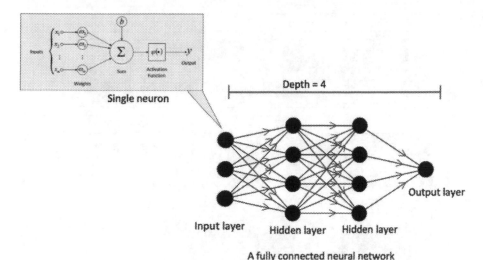

Fig. 7. A fully connected layered neural network with two hidden layers.

In such neural networks, the outputs from all neurons from a previous layer are fed as inputs to all neurons in the next layer. The literature on neural networks often omits the term «layered» and uses the terms fully connected neural network (FCNN) in its place. [20]. When placed parallel to each other, several such neurons form a layer of the neural network. When several layers are stacked one after the other, a feed forward neural network (FFNN) is formed. In this context, stacking refers to passing the output of one function or unit to another. As we increase the stacking, the depth of the neural network increases. The literature on neural networks does not specify a pre-defined threshold for the depth, in order to demarcate deep and shallow networks. Any neural network having more than one hidden layer can be referred to as a deep neural network. A deep neural network can learn more abstract representations of the data compared to a shallow network. The link between depth and abstractions is easily observed when working with image data.

The architecture of the used neural networks is characterized by one input neuron and several output neurons (according to the number of main cycles of the intersection). The input neuron is data about the time of day with a discretization of 1 h. The output neurons are the values of the duration of the main cycles of a particular intersection in seconds. The training was carried out on the example of an array of data characterizing the length of the phases of adaptive traffic light cycles, minimizing the loss of time for vehicles. The back propagation algorithm was used as a learning method. The number of hidden layers and neurons in them is taken in accordance with the following papers [21].

Let us graphically represent the learning results in the form of the optimal duration of the phases (Fig. 8).

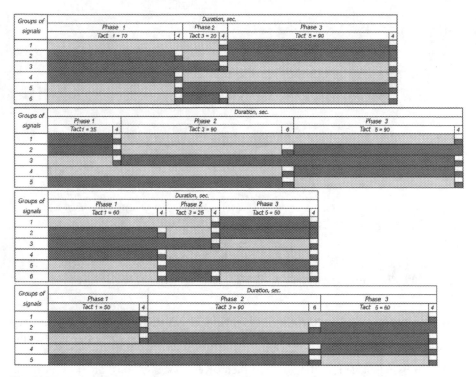

Fig. 8. Optimized durations of the phases of the intersections of the segment under analysis of the road network of Volgograd during periods of peak hours: a) the streets Raboche-Krestyanskaya and Bazisnaya during morning peak hours; b) the same parameter in the evening peak hours; c) the streets Raboche-Krestyanskaya and L. Tolstogo during morning peak hours; d) the same parameter during the evening peak hours.

To analyze the effectiveness of the work done, we will use the relationship between the flow, speed and density (see Fig. 9).

Number of vehicle per unit length of road sector is traffic density.

Percentage of the time during which a point in the road is taken by vehicles is occupancy. Vehicle loop detectors (VLDs) can directly measure occupancy. When the occupancy is homogenous (the length of each vehicle is the same), occupancy is directly proportional to the traffic flow. In practice, the density is most commonly estimated using the fundamental relation between density and speed ($q = k * u$), where q is the flow, k is the density and u is the speed. When traffic stream is heterogeneous, the relationship between occupancy and density is complex [22].

There researchers distinguish the spot speed, space mean-speed and time-mean speed. The spot speed (or instantaneous speed) of a vehicle is the speed that is recorded at a given moment in time and at a specified location. In order to compute mean speed, the aggregation can be done in time or space. Space–mean speed, for a given interval of space, is defined as the ratio between the total distance travelled by all vehicles and the total time taken. Time–mean speed, for a given interval of time, is defined as

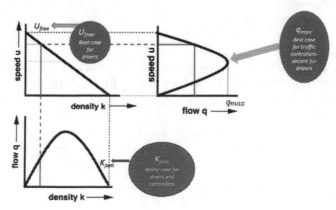

Fig. 9. Representative curves showing the relationship between flow, speed and density. A linear relation between speed and density is assumed here. The two green circles point to maximum speed ($Umax$) and maximum flow ($qmax$) which are the best serviceability conditions w.r.t drivers and traffic controllers respectively. The red circle points to the maximum density or traffic jam ($Kjam$), which implies a lack of serviceability from both perspectives. (Color figure online)

the arithmetic mean of the individual speed of all vehicles. Mathematically, the space–mean speed reduces to the harmonic mean of individual vehicle speeds (v). Assuming N vehicles:

$$space\ mean\ speed = \frac{total\ dist.travelled}{total\ time\ taken} = \frac{N \times D}{\sum_i^N t_i} = \frac{N \times D}{\sum_i^N \frac{D}{u_i}} = \frac{1}{N} \frac{1}{\sum_i^N \frac{1}{u_i}} \quad (6)$$

$$time\ mean\ speed = \frac{1}{N} \sum_i Nu_i \quad (7)$$

The space–mean speed satisfies the fundamental relation between flow, speed and density ($q = k * u$), whereas the time–mean speed does not follow the fundamental equation [23].

In order to calculate disruptions in road networks it is necessary to deal with two extreme values (jam density and free flow speed):

– jam density (k_j): The highest possible value of traffic density; this corresponds to traffic speed = 0 km/h.
– free-flow speed (u_f): The maximum speed at which the vehicles can travel on a given road segment. Under the assumption that drivers respect the speed limit, u_f is the same as the speed limit for the road segment under consideration.

The three variables described above (speed, density and flow) are correlated. However, a generalized equation depicting the relation between these variables has not been established. A simplified linear relationship between speed and density suffices for our discussion here. In Fig. 9, we show the relationship between these variables assuming a linear relationship between speed and density. The various critical points in the three curves in Fig. 9 are highlighted and color-coded to show the level of serviceability for the two most important stakeholders in a transportation system—drivers and traffic controllers. The choice of the target variable is also motivated by taking into account the consumers of the research output. If the research is targeted at optimizing the usage of the transportation network as a system, the focus might be on maximizing the throughput of the network; hence the researchers will focus on predicting the traffic flow accurately. On the other hand, if the research is aimed at improving the user travel time, the focus will be on predicting speed or travel time. For instance, when we use a trip planner to find the optimal route from a starting point to a destination, we often want to figure out the fastest route, we are not concerned with the traffic flow on the roads [24].

4 Analysis of Results and Conclusions

In the end of the paper, the authors carried out a simulation of the traffic in a section of Volgograd street and road network in the morning and evening rush hours. Based on the results of the tests, an array of data was collected and basic equations of the traffic flow were constructed under the existing control regime and under the optimized one which was suggested on the basis of the studies (see Fig. 10).

It is obvious that the introduction of the estimated periods of the main cycles in the morning and evening peak hours significantly improves the traffic capacity of the section of the road network of Volgograd under analysis, increases the average flow rate and reduces the loss of vehicle time. It can be stated that the authors suggested the method for the calculation of the program for traffic lights management during peak periods of time, based on data, adaptive traffic control in the SUMO environment. The suggested methodology allows the following:

1. To develop a software for TLS-objects that significantly reduces the loss of time for road users of the urban road network promptly and with minimal capital expensed, and as a result, to reduce unreasonable economic losses of road users, reduce the noise level, caused by traffic congestion, reduce exhaust emissions.
2. To increase the capacity of the city road network with the consistency of the work of all tls-objects, which in constrained conditions of modern urban agglomerations is a fairly cheap way to reduce the number of accidents.
3. Having collected data characterizing the parameters of traffic on weekends and holidays, periods of unfavorable climatic situation or specific seasons of the year, the suggested methodology can be significantly scaled. As a result, the software for tls-objects can differ not only by the hours of the day, but also by the time of year or days of the week.

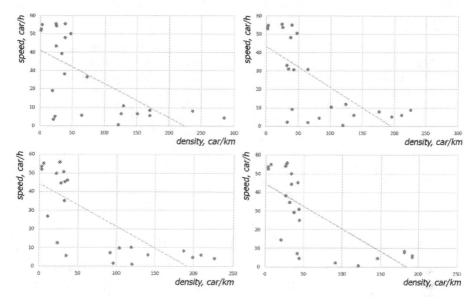

Fig. 10. Effectiveness assessment of the suggested traffic control cycles of the section of Volgograd road network under analysis in comparison with the existing ones: a) current regime (morning); b) suggested mode (morning); c) existing mode (evening); d) suggested mode (evening)

In conclusion, it is worth mentioning that the authors' research confirms that adaptive systems take into account the current traffic situation better and, as a result, the efficiency of their use is much higher than that of traffic lights with a rigidly programmed switching mode. However, in the case of fairly stable traffic, lack of resources to install expensive detectors and cameras, or difficulties in installing them when approaching to the intersection, the approach proposed by the authors can be successfully used.

References

1. Chang, Y.S., Jo, S.J., Lee, Y.-T., Lee, Y.: Population density or populations size. Which factor determines urban traffic congestion? Sustainability **13**(8), 4280 (2021). https://doi.org/10.3390/su13084280
2. Availability of Vehicles. Federal State Statistics Service Homepage. https://rosstat.gov.ru/folder/23455. Accessed 1 Jan 2022
3. Salini, S., Ashalatha, R.: Analysis of traffic characteristics of urban roads under the influence of roadside frictions. Case Stud. Transp. Policy **8**(1), 94–100 (2020)
4. Average speed in Europe's most congested cities in 2017, based on congestion level. Statista Homepage. https://www.statista.com/statistics/264703/average-speed-in-europes-15-most-congested-cities. Accessed 01 Nov 2022
5. Weisbrod, G., Vary, D., Treyz, G.: Economic implications of congestion. Project A2-21 FY'97 (2001)
6. Li, G., et al.: Influence of traffic congestion on driver behavior in post-congestion driving. Accid. Anal. Prev. **141**, 105508 (2020)
7. Barth, M., Boriboonsomsin, K.: Traffic congestion and greenhouse gases. Access Mag. **1**(35), 2–9 (2009)

8. Shepelev, V., Glushkov, A., Almetova, Z., Mavrin, V.: A study of the travel time of intersections by vehicles using computer vision. In: Berns, K., Helfert, M., Gusikhin, O. (eds.) Proceedings of the 6th International Conference on Vehicle Technology and Intelligent Transport Systems. iMLTrans, pp. 653–658 (2020)

9. Feng, Y., Head, K.L., Khoshmagham, S., Zamanipour, M.: A real-time adaptive signal control in a connected vehicle environment. Transp. Res. Part C Emerg. Technol. **55**, 460–473 (2015)

10. Eom, M., Kim, B.I.: The traffic signal control problem for intersections: a review. Eur. Transp. Res. Rev. **12**, 50 (2020). https://doi.org/10.1186/s12544-020-00440-8

11. Hao, Z., Boel, R., Li, Z.: Model based urban traffic control, part I: local model and local model predictive controllers. Transp. Res. Part C Emerg. Technol. **97**, 61–81 (2018)

12. Diakaki, C., Papageorgiou, M., Aboudolas, K.: A multivariable regulator approach to traffic-responsive network-wide signal control. Control. Eng. Pract. **10**(2), 183–195 (2002)

13. Sutton, R.S., Barto, A.G.: Reinforcement Learning: An Introduction. MIT Press, Cambridge (2018)

14. Noaeen, M., Mohajerpoor, R., Far, B., Ramezani, M.: Real-time decentralized traffic signal control for congested urban networks considering queue spillbacks. Transp. Res. Part C Emerg. Technol. **133**, 103407 (2021)

15. Küçükoğlu, İ, Dewil, R., Cattrysse, D.: Hybrid simulated annealing and tabu search method for the electric travelling salesman problem with time windows and mixed charging rates. Expert Syst. Appl. **134**, 279–303 (2019)

16. Glazunov, V.V., Chuvatov, M.V., Chernyshev, A.S., Kurochkin, L.M.: Method and technology for integrating discrete and continuous media models of transport flows in the region. Inform. Telecommun. Manag. **4**, 11–122 (2019)

17. Gasnikov, A.V., Klenov, S.L., Nurminsky, S.L. Nurminsky, E.A., Kholodov, Y.A., Shamray, N.B.: Introduction to Mathematical Modeling of Transport Flows. MIPT, Moscow (2010)

18. Krauß, S., Wagner, P., Gawron, C.: Metastable states in a microscopic model of traffic flow. Phys. Rev. **55**(304), 55–97 (1997)

19. Oertel, R., Wagner, P.: Delay-time actuated traffic signal control for an isolated intersection. In: Proceedings 90st Annual Meeting Transportation Research Board (TRB) (2011)

20. Goodfellow, I., Bengio, Y., Courville, A.: Deep Learning. MIT Press, Cambridge (2016)

21. Stathakis, D.: How many hidden layers and nodes? Int. J. Remote Sens. **30**(8), 2133–2147 (2009). https://doi.org/10.1080/01431160802549278

22. Ramezani, M., Haddad, J., Geroliminis, N.: Dynamics of heterogeneity in urban networks: aggregated traffic modeling and hierarchical control. Transp. Res. Part B Methodol. **74**, 1–19 (2015)

23. Gartner, N.H., Messer, C.J., Rathi, A.: Traffic flow theory-a state-of-the-art report: revised monograph on traffic flow theory (2002)

24. Golledge, R.G.: Path selection and route preference in human navigation: a progress report. In: Frank, A.U., Kuhn, W. (eds.) COSIT 1995. LNCS, vol. 988, pp. 207–222. Springer, Heidelberg (1995). https://doi.org/10.1007/3-540-60392-1_14

Analysis of Numerical Simulation Results in a Symbolic Numerical System for Some Strain Energy Potentials

Yulia Andreeva[1]([✉]), Natalia Asanova[1], and Boris Zhukov[1,2]

[1] Volgograd State Technical University, Lenin Avenue 28, 400005 Volgograd, Russian Federation
ajj308@mail.ru
[2] Volgograd Social Pedagogical University, Lenin Avenue 27, 400005 Volgograd, Russia

Abstract. Rubber-metal shock absorbers are the most common type of shock absorbers used in modern machine-building structures for various purposes. The basis of such shock absorbers is a combination of a technical rubber-like material and a metal shell. The modern nonlinear theory of elasticity, at the moment, cannot provide a generalized equation of state of rubber-like materials, similar to Hooke's law in linear theory. The development of new materials leads to the need to create new mathematical expressions for the deformation energy potentials. Existing commercial packages allow you to calculate a small number of hard-coded deformation models. In this paper, a specialized calculation system is proposed that allows automating the calculation of rubber-metal shear shock absorbers under finite deformations, freely introducing any generalized neo-Hook deformation energy potential and a rather complex configuration of the shock absorber cross section. The results of calculations of the Treloar, Fan and Gent-Thomas potentials are presented. An estimate of time costs has been made.

Keywords: numerical and symbolic integration · antiplane shear deformation · finite antiplane deformation · hyperelastic incompressible material · the potential energy of deformation · exact solution · variational principle · symbol-numerical system

1 Introduction

Solving the problems of nonlinear elasticity theory for rubber-like materials is complicated by the fact that there is no known form of the equation of state describing with acceptable accuracy their behavior under any types of loading, similar to Hooke's law in linear theory. The nonlinearity of the deformation propagation processes leads to the need to introduce additional inequalities that limit the applicability of models. Among such restrictions, we can single out the requirement of monotonicity of the Coleman-Noll stress state, power growth, Drucker conditions and convexity of the specific potential energy of deformations. The fulfillment of these criteria guarantees that the model corresponds to the real behavior of the deformable body. In the well-known reviews of nonlinear defining relations for nonlinear elasticity under finite deformations [1, 2], expressions for almost five dozen known elastic potentials are given.

In common commercial CAE packages, mainly polynomial models of the form are presented

$$W = \sum_{i,j} c_{ij} (I_1 - 3)^i (I_2 - 3)^j$$

Here I_1, I_2 are the main algebraic invariants of the Cauchy strain tensor.

Moreover, almost all packages, with the exception of ABAQUS, are limited to two models for incompressible materials: the phenomenological Mooney-Rivlin model and the Ogden model. There is a package with an open input of the Marc potential, but it also has to be verified for new potentials [3]. For materials described by models expressed in terms of transcendentally or irrationally, it is necessary to develop original numerical packages. To verify the new packages, exact solutions to the problems of nonlinear elasticity theory for the selected material model under conditions of inhomogeneous deformation are required. In addition, it is possible to test new packages and hyperelastic models for compliance with one of the classical sets of experimental data on uniaxial stretching/compression and shear of various elastomers.

Studying The purpose of the work is to test with the help of the Symbolic numerical system some exact solutions to one model problem with different potentials [4, 5]. A problem-oriented specialized calculation system, which is a combination of numerical and symbolic calculation methods developed on the basis of MAPLE and focused on application in the nonlinear theory of elasticity.

In the numerical solution of static problems of nonlinear elasticity theory, the problem of approximation of unknown functions arises at the discretization stage [6]. There are several basic approaches to solving this problem. In the first case, the domain of assignment of unknown functions is decomposed into elementary subdomains. Then, within each subdomain, the desired functions are approximated [7, 8]. This approach is characterized by a flexible approximation system due to the choice of the decomposition configuration and the possibility of approximating functions within the subdomain in different ways [10, 11]. This approach is implemented using finite elements, splines, etc. [3, 6, 8, 12–14]. The positive side of this approach is the adaptation of the configuration of subdomains to the distribution of the desired fields, due to which the high accuracy of the results obtained is achieved. The disadvantage is a large number of unknowns, which means a high order of systems of equations for finding them, which leads to a large expenditure of machine time, especially in problems of nonlinear elasticity theory.

Therefore, this approach is implemented in large commercial packages such as ANSYS, ABAQUS, etc. [3, 7, 13]. These packages implement an incremental approach. That is, a large deformation is divided into a number of small steps, at each of which nonlinear equations are linearized, and then methods for solving linear problems are used [15]. The compromise between a large number of linear problems at small steps and the loss of accuracy due to linearization at large steps requires interactive interaction between the computer and the program [16, 17]. A similar property (that is, a large number of unknowns) possess grid methods, collocation methods and neural approximations [4, 8, 9, 18–20, 26]. An approach in which the desired functions are approximated immediately in the entire task area (a non-local approach) has a significantly smaller number of unknowns, hence a low cost of machine time (by several orders of magnitude). A significant disadvantage of this approach is the inability to adapt the approximation, which limits the accuracy of the solution. Nevertheless, this approach was chosen to build a specialized system, since it is designed for fast calculations with acceptable accuracy.

2   Numerical and Symbolic System Architecture

The Symbolic numerical system (SFS) package is a system with plug-in modules that provides the possibility of upgrading calculation blocks and implementing new features by connecting additional modules to the package [8, 21].

The architecture of the SFS is shown in Fig. 1. It consists of blocks written in the internal programming language MAPLE. All blocks, excluding EqvSolve, are symbolic, the latter includes a numerical component.

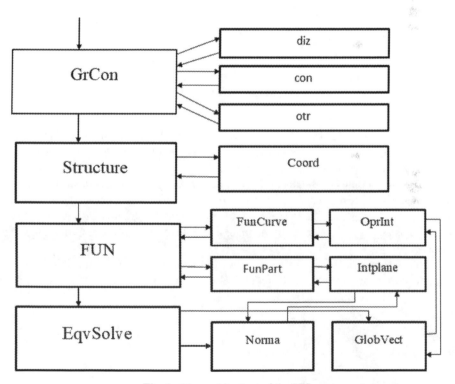

Fig. 1. The architecture of the SFS

3   Comparison of an Exact and Numerical Solution for a Cylindrical Shock Absorber with a Treloar Strain Energy Potential

The task for which it is required to find an exact solution is to shift a circular concentric cage between two rigid cylindrical bushings [22]. In the nonlinear theory of elasticity, this problem is one of the simplest problems, but at the same time it has an applied value, since it is one of the designs of the shear shock [23, 24]. Rubber-metal shear shock absorbers consist of metal clips, between which rubber is firmly fixed [25]. The clips are shifted relative to each other, providing ant flat deformation of the rubber array. The model of incompressible material is considered [26, 27]. A model with the potential of the Treloar strain energy was chosen for testing the SFS [28, 29]. The solution for different materials is known and given in [30, 31]

- Expression for the deplaning function

$$v = \ln(\rho)q$$

- Expression for shear stress

$$\sigma_{rz} = \frac{\mu q}{\rho}$$

- Expression for the stiffness curve

$$\delta = \ln(\kappa)q$$

Here and further we use the notation $v = w/R1$, w is the longitudinal displacement of the points of the shock absorber sleeve. $p = r/R1$ is the dimensionless radial coordinate of the cylindrical coordinate system. $q = Q/(2\pi R1h\mu)$ is the dimensionless shear force, μ is the shear modulus of the linear theory of elasticity. $\delta = \Delta/R1$ is the dimensionless value of the shift of the outer clip relative to the inner one. The parameter $k = R2/R1$ specifies the sleeve size. The longitudinal displacement of the outer cage relative to the inner one is Δ, $R1$, $R2$ - the radii of the inner and outer clips, h is the length of the shock absorber.

Table 1 shows the characteristics of the computational process. Invisible improvements occurred on the Intel(R) Core(TM) Quad CPU Q6600 PC with a frequency of 2.40 GHz and a volume of 2.0 GB.

Table 1. Computational characteristics

No.	The degree of the polynomial approximating the longitudinal shift	The number of nodes of the quadrature formula in the domain	Time to solve a system of equations in seconds	The standard deviation norm of the equilibrium equation
1	4	2500	0.000	2.97
2	8	2500	0.000	1.75
3	10	2500	0.000	1.06
4	10	10000	0.016	0.95
5	10	40000	0.016	0.48
6	10	62500	0.016	0.46

As shown in Fig. 2, the distribution of the relative longitudinal shift $v(p)$ along the radius in the cross section for the exponent values of the approximation polynomial of the longitudinal shift 4 and 8. Parameter values: $k = 2$, $q = 1.4$. From the image, it is easy to see that even with the degree of the polynomial $n = 8$, a high degree of coincidence of the exact values (continuous curve) and the values obtained numerically (points) is achieved [8, 30].

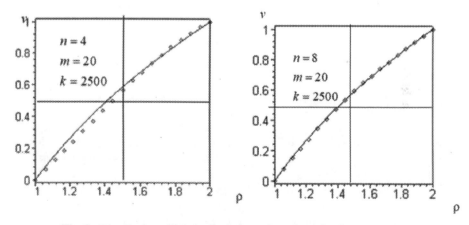

Fig. 2. Distribution of longitudinal shear along the radius in cross section

The distribution of the shear stress $\sigma_{rz}(p)$ along the radius in the cross section is shown in Fig. 3, for the values of the parameters $k = 2$, $q = 1.4$, $\mu = 10$ MPa. The degrees of the approximation polynomial of the longitudinal shift are represented by four values: $n = 4$, $n = 6$, $n = 8$, $n = 10$ at $m = 20$, $k = 2500$. Numerical values correspond to points, and a continuous curve corresponds to exact solutions.

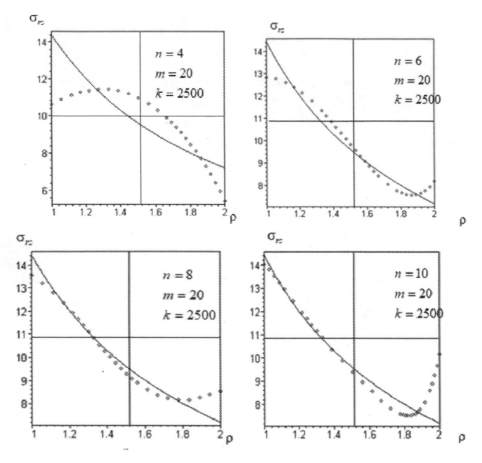

Fig. 3. Distribution of shear stress along the radius in cross section

Figure 4 demonstrates the stability of the process for $n = 10$. First, there is a loss of stability at $n = 10$, $m = 20$, $k = 2500$. But then the stability is restored with an increase in the number of nodes of the quadrature formula in the region [32].

We obtain that with an unknown exact solution, the degree of the approximation polynomial and the number of nodes of the quadrature formula in the domain consistently increases, while the root-mean-square error decreases. This process is limited only by computer resources.

Figure 5 shows a dimensionless stiffness curve $\delta(q)$ at $k = 2$ for the exponent of the approximation polynomial of the longitudinal shift $n = 8$. The graph clearly shows that the exact values (continuous curve) and the values obtained numerically (points) coincide.

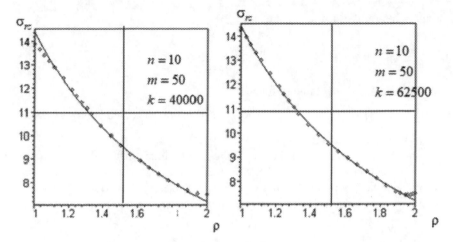

Fig. 4. Restoring resilience

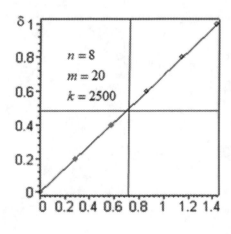

Fig. 5. Stiffness characteristic

4 Comparison of Numerical and Exact Solutions for the Strain Energy Potential of the Fan

The analytical solution was obtained in [30] is represented by the formulas:

- Expression for the deplaning function

$$v(\rho) = q\{e^{-A(\rho)} - e^{-A(1)} + \tfrac{1}{2}[\mathrm{Ei}(1, A(\rho)) - \mathrm{Ei}(1, A(1))]\}$$
$$A(\rho) = \tfrac{1}{2}\mathrm{LambertW}\left(\tfrac{2\beta q^2}{\rho^2}\right)$$

- Expression for shear stress

$$\sigma_{rz} = \frac{\mu q}{\rho}$$

- Expression for the stiffness curve

$$\delta = q\left\{ e^{-A(\kappa)} - e^{-A(1)} + \frac{1}{2}[E_i(1, A(\kappa)) - E_i(1, A(1))] \right\}$$

Here *LambertW(z)* is the Lambert function.

$\text{Ei}(z, a) = \int\limits_1^\infty e^{-tz} t^{-a} dt$ is the exponential integral. The remaining designations coincide with the designations of the previous paragraph.

Figure 6 illustrates the distribution of the longitudinal shift $v(p)$ along the radius in the cross section at $k = 2$, $q = 1.8$, $\beta = 0.2$ for the exponent of the approximation polynomial of the longitudinal shift $n = 8$. The graph clearly shows that the exact values (continuous curve) and the values obtained numerically (points) coincide [30, 32].

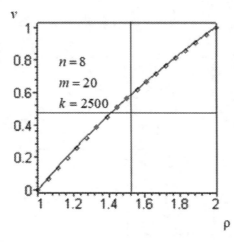

Fig. 6. Distribution of longitudinal shear along the radius in cross section

Figure 7 shows a dimensionless stiffness curve $\delta(q)$ at $k = 2$, $\beta = 0.2$ for the exponent of the degree of approximation of the longitudinal shift $n = 8$. The graph clearly shows that the exact values (continuous curve) and the values obtained numerically (points) coincide.

5   Solution for the Ghent-Thomas Potential

The analytical solution was obtained in [30] is represented by the formulas:

- Expression for the deplaning function

$$v(\rho) = \int\limits_1^\rho \dot{v}(t) dt$$

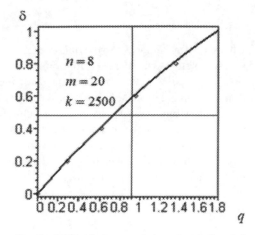

Fig. 7. Stiffness characteristic at $k = 2$, $\beta = 0.2$

- Expression for the stiffness curve

$$\delta = \int_{1}^{\kappa} \dot{v}(\rho)d\rho$$

At $\beta \rightarrow 0$, the Gent-Thomas potential tends to the Treloar potential. Figure 8 shows the curves for $\beta = 1.3$ (curve 1) and $\beta = 1.0$ (curve 2). The hatched line corresponds to the Treloar potential. In all cases $k = 2$. It can be seen that the dependencies are nonlinear and approach the Treloar dependence with decreasing β. Since a detailed analysis of all the characteristics has been presented for a given strain energy potential, it is possible to draw conclusions about a good coincidence of the exact and numerical solutions.

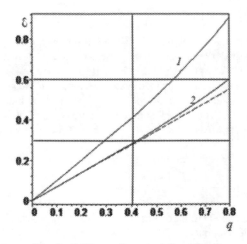

Fig. 8. Stiffness characteristic at $k = 2$

6   Conclusions

Testing of the symbolic numerical system was carried out on exact solutions. Specifically for testing, new more precise solutions with the deformation energy potential of Fan and Thomas-Gent were obtained. Detailed results are presented for the Treloar potential. A good coincidence of numerical and exact solutions for the cross-section deplanation function for the degree of a polynomial approximating this function, starting from order 8, is shown. A similar result is obtained for the dependence of the longitudinal shear of the sleeve on the applied shear force (stiffness characteristic). A comparison of the exact and numerical expressions for the voltage field showed that a good match is obtained when the degree of the polynomial is at least 10 and the number of nodes of the quadrature formula for the integral over the domain is at least 10000. The table shows that calculations take up to 0.0016 s.

References

1. Hossa, L., Marczakb, R.J.: A new constitutive model for rubber-like materials. Comput. Mech. **29**, 2759–2773 (2010)
2. Plotnikov, P.I.: Modeling the isotropic growth of an incompressible neo-Hookean material. Sib. Zh. Ind. Mat. **24**(4), 97–110 (2021). https://doi.org/10.33048/SIBJIM.2021.24.407
3. Korobeynikov, S.N., Oleynikov, A.A., Larichkin, A., Babichev, A.V., Alekhin, V.V.: Numerical realization of Lagrangian formulation of the defining relations of isotropic hyperelastic Genki material. Far Eastern Math. J. **13**(2), 222–249 (2013)
4. Kravets, A.G., Egunov, V.: The software cache optimization-based method for decreasing energy consumption of computational clusters. Energies **15**, 7509 (2022). https://doi.org/10.3390/en15207509
5. Horgan, C.O.: On homogeneous deformations for a new constitutive model for incompressible isotropic hyperelastic soft materials. Mech. Soft Mater. **5**, 3 (2023). https://doi.org/10.1007/s42558-023-00052-x
6. Zhukov, B.A.: Task-oriented system for automized calculation "Mechanic's interface". VSPU, Volgograd (2006)
7. Lychev, S.A., Koifman, K.G., Digilov, A.V.: Nonlinear dynamic equations for elastic micromorphic solids and shells. Part I. Vestn. SamU Estestvennonauchn. Ser. **27**(1), 81–103 (2021). https://doi.org/10.18287/2541-7525-2021-27-1-81-103
8. Andreeva, Y.Y., Zhukov, B.A.: Combined system of numerical and symbolic methods on the basis of MAPLE in the non-linear antiplane shear deformation problems, pp. 237–244 (2016)
9. Zubov, L.M.: Universal solution of nonlinear elasticity for a hollow cylinder with prestressed coatings. Acta Mech. **230**(11), 4137–4143 (2019). https://doi.org/10.1007/s00707-018-2333-x
10. Bondar, V.D.: Modeling of the non-linear antiplane shear deformation of the cylindrical body, pp. 99–109 (2005)
11. Anssari-Benam, A., Horgan, C.O.: A three-parameter structurally motivated robust constitutive model for isotropic incompressible unfilled and filled rubber-like materials. Eur. J. Mech.-A/Solids **95**, 104605 (2022). https://doi.org/10.1016/j.euromechsol.2022.104605
12. Chernykh, K.F. (ed.): Nonlinear Elasticity (Theory and Applications). Solo (2004)
13. Valluri, S.R., Jeffrey, D.J., Corless, R.M.: Some applications of the Lambert W function to physics. Can. J. Phys. **78**, 823–831 (2000)

14. De Pascalis, R., Destrade, M., Saccomandi, G.: The stress field in a pulled cork and some subtle points in the semi-inverse method of nonlinear elasticity. Proc. Roy. Soc. A Math. Phys. Eng. Sci. **463**, 2945–2959 (2007). https://doi.org/10.1098/rspa.2007.0010

15. Horgan, C.O., Murphy, J.G.: Enhancement of protocols for simple shear of isotropic soft hyperelastic samples. J. Elast. **153**, 635–649 (2023). https://doi.org/10.1007/s10659-022-099 08-1

16. Banshchikov, A.V.: Analysis of the dynamics of mechanical systems of large dimension with computer algebra systems. Sib. Zh. Ind. Mat. **12**(3), 15–27 (2009)

17. Grosheva, M.V., Efimov, G.B., Samsonov, V.A.: The history of the use of analytical calculations in problems of mechanics. Edition of the IPM n. a. M.V. Keldysh of the Russian Academy of Sciences (2005)

18. Horgan, C.O., Murphy, J.G.: Incompressible transversely isotropic hyperelastic materials and their linearized counterparts. J. Elast. **143**, 187–194 (2021). https://doi.org/10.1007/s10659-020-09803-7

19. Rvachev, V.L., Sheiko, T.I.: Introduction to the R-functions theory. Mach. Eng. Issues 46–58 (2001)

20. Banshchikov, A.V.: Symbolic-numerical analysis of the necessary stability conditions for the relative equilibria of an orbital gyrostat. Sib. Zh. Ind. Mat. **23**(2) (2020). https://doi.org/10. 1134/S1990478920020015

21. Aladev, V.Z.: Basics of programming in Maple, Tallinn (2006)

22. Horgan, C.O.: Anti-plane shear deformations in linear and nonlinear solid mechanics. SIAM Rev. **37**(1), 53–81 (1995)

23. Ogden, R.W.: Non-Linear Elastic Deformations. Ellis Horwood, Chichester (1997). Reprinted by Dover, New York (1984)

24. Horgan, C.O., Saccomandi, G.: Simple torsion of isotropic, hyperelastic, incompressible materials with limiting chain extensibility. J. Elast. **56**, 159–170 (1999). https://doi.org/10. 1023/A:1007606909163

25. Polignone, D.A., Horgan, C.O.: Pure torsion of compressible nonlinearly elastic circular cylinders. Q. Appl. Math. **49**, 591–607 (1991)

26. Levin, V.A., Zubov, L.M., Zingerman, K.M.: An exact solution to the problem of biaxial loading of a micropolar elastic plate made by joining two prestrained arc-shaped layers under large strains. Eur. J. Mech. A-Solids **88** (2021). https://doi.org/10.1016/j.euromechsol.2021. 104237

27. Mollica, F., Rajagopal, K.R.: Secondary deformations due to axial shear of the annular region between two eccentrically placed cylinders. J. Elast. **48**(2), 103–123 (1997). https://doi.org/ 10.1023/A:1007484731059

28. Zubov, L.M.: On the reduction of some spatial problems of nonlinear elasticity theory to two-dimensional boundary value problems. In: 5th International Conference on Modern Problems of Continuum Mechanics, vol. 1, pp. 83–87. Rostov. State University, Rostov-on-Don (2000)

29. Zingerman, K.M., Zubov, L.M.: Exact solutions to the problems of the theory of multiple superposition of large deformations for bodies formed by a sequential connection of deformed parts. Chebyshev Collection **18**(3), 254–278 (2017). https://doi.org/10.22405/2226-8383-2017-18-3-254-278

30. Andreeva, Y.Y., Zhukov, B.A.: Exact analytical solutions of one problem of the nonlinear theory of elasticity for two potentials of the energy of deformation of an incompressible material. News of higher educational institutions. Volga Reg. Phys. Math. Sci. **2**(46), 64–76 (2018)

31. Root, S.E., et al.: Mechanical properties of organic semiconductors for stretchable, highly flexible and mechanically reliable electronics. Chem. Rev. **117**(9), 6467–6499 (2017)

32. Andreeva, YuYu., Zhukov, B.A., Kalinin, Y.V.: Application of numerical and symbolic system for evaluating stressed state of cylindrical shock absorber. In: Radionov, A.A., Gasiyarov, V.R. (eds.) Proceedings of the 6th International Conference on Industrial Engineering (ICIE 2020): Volume I, pp. 438–445. Springer, Cham (2021). https://doi.org/10.1007/978-3-030-54814-8_52

Intelligent Technologies in Social Engineering. Data Science in Social Networks Analysis and Cyber Security

Digital Integrated Monitoring Platform for Intelligent Social Analysis

Anton Ivaschenko[1](✉), Irina Dubinina[2], Oleg Golovnin[3], Anastasia Golovnina[3], and Pavel Sitnikov[2]

[1] Samara State Medical University, Chapayevskaya Street 89, Samara, Russia
anton.ivashenko@gmail.com
[2] SEC "Open Code", Yarmarochnaya 55, Samara, Russia
[3] Samara National Research University, Moskovskoye Shosse 34, Samara, Russia

Abstract. The paper presents a digital platform for social analysis using the data retrieved from social media. Based on analysis of multiple parameters used to describe social satisfaction and well-being and regional practice of their integrated monitoring for decision-making support there was proposed single indicator called the "level of positivity". This indicator was calculated on the basis of semantic and statistical analysis of time series describing the dynamics of social media members' sentiment changes and estimated using an artificial neural network. Analysis results are visualized by a digital integrated platform in the form of thematic widgets and used to propose countermeasures. Additional attention is given to dynamic analysis of the positivity level deviations in time using approximation models for individuals and groups of social media members. The introduced platform was implemented in practice of the regional ministry of social protection and support and used to identify individuals and groups of people with depressive and deviant behavior in order to conduct timely prevention of negative trends increase the effectiveness of social assistance activities.

Keywords: Social Media Analysis · Smart Society · Digital Transformation · Positivity Level

1 Introduction

Social analysis is a challenging research area nowadays, which covers a wide range of problems of collecting, processing and vitalization of Big Data describing various aspects of human activity. One of the sufficiently informative sources of such data is social media, which reflect reliable information about the reaction of society to ongoing events.

Despite the multiple existing in-depth studies of various trends and aspects of user interaction in social networks, including using artificial intelligence technologies, social monitoring and analysis remain an urgent problem. In the modern world, it is quite difficult to assess the generalized social situation due to the multiplicity of influencing conditions and evaluation criteria.

© The Author(s), under exclusive license to Springer Nature Switzerland AG 2023
A. G. Kravets et al. (Eds.): CIT&DS 2023, CCIS 1909, pp. 365–376, 2023.
https://doi.org/10.1007/978-3-031-44615-3_25

In this regard, the actual task is to create a digital platform for integrated monitoring, allows for a comprehensive social analysis, comparing direct and indirect indicators in the context of various expert opinions and assessments. This paper presents an IT solution that summarizes the experience of analyzing social networks and open sources on the Internet to realize new opportunities for social analysis of modern trends in the development of society.

2 State of the Art

Typically, social analysis is carried out to examine a social problem, issue or trend, often with the aim of prompting changes in the situation being analyzed. Such an analysis can be carried out using various data collecting methods, e.g., surveys, sociological experiments and observations, expert assessments, etc. Among these sociologic technologies social media analysis [1, 2] has certain differences, since they are not specially prepared to clarify specific problems and their causes, but contain general information that reflects the mood of their members as a whole. The advantage of such a data source is that it contains a variety of information and shows the situation as a whole. The disadvantage is the high data noise, the presence of bias in relation to the most popular topics and the relative subjectivity of opinions.

Usually, social media is good for finding out the general background of the situation. Such an analysis can be performed on a number of different indicators that reflect current interests, interaction features, information trends and mood fluctuations in society. However, for ease of interpretation and analysis in dynamics, these indicators are usually generalized to one or two, reflecting the general background mood of the social network.

Social satisfaction is frequently used as a sociologically measurable aggregate indicator related to life satisfaction. Social satisfaction is a set of perceptions and assessments of the conditions of one's social life, quality of life, generalized in the mind of an individual. The main method for calculating this indicator is based on a questionnaire survey. Each expert identifies his own factors influencing the studied indicator. Based on these factors, questions about the degree of satisfaction are formulated. Each degree is assigned a response weight. After the survey, all answers are multiplied by their coefficients, added up and divided by the number of answers. The resulting value is considered satisfaction for one of the factors.

In [3], the methodology for assessing the level of satisfaction is based on the assessment of social and demographic indicators (gender, age, income, health status, education, etc.), socio-psychological indicators (psychological stability, general optimism, self-confidence, etc.), social indicators (the frequency of communication with people, the possibility of spiritual communication, the level of interpersonal trust in society, assessment by others), and macro-factors (i.e. assessment of the performance of the economy, assessment of the performance of the health system, experience of encountering violence, feeling of safety in the neighborhood, anxiety about the possibility of robberies). In [4], a study was made of the index of social satisfaction based on existing methods with minor modifications. Social satisfaction in various areas is associated with civil, socio-economic and educational development activities (the content of one's work, life prospects, services and medical care, leisure activities, etc.).

Social media is also used as a means of exchanging information is added to the factors affecting human satisfaction [5], considering its influence on social overload and social benefits [6]. In [7], the difference between happiness and satisfaction was considered, the methods for measuring satisfaction that were formulated earlier, and whether the priority of factors affecting satisfaction with age changes. In [8], an analysis is made of the correlation of indicators of social satisfaction and social justice. As a result, conclusions are drawn that life satisfaction predicts subsequent perceived social justice, but not vice versa. This effect exists only in people with low incomes.

COVID-19-related self-isolation was investigated, and in [9], the impact of the pandemic as a whole on the level of satisfaction was investigated. Preliminary data revealed an increase in psychological stress due to a decrease in social activity. However, the possibility of using digital technologies slightly softened the decline in satisfaction.

In [10], the influence of subjective socioeconomic status (education, employment, income, human capital, economic status, ability to provide basic necessities, income satisfaction and family opportunities), social capital (social status, self-assessment of health, gender, propensity to individualism, belonging, empathy and trust), self-reported health (physical and psychological) and physical activity on life satisfaction of Iranian residents were investigated.

The concept of social well-being is also considered as a certain state of a person associated with his "comfort—discomfort" of being in society. It includes mental states, various positive and negative assessments that people give to their lives, as well as affective reactions to personal experience [11].

The Organization for Economic Cooperation and Development (OECD) published a report based on an analysis of data on the subjective well-being of the peoples of the world [12]. Among the latest studies [13] there were identified the following parameters that affect social well-being: health, employment opportunities, socioeconomic development, environment, security, politics, the role of human genes, basic and psychological needs, social environment (education, marriage, psychological health), economic environment (income) and political environment (freedom, social trust, quality of governance). As sources for this data, it is proposed to use data from mobile phones, GPS, social networks, electronic health records from mobile applications, news, transactions, Internet search queries, crowdsourcing, surveys.

In [14], social well-being is explored using sentiment analysis, which is a subspecies of natural language processing (NLP) with the help of artificial intelligence. The data sources were social media and retail platforms. In this regard, the results of calculating the value of this indicator can be used as an indicator of the direction of processes in politics and economics, which signals the ongoing fluctuations in the population's assessment of their material and social situation, reacting to significant events in these areas.

In practice, social satisfaction and well-being can be also characterized by indirect parameters like deviant behavior [15, 16]. Based on the experience of analyzing social networks, a technology for identifying and analyzing deviant behavior using modern computing and intelligent technologies was developed in [17]. In this study, we continue the study of possible areas of application of intelligent technologies in the field of social network analysis, started in [18].

One of the manifestations of deviant behavior is depressive and suicidal trends. In [19], the possibilities of deep learning in building a model for detecting suicidal thoughts are explored. The results of experiments show the advantages of models based on C-LSTM in comparison with other classification models based on deep and machine learning [20]. The authors of [21] investigated social media users at risk of suicide using statistical methods and deep learning methods based on their messages, publications, relationships with other users, and posted images. In [22], the classification of social network users into groups was carried out: users who did not show and did not experience deviant behavior in cyberspace; users who have been harmed; users who only exhibited deviant behavior; users who both exhibited and experienced deviant behavior. Such a classification makes it possible to determine the relationship between deviant behavior of users on the Internet and their emotional state: depression, anxiety, loneliness [23].

3 Decision-Making Algorithm

In this study we present the results of digital integrated monitoring platform development for intelligent social analysis. Like in the related papers listed above multiple parameters describing social satisfaction and well-being were reduced to single indicator called the "level of positivity". This indicator was calculated on the basis of semantic and statistical analysis of time series describing the dynamics of social media members' sentiment changes. The main attention was given to identifying people with depressive behavior in order to conduct timely prevention of negative trends.

Decision-making algorithm includes the following steps:

1. Collecting information about social network profiles (uploading to intermediate temporary storage). The platform collects data available to all users if the profile is not private: page ID, first name, last name, nickname, profile photos (avatars), date of birth, city, place of study, gender, status, entries from the page. The platform does not collect personal data of the users and does not identify them personally;
2. Intelligent assessment of signs of depression in publications (posts) using a neural network algorithm;
3. Calculation of the level of positivity and analysis of the digital twin of the social media member;
4. Adding a list of candidates for inclusion in the list of high risk;
5. Expert evaluation and approval of the inclusion of the profile in the list (manually, expertly), periodically (2 times a week);
6. Verification of profiles in the list (confirmation of the reality of the profile);
7. Planning for prevention activities.
8. Constant monitoring and periodic control of profiles in the list.
9. Formation of summary reports (on request).

Based on the results of the analysis of the activity of the user of social networks, the platform builds a model of a digital twin—a virtual personality that imitates the social, behavioral, emotional and cognitive qualities of a person. The digital twin recognizes a typical situation, assesses the specific needs of a person and personalizes an assistance.

The platform has the following limitations:

- the platform works only with open profiles, found profiles must be verified;
- there is no possibility of instant detection of deviant behavior and its warning in real time. The reaction speed of the platform is limited by the need to verify the profile.

Within the framework of the platform, a knowledge base was developed, which is configured in accordance with the rules and templates compiled by expert psychologists. To evaluate posts, an artificial neural network was developed and trained, for training which a sample was collected, consisting of 240 thousand messages downloaded from social networks.

To analyze the risks of depressive behavior the platform introduced the "level of positivity" indicator on a scale from 0 to 5. This indicator is the opposite of the level of depression, respectively, low positivity characterizes a high risk of depressive behavior. This indicator is evaluated for each publication (post) in the social network of a user associated with the region. This assessment is carried out by an intelligent algorithm based on an artificial neural network. The report includes only publications published within the specified time interval.

Then the publications of each user are aggregated, and the degree of positivity of each member of the social network is calculated for the corresponding time interval. Based on the generalization of all users of the social media associated with each region, the degree of positivity of this municipal district or geographical region is calculated. The degree of positivity is displayed on the electronic map and in the report using different color indications.

Since, in this case, a rather strong averaging occurs, and the number of users with a significantly low degree of positivity is not large, several methods have been implemented to calculate the degree of positivity of a municipal district or region:

- absolute assessment of the degree of positivity—strongly averages the results of the assessment and is optimistic (in the reports "everything is fine");
- relative assessment of the degree of positivity—based on the use of ranking and allows for a comparative analysis of selected areas or regions.

Since posts published in a given period of time are used for evaluation, and their detection by the platform occurs with a delay, the received data may change.

The calculation of the level of positivity of the region p_r is performed by calculating the average level of positivity of the found messages p_{pi} of the given region:

$$p_r = \sum_{i=0}^{N} \frac{p_{pi}}{N}, \tag{1}$$

where N is the number of found messages, i.e., messages uploaded to the platform and published in the selected date range.

Similarly, to the previous method, the relative level of positivity is first calculated by formula (1). Then rationing is carried out among the selected municipal districts or

$$m_r = \frac{p_r - \min(p_r)}{\max(p_r) - \min(p_r)} \times d, \tag{2}$$

where $d = 5$ is the maximum value of the level of positivity.

Thus, the degree of positivity, and, consequently, the colors on the map are distributed by the ranking method relative to the selected areas.

For the intellectual analysis of deviant and depressive behavior, as well as the forecast, an artificial neural network was used. It was used for posts sentiment analysis of individuals and social groups. The classifier was trained using a dataset of 100k deviant and 300k regular posts. To obtain a stratified dataset, augmentation was used. Suggestions were extracted from deviant messages using keywords and became separate new posts. Also, errors were added to messages: random replacement of letters, changing letters in places and adding extra spaces in words. Based on the results of augmentation, a dataset was obtained that includes 350k deviant messages and 350k regular ones. For training, it was divided into training and test samples in a ratio of 80% to 20%, respectively.

The pretrained model TFDistilBertForSequenceClassification from the package transformers.modeling_tf_distilbert with two outputs corresponding to the probabilities of deviant and regular messages was used as a classifier for finding deviant messages (see Fig. 1).

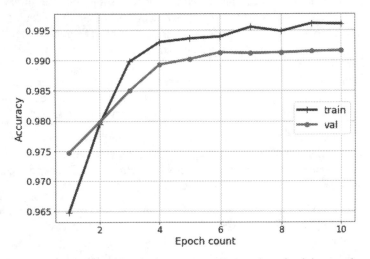

Fig. 1. Graph of dependence of accuracy on the number of training epochs.

The resulting testing dataset accuracy was 0.992. The algorithm was validated using the real dataset including 5671 posts collected and manually tagged during the week. A message was considered deviant if the probability of deviance exceeded 0.5. Classification results are characterized by the precision of 0.716, recall of 1.00 and F1-score of 0.835.

As a result of augmentation of the original dataset, the classifier demonstrates 100% recall with satisfactory precision, which is consistent with the goals of the platform.

4   Implementation

The developed models are implemented by a digital integrated monitoring platform for intelligent social analysis. The platform is designed to detect and prevent deviant and depressive behavior of various population groups.

The platform provides the following main functionality:

- the ability to select a social media to be monitored;
- visualization of monitoring results on the map;
- assessment of users of social networks and published messages according to the degree of positivity;
- automatic updating of the database of profiles of with suspected depressive behavior;
- analysis of profiles of users of social networks;
- preparation of reporting documentation.

The software is implemented in the programming language Python 3.8 in the PyCharm development environment. Additionally, the vue.js framework was used during development to create user interfaces in the reactive programming paradigm and the PostgreSQL. Special tools have been developed for displaying statistics on the map; visual tools designed for specialists to monitor and visualize the results and generate informational reports have been developed.

When working in the platform in the monitoring mode, the following are provided (see Fig. 2):

- setting various parameters for filtering found posts (marker words, data sources, posting period, user gender, age, emotional state level, settlements or municipal districts of the region);
- displaying statistics for the region (the number of posts in total, the number of negative posts, the level of positivity, etc.);
- displaying a map of the region, where the districts are displayed in color, depending on the level of the emotional state of the district (on a scale from 0 to 5, where 0 is red, 5 is green).

The monitoring results are messages that have a low degree of positivity—from 0 to 2.5 inclusive (determined by expert psychologists) (Fig. 3). Messages included in the monitoring results are moderated by the system operator, after which a report is generated based on digital twins (profiles), which is sent to psychologists for examination.

According to the results of an expert evaluation of messages, some of the profiles are considered to have a confirmed risk and are added for further analysis in the following areas (Fig. 4):

- assessment of the dynamics of the user's emotional state. Graph of the dynamics of the emotional state. The X-axis shows the time, the Y-axis shows the values of the degree of positivity of the published messages. The graph is colored depending on the level of profile positivity;
- tracking publication activity. On the graph of publication activity, the X-axis marks the time for which the profile analysis is carried out. Messages are tied to time. The timeline is colored depending on the level of positivity of the message;

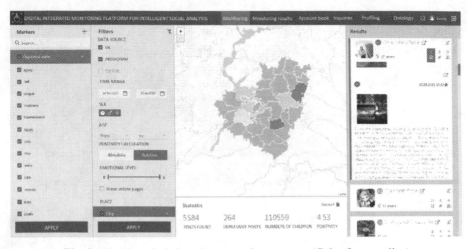

Fig. 2. Social analysis based on open data sources. (Color figure online)

- tape tracking;
- tracking the history of changes to contact information on the page;
- track profile avatars changes.

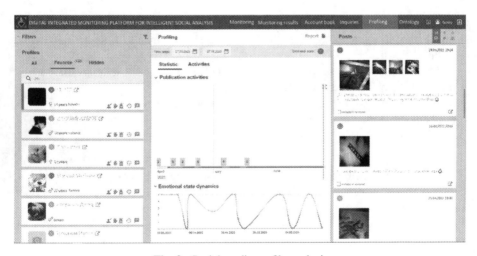

Fig. 3. Social media profile analysis

5 Discussion

As part of the work with the platform, a study was conducted to assess the effectiveness of the work of specialists and psychologists with minors who showed signs of depressive and deviant behavior. From 2019 to the present, the platform has been implemented in the Samara Regional Center for Social Assistance to Families and Children, and its active use has been carried out by the center's specialists supported by SEC "Open Code" since June 2020.

Since that time, 1,482,165 posts have been collected, of which 152,933 have been identified by the platform as depressive. The platform detected 112,348 profiles, of which 12,205 were identified by the platform as depressive.

Studies of the influence of the platform on the detected profiles were carried out to assess the activity of publishing posts and the dynamics of the emotional state of the detected profiles. Figure 4 shows graphs of profile publishing activity for the depressive and control groups. The X-axis on the graph shows dates, the Y-axis shows the number of published posts of the control group. The blue color shows the total number of posts, and the red color shows the depressive ones. It is shown that for the control group posting activity began to decline from September 2020 and reached its minimum in March 2021. For the second control group the frequency of publications in March 2021 is the maximum, but in May 2021 there is already a noticeable downward trend.

For the first control group, the average level of the emotional state of the profiles tends to increase, although it still has not reached the norm. For the second control group the average level of emotional state at the current moment (May 2021) is consistently low, which corresponds to the same observation period for the first control group.

Therefore, it was revealed that the frequency of publications, both depressive and positive, decreased after the discovery and confirmation of profiles in the platform. At the same time, the level of the emotional state of the profiles tends to increase, which may indicate a gradual stabilization of the emotional state.

On the horizon of six months for the control group of confirmed adolescents with signs of depressive behavior, it was found that the activity of profiles in terms of the total number of publications and the frequency of publications of depressive posts has decreased, and the level of emotional state increased on average.

On the horizon of three months for a similar control group, it was established that profile activity in terms of the total number of publications and the frequency of depressive publications remained at the same level, and the level of emotional state slightly decreased.

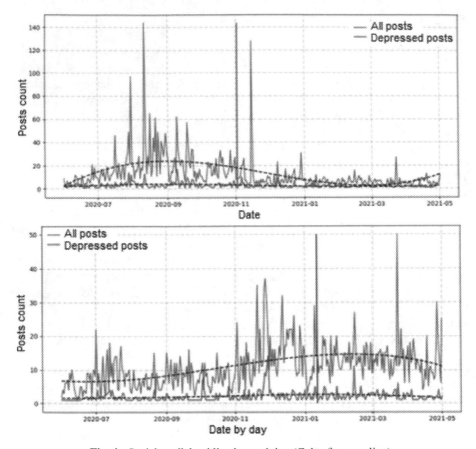

Fig. 4. Social medial publication activity. (Color figure online)

6   Conclusion

The introduced digital platform provides a new approach for integrated monitoring of social satisfaction and well-being using the methods of intelligent social analysis. Advantages of the platform include the ability to analyze the dynamics of changing sentiment trends in social media, match identified trends with social statistics by territory and provide decision-making support to change the social policy in relation to the selected categories of the population. The resulting solution implemented under the framework of social services digital transformation allows improving the effectiveness of social assistance activities.

The "digital twin" model of the social media member makes it possible to summarize the identified cases and identify influencing factors for further work. A methodology for taking into account the results of monitoring in the planning and implementation of preventive measures has been implemented. These opportunities allow using the developed platform on a regular basis for decision-making support for the management of the region.

References

1. Kataev, M., Orlova, V.: Social media event data analysis. In: Proceedings of Tomsk State University of Control Systems and Radioelectronics, vol. 23, pp. 71–77 (2020)
2. Chen, P.-L., Cheng, Y.-C., Chen, K.: Analysis of social media data: an introduction to the characteristics and chronological process. In: Chen, S.-H. (ed.) Big Data in Computational Social Science and Humanities. CSS, pp. 297–321. Springer, Cham (2018). https://doi.org/10.1007/978-3-319-95465-3_16
3. Andreenkova, N.V.: Comparative analysis of life satisfaction and determining factors. Public Opin. Monit. **5**(99), 189–215 (2010)
4. Shamionov, R.M.: The ratio of social activity and satisfaction of basic psychological needs, subjective well-being and social frustration of youth. Siberian J. Psychol. **77**, 176–195 (2020)
5. Dang, V.T.: Social networking site involvement and social life satisfaction: the moderating role of information sharing. Internet Res. **31**(1), 80–99 (2021)
6. Raza, S.A., Qazi, W., Umer, B., Khan, K.A.: Influence of social networking sites on life satisfaction among university students: a mediating role of social benefit and social overload. Health Educ. **120**(2), 141–164 (2020)
7. Ackerman, C.E.: Life satisfaction theory and 4 contributing factors (2021). https://positivepsychology.com/life-satisfaction/
8. Jia, Q., Zhou, J., Huang, M.: Life satisfaction predicts perceived social justice: the lower your life satisfaction, the less just you perceive society to be. Front. Psychol. **11**, 540835 (2020)
9. Ammar, A., et al.: On behalf of the ECLB-COVID consortium. COVID-19 home confinement negative impacts social participation and life satisfaction: a worldwide multicenter study. Int. J. Environ. Res. Public Health **17**(17), 6237 (2020)
10. Bou-Hamad, I., Hoteit, R., Harajli, D.: Health worries, life satisfaction, and social well-being concerns during the COVID-19 pandemic: insights from Lebanon. PLoS ONE **16**(7), e0254989 (2021)
11. Rajabi Gilan, N., Khezeli, M., Zardoshtian, S.: The effect of self-rated health, subjective socioeconomic status, social capital, and physical activity on life satisfaction: a cross-sectional study in urban western Iran. BMC Public Health **21**, 233 (2021). https://doi.org/10.1186/s12889-021-10261-6
12. Shi, Y., Joyce, C., Wall, R.: A life satisfaction approach to valuing the impact of health behaviors on subjective well-being. BMC Public Health **19**, 1–11 (2019)
13. Voukelatou, V., Gabrielli, L., Miliou, I., et al.: Measuring objective and subjective well-being: dimensions and data sources. Int. J. Data Sci. Anal. **11**, 279–309 (2021). https://doi.org/10.1007/s41060-020-00224-2
14. Zunic, A., Corcoran, P., Spasic, I.: Sentiment analysis in health and well-being: systematic review. JMIR Med. Inform. **8**(1), e16023 (2020)
15. Al-Khateeb, S., Hussain, M., Agarwal, N.: Analyzing Deviant Socio-technical behaviors using social network analysis and cyber forensics-based methodologies. In: Big Data Analytics in Cybersecurity, pp. 263–280 (2017)
16. Lee, J.R., Holt, T.J.: The challenges and concerns of using big data to understand cybercrime. In: Big Data, pp. 85–103 (2020)
17. Ivaschenko, A., Krivosheev, A., Stolbova, A., Sitnikov, P.: Approximate analysis of deviant behavior on social media. In: Arai, K. (ed.) Intelligent Computing. LNNS, vol. 283, pp. 539–547. Springer, Cham (2022). https://doi.org/10.1007/978-3-030-80119-9_33
18. Ivaschenko, A., Khorina, A., Sitnikov, P.: Online creativity modeling and analysis based on big data of social networks. In: Arai, K., Kapoor, S., Bhatia, R. (eds.) SAI 2018. AISC, vol. 858, pp. 329–337. Springer, Cham (2019). https://doi.org/10.1007/978-3-030-01174-1_25

19. Sawhney, R., Manchanda, P., Mathur, P., Shah, R., Singh, R.: Exploring and learning suicidal ideation connotations on social media with deep learning. In: 2018 Proceedings of the 9th Workshop on Computational Approaches to Subjectivity, Sentiment and Social Media Analysis, pp. 167–175 (2018)
20. Behera, R.K., Jena, M., Rath, S.K., Misra, S.: Co-LSTM: convolutional LSTM model for sentiment analysis in social big data. Inf. Process. Manag. **58**(1), 102435 (2021)
21. Ramírez-Cifuentes, D., et al.: Detection of suicidal ideation on social media: multimodal, relational, and behavioral analysis. J. Med. Internet Res. **22**(7), e17758 (2020)
22. Nam, S.J.: Deviant behavior in cyberspace and emotional states. Curr. Psychol. **42**, 10751–10760 (2023). https://doi.org/10.1007/s12144-021-02370-7
23. Jasso-Medrano, J.L., Lopez-Rosales, F.: Measuring the relationship between social media use and addictive behavior and depression and suicide ideation among university students. Comput. Hum. Behav. **87**, 183–191 (2018)

Model and Method of Decentralized Secure Storage of Students Digital Portfolios in an Educational Environment Based on Distributed Ledger Technology

Mikhail Deev$^{(\boxtimes)}$ ⓘ, Alexey Finogeev ⓘ, Igor Kamardin ⓘ,
and Alexander Grushevsky ⓘ

Penza State University, Krasnaya Str. 40, 440026 Penza, Russia
miqz@yandex.ru

Abstract. The article discusses the model and method of decentralized secure storage of digital portfolios of students in an open educational environment based on distributed ledger technology. The issues of the formation of a digital portfolio, its composition and structure in the process of continuous training of specialists are considered. The portfolio is a digital trace of educational and professional activities that captures the qualifications and emerging competencies of a future specialist for potential employers and recruitment agencies, which increases the competitiveness of graduates of educational institutions in the regional labor markets. The model of a set of digital portfolios of students in the information space is presented as a set of acyclic digraphs grouped by areas of study, educational programs, groups of competencies being formed, etc. To organize storage and work with digital portfolios, it is proposed to use the following technologies: a distributed registry, hashing, smart contracts, decentralized applications, an interplanetary file system. The main area of research is the creation of a multifunctional platform with smart contracts for the transition from a distributed data registry to a digital portfolio management system with personal data protection and support for the business logic of the educational process of forming professional competencies in the training of specialists in an educational institution. The Ethereum blockchain is used as the base platform. Transactions are implemented by smart contracts that perform the operations of collecting, verifying and authenticating data from sections of the information space associated with the student and adding information to the portfolio. Data processing in the distributed registry of digital portfolios is implemented at three functional levels. The digital portfolio includes public and private parts, which are accessed by multihash.

Keywords: digital portfolio · competencies · data protection · distributed ledger · blockchain · IFPS · smart contract · transactions · multihash · hashing

1 Introduction

A digital portfolio is a set of information with the student's personal data, including information about the educational process, attendance and certification results, project research results, scientific and social activities, etc. During the formation and actualizing of digital portfolios, information about the applicant is transferred after he enters the educational institution into information about the student and then into information about the graduate, his qualifications and acquired competencies during the training.

At the first stage, information about the applicant is entered into the portfolio, including personal and medical data of the applicant, the results of mastering the pre-university educational program, participation in olympiads, competitions and other intellectual competitions, sports and cultural achievements, data on social and social activities, etc. In the course of preparing a specialist in a bachelor's or specialist's program, the results of mastering the university educational program, intermediate and final certification, attendance, the formation of universal, general professional and professional competencies, course and diploma design, reports on practices, publications and scientific achievements, information on additional education, information about practices and work experience in the learning process, information about public, general cultural, volunteer and other social activities, etc. Further, at the stage of training for master's programs, similar information is entered on the learning outcomes and achievements of the future specialist, including the results of mastering the educational program, scientific and practical achievements, publications, data on internships, practical activities and additional education, etc.

The process of further filling and actualizing the digital portfolio continues for graduates who choose to continue their studies in graduate school. In fact, the portfolio is a digital trace of the educational and professional activities of the student, which determines the results of the individual trajectory of specialist training. A digital footprint is a constantly updated set of data blocks with information about the results of training a future specialist in an educational institution. The digital footprint allows you to analyze current information to diagnose the learner's emerging competencies and identify the reasons for insufficiently effective and high-quality training [1].

At the same time, the portfolio is not only a form of accumulating information about the qualifications and competencies of a future specialist, but also a way to assess the results of the educational activities of an educational institution as a whole, thanks to the analysis of statistics with generalized certification results in various areas of specialist training. The availability for potential employers and recruitment agencies of certain information from the portfolio describing the educational achievements of students can motivate future specialists to improve their qualifications and professional rating, and increase the competitiveness of graduates of specific educational institutions in the regional labor markets. Teachers and the administration of educational institutions, by analyzing the learning outcomes and achievements of students in the portfolio, monitor their individual development, and parents and / or persons paying for education can control the learning process.

In particular, the teaching and administrative staff at the levels of departments, deans, institutes and the university as a whole, on the basis of a rating formed on the basis of achievements and learning outcomes, can determine various ways of rewards, such as increased scholarships, funding for participation in events, identifying the best students, selection of candidates for personal scholarships, provision of places in hostels, selection of participants for academic mobility programs, internships, registration for admission to programs of the next level of study, awards and grants for research activities, provision of material assistance and social benefits, etc. In case of academic debts, violations of the order and discipline of the educational institution, etc., such data is also recorded in the digital portfolio and serve as the basis for the application of various types of punishments and disciplinary actions.

Recently, the practice of many educational institutions includes certification for specific competencies formed in the process of training in various disciplines and recorded in the work programs and the matrix of competencies for basic professional educational programs (BPEP). An analysis of the results of such certifications makes it possible to identify problems in the formation of demanded competencies both in general in the direction of training and in specific work disciplines. The inclusion of such results of competency assessments in the digital portfolio of students will allow assessing the quality and effectiveness of the formation of their competencies, which is important for the university administration and potential employers.

Thus, all information in the digital portfolio should be divided into separate information blocks available to different stakeholder groups, namely:

- trainees,
- employees of an educational organization (teachers, methodologists, administrative staff) with access control according to group policy templates in the information and educational environment,
- for potential employers, staffing and recruiting agencies,
- for parents and/or representatives of students,
- for legal entities or individuals paying for education,
- for administrators of the information and educational environment of the university.

For example, a student has full access to his personal account, which is a block with his personal data, learning outcomes and achievements. It includes information of the following nature: personal and passport data, contact information, student data, information about education, medical information, information about the presence of special rights, results of participation in competitions, olympiads and competitions, achievements in sports, scientific achievements, information about knowledge of languages and other additional education, information about social and social activities. Also, during the learning process, such information as academic performance, certification results, a list of disciplines studied and formed competencies, the results of assessment of formed competencies, information about additional educational programs and achievements, information about scholarships, awards and incentives, information about penalties, information about course projects, reports, final qualifying work, etc.

For the employer, access to information about the personal data of the future specialist is not provided, but the opportunity opens up to remotely get acquainted with the results of his educational and scientific-practical activities in the learning process. Such data include information about the direction of training and the main and additional educational programs, about the formed competencies and the results of their assessment, about the student's progress, about abstracts, essays, course and diploma projects, about scientific achievements, about his social and public activities, etc.

Creation and maintenance of an updated base of digital portfolios of students provides the educational institution with the advantages of electronic document management, automation of the learning process and control of students, motivation of students and teaching staff by stimulating the competitive mechanism, ensuring a continuous cycle of training specialists, the possibility of using methods of intellectual analysis and predictive modeling of learning outcomes and so on.

2 Theoretical Review

For reliable storage of information in public networks, blockchain technology is most in demand today [2]. A block chain is an example of a distributed database, where information is written to a block that is linked to the previous block by a hash identifier [3]. The chain is stored on network nodes and forms a distributed data ledger. New blocks are added only at the end of the chain. When a new block is added, copies of all blocks on each node are updated. At the same time, consent to add a new block to the blockchain must be confirmed by the majority of nodes that store copies of the blocks, which is called reaching consensus. Once a block has been added, any modification of records within it is impossible because its hash identifier is calculated based on the integrated data hash of this block and the hash of the identifier of the previous block.

Despite the fact that the development of blockchain technology is a hot topic of research, most of the work is related to its application to work with cryptocurrencies. However, distributed registry technologies, smart contracts and blockchain-based decentralized applications are implemented in various subject areas of human activity. Smart contracts are convenient for establishing trusted contractual relationships between different entities, where the participants' interaction algorithms implemented by them are used to confirm not only the acceptance of the agreement by the parties, but also to confirm the fulfillment of contractual conditions within the established timeframe. Blockchain technology allows you to create registers of records of electronic public services performed by automated systems, which contain data on the lists of services, requests for the provision and payment of services, the results of the provision / non-provision of services, etc. The work [4] shows examples of using the blockchain for the e-government system to simplify the interaction between citizens and government agencies. Article [5] also presents a distributed registry for analyzing public services, supporting the work of the judiciary, and assessing the risks of concluding contracts with private companies through smart contracts.

The introduction of Blockchain technology into the electronic document management system makes it possible to increase the reliability of information, automate the processes of monitoring the execution of contracts, monitor the stages of execution of clauses of the contract, projects and road maps. In particular, the article [6] considers the implementation of technology for managing digital identifiers of electronic documents. The papers [7, 8] analyze the possibilities of using distributed ledger technology and potential solutions in smart city systems, intelligent transport, e-health and other industries.

The actual area of application of the blockchain is the activity of educational institutions [9–11]. The introduction of blockchain technology for the secure storage and presentation of educational data, in particular, was approved back in 2017 by the European Commission. In her report [12], the possibilities of using technology for digital accreditation of academic education were recorded and eight scenarios for using technology to solve problems in the field of education were considered, including the provision of educational loans, payment for tuition, secure electronic document management, licensing of educational services, accreditation of educational institutions, confirmation of the authenticity of educational documents, copyright protection of educational materials, software products, etc.

Examples of implemented projects on the use of technology include: development of a platform for storing and exchanging data on student performance, transferring education documents with confirmation of their authenticity [13], issuing digital diplomas to graduates based on blockchain technology [14, 15]. Penza State University began to provide graduates with electronic diplomas, where the Credentia solution based on the Ethereum blockchain is used for storage and verification [16]. Electronic versions of documents on education, which take into account the qualifications and specialization of students, practice and academic performance, are received by graduates of the Department of Information Support, Management and Production.

To support interactions in the information and educational space, according to [17], the following components of blockchain technology can be used: a distributed ledger, hashing, smart contracts, decentralized applications for data processing. In fact, the main direction of research in this area is the creation of a multifunctional platform with smart contracts for the transition from a distributed data registry to a digital portfolio management system for students and employees with reliable protection of personal data and support for the main functionality of the business logic of the educational process of forming professional competencies as part of the training of specialists. in an educational institution. An example of the results of research in this direction is given in [18], which considers a model of a system for recording the professional competencies of citizens and their development trajectories based on distributed ledger technology and smart contracts for storing and using indicators of the level of competencies in the information environment of interaction between subjects of the economic system.

The main technology for the formation and storage of digital portfolios of students at this stage remains a centralized database with authorized access for different groups of people through the Web interface. However, decentralized storage of information data blocks in the form of a distributed ledger (blockchain) can be considered a more modern approach. The problem is that the problems of centralized data stores are their small cryptographic strength, which decreases over time, as well as exposure to distributed DDoS attacks and spam. In a decentralized database, there is no central storage, data blocks are distributed among network nodes, and new data can be added to blocks through transactional interactions.

The technology of their presentation in the open information space is closely related to data storage. There are various ways to visualize the portfolio of students: in the form of a personal website, in the form of a collection of links to Internet resources, in the form of sections of specialized social networks. Most platforms for creating digital portfolios actually support the basic functionality of a social network, allow you to interact with other users of the system, exchange messages, analyze statistics, set ratings, etc. Thus, the basic model of the digital portfolio system is the model of the social Web network [19]. The rationale for the use of such a model is that the portfolio is primarily created to present the achievements of the student, evaluate and recognize achievements, and, ultimately, to prove the competitive advantages of the future specialist in the labor markets. The digital portfolio social network model is directly embedded in the electronic information and educational environment of an educational institution as one of its central components.

In a number of educational institutions, the Moodle system, which is one of the most demanded learning management systems in the world, is used to form and fill in the digital portfolio of students [20]. The system adapts to specific tasks and features of the organization of the educational process in an educational institution. The digital portfolio, as a subsystem of Moodle, implements the replenishment and accounting of electronic documents that determine the student's achievements in various areas of educational, scientific and social activities. Access to the personal pages of students and personal data in the portfolio is carried out using an account and password authentication provided to the student for the period of study. The placement of information in the digital portfolio is carried out in accordance with the consent to the processing of personal data.

3 Materials and Methods

Simplified, blockchain technology can be viewed as a secure distributed ledger of public data, which implements accounting for data operations (transactions) in a peer-to-peer P2P network. A distributed registry is an effective tool for storing and presenting personal data of students and employees of educational institutions (digital portfolios) in an open information and educational space. The distributed ledger is used to record the history of transactions between network nodes, which are recorded in related information blocks. Blockchain users only see transactions that take place on data they own. The main idea of a distributed registry is to add data records or change information in data blocks in the absence of trust relationships between network nodes and users. The goal is to create a secure transaction log in which users cannot delete or tamper with existing entries. The basic principle is a decentralized mechanism for storing the log (registry) of records and guaranteeing its authenticity with protection against violation of integrity and confidentiality. The main technological components include the synthesis of a tree-like data structure (Merkle tree) with the calculation of hash functions of blocks, the use of transaction timestamps to form chains of related blocks (blockchain), anonymization of stateful transactions, synchronization of chains of information blocks on distributed nodes during data exchange, decentralized storage and exchange of data through a peer-to-peer (P2P) network.

To confirm the reliability of cryptographic calculations during hashing, a costly and energy-intensive algorithm for reaching consensus based on Proof-of-Work (POW) is implemented [21]. Due to this shortcoming, a number of alternative algorithms have been developed, for example, the Proof-of-Stake (POS) algorithm.

In the electronic educational environment, it is proposed to use a distributed registry to organize a system for accounting for digital portfolios of students and control their general professional and professional competencies formed in the process of learning. The platform uses the Ethereum blockchain. This choice is due to the fact that the open source platform solves a wide class of tasks using smart contract technology and allows you to create an updated registry for storing student portfolios at all stages of lifelong education. Records of the facts of obtaining any educational document (certificate, diploma, etc.) with subsequent confirmation of authenticity by a smart contract are registered in the register by the institution that issued the document. A user who has been granted certain access rights to the registry can, upon request, receive information about the achievements of the student recorded in the digital portfolio, in chronological order according to the addition of these records to the blockchain. The authorization problem is solved by using the mechanism of asymmetric cryptography with public and private keys. Similarly, transaction authentication is performed when new data is added to a digital portfolio. Each portfolio has a public and private key pair associated with it. The private key is used in transactions to add data to the portfolio and is used by users with access and permissions to make changes. Public keys are available to users with the right to view the portfolio. Elliptic Curve Digital Signature Algorithm (ECDSA) [22] is used as a hash calculation method for a digital signature.

A digital portfolio is a registry of related blocks of data. To identify each block, the result of the hash function of the previous block is used, which is added to the header along with the current timestamp. The portfolio registry is formed from a set of blocks linked to each other by including the hash of the previous block in the current one. Transactions in this case represent operations for adding new information to the portfolio manually or by collecting data from other sections of the information space associated with a particular student. For example, the collection of data with the results of certification in specific disciplines after grading by teachers in the "electronic dean's office" section. The digital portfolio data may also include graphic files with scanned results of various student-related documents.

Ensuring the integrity of data in the portfolio registry is solved as follows. Let's assume that after the operation to add data, an error is detected: for two consecutive blocks in the blockchain, the hash of the first block does not match the value stored in the second block. This means that the record is corrupted, which is detected after the hashes are calculated and compared. There remains the problem of determining the modified record. The solution uses the double hashing method. Links of successive registry blocks are provided by two hashes, which are calculated for the body of the block and for the metadata. In this case, each of the parts of the block is used to calculate the hash of the other part. Then the resulting hash is inserted into the header of another block, similar to the watermark of an electronic document. If the hash is not found in the block or does not match after calculation, then this means that the block has been modified.

Authentication of digital signatures of data blocks is performed at the portfolio validation step. The procedure is necessary to identify unauthorized, fake or compromised portfolio nodes in order to add them to the blacklist. To authenticate the portfolio, a script is used that implements the linear homomorphic signature (LHS) algorithm [23, 24]. The verifiable portfolio block ID is synthesized by combining two hash functions:

1. H_1 (Id, (T_X)), where the input data is the hash identifier of the previous block Id, the timestamp of its creation (T_X),
2. $H_2(T)$, where T – is a point on an elliptic curve in a finite field with coordinates (x, y):$\{(x, y) \in (F_p)^2 \mid y^2 = x^3 + ax + b \,(mod\,p),\, 4a^3 + 27b^2 \neq 0\,(mod\,p)\} \cup \{0\}$, where F_p is a finite field of integers a, b modulo p, 0 is a point at infinity.

The elliptic curve point is included to increase the security of the real node, to complicate the procedure for possible signature decryption, which is based on the discrete logarithm problem in the group of elliptic curve points. The generated signature can be represented as a combined hash S = (H1(Id, (X, Y)), H2(Tx)) (Fig. 1).

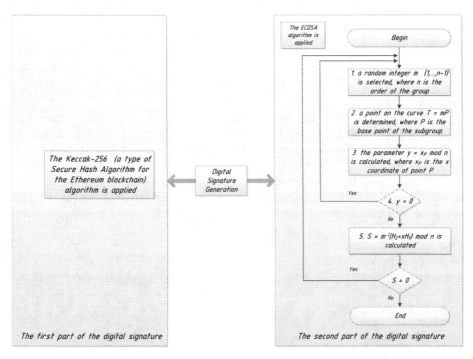

Fig. 1. Digital signature generation algorithm.

To calculate the first part of the digital signature H1(Id, (X, Y)), the Keccak-256 algorithm (a type of Secure Hash Algorithm for the Ethereum blockchain) is used. To synthesize the second part of the H2(Tx) signature, the ECDSA (Elliptic Curve Digital Signature Algorithm) public key algorithm is used defined on a group of points on an elliptic curve. The signature hash is generated iteratively as follows:

1. a random integer $m \in \{1,...,n-1\}$ is selected, where n is the order of the group,
2. a point on the curve $T = mP$ is determined, where P is the base point of the subgroup,
3. the parameter $y = x_P \,mod\, n$ is calculated, where x_P is the x coordinate of point P,
4. if $y = 0$, then choose another number m and go to step 2,
5. $S = m^{-1}\,(H_2 + x\,H_1)\,mod\, n$ is calculated,

6. if $S = 0$, then choose another number m and go to step 2.

The S signature is verified and allows certified users or applications to make transactions to add data to the digital portfolio, and authorized users to access to view it. The Portfolio Registry Authentication Script only allows for a set of valid data processing transactions.

Another task is to validate trusted users in order to confirm access rights and corresponding permissions. It is necessary to detect unauthorized access attempts, fake and compromised accounts. Such accounts and IP addresses of network nodes from which unauthorized access attempts were made are added to the blacklist and entries are made to the security logs. Journaling is both a security measure and a procedure for preparing data for a subsequent audit of an information system.

4 Results

As already mentioned, a system of linked data blocks was chosen to replenish and store digital portfolios. Then the block itself is an independent information unit in the digital portfolio. The same information unit is also used for network transmission. A chain of linked data blocks (digital portfolio) is a directed acyclic graph. Thus, the model of a set of digital portfolios of students in the information space can be represented as a set of acyclic digraphs grouped by areas of study, educational programs, groups of formed competencies, etc.

The order of collecting and forming a set of data blocks for each student's portfolio is implemented using the Ethereum blockchain with adding, reading, controlling and validating data using smart contracts. The block is generated and filled as a result of data collection and verification transactions. After filling, it is replicated between server nodes and its hash is searched (mined) according to the Eth-Hash algorithm. It then connects to the previous block in the registry after calculating the hash function.

The main advantage of Ethereum is the ability to implement and organize the work of smart contracts in the blockchain. A smart contract is a program code that allows you to perform operations on variables and check the conditions for their execution in the form of transactions. A smart contract consists of variables, setter and getter methods with access modifiers. The setter methods change the data, the getter methods only retrieve it. The Ethereum blockchain also allows block data to be stored through smart contract variables. The problem is that such storage requires significant costs, and as the volume of data increases, the cost of uploading transactions to the blockchain increases.

The number of students even in a regional educational institution is quite large and is constantly growing. A set of digital portfolios should be preserved and available at all stages of education, as well as in the case of transferring a student to another educational institution or in the event of a subsequent increase in his qualifications, transition to a new level of education, retraining, etc. Therefore, when using blockchain technology, there is a problem of computational and time costs for storing and processing big data. The downside of the Ethereum blockchain comes from having hard limits on variables to discourage DDoS attacks. In addition, all data must be replicated to all network nodes in the information environment of the educational institution, which is impossible and unacceptable in educational systems.

Therefore, the InterPlanetary File System (IPFS) technology was chosen to store in a network environment a multitude of digital portfolios presented in the form of a blockchain [25, 26].

Since the IPFS network is an open source project, the multi-platform client and other applications for working with it are distributed free of charge. IPFS technology implements a content-addressable model of block storage of digital portfolios of students with the organization of access to content via high-bandwidth hyperlinks. Since the blocks are linked by hash keys, IPFS includes a distributed hash table for decentralized exchange of data blocks. The block exchange protocol is based on the BitTorrent protocol. The digital portfolio namespace is based on public keys and is compatible with the DNS namespace. Block hashes are calculated as a block with new data is added to the chain, based on the hash of the previous block, the timestamp, and the added information. IPFS uses a SHA256 multihash as an identifier for the entire digital portfolio. The multihash includes four parts: hash function identifier, hash size, hash function calculation result, portfolio update timestamp. An example of a digital portfolio multihash in Base58 bitcoin encoding: AmfYx6mKGQAc7tDKLq45Hn8XFxWfBdZpgjsJ3tNXQRFivDmcXf5mKrQAc7tC WLq84Hn7XFxWfBdZpvogJk3tNXQRFiv.

In our case, each portfolio has two multihashes associated with it, which are calculated separately for its open and closed parts. The multihash for accessing the content of the public part is available to a wide range of authenticated persons who can access the system from certified nodes, while the multihash of the private part is available only to portfolio owners and trusted system administrators. Since a block is a separate portfolio unit, when working with the open part, you can get both the full IPFS block get data (multihash) and the data of a separate block. In the second case, the request specifies the portfolio multihash and the hash of a separate IPFS block get data block (multihash&hash). To simplify the search and work with the portfolio, its name and/or DNS name is attached to the multihash. For simple data retrieval from a distributed registry upon request, multihash is embedded in magnet links: magnet:?xt=urn:ipfs:[Base58 bitcoin encoded IPFS multihash].

Blocks of digital portfolios are constantly uploaded to the IPFS network after mining and hashing, and their hashes are stored in the blockchain. The network is a distributed portfolio repository, and the blockchain is a hash registry. To synthesize the blockchain address, an electronic wallet is created that allows you to perform transactions to add new digital portfolio data. To make transactions, smart contracts have been created that search for data by student ID, prepare data, authenticate, calculate the block hash function, place it in the block chain, view transaction results, calculate IPFS multihash for two parts of the portfolio after adding a block of data. Using the IPFS multihash of the open part of the portfolio, you can later access its content in the IPFS network.

5 Discussion and Conclusion

As a result of the research, a model and method for decentralized secure storage of digital portfolios of students in an open educational environment based on distributed ledger technology has been developed. As disadvantages of the proposed approach, it should be noted the computational complexity of implementing the blockchain in full, as is done in the mining of cryptocurrencies, for the synthesis and support of a multitude of digital portfolios of students in the electronic information and educational environment. It is also difficult to implement procedures for ensuring control by supervisory authorities in the field of education. In our case, it is more expedient to use only some components of this technology, in particular, a distributed registry mechanism and a hash of digital portfolio identifiers for organizing a hierarchical NoSQL data warehouse and a digital signature mechanism for certified personal data protection, authentication of stored data in the registry and authenticity of user accounts. In addition, in the developed system, the blockchain technology is implemented by creating an open and closed part of the registry. The closed part of the registry contains personal and medical data of students and employees of the educational institution, and the open part contains data on academic performance, achievements, professional competencies formed in the learning process. The closed part has maximum access restrictions only for owners and administrative staff, and the open part is designed to provide information not only to the administration of the educational institution, but also to potential employers and other interested parties. Each part of the digital portfolio registry defines a different way to access data and supports its own architecture. The advantage of this approach is that there is no need to perform a complex computational, time-consuming and energy-consuming "proof of work" task using the Proof-of-Work algorithm. Instead, simpler algorithms for reaching consensus with authenticated certified participants are used, such as Practical Byzantine Fault Tolerance (PBFT) [27]. A similar technology is discussed in [28], where the public part is defined as a permissioned blockchain in which data processing can be performed by specific individuals with the appropriate rights and permissions. Before performing allowed transactions on such a blockchain, the corresponding smart contract validates the identity of the subject and the network node from which the system is logged in.

To organize such a distributed registry structure, it was decided to use three functional levels of digital portfolio processing. The first level is represented by a cluster of main server nodes that form the private and public parts of the blockchain, which accept transaction requests from groups of trusted users and applications, group transactions into blocks of the public and private parts of the registry, calculate hash identifiers, implement the consensus algorithm and distribute block chains. Portfolio. Server nodes have the rights to register new trusted users and network nodes, maintain group security policies and administer the operation of the blockchain system.

The second level includes a group of caching proxies that are designed to process requests to render available content from the public part of the registry for certified nodes and identified users. These nodes do not participate in the consensus process, but keep a replicated copy of the public part of the registry. They check the operation of the nodes of the first group, work with access control lists, are responsible for authenticating users and certified nodes, forming "black lists" and security logs, and are responsible for load balancing in the network to prevent DDoS attacks and flooding attacks.

The third level includes certified client nodes of users who have the right to send requests for an accessible part of the portfolio. Such nodes store a partial replica of the open part of the student portfolio and have a client application that allows you to monitor changes in the portfolio of selected students with the recording of achievements and competencies. The application can be installed on mobile and stationary platforms for all interested parties, but to access the open part of the portfolio registry, you must register this site and authenticate the user in the system with the appropriate access rights and permissions, and before each new connection to the system, authenticate node and user. To access the public part of the user's registry, a unique hash key is used, which includes the hash of the user's account ID, the hash of the IP address, MAC address, or IMEA host ID. User nodes can store both the data blocks themselves from the public part of the registry, and hashes of digital portfolio data blocks, which are necessary to obtain the required information upon request. The hashed key is used to validate the user and the certified node before a session with the system, as well as to monitor the user's work with it.

The purpose of the research is to create a multifunctional blockchain-based platform with smart contracts and an interplanetary file network environment for the transition from distributed ledger technology to a digital portfolio management system with personal data protection and support for the business logic of the educational process during the formation of general professional and professional competencies with continuous training of specialists in regional educational institutions.

Funding. The research results were obtained with the financial support of the Russian Science Foundation (RSF) and the Penza region (projects No. 22-21-20100).

References

1. Mihajlova, S., Danilova, S., Veselov, A.: Raspredelennaja sistema sbora i analiza cifrovogo sleda obuchajushhegosja vuza. Sovremennye naukoemkie tehnologii **4**, 62–67 (2022)
2. Drescher, D.: Blockchain Basics: A Non-Technical Introduction in 25 Steps. Apress, Frankfurt am Main (2017)
3. Harvey, C.: Cryptofinance. https://papers.ssrn.com/sol3/papers.cfm?abstract_id=2438299. Accessed 05 June 2023
4. Carter, L., Ubacht, J.: Blockchain applications in government. In: Proceedings of the 19th Annual International Conference on Digital Government Research: Governance in the Data Age, pp. 1–2 (2018)
5. Terzi, S.: Blockchain 3.0 smart contracts in E-government 3.0 applications. arXiv preprint arXiv:1910.06092 (2019)
6. Ølnes, S., Jansen, A.: Blockchain technology as s support infrastructure in e-government. In: Janssen, M., et al. (eds.) EGOV 2017. LNCS, vol. 10428, pp. 215–227. Springer, Cham (2017). https://doi.org/10.1007/978-3-319-64677-0_18
7. Mkrttchian, V., Vasin, S., Gamidullaeva, L., Finogeev, A.: The impact of blockchain technology on the smart city industry. In: IV International Scientific and Practical Conference (DEFIN-2021). ACM International Conference Proceeding Series. Association for Computing Machinery, New York, pp. 1–5 (2021). Article 85. https://doi.org/10.1145/3487757.3490940
8. Uddin, M.A., Stranieri, A., Gondal, I., Balasubramanian, V.: A survey on the adoption of blockchain in IoT: challenges and solutions. Blockchain Res. Appl. **2**, 100006 (2021)
9. Bogdanova, D.: Blokchejn i obrazovanie. Distancionnoe i virtual'noe obuchenie **2**(116), 65–74 (2017)
10. Kirilova, D., Maslov, N., Astahova, T.: Perspektivy vnedrenija tehnologii blokchejn v sovremennuju sistemu obrazovanija. Int. J. Open Inf. Technol. **6**(8), 31–37 (2018)

11. Chasovskih, V., Labunec, V., Voronov, M.: Tehnologija blockchain v obrazovanii vuzov i cifrovoj jekonomike. Jeko-potencial **2**(18), 99–105 (2017)
12. Grech, A., Camilleri, A.: Blockchain in education. JRC science for policy report. Publications Office of the European Union, Luxembourg (2017)
13. O'Leary, R.: Malta's government is putting academic certificates on a blockchain. Coindesk. https://www.coindesk.com/maltas-government-putting-academic-certificates-blockchain/. Accessed 05 June 2023
14. Durant, E., Trachy, A.: Digital diploma debuts at MIT. Massachusetts Institute of Technology. http://news.mit.edu/2017/mit-debuts-secure-digital-diploma-using-bitcoin-blockchain-technology-1017. Accessed 05 June 2023
15. Academic Certificates on the Blockchain. https://www.unic.ac.cy/blockchain/free-mooc/. Accessed 05 June 2023
16. Stepanov, D.: V Rossii vpervye vydali cifrovye diplomy na blokchejne. https://cnews.ru/news/top/2020-02-25_rossijskij_vuz_vpervye_vydast. Accessed 05 June 2023
17. Swan, M.: Blockchain: Blueprint for a New Economy. O'Reilly Media (2015)
18. Novikov, S., Miheenko, O., Kulagina, N., Kazakov, O.: Cifrovizacija ucheta professional'nyh kompetencij grazhdan na osnove tehnologij raspredelennyh reestrov i smart-kontraktov. Biznes-informatika **4**(46), 43–53 (2018). https://doi.org/10.17323/1998-0663.2018.4.43.53
19. Sergeev, A., Cherepahina, L.: Razrabotka sistemy jelektronnogo portfolio obuchajushhihsja v social'noj obrazovatel'noj seti. Sovremennye problemy nauki i obrazovanija 6 (2016)
20. Kirillova, V.: Jelektronnoe portfolio kak sovremennaja tehnologija ucheta professional'nogo i lichnostnogo rosta obuchajushhihsja. Molodoj uchenyj **9**(404), 161–164 (2022)
21. Sriman, B., Ganesh Kumar, S., Shamili, P.: Blockchain technology: consensus protocol proof of work and proof of stake. In: Dash, S.S., Das, S., Panigrahi, B.K. (eds.) Intelligent Computing and Applications, vol. 1172, pp. 395–406. Springer, Singapore (2021). https://doi.org/10.1007/978-981-15-5566-4_34
22. Jablon, D.: Standard specifications for public-key cryptography: IEEE P1363 overview. https://csrc.nist.gov/. Accessed 05 June 2023
23. Cheng-Jun, L., Rui, X., Shao-Jun, Y., Xinyi, H., Shimin, L.: Linearly homomorphic signatures from lattices. Comput. J. **63**, 1871–1885 (2020). https://doi.org/10.1093/comjnl/bxaa034
24. Wenbin, C., Hao, L., Ke, Q.: Lattice-based linearly homomorphic signatures in the standard model. Theor. Comput. Sci. **634**, 47–54 (2016). https://doi.org/10.1016/j.tcs.2016.04.009
25. Benet, J.: IPFS - content addressed, versioned, P2P file system. CoRR (2014). https://doi.org/10.48550/arXiv.1407.3561
26. What is IPFS. https://docs.ipfs.tech/install/. Accessed 05 June 2023
27. Lamport, L., Shostak, R., Pease, M.: The Byzantine generals problem. ACM Trans. Program. Lang. Syst. (TOPLAS) **4**(3), 382–401 (1982)
28. Garzik, J.: Public versus private blockchains. https://bitfury.com/content/downloads/public-vs-private-pt1-1.pdf. Accessed 05 June 2023

Optimal Management of Tourism Products Based on the Analysis of User Preferences

Leyla Gamidullaeva$^{(\boxtimes)}$ (ID) and Alexey Finogeev (ID)

Penza State University, Krasnaya Str. 40, 440026 Penza, Russia
gamidullaeva@gmail.com

Abstract. The article considers the issues of planning and managing a tourist product based on the synthesis of the optimal route of movement and visiting tourist sites. A hybrid approach has been developed to manage the process of synthesis of optimal tourist routes. The developed model and method of tourism product management allows taking into account tourist preferences and restrictions along with various external factors that affect the choice of places to visit and route sections. The process of synthesis of alternative tourist routes is carried out at the first stage by a modified ant colony algorithm. At the second stage, the method of analysis of hierarchies was used to select the optimal route from alternatives. The advantage of the approach is the ability to control the route synthesis process in two ways. The first method takes into account the importance of the experience, preferences and limitations of a particular tourist when choosing sites and tourist sites on the route to visit at a particular point in time. The second way is the ability to manage the workload and the number of tourists on route sections and tourist sites, as well as the attractiveness of objects for tourists by changing the degree of importance of the concentration of pheromones when calculating the probability of choosing a site or visiting an object. The process of planning, designing and operating tourist products with the ability to control the process of selecting objects on routes is implemented in a recommender tourist system.

Keywords: Recommender system · multiobjective optimization · tourist route · personalized tourist product · ant colony algorithm · hierarchy analysis

1 Introduction

The tourism industry is becoming one of the rapidly developing industries using info-communication technologies. The introduction of artificial intelligence technologies to help users plan tourist routes opens up a new stage in the development of tourism and increases the competitiveness of tourism business processes. One of the key directions in this area is the tendency to personalize the design of tourist routes through the use of specialized recommender systems [1]. This process is due to various factors, which include federal support for the development of domestic tourism, the emergence and development of high-quality road transport infrastructure, new transport routes to previously hard-to-reach or inaccessible tourist sites, the emergence and development of networks of numerous hotels, guest houses, apartments and other types of places accommodation, chains of cafes, canteens and restaurants, especially in roadside areas, the creation of specialized systems and websites to help tourists in independent planning of tourist routes, booking tours and hotels, excursion services, carsharing and other services necessary in the process of implementing a tourist product.

It should be noted that the creation of travel sites and sites of travel agencies, mobile applications, systems and sites for booking accommodation, meals, excursion services and vehicles, as well as the emergence of many groups, channels and chats in various social networks, sites describing tourist sites and attractions with reviews, dramatically increases the possibility of independent travel planning, increases the ratings of the owners of booked places and visited tourist sites [2]. However, the development of information and software services of this type does not always give the desired result, since in most cases it is not possible to implement a systematic integrated approach to independent planning and design of a tourist product. Partially, the problem can be solved by creating a distributed registry with typed descriptions of tourist sites in the regions, routes between them with a description of various types of communication methods, places of possible stops and stops, as is already done in the main navigation cartographic systems.

New opportunities for organizing personalized regional tourism are opened by a recommender system with artificial intelligence technologies for analyzing and taking into account dynamically changing requirements, preferences and restrictions of travelers, which helps to synthesize individual tourism products with the possibility of modifying them during implementation [3].

Synthesis and/or selection of individual tours in such a system should be carried out on the basis of an intellectual analysis of the preferences and wishes of users, taking into account their capabilities and limitations (financial, temporal, physical, medical, etc.). An object-oriented model for managing the process of forming an optimal tourist product according to specified criteria is designed to synthesize alternative travel routes between tourist sites selected based on user preferences, taking into account temporal, spatial and financial constraints. Tourist preferences and restrictions are presented as a set of formalized quantitative and qualitative semi-structured indicators that are stored in the tourist's digital profile. The finished tourist product is a detailed route with the calculation of time intervals between stops for a particular type of vehicle, with a description of attractions and other tourist sites on the route and next to it, places of food, overnight stays, parking, gas stations, etc.

2 Introduction

Consider some research related to the development of new systems and technologies to help tourists plan and design tourism products. It should be noted that the problem of synthesizing the optimal tourist route based on the analysis of user requirements and taking into account several criteria [4] is the subject of a number of studies.

In [5], for the synthesis of a tourist route, it is proposed to solve the problem of converting the requirements of a tourist from a natural language into a set of criteria taken into account when constructing it. In [6], the issues of creating a recommender system for planning tourism activities and generating tourist routes in an optimization setting are considered. The authors propose a functional model and methodology for the formation of a dynamic tourist route based on multi-criteria optimization for the purposes of educational tourism.

The most famous way to plan and design a tourist route with visits to attractions and other tourist sites specified on the map is to go to the traveling salesman problem and find a Hamiltonian cycle in the graph or an optimal route that passes through the specified points at least once and then returns to the starting point. The optimality criteria are the shortest distance, travel time, traffic congestion, travel cost, etc. Alternative routes are represented by several Hamiltonian cycles with the choice of the optimal one among them according to a given criterion. Since tourist objects have exact geographical locations, the distances between them are known, and the problem is considered geometric (planar or Euclidean). Despite the simplicity of the problem statement, it is NP complete and finding a truly optimal path, especially in the presence of several criteria and many visiting points, is a rather complex computational problem and can be exactly solved only by exhaustive enumeration, and a solution close to optimal can be found by heuristic methods. For example, in [7], a modified ant colony optimization algorithm is used to plan a tourist route using the traveling salesman algorithm with the shortest distance criterion. To take into account the contextual information about tourist sites, their degree of attractiveness, object load, weather conditions and the comfort level of places to visit, the algorithm uses a pheromone update strategy when synthesizing the optimal route. In [8], it was proposed to optimize the accuracy of the optimal solution to the traveling salesman problem using the ant colony algorithm using an entropy-weighted learning strategy. A number of researchers combine several different approaches to solve the problem of designing optimal tourist routes. The article [9] considers the integration of the genetic algorithm with the ant colony algorithm to eliminate the shortcomings of local optimization in order to synthesize the best path with the minimum cost of movement. In [10], the ant colony route search algorithm was combined with the particle swarm algorithm to find the optimal path and improve the rules for updating pheromones through a heuristic function based on particle swarm optimization.

In addition to the ant colony algorithm, other approaches are used to search and synthesize the optimal route, for example, the hybrid evolutionary algorithm [11], the genetic algorithm [12], the particle swarm optimization algorithm [13], the simulated annealing algorithm [14], etc.

The process of choosing the optimal tourist route from alternative solutions obtained as a result of solving the traveling salesman problem can be solved based on the analysis of tourist preferences and constraints. To simplify the task of choice, in a number of works it is proposed to group users into clusters according to the degree of similarity of their preferences, as well as to cluster tourist routes according to various parameters associated with restrictions on their use, for example, comfort level, financial, temporal, transport conditions, etc. Clustering is also used to group attractions, natural places and other tourist sites that are similar in various ways, places of residence and food, short stops, etc. Clustering results make it possible to speed up the process of their selection in the synthesis or selection of a tourist product according to the possibilities, limitations and preferences of tourists. In addition, for new tourists included in the cluster, the system can recommend suitable products and services on the route, as well as predict the attractiveness of tourist sites and products for tourism focus groups with similar interests.

The article [15] proposes a multicriteria algorithm for constructing tourist routes based on a grid spatial model and fuzzy clustering of tourist preferences using the K-means method. The multivariate spatial model is used to obtain a correlation model of routes after analyzing the characteristics of the routes, which are extracted from user data and fuzzy preferences. Adaptive learning of the fuzzy clustering model in the process of analyzing the characteristics for choosing a tourist route is carried out using the hybrid swarm algorithm. Thus, for the synthesis of routes, a system of swarm and intelligence, which prevents suboptimal recommendations for choosing routes.

The clustering technology is used in [16], which considers the methodology for synthesizing routes that combine the most important attractions in the selected region, based on clustering sites with their descriptions to identify similarities between them. The methods of cluster analysis were used by the authors in [17] to process and group tourist places according to their attractiveness for tourists. In [18], it is proposed to use clusters to identify and predict the preferences of tourists in eco-tourism. In [19], the clustering algorithm is used to classify cities based on data from tourist destinations in order to predict the competitiveness of tourism development in them.

3 Materials and Methods

Today, on the market of tourist services and applications, there are practically no recommender systems with elements of artificial intelligence, which, based on the analysis of a fuzzy description of tourist preferences, can form offers of possible tourist products in a given direction with a description of a synthesized route compiled on the basis of possible options for traveling by one's own (car, motorcycle)., bicycle, boat, etc.) or by public means of transport (passing cars, commuter or long-distance trains, airplanes, water modes of transport). Moreover, such a route should not simply offer the shortest route to the final selected point, as modern navigation services do. The recommender system should offer several alternative tourism products for the selected destination according to a fuzzy description.

Each product here is presented as a route on a digital map and should include descriptions of places of interest and stopping places along the route (food, toilets, overnight stays, short rest, playgrounds, natural beautiful places, etc.) both along the route, and near with access within a given time interval. The formation of tourism products is implemented according to the methodology proposed by the authors in [20].

The initial data for the formation of possible alternative tourism products are the personal data and preferences of the user of the recommender system, as well as the possibilities determined by him, which should narrow and limit the range of routes and tours recommended to him by the system. In fact, a part of personal data (for example, some medical indicators, preferences and opportunities (financial, physical, family and others) determine a set of many criteria, based on the analysis of which the problem of multi-criteria selection of the optimal tourism products for a particular user is solved [21].

A feature of the proposed recommender system is the ability to analyze fuzzy preferences and restrictions, and, accordingly, to assess their degree of similarity with sets of criteria received from other tourists, a previously developed fuzzy clustering algorithm is used [22].

The process of synthesizing a new tourist product according to the generalized and fuzzy wishes of the tourist is the most difficult task. That is why most travel services require the user to clearly define the criteria for searching and choosing tours, indicating specific dates (with a small range of variations) and places of residence. Moreover, such systems are often focused on offers of early booking of tours, which forces users to try to plan their trips many days or even months in advance, which does not allow obtaining guarantees for the implementation of the purchased tourist product without problems. Often personal/family circumstances or external factors (natural disasters, congestion of tourist sites, lack of tickets, weather conditions, employment, health problems, etc.) do not allow the purchased tour to be realized, which leads to significant financial losses. The best option here is to plan your trip yourself with a choice of hotels and transport, as booking services often offer the possibility of free cancellation up to a certain time. Unfortunately, transport companies do not always provide such an opportunity to their passengers (this is especially true for low-cost air carrier fares).

The main point in the work of the advisory tourist service is the intelligent planning of alternative tourist routes with the most complete visits to the selected attractions for a given time interval, taking into account the road infrastructure, type of vehicle, the degree of congestion of tourist facilities (number of visitors, the presence of queues and lack of tickets), financial, temporary, meteorological, medical, family and other factors, taking into account the time for long and short stops, for possible visits to unplanned tourist sites on the route, etc. The result is a synthesis or selection of a tourist route, which is associated with visiting a certain number of attractions in a given period of time with the choice of methods of movement between stops along the way with the optimization of heterogeneous criteria. The conditions for solving a multi-criteria problem can lead to the synthesis of different routes that are the best only from the point of view of fulfilling a specific criterion. The synthesis or choice of a tourist route is complicated by the fact that often the preferences and possibilities of a tourist change during preparation for a trip and / or during movement between stops due to external factors (for example, the presence of large queues and lack of tickets to visit), changes in their own priorities and wishes. Therefore, the process of planning and designing a tourist product can be divided into five stages:

- The stage of planning and synthesis of the travel route. The synthesis of the route is carried out taking into account the choice of the mode of transport, the choice of attractions and other places to visit, with the reservation of places of residence on the planned dates for the implementation of the tourist product.
- The stage of iterative adjustment of the planned route before the start of movement. This adjustment process may be performed several times due to various changes in travel conditions (changes in preferences, composition, dates, financial conditions, weather conditions and other factors).
- The stage of dynamic adjustment of the tourist product during the route, depending on external factors and personal preferences.

- The stage of implementing a tourist product (planned or dynamically changing) with fixation of geospatial locations, photo and video materials about sights, places of visits and stops along the route.
- The stage of the final description and evaluation of the tourist product with the addition of reviews, additional photo and video materials to help other tourists in choosing a route.

As shown earlier, the process of synthesizing alternative optimized routes, taking into account many criteria, is reduced to solving the geometric traveling salesman problem or searching for Hamiltonian cycles in a graph with geospatial binding of visiting points. There are no exact algorithms for finding the optimal solution to this multicriteria problem, so researchers offer many heuristic approaches to solve it. In our system, the traveling salesman problem is solved using a hybrid approach that combines the ant colony algorithm [8] for finding alternative paths and the hierarchy analysis method for choosing the most optimal tourist route from alternatives. The ant colony algorithm belongs to swarm intelligence methods and is widely used in path planning [23], for solving logistical problems [24], for routing in networks [25], for scheduling [26], for controlling the movement of underwater robots [10], for planning tourist trips [27], etc.

Consider the application of this algorithm to solve the problem of designing alternative tourist routes with planned visits to selected tourist sites. Let m tourist objects be given with distances between them (determined using the navigation system) d_{ij}, where $i,j = 1,2...,m$, are pairs of objects on the map, $w_{ij}(t)$ is the weight of the section of the path between the objects at time t, which is defined as a convolution of the criteria or values of pheromones left on the site by ants of the first type, $k_{ij}(t)$ is the number of pheromones on the path section. Then the probability of choosing a site by an ant of the second type will be equal to:

$$p_{ij} = \frac{k_{ij}^{\alpha} + \frac{1}{w_{ij}^{\beta}}}{\sum_{l \in S_i}(k_{ij}^{\alpha} + \frac{1}{w_{ij}^{\beta}})},$$

where α, β are the coefficients defining the degree of importance of the concentration and weights of pheromones (criteria), l is the section of the alternative route S_i.

The coefficients is determined through the expert opinion of tourists based on their tourist experience.

The process of synthesizing alternative routes is carried out by simulating the process of searching for food by a set of ants of the first type, and the shortest route is selected due to the information transfer mechanism. In the process of finding a path, the ants of the first type leave pheromones, by which the ants of the second type choose the path. Pheromones model the criteria for choosing the optimal section of the path. Since there are several criteria, each criterion has its own type of pheromone. Ants of the first type move in groups between given waypoints, each of which carries its own type of pheromone. The ants evaluate the segments of the path and, at the most optimal of them for a particular criterion, leaves a given type of pheromone or a label of optimality of the segment. The ants remember the sections of the path they have traveled and cannot repeat them until they return to the starting point of the route. After returning, the list of segments of the traversed path for such ants is reset to zero. The greater the concentration of pheromones of different types remains on the segment of the route after the passage of ants of all groups, the higher the probability of choosing a site at a given time.

After passing through all groups of the ant colony, a path is synthesized from the selected sites. To synthesize the path based on the concentration and weight of pheromones, ants of the second type are used, which do not have pheromones and make up a route from lists of sites with the maximum probability of including sites in the route, which is determined by the maximum degree of pheromone concentration and their maximum weight. Since, in the general case, the concentration and integral weight of pheromones in different areas can coincide, several alternative routes (lists of areas) can be obtained, from which the most optimal route is then selected by the hierarchy analysis method.

The number and values of the criteria that affect the route synthesis process may vary depending on the preferences and experience of the tourist, as well as on the time of travel along the route. To take into account the time factor, all criteria, and therefore pheromones, are divided into two groups, a) static (for example, the distance between waypoints does not change), b) dynamic (for example, travel time between waypoints changes due to road conditions and traffic jams). At each section of the path, the process of reducing the concentration of pheromones is realized, since dynamic pheromones evaporate after the synthesis of alternative routes by ants of the second type. Next, new coefficients of importance of the criteria for their concentration are set, and a new path search is performed. Groups with pheromones of the first type do not participate in the new search, since static pheromones remain on the sites as their permanent characteristics and are recorded in the route register. The algorithm implements two ways of adaptive setting of the tourist route:

1. a mechanism for changing the degree of importance of specific factors and restrictions of tourists, which allow taking into account the experience, preferences and capabilities of users when choosing a path in a specific period of time (for example, when visiting natural tourist sites, it is necessary to increase the degree of importance of the weather passability (attractions, museums, etc.) the factor of the number of tourists at the time of visiting is important),
2. a mechanism for changing the degree of importance of the concentration of pheromones, which affects the number of selected sections of the path and allows you to regulate the congestion of roads and tourist sites, which affects the number of visitors, the length of queues, the availability of tickets to visit, etc. Also, increasing the importance of the concentration of pheromones on the way to the attraction helps to increase its attractiveness for tourists.

At the second stage of the hybrid approach, to select the optimal route from alternatives, it is advisable to use the hierarchy analysis method (Saaty method) [28, 29]. This approach is used to make decisions in conditions of certainty and multi-criteria. Each route here is considered as a simple hierarchy that has:

- goal in the form of a list of tourist sites on the route planned to be visited,
- alternative ways and means of transportation between points on the route,

- criteria for achieving the goal and assessing the quality of alternative routes and methods of travel between waypoints, including well-defined quantitative criteria (minimum number of intermediate stops, shortest distance between waypoints, maximum number of attractions planned for sightseeing, minimum travel time between stops, minimum cost of travel between waypoints, etc.) and vaguely defined criteria for qualitative assessment (quality of overnight stay and assessment of service quality, assessment of food quality on the route, assessment of the quality of excursion support when sightseeing, assessment of the quality of intermediate stops, etc.).

According to the hierarchy analysis method, the first step is to select a qualitative model of a tourist route, which includes a goal, a set of alternatives for moving between points, and a set of criteria for evaluating alternatives.

To set the priorities of quantitative criteria and obtain qualitative estimates of alternative ways and means of movement, the method of pairwise comparisons (benchmarking) is used, the result of which is the matrix of pairwise comparisons of alternatives $A = \|a_{ij}\|$, where $a_{ij} = w_i/w_j$, w_i and w_j are the weights of the i-th and j-th elements of the hierarchy.

At the same time, quantitative criteria for alternative route paths are set at the first stage of selection and refined at the second stage of route correction. Qualitative estimates of alternatives can be obtained in two ways. The first method is used if the route is new and there are no quality ratings for its alternative steps from other tourists who could already evaluate them. In this case, the synthesis of the entire route from alternative steps is performed only on the basis of the analysis of hierarchies according to quantitative criteria, which are extracted from known navigation services.

To solve the choice of route, taking into account only quantitative criteria, in the recommender system, the locations of tourist sites and stopping points on the route are written in the form of a matrix, where the rows correspond to the points of departure, and the columns correspond to the places of arrival. They are vertices of the route graph with edges that define alternative travel paths between points. The edges of the graph are weighted according to the quantitative estimates of alternative routes, such as distance, travel time, fuel consumption with estimated cost, number of stops, and so on. Thus, for each edge, a vector of quantitative criteria is formed, which are used as estimates of alternatives in the analysis of hierarchies. Each graph is linked to a digital map, where waypoints have specific latitude and longitude coordinates.

Qualitative assessments are added by the tourist at stages 3 and 4 in the course of dynamic adjustment and implementation of the selected route. For a qualitative assessment of each alternative route according to various criteria, a ten-point scale is used. After the final fixation of ratings at the last 5th stage with writing reviews and scoring for each alternative step, these ratings become available to other users in the process of synthesizing a similar tourist product in a recommender system. The choice of a route by a new user is carried out taking into account the qualitative assessments of individual steps. After the tourist sells the received product with visits to similar tourist sites, but moving along new alternative routes and subsequent evaluation, new quality assessments are added to the route register and then used in the selection process. Thus, the system is trained in the process of using the same tourist product by new users.

In the general case, the number of paired comparison matrices is determined by the number of available alternatives for each tourist route and the number of criteria for evaluating alternatives. Since the number of criteria and alternatives can increase with each new operation of the product and the addition of new estimates, the number of matrices will increase at the stage of system training. This is due to the fact that in a simple hierarchy, the total number of matrices is equal to the number of criteria, since the matrices are built to compare alternatives for each of them, plus the comparison matrix of the criteria themselves.

The time lag for the implementation of a separate stage of the tourist route, which includes several alternative ways of transportation for automobile, motorcycle or bicycle transport, is considered by default to be daylight hours. For rail or water transport, one step of the route may include night time, since often the movement between stops on the route occurs at night, and daytime is spent on visiting tourist sites located at one stop. At the same time, transport plays the role of places to spend the night and eat. It should also be noted that the number of alternative ways of movement depends on the degree of freedom of the vehicle. The maximum degree of freedom is considered to be personal transport, which does not depend on rigidly defined routes for the transportation of passengers by public transport. Here, the degree of freedom is determined by the possibility of choosing the type of transport by the tourist and the availability of tickets for the selected routes, dates, times and type of vehicle.

For each matrix, vectors of local priorities of alternatives are also synthesized. Local priorities are the relative weights of alternative travel routes between tourist sites along the route. Priorities can take values from zero to one. The higher the priority value, the more significant is the corresponding alternative path. When calculating the criteria for each row of the matrix, the geometric mean of its elements is calculated:

$$\overline{s} = \sqrt[n]{s_1 \cdot s_2 \cdot \cdots \cdot s_n},$$

where n is the number of criteria. Next is the sum of all geometric means. To calculate the relative weight, the geometric mean of each row of the matrix is divided by this sum. The resulting weight (local alternative priority) is an estimate of the alternative travel path between the selected tourist sites along the route.

The priority value depends on the quantitative assessments of the alternative (for example, the cost of fuel, the price of a check in a cafe, travel time, etc.) and the qualitative subjective assessments by the tourist of the elements of the alternative route (traffic conditions, road quality, fuel quality at gas stations, weather conditions at route, the quality of food and service in cafes, the degree of cleanliness at short-term stops, etc.). The local priorities of the alternatives are multiplied by the priorities of the corresponding criteria of the previous hop and then summed over each element according to the criteria. As a result, the final estimate of the alternative route step is calculated, which is its weight, calculated as a convolution of the weights of local criteria for all route steps.

Also, for each matrix, the index of consistency of estimates is calculated:

$$I = \frac{\mu_{max} - n}{n - 1},$$

where n is the dimension of the pairwise comparison matrix, and to calculate μmax, the sums of elements in the columns of the pairwise comparison matrix are multiplied by the local priority vector in each row and the resulting product results are added.

This consistency index is necessary to check the consistency of estimates of the same steps of a tourist route according to different criteria. To do this, the consistency indices are compared with random consistency values by calculating the consistency ratio. The values of the consistency ratio must be greater than 0.1, otherwise it is considered that the criterion estimates of alternative paths between waypoints are highly mismatched, since the matrices of pairwise comparisons are filled in erroneously.

Then, based on the obtained vectors of local priorities for the alternatives of each step of the routes and the consistency indices of tourists' assessments of the quality of services, they determine the vector of priorities for the goals of the entire tourism product and activities to provide quality services to tourists along the entire route. To do this, the local priorities of the alternatives at each step of the route are multiplied by the priorities of the corresponding step criteria and summed for each element in accordance with the criteria. As a result, the global priorities of all alternative routes are determined taking into account the priorities of the criteria by the multiplicative convolution method. The maximum rating will correspond to the selected tourist route with the highest global priority. Such a route is considered the most optimal for the selected criteria and implementation conditions, given the preferences and restrictions of the tourist.

4 Discussion and Conclusion

In the course of the research, a hybrid approach has been developed to manage the process of synthesis of optimal tourism products. The proposed method allows planning and designing tourist routes taking into account several criteria with the possibility of adaptive control of this process. The developed model and method of managing a tourist product during its synthesis and selection allows taking into account tourist preferences and restrictions together with various external factors that affect the choice of places to visit and sections of routes to them.

The advantage of the proposed approach is the ability to control the route synthesis process in two ways. The first method allows taking into account the importance of the experience, preferences and limitations of a particular tourist or group when choosing sites and tourist sites on the route to visit at a specific period or point in time. At the same time, you can manage the priorities for selecting tourist attractions or objects. For example, when visiting natural tourist sites, weather conditions may be a priority, and when visiting sites with low traffic, such as museums, attractions, restaurants, hotels, etc. the main priority is the number of tourists, which determines the availability of the object. The second way is to manage the traffic and number of tourists on route sections and tourist sites, as well as the attractiveness of objects for tourists, by changing the degree of importance of the concentration of pheromones to calculate the probability of choosing a road section or the probability of visiting a site.

Although the ant colony algorithm has the advantages of strong adaptability and dynamic feedback optimization, it has the disadvantages of long convergence time and the probability of obtaining a locally optimal solution. In addition, incorrect selection of the pheromone concentration coefficient can lead to mass synthesis of the same route for many tourists in one time interval, which will lead to congestion of a road section or tourist site.

Therefore, to improve the multicriteria procedure for synthesizing the optimal tourist route, the recommender system uses the method of analyzing hierarchies. The method is implemented at the second stage and is used to select the most optimal route from the synthesized alternatives. It also has advantages unlike the others, as it contains a mechanism for evaluating the received routes according to several criteria. The method corresponds to the tourist's intuitive ideas about the recommended tourist route. The procedure for synthesizing a tourist product in a recommender system with the possibility of a multi-criteria selection of route sections and changing priorities when taking into account various criteria in an iterative mode allows tourists to receive personalized tourist offers based on their own preferences and capabilities.

After selecting the optimal route, the tourist receives detailed information about the route and stopping points with its visualization on the map. The route includes a list of sights that it links, a list of possible stops on the route (overnight stays, places of food, places of rest, etc.) with a calculation of time for the average speed of movement of a given type of transport. You can also see a set of criteria for choosing a tourist route and certain degrees of importance for each of them, which determine the priority of choosing route sections and tourist sites to visit. By changing the pheromone concentration coefficients and their weights in the ant colony algorithm, the user can change his tourist route during its adjustment before the start or during its direct implementation. Thus, on the platform of the recommender system, the process of planning, designing and operating tourist products is modeled with the ability to control the process of selecting sites and objects along the routes in a sliding mode. The optimization of tourism products is carried out in accordance with user preferences, attributive characteristics of user clusters and external factors affecting the tourism product in the planned time interval of its operation.

Acknowledgment. The study was supported by the grant of the Russian Science Foundation No. 22-28-20524 "Digitalization of the life cycle management of an internal regional tourism product based on blockchain technology". https://rscf.ru/project/22-28-20524.

References

1. Zheng, W., Liao, Z.: Using a heuristic approach to design personalized tour routes for heterogeneous tourist groups. Tour. Manage. **72**, 313–325 (2019)
2. Cenamor, I., de la Rosa, T., Núñez, S., Borrajo, D.: Planning for tourism routes using social networks. Expert Syst. Appl. **69**, 1-9 (2017)
3. Sumardi, M., Wongso, R., Luwinda, F.A.: "TripBuddy" travel planner with recommendation based on user's browsing behavior. Procedia Comput. Sci. **116**, 326–333 (2017)
4. Sharafutdinov, E.F., Evseeva, E.F.: A system for constructing optimal routes on the map, taking into account several criteria: architectural technological solutions. Appl. Inf. Syst. S. 259–264 (2015)
5. Pestun M.V.: Cognitive navigation and an algorithm for constructing a text description of the route in a human-friendly form. Softw. Prod. Syst. No. 1, pp. 28–33 (2015)

6. Kotsyuba I.Y., Nazarenko A.E.: Development of a recommender system for planning tourist routes in an optimization setting modeling, optimization and information technology. **8**(2) (2020). https://moit.vivt.ru/wpcontent/uploads/2020/05/KotsyubaNazarenko_2_20_1.pdf. https://doi.org/10.26102/2310-6018/2020.29.2.021

7. Liang, S., Jiao, T., Du, W., Qu, S.: An improved ant colony optimization algorithm based on context for tourism route planning. PLoS ONE **16**(9), e0257317 (2021). https://doi.org/10.1371/journal.pone.0257317

8. Yang, K., You, X., Liu, S., Pan, H.: A novel ant colony optimization based on game for traveling salesman problem. Appl. Intell. **50**(12), 4529–4542 (2020)

9. Liang, Y., Wang, L.: Applying genetic algorithm and ant colony optimization algorithm into marine investigation path planning model. Soft Comput. **24**(11), 8199–8210 (2020)

10. Che, G., Liu, L., Yu, Z.: An improved ant colony optimization algorithm based on particle swarm optimization algorithm for path planning of autonomous underwater vehicle. J. Ambient. Intell. Humaniz. Comput. **11**(8), 3349–3354 (2020)

11. Lu, Y., Benlic, U., Wu, Q.: A highly effective hybrid evolutionary algorithm for the covering salesman problem. Inf. Sci. **2021**(564), 144–162 (2021)

12. Ahmed, Z.H.: Genetic algorithm for the traveling salesman problem using sequential constructive crossover operator. Int. J. Biometrics Bioinform. (IJBB) **3**(6), 96–105 (2010)

13. Liu, Z., Huang, L.: A mixed discrete particle swarm optimization for TSP. In: 2010 3rd International Conference on Advanced Computer Theory and Engineering (ICACTE), vol. 2, pp. V2–208. IEEE (2010)

14. Hao, M., Xin, G.: UAV route planning based on the genetically simulated annealing algorithm. In: International Conference on Mechatronics and Automation (2010)

15. Li, Y.: Multicriteria recommendation method of tourist routes based on tourist clustering. Mob. Inf. Syst. (2022). https://doi.org/10.1155/2022/9168899

16. Duarte, J., Talero, L., Rodriguez, C.: Methodological proposal for the identification of tourist routes in a particular region through clustering techniques. Helion **7**, e06655 (2021). https://doi.org/10.1016/j.heliyon.2021.e06655

17. Gosal, A.S., Geijzendorffer, I.R., Václavík, T., Poulin, B., Ziv, G.: Using social media, machine learning and natural language processing to map multiple recreational beneficiaries. Ecosyst. Serv. **38**, 100958 (2019). https://doi.org/10.1016/j.ecoser.2019.100958

18. Nilashi, M., et al.: Preference learning for eco-friendly hotels recommendation: a multicriteria collaborative filtering approach. J. Cleaner Prod. **215**, 767–783 (2019). https://doi.org/10.1016/j.jclepro.2019.01.012

19. Guo, S., Jiang, Y., Long, W.: Urban tourism competitiveness evaluation system and its application: comparison and analysis of regression and classification methods. Procedia Comput. Sci. **162**, 429–437 (2019). https://doi.org/10.1016/j.procs.2019.12.007

20. Gamidullaeva, L., Finogeev, A., Kataev, M., Bulysheva, L.: A design concept for a tourism recommender system for regional development. Algorithms **16**(1), art. no. 58 (2023). https://doi.org/10.3390/a16010058

21. Gamidullaeva, L., Finogeev, A.: A multi-criteria method for the synthesis of regional and interregional tourism routes. In: Silhavy, R., Silhavy, P. (eds.) Software Engineering Research in System Science. CSOC 2023. Lecture Notes in Networks and Systems, vol. 722, pp. 141–151. Springer, Cham (2023). https://doi.org/10.1007/978-3-031-35311-6_16

22. Gamidullaeva, L.A., Finogeev, A.G.: Methodological approaches to managing the development of industry ecosystems (on the example of the tourism industry). π-Economy, **16**(2), 7–23 (2023). https://doi.org/10.18721/JE.16201

23. Akka, K., Khaber, F.: Mobile robot path planning using an improved ant colony optimization. Int. J. Adv. Rob. Syst. **15**(3), 1–7 (2018)

24. Feng, Y.J., Zhang, X., Liu, X.H.: Research on the optimization of the enterprise logistics distribution based on ACO algorithm. In: Advanced Materials Research, vol. 912, pp. 1900–1903. Trans Tech Publications (2014)
25. Maheshwari, P., Sharma, A.K., Verma, K.: Energy efficient cluster based routing protocol for WSN using butterfly optimization algorithm and ant colony optimization. Ad Hoc Netw. **110**, 102317 (2021)
26. Deng, W., Xu, J., Zhao, H.: An improved ant colony optimization algorithm based on hybrid strategies for scheduling problem. IEEE access. **7**, 20281–20292 (2019)
27. Huang, H.C.: The application of ant colony optimization algorithm in tour route planning. J. Theor. Appl. Inf. Technol. **52**(3), 343–347 (2013)
28. Bachtiar, A.S.A., Nurwatik: Alternative route planning analysis of tourism transport using analytical hierarchy process (AHP) and network analysis methods (Case Study: Jember Regency). In: IOP Conference Series: Earth and Environmental Science, vol. 1127, no. 1, p. 012046 (2023). https://doi.org/10.1088/1755-1315/1127/1/012046
29. Basak, I., Saaty, T.: Group decision making using the analytic hierarchy process. Math. Comput. Model. **17**(4–5), 101–109 (1993). https://doi.org/10.1088/1755-1315/1127/1/012046

Intelligent Technologies in Social Engineering. Creativity and Game-Based Learning

Lattice-Based Adaptation Model for Developing Adaptive Learning Games

Olga Shabalina[1]([✉]) [iD], Alexander Khairov[1] [iD], Alexander Kataev[1] [iD],
and David C. Moffat[2]

[1] Volgograd State Technical University, Volgograd, Russia
o.a.shabalina@gmail.com
[2] Glasgow Caledonian University, Glasgow, UK
d.c.moffat@gcu.ac.uk

Abstract. Adaptive learning applications that provide personalization of the learning process are one of the fastest growing types of educational software. The article analyzes the models and methods of adaptation for the development of adaptive learning games in which the learning process is implemented in a game context. A portable adaptation model is proposed, applicable for the development of adaptive learning games of various genres. The learning course for adaptive learning games is represented by a space, formed by embedding the initial course structure into the lattice, the structural ordering of which allows the formation of personalized learning strategies determined by the current state of the learner and the structure of the space itself. An approach for dynamic content matching of non-linear learning scenarios and gameplay is proposed, which preserves the logic of both the learning process and the game process. An embedded adaptation module for adaptive learning games has been designed and implemented, which makes it possible to reduce the complexity of development and improve the quality of such games in terms of the effectiveness of the learning process. An example of applying the proposed module to the development of an adaptive game for studying the object-oriented paradigm and the C# language is described.

Keywords: Adaptation Model · Adaptation Method · Adaptation Technique · Knowledge Domain Model · User Model · Adaptive Learning Game · Learning Strategy · Training Course · Lattice-Based Approach · Knowledge Space

1 Introduction

In the context of the development of e- and distance learning, the introduction of a system of continuous education, advanced training and retraining of the educational sphere as a whole, the demand for training systems designed to teach and train skills in various fields of knowledge is increasing [1]. Educational software (software) is one of the most dynamically developing types of software, the sphere of development of educational systems is actively developing, well systematized, models, methods and technologies used to implement the learning process in such systems have been developed.

A. G. Kravets et al. (Eds.): CIT&DS 2023, CCIS 1909, pp. 405–419, 2023.
https://doi.org/10.1007/978-3-031-44615-3_28

Modern trends in software development are associated with the personification of the processes of user interaction with the system, which has led to the emergence of a new class of learning systems - adaptive learning systems that are able to observe user actions and adapt to their capabilities and needs. The task of finding adaptive software solutions is especially relevant for learning systems, since the quality of learning outcomes, and, accordingly, the quality of the system itself, directly depends on this [2–4].

One of the most promising approaches to improving the effectiveness of learning is the use of computer games in learning (Digital Game Based Learning, DGBL [5–7]. Educational computer games are learning systems in which the learning process is implemented in a game context [8].

A new step in the development of educational games is the personification of the learning process in a game context, i.e. development of adaptive learning games [9–12]. Currently, adaptive learning games are considered as an independent class of software that requires the development of original models, methods and technologies that take into account the specifics of this class.

Known adaptation models specifically designed for adaptive learning games are built-in ad-hoc models tied to the implementation of a single game. In addition, the development of adaptive learning games is mainly carried out not by specialized companies, but by educational communities and/or individual developers who do not have sufficiently high qualifications, and this affects both the speed of developing such games and the quality of the games developed. Solutions. Therefore, the task of developing portable adaptation models and their software implementations that can be integrated into game projects, allowing to automate the process of designing adaptive learning games, and thus reducing the complexity of developing such games and improving their quality from the point of view of the effectiveness of the learning process in the game, is an urgent task. Context.

2   Analysis of Adaptation Models for Adaptive Learning Games

Modern approaches to the development of adaptive learning systems are based on the allocation of three components of the adaptation model: the domain model (Knowledge Domain model), the learner model (Learner model) and the adaptation method (Adaptation technique). The domain model is usually represented as a general graph that defines a finite set of fragments that make up the content of the knowledge area, and links between fragments that reflect the logic of its development. To reflect the structural features of the knowledge area, the graph can be endowed with additional properties. The learner model (Learner model, Learner profile) stores some of its characteristics, which are taken into account during adaptation. Most systems use the current knowledge of the learner as a characteristic of the learner; some learner models also store such characteristics of the learner as learning style, interests, previous experience, etc. The adaptation method determines how to change some parameters of the learning process based on monitoring the change in the student's state in the process of his interaction with the learning system. Known adaptation methods are mostly based on rules, cause-and-effect relationships, i.e. methods based on the mechanisms of logical inference. The definition of the logic of adaptation depends on the chosen model of the learner.

Computer games are an independent category of software. Game content according to its purpose corresponds to the domain model; the player's profile and game statistics, which store data about the player, correspond to the student's model; game mechanics can be correlated with the learning process model. Adaptive computer games, in addition to the components of conventional games, have built-in mechanisms for changing the behavior of the game depending on the user's current gaming results. Changes may be made to the parameters of the game, the scenario of the passage, the content of the game.

Adaptive learning computer games are a combination of adaptive learning systems and computer games. The development of adaptive learning games requires the development of methods for modeling the learning process in a game context and the development of an adaptation model that ensures the preservation of the logic of both learning and game scenarios.

The development of domain models for adaptive learning games requires, in most cases, serious efforts of experts in developing the model and updating player profiles [13]. In [14], methods for automatically searching for student models for creating domain models based on the Q-matrix method are proposed. The Q-matrix is built on the basis of student test scores. In [15], a method was developed for automatically creating a domain model (e-Learning domain) based on the application of text mining technology to journal and conference articles used as data sources. However, the proposed method does not take into account the results of the interaction of students with the subject area. In [16], it is proposed to use learning curves to build a domain model. A similar approach was proposed in [17], in which possible spaces of alternative models of the subject area are searched and the best model according to some given attribute is found. However, the addition of new concepts and relations of the subject area is not provided. In the latest works, the use of concept maps (concept maps) [18, 19] and ontologies [20] is proposed for the development of a domain model.

The paper [21] proposes various student (player) models developed for adaptive games. Adaptation models for adaptive learning games use approaches based on pedagogical agents [22–24], technologies based on game tracks and analysis of aggregated data [25]. In [26], an adaptation model based on an adaptive scenario (adaptive digital storytelling) is proposed, in [27] a method for constructing adaptive learning strategies in a game.

The well-known adaptation models developed specifically for use in adaptive learning games differ in the information collected by the system during the student's interaction with the game, in the ways of obtaining it, and in the methods of adapting the learning process to the current values of the user's characteristics. In [28, 29], the ALIGN model is described, which allows you to adapt to the skills of the student using an implicit method of collecting information during the game. The adaptation method in this model is based on the change in the flow of information from the interpretation of the choice of tasks is trainable and is implemented in the Elektra game. Honey and Mumford's LSQ model is featured in Minerva [30]. The adaptation method in this model is based on changing the level of complexity of game tasks and types of prompts. Information about the learner is collected explicitly with the help of questions, and implicitly with the help of tracking the actions of the learner during the game. The work [31] describes the

Triage model implemented in the Code Red game. This model allows you to implicitly adapt to the knowledge and skills of the trainee.

3   Methodology

3.1   A Lattice-Based Approach for Modeling in Adaptive Learning Systems

The learning process is considered as a process of interaction of a learner with the knowledge domain. Correspondingly, the learning process model is represented by three models: knowledge domain model, learner model and a model of the learner interaction with the knowledge domain (as shown in Fig. 1).

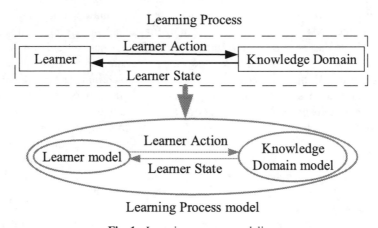

Fig. 1. Learning process modeling

3.2   Knowledge Domain Model

Knowledge structure is customary to represent by a finite set of related fragments of knowledge that make up the content of the corresponding knowledge domain:

$$KnowledgeStructure = < Concepts, \leq >, \qquad (1)$$

where $Concepts = \{c_1, \ldots, c_i, \ldots, c_n\}$ – a set of fragments of knowledge, $\leq$ - binary relations between the fragments, reflecting the logic of their mastering.

The graph representation (1), as the most general representation of binary relations, is sufficient for modeling knowledge domain structure. But for the organization of the process of mastering knowledge, it is necessary that the knowledge domain model allows calculating the knowledge accumulated by each learner while mastering the knowledge domain. For this the initial knowledge structure KD is embedded in the algebraic structure (lattice), which keeps the partial order of the initial structure, but on which two binary operations ($*$, $\oplus$) are defined. The presence of operations on the lattice allows to calculate the level of knowledge acquired by the learner, which determines his current state while mastering the knowledge domain. In terms of Knowledge Space Theory (KST), a structure reflecting the learner state represents a knowledge space (KS) [34]. Thus, the knowledge domain model is represented as shown in Fig. 2:

$$KS = < S, (*, \oplus) >, \qquad (2)$$

where KS – knowledge space, $S \supset Concepts$ – a set of knowledge space elements, ($*$, $\oplus$) – binary operations on the space.

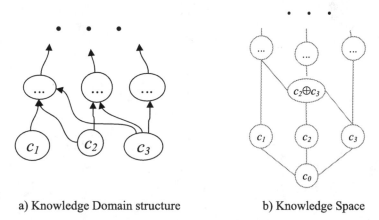

a) Knowledge Domain structure   b) Knowledge Space

Fig. 2. Knowledge Space as Embedding the Knowledge Domain structure in a lattice

As a result of embedding the knowledge structure in the lattice in general case, new elements might appear in the resulting structure (ex. $c_2 \oplus c_3$), which ensure structural ordering ("structural completeness") of the knowledge space. Fragments of knowledge and learner actions as well to these elements are not matched, but can be matched by the knowledge domain developer on order to provide the "content completeness" of the knowledge space (see "Appendix 1" for detailed description of the knowledge space properties).

3.3 Learner Model

Interaction between the learner and the knowledge space KS is considered as performing by the learner actions that are needed to be done for mastering corresponding fragments of knowledge (for example, reading some knowledge fragment, solving a problem, passing a test, etc.). The results of performing the actions $la(x)$ are assessed on some selected scale $\Lambda_\varphi = \{\lambda_{min}, \ldots, \lambda_i, \ldots, \lambda_{max}\}$ and define the learner state on the knowledge space. Thus, the learner state $\varphi \in$ on the knowledge space KS is a mapping:

$$\varphi \in LS \leftrightarrow \varphi : KS \rightarrow \Lambda\varphi, \tag{3}$$

where LS is a set of possible learner states on the knowledge space.

Before the learner start to mastering the KS each element $x \in KS$ is associated with the initial state of the learner φ^0 and the threshold state $\varphi^*(x) = \lambda$, which is considered as sufficient level of mastering x for this learner. Each action $la(x)$ performed by the learner and assessed as $\lambda \geq \varphi^*(x)$ changes the state of the learner on the knowledge space:

$$la \in LA \leftrightarrow la : \Phi(KS, \Lambda_\varphi) \rightarrow \Phi(KS, \Lambda_\varphi), \tag{4}$$

where LA is a set of possible learner states on the knowledge space.

Thus, la is represented as an operator acting on the state space Φ and possessing the property such that no one action reduces the level of mastering of the corresponding element: $la\ (\varphi)\ (x) \geq \varphi\ (x)$.

The learner model (Fig. 3) is represented as a tuple:

$$Learner = < LS, LA >, \tag{5}$$

where $LS-$ a set of learner states, LA – a set learner actions.

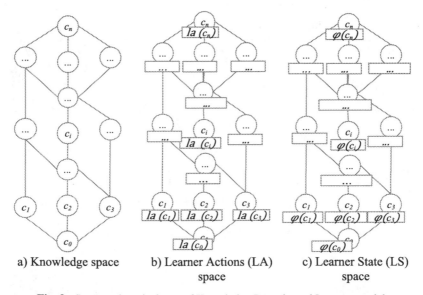

a) Knowledge space   b) Learner Actions (LA)   c) Learner State (LS)
                           space   space

Fig. 3. Structural equivalence of Knowledge Domain and Learner models

3.4   Modeling Learner and Knowledge Domain Interaction

The model of learner interaction with knowledge space is represented as evolution of the learner state on the knowledge space (Fig. 4):

$$\varphi_{i+1} = la_{i+1}(\varphi_i), \tag{6}$$

where φ_{i+1} – the state the learner goes into after the action la_{i+1}, determined by the previous state φ_i and assessed as $\lambda \geq \varphi^*(x)$, $\varphi \in LS$, la $\in LA$, where LS and LA are determined by the learner model (5).

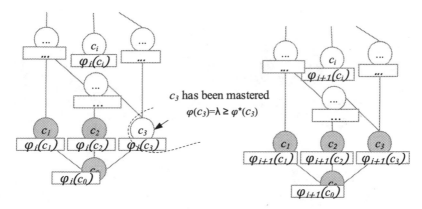

Fig. 4. Learner-Knowledge Domain Interaction model

Thus, each learner state φ factorizes the space KS into three subspaces:

$$KS = KS_{masered} \cup KS_{ready-to-master} \cup KS_{unmastered}, \tag{7}$$

where $KS_{masered} : x \in KS_{masered} \leftrightarrow \varphi(x) > \varphi^*(x)$;
$KS_{lunmastered} : x \in KS_{unmastered} \leftrightarrow J(x, \varphi) < J^*(x)$;
$KS_{ready-to-master} : x \in KS_{ready-to-master} \leftrightarrow J(x, \varphi) > J^*(x)$ and $< \varphi(x) < \varphi^*(x)$.

A set of ready-to-master elements defines a subspace, on which the learner can chose any element x for mastering. The results of mastering are assessed and if element x is considered as mastered, the learner state on the knowledge space changes and new elements. The learner interaction with the knowledge space lasts until the learner reaches some certain state φ^{goal}, that meets the required learning outcomes:

$$\varphi_0 \xrightarrow{la_1} \varphi_1 \xrightarrow{la_2} \cdots \xrightarrow{la_i} \varphi_i \xrightarrow{la_{i+1}} \cdots \xrightarrow{la_n} \varphi^{goal}$$

$$\downarrow\downarrow\downarrow\downarrow$$

$$KS(\varphi_0) \subset KS(\varphi_1) \subset \cdots \subset KS(\varphi_i) \subset \cdots \subset KS\left(\varphi^{goal}\right) \tag{8}$$

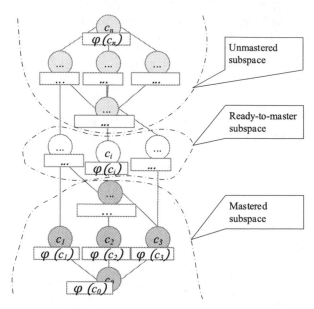

Fig. 5. Knowledge space subspaces

The learner interaction with the knowledge space is an expansion in the space KS of the subspace $KS_{masered}$ as a result of performing by the learner actions related to the corresponding elements $x \in KS_{ready-to-master}$ (Fig. 5).

Such a process can be considered as a logical analogy (analogy of mechanisms) of propagation in discrete space KS of a single wave (soliton) carries energy (the knowledge accumulated by the learner), until the wave front ($KS_{ready-to-master}$) completely covers the space KS, which, in turn, means successful mastering of the knowledge space and achievement by the learner the state φ^{goal} (Fig. 6).

While mastering the knowledge space each learner is free to perform any action la matched to corresponding $x \in KS_{ready-to-master}$ determined by his current state φ. In such a way he creates his personal learning path as a sequence of actions he performs for the mastering the knowledge space, such that none of the possible paths violate the knowledge space logic (Fig. 7).

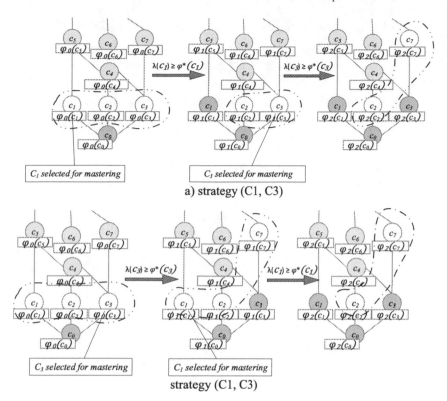

a) strategy (C1, C3)

strategy (C1, C3)

Fig. 6. Wave-like personified knowledge space mastering process

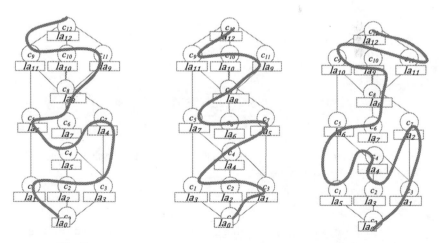

Fig. 7. Examples of possible learning paths on the knowledge space

3.5   Integration of the Lattice-based Models to a Game Context

3I-Approach. Combining the learning process and the gameplay requires integration of knowledge domain model, learner model and model of learner and knowledge domain interaction into the game context [35].

Combining Learning and Game Scenario. While interacting with the game the player performs game actions ga_i provided by the game scenario:

$$GamePath = \{ga_1, \ldots, ga_i, \ldots, ga_m\}. \tag{9}$$

Implementation of the 3i-aproach requires that learning and game actions to be performed simultaneously, i.e. merged in one action la_i/ga_i (Fig. 8):

$$LeanringPath_{inGame} = \left\{ \frac{la_1}{ga_1}, \ldots, \frac{la_i}{ga_i}, \ldots, \frac{la_n}{ga_n} \right\} \tag{10}$$

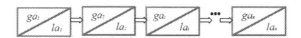

Fig. 8. Combined linear scenario model

To ensure the compatibility of nonlinear learning and game scenarios, for any sequence of unrelated learning actions matched to corresponding ready-to-master knowledge subspace (Fig. 9a), it is necessary provide a predefined sequence of the game actions (Fig. 9b).

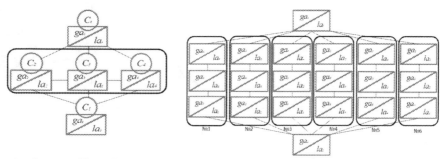

a) subspace of knowledge space   6) possible variants of gameplay corresponding
integrated in a game context   the subspace

Fig. 9. Compatibility of nonlinear learning and game scenarios

In the general case, more than one game action can be associated with each learning action, which can be selected based on the game situation (Fig. 10).

This allows you to expand the game scenario and increase game attractiveness without losing the knowledge space logic.

This allows you to expand the game scenario and increase game attractiveness without losing the knowledge space logic.

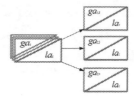

Fig. 10. " One-to-many" combined game scenario (fragment)

4 Adaptive Learning Game for Mastering OOD and Programming Language C#

As a prototype a role-playing game "Kammy" for learning object-oriented design (OOD) and the C # language with hierarchical knowledge domain and linear game scenario was taken. Knowledge domain includes the following sections: data types, classes, objects, properties and methods, class inheritance and polymorphism, access modes, design patterns, class libraries. A virtual world based on these concepts has been developed.

The main character of the game is "Professor Kamaev"[1], who occasionally destroys his research laboratory and due to an explosion turns into Kammy – a small transformer, consisting of 16 round pieces. Kammy, as a game character with which the learner, acting as a player, associates himself, has to adapt to his new appearance to survive in the unknown world and to reach and recover his laboratory in order to become a human again.

The knowledge domain is represented as a structure which embedded in the lattice. A fragment of the structure of the training course and the corresponding fragment of the game scenario are presented in Figs. 11, 12.

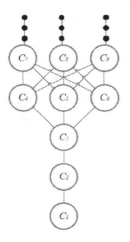

Fig. 11. Fragment of the structure of the training course

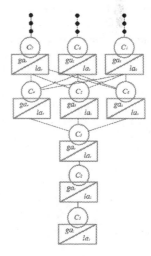

Fig. 12. Fragment of the game script

The description of the game content associated with the fragment of the game scenario is given in Table 1.

Table 1. Description of the game content associated with the fragment of the game scenario.

Knowledge space fragment identifier	Job fragment theme	Learning action, *la*	Game event, *ga*
C1	Exploring data types	Selecting data types	Player identification
C2	Creating classes and class objects	Creating a class and class object	Creating the main character of the game Kammy
C3	Exploring class methods	Development of a class method for moving forward	Teaching a character to move forward
C4–C7	***	***	***
C8	Exploring one-dimensional arrays	Declaring and initializing a one-dimensional array	Character Transformation into Serpent form
C9	Exploring three-dimensional arrays	Declaration and initialization of a three-dimensional array	Transformation of the character into the form of Kettlebell

The knowledge space includes logically unrelated elements, defining the fragments of knowledge that can be studied in any order. For example, to study class methods, the fragments of knowledge associated with development of functions for moving forward, backward, left, and right can be mastered in any order. But, not to include in each element a description of how to write the class methods, this information block is included only to the task for the development of the forward movement function, and this element precedes the elements related to the development of the rest of the movement function. This seems also logical in the context of the game, as the player will most likely select to start teaching Kammy how to move forward first. The game screenshots are shown in Fig. 13.

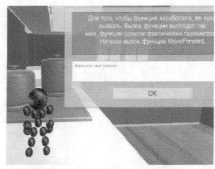

a) Kammy is located on the kitchen set and he can't move

b) Kammy has learned to move forward but he ran into a pot

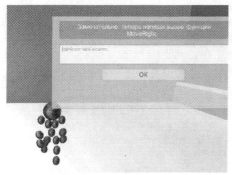

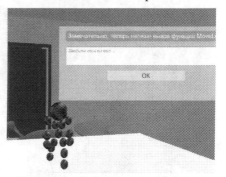

c) Kammy has learned to move back, but ran into a wall.

d) Kammy will fall from the kitchen if he does not learn to move to the left.

Fig. 13. Screenshots of the game

5 Conclusion

The paper describes a lattice-based approach for modeling in adaptive learning systems and its application to the development of adaptive learning games. A method has been developed for implementing the method of dynamic content matching of non-linear training and game scenarios in a training role-playing game, which ensures the development of a training course for any game strategy formed by the player. The proposed method is applicable to the development of adaptive role-playing learning games with a non-linear scenario.

Currently, work is underway to develop an adaptation module that can be integrated into adaptive learning games developed on Unity. The module will include algorithms that ensure the operation of the user interface and the dialog system, control of script execution based on triggers, evaluation and adaptation algorithms. To build a space according to a given course structure, a set of tools is provided that provides effective management of the course structure and its elements of the course and automatic generation of the necessary data in the game.

The use of the module in the development of adaptive learning games will improve the process of their development at the stages of design and implementation, significantly reduce the complexity of development, as well as improve their quality in terms of the learning process.

References

1. Burac, M.A., Fernandez, J., Cruz, M., Dela, C.J.: Assessing the impact of e-learning system of higher education institution's instructors and students. In: IOP Conference Series: Materials Science and Engineering, vol. 482 (2019)
2. Mirata, V., Hirt, F., Bergamin, P., Van der, W.: Challenges and contexts in establishing adaptive learning in higher education: findings from a Delphi study. Int. J. Educ. Technol. High. Educ. **17** (2020)
3. Shuai, W., et al.: When adaptive learning is effective learning: comparison of an adaptive learning system to teacher-led instruction. Interact. Learn. Environ. **31**, 793–803 (2020)
4. El-Sabagh, H.A.: Adaptive e-learning environment based on learning styles and its impact on development students' engagement. Int. J. Educ. Technol. High. Educ. **18**(1), 1–24 (2021). https://doi.org/10.1186/s41239-021-00289-4
5. Lee, Y., Zhu, M.: Digital game-based learning can develop students' literacy skills and meet learning standards in the US. Comput. Sch. **39**, 1–23 (2022)
6. Tay, J., Goh, Y.M., Safiena, S., Bound, H.: Designing digital game-based learning for professional upskilling: a systematic literature review. Comput. Educ. **184**, 104518 (2022)
7. Forrest, C., Moffat, D.C., Shabalina, O.: Gamification in a high school class improved motivation and grades. In: Proceedings of the 14th International Conference on Game Based Learning. Brighton, United Kingdom, vol. 14, pp. 168–176 (2020)
8. Shabalina, O., Malliarakis, C., Tomos, F., Mozelius, P.: Game-based learning for learning to program: from learning through play to learning through game development. In: Proceedings of the 11th European Conference on Games Based Learning. Graz, Austria, vol. 11, pp. 571–576 (2017)
9. Vanbecelaere, S., Berghe, K., Cornillie, F., Sasanguie, D., Reynvoet, B., Depaepe, F.: The effectiveness of adaptive versus non-adaptive learning with digital educational games. J. Comput. Assist. Learn. **36**, 502–513 (2020)
10. Adcock, A., Van, E.R.: Adaptive game-based learning. In: Seel, N.M. (eds.) Encyclopedia of the Sciences of Learning, pp. 106–110. Springer, Boston (2012) https://doi.org/10.1007/978-1-4419-1428-6_4
11. Darwesh, A.: Serious games in adaptive learning. J. Univ. Hum. Develop. **2**, 418–423 (2016)
12. Mozelius, P., et al.: Game-based technologies in teaching programming in higher education: theory and practices. Recent Pat. Comput. Sci. **08**, 1 (2015)
13. Plamondon, K.E., Donovan, M.A., Pulakos, E.D., Arad, S.: Adaptability in the workplace: development of a taxonomy of adaptive performance. J. Appl. Psychol. **85**, 612–624 (2000)
14. Barnes, T.: The Q-matrix method: mining student response data for knowledge. In: AAAI Workshop - Technical Report vol. 5, no. 2, pp.39–46 (2005)
15. Chen, N.-S., Kinshuk, D., Wei, C.-W., Chen, H.-J.: Mining e-learning domain concept map from academic articles. Comput. Educ. **50**, 1009–1021 (2008)
16. Martin, B., Mitrovic, A., Koedinger, K.R., Mathan, S.: Evaluating and improving adaptive educational systems with learning curves. User Model. User-Adap. Inter. **21**(3), 249–283 (2011)
17. Cen, H., Koedinger, K., Junker, B.: Learning factors analysis – a general method for cognitive model evaluation and improvement. In: Ikeda, M., Ashley, K.D., Chan, T.W. (eds.) Intelligent Tutoring Systems. ITS 2006. Lecture Notes in Computer Science, vol. 4053, pp. 164–175. Springer, Heidelberg (2006). https://doi.org/10.1007/11774303_17

18. Chen, S., Sue, P.-J.: Constructing concept maps for adaptive learning systems based on data mining techniques. Expert Syst. Appl. **40**(7), 2746–2755 (2013)
19. Chrysafiadi, K., Virvou, M.: A knowledge representation approach using fuzzy cognitive maps for better navigation support in an adaptive learning system. SpringerPlus **2**, 81 (2013). https://doi.org/10.1186/2193-1801-2-81
20. Lopes, R., Bidarra, R.: Adaptivity challenges in games and simulations: a survey. IEEE Trans. on Comput. Intell. AI Games **3**(2), 85–99 (2011)
21. Houlette, R.: Player modeling for adaptive games. In: AI Game Programming Wisdom, vol. 2, pp. 557-561 (2003)
22. Hussaan, A.M., Sehaba, K., Mille, A.: Tailoring serious games with adaptive pedagogical scenarios: a serious game for persons with cognitive disabilities. In: Proceedings of the 2011 11th IEEE International Conference on Advanced Learning Technologies. Washington, United States, pp. 486–490 (2011)
23. Tumenayu, O., Shabalina, O., Kamaev, V., Davtyan, A.: Using agent-based technologies to enhance learning in educational games. In: Proceedings of the International Conference e-Learning 2014 - Part of the Multi Conference on Computer Science and Information Systems. Lisbon, Portugal, pp. 149–155 (2014)
24. Tumenayu, O., Shabalina, O.: Digital educational games: adopting pedagogical agent to infer leaner's motivation and emotional state. In: Proceedings of the 7th European Conference on Games Based Learning. Porto, Portugal, pp.546–552 (2013)
25. Reuter, C., Mehm, F., Göbel, S., Steinmetz, R.: Evaluation of adaptive serious games using playtraces and aggregated play data. In: Proceedings of the 7th European Conference on Games Based Learning. Porto, Portugal, vol. 2, pp.504–511 (2013)
26. Göbel, S., Mehm, F., Radke, S., Steinmetz, R.: 80 days: adaptive digital storytelling for digital educational games. In: CEUR Workshop Proceedings, 498 (2009)
27. Morizane, M., Nakano, Y., Shimohara, K., Tanev, I.: Personalized adaptive strategies in human-PC learning game. In: Proceedings of the ICCAS-SICE 2009. Fukuoka, Japan, pp. 2728–2731 (2009)
28. Peirce, N., Wade, V.: Personalised learning for casual games: The'Language Trap'Online language learning game. In: Proceedings of the 4th European Conference on Games Based Learning. Copenhagen, Denmark (2010)
29. Peirce, N., Conlan, O., Wade, V.: Adaptive educational games: providing non-invasive personalised learning experiences. In: Proceedings - 2nd IEEE International Conference on Digital Game and Intelligent Toy Enhanced Learning. Washington, pp. 28–35 (2008)
30. Lindberg, R., Hasanov, A., Laine, T.: Improving play and learning style adaptation in a programming education game, pp. 450–457 (2017)
31. Oostendorp, H., Spek, E., Linssen, J.: Adapting the complexity level of a serious game to the proficiency of players. EAI Endorsed Trans. Serious Games **14**, 1–8 (2014)
32. Lavieri Jr, E.D.: A study of adaptive learning for educational game design. Colorado Technical University (2014)
33. Calongne, C., Stricker, A., Truman, B., Murray, J., Lavieri, E.: Slippery rocks and ALGAE: a multiplayer educational roleplaying game and a model for adaptive learning game design. In Proceedings of TCC, pp. 13–23 (2014)
34. Shabalina, O.A., Erkin, D.A., Davtyan, A.G., Sadovnikova, N.P.: A lattice-theoretical approach to modeling naturally ordered structures. In: Proceedings of the 2016 Conference on Information Technologies in Science, pp. 158–161 (2016)
35. Shabalina, O., Vorobkalov, P., Kataev, A., Tarasenko, A.: 3I-Approach for IT Educational Games Development. In: Proceedings of the 3rd European Conference on Games-Based Learning, Graz, Austria, 12–13 October 2009, pp. 339–344 (2009)

Can a Robot Companion Help Students Learn Chinese Tones? The Role of Speech and Gesture Cues

Anna Zinina[1,2,3](✉) ⓘ, Artemiy Kotov[1,2] ⓘ, Nikita Arinkin[1,2] ⓘ, and Anna Gureyeva[3]

[1] National Research Center "Kurchatov Institute", Moscow, Russia
zinina_aa@nrcki.ru
[2] Russian State University for the Humanities, Moscow, Russia
[3] Moscow State Linguistic University, Moscow, Russia

Abstract. The paper examines the possibility of using companion robots (F-2 robot, as the example) to assist humans in learning the tonal system of Chinese. The experiment compares the effectiveness of supportive cues via speech and gestures. The results of the experiment (N = 20, 4 males, mean age 24,5) show that the learning is effective – subjects learn the pronunciation of Chinese syllables with the given tones. At the same time the effectiveness of speech cues is higher than of the gestural cues. It is the speech cue that seems to be more understandable during the subjects pass the introduction to the system of Chinese tones. In general, a combination of conditions in the experiment is effective when subjects learn Chinese phonetics with gestural cues and with speech cues – in any order of conditions. In addition, the robot with gesture cues is perceived by the participants as more natural and engaging, eliciting more sympathy. The results suggest that companion robots with gestural behavior can be used to support the educational process and increase students' engagement.

Keywords: Social Robots · Learning · Human-Machine Interaction · Chinese

1 Introduction

The phonetics of the Chinese language is one of the most difficult aspects in its study, since it is here that a large number of linguistic phenomena that have no analogues in Indo–European languages are concentrated. Tone in Chinese has a semantic function: a syllable consisting of a given set of phonemes, when pronounced in different tones, corresponds to different characters and has different meanings. Different dialects of Chinese have diverse tonal systems. In normalized Mandarin Putonghua there are four tones, contrasted by pitch and voice movement pattern: (a) high, even; (b) rising; (c) falling-rising; (d) falling. For example, the syllable *tu* has at least four different lexical meanings depending on its tonal pattern: the first tone *tū* would mean 'suddenly' (突), the second *tú* would mean 'image' (图), the third *tǔ* would mean 'soil' (土), and the fourth *tù* would mean 'hare' (兔). The fifth, or zero tone is not considered as independent, as it is pronounced neutrally and is not opposed to other tones neither phonetically nor

A. G. Kravets et al. (Eds.): CIT&DS 2023, CCIS 1909, pp. 420–432, 2023.
https://doi.org/10.1007/978-3-031-44615-3_29

semantically [Panov, 1967; Speshnev, 1980; Susov, 2008]. A description of the voice patterns in Chinese tones can be represented in Fig. 1.

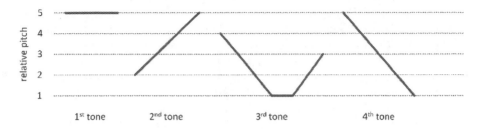

Fig. 1. Voice frequency patterns of Chinese tones.

The melody of the first tone is high, smooth, long, with regular intensity and only some decrease to the end (it may give an impression of an unfinished statement to a European listener). The melody of the second tone is short, rapidly rising, with maximum intensity at the end of the syllable; it gives an impression of interrogation. The third tone is low, long, and has a falling-rising pattern, with maximum intensity on the low note. The fourth tone is short, sharply falling from the highest point to the lowest. The falling tone is accompanied by a sharp decrease of intensity (the melody of the fourth tone gives an impression of a categorical command) [Zadoenko, Huang, 1993; Aleksakhin, 2006].

The phonetic system of Chinese differs significantly from European languages. Speakers of tonal and non-tonal languages have significantly different abilities to learn the phonetics of Chinese [Francis et al., 2008]. Therefore, when European students learn Chinese, phonetics is given significant time in the first months of the curriculum. As a rule, European students do not pay enough attention to the change of pitch: in most cases speakers of non-tonal languages use pitch only for lexical and phrasal emphasis, to express emotions or to choose the focus of a statement [Malyshev, Kiselevich et al., 2018]. In the process of learning, students should pay attention to the tone contour and learn to recognize and pronounce Chinese syllables with a given tone. To do this, the teacher must use special cues to direct the student's attention to phonetic processes. McGuiness [1997] emphasizes the difficulties of learning tones in Chinese, noting that most native English learners of Chinese consider the concept of using tones to change word meaning as so distant from their native English that learning tones becomes problematic, neglected, or both. In [Xu, 2011] was shown that the presence of tones is the linguistic aspect that causes the most difficulty for learners – for example, when pronouncing tones, students confuse them with stresses. It is also noted that a common mistake is the incorrect pitch of the beginning of the tones and the addition of extra stress to Chinese words, leading to a disruption of syllable equivalence. In the survey on the evaluation of difficulties in learning Chinese [Chiang, 2002], the students who participated in the survey – 26 2nd year students – most often mentioned difficulties with the study of tones: students would like to get more explanations on this topic at the elementary level, in the first year of study.

1.1 The Role of Gestures in Learning a Foreign Language

To solve the difficulties in learning Chinese phonetic system, teachers can use different exercises and means to direct students' attention to phonetic phenomena, for example – use iconic gestures [Francis et al., 2008]. Gestures can enhance comprehension and memorization by supporting verbal messages, helping to illustrate concepts, conveying additional information, and providing cues. Indirect benefits of using gestures are capturing the listener's attention and creating a comfortable, trusted atmosphere. Therefore, teachers often use gestures in the classroom, even when explaining abstract concepts or phonetic phenomena that have no spatial representation. This directs the attention of the learners. The interaction of words and gestures is important, as well as their optimal ratio: a lack of gestures by the lecturer gives the impression of stiffness and insecurity. Their excessive use is perceived as unnatural and intrusive behavior.

Iconic gestures are a particular type of the iconic signs, where the signifier is in some aspect similar to the signified [Peirce, 2000]. Iconic gestures can denote an action, an event, or an object by reproducing the way of performing the action, the trajectory of the action, the shape of the object, or the way of interacting with the object (affordance). Iconic gestures are natural and common part of spoken language, visually representing the concepts to which they refer [Peirce, 2000]. We can consider Chinese tone gestures as iconic: in such a gesture, a person may represent the shape of the tone outlined with his hand, where the height at which the hand is positioned denotes the pitch of the sound. In addition to conveying iconic meaning, gestures can also be used to represent abstract metaphors [McNeill, 1992], and in these circumstances the gesture is classified as metaphorical. For example, if a student says that his grades have improved and at the same time points upward, he is using a metaphorical gesture where the upward movement symbolizes the improvement. From this perspective, the iconic gesture indicating tone can be seen as metaphorical because of the abstract correspondence between the height of the hand placement and the height of the sound.

Iconic gestures are known to affect the learning of foreign words [Kelly et al., 2009; Hirata et al., 2014; Dargue et al., 2019]. There is also evidence that people use head and hand gestures to project the tones of hieroglyphs that makes is easier to distinguish similar-sounding hieroglyphs [Chen, Massaro, 2008; Baills et al., 2019; Morett, Chang, 2015].

1.2 Using Robots for Foreign Language Learning

In this study, we used a companion robot F-2 that interactively assisted humans in learning the tonal system. It is known that robots have long been used in education [Golonka et al., 2014; Young et al., 2012; van Ewijk, 2020]. Physically embodied robots can be used for educational programs that require interaction with the surrounding physical world; they are able to add social interaction to learning, that stimulates student engagement in the educational process, increasing its effectiveness [Kidd, Breazeal, 2004; Han et al., 2008]. Physically embodied robots are perceived with more enthusiasm and interest, as compared to virtual agents. Also, with them, users show higher learning results [Belpaeme et al., 2018]. With their ability to support natural communication, robots are an effective tool for language learning [van den Berghe et al., 2019; Belpaeme et al., 2018;

Kennedy et al., 2016; Alemi et al., 2014]. This rapidly growing area is referred to as – Robot-Assisted Language Learning (RALL) [van den Berghe et al., 2019]. Although this technological field is quite young, it is also very promising: social robots seem extremely appropriate for use in language learning due to their inherently social design [Randall, 2019].

There is not much experience in the use of robots for learning Chinese [Hao, 2012]. There are studies indicating the influence of iconic [de Wit et al., 2018] and rhythmic [Gluhareva, Prieto, 2017] robot gestures on foreign word memorization. However, there is practically no research on whether robots as teachers using head and hand gestures (i.e., pitch indicators) can improve the learning of different tones in Chinese. In [Zhang, de Haas, 2020], there are some preliminary results indicating the effectiveness of gesture cues in learning Chinese tones. The paper showed that the robot, which does not use gestures when teaching Chinese tones, increased the efficiency of learning, but only if the participants were previously introduced to the Chinese characters by the robot using gestures. In general, the authors do not deny the prospects of using a social robot to learn Chinese tones. In our study, we will not only consider the impact of the social robot on learning Chinese tones, but also compare the iconic gesture-based cueing of Chinese tones with the voice-based cueing.

2 Experimental Research

As part of the study, an experiment was conducted in which students were learning Chinese tones using two F-2 robots. Both robots explained the concept of Chinese tones, and the explanation of one of them (condition 1) was supported by gestures illustrating the pattern of voice movement when playing the tone, while the other explained it only in speech (condition 2). For the following questioning, the robots were differentiated by labeling: the robot with gesture cues was marked with a triangle, and the robot using only speech cues was marked with a square.

Each subject learned tones with each of the robots – in random order. Each robot's learning session consisted of two stages – the introduction stage and the training stage. In the introduction stage, the robot briefly explained the concept and function of tones in Chinese, and then – demonstrated the difference of tones by reproducing one syllable in different tones. The robot's speech was synthesized using Yandex Speech API (state of the art text synthesis software), and the syllables in Chinese were recorded by a native speaker – university teacher. Both robots used speech description of tone (*Here is the first tone. The voice is high, goes straight…*) when demonstrating syllable differences. A robot using gestures also demonstrated a gesture depicting the tone pattern. Also, both robots voiced the translation of each tonal syllable, thereby illustrating the semantic differentiating nature of the tones. Then, at the training stage, the students were asked by the robot to pronounce given syllables themselves with a specific tone. Further, Fig. 2 shows the structure of the tone training stage.

The scheme shows that the robot sequentially named different syllables and asked the subject to pronounce them with a certain tone (*Say the first tone "ma"…*). When an incorrect answer was received, or in case the answer was not received within 5 s, the robot played a hint: the robot with gestures used a gesture to represent the voice

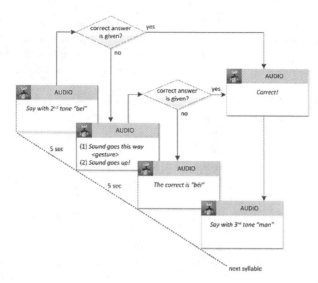

Fig. 2. Schematic representation of the training stage

movement of the required tone as a cue (condition 1). The other robot (condition 2) illustrated the required voice movement in speech, for example: *The voice is high, it goes straight, The voice falls*, etc. If the participant then made a mistake in tone or did not give an answer within the next 5 s, an audio recording with the correct pronunciation by the native speaker was played. Table 1 shows the robot's gestures and actual cues for a particular tone of Chinese.

The syllable sets used by the robots in the explanation and training stages differed between the two robots, but were similar in structure and complexity (example: *lan – man, mu – lu*; with different initials but similar or identical finals and identical tones). The syllable sets had the same size, 20 units. In the training stage, the student first had to pronounce the syllable suggested by the robot alternately in four tones. First, a syllable from the training stage was used (in the first condition, the syllable *ma*; in the second condition, the syllable *lu*), then another syllable (in the first condition, the syllable *du*; in the second condition, the syllable *mu*). After that, the robot instructed the student to pronounce the suggested syllable in a new tone (syllables and tones were given in different order, but the syllable structure and tone were similar for the two conditions). Correctness of pronunciation was controlled by an assistant experimenter (a specialist in Chinese linguistics) from another room according to the Wizard-of-Oz scheme. During the evaluation, special attention was paid to the tonal pattern of the syllable. Due to the fact that the pronunciation rules in Chinese and Russian differ significantly, during the experiment subjects were allowed to pronounce inaccurately the syllables suggested by the robot (i. e. with incorrect pronunciation of the initial – the starting consonant of a syllable, or of the final – the end of it). It was the correctness of the tonal pattern that was in the focus of attention.

A within-subject experimental design was used: each participant of the experiment was learning from both robots in turn, and the order in which the learning took place was

Table 1. Robot cues in the training phase for two experimental conditions.

	Condition 1. A robot using gestures as a cue[1]	Condition 2. A robot using speech as a cue
The first tone:	*Sound goes this way...*	*The voice is high, and goes straight.*
The second tone:	*Sound goes this way...*	*The voice rises from the bottom up*
The third tone:	*Sound goes this way...*	*The voice falls smoothly down, then up*

(continued)

Table 1. (*continued*)

The fourth tone:	*Sound goes this way...*	The voice falls straight down

randomized in order to achieve maximum objectivity in the evaluation. In the experimental instruction, the investigator explained to the subject that both robots were to help the person learn Chinese phonetics, and the subject would be trained with each robot to compare them afterwards. After completing the training with each robot, the subject filled out a questionnaire to rate their impressions using a semantic differential scales and chose the preferable robot.

The subjects were students – 20 people (men 4, women 16; mean age – 24,5 years). None of the subjects had studied Chinese before. Each experimental interaction was recorded on camera.

3 Results

On the basis of summarized statistics, we can conclude that the learning of Chinese tones is more effective with the robot using speech cues (Wilcoxon matched pairs test, $p < 0,005$). However, it is more correct to continue further analysis considering the order of presentation. It can be observed that the efficiency of correct tone reproduction increases by the second presentation, regardless of the type of condition – hence, the learning of Chinese tones was successful. The difference in the progress of correct answers is statistically significant (Wilcoxon matched pairs test, $p < 0,001$).

When analyzing the data, we can also observe that if the first condition was with a gesture cue, the learning efficiency was slightly lower than if the first condition was with a speech cue, this difference is significant (Wilcoxon matched pairs test, $p < 0,001$).

If we look at the graphical representation of the results (Fig. 3), we can conclude that the verbal cues work better: test subjects recognize and understand the voice cue quickly, while the gesture cue is sometimes misread. The graph shows a trend: in the first presentation, the gesture cue works only 8% of the time, while the speech cue works 20,5% of the time.

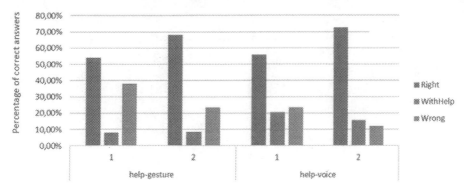

Fig. 3. Percentages of *Right*, *Wrong*, and *WithHelp* (after a hint) answers in the first (1) and second (2) presentations of the corresponding condition.

This can be compared to the fact that according to the post-experiment survey, 20% of participants perceived the iconic gestures depicting the tone contour as rhythmic gestures of the robot, which did not carry any semantic meaning, although the robot accompanied them with the words *Sound goes like this...* This implies the need to accompany gestural cues with more clear verbal explanations, focusing more attention on them.

The results of the repeated-measures ANOVA indicate that both the condition factor (gestures or speech) and the presentation factor (first and second presentation of the condition) are significant (Wilks lambda = 0,92146, $F(2, 397) = 16,920$, $p < 0,001$) for learning Chinese tones.

An analysis of the efficiency of learning each Chinese tone indicates that the subjects learned the 4th tone significantly easier, the worst of all the subjects learned the 1st tone (Fig. 5). In Chinese phonetics the 1st tone is considered the easiest to learn: it has a flat tonal pattern. However, according to the results of the experiment, we can say that the interaction with the robots with different types of cues is not enough for its learning. The supposed reason for this result is the insufficient separation by the robot of the phase of raising the arm to the starting point and the phase of the tone image (flat hand movement at a high level). Based on this, further research is required to attract more attention to the development of a gesture cue system for the robot.

Figure 4 also shows the effectiveness of different types of cues in learning different tones of Chinese: it can be concluded that the speech cue is significantly ($p < 0,05$) more effective for learning the 2nd tone. This may also be due to the fact that the speech cue *Sound rises up* is more effective than the diagonal raising of the robot hand, which students could perceive as an assistive movement and not as an iconic gesture.

After the experiment, we asked the subjects if they noticed a difference between the robots and their behavior: only 10 subjects (50%) could correctly identify the difference between the two conditions. Some of the subjects perceived iconic gestures as rhythmic robot gestures that carried no semantic meaning. At the same time, a person's inability to describe the difference between robots in the aspect of gestural behavior does not mean that the gestures had no influence on them: robot gestures can influence a person, even if the person does not describe it in the final report [Zinina et al., 2019].

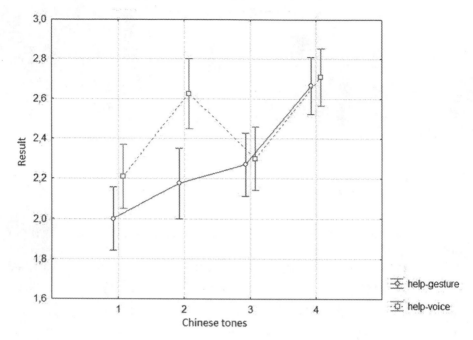

Fig. 4. The effectiveness of learning 1st, 2nd, 3rd and 4th Chinese tones depending on the cue type.

Based on the questionnaire data, it is not possible to identify the subjects' preferred type of cues: 11 subjects preferred learning with a robot that used verbal cues (55%), 9 people (45%) preferred a robot with gestural cues.

According to the questionnaire, the robot with gestural prompts seemed more engaging (2,95 out of 5 on the semantic differential scale) and comfortable (2,7 out of 5), but participants noted that this robot was also more distracting (1,9 out of 5 – compared to 1,6 out of 5 for the second condition). It was also found that subjects perceived its cues to be more confusing (1,6 points out of 5), as compared to the robot with speech cues (1,35 points out of 5).

The learning behavior of the robot with verbal cues was perceived by the subjects as more understandable (4,7 out of 5) and useful (4,35 out of 5) – the difference in this parameter was statistically significant (T-test, $p < 0,05$), see Fig. 5.

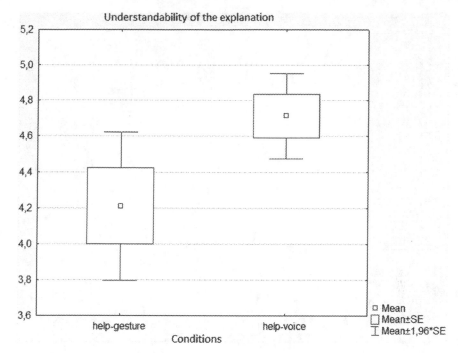

Fig. 5. Differences in the subjective evaluation of the understandability of the explanation of Chinese tones in the robot with gesture and speech cues.

According to the subjective evaluation of the effectiveness of the cues of each robot, the most effective were the speech cues (2,4 points out of 5).

A more detailed analysis of the results shows that the type of cues significantly affects the success specifically in the first introduction to the Chinese tones – this is confirmed not only in the evaluation of learning effectiveness, but also in the self-evaluation by the subjects after interaction with the robots (Fig. 6) – (T-test, p < 0,05).

Based on their subjective evaluation of the understandability of the explanation of Chinese tones, subjects identified speech cues as more comprehensible – but the difference in the second turn of the presented conditions is small: it shows that subjects equally well learned to pronounce syllables in the correct tone, regardless of the order of the experimental conditions.

The insufficient effectiveness of gestural iconic cues in the first stage can be explained by the novelty effect when meeting the robot, the limitations of the robot's body model, the requirements to better separate the preparatory and iconic gesture stages, and the need to better focus the student's attention on the robot's iconic gesture. Based on the frequent misreading of gesture cues by test subjects, more attention should be paid at the design the robot gesture cue system, making it more explicit to the learners.

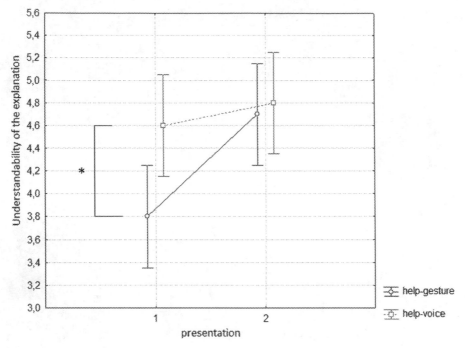

Fig. 6. Differences in subjective assessment of the understandability of the explanation of Chinese tones (a) in the robots with gestural or speech cues, (b) within the first and second presentation.

4   Conclusion

Based on the results of the experimental study, it has been demonstrated that the gestural iconic cues of companion robots are not as effective as the speech cues in the context of primary Chinese language tone teaching. However, the use of gestures allows the robot to better establish emotional contact with the learner: the robot with gestural cues was perceived by the participants as more natural and engaging, eliciting the greatest sympathy.

After passing the two conditions, the subjects learned the topic of Chinese tones equally well, and the learning efficiency did not depend on the order in which the conditions were presented. This may indicate that the use of verbal and gestural cues creates a complex effect that allows the student to learn the topic after passing the training with these two types of learning methods.

The most important result of the experiment was the confirmation of the fact that a social robot can be used to teach the Chinese tones. Further research will focus on finding the optimal learning strategies that specifically combine the different types of cues: speech and gestures. The result seems to be extremely important because learning Chinese is a complex process in which any means of optimization will be in demand. That is why it is important to develop training communication strategies for companion robots in this way, in order to maximize the effectiveness of learning with robots.

Acknowledgements. The project is in part supported by the Russian Science Foundation, project No 19-18-00547, https://rscf.ru/project/19-18-00547/.

References

Aleksakhin, A.N.: Theoretical Phonetics of the Chinese Language. AST: Vostok-Zapad, Moscow (2006)

Alemi, M., Meghdari, A., Ghazisaedy, M.: Employing humanoid robots for teaching English language in Iranian junior high-schools. Int. J. Humanoid Rob. **11**, 1450022-1–1450022-25 (2014). https://doi.org/10.1142/S0219843614500224

Baills, F., Suárez-González, N., González-Fuente, S., Prieto, P.: Observing and producing pitch gestures facilitates the learning of Mandarin Chinese tones and words. Stud. Second. Lang. Acquis. **41**(1), 33–58 (2019)

Belpaeme, T., Kennedy, J., Ramachandran, A., Scassellati, B., Tanaka, F.: Social robots for education: a review. Sci. Robot. **3**(21), eaat5954 (2018)

Chen, T.H., Massaro, D.W.: Seeing pitch: visual information for lexical tones of Mandarin-Chinese. J. Acoust. Soc. Am. **123**(4), 2356–2366 (2008)

Chiang, M.H.: An investigation of students' perspective on Chinese language learning. J.-Chin. Lang. Teach. Assoc. **37**(1), 43–64 (2002)

Dargue, N., Sweller, N., Jones, M.P.: When our hands help us understand: a meta-analysis into the effects of gesture on comprehension. Psychol. Bull. **145**(8), 765 (2019)

de Wit, J., et al.: The effect of a robot's gestures and adaptive tutoring on children's acquisition of second language vocabularies. In: Proceedings of the 2018 ACM/IEEE International Conference on Human-Robot Interaction, pp. 50–58, February 2018

Francis, A.L., Ciocca, V., Ma, L., Fenn, K.: Perceptual learning of Cantonese lexical tones by tone and non-tone language speakers. J. Phon. **36**(2), 268–294 (2008)

Gluhareva, D., Prieto, P.: Training with rhythmic beat gestures benefits L2 pronunciation in discourse-demanding situations. Lang. Teach. Res. **21**(5), 609–631 (2017)

Golonka, E.M., Bowles, A.R., Frank, V.M., Richardson, D.L., Freynik, S.F.: Technologies for foreign language learning: a review of technology types and their effectiveness. Comput. Assist. Lang. Learn. **27**(1), 70–105 (2014). https://doi.org/10.1080/09588221.2012.700315

Han, J.H., Jo, M.H., Jones, V., Jo, J.H.: Comparative study on the educational use of home robots for children. J. Inf. Process. Syst. **4**(4), 159–168 (2008)

Hao, Y.C.: Second language acquisition of Mandarin Chinese tones by tonal and non-tonal language speakers. J. Phon. **40**(2), 269–279 (2012)

Hirata, Y., Kelly, S.D., Huang, J., Manansala, M.: Effects of hand gestures on auditory learning of second-language vowel length contrasts. J. Speech Lang. Hear. Res. **57**(6), 2090–2101 (2014)

Kelly, S.D., McDevitt, T., Esch, M.: Brief training with co-speech gesture lends a hand to word learning in a foreign language. Lang. Cognit. Process. **24**(2), 313–334 (2009)

Kennedy, J., Baxter, P., Senft, E., Belpaeme, T.: Social robot tutoring for child second language learning. In: 2016 11th ACM/IEEE International Conference on Human-Robot Interaction (HRI), pp. 231–238. IEEE, March 2016

Kidd, C.D., Breazeal, C.: Effect of a robot on user perceptions. In: 2004 IEEE/RSJ International Conference on Intelligent Robots and Systems (IROS) (IEEE Cat. No. 04CH37566), vol. 4, pp. 3559–3564. IEEE, September 2004

Malyshev, G.I., Kiselevich, Y.E., Mitchell, P.D.: Difficulties in studying phonetics of Chinese by Russian-speaking students: the main mistakes and the ways to fix them. Bull. Tambov Univ. Humanit. Ser. **23**(173), 43–48 (2018)

McGinnis, S.: Tonal spelling versus diacritics for teaching pronunciation of Mandarin Chinese. Mod. Lang. J. **81**(2), 228–236 (1997)

McNeill, D.: Hand and Mind: What Gestures Reveal About Thought. The University of Chicago Press, Chicago, IL (1992)

Morett, L.M., Chang, L.Y.: Emphasising sound and meaning: pitch gestures enhance Mandarin lexical tone acquisition. Lang. Cognit. Neurosci. **30**(3), 347–353 (2015)

Panov, M.V.: Russian phonetics. Prosveshcheniye (1967)

Peirce, C.: The Beginnings of Pragmatism. Translation from English, foreword by V. V. Kiryushchenko, M. V. Kolopotin. St. Petersburg: Laboratory of Metaphysical Research of the Philosophical Faculty of St. Petersburg State University, Aletheia (2000)

Randall, N.: A survey of robot-assisted language learning (RALL). ACM Trans. Hum.-Robot Interact. (THRI) **9**(1), 1–36 (2019)

Speshnev, N.A.: Phonetics of the Chinese language. Leningrad University Publisher (1980)

Susov, I.P.: Introduction to Linguistics: Textbook for Students of Linguistic and Philological Specialties. Tver State University. AST: Vostok – Zapad, Moscow (2008)

Van den Berghe, R., Verhagen, J., Oudgenoeg-Paz, O., Van der Ven, S., Leseman, P.: Social robots for language learning: a review. Rev. Educ. Res. **89**(2), 259–295 (2019)

van Ewijk, G., Smakman, M., Konijn, E.A.: Teachers' perspectives on social robots in education: an exploratory case study. In: Proceedings of the Interaction Design and Children Conference, pp. 273–280, June 2020

Xu, S.Y.: Problems of teaching phonetics of Chinese language to Russian students. Scientist **12**(35), 141–144 (2011)

Young, M.F., et al.: Our princess is in another castle: a review of trends in serious gaming for education. Rev. Educ. Res. **82**(1), 61–89 (2012)

Zadoenko, T.P., Huang, S.: Fundamentals of Chinese. An Introductory Course, 2nd ed. Nauka, Oriental Literature Publishing House, Moscow (1993)

Zhang, P., de Haas, M.: Effects of pitch gestures on learning Chinese orthography with a social robot. In: Companion of the 2020 ACM/IEEE International Conference on Human-Robot Interaction, pp. 180–182, March 2020

Zinina, A., Arinkin, N., Zaydelman, L., Kotov, A.: The role of oriented gestures during robot's communication to a human. Comput. Linguist. Intellect. Technol. **18**(25), 800–808 (2019)

Interaction with Virtual Objects in VR-Applications

Alla G. Kravets[1,2](✉) ⓘ, Ivan D. Pavlenko[1], Vitaly A. Egunov[1], and Evgeny Kravets[3]

[1] Volgograd State Technical University, 28 Lenin av., Volgograd 400005, Russia
allagkravets@yandex.ru, vn-pavlenko@bk.ru, vegunov@mail.ru
[2] Dubna State University, 19 Universitetskaya st., Dubna, Moscow Region 141982, Russia
[3] Volgograd Academy of the Russian Ministry of Internal Affairs, 130, Istoricheskaya str., Volgograd 400089, Russia
80kravez@gmail.com

Abstract. The paper investigates the effectiveness of methods of interaction with virtual objects in a virtual reality environment. We consider the role of various input devices, such as virtual reality gloves and vests, in providing a more realistic and immersive user experience, analyze the advantages and applications of these devices in various industries, including medicine, education, the gaming industry and others. We also describe the development of a VR simulator for modeling emergency scenarios, consider the implementation of realistic physics of objects in the virtual world, taking into account the use of Configurable Joint and Rigidbody.

Keywords: Virtual Reality · VR · VR Interaction · Realistic VR Physics · Configurable Joint · Rigidbody · VR Simulator

1 Introduction

Virtual Reality (VR) is an exciting and innovative technology that allows users to immerse themselves in completely new virtual worlds and interact with virtual objects. Currently, there is a surge in the popularity of VR technologies. In addition to video games, analysts at the investment bank Goldman Sachs identified eight key industries: healthcare [1], real estate [2, 3], trade [4], entertainment events [5], video [6], education [7, 8], engineering [9, 10], the army [11, 12]. Modern VR technologies are increasingly penetrating into our lives. Optimal interaction with virtual objects plays a key role in creating more efficient and realistic virtual environments for these applications.

In this regard, the development of effective methods of interaction with virtual objects in virtual reality is one of the key tasks to achieve a more realistic and exciting user experience [13]. Understanding the theoretical foundations of interaction and their practical implementation in VR applications are important for developers, researchers and professionals in the field of VR. The development of interaction with virtual objects has the potential to increase efficiency and meet user needs in various tasks and scenarios. Creating more intuitive and natural ways to interact with virtual objects will allow users to maximize the possibilities of VR and open up new horizons for their creativity and interaction with virtual content.

In this paper, we explore the theoretical foundations of interaction with virtual objects and present the practical implementation of this interaction in a VR application. We consider important aspects that allow users to actively and naturally interact with virtual objects, and also present a concrete example of a developed application demonstrating these principles. The further development of virtual reality is expected to be more widely used in various fields, and research on interaction with virtual objects plays a key role in creating more realistic and exciting virtual environments.

The rest of the paper is organized as follows. Section 2 describes the basic principles and methods that provide control and manipulation of virtual objects, analyzes visual and tactile perception, as well as new technologies that create more natural and intuitive ways of interaction. Section 3 describes the development of a VR simulator for modeling emergency scenarios, examines the architecture of the application, its main functions and the implementation of interaction with virtual objects. The presented examples of use cases will help demonstrate the effectiveness and potential of interaction with virtual objects in practical applications. Section 4 describes the development of realistic physics of virtual world objects.

2   VR Interactions Types

To implement VR interaction, developers use various input devices that are used for different purposes. The first-generation input devices in virtual reality can be considered motion sensors. These sensors are built into the head units and register the position of the user's head to change the virtual scene. However, with the development of software, it became possible for the user to interact with the virtual world with the help of hands. In the 1990s, various pointing devices were developed, including special gloves that allow the user to manipulate virtual objects with their hands. The advent of wireless and camera tracking, such as Leap Motion [14] and similar technologies without tactile feedback, has significantly improved the level of interactivity.

2.1   Face Capturing Methods

Until recently, the technology of tracking the direction of the gaze was expensive and was intended mainly for academic research. However, now it is becoming more accessible and allows for more realistic interaction between the user and virtual characters. In addition to eye tracking technology, speech recognition can be added, which allows the user to give categorical commands, for example, to say "open" when looking at the door (Fig. 1). Large companies have already acquired such technologies that recognize facial expressions, which are an important aspect of the interaction of virtual and augmented reality.

To visualize the lower part of the face, developers use head-mounted devices with connected depth cameras (Fig. 2). However, it is not yet clear whether this method will be widely used in the future. Possible reasons why this approach may be problematic are related to issues of human interaction with the system, ergonomics, computing requirements and battery life.

Fig. 1. Eye tracker from Vive company

Some studies show that the information transmitted through the face during face-to-face interaction is maximally concentrated in the eye area. Delight, anger, disgust and a smile require the visibility of areas of the face that are usually hidden under head devices. One of the companies, Oculus [15], has integrated stretching sensors into the headset material adjacent to the user's skin in order to receive data about emotions and transmit them for further processing. It will be interesting to see how this technology will develop in the final version.

Fig. 2. Depth camera for fixing the lower part of the face.

However, along with face capture technologies in virtual reality, other ways of direct interaction with virtual environment objects are also developing.

2.2 Controllers and Tracking Systems

Controllers and hand tracking systems are becoming increasingly popular and are widely used in VR applications. Controllers are devices that the user holds in his hands and which allow precise control and manipulation of virtual objects. They provide direct and accurate interaction, allowing the user to perform actions similar to real interactions.

Hand tracking systems, such as sensors or cameras, track the movements and poses of the user's hands. This allows the virtual environment to more accurately display hand movements and gestures, which creates even greater immersion and realistic interaction. Hand tracking systems, such as Leap Motion, track fingers and accurately reproduce the movements of the user's hands. Such systems allow users to interact with objects in a more realistic and tactile way. Users can imagine their hands in a virtual environment, perform gestures and instantly interact with three-dimensional objects using finger tracking.

Traditional virtual reality controllers and joysticks give users the ability to interact with artificial objects by squeezing knobs and moving triggers. However, the idea of a controller is limited to two-dimensional interaction. This can be useful when working with objects such as brushes, markers, balls or baseball bats that can be picked up in the hand, but they do not provide flexibility and precision of hand movements and, in particular, fingers.

Practical reproduction and control of hand and finger movements improves the sense of reality and makes the virtual environment more intuitive. The VRfree [16] glove system allows users to interact with virtual space as if they are in the real world. This system uses various inertial measurement modules (IMU) located at the fingertips, which fully track the three-dimensional position of fingers and hands.

Fig. 3. VRfree gloves fingers tracking system

Thanks to the finger tracking system in VR and the use of VRfree gloves, users are able to interact more naturally and accurately with virtual objects (Fig. 3). This creates a more convincing and realistic feeling of the virtual environment, allowing users to embody their movements and gestures in the virtual world.

The combination of controllers and hand tracking systems in VR applications allows users not only to interact with virtual objects, but also to precisely control them. Users can compress and expand objects, drag them, perform gestures and manipulations similar to those they do in the real world. This creates an even greater degree of engagement and satisfaction from interacting with virtual objects.

Modern virtual reality technologies not only provide an opportunity to manage virtual objects, but also make this process more intuitive and natural. Thanks to the development of controllers and hand tracking systems, users can interact more freely and accurately with virtual objects, opening up huge opportunities for research, entertainment and learning.

2.3   VR Gloves

VR gloves, visually similar to ordinary cycling gloves made of durable fabric, have some distinctive features. They have a small unit on the wrist where the electronics and battery are located. However, there are also unusual models, such as Plexus [17] gloves, which are worn on top of the fingers and leave the lower part of the palm open.

Each glove is equipped with a set of sensors, including accelerometers, magnetometers, gyroscopes, barometers and sensors capable of recognizing hand and finger movements. This data is transmitted to the VR application, allowing the user to interact with the virtual environment. Gloves are widely used not only in games, but also in smart home systems, professional training and training programs, specialized applications and augmented reality devices.

Fig. 4. Plexus gloves fingers tracking system

VR gloves are a complex device (Fig. 4). They are equipped with a variety of sensors that track the movements of your hands and fingers. Some advanced models can even register finger bends in the phalanges. A microprocessor, a wireless communication module and a battery are usually placed on the wrist, although in some cases gloves can be connected to a computer or console via a cable, and a battery is not required.

Despite the complex technical design, the principle of operation of the gloves is quite simple. When the user changes the position of the hand, finger or fingers, or performs certain actions or gestures, information about the new coordinates is transmitted to the application on the PC. The virtual image in the helmet changes dynamically, allowing the user to see a virtual display of his hands repeating his movements in the real world. For example, if a user opens a door with his hand in reality, a virtual door opens in a VR application. Gyroscopes, magnetometers and accelerometers are used to track the movements of the user's hands and fingers, as well as to measure the speed of these movements. The presence of a barometer in the device assess the degree of pressure created by the user's hands or fingers.

In modern models, all sensors are hidden inside gloves, which makes them look like ordinary gloves. Early models used IR sensors located on each finger, and a special IR camera received data on the movement of sensors. New devices are not equipped with external sensors and cameras.

Models for gamers are increasingly equipped with small vibration motors that create tactile feedback. For example, when shooting in shooters, such feedback can manifest itself in the form of recoil. Some devices are also equipped with thermal sensors that transmit heat to the user's hands.

2.4 VR Vest

In addition to the already mentioned methods of interacting with virtual objects, such as face capture devices, controllers and finger tracking systems, there is another important method - virtual reality vests.

Virtual reality vests are devices that are put on the user's body and have built-in sensors and vibration motors. They create a sense of physical contact and immersiveness of the virtual environment by transmitting tactile sensations and physical effects to the user's body.

VR vests are usually equipped with a variety of vibration motors located in various areas of the body, such as the back, shoulders, chest and even in the abdomen. These vibration motors create various sensory sensations, such as shocks, vibrations, pressure and other physical effects synchronized with the actions of the virtual environment.

When interacting with virtual objects, VR vests can convey a sense of contact, such as a blow from a falling object or a feeling of heat from a fire source. They can also create immersion effects, for example by transmitting vibrations from vehicle movement or pulsations from explosions in the game.

VR vests complement and expand the virtual reality experience, making it more realistic and complete. They allow users to immerse themselves more deeply into the virtual environment and experience the physical effects, which can significantly increase the level of engagement and emotional perception.

Fig. 5. VR Vest

Various models of virtual reality vests are available on the market, each of which has its own characteristics and advantages (Fig. 5).

One of the options is the Hardlight Suit vest [18], which contains 16 modules for tracking movements in the game and provides high-quality feedback. Each module monitors individual muscles, allowing players to feel all the touches of the virtual world. The vest supports USB 2.0/3.0 and is currently compatible with some popular virtual reality helmets. It is planned to expand compatibility and introduce a wireless module for autonomous operation.

The Kor FX wireless vest [19] has sensors on the chest and shoulder joints. Its main task is to convey the sensations of light blows and strong shocks, especially when bullets hit. In the vest, you can adjust the feedback and adjust the power of the impact on the body. It is wireless and is supported by various game consoles and virtual reality helmets.

The VR Vest Pro Woojer vest [20] provides tactile interaction with the player's body. It contains 8 feedback sensors that are located on the most sensitive muscles. The vest is connected via a 3.5 mm jack or Bluetooth and has autonomous operation for up to 8 h. It is compatible with various game consoles and virtual reality helmets.

TactSuit X40 [21] is a project of a South Korean company that provides a real immersion in virtual reality. The vest weighs 1.7 kg and contains 40 special vibration systems located at the front and back of the case. Each sensor is able to respond to the pulse individually. The vest has a 9800 mAh battery and can work autonomously for up to 18 h. It can be connected via 3.5 mm jack or Bluetooth.

Of course, these are just a few examples of available models of virtual reality vests, there are other options. Some models may be more affordable, but may have less performance. The choice of a vest depends on the individual preferences of the user and the requirements for interaction with virtual objects.

3   VR Application Development

We have developed a VR application that provides the user with the opportunity to interact with various objects. Within the framework of the application, we have developed innovative methods of interaction, including moving objects such as a stick, a fire extinguisher, an emergency sign and others. To achieve maximum realism and immersion in a virtual environment, a special script was developed that provides realistic behavior of a complex object. The main focus in the development of the application was made on the possibilities of interaction with various virtual reality objects in order to provide the user with the most interactive and realistic experience.

Fig. 6. Development of a virtual environment for the scenario "A person falling into a pit or well"

To create a realistic atmosphere and effects, we used various techniques, such as texturing, lighting and the use of particles to emulate fire, smoke and other effects, we will describe them in detail below (Fig. 6).

We have carefully worked out and checked each scene for compliance with real situations to ensure the most realistic experience for pilots. This allows them to better understand and apply the right skills in case of emergencies. For example, a pilot can interact with a rope. Virtual controllers or gestures allow the player to grab the rope and hold it in his hands (Fig. 7).

Fig. 7. Interaction with the rope object

This interaction can be implemented through special buttons on the controllers or gesture interaction using motion sensors.

The C# programming language and the Unity environment were used to develop the application. A special class was created to implement the interaction between the user and virtual objects. This class is part of the application we developed and is responsible for managing the interaction of the user's hand with objects in a virtual environment. It can capture, move and detach objects in real time.

Below is the class code implementing the described functionality.

```
public class Interaction: MonoBehaviour {
    private Hand.AttachmentFlags attachmentFlags =
Hand.defaultAttachmentFlags &
(~Hand.AttachmentFlags.SnapOnAttach) &
(~Hand.AttachmentFlags.DetachOthers) &
(~Hand.AttachmentFlags.VelocityMovement);
    private Interactable interactable;

    void Start () {
        interactable = this.GetComponent<Interactable>();
    }
    private void HandHoverUpdate(Hand hand)
    {
        GrabTypes startingGrabType =
hand.GetGrabStarting();
        bool isGrabEnding =
hand.IsGrabEnding(this.gameObject);
        if (startingGrabType != GrabTypes.None)
        {
            hand.HoverLock(interactable);
            hand.AttachObject(gameObject, startingGrab-
Type, attachmentFlags);
        }
        else if (isGrabEnding)
        {
            hand.DetachObject(gameObject);
            hand.HoverUnlock(interactable);
        }
    }
}
```

The *Interaction* class uses the capabilities of the C# language and the Unity library to ensure smooth and natural user interaction with virtual objects. The system uses this class to interact with objects in a virtual environment, creating a more realistic and immersive experience.

This code is part of the *Interaction* class [22], which is inherited from the *MonoBehaviour* class in Unity. This class provides functionality for working with controllers and interacting in a virtual environment. Flags (*attachmentFlags*) are defined inside the class, which are used to control interaction with the object. They can limit the movement of an object at a certain speed and detach other objects when it is captured. The *Start* method initializes the *interactable* variable, which gets access to the *Interactable* component on the same object. The main method in this class is *handoverupdate*(Hand hand). It is called every time the hand is over the object. Inside the method, there is a check for the beginning of the object capture (*startingGrabType*) and the completion of the capture (*isGrabEnding*). If the capture starts (*startingGrabType* is not equal to None), then the hover of the hand is blocked and the object (*GameObject*) is attached to the hand with the specified capture type (*startingGrabType*) and the specified interaction flags (*attachmentFlags*). If the capture is completed (*isGrabEnding* is true), then the object is detached from the hand (*DetachObject*) and the hover is unlocked (*HoverUnlock*). This code handles the interaction between the object and the virtual reality controller, can grab and release the object using the controller.

To provide the player with various options for interacting with the rope, an action selection menu can be implemented (Fig. 8). The player can open the menu using controllers or gestures and select one of the available actions related to the rope. For example, it can be an option to "tie a rope to yourself", using a rope for traction, or tying other objects with a rope.

Fig. 8. Interaction of an object with another object

3.1 The Particle System

The particle system in Unity provides powerful tools for creating a variety of visual effects that can enliven scenes and add realism to them.

To create the snow effect (Fig. 9) using the particle system in Unity, you can use various parameters and settings. For example, you can adjust the shape, size, speed and behavior of snowflakes using particle emitters. Snowflakes can have different textures, colors and transparency to create a natural and atmospheric effect of snowfall.

Using the particle system in Unity to create a fire effect also provides many possibilities. Particle emitters can generate various types of particles that simulate fire, sparks and smoke (Fig. 10). The size, speed, color and transparency of the particles can be customized to create a convincing and realistic visual fire effect. In addition, the particle system adds animation and interaction with surrounding objects to make the fire effect more dynamic and lively.

Fig. 9. Snow particles in the scenario of "A person falling into a pit or well"

Fig. 10. Fire particles in the "Kitchen Fire" scenario

Developers can experiment with parameters, settings, and particle textures to achieve the desired effect and atmosphere in their scenes.

4   Realistic Physics of Virtual World Objects

The rope is a rather complex object to implement in a virtual reality simulator, since it is required to achieve the most realistic appearance and behavior. In each part of Fig. 11, changes in the geometry and behavior of potential rope knots are demonstrated.

To achieve realism, a special script has been implemented that maintains the shape of colliders, components used in the game development environment to determine the boundaries and areas of collision of objects in virtual space. The script provides the rope with its flexibility and ability to interact with surrounding objects. This creates the impression that the rope virtually touches and reacts to physical forces, similar to a real rope. This approach helps achieve a high degree of realism and bring the virtual experience closer to the real situation (Fig. 11).

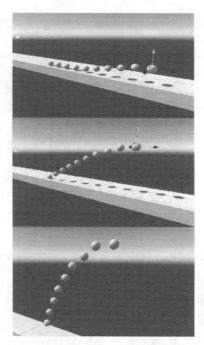

Fig. 11. Rope prototype works in a test project

To achieve realistic rope behavior, the "Configurable Joint" component was used [23]. This component links objects in the scene, in this case rope blocks, and control their physical interaction. The "Configurable Joint" component has a wide range of settings that help to set stiffness, movement restrictions and other physical properties of the joint. It creates a flexible and realistic rope behavior. With the help of the "Configurable Joint" component, each rope block was connected to neighboring blocks, forming a sequence of nodes. This allows the rope to react to physical forces, transmit movement and deform depending on the environmental impact.

The following is the code that manages the connection between two objects using Configurable Joint and Rigidbody [24].

```
public class pipe : MonoBehaviour
{
    public ConfigurableJoint j;
    public Rigidbody c;
    // Start is called before the first frame update
    void Start()
    {}

    void Update()
    {
        j.xMotion = ConfigurableJointMotion.Locked;
        j.yMotion = ConfigurableJointMotion.Locked;
        j.zMotion = ConfigurableJointMotion.Locked;
        j.angularZMotion = ConfigurableJointMo-
tion.Limited;
        j.angularYMotion = ConfigurableJointMo-
tion.Limited;
        j.angularXMotion = ConfigurableJointMo-
tion.Limited;
        j.projectionMode = JointProjec-
tionMode.PositionAndRotation;
        j.enablePreprocessing = false;
        j.connectedBody = c;
    }
}
```

The pipe class inherits *MonoBehaviour* and contains two public variables: *j* (of the *ConfigurableJoint* type) and *c* (of the *Rigidbody* type). Initialization occurs in the *Start* method, but in this case it is empty and does not perform any actions. The *Update* method is called every frame. The *ConfigurableJoint* parameters are set inside the method to restrict the movement and rotation of the joint.

With the help of *j.xMotion, j.yMotion* and *j.zMotion*, a lock is set on the X, Y and Z axes, respectively, to prevent the object from moving in these directions. Using *j.angularZMotion, j.angularYMotion* and *j.angularXMotion*, the rotation limit is set on the Z, Y and X axes, respectively. *j.projectionMode* sets the connection projection mode to the position and rotation of the object. *j.enablePreprocessing* is set to false, which disables connection preprocessing. *j.connectedBody* is set to c, which means Binds the *ConfigurableJoint* to the specified *Rigidbody* object.

This code controls the connection parameters between objects to restrict their movement and rotation using *ConfigurableJoint* in Unity.

In addition to the rope, a realistic representation of the object was given to the water. Water Pro [25] was used for this. Water Pro in Unity is a component that creates realistic visualization of the water surface and fluid effects in the virtual world. It provides various options for configuring and controlling the appearance and behavior of water, and also uses a special material and shader to determine the appearance of water. The material contains textures, colors and other parameters, and the shader provides reflection, refraction and illumination, creating a realistic look.

Water Pro uses a mesh to determine the shape and geometry of the water surface. The mesh consists of vertices and triangles that define the shape of the water. With the help of settings and parameters, the mesh can be dynamically changed, creating the effects of waves and deformations (Fig. 12).

Fig. 12. Deformation of water meshes under the influence of a solid object with a collider

Rendering of the water surface is carried out through the Unity rendering system. It goes through shaders and materials to create a visual representation of water. Water Pro also contains physics components such as colliders and a solid that determine the physical behavior of water, including collisions and buoyancy.

Water Pro helps to interact with other objects and components in the scene. For example, objects can create waves and destruction effects upon contact with the water surface. The parameters and settings of Water Pro are using by developer to control the appearance and behavior of water, including wave height, speed, transparency, reflection, refraction and other properties.

Water Pro provides developers with a convenient way to create realistic water surface effects and fluid effects in Unity. Using a combination of materials, shaders, physical simulation and settings, developers can achieve a high degree of realism and interactivity of water in their projects.

In addition to Water Pro, Unity has a Water4 [25] component, but within the framework of the created application we used Water Pro. The use of a more powerful component was not necessary. The water display in Water4 is much more realistic than in Water Pro. Water4 in Unity is a component that creates realistic water surface effects in a game environment, and also provides developers with the ability to create visually attractive water effects such as oceans, rivers, lakes and other bodies of water. Water4 has a number of settings and parameters that allow developers to control the appearance and behavior of the water surface. Settings include wave height, movement speed, transparency, color, reflection, refraction, and other properties that can be customized to achieve the desired visual effect.

Water4 components also support physical interaction with other objects in the scene. They can detect collisions and interact with objects, buoyancy and dynamic effects such as waves and destruction.

Water4 offers a more realistic visualization of water with more accurate refraction, reflection and illumination than Water Pro. Water4 has more flexibility of settings, providing developers with more parameters to control the appearance and behavior of the water surface. Developer can adjust the height of the waves, the speed of movement, color, transparency and other properties of the water with greater accuracy. Water4 supports physical interaction with objects in the scene, including collision detection. This creates the effects of buoyancy, waves and destruction, adding realism and interactivity to the water scenes.

Water4 is a newer version and probably has more active support and updates from developers. This may mean that Water4 can offer more up-to-date features, bug fixes and updates, which is important for projects that require up-to-date features and improvements.

The specific benefits may depend on the requirements and needs of the project, as well as on the versions of Water4 and Water Pro.

5 Conclusions

The results of the study of interaction with virtual objects and the implementation of realistic physics in the virtual world, presented in this article, are an important step in the development of virtual reality applications. They open up new opportunities for creating fascinating and immersive virtual scenarios that can be applied in various fields, from the gaming industry to education and medicine.

We consider various methods of interaction with virtual objects, such as gloves, vests and other devices that add a sense of presence and realism when interacting with a virtual environment. The practical implementation of the principles of interaction in the developed virtual reality application has confirmed the effectiveness of these methods and their potential for creating exciting virtual scenarios.

Particular attention was paid to the development of realistic physics of virtual world objects, including the creation of a rope using Unity software tools. This made it possible to achieve a more accurate simulation of the physical behavior of objects, their strength and interaction with the environment. Such details and mechanics add depth and realism to virtual scenarios, improving user engagement.

The results of the research and practical implementation showed the potential and prospects for the development of virtual reality in the future. The ongoing progress in virtual object interaction and physical simulation opens up new opportunities for creating more realistic and exciting virtual worlds.

References

1. Mangina, E., McGirl, T., Ryan, G., Murphy, J., McAuliffe, F.: Experience API (xAPI) for virtual reality (VR) education in medicine. In: Auer, M.E., Pester, A., May, D. (eds.) Learning with Technologies and Technologies in Learning. LNNS, vol. 456. Springer, Cham (2022). https://doi.org/10.1007/978-3-031-04286-7_16

2. Gleb, B.: Five Innovative Ways You Can Use Virtual Reality in the Real Estate Business (2020). https://rubygarage.org/blog/virtual-reality-in-real-estate

3. Lunas 3D, 2020. Interactive VR Tours Boosting Estate and Developers Market. https://www.lunas.pro/interactive-virtual-reality-tour.html

4. Rumiński, D., Maik, M., Walczak, K.: Mixed reality stock trading visualization system. In: De Paolis, L., Bourdot, P. (eds.) Augmented Reality, Virtual Reality, and Computer Graphics. AVR 2018. LNCS, vol. 10850. Springer, Cham (2018). https://doi.org/10.1007/978-3-319-95270-3_25

5. Onderdijk, K.E., Bouckaert, L., Van Dyck, E., et al.: Concert experiences in virtual reality environments. Virtual Reality (2023).https://doi.org/10.1007/s10055-023-00814-y

6. Spiess, F., Gasser, R., Heller, S., Rossetto, L., Sauter, L., Schuldt, H.: Competitive interactive video retrieval in virtual reality with vitrivr-VR. In: Lokoč, J., et al. (eds.) MultiMedia Modeling. MMM 2021. LNCS, vol. 12573. Springer, Cham (2021). https://doi.org/10.1007/978-3-030-67835-7_42

7. Heyward, M.: VR and Screen Education: An Approach to Assist Student Understanding of Narrative Emphasis, Spatiality and Structural Elements within Narrative VR. In: Batty, C., Berry, M., Dooley, K., Frankham, B., Kerrigan, S. (eds.) The Palgrave Handbook of Screen Production, pp. 443–458. Palgrave Macmillan, Cham (2019). https://doi.org/10.1007/978-3-030-21744-0_34

8. Jing, Y.: VR, AR, and Wearable Technologies in Education: An Introduction. In: Zhang, Y., Cristol, D. (eds.) Handbook of Mobile Teaching and Learning. Springer, Singapore (2019). https://doi.org/10.1007/978-981-13-2766-7_109

9. Sampaio, A.Z., Ferreira, M.M., Rosário, D.P., Martins, O.P.: CAD and VR technologies used in civil engineering education. In: Luo, Y. (eds.) Cooperative Design, Visualization, and Engineering. LNCS, vol. 6240, pp. 207–210. Springer, Berlin, Heidelberg (2010). https://doi.org/10.1007/978-3-642-16066-0_31

10. Probst, J.M., Orsolits, H.: Experts' view on AR/VR in engineering education at universities. In: Auer, M.E., Pachatz, W., Rüütmann, T. (eds.) Learning in the Age of Digital and Green Transition. ICL 2022. LNNS, vol. 634, pp. 1010–1022. Springer, Cham (2023). https://doi.org/10.1007/978-3-031-26190-9_103

11. Girardi, R., de Oliveira, J.C.: IMEVR: an MVC framework for military training VR simulators. In: Chen, J.Y.C., Fragomeni, G. (eds.) Virtual, Augmented and Mixed Reality. HCII 2021. LNCS, vol. 12770, pp. 582–594. Springer, Cham (2021). https://doi.org/10.1007/978-3-030-77599-5_40

12. Zhong, H.: Analysis on the application of VR technology in military psychological training in 5g era. In: Pei, Y., Chang, JW., Hung, J.C. (eds.) Innovative Computing. IC 2022. LNEE, vol. 935, pp. 1141–1146. Springer, Singapore (2022). https://doi.org/10.1007/978-981-19-4132-0_156

13. Bhowmick, S., Kalita, P.C., Sorathia, K.: Tiny hands are cute: adaptive virtual hands to accurately select nail-size arm's reach virtual objects in dense immersive VR. In: Stephanidis, C., Antona, M., Ntoa, S., Salvendy, G. (eds.) HCI International 2022 – Late Breaking Posters. HCII 2022. CCIS, vol. 1654, pp. 520–527. Springer, Cham (2022). https://doi.org/10.1007/978-3-031-19679-9_65

14. Nandy, A.: Introduction to Leap Motion. In: Leap Motion for Developers. Apress, Berkeley, CA (2016). https://doi.org/10.1007/978-1-4842-2550-9

15. Hillmann, C.: Comparing the Gear VR, Oculus Go, and Oculus Quest. In: Unreal for Mobile and Standalone VR. Apress, Berkeley, CA (2019). https://doi.org/10.1007/978-1-4842-4360-2_5

16. Manfredi, G., Capece, N., Erra, U., Gilio, G., Baldi, V., Di Domenico, S.G.: TryItOn: a virtual dressing room with motion tracking and physically based garment simulation. In: De Paolis,

L.T., Arpaia, P., Sacco, M. (eds.) Extended Reality. XR Salento 2022. LNCS, vol. 13445, pp. 63–76. Springer, Cham (2022). https://doi.org/10.1007/978-3-031-15546-8_5

17. Kim, S., Gu, S., Kim, J.: Variable shape and stiffness feedback system for VR gloves using SMA textile actuator. Fibers Polym. **23**(3), 836–842 (2022). https://doi.org/10.1007/s12221-022-3349-3

18. Thalmann, D.: Sensors and actuators for HCI and VR: a few case studies. In: Prabaharan, S., Thalmann, N., Kanchana Bhaaskaran, V. (eds.) Frontiers in Electronic Technologies. LNEE, vol. 433, pp. 65–83. Springer, Singapore (2017). https://doi.org/10.1007/978-981-10-4235-5_4

19. Börsting, I., Fischer, B., Gruhn, V.: AR scribble: evaluating design patterns for augmented reality user interfaces. In: De Paolis, L.T., Arpaia, P., Bourdot, P. (eds.) AVR 2021. LNCS, vol. 12980, pp. 169–177. Springer, Cham (2021). https://doi.org/10.1007/978-3-030-87595-4_13

20. Börsting, I., Shulikina, E., Gruhn, V.: Interdisciplinary collaboration in augmented reality development - a process model. In: De Paolis, L.T., Arpaia, P., Bourdot, P. (eds.) Augmented Reality, Virtual Reality, and Computer Graphics. AVR 2021. LNCS, vol. 12980, pp. 178–194. Springer, Cham (2021). https://doi.org/10.1007/978-3-030-87595-4_14

21. Becerra, M., Ierache, J., Abasolo, M.J.: Interoperable dynamic procedure interactions on semantic augmented reality browsers. In: De Paolis, L.T., Arpaia, P., Bourdot, P. (eds.) Augmented Reality, Virtual Reality, and Computer Graphics. AVR 2021. LNCS, vol. 12980. Springer, Cham (2021). https://doi.org/10.1007/978-3-030-87595-4_15

22. Blackman, S.: Unity UI Basics—Getting Started. In: Beginning 3D Game Development with Unity. Apress, Berkeley, CA (2011). https://doi.org/10.1007/978-1-4302-3423-4_2

23. Blackman, S., Tuliper, A.: The Unity Editor. In: Learn Unity for Windows 10 Game Development. Apress, Berkeley, CA (2016). https://doi.org/10.1007/978-1-4302-6757-7_1

24. Blackman, S., Tuliper, A.: Unity Basics. In: Learn Unity for Windows 10 Game Development. Apress, Berkeley, CA (2016). https://doi.org/10.1007/978-1-4302-6757-7_2

25. Blackman, S., Tuliper, A.: Creating the Environment. In: Learn Unity for Windows 10 Game Development. Apress, Berkeley, CA (2016). https://doi.org/10.1007/978-1-4302-6757-7_7

The Structure Oriented Evaluation of Five Courses Teach by the Single Teacher

Gantsetseg Sukhbaatar[1], Selenge Erdenechimeg[2], Bazarragchaa Sodnom[2], and Uranchimeg Tudevdagva[3](✉)

[1] Sports Theory and Methodology Department, School of Physical Education, Mongolian National University of Education, Ulaanbaatar, Mongolia
[2] Graduate School, Mongolian University of Pharmaceutical Sciences, Ulaanbaatar, Mongolia
[3] Computer Science Department, Chemnitz University of Technology, Chemnitz, Germany
uranchimeg.tudevdagva@informatik.tu-chemnitz.de

Abstract. In Mongolian National University of Education sometime need to teach a single teacher several courses in parallel during one academic semester. In this paper describes the evaluation process and data analyze of the five different courses teach by the single teacher. For evaluation process is applied the structure-oriented evaluation model. 69 students responded to survey checklist. All evaluation scores were higher than 0.73 but less than 0.87 which confirmed prediction of evaluator teacher. The teacher is predicted that evaluation results cannot but enough high due to the complex of teaching many different courses in parallel. Main aim of this study was figure out opinions of students and compare the evaluation result with prediction of the teacher. Based on this fact make in light some teaching issues to stakeholders.

Keywords: evaluation goal structure · adapted checklist · SURE score

1 Introduction

The Mongolian National University of Education (MNUE) was established in 1951 and is a state-owned university with nine school branches university. The School of Physical Education (SPE.1955), a branch school of the Mongolian National University of Education, has been conducted sports journalism training since 1996 and has the advantage of implementing this bachelor's program solely in Mongolia [1].

"The profession of "Sports Journalist" (SJ) has a social responsibility to disseminate and raise awareness of sports, public sports, and healthy living, and can be converted to work in the sector of sports journalism. As of 2020, more than 300 students graduated from SPE nationwide, and working as sports journalists, reporters, commentators, producers, and editors. Moreover, they specialized in sports, as well as working as a public relations specialist, manager, physical education teacher and methodologist in sports organizations, associations, and clubs [2].

With the spread of the pandemic in early 2020, many problems have arisen around the world, and many unprepared industries have been forced to make electronic changes in a very short period of time. One of the sectors that needed to be transformed immediately was the education sector, where the traditional classroom environment made it impossible for all levels of education to move to electronic form.

A "hybrid" approach to both classroom and web-based instruction is optimal [3]. A review 22 research articles on these courses since 2000 clearly shows that interests learners have already shifted to e-learning, and it is clear that they prefer hybrid and blended learning over e-learning alone [4]. Hartman and others define blended learning as a combination of pedagogy efficiency learning advancements in technology [5]. Summarizing the concepts and proposals put forward by most researchers about the hybrid form, the course is flexible, it can be conducted in a serial and synchronous environment regardless of time and space, and student's ability to work independently, find information, and work with information. Despite the advantages of developing and responsible learning, problems such as the lack of live communication between teachers and students, time-consuming development of course materials, and technical equipment problems were mentioned [6]. Most higher education institutions are highlighting the potential benefits of internet-based learning [7].

Studying the quality and accessibility of e-learning is of great importance for the further successful development of e-learning. E-learning is a relatively young field compared to traditional learning, and methods for evaluating the quality of e-learning are still evolving today, and new methodologies and models are being developed. The National Agency's model for assessing quality in e-learning – Elearning quality (ELQ) – comprises ten quality aspects which, in our view, are central to such assessments: structure/virtual environment; flexibility and adaptability; support (student and staff) [8]. A review by the World Health Organization (WHO) [9] examined on e-education shows that online learning can be viewed holistically as a teacher, learner, and organization [10]. The effectiveness of distance learning has been evaluated under comparing it with traditional approaches [11]. Lately, e-learning quality assessment has expanded in Europe [12], and quality criteria and evaluation guidelines [13] have been developed.

The Ministry of Education and Culture of Mongolia began to pay attention to the provision of quality education [14], to improve the digital skills of teachers, and to improve ICT [15]. A common issue in Mongolian e-learning is the development of an environment for distribution, monitoring and activation of online content [16].

It does not reflect individual knowledge, skills, and practices when evaluating the quality of education [17]. If this information is collected, it will greatly influence the decision-making of educational administrators [18].

Formative assessment can be used as a feedback loop between the learner and the teacher [19]. Assessment of learning is described by Wolff (1987) as general assessment; by Coldeway (1988) the act of evaluating the importance of anything; by Scriven (1993) benefits of learning activities; Stufflebeam & Shinkfield (2007) described it as providing cost-effectiveness and reliability [20].

Due to the global pandemic, Mongolia went into a public state of emergency on November 11, 2020 [21], and classroom learning at universities were temporarily suspended and transferred to an electronic format, which lasted until February 14, 2022.

It's been seven years since the school introduced LMS 3.0 Training Management Information System for students (TMIS) in its education. During the pre-epidemic classroom training, the TMIS was used by teachers to keep track of class schedules, e-journals, student assessments, and time sheets, while students used information on course selection, course assessments, and tuition fees. With the advent of e-learning, teachers and students are using LMS more widely.

In the first quarter of 2019–2020, when MSUE teachers fully switched to electronic, all subjects (lectures, seminars, laboratories, practices) were posted on the TMIS training website, regardless of the format, and students viewed and studied according to the course schedule. (Office, 2019) In the next semester of e-learning (2020–2021), teachers began to teach all types of lessons directly with their students during class hours using the 'Teams' learning platform. (In accordance with the guidelines approved by the Order A/16 of the Director of the Mongolian State University of Education on January 13, 2021, the Quality Assurance, Monitoring and Evaluation Office organized an evaluation of the implementation of e-learning).

According to the above assessment, the number of e-learning courses for SPE teachers and the number of students who have chosen and attended the course have increased. Starting from the second semester of the full transition to e-learning, in addition to the TMIS, "Teams" for undergraduate students studying domestically and "VOOV" for international students studying for a master's degree have been made available. The use of Teams by all teachers in the classroom significantly improved student engagement. For example, student attendance increased from 40% in the first 3 weeks to 60% after 2 weeks.

In the field of "Teacher Development and Teaching Methodology" for the 2020–2021 academic year, main focus was on the implementation of Teachers' Development Plan and the Methodology of Developing Online Courses of SPE. In the winter of 2020, 33 teachers from SPE and in the spring of 2021, 38 teachers participated in 10 time's e-learning courses organized by the Distance Learning Office.

During the two years of e-learning, 51 courses of 107 credit hours have been taught online to 1–4-year students in in the CC class. As of the fall semester of 2020–2021, a total of 735 students are studying at the SPE, of which 72 are majoring in sports journalism.

2   Materials and Methods

These five subjects are included in the curriculum approved by the order of the director of the Mongolian National University of Education [22] and were taught by the teacher before the e-quarantine period. These programs are implemented by the basic professional teacher involved in the survey. During the semester, the format of the training was changed to online, but the credits, format, and teachers' hour-norms remained the same.

A. *Journalism research methodology:* Basic professional course in the form of a seminar. Using sociological research theory and methodology, they will be able to select the appropriate research methodology for each field, conduct research, prepare reports, use professional books, journals and research materials, collect research documents and information, and analyze them.

B. *Sports Journalism:* A professional course in the form of lectures and seminars. They will be proficient at research subjects of sports journalism, and types, features, and sources of information of public or social media, position of sports journalism in society, recognition of social goals to address, role of traditional and modern sports journalism, values, goals, social goals to be solved, labor and organization of sports journalism, methods of working on their texts, master writing methods, write and publish on sports journalism using information and communication technologies.

C. *Practical Sports Journalism-II:* A professional course in the form of a seminar. Develop a practical approach to writing and preparing physical education and sports topics in analytical texts.

D. *Interpreter Skills-I:* A professional course that takes the form of lectures and seminars. Provides the ability to articulate the specifics and requirements of sports program interpretation, correct pronunciation of sports vocabulary and terminology, and to present sports topics and athlete profiles in a professional manner.

E. *Mass Communication Media Advertising:* A professional elective course that takes the form of lectures and seminars. Knowledge of the origin and development, types, classification, importance of advertising, advertising ethics, legal environment, ability to classify advertising by types, and consider its importance and impact in the preparation of advertising.

The structure-oriented evaluation (SURE) model was selected as basic evaluation methodology for this evaluation process.

2.1 Short Overview of Selected Model

The selected model first presented in the conference for e-learning in 2012 was presented idea of new evaluation model which is developed based on logical structures like in electronic schemes [23]. The developed version presented as thesis in July 2014 to Chemnitz University of Technology [24]. Later evaluation model applied for measurement of faculty member achievements and result of this study applied for ranking of faculty members [25]. Extended version of the evaluation model published in Springer in 2020 for evaluation of complex systems [26].

2.2 Practical Application of the SURE Model

For data processing, used online calculator of the SURE model [27].

1. The evaluation of online course

Sixty-nine students who studied five e-learning courses taught by one instructor, including "Journalism Research Methodology", "Sports Journalism", "Sports Practical Journalism- II", "Commentator Skills -I", and "Mass Media Advertising" were surveyed online using a Google form. Twenty three percent of all students who participated in the study were studying in the first year, 23 percent in the second year, 25 percent in the third year, and 29 percent in the fourth year. The class with the largest number of students was the fourth year.

2. Step from one to three

These steps are focused on definition and confirmation of evaluation goals.

- Definition of key goals. Based on discussion of evaluators we defined four key goals:

– Lecture quality (B_1),
– Seminars/Practices/Laboratories quality (B_2),
– Learning environment (B_3),
– Teacher skills for e-learning (B_4) (Fig. 1).

Fig. 1. Key goal structure

- Definition of sub goals. To reach defined key goals here described sub goals (Fig. 2):

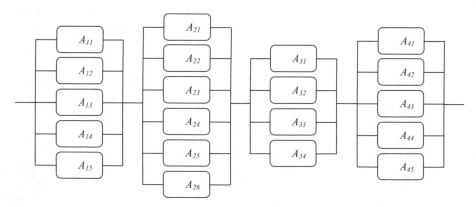

Fig. 2. Sub goal structure

– Lecture quality (B_1):

- Content of lecture (A_{11}),
- Lecture lesson (A_{12}),
- Time management of teacher during lecture (A_{13}),
- Online synchronic lecture (A_{14}),
- Offline video lecture (A_{15}).

– Seminars/Practices/Laboratories quality (B_2):

- Knowledge (A_{21}),
- Practical skills (A_{22}),
- Learner centred learning (A_{23}),
- Understanding the profession (A_{24}),
- Online synchronic practice (A_{25}),
- Offline video practice (A_{26}).

– Teacher instruction (B_3):

- Preparation level (A_{31}),
- Teaching method (A_{32}),
- Oral skills (A_{33}),
- Technical skills (A_{34})

– Teacher skills for e-learning (B_4):

- Online lesson preparation (A_{41}),
- Files for lessons (A_{42}),
- Motivation (A_{43}),
- Communication skill (A_{44}),
- Advice (A_{45})

- Confirmation of goals structures. The SURE evaluation expert and professors who teach courses confirmed the goal structures.

3. Step four and five

   The focuses of these steps are questionnaire.

- In step four questions based on sub goal's structure have to be formulated. Example of questions is showed in Table 1.

Table 1. Example of question and scaling

№	Evaluation indicators	Disagree at all (0)	Up to 30% agree (1)	31–50% agree (2)	51–75% agree (3)	76–100% agree (4)
1.	The content of the lecture was clear					
2.	Lecture is comprehensible					
3.	The teacher was able to use the class time perfectly for the lecture content					
4.	It was convenient to teach the lecture online directly in accordance with the schedule					
5.	It was convenient to watch the lecture on video and study it independently					

- Formulated questions should be checked and controlled by all interested groups of evaluation results. Only tested and accepted questionnaires can be used for data collection.

4. Step six

Data collection is a very important part of any evaluation process. Objectively in good time collected data can increase probability of final evaluation score. For objective data collection we applied Google Form as online tool (Fig. 3).

5. Step seven

Data collected by Google form in original is shown in Fig. 4.

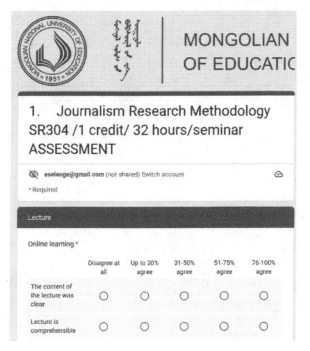

Fig. 3. Online data collection

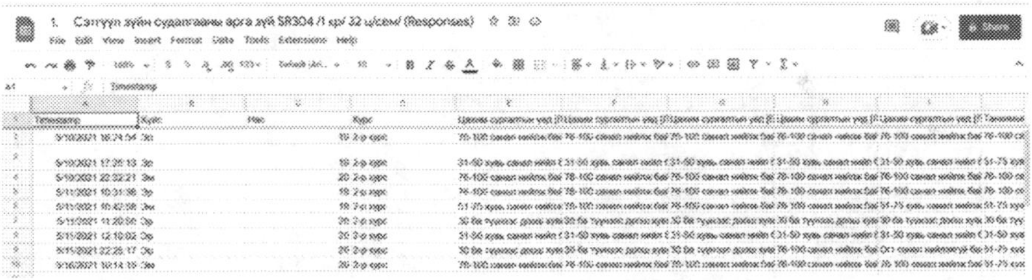

Fig. 4. Original data Excel sheet

The collected data should be processed by the SURE evaluation rules. Main mathematic rules defined based on goal structures [27]. To process the collected data (Fig. 5) by online calculator the original data should be transferred to comma separated vector (CSV) files (Fig. 6).

The CSV file should be entered to online calculator of the SURE model (Fig. 6).

6. Step eight

The SURE model calculated four different evaluation scores. In case "Journalism research methodology".

- Main evaluation score. $Q^*_e(C) = 0.81$
- Evaluation scores of key goals.

...

```
5,5,5,5,5,5,5,5,5,5,5,5,5,5,5,5,5,5,5,5,5,5,
3,3,3,3,3,3,3,3,3,3,3,3,3,3,3,3,3,3,3,3,3,3,
3,3,3,2,3,3,3,3,3,3,3,3,3,3,3,3,3,3,3,3,3,3,
2,2,2,3,3,2,2,2,2,2,2,1,1,2,2,2,2,1,2,2,
4,4,4,4,4,4,4,4,4,4,4,4,4,4,4,5,5,5,5,5,
2,2,2,2,2,2,2,2,2,2,2,2,2,2,2,2,2,2,2,2,
5,5,4,5,5,5,4,5,4,5,4,5,5,5,5,4,4,4,5,5,
5,5,5,5,4,4,4,5,5,5,5,5,5,5,5,5,5,5,5,5,
3,2,3,2,1,3,2,2,3,2,1,2,2,3,2,3,2,2,1,2,
5,5,5,5,5,5,5,5,5,5,5,5,5,5,5,5,5,5,5,5,
```

...

Fig. 5. Part of CSV file

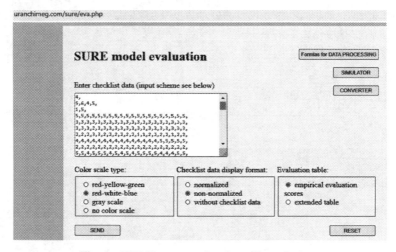

Fig. 6. CSV file as enter data for online calculator

- $B_1 = 0.81$;
- $B_2 = 0.82$;
- $B_3 = 0.8$;
- $B_4 = 0.83$.

- Evaluation scores of sub goals.

- $A_{11} = 0.69$; $A_{12} = 0.72$; $A_{13} = 0.72$; $A_{14} = 0.81$; $A_{15} = 0.67$;
- $A_{21} = 0.75$; $A_{22} = 0.75$; $A_{23} = 0.78$; $A_{24} = 0.78$; $A_{25} = 0.83$; $A_{26} = 0.78$
- $A_{31} = 0.81$; $A_{32} = 0.81$; $A_{33} = 0.81$; $A_{34} = 0.78$;
- $A_{41} = 0.83$; $A_{42} = 0.81$; $A_{43} = 0.81$; $A_{44} = 0.81$; $A_{45} = 0.81$;

The given data will be processed by online tool and as outcome from online tool table with evaluation scores will be returned (Fig. 7).

		B_1					B_2						B_3				B_4					
	k	A_{11}	A_{12}	A_{13}	A_{14}	A_{15}	A_{21}	A_{22}	A_{23}	A_{24}	A_{25}	A_{26}	A_{31} A_{32} A_{33} A_{34}				A_{41} A_{42} A_{43} A_{44} A_{45}					$Q_e*(C)$
JRM	$Q*(A_{ij})$	0.69	0.72	0.72	0.81	0.67	0.75	0.75	0.78	0.78	0.83	0.78	0.81 0.81 0.81 0.78				0.83 0.81 0.81 0.81 0.81					$Q_e*(C)= 0.8124$
	$Q_e*(B_i)$	0.81					0.82						0.80				0.83					
	k	A_{11}	A_{12}	A_{13}	A_{14}	A_{15}	A_{21}	A_{22}	A_{23}	A_{24}	A_{25}	A_{26}	A_{31} A_{32} A_{33} A_{34}				A_{41} A_{42} A_{43} A_{44} A_{45}					$Q_e*(C)$
SJ	$Q*(A_{ij})$	0.75	0.75	0.75	0.72	0.78	0.67	0.69	0.73	0.73	0.73	0.75	0.63 0.70 0.77 0.75				0.80 0.77 0.73 0.77 0.75					$Q_e*(C)=0.7343$
	$Q_e*(B_i)$	0.87					0.75						0.76				0.80					
	k	A_{11}	A_{12}	A_{13}	A_{14}	A_{15}	A_{21}	A_{22}	A_{23}	A_{24}	A_{25}	A_{26}	A_{31} A_{32} A_{33} A_{34}				A_{41} A_{42} A_{43} A_{44} A_{45}					$Q_e*(C)$
MMA	$Q*(A_{ij})$	0.82	0.71	0.77	0.82	0.64	0.79	0.80	0.80	0.86	0.86	0.80	0.70 0.80 0.82 0.82				0.88 0.86 0.80 0.80 0.79					$Q_e*(C)=0.7646$
	$Q_e*(B_i)$	0.82					0.83						0.81				0.85					
	k	A_{11}	A_{12}	A_{13}	A_{14}	A_{15}	A_{21}	A_{22}	A_{23}	A_{24}	A_{25}	A_{26}	A_{31} A_{32} A_{33} A_{34}				A_{41} A_{42} A_{43} A_{44} A_{45}					$Q_e*(C)$
SPJ	$Q*(A_{ij})$	0.87	0.87	0.79	0.83	0.77	0.79	0.83	0.85	0.88	0.79	0.85	0.77 0.77 0.79 0.81				0.88 0.90 0.90 0.90 0.90					$Q_e*(C)=0.8677$
	$Q_e*(B_i)$	0.89					0.88						0.81				0.91					
	k	A_{11}	A_{12}	A_{13}	A_{14}	A_{15}	A_{21}	A_{22}	A_{23}	A_{24}	A_{25}	A_{26}	A_{31} A_{32} A_{33} A_{34}				A_{41} A_{42} A_{43} A_{44} A_{45}					$Q_e*(C)$
CS	$Q*(A_{ij})$	0.85	0.87	0.90	0.90	0.81	0.85	0.87	0.87	0.87	0.84	0.81	0.72 0.79 0.87 0.85				0.90 0.90 0.90 0.91 0.90					$Q_e*(C)=0.8723$
	$Q_e*(B_i)$	0.91					0.86						0.87				0.90					

Fig. 7. The evaluation results

3   Results

In the study of five courses taught online by one teacher, 69 students out of 78 students who are studying sports journalism participated in the study, which is 88% of the total enrollment. 54% of participants are female and 46% are male students.

The overall scores for the five different subjects ranged from 0.73 to 0.87. The main objectives were evaluated such as $B_1 = 0.64$–0.81, $B_2 = 0.67$–0.81, $B_3 = 0.63$–0.78, $B_4 = 0.73$–0.90. The sections (B_2), (B_3), and (B_4) in SJ course were evaluated with lower scores than other courses in the.

For the main objectives of each of the five subjects, the JRM course had a rating of 0.67 to 0.81, with participants giving the lowest score of B_1 and the highest score of B_4. The lowest and highest scores were given to B_3 and B_4, while the SJ course was evaluated between 0.63 and 0.73, the MMA course was evaluated between 0.64 and 0.79, and the lowest score was given to B_1 and the highest score was given to B_2 and B_4. On the other hand, the SPJ course was evaluated as 0.77–0.88, while B_1 and B_3 were given the lowest and B_4 the highest. CS was graded between 0.72 and 0.90, with B_3 being the lowest and B_4 the highest.

Results of the sub-objectives: The best evaluation score of 0.91 was associated with the response of the CS course, "It was easy to communicate with the teacher who taught the e-course (A_{44})", while the best evaluation score of the SPJ course was 0.90, and the presentation files were structured (A_{42}); was able to encourage and motivate students to study during e-learning (A_{43}); It was highly appreciated that he was easy to communicate with (A_{44}), promptly answered questions and gave useful advice (A_{45}).

The highest rating for the MMA course was 0.88, and the e-course was well prepared (A_{41}); The high rating of the JRM course was 0.83, which is due to the high rating of sub-objectives such as it was convenient to directly connect the practice course online (Teams) according to the schedule (A_{25}), and the teacher prepared the online course well (A_{41}). The highest evaluation score for the SJ course was 0.78, the lecture-style course was viewed on the educational web (econtent.msue.edu.mn) and self-study was convenient (A_{15}).

A_{15} scored the worst, ranging from 0.64 to 0.81 under compared to other sub-objectives in SPJ, CS, and MMA. 11 of the 78 students who gave the survey gave a low score or 0 in the B_3 main objective; 2 students gave 0 points out of 1 point. In B_4,

5 students gave low points or 1 point. Out of each of the five subjects, the maximum number of students in B_3, 5 students, gave 1 point in MMA. In B_4, 2 students scored 1 point or were unsatisfied with the SJ course.

Of the nine students who participated in the JRM study, one student gave the same score to all sub-objectives (A_{11}- A_{45}). Another student gave 0 points to A_{15}. Of the 16 students who evaluated the SJ course, one student gave zero points to A_{11}- A_{14}, A_{21}- A_{25}, A_{31}- A_{34}, or 13 of the 20 sub-objectives. Also, one student gave the same score (1) for all sub-objectives (A_{11}- A_{45}), while another participant gave 0 points for all sub-objectives A_{31}- A_{34} and 1 point for all sub-objectives A_{41}- A_{45}. A total of 14 students participated in the study of the MMA course, one student gave 1 point for all sub-objectives (A_{11}-A_{45}), another participant gave 0 points for all sub-objectives A_{11}- A_{15}, and another 4 students gave 1 point each for A_{31}.

Of the 13 students who evaluated the SPJ course, one student gave a low score of 1 or 0 for A_{13}- A_{15}, A_{21}, and another student gave one score for A_{11}- A_{13}, A_{15}, A_{21}- A_{26}, A_{31}- A_{34}, A_{43}, A_{45} or 16 sub-objectives. A total of 17 students participated in the CS study, one student gave 0 points for A_{15} and A_{26}, one student got 1 point for A_{31}, another student got 0 and 1 point for A_{31} and A_{34}, and one student gave one point for A_{41}- A_{43} and A_{45}.

4 Discussion

Assessment has become, over the years, an essential key [28] to the improvement of the quality of education. It is one of the most reliable ways of identifying problems at the all levels of education system [29].

If the overall score of 0.73–0.87 for five different courses taught online by the same teacher is compared to the individualized scores used to evaluate students' academic performance, the letter grade and the numerical GPA, the 0.73 score is 71–73, C-, 1.7; A score of 0.87 corresponds to an 84–87, B, and 3.0 GPA. $B_1 = 0.64$–0.81, $B_2 = 0.67$–0.81, $B_3 = 0.63$–0.78, $B_4 = 0.73$–0.90 students' evaluations according to the letter grade that they are evaluated according to the main objectives of the research: $B_1 = $ D-B-, $B_2 = $ D-B-, $B_3 = $ D- -C +, $B_4 = $ C- -B + is rated.

The students were most satisfied with the ease of communication with the instructor in the two courses "Commentator's Skills" and "Practical Journalism of Sports ", which received the highest scores out of the five courses. These courses are specialized courses in the 3rd year, and in this course, the teacher has previously taught other courses in the classroom. Also, students who studied both MMA and JRM courses are highly satisfied with the skills of the teacher who taught the online course. Among the subjects, SPJ was the one subject in which students rated the most sub-objectives, or four, highly. These were questions designed to clarify the teacher's skills. The teacher who led the e-course prepared his presentations in a clear structure, encouraged and motivated the students, made it easy to communicate, answered questions quickly, and gave useful advice. When the teacher taught this lesson, by creating a Facebook group for that lesson, the tasks could be easily completed in video form using mobile phones, the class could discuss and talk freely, the teacher gave advice, wrote comments that were open to other students, freely discussed their opinions, and planned a creative discussion. However, in the other four courses, no special Facebook group was opened, and each topic of each course was prepared in advance as a PPT file according to the credit hours of the course.

As planned by the school administration, the teacher connected all the lessons directly according to the schedule using the Teams program, and as soon as the lesson was over, the lectures and seminars were uploaded to the training web. Another sub-objective with high satisfaction was students' high scores for self-study of SJ course lectures on the school web and scheduled JRM seminar courses online.

Dissatisfaction with the organization of the "Sports Journalism" course and the skills of the teacher who led the e-course is reflected in the fact that the SJ course received the lowest rating among the other four courses. It is a professional fundamental course for the 2nd year, and it is the first time that the students attended this teacher's class, and the courses of the first 1st and 2nd years weren't conducted in the classroom.

Analyzing the main objectives of each lesson; participants in the three courses JRM, MMA, and SPJ were not satisfied with the "Lecture quality" goal, and the participants in the three courses SJ, SPJ, and CS were less satisfied with the "teacher instruction" goal.

Out of the five subjects, the surveyed students gave low grades of inadequate preparation in four subjects: SJ, MMA, SPJ, and CS. In the JRM course, the questionnaire "whether the teacher's ability to work with technology was good" was rated the lowest. Analyzing the results of the "teacher instruction (B_3), (B_4) questionnaires to directly connect with the teacher from the 4 main objectives of each lesson; among the main objectives of each of the 5 courses, the highest score was given to the teaching skills for e-learning section of the CS course, or students are highly satisfied with this section. The second on the list, students who attended the SPJ course also rated the teacher's skills highly.

It is worth noting that the main objective "teacher's ability taught e-courses" was rated the highest among the other three objectives in all five subjects.

5 Conclusions

In conclusion the sub-objectives; among the sub-objectives of the five courses, the questionnaire "It was easy to communicate" in the "Commentator's Skills" course received the highest rating, showing that the students were satisfied. Also, the 2nd highest rating was "The presentation files have an understandable structure", "I was able to inspire and motivate students to learn during e-learning", "It was easy to establish a connection and communicate", and "They answered questions quickly and gave useful advice". The worst-rated sub-objective in the three courses JRM, SPJ, and MMA indicates that the students were not satisfied that the lecture format was suitable for viewing the lecture format on the learning web (econtent.msue.edu.mn) and independent study under comparison to the other sub-objectives. Also, in the question of whether the teacher's preparation during the e-learning period was sufficient, SJ and CS were given the worst grades, which indicate that it is necessary to study the workload of teachers who take many courses and the time to prepare lessons. More detailed research is needed to find out why these scores are the worst and how they can be improved in future courses /determining the demand and needs of teaching assistants/.

References

1. Erdenechimeg, L.: Erdmiin ikh urguu-Mongolian National University of Education. Jikom Press, Ulaanbaatar (2021)
2. Gantsetseg, S., Sarantuya, J., Batzaya, B.: Sports journalism, vol 1. Soyombo printing, Ulaanbaatar (2021)
3. Black, G.: A comparison of traditional, online and hybrid methods of course delivery. Bus. Adm. Online 1(1), 1–9 (2002)
4. Hemsley-Brown, J.: Universities in a competitive global marketplace: a systematic review of the literature on higher education marketing. Int. J. Public Sect. Manag. 19(4), 316–338 (2006)
5. Poon, J.: Blended learning: an institutional approach for enhancing students' learning experiences. MERLOT J. Online Learn. Teach. 9(2), 271–289 (2013)
6. Seifert, T.: What students really think about online lessons?. In: Site-2017-Austin, USA, p. 1792 (2017)
7. Qandil, A., Abdel-Halim, H.: Distance e-learning is closer than everybody thought: a pharmacy education perspective. Health Prof. Educ. 6(3), 301–303 (2020)
8. Eva, Å.: E-learning quality aspects and criteria for evaluation of e-learning in higher education. Swedish National Agency for Higher Education, 11R (2008)
9. Al-Shorbaji, N., Atun, R., Car, J., Majeed, A., Wheeler, E.: eLearning for undergraduate health professional education. World Health Organization
10. Olasile, B.A., Emrah, S.: Covid-19 pandemic and online learning: the challenges and opportunities. Interact. Learn. Environ. 31, 863–875 (2020). https://doi.org/10.1080/10494820.2020.1813180
11. Frehywot, S., Vovides, Y., Talib, Z., Mikhail, N., Ross, H., Wohltjen, H.: E-learning in medical education in resource constrained low- and middle-income countries. BMC Hum. Resour. Health 11(4), 1–15 (2013). https://doi.org/10.1186/1478-4491-11-4
12. Michele, S., Maria, S.: Quality Assurance of E-learning, European Association for Quality Assurance in Higher Education, Helsinki, Workshop report (2009)
13. Olaf, Z.-R., Terry, A.: Online Distance Education. AU Press, Athabasca University (2014)
14. Vision 2050, a project to be implemented within the framework of Mongolia's long-term development policy, Package Discussion of the Education, Government of Mongolia, Ulaanbaatar (2019)
15. "Vision-2050" On approving Mongolia's long-term development policy, Government of Mongolia, Ulaanbaatar, [12]Resolution No. 52 of the Parliament of Mongolia (2020)
16. Munkhchimeg, B.: A study of the use of data mining in training management systems for electric learning assessment (2015)
17. Alumni Tracking Survey and Employer Satisfaction Survey Handbook. Higher Education Reform Project (2015)
18. Ganbold, D.: Evaluation reform or evaluation of student learning, Ulaanbaatar (2017)
19. Purevdorj, C.: Teaching Management, "Munkhiin useg", Ulaanbaatar, vol. 6, pp 10–11 (2010)
20. Ariunbolor, D., Myadagmaa, R., Tuul, P., Bulga, P., Batbayar, D.: Handbook-Methodological recommendations for updating and evaluating the training process
21. Uranchimeg, T., Bazarragchaa, S., Selenge, E.: E-learning: evaluation based on sure model for pharmacy training. High. Educ., 95–99 (2021)
22. Mandakh, D.: Curriculum for the sports journalism program at the school of physical education of the Mongolian National University of Education (2022)
23. Tudevdagva, U., Hardt, W.: A measure theoretical evaluation model for e-learning programs, presented at the IADIS on e-Society, Berlin, Germany (2012)

24. Tudevdagva, U.: Structure Oriented Evaluation Model for E-Learning". Universitätsverlag Chemnitz, Wissenschaftliche Schriftenreihe Eingebettete Selbstorganisierende Systeme (2014)
25. Tudevdagva, U., Bayar-Erdene, L., Hardt, W.: A self-assessment system for faculty based on the evaluation SURE model. In: 5th International Conference on Industrial Convergence technology, Asan, Korea (2014)
26. Tudevdagva, U.: Structure-Oriented Evaluation an Evaluation Approach for Complex Processes and Systems. Springer, Switzerland (2020)
27. Online calculator of the SURE model (2021). http://uranchimeg.com/sure/eva.php
28. Kellaghan, T., Greaney, V.: Using assessment to improve the quality of education, UNESCO (2001)
29. Smith, E.R., Tyler, R.W.: Appraising and recording student progress (1942)

Intelligent Technologies in Social Engineering. Intelligent Technologies in Medicine and Healthcare

Two-Dimensional Walsh Spectral Transform in Problems of Automated Analysis of Ultrasound Images

Alexander Kuzmin[✉] ⬤, Hasan Chasib Al-Darraji⬤, Artem Sukhomlinov⬤, and Sergei Filist⬤

Southwest State University, Kursk, Russian Federation
kuz.a.u@yandex.ru

Abstract. The scanning window with the calculation of the local two-dimensional Walsh transform in it is proposed to be used for automated systems of processing ultrasound images. Preliminary studies of the computational capacity of such a process have been carried out and the high speed of this approach has been shown. Frequencies are selected on the spectral two-dimensional plane. The analysis of these frequencies makes it possible to determine the degree of echogenicity in the scan area, as well as to detect the edges of ultrasound image objects. The architecture of the ultrasonic image pixel state detector is proposed based on a two-dimensional scanning windowed Walsh transform, a significant frequency selector, and a neural network tuned to classify the pixel state. The detector was tested both on simulated images and on ultrasound images of phantoms and real medical ultrasound examinations of the human abdominal cavity.

Keywords: ultrasound imaging · Walsh transform · edge detector

1 Introduction

According to the latest data published by the World Health Organization (WHO), pancreatic cancer mortality in Russia reached 20,282 or 1.23% of total deaths in 2020 [1]. The age-adjusted death rate is 8.15 per 100,000 population, placing Russia 20th in the world. In Russia, it was indicated that men are more likely to get pancreatic cancer than women [2]. This is due to the fact that men consume excessive amounts of alcohol. Pancreatic cancer begins from two types of pancreatic cells: exocrine cells and neuroendocrine cells. The most common is exocrine, usually found in advanced stages. In general, mortality from pancreatic cancer is quite high, since the majority of patients (>80%) do not show symptoms characteristic of cancer until the advanced stages. According to [3], the survival rate of patients with pancreatic adenocarcinoma in the world for five years is only 6%. Unfortunately, pancreatic cancer often manifests late, and only 20% of patients with pancreatic cancer have resectable disease at the time of presentation. For patients who can undergo successful surgical resection, the 5-year survival rate is 27%.

Diagnosis of a pancreatic tumor typically involves several steps: image screening, pancreatic location, pancreatic segmentation, and pancreatic tumor classification. Due

A. G. Kravets et al. (Eds.): CIT&DS 2023, CCIS 1909, pp. 467–477, 2023.
https://doi.org/10.1007/978-3-031-44615-3_32

to the anatomical location of the pancreas and the variability of its shape and volume in the abdominal cavity, automatic segmentation of the pancreas on radiological images is a challenge. However, computed tomography (CT) screening, preoperative diagnosis, and pancreatic quantification are required to develop an effective treatment plan. Once segmentation is performed on images containing the pancreas, it generally provides a more reliable quantitative representation than manual cross-sectional measurements. In addition, automated, reliable, fast, and accurate pancreatic segmentation processing thousands of scanned images can provide new diagnostic information, assist in preoperative surgical planning, and be adopted in clinical practice. In the context of efficient segmentation of the pancreas, the process of applying machine learning algorithms to obtain or extract meaningful information and automating image analysis processes from computed tomography (CT) or magnetic resonance imaging (MRI) has become a very active area of research. This process allows non-invasive characterization of lesions and assessment of their progression and possible response to therapy.

As mentioned above the first step to effective treatment of pancreatic cancer is to obtain an image for quantification. Computed tomography, magnetic resonance imaging, ultrasound are widely used for this purpose. Of all these methods, ultrasound is the cheapest and most accessible method.

Ultrasound diagnostics is one of the most common methods for detecting diseases in clinical practice. There are many advantages of ultrasound imaging such as safety, convenience and low cost. However, years of experience and training are required to master the technique of interpreting ultrasound images. A variety of ultrasound computer diagnostic systems have been developed to support the diagnostic process. Currently, various methods, models and algorithms have been developed to solve the problem of identification and classification of pancreatic ultrasound images.

Ultrasound images are complex unstructured images with a high level of noise and a very low signal-to-noise ratio [4]. Very often, ultrasound scanners form a picture visually on the verge of being distinguishable, and only doctors with extensive experience in reading ultrasound pictures become able to carry out diagnostics. The main tasks of automated systems for processing ultrasound images are to increase the signal-to-noise ratio, search for objects in pictures and measure the characteristics of objects (number of objects, size, brightness, etc.) [5–8]. To increase the signal-to-noise ratio, special filters have long been used in technology, which purposefully change the spectrum of the processed signal - the filters pass the useful frequency components, and the filters suppress the frequency components of the noise [9]. Naturally, the filters work fine only if the spectral range of the useful signal and the spectral range of the noise are different. Sometimes the spectral range of interference is localized around a certain frequency, which is included in the spectral range of the useful signal. For example, an electrical network interference frequency of 50 Hz is included in the useful frequency range of an electromyosignal (EMG), which occupies a frequency band from units to hundreds of hertz. In this case, to eliminate network interference, system developers distort the useful signal and still filter the frequency component of 50 Hz.

Frequency transforms such as Fourier, Hartley, Walsh, etc. widely used for frequency filtering and various frequency transformations in signals, including two-dimensional signals such as images. The calculation of the Fourier transform on a computer is associated with operations with complex numbers, which is quite expensive in terms of memory and computing resources. The Hartley transform, for example, is already carried out in the domain of real numbers, but to calculate the kernel of the Hartley transform, you still need to calculate trigonometric functions. The Walsh transform compares favorably with the above transforms in that the Walsh functions are sequences of single pulses with a single (possibly both positive and negative) polarity. Those to calculate the Walsh transform, there is no need to calculate trigonometric functions, which leads to a significant increase in the performance of systems based on them. Thus, according to our data, the calculation of the two-dimensional Walsh transform in a window of 8×8 pixels on a conventional educational computer with a 2 GHz Celeron processor takes less than a microsecond. This means that if for each pixel of a megapixel image we calculate our two-dimensional Walsh transform, then the total time will take less than a second. This is quite acceptable time even for real-time image processing.

2 Methods

Let's take a closer look at the properties of two-dimensional Walsh frequencies for building image processing systems based on the spectral two-dimensional Walsh transform.

For example, the zero frequency (the frequency with coordinates 0.0) according to the Walsh transform formula [10] is the arithmetic mean of the brightness of the pixels in the transform window. Or, if the transformation window is significantly smaller than the image dimensions, then the local average brightness of the image is calculated at zero frequency. For ultrasound image processing this is a very important knowledge, since it is known that a number of objects on ultrasound images have a certain echogenicity: there are objects with reduced echogenicity (usually filled with fluids - arteries, veins, etc., with an average echogenicity - various tissues, and with high echogenicity - walls, surfaces, etc.) Visually, echogenicity is perceived as the brightness of a point in the ultrasound picture. Thus, to determine the aortic section in the pancreas image, it is necessary to look for a sufficiently large area with reduced echogenicity (low average brightness) in a certain place of the ultrasound image (Fig. 1).

The frequency with coordinate 1.0 is responsible for the vertical boundaries (see Fig. 2). In this figure, the vertical brightness difference is shown from the maximum value to the minimum value, which occurs exactly in the middle (at x = 0.5*max = const) of the window (Fig. 2a). This pattern corresponds to the values of the Walsh frequencies shown in Fig. 2c in numbers (modulus of numbers is shown) and in Fig. 2b in grayscale form. If the brightness difference did not occur exactly in the middle of the image, then non-zero numbers corresponding to phase distortions would appear in other frequencies other than 0.0 and 1.0. However, the overall halftone pattern would not change much and the dominant frequencies of 0.0 and 1.0 would retain their position. The same picture would be observed when replacing a flat vertical line with an any arc, for example, from the vertical part of the circle - with the vertical nature of the transition boundary, the frequency with coordinate 1.0 dominates (Fig. 3). With an inverse input pattern, when there is a vertical drop in brightness from the minimum value to the

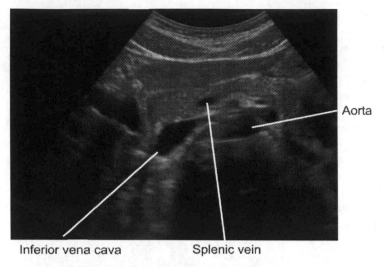

Aorta

Inferior vena cava   Splenic vein

Fig. 1. The main veins and arteries in the ultrasound image of the abdominal cavity

	0	1	2	3	4	5	6	7
	8160	8160	0	0	0	0	0	0
	0	0	0	0	0	0	0	0
	0	0	0	0	0	0	0	0
	0	0	0	0	0	0	0	0
	0	0	0	0	0	0	0	0
	0	0	0	0	0	0	0	0
	0	0	0	0	0	0	0	0
	0	0	0	0	0	0	0	0

a)   b)   c)

Fig. 2. Vertical gradient of brightness (a) and its Walsh transform in halftone (b) and in numbers (c).

maximum value, which occurs exactly in the middle of the window, the values of the Walsh frequencies will be the same, but with a another sign. Therefore, the sign in the numbers in Fig. 1b is discarded and only the frequency amplitudes are given.

Similar to the frequency with coordinate 0.1, the frequency with coordinate 1.0 is responsible for the horizontal boundaries (see Fig. 4). In this figure, the horizontal brightness difference from the maximum value to the minimum value is shown, which occurs exactly in the middle of the window, at $y = 0.5*max = const$ (Fig. 4a). This picture also corresponds to the values of the Walsh frequencies, shown in Fig. 4c in numbers (the modulus of numbers is given) and in 4b in grayscale form. Similar reasoning can be given for phase shifts of the input pattern, as well as when there are "irregularities" of the lines. And we can draw a similar conclusion: with the horizontal nature of the transition's border of the image's brightness, the frequency with the coordinate 0.1 dominates.

Thus, the analysis of three Walsh transform frequencies in a window can lead to the recognition of several states of each specific pixel: a pixel can belong to an area with a

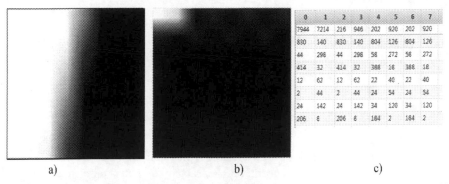

0	1	2	3	4	5	6	7
7944	7214	216	946	202	920	202	920
830	140	830	140	804	126	804	126
44	298	44	298	58	272	58	272
414	32	414	32	388	18	386	18
12	62	12	62	22	40	22	40
2	44	2	44	24	54	24	54
24	142	24	142	34	120	34	120
206	6	206	6	184	2	184	2

a)   b)   c)

Fig. 3. An uneven vertical brightness gradient (a) and its Walsh transform in halftone (b) and in numbers (c).

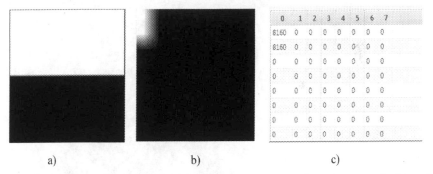

0	1	2	3	4	5	6	7
8160	0	0	0	0	0	0	0
8160	0	0	0	0	0	0	0
0	0	0	0	0	0	0	0
0	0	0	0	0	0	0	0
0	0	0	0	0	0	0	0
0	0	0	0	0	0	0	0
0	0	0	0	0	0	0	0
0	0	0	0	0	0	0	0

a)   b)   c)

Fig. 4. Horizontal brightness difference (a) and its Walsh transform in grayscale (b) and in numbers (c).

certain (low, medium, high) echogenicity, a pixel can be the boundary of a vertical or horizontal transition of echogenicity. For decision-making in image processing, including ultrasound, neural networks are widely used [11–14]. In our work, we also use the work of a neural network, to the inputs of which we will supply the values of the Walsh transform frequencies, and from the output we will take numerical data corresponding to decisions about the state of each pixel (Fig. 5). Block "2D Walsh Transform Calculator" calculates the required set of two-dimensional Walsh frequencies. Moreover, if standard fast Walsh transform modules are used (for example, inside DSPs), all window frequencies are calculated. To increase performance, you can configure the block to calculate only the required frequencies. This set of frequencies is fed to the input of the frequency selector, which operates on the principle of a multiplexer and selects only the necessary frequencies from the entire set of frequencies. The architecture of a neural network (block "Neural Network") can be simplified to ones neurons, and then the process of learning such a network is reduced to the correct setting of threshold levels. We used similar solutions for other tasks where they showed high efficiency [15–20].

To illustrate the operation of the vertical edge detector, we will generate a test image containing a rectangle, a slanted rectangle, and a circle (Fig. 6a). Let's choose the Walsh

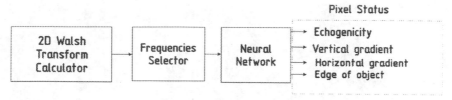

Fig. 5. Architecture of the pixel state detector based on the 2D Walsh windowed transform.

transform window size of 8 × 8 pixels and adjust the input of the neural network to the frequency with coordinate 1.0. Sequentially, for each pixel of the source image, we will fill a square window of 8 × 8 in size from pixels to the right and below the source pixel. In this window, we find the Walsh transform and pass the frequency value with coordinate 1.0 to the neural network, which in this case plays the role of an amplitude detector. The result of the neural network is shown in Fig. 6b. As we can see in this figure, vertical brightness gradients are detected, but horizontal ones (the top and bottom edges of the rectangle, as well as the top and bottom points of the circle) are not.

Similarly, you can make a detector of horizontal brightness differences, but at a frequency of 0.1 of the two-dimensional Walsh transform. The result of the operation of such a detector is shown in Fig. 7. Similar conclusions can be drawn, but for horizontal brightness differences.

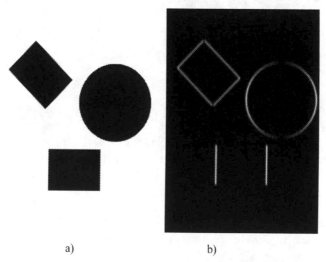

a)   b)

Fig. 6. Operation of the vertical edge detector: a) - the original model image, b) - the result of the detector operation

Finally, if we combine the work of the two above detectors and apply two frequencies with coordinates 1.0 and 0.1 to the input of the combined neural network, then we can get a common edge detector of objects in the image. In this case, the combined neural network plays the actual role of the adder. The result of the operation of such a detector on model data is shown in Fig. 8.

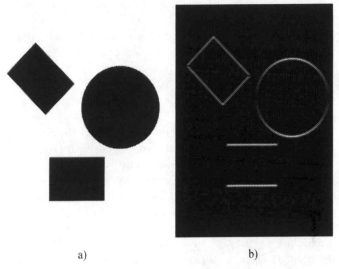

a)   b)

Fig. 7. The operation of the horizontal edge detector: a) - the original model image, b) - the result of the detector operation

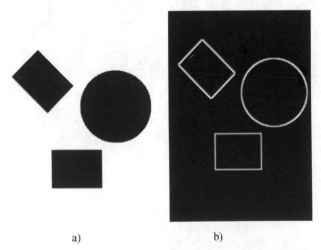

a)   b)

Fig. 8. The operation of the edge detector at two frequencies: a) - the original model image, b) - the result of the detector operation

3   Results

Doctors are taught the technique of ultrasound studies on specialized phantoms, which are a collection of materials with different echogenicity. As a result, images are obtained that can be characterized, on the one hand, as model ones, with relatively clear boundaries. On the other hand, a sufficiently large proportion of the noise introduced by the scanning system of the ultrasound scanner is already present in these images.

An example of an ultrasound image of a phantom is shown in Fig. 9a. The application of the developed edge detector on the ultrasound image of the phantom is shown in Fig. 9b. As you can see from this figure, the edges of the phantom objects are usually well recognized in the resulting image.

Real ultrasound images, for example, of the abdominal cavity are characterized by a rather large amount of noise. For visual search of objects in the image, as well as for tasks of automated measurements, the original image must be freed from noise, i.e. increase the signal-to-noise ratio. The boundaries of objects are often used as a useful signal, so the search for the boundaries of objects can be considered as a procedure for filtering unwanted noise. Figure 10a shows an ultrasound image of the abdominal cavity. The application of the developed edge detector on the ultrasound image of the abdominal cavity is shown in Fig. 10b. As you can see from this figure, the edges of the abdominal objects are highlighted, which leads to an improvement in the visual perception of the image, and also facilitates automated measurements on the ultrasound image.

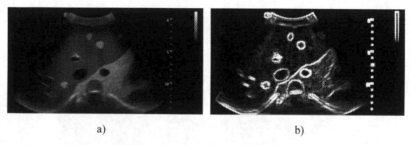

a)   b)

Fig. 9. Ultrasound image of the phantom: a) - the original image, b) - the result of the detector

We compared the obtained results of using the developed edge detector on an ultrasound image with the known methods for searching for edges on an image: with the Sobel, Sharr, Prewitt operator [21]. From a mathematical and practical point of view, these methods are similar to the proposed method, but instead of the spatial Walsh functions they use the Sobel, Scharr, Prewitt basis kernels with different weight coefficients. Since the proposed method contains a neural network with thresholding, it can be concluded that the developed edge detector includes image post-processing, which leads to more contrasting results. The results of the developed detector are close to the Canny method [22], which uses a Gaussian filter, the Sobel operator, and hysteresis threshold post-processing. Quality results are highly dependent on correctly set threshold levels, both in our case and in the case of applying the Canny method.

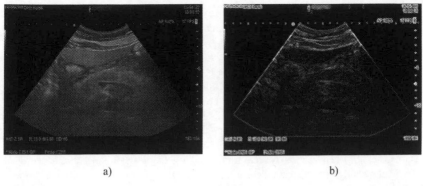

a)   b)

Fig. 10. Ultrasound image of the abdominal cavity: a) - the original image, b) - the result of the edge detector

4 Conclusion

So, in this article, a scanning window with the calculation of the local two-dimensional Walsh transform in it is proposed to be used for automated systems for processing medical ultrasound images. Preliminary studies of the computational capacity of such a process have been carried out and the high speed of this approach has been shown. On the spectral two-dimensional plane, we have identified frequencies, the analysis of which allows us to determine the degree of echogenicity in the scanning area, as well as to detect the edges of ultrasound image objects.

The architecture of the ultrasonic image pixel state detector is proposed based on a two-dimensional scanning windowed Walsh transform, a significant frequency selector, and a neural network tuned to classify the pixel state. The detector was tested both on simulated images and on ultrasound images of phantoms and real medical ultrasound examinations of the human abdominal cavity. Comparison of the proposed ultrasonic image pixel state detector based on the scanning windowed two-dimensional Walsh transform with existing methods showed good results with a moderate computational load on the computer.

The proposed detector can be used in systems for processing ultrasound medical images, in particular in systems for the classification of pancreatic ultrasound images.

References

1. Zemlyakova, S.S., Kiseleva, Y.V., Zharikova, T.S., Antonyan, S.G., Tupikin, K.A., Nikolenko, V.N., et al.: Pancreatic cancer: statistics and treatment in the Russian Federation. Russ. Open Med. J. **9**(4), 415 (2020)
2. Razvodovsky, Y.E.: Alcohol consumption and pancreatitis mortality in Russia. JOP. J. Pancreas **15**(4), 365–370 (2014)
3. McGuigan, A., Kelly, P., Turkington, R.C., Jones, C., Coleman, H.G., McCain, R.S.: Pancreatic cancer: a review of clinical diagnosis, epidemiology, treatment and outcomes. World J. Gastroenterol. **24**(43), 4846 (2018)

4. Filist, S.A., Tomakova, R.A., Shatalova, O.V., Kuzmin, A.A., Ali Kassim, K.D.: Method of classification of complex structured images based on self-organizing neural network structures. Radiopromyshlennost' = Radio Ind. **4**, 57–65 (2016). (In Russ.)

5. Săftoiu A., et al.: Efficacy of an artificial neural network–based approach to endoscopic ultrasound elastography in diagnosis of focal pancreatic masses. Clin. Gastroenterol. Hepatol. **10**(1), 84–90 (2012). The Official Clinical Practice Journal of the American Gastroenterological Association. https://doi.org/10.1016/j.cgh.2011.09.014

6. Ozkan, M., et al.: Age-based computer-aided diagnosis approach for pancreatic cancer on endoscopic ultrasound images. Endoscopic Ultrasound. **5**(2), 101 (2016). https://doi.org/10.4103/2303-9027.180473

7. Tian, G., et al.: Deep learning for real-time auxiliary diagnosis of pancreatic cancer in endoscopic ultrasonography. Front. Oncol. **12**, 973652 (2022). https://doi.org/10.3389/fonc.2022.973652

8. Udriştoiu, A.L., et al.: Real-time computer-aided diagnosis of focal pancreatic masses from endoscopic ultrasound imaging based on a hybrid convolutional and long short-term memory neural network model. PLoS ONE **16**(6), e0251701 (2021). https://doi.org/10.1371/journal.pone.0251701

9. Filist S.A., Kondrashov D.S., Sukhomlinov A.Y., Shulga L.V., Al-Darraji Ch.H., Belozerov V.A.: Automated system for classifying pancreatic ultrasound images based on the segment spectral analysis method. Model. Optim. Inf. Technol. **11**(1) (2023). https://moitvivt.ru/ru/journal/pdf?id=1302, https://doi.org/10.26102/2310-6018/2023.40.1.021. (In Russ.)

10. Golubov, B., Efimov, A., Skvortsov, V.: Walsh series and transforms-Theory and applications. Kluwer Academic Publishers Dordrecht, Boston, London, p. 368. ISBN: 9780792311003

11. Kudryavtsev P.S., Kuzmin A.A., Filist S.A.: Development of boosting methodology for classification of chest fluorograms. Biomeditsinskaya radioelektronika = Biomedical radioelectronic **9**, 10–15 (2016). (In Russ.)

12. Kudryavtsev, P.S., Kuzmin, A.A., Savinov, D.Yu., Filist, S.A., Shatalova O.V.: Modeling of morphological formations on chest radiographs in intelligent diagnostic systems for medical purposes. Prikaspiiskii zhurnal: upravlenie i vysokie tekhnologii = Caspian journal: management and high technologies **3**, 109–120 (2017). (In Russ.)

13. Filist, S.A., Ali Kassim, K.D., Kuzmin, A.A., Shatalova, O.V., Alyabev, E.A.: Formation of a feature space for classification problems of complex structured images based on spectral windows and neural network structures. Izvestiya Yugo-Zapadnogo gosudarstvennogo universiteta. Seriya: Upravlenie, vychislitel'naya tekhnika, informatika. Meditsinskoe priborostroenie = Proceedings of the South-West State University. Series: Control, computer engineering, information science. medical instruments engineering, vol. 4, pp.56–68 (2016). (In Russ.)

14. Filist, S.A., Dabagov, A.R., Tomakova, R.A., Malyutina, I.A., Kondrashov, D.S.: Multilayer morphological operators for segmentation of complex structured raster halftone images. Izvestiya Yugo-Zapadnogo gosudarstvennogo universiteta. Seriya: Upravlenie, vychislitel'naya tekhnika, informatika. Meditsinskoe priborostroenie = Proceedings of the South-West State University. Series: Control, computer engineering, information science. medical instruments engineering, vol. 9, no. 3, pp.44–63 (2019). (In Russ.)

15. Myasnyankin, M.B., Kuzmin, A.A., Filist, S.A.: Neural network classifiers with descriptors obtained on the basis of analysis of the system rhythms in intellectual prediction systems for non-hospital pneumonia. In: Journal of Physics: Conference Series. "International Scientific Conference Artificial Intelligence and Digital Technologies in Technical Systems 2020, AIDTTS 2020", vol. 1801 (2021)

16. Filist, S.A., Myasnyankin, M.B., Safronov, R.I., Kuzmin, A.A.: Multimodal neural network classifier of the functional state of the respiratory system. In: Journal of Physics: Conference

Series. Krasnoyarsk Science and Technology City Hall of the Russian Union of Scientific and Engineering Associations. Krasnoyarsk, Russia, p. 32064 (2021)

17. Belykh, V.S., Efremov, M.A., Filist, S.A.: Development and research of a method and algorithms for intelligent classification systems for complexly structured images. In: Izvestiya Yugo-Zapadnogo gosudarstvennogo universiteta. Seriya: Upravlenie, vychisli-tel'naya tekhnika, informatika. Meditsinskoe priborostroenie = Proceedings of the South-West State University. Series: Control, computer engineering, information science. medical instruments engineering, vol. 2, pp.12–24 (2016). (In Russ.)

18. Filist, S.A., Dabagov, A.R., Tomakova, R.A., Malyutina, I.A., Kondrashov, D.S.: Method of cascade segmentation of breast radiographs. In: Izvestiya Yugo-Zapadnogo gosudarstvennogo uni-versiteta. Seriya: Upravlenie, vychislitel'naya tekhnika, informatika. Meditsinskoe pri-borostroenie = Proceedings of the South-West State University. Series: Control, computer engineering, information science. medical instruments engineering, vol. 9, no. 1, pp.49–61 (2019). (In Russ.)

19. Tomakova, R.A., Filist, S.A., Pykhtin, A.I.: Development and research of methods and algorithms for intelligent systems for complex structured images classification. J. Eng. Appl. Sci. **12**(22), 6039–6041 (2017)

20. Filist, S.A., Shevtsov, M.V., Belozerov, V.A., Kondrashov, D.S., Gorbachev, I.N., Korsun-sky, N.A.: Automated system for classifying video stream snapshots. In: Izvestiya Yugo-Zapadnogo gosudarstvennogo uni-versiteta. Seriya: Upravlenie, vychislitel'naya tekhnika, informatika. Meditsinskoe priborostroenie = Proceedings of the South-West State University. Series: Control, computer engineering, information science. medical instruments engineering, vol. 11, no. 4, pp. 85–105 (2021). (In Russ.)

21. Krig, S.: Computer Vision Metrics. Survey, Taxonomy and Analysis of Computer Vision, Visual Neuroscience, and Deep Learning, p. 637. Springer Cham (2016). https://doi.org/10. 1007/978-3-319-33762-3

22. Canny, J.: A computational approach to edge detection. IEEE Trans. Pattern Anal. Mach. Intell. **Pami-8**(6) (1986)

A System for Management of Adaptable Mobile Applications for People with Intellectual Disabilities

Vladislav Guriev[1]($\boxtimes$), Angelina Voronina[1], Alexander Kataev[1,2], and Tatyana Petrova[2]

[1] Volgograd State Technical University, Volgograd, Russia
vladgurjev@mail.ru

[2] Volgograd State Socio-Pedagogical University, Volgograd, Russia

Abstract. One of the trends in the development of modern mobile applications is adaptability, which makes it possible to increase the accessibility of mobile applications for various categories of users. The article is devoted to the study of approaches to the development of adaptable mobile applications and software development tools for such applications. The possibilities of using CALS-technologies to support various stages of the MA life cycle are considered. A technology for the development of MA, the interface of which can be adapted at the maintenance stage, and ways of adapting the interfaces of the developed MA for the end users are proposed. A system has been developed that combines the typical capabilities of mobile application management systems at the stages of implementation and maintenance, and expands them by adding functions that provide the ability to adapt the MA user interface. MA development is based on a multi-module architecture, which makes it possible to use MA components for reuse in other MAs. A template-based technology for adapting the MA interface and a method for adapting the interface using a built-in configuration panel (CP) have been developed. A method of using the system for developing adaptable MA is described. It is shown that the proposed technology makes it possible to increase accessibility of MA and applicability for different people with intellectual disabilities by customizing the interface for each user in accordance with his/her capabilities and limitations and significantly reduce the overall development time of MA through the use of a unified multi-module architecture and the inclusion into the MA project of ready-made modules, as well as the generation of CPs for adapting the MA interface.

Keywords: adaptable mobile application · mobile application development · mobile application management · CALS technology · adaptable interface · configuration panel · modularization

1 Introduction

The number of mobile applications (MA) released to the software (SW) market is constantly growing, and the fields of application of MA cover all new areas of human life [1–4]. SEs are increasingly penetrating the corporate environment, providing new competitive advantages to companies [5]. Calculation of the number of developers creating

© The Author(s), under exclusive license to Springer Nature Switzerland AG 2023
A. G. Kravets et al. (Eds.): CIT&DS 2023, CCIS 1909, pp. 478–487, 2023.
https://doi.org/10.1007/978-3-031-44615-3_33

MAs focused on solving certain professional problems, and the number of companies using such MAs for their own needs. One of the trends in the development of MA is adaptability, i.e. the ability to adjust certain MA functionality and visual display for the end user [6–8]. Many adaptable MAs provide one or another option for customizing the MA, in most cases these are interface settings (fonts, color palette, sound, etc.). In this case, it is assumed that the user of the MA should configure the interface himself. However, for some categories of users (for example, users with intellectual disabilities), a more personal adaptation of the interface is required (number of controls, use of icons, use or not use of text). In addition, many users with intellectual disabilities will not be able to configure the interface on their own, in such cases, the interface can be adapted by the parents and/or guardians of these users, who know the capabilities and limitations of their wards [9, 10]. Such MA capabilities should be provided immediately at the development stage, because this may require changes in the program code.

The development of high-quality solutions with wide functionality requires high qualifications from MA developers, because it is necessary to understand development methodologies, meaningful application of technology, conduct various types of software testing, professional knowledge of the required programming languages and related tools. The development of MA for people with intellectual disabilities is carried out not only by specialized companies, but also by individual developers who do not have a sufficiently high qualification, and this affects both the speed of development of such MA and the quality of the developed solutions. To create high-quality MAs with an adaptable interface accessible to people with intellectual disabilities, specialized software tools are required to support the development of such MAs and the ability to adapt their interface to the end user.

2 Modern Approaches to Mobile Application Development Management

Currently, specialized software tools (Mobile Application Development Management, MADM) are widely used to manage the development of MAs. The typical functionality of the MADM system includes an interface designer, a functionality for refining the program code, and publishing MA updates. The use of the MADM system makes it possible to reduce the complexity in the development of the MT, as well as to improve its quality. To administer MAs designed for use in various types of professional activities and manage users of such MAs, MA management systems (Mobile Application Management, MAM) are used. Typical functionality of the MAM system: adaptation of the MA interface for the end user, user account management, statistics collection. The use of the MAM system makes it possible to simplify user management and MA configuration [11].

Thus, MADM systems provide support for MA at the development stage, and MAM systems at the operational stage. MA development can be carried out using the MADP platform (Mobile Application Development Platform). MADP includes MA management functions as if they were hosted on a service for download by users, as well as MA management tools for deploying and protecting applications [12].

3   Application of CALS Technology for Software Development

MA development support tools that provide the ability to adapt their interface to the end user should combine the typical capabilities of MA control systems at the stages of development and operation, as well as expand them by adding interface adaptation functions for the developed MA. Currently, CALS (Continuous Acquisition and Life Cycle Support) technologies are used for information support of various stages of the software life cycle. From the point of view of a software developer, this is a unified data transfer protocol, specialized sets of pre-developed components and libraries to support development, unified testing methods, inheritance support and access restriction (components can have the status of protection against unauthorized access).

The use of CALS to create high-tech applications, such as software, allows you to effectively, in a single way, solve the problems of ensuring the quality of products [13]. To support different stages of the software life cycle, various software tools are used. For each category of software, its own software tools have been developed that are focused on the specifics of this category of software.

MAs constitute an independent category of software designed to run on smartphones, tablets and other mobile devices and developed for a specific platform (iOS, Android, Windows Phone, etc.). A number of support tools at the requirements analysis and design stages are independent of the software category. However, at the stages of implementation, testing, operation of the MA, tools are developed that are focused on supporting this particular category of software, such as, for example, Android Studio, Visual Studio.

Most of the MA life cycle support tools used in the development of MA support only one stage of the life cycle, the execution of the remaining stages of the life cycle is implemented in other systems or programs that are not interconnected. There are a number of support tools that support the two stages of the MA life cycle (implementation, operation): appery.io (Appery developer), TheAppBuilder Thrive.App developer), iBuildApp (iBuildApp developer). However, such systems are focused on the development of business-oriented MA. MA support during the operation phase mainly consists in collecting statistics, managing the access rights of MA users and other functions intended for MA administrators.

4   Development of a Mobile Application Management System with an Adaptable User Interface

The concept of the MA control system with an adaptable user interface has been developed. The system combines the typical capabilities of MADM and MAM systems, and also expands them by adding functions that provide the ability to adapt the MA user interface. To implement such a system, methods have been developed for developing MAs with an adaptable interface and adapting interfaces of developed MAs for end users at the stage of MA operation.

The MA development method is based on modularization technology, i.e. allocation of some functionality of the program into logically complete, maximally independent modules that solve a specific user problem, with clearly marked external dependencies [14]. MA development is based on a multi-module architecture that includes three levels of modules: application module (APP), functional modules (Feature), library modules (Library). Developed modules can be stored in the modules repository as components for reuse in other MAs.

A technology for adapting the MA interface based on templates and a method for adapting the interface using a configuration panel (CP) built into the MA control system have been developed [15]. Interface templates developed at the interface design stage display the location of required and optional screen elements (controls, text fields, etc.) and options for their possible images. The configuration panel includes a settings area that contains widgets for setting up the interface elements of the configured MA and an area that displays the current page of the MA interface.

Interface customization includes the selection of interface elements to display from and their images on the MA screen (pictograms or other graphic illustrations). The process of generating the CP is based on validation, parsing the description of the MA interface and building a block of controls and a block of presentation elements based on tags and the information contained in them. The editor, which is also a part of the developed module, allows you to pre-generate a CP based on the prepared description and check the description file for errors.

The main functionality of the MADM subsystem includes viewing the repository of modules, selecting and connecting a single module to the project of the developed MA, adding a file describing the MA page templates, generating and editing the configuration panel for the MA. After testing the developed MA, modules determined by the developer as applicable for reuse can be added to the modules repository. Generation of MA interfaces in a web application includes the following features: adding an application to the web system (performed by the MA developer), with the name and description of the application, as well as a file describing the interface; interface descriptions must be done using JSX; editing the downloaded application; view the list of applications in the system; application deletion.

The main functionality of the MAM subsystem implements the configuration of MA screen templates for a specific user using the CP generated for this MA. The architecture of the MADM/MAM system is shown in Fig. 1.

The system is built on the REST architectural style, which establishes a one-to-one correspondence between the operations used when working with persistent data stores and HTTP methods, and thus ensures the independence of the way the MA connects to the database.

The MA control algorithm with an adaptable interface at the development and operation stages is shown in Fig. 2.

MADM/MAM system is implemented as a web application. Node.js platform was chosen for back-end development, HTML, CSS, JavaScript were used for front-end development. MongoDB is used as a database. To organize the interaction of the MA with the server, the HTTP protocol was used, to support the development of the MA, specialized sets of pre-developed components and libraries were used, support for inheritance and restriction of access to certain system components was implemented.

A client-side interface has been developed for visual management of the process of supporting the development of MA and adaptation of the developed MA for the end user.

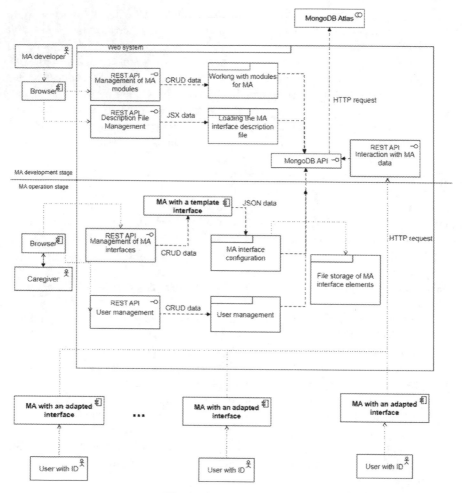

Fig. 1. System architecture

The screen for selecting modules from the repository of ready-made solutions for the developed MA includes forms for searching for a module by name and adding a module to the system. The code of the selected module is displayed on the screen for describing and adding a module to your own MA project. An example of screen forms for working with the repository of modules is shown in Fig. 3.

In the CP selection and addition mode, a list of previously developed CPs is displayed, which can be edited to configure the interface of the developed MA, and the option to add a new CP, if no suitable CP prototypes are found. The screen form of the page for generating the CP includes the visual presentation area of the CP for the MA and the CP editor (Fig. 4).

The screen form for selecting an overview and adding users includes a list of users for whom adaptation of the MA is required, and a form for adding new users (Fig. 5).

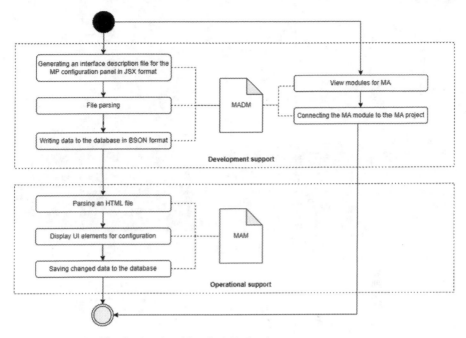

Fig. 2. An algorithm for MA development management

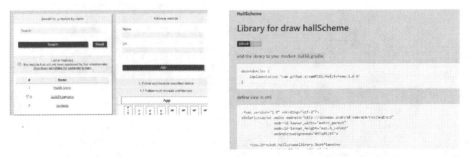

a) Module selection screen and   b) Screen form for adding a module to your
   module list view   own project

Fig. 3. Screen forms for working with module storages

The screen form of detailed viewing and editing of information about the user with the choice of MA for configuration includes a form for changing user data and selecting the MA for configuration (Fig. 6).

Fig. 4. Screen form for CP generation

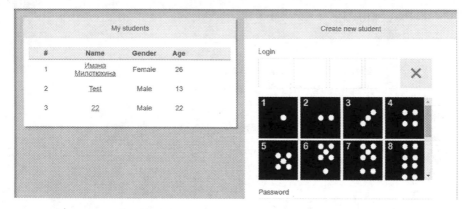

Fig. 5. Screen form for viewing and adding users

5   An Example of Developing an Adaptable MA in the System

The process of developing MA in the system includes the following steps: development of MA functionality; development of MA interface templates; creation of the MA project; search for modules in the repository of ready-made solutions that implement the required functions of the developed MA; connecting the selected modules to the MA project; implementation of the MA project; loading a file describing interface templates for generating CPs; adaptation of the interface for a specific user using the CP.

The system was applied to develop a mobile game "MoneyGame" to develop shopping skills for people with intellectual disabilities [16]. The MA project was developed on the basis of a multi-module architecture. Since the MA is intended for people with intellectual disabilities who cannot read and write, for self-authorization of users, a user authorization module using icons, developed in the framework of another project,

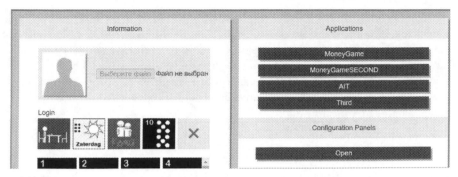

Fig. 6. Screen form of detailed viewing and editing of the user with the choice of MA for configuration

selected from the model repository, was included in the project. Screen forms are shown in Fig. 7.

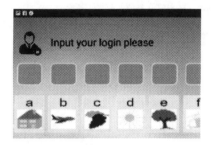 

a) On-screen authorization form using icons b) Screen form "Wallet filling"

Fig. 7. Screen forms of the game "MoneyGame"

At the development stage of the project, templates for the screen forms of the game were created. The description of screen form templates contained lists of required and optional interface elements and sets of pictogram options for representing controls and graphical objects of the MA game interface.

The developed game was tested with clients of the MAI Osterloo Medical Center, Belgium (https://www.mpi-oosterlo.be/) for people with intellectual disabilities. The center's employees configured the MA interface for each client, taking into account its capabilities and limitations. Testing showed that MAs with an interface adapted for end users were suitable for use by this category of people.

To evaluate the effectiveness of the MADM/MAM system, an analysis was made of the actual development time of the game using the MADM/MAM system and the time required to develop a "MoneyGame" level game without external integrations. The approximate time required to develop the MA and customize the UI of the MA was determined by experts in the field of MA and web development. The use of the developed system made it possible to reduce the development time of the MA interface by almost 4 times, and the MA itself by almost 2 times.

6 Conclusion

The use of the MADM/MAM system for developing MA for people with intellectual disabilities made it possible to increase the MA accessibility and applicability for different people with intellectual disabilities by customizing the interface for each user in accordance with its capabilities and limitations and significantly reduce the total time for MA development through the use of a unified multi-module architecture and the inclusion of ready-made modules in the MA project, as well as the generation of CPs for adapting the MA interface.

To improve the effectiveness of the proposed system, it is necessary to involve MA developers for people with intellectual disabilities in the development of MA using the system. This will allow you to replenish the storage of modules available for connection to new projects, and thus expand the capabilities of the system. As part of further work, it is planned to develop methods for collecting and analyzing data on user interaction with MAs developed using the system, and improving methods for adapting MAs to increase their accessibility for different categories of users.

References

1. Mobile App Statistics 2021: Downloads, Trends and Industry Profitability. https://vc.ru/mar keting/245003-statistika-mobilnyh-prilozheniy-2021-zagruzki-trendy-i-dohodnost-industrii. Accessed 10 June 2023]
2. Stocchi, L., Pourazad, N., Michaelidou, N., et al.: Marketing research on mobile apps: past, present and future. J. Acad. Mark. Sci. **50**, 195–225 (2022)
3. Chandran, V.P., Balakrishnan, A., Rashid, M., Pai Kulyadi, G., Khan, S., Devi, E.S., et al.: Mobile applications in medical education: a systematic review and meta-analysis. Proceedings PLoS One (2022). https://doi.org/10.1371/journal.pone.0265927
4. Thomas, C.G., Jayanthila Devi, A.: A study and overview of the mobile app development industry. Int. J. Appl. Eng. Manage. Lett. (IJAEML) **5**(1), 115–130 (2021). https://doi.org/10.5281/zenodo.4966320
5. Angelova, N.: Mobile applications for business. Trakia J. Sci. **17**, 853–859 (2019). https://doi.org/10.15547/tjs.2019.s.01.140
6. Lee, K.B., Lee, J.W.: Development of mobile adaptive learning application using adaptation layer. Int. J. Eng. Res. Technol. **11**(3) 2022
7. Grua, E. M., Malavolta, I., Lago, P.: Self-Adaptation in mobile apps: a systematic literature study 51–62 (2019). https://doi.org/10.1109/SEAMS.2019.00016
8. Kultsova, M., Potseluico, A., Zhukova, I., Skorikov, A., Romanenko, R.: A two-phase method of user interface adaptation for people with special needs. In: Kravets, A., Shcherbakov, M., Kultsova, M., Groumpos, P. (eds.) CIT&DS 2017. CCIS, vol. 754, pp. 805–821. Springer, Cham (2017). https://doi.org/10.1007/978-3-319-65551-2_58

9. Shabalina, O., Guriev, V., Kosyakov, S., Voronina, A., Moffat, D.C.: Adaptable mobile soft-ware for supporting daily activities of people with intellectual disabilities. In: Kravets, A., Groumpos, P., Shcherbakov, M., Kultsova, M. (eds) Creativity in Intelligent Technologies and Data Science. CIT&DS 2019 Communications in Computer and Information Science, vol. 1084, pp. 474–484 (2019). https://doi.org/10.1007/978-3-030-29750-3_37

10. Bos, A., Dekelver, J., Niesen, W., Shabalina, O.A., Skvaznikov, D., Hensbergen, R.: LIT: labour interest test for people with intellectual disabilities. In: Kravets, A., Shcherbakov, M., Kultsova, M., Groumpos, P. (eds.) CIT&DS 2017. CCIS, vol. 754, pp. 822–832. Springer, Cham (2017). https://doi.org/10.1007/978-3-319-65551-2_59

11. Adinugroho, T.Y., Gautama, J.B.: Review of multi-platform mobile application development using webview: learning management system on mobile platform. Proc. Comput. Sci. **59**, 291–297 (2015). https://doi.org/10.1016/j.procs.2015.07.568

12. Darren, H., Francesco, C., Nhien, A.: An effective approach to mobile device management: security and privacy issues associated with mobile applications. Digital Bus. **1**(1), 100001 (2020). https://doi.org/10.1016/j.digbus.2020.100001

13. The concept of "CALS", goals and areas of application of CALS-technologies. https://studfile.net/preview/577482/page:12/. Accessed 10 June 2023

14. Kosyakov S.V., Guryev V.V., Shabalina O.A. Mobile applications modularization technologies. In: Berestneva, O.G., Mitselya, A.A., Spitsyna, V.V., Gladkova, T.A. (eds.) V International Scientific Conference Information Technologies in Science, Management, Social Sphere and Medicine. In 2 parts, pp. 297–302 (2018)

15. Shabalina, O., Guriev, V., Kosyakov, S., Dmitriev, N., Davtian, A.: MADM system for the development of adaptable mobile applications for people with intellectual disabilities. In: Proceedings of the 11th International Conference on Information, Intelligence, Systems and Applications, pp. 1–8 (2020)

16. Shabalina, O., Voronina, A., Davtian, A., Delekelver, J., Peeters, E., Hensbergen, R.: A mobile game for training shopping skills for people with intellectual disabilities. In: Proceedings of the 12th European Conference on Game-Based Learning, ECGBL, pp. 565–573 (2018)

Models and Methods for Processing Heterogeneous Data for Assessing the State of a Human

Angelina Voronina[1]($\boxtimes$), Vladislav Guriev[1], David C. Moffat[2], and Irina Molodtsova[3]

[1] Volgograd State Technical University, Volgagrad, Russia
angelina.vaa@gmail.com
[2] Glasgow Caledonian University, Glasgow, UK
d.c.moffat@gcu.ac.uk
[3] Volgograd State Medical University, Volgograd, Russia

Abstract. The article discusses the concept of the human state, its types, methods of assessment. The state is a reaction of the body and psyche to external influences. The human state is the most important part of the entire mental regulation, play an essential role in any kind of activity and behavior. Considered types of functional states that affect human activity: fatigue; monotony; mental overstrain; tension/stress. The study presents the main technologies that can be used to assess a human state such as oculography and emotion recognition, the input parameters used for this and the ways to collect them. The main approaches of emotion recognition are considered, such as emotion recognition based on facial expressions; speech-based emotion recognition; emotion recognition based on physiological signals; gesture-based emotion recognition. As well as the main approaches of oculography: electrooculography; videooculography.

Keywords: human state · state assessment · methods of state assessment · assessing professional activity · electrooculography · videooculography · speech-based emotion recognition · emotion recognition based on physiological signals · gesture-based emotion recognition

1 Introduction

The assessment of a human state can be used for optimal construction of the production process, labor rationing, determining adequate physical and neuropsychic loads, and increasing neuropsychic stability, and carrying out preventive measures to combat various diseases. The optimal condition provides the possibility of successful and effective performance of a particular type of activity. The normal state of a person is an important part of any kind of activity.

2 Analysis of Ways to Assess a Human's State

2.1 Human State

The human state is considered in various studies. In [1] it is described that the human state is characterized by three levels:

A. G. Kravets et al. (Eds.): CIT&DS 2023, CCIS 1909, pp. 488–499, 2023.
https://doi.org/10.1007/978-3-031-44615-3_34

- physiological;
- psychophysiological;
- mental.

The set of possible human states can be different:

- relaxation;
- optimal working condition;
- fatigue;
- the state of neuropsychic tension;
- stress;
- borderline mental states caused by a violation of both the somatic and mental spheres, etc.

At the same time, the state is a reaction of the body and psyche to external influences [1].

In [2], the mental state of a person is defined as "an integral characteristic of mental activity over a certain period of time, showing the peculiarity of the course of mental processes depending on the objects and phenomena of reality, the previous state and personality properties."

The functional state is defined as "a relatively stable structure of the means of activity actualized by the subject in a specific situation, which reflects the specifics of the mechanisms of regulation of activity that have developed at the current time and determines the effectiveness of solving labor tasks" [3].

Some studies indicate that mental and functional state are interrelated. "The mental is based on the functional state of the brain. At the same time, if the mental state is a holistic integral characteristic of the activity of all elements involved in the mental act, then the functional state characterizes the processes of regulation in physiological systems that provide mental activity" [4].

2.2 Human State as a Way of Assessing Professional Activity

In [4] it is stated that "states are the most important part of the entire mental regulation, play an essential role in any kind of activity and behavior." In [5], the functional state is defined as an integral characteristic of the qualities and properties of a person, which determines the effectiveness of his activity and behavior. There are the following types of functional states that affect human activity [5]:

- fatigue;
- monotony;
- mental overstrain;
- tension/stress.

Fatigue is understood as a state in which there is a temporary decrease in performance, accompanied by a violation of coordination and exhaustion. The state of monotony is defined as a decrease in conscious control over activity. With mental overstrain, "a person does not accept uninteresting and meaningless activities" [5]. Stress is understood as a state of increased mobilization of "psychological and energy resources that develop in response to an increase in the complexity or subjective significance of activities" [3].

In [2] it is stated that the mental states of a person differ from functional states in that they reflect the attitude of the subject, his real life and work situation, involve mental processes and personal properties (motivational and emotional-volitional sphere, characterological traits) in the process of solving a problem situation.

2.3 Methods of Assessing the Human State

An assessment is understood as an action or an example of making a judgment about something [6]. Accordingly, the assessment of the state is usually understood as making a judgment about the state.

In [7], various groups of methods for assessing the human state are identified:

- self-report;
- observation of external manifestations (including using photo and video equipment);
- experiment in natural or laboratory conditions (simulation of a situation in which states may manifest themselves);
- projective methods (presenting a weakly structured stimulus material to a person for the projection of experiences, feelings and subsequent analysis of associations);
- psychophysiological methods (registration of psychophysiological changes that occur as a result of exposure to mental stimuli).

In some studies [8–11], emotion recognition and oculography are used as methods of observing external manifestations. Since software is used for these methods, the category of a person is a software user. Either a person (an expert) or a state assessment system (software) can interpret the results of the human state assessment. There are various human state assessment systems that use methods of assessing a human state, differing in the ways of data collection and methods of their interpretation. The process of assessing the human state in the IDEF0 notation is shown in the Figs. 1, 2.

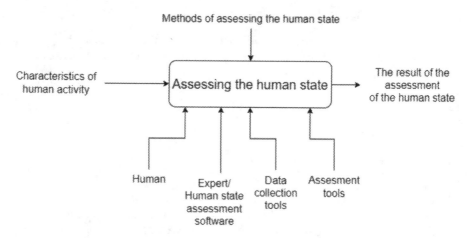

Fig. 1. The process of assessing the human state

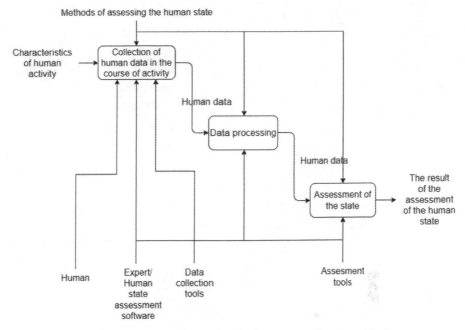

Fig. 2. The process of assessing the human state (decomposition)

In the software, either self-report methods or methods of external observation are used to assess a human state, presented in the information space. Self-reporting methods include online questionnaires, forms. With their help, the human (user) whose state needs to be assessed independently answers a number of questions. After processing the results of the responses, they receive a final assessment of the human state. Methods of external monitoring of users are implemented on the basis of oculographic data and analysis of user emotions. With the help of these methods, user data is collected in the course of his activity, and according to the data obtained, the software evaluates the human state. Thus, a human either evaluates his state himself, or does it by software. The input data in such systems are images/videos of the user's face or eyes, body movements, speech. To receive data from the user of the system, a video camera, microphone or various sensors (EEG, heart rate monitor) are used. The input data for assessing a human state using software and how to collect them are shown in Table 1.

The classification of software for assessing the human state according to the methods used is shown in Fig. 3.

2.4 Recognition of Emotions of the Software User

The following approaches to emotion recognition are distinguished [12]:

- emotion recognition based on facial expressions;
- speech-based emotion recognition;
- emotion recognition based on physiological signals;
- gesture-based emotion recognition.

Table 1. Input data and ways to collect them

Method	Input data	Collection method
Self-report	User responses	Online questionnaire, online forms
Emotion recognition	Video	Video camera
	Speech	Microphone
	EEG	Electroencephalograph
	Body movement	Video camera
Oculography	Potential difference	Electrodes
	Image of a human face	Video camera
	Image of human eyes in high resolution	Video camera

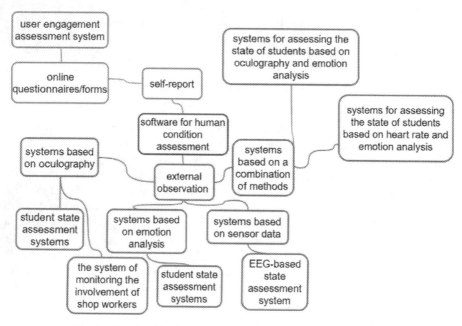

Fig. 3. The classification of software for assessing the human state

To solve the problem of emotion recognition, deep Learning algorithms (DL) of convolutional neural networks (CNN) are used [13]. DL methods allow for end-to-end learning directly from input images. CNN usually has three layers: convolution layer, subsampling layer, fully connected layer, FC layer, which perform activation volume transformation using a differentiable function. CNN takes an image as input data and combines this input data with a series of filter blocks to create maps of objects reflecting the spatial structure of the face image. Implementing one of the approaches to unification, i.e. maximum unification, minimum unification, or average unification, the second type of layer, called subsampling, is responsible for reducing the specified maps of objects. The last FC level of the CNN architecture calculates the probability that the entire input image belongs to a class. Thus, it is possible to determine the current emotional state of the user by the image of the user's face.

In [14], a three-dimensional CNN model for recognizing micro-images based on video is proposed, which extracts deeply studied features capable of characterizing the flow of small movements resulting from the smallest facial movements.

In [15], the implementation of the emotion recognition method based on the user's speech from images is presented. Since most of the existing pre-trained neural networks are designed to classify images, and the database of marked speech samples for emotion recognition is quite small, the paper proposes to solve the problem of emotion recognition based on speech as an image classification problem. To achieve this, the tagged speech samples were buffered into short-term blocks. A matrix of spectral amplification spectrograms was calculated for each block, converted to RGB (Red, Green, Blue) image format and transmitted as input data to a pre-trained CNN. After a relatively short training, CNN can be used to recognize emotions from unmarked (streamed) speech using the same process of converting speech into an image. The algorithm proposed in the paper is shown in the Fig. 4.

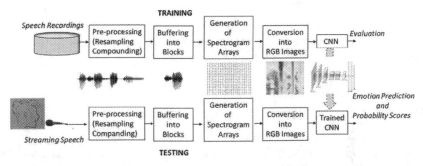

Fig. 4. Emotion recognition algorithm based on speech from [15]

An approach to speech-based emotion recognition using Deep Neural Networks (DNN) is proposed in [16]. The input signal is divided into segments, characteristics for DNN training are extracted from the segments. The trained DNN calculates the distribution of emotional state for each segment. From these distributions of emotional states, the emotional state of the entire expression is determined at the segment level. The speech-based emotion recognition algorithm proposed in the paper is shown in the Fig. 5.

A real-time emotion recognition system based on an electroencephalogram (EEG) was proposed in the study [17]. The paper uses a discrete wave transformer to extract the characteristics of the time-frequency domain and time windows of several seconds to perform classification by the developed system. The emotion classification problem is modeled as two separate binary classifiers: one for latency (low or high) and one for arousal (low or high). The output of both classifiers can then be combined to obtain the emotion category of one of the four quadrants of the Russell circular affect model. The

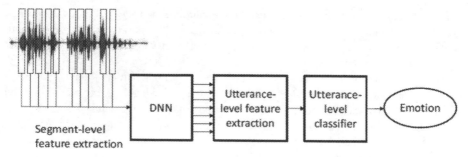

Fig. 5. The speech-based emotion recognition algorithm from [16]

characteristics for emotion recognition are extracted using a discrete wave transformer. The obtained characteristics are used to obtain the emotional state of a person using machine learning methods.

The study [18] suggests an approach to emotion recognition using deep learning based on the analysis of human body movements. For emotion recognition, a convolutional deep neural network of direct propagation (Feedforward Deep Convolution Neural Network, FDCNN) is used. As an input parameter for the approach, video is used, which is converted into frames. The received frames are saved as a training set and a set for checking the received recognition result. So the raw images are the input data for the first layers of the neural network. Three layers of the neural network are used for image processing, a semi-connected layer is used for emotion prediction. Two detesets are used in the work:

– emotional;
– The Geneva Multimodal Emotion Portrayals, GEMEP.

The first dataset contains five emotions (happiness, anger, sadness, insecurity and fear) and actions (jumping, sitting, walking), represented by twenty-nine actors. The second dataset is a set of audio and video recordings. Five main emotions (anger, joy, fear, sadness and pride) expressed by ten actors were used for the work. The recorded videos have a resolution of 720×576, and each video has a frame rate of 25 frames per second.

A system for recognizing emotions based on human body movements was proposed in [19]. The system recognizes five basic emotions: happiness, sadness, fear, anger and neutrality. The recording of body movements of non-professional actors is used as a dataset. Motion characteristics for determining the emotional state are calculated either for a single frame or for a sequence of frames stretched over a short period. As a result, the calculated motion characteristics characterize various aspects of human movement, such as trajectories or geometric properties of poses. To extract the characteristics of movements and emotion recognition based on them, variance analysis, multivariate variance analysis and a genetic algorithm based on binary chromosomes are used to select a subset of signs from the corresponding list of characteristics.

Table 2 shows the systems, models of emotion recognition and the input data used in them.

Table 2. Systems, models of emotion recognition with the input data used

System/model	Input data	Collection method
CNN model[14]	Video	Video camera
System [15]	Speech	Microphone
System [16]	Speech	Microphone
System [17]	EEG	Electroencephalograph
System [18]	Body movement	Video camera
System [19]	Body movement	Video camera

The easiest way to collect data is a video camera due to its availability. Most of the existing datasets are designed to work with images or videos of the user [13].

2.5 Oculography

Oculography is a method of tracking human eye movements. Two main types of oculography are described in [20]:

- electrooculography;
- videooculography.

Electrooculography is a method that uses sensors mounted on both sides of the eye, measuring the difference in position between them and identifying any type of movement in the eye. In electrooculography, an electrode consisting of two poles is used: a positive pole concentrated in relation to the cornea, and a negative pole concentrated in relation to the retina. A potential difference of 1 mV is created between the two poles, and the electric field is created due to the corneoretinial potential in front of the head. This is due to a change in the orientation of the head when the eyeballs rotate. The electrodes track eye movements in two possible directions, such as horizontal and vertical positions.

Video oculography is a method in which a camera is used to track eye movement. In this technology, one webcam is used to detect eye gaze based on the extraction of geometric features.

There are several methods of video oculography [21]:

- methods based on the appearance of the subject;
- methods based on the traits/characteristics of the subject;
- methods of analyzing the movement of the subject's head.

In methods based on the appearance of the subject, the problem of gaze assessment is solved through the function of displaying eye images in the direction of gaze. The pixel values of all eye areas in the image are used as input data. The output of the method is the direction of the gaze, which can be represented as coordinates (x; y) on the screen where the gaze falls, or the angles of rotation of the eye relative to the position of the subject's head. The display function allows you to associate the raw input image with the coordinates of the direction of view. The mapping function is trained on images of eyes with a known gaze direction using various regression methods, neural networks, local interpolation or Gaussian process. Input parameters and methods of their collection for oculography are presented in Table 3.

Table 3. Input parameters and methods of their collection for oculography

Input data	Collection method
Head movement	Video camera
Traits/characteristics	Video camera
Face image	Video camera
Difference in position between eyes	Electrodes, sensors

2.6 Application Areas

Health assessment can be used as a way to assess professional activity. States are the most important part of all mental regulation, play an essential role in any kind of activity and behavior.

In studies [22, 23], the assessment of the state is used to analyze the efficiency and effectiveness of employees of companies.

The assessment of the condition is also considered in the context of the learning process. In [24, 25], students' states are associated with their satisfaction, perceived learning and the quality of experience.

In [26], it is proposed to use the monitoring of the state of involvement of machine tool workers to analyze their behavior during visual inspection of machine tools.

Mind map of the human state is shown in Fig. 6.

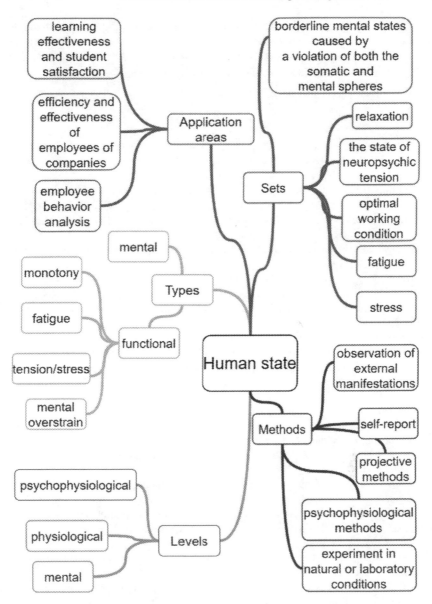

Fig. 6. Mind map of the human state

3   Conclusion

In this work, the concept of the human state is considered, its classification is given. The human condition is a complex characteristic, which involves various aspects, classifications. There are different methods of assessing human conditions. The methods of assessing the human state are considered. The paper also analyzes existing models and approaches to the recognition of human emotions and oculography using software tools, input parameters used in the approaches, and ways to collect them.

The assessment of a human state is applicable in various fields, for example, to assess the effectiveness of professional activity, to identify burnout of employees.

References

1. Druzhilov, S.A., Oleshchenko, A.M.: Mental states of a person at work: theoretical analysis of relationships in the system "Personality Properties - States - Processes": Psychological research, vol. 7(34), p. 10 (2014). (in Russian)
2. Levitov, N.D.: On the mental states of a person, p. 20 (1964). (in Russian)
3. Leonova, A.B., Kuznetsova, A.S.: Functional states and working capacity of a person in professional activity: Labor Psychology, Engineering Psychology Ergonomics, pp. 319–346 (2015). (in Russian)
4. Khvatova, M.V.: Human functional state as an integral characteristic: Bulletin of TSU, vol. 3(59), pp. 22–27 (2008). (in Russian)
5. Lavrova, M.S., Anikeeva, N.V.: Functional states as regulators of the success of professional activity: Psychology and pedagogy of service activities, vol. 1, pp. 53-55 (2019). (in Russian)
6. Merriam-Webster. https://www.merriam-webster.com/dictionary/assessment. Accessed 16 Nov 2021
7. Raspopin, E.V.: Methods of study and evaluation of mental states: Bulletin of the Ural Federal University, vol. 22(4), pp. 129–136 (2016). (in Russian)
8. Whitehill, J., et al.: The faces of engagement: automatic recognition of student engagement-from facial expressions. IEEE Trans. Affect. Comput. 5(1), 86–98 (2014). https://doi.org/10.1109/TAFFC.2014.2316163 (2014)
9. Mohamad Nezami, O., Dras, M., Hamey, L., Richards, D., Wan, S., Paris, C.: Automatic recognition of student engagement using deep learning and facial expression. In: Brefeld, U., Fromont, E., Hotho, A., Knobbe, A., Maathuis, M., Robardet, C. (eds.) ECML PKDD 2019. LNCS (LNAI), vol. 11908, pp. 273–289. Springer, Cham (2020). https://doi.org/10.1007/978-3-030-46133-1_17
10. Sharma, P. et al.: Student engagement detection using emotion analysis, eye tracking and head movement with machine learning. In: Reis, A., Barroso, J., Martins, P., Jimoyiannis, A., Huang, R.YM., Henriques, R. (eds.) Technology and Innovation in Learning, Teaching and Education. TECH-EDU 2022 Communications in Computer and Information Science, vol. 1720, pp. 52–68. Springer, Cham (2019). https://doi.org/10.1007/978-3-031-22918-3_5
11. Mido, J. A.: A Model to measure online student engagement using eye tracking and body movement analysis: MSIT Theses and Dissertations (2021)
12. Song, Z.: Facial expression emotion recognition model integrating philosophy and machine learning theory. Front. Psychol., Sec. Emotion Sci. 12 (2021). https://doi.org/10.3389/fpsyg.2021.759485
13. Khan, A. R.: Facial Emotion Recognition Using Conventional Machine Learning and Deep Learning Methods: Current Achievements, Analysis and Remaining Challenges: Artificial Intelligence & Data Analytics (AIDA) Lab, CCIS Prince Sultan University, Saudi Arabia
14. Li, J., et al.: Micro-expression recognition based on 3D flow convolutional neural network. Pattern Anal. Appl. 22, pp. 1331–1339 (2019). https://doi.org/10.1007/s10044-018-0757-5
15. Lech, M., Stolar, M., Best, C.: Real-time speech emotion recognition using a pre-trained image classification network: effects of bandwidth reduction and companding. Front. Comput. Sci. 2, 14 (2020). https://doi.org/10.3389/fcomp.2020.00014

16. Han, K., Yu, D., Tashev, I.: Speech emotion recognition using deep neural network and extreme learning machine. In: Interspeech (2014)
17. Bajada, J., Bonello, F.B.: Real-time EEG-based emotion recognition using discrete wavelet transforms on full and reduced channel signals (2021)
18. Santhoshkumar, R., Kalaiselvi, G.M.: Deep learning approach for emotion recognition from human body movements with feedforward deep convolution neural networks. Procedia Comput. Sci. **152**, 158–165 (2019)
19. Ahmed, F., Bari, A.S.M.H., Gavrilova, M.L.: Emotion recognition from body movement. IEEE Access, **8**, 11761–11781 (2020). https://doi.org/10.1109/ACCESS.2019.2963113
20. Asha, N.H., Ashwini, A., Harshitha, A.S.: Deepthi Chengappa Oculography: A review: perspectives in communication, embedded-systems and signal-processing (PiCES). Int. J. 3 (2019)
21. Larrazabala, A.J., Garcıa Cenab, C.E., Martinez, C.E.: Video-oculography eye tracking towards clinical applications: a review. Comput. Biol. Med. **108**, 57–66 (2019)
22. Marrelli, A.F.: Employee engagement and performance management in the federal sector. Performance Improvement **50**, 5–13 (2011)
23. Shrotryia, V.K., Dhanda, U.: Development of employee engagement measure: experiences from best companies to work for in India. Measuring Bus. Excellence **24**(3), 319–343 (2020)
24. Holmes, N.: Engaging with assessment: increasing student engagement through continuous assessment. Act. Learn. High. Educ. **19**(1), 23–34 (2017)
25. Gray, J.A., DiLoreto, M.: The effects of student engagement, student satisfaction, and perceived learning in online learning environments. Int. J. Educ. Leadersh. Prep. **11**, 89–119 (2016)
26. Bektas, K., et al.: EToS-1: eye tracking on shopfloors for user engagement with automation. In: Proceedings of the Workshop on Engaging with Automation (AutomationXP) co-located with the ACM Conference on Human Factors in Computing Systems (CHI 2022). New Orleans, LA, vol. 3154 (2022)

Comprehensive Assessment of the Driver's Functional Readiness Before the Trip

Maksim Dyatlov[1]([⊠]) [iD], Rodion Kudrin[2] [iD], Aleksej Todorev[1],
and Konstantin Katerinin[1] [iD]

[1] Volgograd State Technical University, Volgograd, Russia
makdyatlov@yandex.ru
[2] Volgograd State Medical University, Volgograd, Russia

Abstract. In urban passenger transportation (bus or trolleybus), the most common traffic situations are exit from the traffic flow and embedding in it, as well as the passage of regulated and non-regulated intersections. It is on the clear and skillful actions of the driver in these traffic situations that the safety in urban passenger transport mainly depends. In connection with the responsibility for the lives of passengers and other road users, the work of a driver is associated with high neuro-emotional stress. The intensity of the work of the driver of urban passenger transport is explained by the complexity of driving a vehicle in conditions of heavy traffic, shift work schedule, regulated time and speed along the route, and other factors. The high level of functional readiness of the driver before the trip is an important component of safety in the implementation of urban passenger transportation. In order to increase the prognostic significance of this approach, the key factors that reduce the level of pre-trip performance and significantly affect the level of the driver's functional readiness are identified. Simple and publicly available methods for assessing the functional state have been developed and selected, original and existing test tasks have been used to diagnose the degree of development of professionally important qualities of a driver. Software for personal computers has been developed, which makes it possible to carry out express diagnostics of the functional states of drivers based on the analysis of the obtained test values.

Keywords: Driver of Urban Passenger Transport · Simulation Test Tasks · Methods of Functional Express Diagnostics · Evaluation of the Driver's Pre-Trip Performance · Methods for Assessing the Driver's Functional Readiness

1 Introduction

Currently, there is a pronounced tendency to increase the car park and the intensity of traffic in the urban environment. At the same time, the energy saturation and dynamism of the car increase, and for the driver, the complexity of orientation in a traffic situation increases. Simultaneously the time for making a decision on the required maneuver (rearrangement, overtaking, turning, accelerating, decelerating or braking to a complete stop) is reduced. An increasing number of amateur drivers with insufficient qualifications and experience are involved in road traffic, and professionals (and amateurs with experience), unfortunately, do not always strictly comply with the rules of the road traffic rules (RTR) [1–4]. In addition, it should be borne in mind that a number of factors (fatigue, acute and chronic diseases, alcohol and other types of intoxication, stressful effects) have a negative effect on the driver, reducing his psychophysiological reliability. Increased demands on the driver have caused the need for preventive measures.

2 Analysis of Factors Affecting the Level of Performance of the Driver of the Vehicle and Diagnostic Tools

Of great importance in assessing the functional readiness of a driver before a trip are technical means for recording such physiological parameters as pulse rate and respiratory rate, blood pressure and other indicators that are used in assessing the current functional state of operators' professions (Fig. 1).

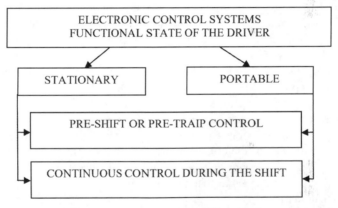

Fig. 1. Electronic systems for monitoring the functional state of the driver

The automated system of pre-trip medical examination (ASPTME) from the company «System Technologies» was created on the basis of pulse diagnostics and developments in space medicine. This company has developed equipment that allows you to track the first symptoms of diseases in drivers on the route. On prototypes, diagnostics was carried out according to 35 parameters, checking the effect of alcohol and various medications on physiological parameters, as well as stress and other factors. First of all, the work of the cardiovascular system was analyzed, in particular, changes in heart rate. Thanks to pulse wave research, it was possible to determine at what point a person loses the concentration and reaction speed necessary to drive a vehicle. Currently, ASPTME checks more than 40 indicators, which greatly simplifies the task of a health worker conducting a pre-trip inspection [5].

The remote pre-trip medical examination complex is a software and hardware complex for collecting information about the driver's condition. Includes work with the program and equipment for remote inspection. The medical worker receives the data when checking the health of the driver and makes a decision on admission to driving. The examination of the driver is carried out in several stages: 1) the driver enters his identification number and presses the button «Start inspection»; 2) personal data appears on the screen, and the driver needs to check them and select the type of inspection (pre-trip, post-trip, post-shift, etc.); 3) the driver measures blood pressure, for which the «Start» button on the tonometer is pressed; 4) body temperature is measured through a non-contact thermometer, for which you need to point the device at the forehead; 5) after that, it is necessary to determine the presence of alcohol vapor in the exhaled air, for which the driver activates the device and blows into the breathalyzer; 6) then you need to answer questions about how you feel (for example, «Are you feeling well?»); 7) the medical specialist receives the data and makes a decision on admission to the trip, confirming the conclusion with a personal signature [6].

The state of mental and physical health is an essential factor that makes it possible to predict the success of educational and professional activities, social adaptation of a person, correctional and developmental work with him. With the help of computer programs included in the psychodiagnostics module of the current state of a person of the complex «Psychology in personnel management» by the company «EFFECTON», it is possible to determine the current psychological state of a person, his emotional background, the degree of mobilization of physical and mental resources and other parameters [7].

The universal psycho-diagnostic complex – mobile complex «Avtopredpriyatie» (UPDK-MC «Avtopredpriyatie»), developed by the company «Neurocom», is designed to conduct a psychophysiological examination of drivers of motor transport enterprises. Testing is carried out according to an exclusive set of methods for various types of vehicles and modes of transportation. This procedure requires the presence of a professional psychologist on the staff of the organization. In order to increase the effectiveness of training, the software psychophysiological simulator «HORIZONT-2» was included in the UPDK-MC «Avtopredpriyatie» to train and increase the level of psychophysiological qualities of the driver [8].

The functional state of the driver before the trip depends on a large number of factors, under the influence of which his performance can significantly change [9] (Fig. 2).

When studying the factors that affect the psycho-physiological state of the driver and, accordingly, the safety and faultlessness of his work, special attention should be paid to those that lead to a clear decrease in functionality, but may not be felt or realized by a person. In such cases, the driver's pulse rate and blood pressure may be within acceptable limits (certain mental states, the initial stages of acute respiratory viral infections, the influence of biological rhythms, atmospheric phenomena, etc.).

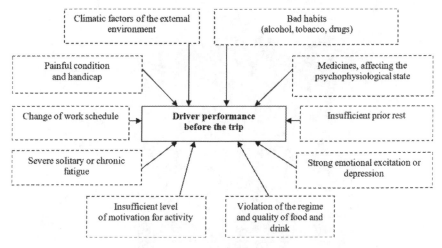

Fig. 2. The main factors that reduce the driver's performance before the trip

3 Determining the Level of Sensorimotor Reactions of the Driver Under Conditions of Computer Simulation of Traffic

The diagnostic capabilities of simulation test tasks were determined based on the results of expert assessments on a three-point scale, based on the following conditions: 3 points – the degree of development of this professionally important feature primarily affects the success of the given test; 1 point – the degree of development of this professionally important feature also affects the success of the given test, but is not decisive; 2 points – average value; 0 points – a professionally important feature does not affect the success of the test task. Experts could also use fractional scores. The results of the experts' answers on determining the most significant professionally important features for the effective implementation of the developed simulation test tasks are shown in Table 1 (Figs. 3 and 4).

To calculate the assessment of the success of the simulation test task, a generalized criterion for the reliability of maneuvering is proposed:

$$R = \frac{a_1 \cdot R_{PO} + a_2 \cdot R_{PK} + a_1 \cdot R_{DO} + a_2 \cdot R_{DK}}{2 \cdot a_1 + 2 \cdot a_2},$$

where a_1, a_2 are the coefficients of significance of the maneuvering criteria.

Since the main task of the simulation test tasks studied during the execution was to exclude the intersection of critical areas of the road and obstacles (which is considered the necessary conditions for road safety), then the values of the parameters R_{PK} and R_{DK} will largely affect the generalized assessment of success passing the test [10, 11].

As a result of the analysis of statistical data on various types of violations of the rules of the road by drivers of vehicles and the severity of the consequences of road accidents, the following values of the coefficients of significance of the maneuvering criteria were proposed: a1 = 0.2; a2 = 0.8.

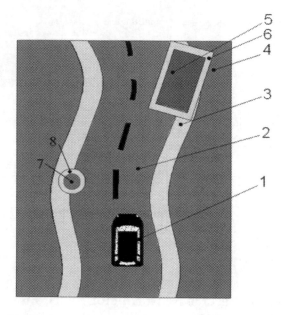

1 – «car» of the subject;

2 – «road» (safe zone);

3 – the contour of the «roadside» (dangerous zone);

4 – «near-road space» (critical zone);

5 – fixed or movable obstacles (critical zone);

6 – contour of a dangerous distance along the perimeter of a fixed or movable obstacle (danger zone);

7 – «road pit» (critical zone);

8 – contour of the dangerous distance along the perimeter of the «road pit» (danger zone).

Fig. 3. The layout of the objects of the simulation test task «Movement on a road with fixed obstacles» [10, 11]

A hardware-software complex for simulating traffic has been developed that implements the following functionality: testing a test subject in a virtual three-dimensional space using a «computer steering wheel»; registration of errors made by the user during the execution of the simulation test task; calculation of maneuvering criteria with respect to dangerous and critical zones of objects of the simulation test task, as well as the resulting maneuvering reliability criterion. Implementations of the model have been developed: «Movement along an empty road», «Movement along a road with fixed obstacles». The subject controls the «car» object with the help of the «computer steering wheel» manipulator.

Numerical intervals of values of the maneuvering reliability criterion according to the levels of functional readiness of drivers of urban passenger transport (bus, trolley bus) are proposed (Table 2).

Table 1. Diagnostic capabilities of the simulation test task «Driving on a road with fixed obstacles».

No. of professional quality in terms of importance	Professionally important feature of a driver	Leading Psychophysiological system	Diagnosed professionally important features of a driver, arithmetic mean values, points
1	Movement accuracy	Sensorimotor reactions	2,8
2	Reaction to a moving object	Sensorimotor reactions	2,6
3	Complex sensorimotor reactions	Sensorimotor reactions	2,6
4	Movement perception	Properties of visual, motor, vestibular, auditory analyzers	2,6
5	Concentration of attention	Attention properties	2,4
6	Movement coordination	Sensorimotor reactions	2,4
7	Distribution of attention	Attention properties	2,4
8	Simple sensorimotor response	Sensorimotor reactions	2,2
9	Perception of space	Properties of visual analyzer	2,1
10	Operational thinking	Properties of thinking	2

Thus, the method for determining the level of functional readiness according to the level of professionally important features of the person under study in the conditions of traffic simulation includes the following steps:

– adaptation of the test equipment under study to the ergonomics and the conditions of the virtual environment of the hardware-software complex when performing trial attempts of simulation test tasks;
– execution by the studied set of simulation test tasks in the environment of the hardware-software complex;
– calculation of the criterion of reliability of maneuvering, which determines the success of the execution of the studied simulation test tasks in the environment of the hardware-software complex.

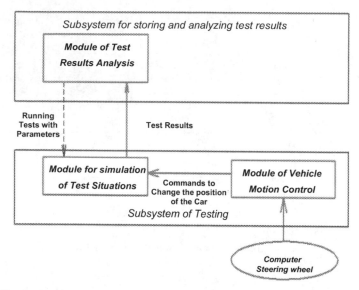

Fig. 4. Architecture of the hardware-software complex for traffic simulation

Table 2. Proposed numerical intervals of values of the criterion of reliability of maneuvering and the reduced criterion of maneuvering by levels of functional readiness.

Maneuvering reliability criterion R, points	Reduced maneuvering coefficient K_{CS}, points	Level of functional readiness
0–0,499	0–4,99	Very low
0,5–0,699	5–6,99	Low
0,7–0,849	7–8,49	Average
0,85–0,949	8,5–9,49	High
0,95–1	9,5–10	Very high

4   Comprehensive Assessment of the Functional Readiness of the Driver of Urban Passenger Transport Before the Trip

4.1   Methods for Assessing the Levels of Functional Readiness of the Driver

For effective activity in the «Man» – «Machine» – «Sign» system, sensory-perceptual-motor qualities (perception, attention, reaction) and intellectual (information processing, decision-making) are important. Various methods can be used to assess these qualities. The authors of the work propose to use the «Tables of Schulte» for express assessment of attention. When testing, the subject needs to visually find digital values and click on the corresponding images in the virtual space in ascending order. Samples can be repeated with different tables – one, two or more. The main indicator of the task completion is the execution time.

To process and interpret the test results, the indicators proposed by A. Yu. Kozyreva [12–14] were used: work efficiency (WE), degree of workability (DW), psychic stability (PS). The efficiency of work is estimated by the average work time in seconds:

$$WE = (T1 + T2 + T3 + T4 + T5/5),$$ (1)

where: T1–T5 — time of work with tables.

The degree of workability (DW) is calculated by the formula:

$$DW = T1/WE,$$ (2)

where: T1 — time of work with the 1st table, WE — work efficiency.

The result is less than 1 — an indicator of good workability, respectively, the more the indicator exceeds 1, the more the subject needs to prepare for the main work.

Psychic stability (resistance) is calculated by the formula:

$$PS = T4/WE,$$ (3)

where: T4 — work time with the 4th table, WE — work efficiency.

The proposed estimated values of the success of the test tasks in points are presented in Table 3.

Table 3. Proposed numerical intervals of success values for the performance of test tasks «Tables of Schulte» by levels of functional readiness.

Task execution time, s	310 and more	309-290	289-270	269-250	249-230	229-210	209-190	189-170	169-150	149 and less	310 and more	309-290
Estimated values, points	1	2	3	4	5	6	7	8	9		10	
Level of functional readiness	Very low		Low				Medium		High		Very High	

To assess the level of functioning of the cardiovascular system – the leading homeostatic system of the body – R. M. Baevsky [15] developed a special indicator called the index of functional changes (IFC) presented in Table 4. It is calculated in points according to the following formula [16]:

$$IFC = 0,011 \cdot HR + 0,014 \cdot SBP + 0,008 \cdot DBP + 0,014 \cdot A + 0,009 \cdot BW - 0,009 \cdot H - 0,27,$$ (4)

where HR is the heart rate in beats/min., SBP and DBP are systolic and diastolic blood pressure in mm Hg, A – age in years, BW – body weight in kg, H – height in cm.

The index of functional changes of differs from many similar indicators in those even small changes in frequently measured indicators, such as heart rate, blood pressure, body weight, change the value of this integrative indicator, indicating the direction of the shift

Table 4. Assessment of the degree of adaptation of the circulatory system.

Assessment of the degree of adaptation of the circulatory system	Values of IFC	Estimated values, points	Level of functional readiness
Satisfactory adaptation	Up to 2,59	9–10	High
Tension of adaptation mechanisms	2,60–3,09	6–8	Medium
Unsatisfactory adaptation	3,10–3,49	3–5	Low
Adaptation failure	3,50 and more	1–2	Very Low

in the functional state of the body. The information content of this parameter has been proven during mass surveys of many thousands of employees of various enterprises [16].

The authors of the work analyzed and selected factors that reduce the level of efficiency of the driver of a vehicle before going on a trip. An original questionnaire was developed, which contains 15 questions, including all the considered characteristics of reducing the level of pre-trip performance of the driver.

4.2 Computer System of Express Diagnostic

The concept proposed by the authors of the work is implemented in the system of pre-trip computer express diagnostics of the driver, which is intended for employees of motor transport enterprises responsible for the readiness of drivers for work. After passing a certain number of tests, the program compiles a psychophysiological portrait of the user's personality. The obtained values can be compared with previous results, thereby analyzing the values of possible deviations from the average for a given subject. The system is implemented as a three-level client-server application. The core of the system is a database server, which is an application that interacts with data (performs queries, stores and backs up data, monitors data integrity, checks user rights and privileges, keeps a transaction log). Any device with the ability to connect to the server via the Internet can be used as a client workplace. Choosing a client-server architecture allows you to reduce network traffic when making requests. Storing business rules on the server side avoids code duplication in applications connected to a shared database. The system does not impose serious requirements on workstations due to the possibility of storing various procedures on the server. The server is responsible for user interaction with the database and is the initiator of the testing process. On the client side, the functionality associated with providing the user with an interface for viewing and editing is implemented. However, the system also has the ability to store data on the client side through the TaffyDB library. This feature allows you to use the offline version of the application without requiring an Internet connection [10, 17]. Screen forms of the system are shown in Fig. 5–7.

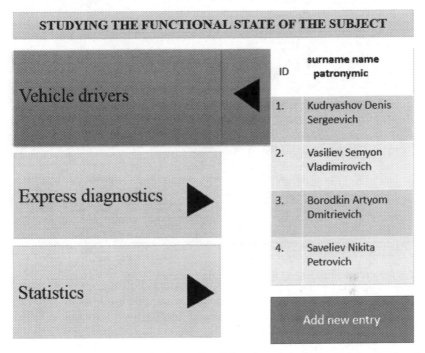

Fig. 5. Screen form of the system in the mode of choosing methods for studying the functional state of the subject.

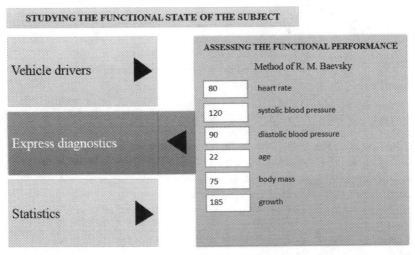

Fig. 6. Screen form of the system in the mode of assessing the functional performance of the researched according to the method of R. M. Baevsky.

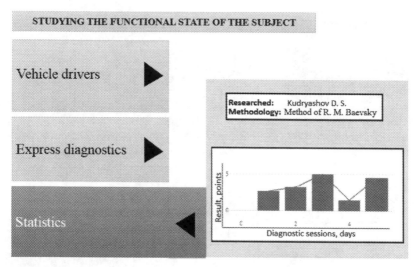

Fig. 7. Screen form of the system in the mode of displaying statistics of the results of test tasks performed by the subject.

Using the web application allows the driver to perform test tasks online, which, as a result of interactive interaction with a medical worker, makes it possible to receive generalized recommendations on readiness for work.

Each of the proposed methods can be used alone or in combination with others. This allows the medical worker to select the necessary, in his opinion, the number of tests and calculated characteristics in addition to the main procedures currently used at the stage of pre-trip express diagnostics of drivers.

4.3 Recommendations for the Use of Test Tasks at the Stage of Pre-trip Express Diagnostics of Drivers

The methodology for a comprehensive assessment of the functional readiness of an urban passenger transport driver is formed from the following test methods:

- determination of the level of professionally important qualities in the conditions of traffic simulation on the hardware-software complex of traffic simulation. At the first stage, the subject performs the task under the conditions of the «Empty Road» test in order to adapt to the testing conditions. Further, the researcher is invited to perform two attempts of the test task «Road with fixed obstacles». The final value of the maneuvering reliability criterion is determined by the choice of the most successful result of the simulation test task. The duration of testing is about 10 min;
- determination of the stability of attention and a simple sensorimotor reaction using the test task «Tables of Schulte». The researcher is offered five tables in turn, on which numbers from 1 to 25 are arranged in random order. The researcher searches on the monitor screen and points with the mouse cursor to rectangular areas with numbers in ascending order. Testing is carried out with five different tables. The duration of testing is about 3–5 min;

– determination of the level of functioning of the cardiovascular system using the index of functional changes. The indicators necessary to calculate the index are measured: heart rate in beats per minute; systolic and diastolic blood pressure in mm Hg. Indicators such as age in years, body weight in kg, height in cm, after the first test, are stored in the database of the subject and can be used in further interpretation of the measurement results.

5   Conclusion

The proposed method of pre-trip computer assessment of the functional readiness of an urban passenger transport driver makes it possible to analyze and evaluate the driver's readiness for an extended set of characteristics that affect the efficiency of labor activity. A comprehensive assessment of the psychophysiological status of the subject, based on a multidimensional analysis of various characteristics of professionally important qualities, taking into account the possibility of assessing the level of their development and training. Only a multi-component assessment makes it possible to obtain a complete picture of the functional readiness of an urban passenger transport driver in the context of his professional activity.

The implementation of the proposed methodology in the pre-trip diagnostics system allows using it as one of the elements of a comprehensive assessment of the safety level of the «Driver» – «Car» – «Road» – «Environment» system, as well as for making a decision on the driver's functional readiness for working activities.

References

1. Ageev, E.V., Vinogradov, E.S., Novikov, A.N.: Methodology for determining the professional qualities of motor vehicle drivers. In the collection: IOP Conference Series: Materials Science and Engineering. Ser. "International Conference on Modern Trends in Manufacturing Technologies and Equipment, ICMTMTE 2020 – Machine Science, Mechanization, Auotomatization and Robotics", pp. 052–078 (2020)
2. Kuryanova, O., Zhankaziev, S., Gavrilyuk, M., Rubtsov, M.: A method of performance audit of constituent entities of the Russian Federation to prevent road accident injuries. In: Thirteenth International Conference on Organization and Traffic Safety Management in Large Cities (SPbOTSIC 2018). Elsevier, Transportation Research Procedia, vol. 36, pp. 398–403 (2018)
3. Liu, F., Chen, C., Dong, G.: Example verification of a safety evaluation model for road passenger transportation. In: Jain, L.C., Kountchev, R., Hu, B., Kountcheva, R. (eds.) Smart Communications, Intelligent Algorithms and Interactive Methods. SIST, vol. 257, pp. 223–232. Springer, Singapore (2022). https://doi.org/10.1007/978-981-16-5164-9_27
4. Mexquititla, V.M.C., Rivera-Hernández, M.A., Torres-San Miguel, C.R.: Intercity bus occupant safety. In: Quaglia, G., Gasparetto, A., Petuya, V., Carbone, G. (eds.) I4SDG 2021. MMS, vol. 108, pp. 182–192. Springer, Cham (2022). https://doi.org/10.1007/978-3-030-87383-7_20
5. Williamson, A., Lombard, D.A., Folkard, S., et al.: The link between fatigue and safety. Accid. Anal. Prev. **43**(2), 498–515 (2011)
6. Baek, H.J., Cho, J.: Novel heart rate variability index for wrist-worn wearable devices subject to motion artifacts that complicate measurement of the continuous pulse interval. Physiol. Meas **40**(10), 1050–1010 (2019). https://doi.org/10.1088/1361-6579/ab4c28

7. Zelikov, V.A., Klimova, G.N., Strukov, Y.V., Artemov, A.Y., Likhachev. D.V.: Increasing psychological stability of vehicle drivers. In: Popkova, E. (eds.) Ubiquitous Computing and the Internet of Things: Prerequisites for the Development of ICT. Studies in Computational Intelligence, vol. 826, pp. 1129–1136. Springer, Cham (2019). https://doi.org/10.1007/978-3-030-13397-9_115

8. Complex UPDK–MK «Avtopredpriyatiye». https://www.neurocom.ru/products/professio nal-systems/avtopredpriyatie/. Accessed 20 June 2023

9. Zhang, T., Limin, J., Zhao, C., Wang, Y.: Research on the construction of human-factor complex risk network model for urban rail transit operation. In: Qin, Y., Jia, L., Liang, J., Liu, Z., Diao, L., An, M. (eds) Proceedings of the 5th International Conference on Electrical Engineering and Information Technologies for Rail Transportation (EITRT) 2021. EITRT 2021. LNEE, vol. 868, pp. 146–152. Springer, Singapore (2022). https://doi.org/10.1007/ 978-981-16-9913-9_17

10. Dyatlov, M., Shabalina, O., Todorev, A., Kudrin, R., Sentyabryov, N.: Method of preliminary computer evaluation of professional readiness of the vehicle driver. In: Kravets, A.G., Groumpos, P.P., Shcherbakov, M., Kultsova, M. (eds.) CIT&DS 2019. CCIS, vol. 1084, pp. 378–392. Springer, Cham (2019). https://doi.org/10.1007/978-3-030-29750-3_30

11. Dyatlov, M., Shabalina, O., Todorev, A., Kudrin, R., Komarov, Y., Katerinin, K.: Development of specialized methods and algorithms for preventive monitoring of reliability. In: Kravets, A.G., Shcherbakov, M., Parygin, D., Groumpos, P.P. (eds.) CIT&DS 2021. CCIS, vol. 1448, pp. 598–611. Springer, Cham (2021). https://doi.org/10.1007/978-3-030-87034-8_44

12. Torrance, E.P.: The nature of creativity as manifest in the testing. In: Sternberg, R., Tardif, T., (eds.) The Nature of Creativity.: Cambridge, Press, pp. 43–75 (1988)

13. Schneider, R.A.: Test too far. OECD Obs. **242**, 12–15 (2004)

14. Sagar, S., Stamatiadis, N., Wright, S., Cambron, A.: Identifying high-risk commercial vehicle drivers using sociodemographic characteristics. Accid. Anal. Prev. **143**, 105582 (2020)

15. Bayevskiy, R.M.: Predicting the state on the verge of norm and pathology. Moskva, p. 298 (1979)

16. Neureiter, E., et al.: An introduction to the «Psycho-Physiological-Stress-Test» («PPST») – a standardized instrument for evaluating stress reactions. https://journals.plos.org/plosone/art icle?id. https://doi.org/10.1371/journal.pone.0187859. Accessed 02 Mar 2019

17. Beskishkin, A.S., Shabalina, O.A., Dyatlov, M.N.: The system of pre-trip express diagnostics of drivers of passenger vehicles. Eng. Bull. Don: Electron. Sci. J. 5, 12 (2019). http://ivdon. ru/ru/magazine/archive/n5y2019/5965

Exploring the Interaction Between Daytime and Situational Sleepiness: A Pilot Study Analyzing Heart Rate Variability

Valeriia Demareva$^{(\boxtimes)}$, Nikolay Nazarov , Inna Isakova , Andrey Demarev ,
and Irina Zayceva

Lobachevsky State University, Nizhny Novgorod 603022, Russia
valeriia.demareva@fsn.unn.ru

Abstract. Nowadays, sleepiness research is particularly relevant in fields like transportation, where drowsiness can lead to accidents and fatalities. Developing an accurate sleepiness detector requires a deep and fundamental understanding of sleepiness processes and mechanisms. The purpose of the current study was to investigate the features of evening-night situational sleepiness and heart rate metrics in individuals with different levels of daytime sleepiness. A collection of 32 recordings was gathered from the Subjective Sleepiness Dynamics Dataset. Daytime sleepiness was assessed using the Epworth Sleepiness Scale, while various domain heart rate variability (HRV) metrics and situational sleepiness (measured by the Karolinska and Stanford Sleepiness Scales) were assessed at 8 PM and 10 PM. The study results demonstrated that situational sleepiness increased from 8 PM until 10 PM only in individuals with lower normal daytime sleepiness, which was accompanied by a decrease in TINN, possibly indicating an increase in fatigue. On the other hand, individuals with higher normal daytime sleepiness did not experience a change in subjective sleepiness, but their sympatho-vagal index decreased, and fragmentation heart rate metrics increased from 8 PM to 10 PM. Thus, the results confirmed the hypotheses regarding a significant increase in subjective sleepiness in individuals with lower daytime sleepiness from evening till night, and the different dynamics of HRV metrics from evening till night in individuals with different daytime sleepiness levels.

Keywords: Daytime Sleepiness · Situational Sleepiness · Heart Rate Variability

1 Introduction

Information saturation and life under conditions of technogenic stress make the problem of monitoring human condition increasingly relevant. This becomes particularly significant for professionals whose work is associated with the risks of serious consequences due to human factors. Decreased productivity and an increase in the number of errors are traditionally linked to fatigue [1]. Many authors also consider the influence of sleepiness or drowsiness on cognitive abilities, performance, and the number of errors in task execution [2, 3]. The impact of these factors was assessed in studies of optimal and extreme

A. G. Kravets et al. (Eds.): CIT&DS 2023, CCIS 1909, pp. 513–524, 2023.
https://doi.org/10.1007/978-3-031-44615-3_36

human conditions while driving a car [4–6], in aviation [7], in maritime operations [3], and in railway transport management [8, 9]. Fischer et al. use a 'risk index' related to four components of work schedule: working time duration, shift type (night or day), number of short breaks, and presence of a full rest break, to create a model for predicting accidents in the workplace [1]. However, the same authors' research showed that the distribution of error risk during work throughout the day was associated with age. Similar data exist in other studies: age-related changes occurred in the daily dynamics of sleepiness [10]. Rabat et al. concluded that the degree of impairment of performance and the time required for recovery also depended on individual factors, such as the initial condition and the ability to remain actively engaged in the process [11]. Thus, it is evident that creating a predictive model for critical situations considering all possible personal characteristics of different population groups is not feasible.

The optimal solution here is to develop technologies that allow real-time monitoring of human conditions characterized by reduced cognitive functions, attention loss, performance, and vigilance. And in this case, sleepiness is an important concept for research. Sleepiness became the focus of scientific inquiry during the 20th century. The structured methods of sleepiness assessment emerged initially within medical research and the study of the effects of drugs on sleep [16, 19]. In 1973, the Stanford Sleepiness Scale (SSS) was proposed as a new approach to sleep assessment and has become the gold standard for many studies of situational sleepiness [20]. The SSS is a self-assessment scale that is used to quantify and situationally assess progressive stages of sleepiness. In 1990, the Karolinska Sleepiness Scale was proposed [21], which is also often used in situational sleepiness research. The next round of sleep studies is associated with the introduction of the Epworth Sleepiness Scale (ESS) into research practice [22]. The ESS is a simple, self-administered questionnaire that measures the subject's general (not situational) level of daytime sleepiness. The scales are still used in most studies on sleep and sleepiness, but authors haven't found any studies discovering the influence of daytime sleepiness on situational evening sleepiness.

As physiology and psychology advanced, along with a burgeoning understanding of the nervous system's structure and operations, specific facets of sleepiness became amenable to objective examination. Analysis of physiological indicators involves using methods such as electroencephalography, electrocardiography, photoplethysmography, electrooculography, electromyography, and conclusions can be drawn based on the study of breathing characteristics. Physiological indicators remain the most accurate way to determine a person's condition in the 'drowsiness-vigilance' paradigm. One of the common solutions related to monitoring a person's condition is the use of technologies that involve collecting and analyzing data about heart activity. Portable wearable sensors allow for the recording of electrocardiographic signals and inference of the human nervous system's function based on heart rate, heart rate variability, frequency domain metrics, and others [12]. Another widely used method in research to obtain similar information is photoplethysmography, which does not only provides information on essential parameters such as pulse wave transit time [13] but also allows for the reconstruction of the actual electrocardiographic signal based on this data [14]. Additionally, in recent years, attempts have been made to obtain non-invasive information about heart activity using the analysis of the distance between the sensor and the person. This includes the use of Time-of-Flight cameras [15] and Doppler radar [16]. However, Kim et al. were only able to obtain data on heart rate using Doppler radar, and the accuracy for heart rate variability analysis proved insufficient. Technologies related to heart rate data collection can be applied for monitoring various conditions, such as driver sleepiness or drowsiness [17].

But the level of human sleepiness varies throughout the day. Studies show that the early morning hours are characterized by high subjective sleepiness, which then decreases during the day, followed by a steady increase in subjective sleepiness after 8 p.m. [23–25]. In experiments involving sleep deprivation, the baseline night typically exhibits a classical pattern, the deprivation period shows fluctuations in sleepiness levels above average, and the recovery time shows a pattern of daytime sleepiness returning towards the initial level, though some level of sleepiness remains elevated [25]. It would be reasonable to assume that individuals with sleep disturbances or engaged in shift work, alternating between day and night shifts, may experience different dynamics of subjective sleepiness.

Johns, while developing a new model for human sleepiness and alertness states, suggested that measuring the level of sleepiness requires new parameters that need to be distinguished from situational sleepiness or the average propensity to sleep [26]. In addition to the time of day and the amount of previous sleep, he introduced the third factor into the model, referred to as 'Process A,' which is related to individual characteristics of the nervous system in responding to a specific pattern of sensory signals. Johns noted that further research is needed to explain the physiological basis of sleepiness scales [27]. Krylova et al. associated levels of alertness with microstates of the brain, recorded using EEG. Sleepiness was characterized by increased power in delta and theta rhythms, while wakefulness is associated with alpha rhythms in the occipital regions of the brain, and the transition from wakefulness to sleepiness is accompanied by a shift of alpha rhythms towards frontal areas [28].

There have also been attempts to compare sleepiness scales' scores with physiological data. In a study by Taranto Montemurro et al., patients with chronic obstructive syndrome and excessive daytime sleepiness, according to the ESS, had different heart rate variability compared to those without excessive daytime sleepiness [29]. Ha et al., while studying heart rate variability in people with chronic obstructive apnea, found a correlation between the ESS score and increased sympathetic activity and reduced parasympathetic activity [30]. In patients with renal insufficiency, the total ESS score did not show significant correlation with heart rate variability [31].

We could not identify any studies that compare levels of subjective sleepiness with various physiological indicators of nervous system activity in healthy individuals. However, objective data related to daytime sleepiness are crucial for better understanding this phenomenon and for the development of more accurate systems for detecting situational sleepiness. High ESS scores may indicate sleep disorders [27]. Moreover, sleepiness, being a significant factor influencing a person's decision to go to sleep, serves as an important signal for maintaining a stable sleep pattern [24]. It is conceivable that a relatively high level of daytime sleepiness in some individuals may be due to their low sensitivity to subjective sleepiness, leading to sleep schedule disturbances or being a consequence of sleep disruptions. Individuals might struggle with sleepiness throughout the day, expending more resources in the process, which can subsequently affect their evening state and the transition to sleep.

We tested two hypotheses in our pilot study:

1. Subjective sleepiness will increase more in people with lower daily sleepiness from evening till night.
2. Heart rate metrics will demonstrate different dynamics from evening till night in people with different daytime sleepiness.

The main objective of the current study was to investigate the differences in body functioning among people with different daytime sleepiness levels.

2   Materials and Methods

2.1   Study Sample

Recordings from 32 participants were obtained from the Subjective Sleepiness Dynamics Dataset (SSDD [32]). These participants went to bed between 10:30 PM and 11:00 PM, and their heart rate data were gapless and artifact-free for a minimum of 4 min around each of the 8 PM and 10 PM time points.

SSDD contains heart rate, social-demographic, and sleepiness data. The full description of the experimental design is provided in [32] and is illustrated in Fig. 1.

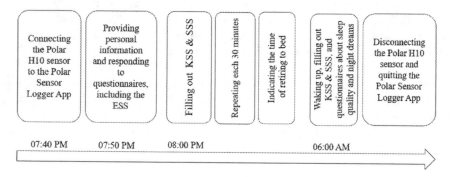

Fig. 1. Experimental design.

Participants initiated the data collection process by connecting the Polar H10 sensor to the Polar Sensor Logger App at 07:40 PM. Then they provided personal information and responded to various questionnaires, including the ESS, using the UnnCyberpsy web-application created by authors. Subsequently, at 08:00 PM and every 30 min thereafter, they completed cyclic tests (the KSS and the SSS) until they retired to bed. Thus, UnnCyberpsy uses a branching algorithm. The participant completes cyclic KSS and SSS tests every half an hour, but if they indicate that they have gone to sleep, UnnCyberpsy stops the cyclicity. The next login to the system is possible at 06:00 AM to complete the final stage of the experiment. The operation of the branching algorithm in UnnCyberpsy is demonstrated in Fig. 2.

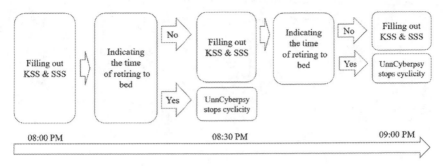

Fig. 2. Branched algorithm demonstration implied in UnnCyberpsy.

2.2 Data Analysis

The data were preprocessed using Jupyter Notebook (Python). For data filtering, NN intervals lasting less than 400 ms or exceeding 1300 ms, as well as those deviating more than 70% from the median of the five preceding intervals, were excluded from the analysis. Subsequently, 4-min heart rate recordings (NN intervals) were chosen for each participant at 8 PM and 10 PM time points. The 'neurokit2' module was used to calculate the time, frequency, and nonlinear domain metrics, as well as fragmentation metrics [33] within each time point. To calculate the dynamics indices of heart rate metrics between 8 PM and 10 PM, the following formula was used:

$$(10\,\text{PM value} - 8\,\text{PM value})/8\,\text{PM value} \tag{1}$$

Statistical analysis was performed using the 'scipy.stats' module in Jupyter Notebook. The Mann-Whitney U test was used to assess differences in situational sleepiness scores and heart rate variability metrics between different levels of daytime sleepiness at 8 PM and 10 PM time points. The Wilcoxon signed-rank test was used to assess differences in sleepiness scores and heart rate metrics between the 8 PM and 10 PM time points within different levels of daytime sleepiness.

3 Results

3.1 Grouping the Sample by Daytime Sleepiness Level

According to the ESS manual, the scores on the ESS were marked based on the level of daytime sleepiness. The resulting distribution is presented in Table 1.

As only three participants had a daytime sleepiness level classified as 'moderate excessive' or 'mild excessive,' only participants with 'lower normal' (N = 17) and 'higher normal' (N = 12) were included for further comparative analysis. In the sections below, we analyzed the situational sleepiness and heart rate metrics at 8 PM and 10 PM in these two groups.

Table 1. Daytime Sleepiness Level Distribution within the sample.

Daytime Sleepiness Level	Count
'lower normal'	17
'higher normal'	12
'moderate excessive'	2
'mild excessive'	1

3.2 Subjective Sleepiness Comparison within Different Daily Sleepiness Levels at 8 PM and 10 PM

Tables 2 and 3 present information on the differences in the KSS and SSS scores within 8 PM and 10 PM in 'lower normal' and 'higher normal' daytime sleepiness.

Table 2. KSS Scores Comparison within 8 PM and 10 PM in Different Levels of Daytime Sleepiness ('lower normal' and 'higher normal') (U – the value of Mann-Whitney U test, W – the value of Wilcoxon signed-rank test, p – p-value).

Time point	'lower normal' N = 17	'higher normal' N = 12	U	p
8 PM	4.3	5.3	71	0.169
10 PM	5.9	5.8	96	0.804
W	4	17		
p	0.002	0.511		

Table 3. SSS Scores Mean Values within 8 PM and 10 PM in Different Levels of Daytime Sleepiness ('lower normal' and 'higher normal') (U – the value of Mann-Whitney U test, W – the value of Wilcoxon signed-rank test, p – p-value).

Time point	'lower normal' N = 17	'higher normal' N = 12	U	p
8 PM	2.4	3.0	74	0.207
10 PM	3.5	3.7	89.5	0.575
W	0	13.5		
p	0.003	0.282		

The data in Tables 2–3 demonstrate that significant differences in situational sleepiness between 8 PM and 10 PM were found only for 'lower normal' daytime sleepiness for the KSS (W = 4; p = 0.002) and for the SSS (W = 0; p = 0.003). No significant differences were observed between 'lower normal' and 'higher normal' daytime sleepiness for any situational sleepiness scale, neither at 8 PM nor at 10 PM.

3.3 Heart Rate Metrics Comparison within Different Daily Sleepiness Levels at 8 PM and 10 PM

Only two heart rate variability time or frequency domain metrics appeared to demonstrate significant differences in 'lower normal' and 'higher normal' daytime sleepiness at 8 PM and 10 PM – TINN (baseline width of the minimum square difference triangular interpolation) and LF/HF (a ratio of low frequency to high frequency band power). Tables 4 and 5 contain information about the differences in the TINN and LF/HF metrics between 8 PM and 10 PM in 'lower normal' and 'higher normal' daytime sleepiness.

Table 4. TINN Mean Values at 8 PM and 10 PM in Different Levels of Daytime Sleepiness ('lower normal' and 'higher normal') (U – the value of Mann-Whitney U test, W – the value of Wilcoxon signed-rank test, p – p-value).

Time point	'lower normal' N = 17	'higher normal' N = 12	U	p
8 PM	189.8	212.9	86	0.491
10 PM	149.4	205.1	76.5	0.268
W	34	37		
p	0.045	0.910		

Thus, TINN was lower at 10 PM compared to 8 PM in 'lower normal' daytime sleepiness (W = 34; p = 0.045). TINN didn't differ from 8 PM to 10 PM in 'higher normal' daytime sleepiness (W = 37; p = 0.910). Additionally, no differences were found for between-sample comparison – neither at 8 PM (U = 86; p = 0.491), nor at 10 PM (U = 76.5; p = 0.268).

Table 5. LF/HF Mean Values at 8 PM and 10 PM in Different Levels of Daytime Sleepiness ('lower normal' and 'higher normal') (U – the value of Mann-Whitney U test, W – the value of Wilcoxon signed-rank test, p – p-value).

Time point	'lower normal' N = 17	'higher normal' N = 12	U	p
8 PM	5.8	4.41	101	0.982
10 PM	4.2	2.7	91	0.642
W	52	11		
p	0.263	0.027		

LF/HF decreased from 8 PM to 10 PM in 'higher normal' daytime sleepiness (W = 11; p = 0.027). LF/HF didn't differ from 8 PM to 10 PM in 'lower normal' daytime sleepiness (W = 52; p = 0.263). Additionally, no differences were found for between-samples comparison – neither at 8 PM (U = 101; p = 0.982), nor at 10 PM (U = 91; p = 0.642).

As for fragmentation metrics, significant differences between 8 PM and 10 PM were found only for 'higher normal' daytime sleepiness. These differences were observed in PIP (percentage of inflection points of the RR intervals series), IALS (inverse of the average length of the acceleration/deceleration segments), and PSS (percentage of short segments) – see Table 6.

Table 6. PIP, IALS, and PSS Mean Values at 8 PM and 10 PM in 'higher normal' Daytime Sleepiness (W – the value of Wilcoxon signed-rank test, p – p-value).

Metrics	8 PM	10 PM	W	p
PIP	0.469	0.552	6	0.007
IALS	0.457	0.542	8	0.012
PSS	0.701	0.816	6	0.007

The data in Table 6 demonstrate that all the mentioned fragmentation metrics (PIP, IALS, and PSS) increased from 8 PM to 10 PM in participants with 'higher normal' daytime sleepiness.

3.4 HRV Dynamics Comparison within Different Levels of Daytime Sleepiness

Only the dynamics indices of fragmentation metrics (calculated as described in (1)) appeared to demonstrate significant differences in 'lower normal' and 'higher normal' daytime sleepiness. In addition to the metrics presented in Table 6, the dynamics of PAS (Percentage of NN intervals in alternation segments) also changed - see Table 7.

Table 7. Fragmentation Metrics' Dynamics in 'lower normal' and 'higher normal' Daytime Sleepiness (U – the value of Mann-Whitney U test, p – p-value).

Metrics	'lower normal' N = 17	'higher normal' N = 12	U	p
PIP	-0.01	0.23	45	0.012
IALS	0.00	0.24	46	0.014
PSS	-0.01	0.18	35	0.003
PAS	0.18	1.25	52	0.028

Thus, the PIP index (U = 45; p = 0.012), IALS index (U = 46; p = 0.014), PSS index (U = 35; p = 0.003), and PAS index (U = 52; p = 0.028) increased from 8 PM to 10 PM in 'higher normal' daytime sleepiness.

4   Discussion

In our study, we were able to distinguish two groups of participants - with 'lower normal' and 'higher normal' daytime sleepiness. Although we could not identify extreme cases of severe daytime sleepiness, we were able to find distinctive features in situational sleepiness and heart rate variability metrics for these two groups.

For individuals with 'lower normal' daytime sleepiness, subjective sleepiness increased from 8 PM to 10 PM. This pattern is consistent with the findings of other studies [21, 24, 25] that subjective sleepiness increases after 8 PM. However, at the same time, we did not observe such a pattern for individuals with 'higher normal' daytime sleepiness. This may suggest that the results of sleepiness studies should take into account the factor of participants' overall daytime sleepiness.

Also, for individuals with 'lower normal' daytime sleepiness, TINN decreased from 8 PM to 10 PM. Previous studies have associated TINN with physical fatigue detection [34, 35]. Thus, the decrease in TINN for people with 'lower normal' daytime sleepiness from 8 PM to 10 PM may indicate an increase in fatigue from evening till night. In other words, low daytime sleepiness led to an increase in situational sleepiness and fatigue from evening till night. One could have expected that the reduction in alertness and increase in sleepiness would be accompanied by a decrease in the activity of the sympathetic component of heart rate modulation [29], but such results were not obtained. Perhaps increasing the sample size will provide more detailed results. However, at the same time, in the study [29], it is noted that increased activity of the sympathetic component of heart rate modulation is observed during heightened alertness in individuals with severe obstructive sleep apnea and without excessive daytime sleepiness. In our case, we had a sample of conditionally healthy individuals without sleep disorders.

On the other hand, individuals with 'higher normal' daytime sleepiness demonstrated a decrease in LF/HF from 8 PM to 10 PM, while their situational sleepiness showed no significant dynamics. This suggests that their evening-night condition dynamics differ from those with 'lower normal' sleepiness. Previous studies have reported various dynamics of LF/HF in relation to situational sleepiness or fatigue, with some showing a decrease [4, 36], while others show an increase if a person resists sleep [37, 38]. We may speculate that people with 'higher normal' daytime sleepiness resist sleep less at 10 PM compared to 8 PM.

Moreover, fragmentation metrics showed an increase in 'higher normal' daytime sleepiness from 8 PM to 10 PM. These heart rate variability metrics are rarely analyzed within psychophysiological research and are usually calculated within long windows. However, a study [39] used a 5-min window. Heart rate fragmentation was reported to be related to decreased global cognitive performance [40]. In our study, we found that heart rate fragmentation closer to bedtime increased in those who were sleepier during the day. Higher daytime sleepiness may be associated with worse daytime cognitive performance, but this needs to be tested in future studies.

5   Conclusions

Situational sleepiness from 8 PM till 10 PM changed only in people with lower normal daytime sleepiness which was accompanied by the TINN decrease possibly related to fatigue increase. This may indicate that such people are more sensitive to changes in their situational sleepiness from evening till night. In people with higher normal daytime sleepiness, the subjective sleepiness score didn't change, but the sympatho-vagal index decreased, and fragmentation heart rate metrics increased from 8 PM till 10 PM. This suggests that their transition from evening to night mode requires a body and cognitive tension decrease.

Acknowledgements. This research was funded by the Russian Science Foundation, grant number 22–28-20509.

References

1. Fischer, D., Lombardi, D.A., Folkard, S., Willetts, J., Christiani, D.C.: Updating the 'risk index': a systematic review and meta-analysis of occupational injuries and work schedule characteristics. Chronobiol. Int. **34**(10), 1423–1438 (2017). https://doi.org/10.1080/074 20528.2017.1367305
2. Kecklund, G., Axelsson, J.: Health consequences of shift work and insufficient sleep. BMJ **355**, i5210 (2016). https://doi.org/10.1136/bmj.i5210
3. Abrahamsen, A., Weihe, P., Debes, F., van Leeuwen, W.M.: Sleep, sleepiness, and fatigue on board Faroese fishing vessels. Nat. Sci. Sleep **14**, 347–362 (2022). https://doi.org/10.2147/NSS.S342410
4. Awais, M., Badruddin, N., Drieberg, M.: A Hybrid approach to detect driver drowsiness utilizing physiological signals to improve system performance and wearability. Sensors **17**(9), 1991 (2017). https://doi.org/10.3390/s17091991
5. Arefnezhad, S., Eichberger, A., Frühwirth, M., Kaufmann, C., Moser, M., Koglbauer, I.V.: Driver monitoring of automated vehicles by classification of driver drowsiness using a deep convolutional neural network trained by scalograms of ECG signals. Energies **15**(2), 480 (2022). https://doi.org/10.3390/en15020480
6. Antunes, A.R., Braga, A.C., Gonçalves, J.: Drowsiness transitions detection using a wearable device. Appl. Sci. **13**(4), 2651 (2023). https://doi.org/10.3390/app13042651
7. Flaa, T.A., et al.: Sleep and sleepiness measured by diaries and actigraphy among Norwegian and Austrian helicopter emergency medical service (HEMS) pilots. Int. J. Environ. Res. Public Health **19**(7), 4311 (2022). https://doi.org/10.3390/ijerph19074311
8. Kazemi, Z., Mazloumi, A., Nasl Saraji, G., Barideh, S.: Fatigue and workload in short and long-haul train driving. Work **54**(2), 425–433 (2016). https://doi.org/10.3233/WOR-162328
9. Yan, R., Wu, C., Wang, Y.: Exploration and evaluation of individual difference to driving fatigue for high-speed railway: a parametric SVM model based on multidimensional visual cue. IET Intel. Transport Syst. **12**(6), 504–512 (2018). https://doi.org/10.1049/iet-its.2017.0289
10. Dijk, D.J., Groeger, J.A., Stanley, N., Deacon, S.: Age-related reduction in daytime sleep propensity and nocturnal slow wave sleep. Sleep **33**(2), 211–223 (2010). https://doi.org/10.1093/sleep/33.2.211

11. Rabat, A., et al.: Differential kinetics in alteration and recovery of cognitive processes from a chronic sleep restriction in young healthy men. Front. Behav. Neurosci. **10**, 95 (2016). https://doi.org/10.3389/fnbeh.2016.00095

12. Rogers, B., Schaffarczyk, M., Gronwald, T.: Estimation of respiratory frequency in women and men by Kubios HRV software using the polar H10 or movesense medical ECG sensor during an exercise ramp. Sensors **22**(19), 7156 (2022). https://doi.org/10.3390/s22197156

13. Bridges, J., Shishavan, H.H., Salmon, A., Metersky, M., Kim, I.: Exploring the potential of pulse transit time as a biomarker for sleep efficiency through a comparison analysis with heart rate and heart rate variability. Sensors **23**(11), 5112 (2023). https://doi.org/10.3390/s23115112

14. Tang, Q., Chen, Z., Ward, R., Menon, C., Elgendi, M.: PPG2ECGps: an end-to-end subject-specific deep neural network model for electrocardiogram reconstruction from photoplethysmography signals without pulse arrival time adjustments. Bioengineering **10**(6), 630 (2023). https://doi.org/10.3390/bioengineering10060630

15. Guo, K., et al.: Contactless vital sign monitoring system for in-vehicle driver monitoring using a near-infrared time-of-flight camera. Appl. Sci. **12**(9), 4416 (2022). https://doi.org/10.3390/app12094416

16. Kim, J.-Y., Park, J.-H., Jang, S.-Y., Yang, J.-R.: Peak detection algorithm for vital sign detection using doppler radar sensors. Sensors **19**(7), 1575 (2019). https://doi.org/10.3390/s19071575

17. Li, R., Chen, Y.V., Zhang, L.: A method for fatigue detection based on driver's steering wheel grip. Int. J. Ind. Ergon. **82**, 103083 (2021). https://doi.org/10.1016/j.ergon.2021.103083

18. Barmack, J.E.: Studies on the psychophysiology of boredom: part I. The effect of 15 mgs. of benzedrine sulfate and 60 mgs. of ephedrine hydrochloride on blood pressure, report of boredom and other factors. J. Exp. Psychol. **25**(5), 494–505 (1939). https://doi.org/10.1037/h0054402

19. Hollister, L.E., Clyde, D.J.: Blood levels of pentobarbital sodium, meprobamate, and tybamate in relation to clinical effects. Clin. Pharmacol. Ther. **9**(2), 204–208 (1968). https://doi.org/10.1002/cpt196892204

20. Carskadon, M.A., Dement, W.C.: Sleepiness and sleep state on a 90-min schedule. Psychophysiology **14**(2), 127–133 (1977). https://doi.org/10.1111/j.1469-8986.1977.tb03362.x

21. Åkerstedt, T., Gillberg, M.: Subjective and objective sleepiness in the active individual. Int. J. Neurosci. **52**, 29–37 (1990). https://doi.org/10.3109/00207459008994241

22. Johns, M.W.: A new method for measuring daytime sleepiness: the epworth sleepiness scale. Sleep **14**(6), 540–545 (1991). https://doi.org/10.1093/sleep/14.6.540

23. Åkerstedt, T., Axelsson, J., Lekander, M., Orsini, N., Kecklund, G.: The daily variation in sleepiness and its relation to the preceding sleep episode-a prospective study across 42 days of normal living. J. Sleep Res. **22**(3), 258–265 (2012). https://doi.org/10.1111/jsr.12014

24. Shochat, T.N., Santhi, N., Herer, P., Dijk, D., Skeldon, A.C.: Sleepiness is a signal to go to bed: data and model simulations. SLEEPJ **44**(10), zsab123 (2021). https://doi.org/10.1093/sleep/zsab123

25. Hoddes, E., Zarcone, V., Smythe, H., Phillips, R., Dement, W.C.: Quantification of sleepiness: a new approach. Psychophysiology **10**(4), 431–436 (1973). https://doi.org/10.1111/j.1469-8986.1973.tb00801.x

26. Johns, M.W.: A sleep physiologist's view of the drowsy driver. Transp. Res. Part F Traffic Psychol. Behav. **3**, 241–249 (2000). https://doi.org/10.1016/S1369-8478(01)00008-0

27. Johns, M.W.: A new perspective on sleepiness. Sleep Biol. Rhythms **8**(3), 170–179 (2010). https://doi.org/10.1111/j.1479-8425.2010.00450.x

28. Krylova, M., et al.: Evidence for modulation of EEG microstate sequence by vigilance level. Neuroimage **224**, 117393 (2021). https://doi.org/10.1016/j.neuroimage.2020.117393

29. Taranto Montemurro, L., et al.: Relationship of heart rate variability to sleepiness in patients with obstructive sleep apnea with and without heart failure. J. Clin. Sleep Med. **10**(3), 271–276 (2014). https://doi.org/10.5664/jcsm.3526

30. Ha, S.-S., Kim, D.-K.: Diagnostic efficacy of ultra-short term HRV analysis in obstructive sleep apnea. J. Pers. Med. **12**, 1494 (2022). https://doi.org/10.3390/jpm12091494

31. Wei, C.Y., Chung, T.C., Wu, S.C., Chung, C.F., Wu, W.P.: The subjective sleep quality and heart rate variability in hemodialysis patients. Ren. Fail. **33**(2), 109–117 (2011). https://doi.org/10.3109/0886022X.2010.541578

32. Demareva, V., et al.: Temporal dynamics of subjective sleepiness: a convergence analysis of two scales. Biol. Rhythm. Res. **54**(4), 369–384 (2023). https://doi.org/10.1080/09291016.2023.2193791

33. Costa, M.D., Davis, R.B., Goldberger, A.L.: Heart rate fragmentation: a new approach to the analysis of cardiac interbeat interval dynamics. Front. Physiol. **8**, 255 (2017). https://doi.org/10.3389/fphys.2017.00255

34. Ni, Z., Sun, F., Li, Y.: Heart rate variability-based subjective physical fatigue assessment. Sensors **22**(9), 3199 (2022). https://doi.org/10.3390/s22093199

35. Anwer, S., et al.: Identification and classification of physical fatigue in construction workers using linear and nonlinear heart rate variability measurements. J. Constr. Eng. Manag. **149**(7), 04023057 (2023). https://doi.org/10.1061/JCEMD4.COENG-1310

36. Patel, M., Lal, S.K.L., Kavanagh, D., Rossiter, P.: Applying neural network analysis on heart rate variability data to assess driver fatigue. Expert Syst. Appl. **38**, 7235–7242 (2011). https://doi.org/10.1016/j.eswa.2010.12.028

37. Furman, G.D., Baharav, A., Cahan, C., Akselrod, S.: Early detection of falling asleep at the wheel: a heart rate variability approach. In: Computers in Cardiology 2008, pp. 1109–1112. IEEE, Bologna, Italy (2008). https://doi.org/10.1109/CIC.2008.4749240

38. Zhang, N., Fard, M., Bhuiyan, M.H.U., Verhagen, D., Azari, M.F., Robinson, S.R.: The effects of physical vibration on heart rate variability as a measure of drowsiness. Ergonomics **61**(9), 1259–1272 (2018). https://doi.org/10.1080/00140139.2018.1482373

39. Romero, D., Jane, R.: Non-linear HRV analysis to quantify the effects of intermittent hypoxia using an OSA rat model. In: 41st Annual International Conference of the IEEE Engineering in Medicine and Biology Society (EMBC), pp. 4994–4997. IEEE, Berlin, Germany (2019). https://doi.org/10.1109/EMBC.2019.8857636

40. Costa, M.D., Redline, S., Hughes, T.M., Heckbert, S.R., Goldberger, A.L.: Prediction of cognitive decline using heart rate fragmentation analysis: the multi-ethnic study of atherosclerosis. Front. Aging Neurosci. **13**, 708130 (2021). https://doi.org/10.3389/fnagi.2021.708130

Intelligent Technologies in Social Engineering. Intelligent technologies in Urban Design and Computing

The Concept of Complex Assessment System for Territories

Aleksander Bershadsky[ID], Pavel Gudkov[(✉)][ID], and Ekaterina Podmarkova[ID]

Penza State University, Krasnaya Str. 40, 440026 Penza, Russia
p.a.gudkov@gmail.com

Abstract. The concept of a system for collecting and analyzing data by region is proposed, and as a result, obtaining an integral indicators system that allow a comprehensive assessment of the individual regions state. Possible areas of such system application are considered, ranging from the tasks of general resource planning for optimizing the socio-economic well-being of individual regions, and ending with the tasks of zoning on an administrative-territorial basis. An algorithm for such problems solving is described. The features that must be taken into account for the Russian Federation subjects are listed. Key research methods are identified and it is noted that an important component of the solving this problem process is proactive modeling, which makes it possible to predict some consequences of infrastructure changes, the economy and the social sphere in a particular territory. An important advantage of the described in this paper system is that the data obtained from different sources and fed to the neural network input are naturally integrated with each other, allowing for a comprehensive assessment of the regions state.

Keywords: administrative-territorial division · regions · proactive modeling · neural networks · algorithm

1 Introduction

Comprehensive assessment is one of the most important management tools that can help the manager make informed decisions and determine the most effective strategy for the development of the region. It allows you to get an objective picture of the state of the region, identify problem areas, offer options for solving the problem.

The implementation of the procedure for a comprehensive assessment of the state of the regions is necessary in various areas of human activity:

- to assess the state and prospects for the development of individual regions,
- to determine the priorities and strategies for the development of the region,
- to take into account the information and legal aspects of sustainable development of the region,
- to determine the budgetary policy of the region,
- to manage the region's strategic competitiveness,

- to take into account the specifics of the economy and manage the reproduction process in the region's agriculture,
- to manage the attractiveness of the region on the basis of strategic partnership,
- to determine the effective investment policy of the region,
- to form and assess the competitiveness of municipalities in the region,
- to assess the resource potential and constraints on the development of the region's economy,
- to study the mechanisms of interaction between economic entities in the innovative development of the regional economy,
- for state management of structural transformations in the economy of the region,
- to form a favorable business environment in the region,
- to ensure the food security of the regions
- etc.

Thus, at present there are many areas of application in which a comprehensive analysis of the state of regions is required, ranging from the tasks of general resource planning to optimize the socio-economic well-being of individual regions, and ending with the tasks of zoning on an administrative-territorial basis.

The solution of this kind of problems can be expressed in the search for and association of regions with lower indicators of the level of socio-economic development with more competitive and economically stronger ones. The solution algorithm boils down to the following: a large amount of information about the region is collected from open and closed sources of information, which are official government and statistical Internet resources, as well as data from the media and various manipulations are performed on them. All of this data is mostly unstructured. After processing and purification, it becomes possible to gradate according to a variety of indicators. Based on this, it seems possible to carry out the consolidation, if this is the task of zoning. But it also becomes possible in this way, by varying a certain set of indicators, to solve smaller problems of local significance. These criteria can include a variety of indicators, sometimes unrelated, such as geographical location, socio-economic indicators, availability of infrastructure, etc.

Performing a comprehensive assessment of the state of the regions, the following socio-economic indicators are taken as a basis by the authors [1]:

- the standard of living of the population, which consists of the opportunities provided to the population to receive quality education, medical, cultural and leisure services,
- infrastructure provision of territories,
- transport accessibility of territories,
- scientific, technical and educational potential of the region,
- the presence of territorial production clusters focused on high-tech industries in priority sectors of the economy,
- the presence of territorial production clusters focused on deep processing of raw materials and energy production using modern technologies,
- level of tourist services,
- throughput capacity of the region's transport system, divided into cargo and passenger flows,

- the level of inter-regional and intra-regional differentiation of the social environment and incomes of the population,
- the dynamics of economic growth due to the influx of population and investments,
- etc.

At the same time, it is necessary to take into account the following key aspects specific to the constituent entities of the Russian Federation [2–5]:

- The area of territories of the subjects varies greatly. These differences far exceed the scope of territorial differences in most other states [6].
- The values of the population of the constituent entities of the Russian Federation vary considerably. Russia surpasses most other countries in this parameter, and is second only to Argentina, which has a population variation coefficient value of 10.2. For Russia, the value of this coefficient is 8.5.
- Great differences in the values of economic indicators of the regions. The values of the gross regional product per capita of many subjects vary greatly among themselves.
- Status asymmetry of the federal structure of the country [7], which consists in the existence of various types of state, republican and "ordinary" subjects of the Russian Federation.
- 32 constituent entities of the Russian Federation were formed on national and ethnic grounds, without taking into account the economic component.
- Structural disorder–several independent subjects of the Russian Federation are part of other independent subjects of the Russian Federation, and two subjects of the Russian Federation have administrative centers on the territory of other subjects.
- High imbalance of needs and own resources for the implementation of the status powers of the authorities of the constituent entities of the Russian Federation.
- Excessive personification of real federative relations–the possibility of violations of the general order (in the political, budgetary and financial, national and ethnic spheres), dependence on the personality of the regional leader and his personal relationship with the center region (Moscow).

To take into account the many features of the Russian Federation and develop the concept of a proactive approach to complex assessment to solve many problems, the authors suggest using data mining technologies to analyze the collected information [8]. This will allow modeling the optimal solution to the required task, in particular, directing the necessary resources to the regions that require the most attention in terms of financial investments, solving personnel and other issues.

Proactive modeling is also an important tool in solving the problem of territorial restructuring, as it allows you to predict the possible consequences of changes and make informed decisions based on data analysis. Such modeling can be used to identify the most effective strategies for the development of the territory–to determine what changes in infrastructure will be most beneficial for economic development and improving the quality of life of the population.

2 Method

A comprehensive assessment of the region may include various aspects, such as the financial condition of its constituent enterprises, production indicators, the level of product quality, customer and employee satisfaction, social responsibility, environmental safety, etc.

To conduct a comprehensive assessment, it is necessary to have access to various sources of information, such as financial documents, production data, reviews posted on the Internet, statistical data, etc.

Evaluation can be performed both fully automatically and with the help of involved experts. As a result, a general picture of the economic activity of the region is formed, which can be used to make managerial decisions and develop a strategy for the development of the region.

It usually begins with the definition of the goals and objectives of the assessment. At this stage, the main criteria and their weighting coefficients are determined, which will be used in the calculation of the comprehensive assessment. Then the information is collected and analyzed. This is followed by the stage of interpreting the results and making managerial decisions to develop a strategy for the development of the region.

Different analysis methods have their own advantages and disadvantages, and the choice of method depends on the specific task and available resources. Therefore, from the whole set of methods for studying complex systems, the following were chosen to solve the problem posed in this work:

- methods of computer modeling, in particular proactive modeling, which allow creating mathematical models of complex systems and analyzing their behavior under various conditions.
- methods of text mining, allowing you to view large amounts of textual information and find hidden patterns. The need to use these methods is due to the constantly growing volume of unstructured or semi-structured heterogeneous information about the regions.
- machine learning methods that allow you to combine many disparate factors about the region in question into a single whole.
- methods of statistical data analysis that allow assessing the socio-economic situation in the regions, identify problem areas and determine priority areas for development.

Let's consider them in more detail. Proactive modeling methods are methods for predicting the future development of a region based on the creation of mathematical models that take into account various factors and conditions that affect the development of the region. These methods make it possible to analyze future scenarios for the development of the region and determine the most optimal ones among them. They include methods of system analysis, economic modeling, forecasting, etc.

The use of proactive modeling methods allows not only to determine the most optimal ways for the development of the region, but also to assess possible risks and obstacles on the way to achieving the goals. In addition, these methods can be used to evaluate the effectiveness of various development strategies and programs, as well as to make informed decisions in the face of uncertainty and risk.

Text Mining methods (text analysis) are a set of technologies and methods that are used to automatically extract information from text data. They allow you to process large amounts of textual information and reveal hidden connections, themes, semantic relationships, etc. in it. These methods are widely used in various fields for the analysis of non-structured textual information.

Text Mining methods are named by analogy with Data Mining methods–a set of algorithms and methods used to automatically extract useful information from large amounts of data. They allow you to discover hidden patterns, connections and trends in data that can be used by decision makers.

Data mining methods include techniques such as cluster analysis, classification, regression analysis, associative analysis, etc. However, when using these methods, it is necessary to take into account the possibility of errors due to inaccuracies in the data, as well as the need to evaluate the results and adjust models based on real data and experience.

Big Data is a technology for processing and analyzing large amounts of data that cannot be processed using traditional methods. Big Data uses special tools and technologies that allow you to process data in real time and reveal hidden patterns and trends in them. These methods are applied in various fields such as finance, healthcare, marketing, etc. One of the main advantages of Big Data is the ability to make more accurate decisions based on more data.

Neural networks are machine learning models that mimic how the human brain works. They consist of many interconnected neurons that process input data and produce a result. Neural networks are used to solve problems of pattern recognition, classification, prediction, etc.

In general, machine learning methods play an important role in the creation of neural networks and allow you to create models that can be trained on large amounts of data and solve complex problems.

It should also be noted that the combination of different methods can also give a more complete picture and help in making informed decisions on the development of the region. For example, if experts are available, it is possible to expand the recommendatory base by applying SWOT analysis methods, which allow assessing the strengths and weaknesses of the region, as well as opportunities and threats that may affect its development, economic analysis methods, including the analysis of financial statements, calculation of economic indicators and investment efficiency assessment, methods of sociological research, allowing to assess the opinion and needs of the population of the region, as well as identify socio-economic problems.

Advances in technology and improvements in data mining methods are now making it possible to obtain increasingly accurate and useful results in the study of complex systems.

If we perform a comprehensive assessment of the state of the regions for the purpose of their subsequent restructuring, then an additional task arises to compare specific options for their enlargement. The choice of the optimal variant of the administrative-territorial division from the entire set of obtained options is made by multi-criteria optimization, for which the objective function $f(h)$, reflecting the spread of values of socio-economic indicators of the region's development, tends to a minimum [9–11]:

$$f(h) = \sum_{i=1}^{4} P_i^h \cdot \omega_i \to \min$$

where P_i^h are the normalized values of the indicators used; ω_i are the weight coefficients set by experts.

The function $f(h)$ calculates the integral indicator of the socio-economic efficiency of the region, based on the socio-economic and spatial indicators for this variant of the administrative-territorial division –h. . This takes into account a set of four partial indicators: the spread of surplus values of the united districts (P_1), the spread of the number of districts in each group (P_2), the spread of the population in each group (P_3), and the maximum remoteness of settlements within the group (P_4). The choice of this set of indicators is due to the requirements of the Federal Law of the Russian Federation of October 6, 2003 No. 131-FZ "On the General Principles of Organizing Local Self-Government in the Russian Federation".

The specified partial indicators are calculated according to the following formulas for determining the root mean square value:

$$P_1 = \sqrt{\frac{1}{N} \cdot \sum_{j=1}^{N} \left(\sum_{i=1}^{L_j} C_{ij} \right)^2}$$

$$P_2 = \sqrt{\frac{1}{N} \cdot \sum_{j=1}^{N} L_j^2}$$

$$P_3 = \sqrt{\frac{1}{N} \cdot \sum_{j=1}^{N} \left(\sum_{i=1}^{L_j} S_{ij} \right)^2}$$

$$P_4 = \max_{1 \le j \le N} Q_j$$

where

- C_{ij}–normalized value of surplus for the i-th district in the j-th group;
- S_{ij}– normalized value of the population living in the i-th district in the j-th group;
- Q_{ij}– normalized value of the maximum distance on the roads between the settlements of the j-th group;
- L_j– number of districts in the j-th group;
- N– number of groups.

The boundary conditions are the requirements for the number of groups of districts ($N_{\min}$ and N_{max}), the maximum number of districts in a group (L_{max}), the adjacency of districts in a group:

$$L_j \le L_{\max}, \, 1 \le j \le N, N_{\min} \le N \le N_{\max}$$

where the values N_{min}, N_{max} and L_{max} are set by the user.

3 Results

The authors propose to single out the following stages of analysis:

1. Automated collection of data from open sources for subsequent obtaining a complete picture of the state of the region. This step will automatically scan sites in search of the required information.
2. Application of Text Mining and Big Data methods for processing large volumes of unstructured textual information [12].
3. Using neural networks to perform spatial analysis of the collected information and its further visualization.

Automated data collection from websites is the process of collecting information from web pages using special software tools. This process can be especially useful for obtaining a large amount of information that can be used for various purposes, such as market analysis, competitor monitoring, customer research, etc.

Various technologies and tools are used to automatically collect data from websites, such as web scraping, page HTML code parsing, API requests, etc. Web scraping is the process of extracting data from web pages by parsing the page's HTML code. HTML parsing allows you to extract information from certain page elements such as headings, text, images, and so on. Some web resources provide the ability to receive information using API requests–the application programming interface–storing data from the server directly, without intermediate web pages.

Consider a possible variant of analysis using the proposed approach. As shown by a analysis of the research domain, most of the population of Russia is concentrated in its central part (Fig. 1). Individual dots in this figure are settlements.

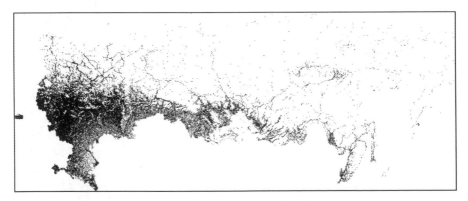

Fig. 1. Territorial distribution of settlements

Therefore, to test the efficiency of the algorithm proposed by the authors, the area of 50° - 60° north latitude and 30° - 60° east longitude was chosen, including such Russian cities as Moscow, St. Petersburg, Penza, Samara, etc. (Fig. 2). Unshaded areas along the edges are the adjacent territories of Belarus, Ukraine and Kazakhstan.

To identify the territories of regions that are similar in their socio-economic indicators, the authors propose to use the following algorithm:

Fig. 2. Central part of the Russian Federation

- The algorithm is based on the convolutional neural network, the input of which is the next fragment of a geographic map [13, 14].
- A passage is made over the entire area under study with a certain specified vertical and horizontal step. The input parameters of the neural network are the geographical coordinates of settlements, indicators that characterize them (for example, population), etc.
- The output forms a grid of values, overlaying which on a geographical map, decision makers can get some recommendations regarding adjacent regions. For example, that these regions should be merged to improve their economic performance.
- Types of recommendations depend on how the neural network underlying the proposed algorithm is trained.

Figures 3 and 4 show examples of grids of indicators generated at the output of the neural network. The coordinates of the axes of the figures correspond to the geographic coordinates of latitude and longitude shown above in Fig. 2.

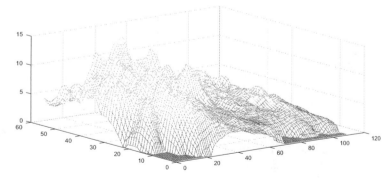

Fig. 3. The result of the neural network (example 1)

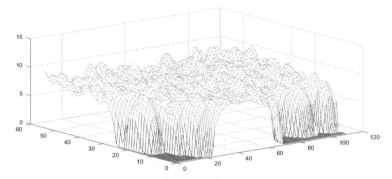

Fig. 4. The result of the neural network (example 2)

The first example shows a situation where the emphasis in training the neural network was on the number of settlements and their uniform territorial distribution - bursts of the objective function are visible near Moscow. The second figure shows an example of training a neural network with a focus on the number of people living in a certain area. Therefore, the extrema of the objective function correspond to the geographical coordinates of large settlements, which is in good agreement with the results of the experiment.

To provide the results to the end user, it is possible to overlay the values obtained at the output of the neural network on the cartographic substrate, thereby giving the decision maker the opportunity to compare several options for solving the problem.

4 Discussion

An important component of the process of solving this problem is proactive modeling, which makes it possible to predict the possible consequences of changes in the infrastructure, economy and social sphere in a particular territory. It helps to make decisions based on data mining and predicting future events. Since the material and material structure of products consumed in the territory of one region in most cases does not coincide with the material and material structure of production, this leaves its mark on the modeling processes - the relationship of a separate territory as a subsystem with the entire system or other subsystems is diverse and rather complex. They affect almost all aspects of the industrial, socio-cultural and scientific life of a region or district.

It should also be noted that when restructuring regions, it is necessary to take into account not only socio-economic indicators and features of the material structure of production and consumption in a given territory, but also the opinion of the living population, which may be against merging with other regions due to cultural, historical or other reasons [15, 16].

5 Conclusion

The development of the concept of proactive modeling in intelligent decision support is determined by the requirements of simultaneous consideration of many diverse factors, which follows from the existing territorial division of labor, which aims to reduce the socially necessary costs of production and circulation of products and increase production efficiency. The spatial gap between production and consumption will continue to widen.

The organization of the system proposed by the authors will make it easy to change the scale of the problems being solved. For example, when solving the problem of restructuring an urban area to assess the impact of certain factors on the life of citizens, economic activity and business development, proactive modeling can be used to analyze changes in the transport infrastructure, residential areas, green areas, accessibility of public places, etc.

An important advantage of the system described in this paper is that the data obtained from different sources and fed to the input of the neural network are naturally integrated with each other, allowing a comprehensive assessment of the state of the regions.

The approach proposed in this article is planned to be implemented and tested at the Department of Computer-Aided Design Systems, Penza State University.

References

1. Morozova, G.A., Maltsev, V.A., Maltsev, K.V.: Sustainable development of the region: monograph. Nizhny Novgorod, NRU RANEPA (2012)
2. Korytny, L.: Administrative-territorial division of Russia: a basin version. Geogr. Nat. Resour. 4 (2006)
3. Parson, H.E.: Regional trends of agricultural restructuring in Canada. Can. J. Reg. Sci. 22(3), 343–356 (1999)
4. Lagendijk, A., Giunta, A., Pike, A.: Introduction: scalar interdependencies between industry and territory. In: Restructuring Industry and Territory: The Experience of Europe's Regions, pp. 3–21 (2000)
5. Swianiewicz, P.: territorial fragmentation as a problem, consolidation as a solution? In: Swianiewicz P. (ed.), Territorial consolidation reforms in Europe, pp. 1–23, Budapest: Local Government and Public Service Reform Initiative, Open Society Institute (2010)
6. Kolosov, V.A., Myronenko, N.S.: Geopolitics and Political Geography. Aspect Press, Moscow (2002)
7. Sulakshin, S.S.: Regional Dimension of the State Economic Policy of Russia. Scientific expert, Moscow (2007)
8. Russell, S., Norvig, P.: Artificial Intelligence: A Modern Approach. Prentice Hall (2010)
9. Podmarkova, E.M.: Convolution algorithm socio-economic indicators in finding the optimal variant of the restructuring of the territorial units. In: Scientific and scientific-pedagogical personnel of innovative Russia in the 2009/2013 years: Research in the Modern World: Problems, Prospects and Challenges: Proceedings of the II Intern. youth researcher. Conf. Part I. Ufa, pp. 70–75 (2012)
10. Podmarkova, E.M., Gudkov, P.A.: The methods and algorithms for automated formation of the training courses structure. In: University education, XVIII International Scientific Conference (2014)
11. Podmarkova, E.M.: Mathematical and algorithmic support for the formation and evaluation of options for the administrative-territorial division of the region. Thesis of a candidate of technical sciences: 05.13.10, 05.13.01. Penza State University, Penza (2013)
12. Barseghyan, A.A., Kupriyanov, M.S., Kholod, I.I., Tess, M.D., Elizarov, S.I.: Analysis of data and processes. St. Petersburg, BHV-Petersburg (2009)
13. Dua, A., Ayub, U.: Beginning with Machine Learning. BPB Publications (2022)

14. Kreyman, G.: Biological and Computer Vision. DMK Press (2022)
15. Korytny, L., Artobolevsky, S., Sintserova, L.: On the necessity and the possibility of reforming the administrative-territorial division of Russia. In: Proceedings of the XXV session MARS, Institute of Geography, Russian Academy of Sciences, Moscow, pp. 5–15 (2008)
16. Swianiewicz, P.: If territorial fragmentation is a problem, is amalgamation a solution?–ten years later. Local Gov. Stud. **44**(1), 1–10 (2018)

Balance Model of Interests of a Transport Company and Passengers in Urban Transportation by Automatic Transport

Vasily Shuts[(✉)] and Alena Shviatsova

Brest State Technical University, Belarus, 267 Moskovskaya, 224016 Brest, Belarus
lucking@mail.ru, helengood@internet.ru

Abstract. The paper investigates the technology of organizing the transportation process in the passenger urban transport system based on unmanned automatic vehicles. Recently, research has been intensively conducted in the field of development of unmanned vehicles in many countries of the world. On the basis of these vehicles, fully automatic transport systems should be developed in the future, excluding the human dispatcher from the control loop of urban passenger transportation. Such systems have parameters and capabilities far superior to modern urban transport systems.

Keywords: automatic transport · information and transport system · transportation organization · correspondence matrix · transportation organization algorithm · infobus

1 Introduction

The development of information technologies makes it possible to revise the concept of organization and management of modern urban transport [1–5]. At the same time, the whole variety of urban passenger vehicles can be canceled and reduced to one transport unit of nominal capacity - the infobus.

Infobus is an unmanned electric vehicle with a small capacity of up to thirty passengers, Fig. 1. Depending on the intensity of passenger traffic on the route, the control computer (coordinating server) sends such a number of infobuses to the route that their total volume is equal to the volume of passenger traffic or slightly exceeds it. At the same time, infobuses can be assembled into cassettes consisting of a different number of vehicles. A different number of infobuses can be collected in the cassette, Fig. 1.

Now it is possible to quickly and inexpensively assemble a vehicle of any capacity required on the route, since there are no mechanical connections in the cassette. The connection is virtual, as in road trains [6]. Thus, infobus cassette represents a vehicle with divisible parts [7, 8].

Modern cities are characterized by a high population density, which requires a change in approaches to urban mobility management. The organization of urban passenger transportation is transferred from a human to information systems, since it (information systems), unlike a human, are able to permanently record and collect data about the processes occurring in the passengers transportations and, based on the analysis of big data, make decisions.

Fig. 1. The movement of infobuses independently and in a cassette

The fusion of information technology and passenger transportation technologies has created a new kind of system: information - transport systems. Due to the high speed of information processing, such passenger transportation management systems are able to adapt to changes in the intensity of passenger flows [9–13], sending vehicles of optimal capacity for passenger transportation.

And one of the tasks of information and transport systems is to maintain a balance of interests of the transport company and passengers when organizing transportation. This paper proposes a model that describes balance of interests of the transport company and passengers in urban passenger information-transport system.

The considered information - transport system of passenger transportation must to include:

- a dedicated line for the movement of vehicles. e.g. a rail track, which gives vehicles the highest priority. Crossroads in this case can be overcome through underground tunnels or elevated overpasses, Fig. 1;
- a route with k passengers stops in two directions, Fig. 2. At the end of the route there are Assembly Points for charging vehicles;
- the stopping points for embarkation and disembarkation of passengers are equipped with turnstiles for ordering transportation and paying for it, Fig. 3.

- fleet of unmanned vehicles (infobus), fixed small capacity (up to 30 passengers), connected with the coordinating server, whose teams are trained by the vehicle;
- information server that coordinating the work of the entire information - transport system. It collects passenger requests for transportation from stops, analyzes the collected data and organizes passenger transportation in real time;

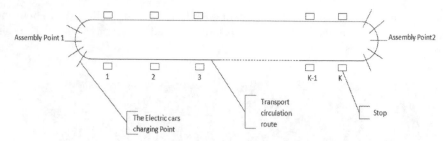

Fig. 2. Route from k stations in two directions

Fig. 3. The stopping points

- correspondence matrix, which is the information basis for the organization of transportation:

$$M_Z = \begin{pmatrix} 0 & m_{12} & m_{13} & \dots & \dots m_{1j} & \dots & m_{1k} \\ 0 & 0 & m_{23} & \dots & \dots m_{2j} & \dots & m_{2k} \\ \dots & \dots & \dots & \dots & \dots \dots & \dots & \dots \\ 0 & \dots & 0 & m_{ii+1} & \dots m_{ij} & \dots & m_{ik} \\ \dots & \dots & \dots & \dots & \dots \dots & \dots & \dots \\ 0 & \dots & \dots & \dots & \dots \dots & 0 & m_{k-1k} \\ 0 & \dots & \dots & \dots & \dots \dots & & 0 \end{pmatrix}$$

In the matrix of correspondences M_z, $Z = 1, 2, \dots$. Each element m_{ij} defines the number of passengers traveling from stop i to stop j, $i = 1, \dots, k-1$, $j = 2, \dots, k$ [14, 15]. Here k is the number of stops in one (direct or reverse) direction' of the route, Fig.2.

The process of functioning of the information-transport system is cyclical and consists of repeated procedures:

- accumulation of information about the passengers arriving at the stopping points;

- determination of the moment of sufficient accumulation of passengers for transportation;
- development of a delivery plan for transportation and the implementation of this plan.

The transportation plan - is a procedure of assignment number for each infobus that will be sanded to rout line and sequential sending of numbered infobuses from Assembly Points to the route line with indicating the final destination station and, perhaps, several intermediate stopping points for each numbered infobus individually.

The information- transport system works as follows. The passenger, passing through the turnstile of the stopping point, and paying for the fare, also indicates the stop to which he should go. By this, he initializes his appearance in the system with a request for service and, at the same time, mainly non-stop, or with a minimum number of intermediate stops from the point of departure to the point of destination.

Information from the terminals is sent to the coordinating server and is stored in a database, Fig. 4.

ID 🔒 integer	Origin 🔒 integer	Destination 🔒 integer	SeatsNumber 🔒 integer	TimeRequest 🔒 timestamp without time zone
109122	3	7	1	2021-06-16 00:07:57.07
109130	8	10	1	2021-06-16 00:08:11.08
109131	2	7	1	2021-09-02 10:18:09.18
109135	4	7	1	2021-09-02 10:18:18.18
109137	4	10	1	2021-09-02 10:18:23.18
109141	1	5	1	2021-09-02 10:40:51.4
109142	8	9	1	2021-09-02 10:40:55.4

Fig. 4. Passenger request metrics are stored in the database

Based on this information a correspondence matrix is generated in which each passenger arriving at the stop is recorded, Fig. 5.

The plan of passenger transportation begins to form after some time when information about some number of passengers has be accumulated in the matrix of correspondences.

The moment when the process of accumulation in the correspondence matrix of information about requests for transportation stops is determined by the condition

$$m_{ij} \geq a * V, a \in (0.8, 1), i = \overline{1, k-1}, j = \overline{1, k},$$

where m_{ij} is some element of the matrix containing information about requests for transportation from stop i to stop j;

V - vehicle volume;

a - coefficient of elasticity. This coefficient is used to ensure also those passengers, who will appear at the stop for the period from the start of transportation to the moment the vehicle appears at the stop.

The information server (Fig. 6) constantly scans the correspondence matrix for the fulfillment of this condition.

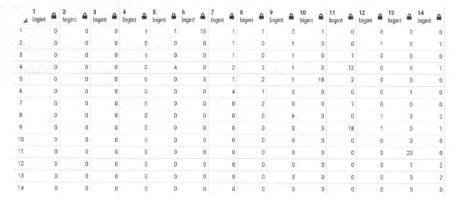

	1 bigint	2 bigint	3 bigint	4 bigint	5 bigint	6 bigint	7 bigint	8 bigint	9 bigint	10 bigint	11 bigint	12 bigint	13 bigint	14 bigint
1	0	0	0	1	1	15	1	1	2	1	0	0	0	0
2	0	0	0	0	0	0	1	0	1	0	0	1	0	1
3	0	0	0	1	0	0	1	0	1	0	1	0	0	0
4	0	0	0	0	4	0	2	2	1	0	12	0	0	1
5	0	0	0	0	0	3	1	2	1	18	2	0	0	0
6	0	0	0	0	0	0	4	1	0	0	0	0	1	0
7	0	0	0	0	0	0	0	2	0	0	1	0	0	0
8	0	0	0	0	0	0	0	0	6	0	0	1	0	2
9	0	0	0	0	0	0	0	0	0	0	18	1	0	1
10	0	0	0	0	0	0	0	0	0	0	0	0	0	0
11	0	0	0	0	0	0	0	0	0	0	0	0	20	0
12	0	0	0	0	0	0	0	0	0	0	0	0	1	2
13	0	0	0	0	0	0	0	0	0	0	0	0	0	2
14	0	0	0	0	0	0	0	0	0	0	0	0	0	0

Fig. 5. Correspondence matrix generated by the information server

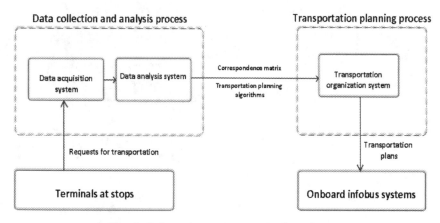

Fig. 6. Information server organization scheme

As soon as the condition is met, the current matrix of correspondence is fixed and the formation of a transportation plan for it begins.

Also, the server immediately starts collecting applications for the next matrix of correspondence.

To form a transportation plan, the information server uses various algorithms for processing the correspondence matrix, each time choosing the optimal one in this case.

The transportation plan defines the number of participating vehicles, the schedule for them, the stops that the vehicle will visit. Each infobus is also assigned an identification number. According this information infobuses will sent to transport passengers to the destination stations.

Each arriving infobus on departure station has information on own display about destination points also this information is shown on monitor of departure station. Passengers, which have as the final destination the proposed set of stops, take places in this infobus. The other passengers wait for their infobus.

After receiving a report from the infobuses on the completion of the transportation of passengers, the information server performs the calculation of the transportation efficiency.

Structurally, the information server consists of three subsystems:

- Data acquisition system collects applications from passengers for transportation from terminals at stops through telecommunications.
- Data analysis system performs scanning and fixing according to the condition of the correspondence matrix, analysis of the accumulated data, selection of the transportation organization algorithm.
- Transportation organization system processes the correspondence matrix in accordance with the selected algorithm.

In the functioning of the information server, one can single out such processes as: data collection and analysis process and transportation planning process. Both processes proceed in the system continuously and cyclically, ensuring the efficient functioning of the system with minimal human intervention.

Such a transport system is adaptive to passenger traffic. It able to changes in a timely and prompt manner, and adjusts to the passenger flow.

2   Balance Model of Interests

There are two types of losses in the transportation process:

- losses of the motor transport enterprise (MTE), L_{MTE}
- losses of a passenger, L_{Pass}

The losses of the MTE consist of the vehicle underloading during following on the route. The total volume of the vehicle is V passengers (passenger capacity). The volume of the vehicle is allocated per passenger $1/V$. . If r passengers ($r < V$) go to the vehicle, then the underload of the vehicle is (V - r). It possible to express the vehicle losses in terms of passengers following way: $L_{MTE} = V - r$. Using multiplying L_{MTE} by the fare, we get these losses in monetary terms. Figure 7 shows a chart of MTE losses.

In this transport system the transportation of passengers from stop $i, i = 1,...,k-1$ to stop $j, j = 2, ..., k$ is carried out mainly without intermediate stops, or with a minimum number of them [16, 17].

The Fig. 7 shows the process of reducing losses as the vehicle fills up, which will carry passengers non-stop from stop i to j.

The chart of MTE losses is stepped. The size of the step equals $1/V$ and indicates the decrease in MTE losses by this amount since the next passenger has arrived at stop i for traveling to stop j.

Thus, the first passenger arrives at stop i at time t_1 (he is fixed in element ij of the correspondence matrix M_z). At time t_2 two passengers, who indicated stop j as the final destination of the trip, approached to stop i. The chart of MTE losses immediately dropped by two steps (Fig. 8), and so on.

Passengers that arrive at stop i are recorded in the i-line of the correspondence matrix M_z. At some point in time t_r at stop i, the number of passengers going to stop j is equal

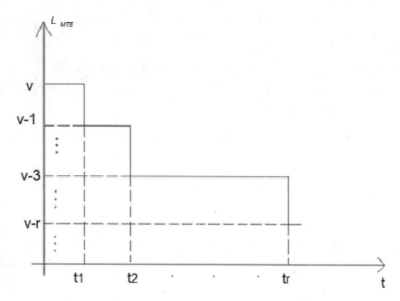

Fig. 7. The MTE losses

to $r = m_{ij} = a \times V, a \in [0.8, 1)$. This is a criterion and a signal to start transportation, because the vehicle will be quite fully loaded with passengers of one destination stop j and the losses of the MTE (L_{MTE}) are minimal and amount to V- r. The loss measurement unit is one passenger (pass.).

The coefficient a regulates the level of occupancy of the vehicle with passengers on the route ij. When the required filling level of the cabin is reached, transportation begins. Let's suppose, that if $a = 0.8$ is set, then at 80% of the vehicle cabin filling and the transportation process starts from stop i to j.

Consider the loss L_{Pass} of vehicle users (passengers). Losses of passengers consist of the loss of time waiting for the vehicle. L_{Pass} grows in proportion to the waiting time with a given proportionality coefficient. Also, these losses increase with the number of passengers waiting at the stop.

Figure 8 shows a chart of the passenger's losses. The starting point of the chart in Fig. 9 (as well as on the graph in Fig. 8) is the moment of zeroing the cell ij of the correspondence matrix M_z, i.e. the vehicle was loaded with passengers that travel from i to j and set off with passengers along the route ij (from i to j). Passengers from stop i to stop j pass without intermediate stops. After sending the vehicle (infobus) from stop i to j, a new cycle begins and a new collection of passengers into cell ij of the correspondence matrix M_z.

Let at the time t_1 from the begin of count the first passenger enters the system, which is fixed by the system in the ij cell of the correspondence matrix M_z. If the system server needs the data of the correspondence matrix M_z to calculate the losses of the transport enterprise, then in case of calculating passenger's losses it is necessary to enter the matrix of events M_{Ev}. Each ij cell of events matrix the times of passenger's arrival of the route

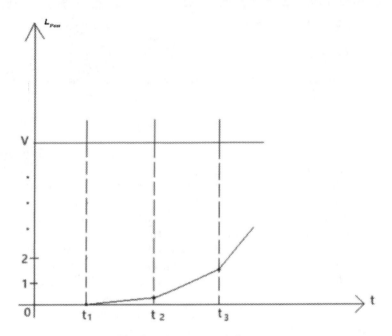

Fig. 8. The passenger's losses

ij at the i-stop will be recorded. Based on these data, a special program will calculate the costs of L_{Pass} for each individual cell of the matrix M_{Ev}.

Passenger losses measured by the unit of time will be reduced to the unit of measurement «pass» (passenger). Let us designate the maximum of «patient waiting time» for a transport by a passenger as T. T can be in the range from 10 to 20 min. It is also one of the set parameters of the multicriteria problem that defines the contours of the automatic transport system.

The second parameter is the coefficient of proportionality, which establishes the preference (ratio) between the losses of the vehicle enterprise and passengers. This coefficient k follows directly from the conversion of losses per unit of time (minute) into the loss unit «pass». For example, let 20 min be equivalent to 0.25 «pass». Here «pass» will be the unit of loss. Then the coefficient k will be equal to $0.25/20 = 0.0125$. Thus, the time of arrival t_1 (Fig. 9) of the first passenger ij (the trip from stop i to j) is recorded in the ij cell of the matrix M_c. It possible to write the equation for the growth of losses over time for the first passenger:

$$L_{Pass_1} = k(t - t_1), T \geq t \geq t_1 \tag{1}$$

At time t_2, the second passenger was added to the first one (Fig. 9). Now two passengers determine the growth of losses. Loss equation for the second passenger:

$$L_{Pass_2} = k(t - t_2), T \geq t \geq t_2 \tag{2}$$

The equation for the joint growth of losses after the event t_2 has the form:

$$L_{Pass_{12}} = k(t_2 - t_1) + 2k(t - t_2), T \geq t \geq t_2 \tag{3}$$

At time t_3, a third passenger arrives and the total loss equation becomes:

$$L_{Pass_{123}} = k(t_2 - t_1) + 2k(t_3 - t_2) + 3k(t - t_3), T \geq t \geq t_3 \qquad (4)$$

Similarly, it possible to write the general loss equation for r passengers who arrived at the stop by the time t_r:

$$L_{Pass_{12...r}} = k(t_2 - t_1) + 2k(t_3 - t_2) + 3k(t_4 - t_3) + \ldots + rk(t - t_r), T \geq t \geq t_r \quad (5)$$

Transport system has two components: MTE and passengers. The interests of the MTE and the passenger are opposite. Thus, an increase in the waiting time for a passenger transport leads to an increase in the occupancy of the vehicle, and vice versa. The task of effective management is to ensure a balance between these parts of the system so that the interests of each component are taken into account as much as possible.

From the chart in Fig. 9 it can be seen that the losses of the transport enterprise decrease with each new passenger, and the losses of passengers increase with the increase in waiting time. Let's consider options for possible cases relatively the time T of «patient waiting» for a transport by a passenger. Time T is the time after which the vehicle will be delivered to the passenger guaranteed. Let's consider possible cases.

Let's the «patient waiting time» be equal to T_1, as shown in Fig. 9. Consequently, after its expiration, the vehicle will be delivered to the passengers at the time t_4, $(t_4 - t_1)$ $= T_1$ (Fig. 9). At the moment t_4 of the vehicle departure from stop i to stop j, the loss of MTE is higher than the loss of passengers $(G_1G_3 > G_2G_3)$.

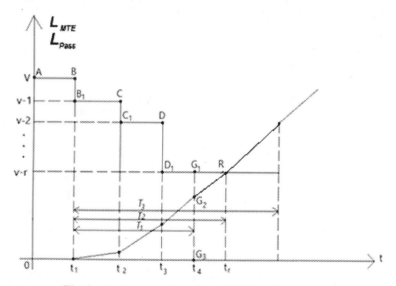

Fig. 9. The combined loss chart of MTE and passengers

If the vehicle is brought to stop i after the «patient waiting time» T_2 $(T_2 > T_1)$, then the losses of the vehicle and passengers will become equal (point R). Point R is the equilibrium point, where $L_{MTE} = L_{Pass}$.

In case of further increasing of «patient waiting time» ($T_3 > T_2$) passengers losses will exceed MTE losses. Thus, by varying the time T after which the vehicle will be sent to stop i to take passengers to stop j, it possible to get different results of losses between the MTE and passengers.

Let's explore the balance point R. Let's determine the time of the event t_r, when the losses of the vehicle and passengers are in balance (balance point R in Fig. 9). The balance point R is the intersection of charts L_{MTE} and L_{Pass} (horizontal V-r).

At point R, the number of passengers coming from stops i to j is r is m_{ij}. So, at point R:

$$L_{Pass} = L_{MTE} = V - r = k(t_2 - t_1) + 2k(t_3 - t_2) + ... + (r - 1)k(t_r - t_{r-1}) + rk(t - t_r) \tag{6}$$

The last term of the polynomial (on the right side of the relation) at $t = t_r$ is equal to zero. From Eq. (6) we calculate the time t_r:

$$t_r = \frac{(V - r) - k(t_2 - t_1) - 2k(t_3 - t_2) - ... + (r - 1)kt_{r-1}}{(r - 1)k} \tag{7}$$

The closer the point R is to the abscissa axis $0t$ (segment Rt_r), the better the result of transportation for both side (MTE and passengers). The total loss at point R is $2(V$-$r)$. Thus, it is possible to establish a balance of losses between the vehicle and passengers by setting the coefficient k and the «patient waiting time» T.

3 Conclusion

A model is proposed that allows, based on the calculations of losses incurred by the parties to the transportation process (carrier and passenger), to determine the optimal balance of their interests. And on the basis of the information received, to organize the optimal passenger transportation.

References

1. Schwedes, O., Ringwald, R.: Public services and public mobility: the role of the state as guarantor. In: Schwedes, O. (eds.) Public Mobility. Springer, Wiesbaden (2023). https://doi.org/10.1007/978-3-658-39579-7_2
2. Von Schneidemesser, D.: Public mobility and new forms of governance: the example of the berlin bicycle referendum. In: Schwedes, O. (eds.) Public Mobility. Springer, Wiesbaden (2023). https://doi.org/10.1007/978-3-658-39579-7_6
3. Wolking, C.: Public mobility and new mobility services: contextual conditions and perspectives for design. In: Schwedes, O. (eds.) Public Mobility. Springer, Wiesbaden (2023). https://doi.org/10.1007/978-3-658-39579-7_5
4. Hoor, M.: Public mobility and a new mobility culture: foundations, developments and paths to a cultural transport turnaround. In: Schwedes, O. (eds.) Public Mobility. Springer, Wiesbaden (2023). https://doi.org/10.1007/978-3-658-39579-7_7
5. Schwedes, O.: Conclusion: transport science as a social science. In: Schwedes, O. (eds.) Public Mobility. Springer, Wiesbaden (2023). https://doi.org/10.1007/978-3-658-39579-7_12

6. Safe Road Trains for the Environment (2023). Wikipedia. http://en.wikipedia.org/wiki/Safe_R oad_Trains_for_the_Environment

7. Shviatsova, E.V., Shuts, V.N.: The intellectual transport with divisible parts. In: Kravets, A.G., Bolshakov, A.A., Shcherbakov, M. (eds.) Society 5.0: Human-Centered Society Challenges and Solutions. SSDC, vol. 416, pp. 265–274. Springer, Cham (2022). https://doi.org/10.1007/978-3-030-95112-2_22

8. Shuts, V., Prolisko, E., Shvetsova, A.: Automated management system for split passenger transport. Reports of the XVIII International Conference "Development of Informatisation and State System of Scientific and Technical Information", pp. 176–180 (2019)

9. Mitteregger, M., et al.: Connected and automated transport in the long level 4. In: AVENUE21. Connected and Automated Driving: Prospects for Urban Europe. Springer Vieweg, Berlin, Heidelberg (2022). https://doi.org/10.1007/978-3-662-64140-8_4

10. Soteropoulos, A., et al.: Automation, public transport and mobility as a service: experience from tests with automated shuttle buses. In: Mitteregger, M., et al. (eds.) AVENUE21. Planning and Policy Considerations for an Age of Automated Mobility. Springer Vieweg, Berlin, Heidelberg (2023). https://doi.org/10.1007/978-3-662-67004-0

11. Alessandrini, A., Holguín, C., Stam, D.: Automated road transport systems (ARTS)—the safe way to integrate automated road transport in urban areas. In: Meyer, G., Beiker, S. (eds.) Road Vehicle Automation 2. LNM, pp. 195–203. Springer, Cham (2015). https://doi.org/10.1007/978-3-319-19078-5_17

12. Gora, P., Wasilewski, P.: Adaptive system for intelligent traffic management in smart cities. In: Ślęzak, D., Schaefer, G., Vuong, S.T., Kim, Y.S. (eds.) Active Media Technology. AMT 2014. LNCS, vol. 8610. Springer, Cham (2014). https://doi.org/10.1007/978-3-319-09912-5_44

13. Malucelli, F., Nonato, M., Pallottino, S.: Demand adaptive systems: some proposals on flexible transit1. In: Ciriani, T.A., Gliozzi, S., Johnson, E.L., Tadei, R. (eds.) Operational Research in Industry. Palgrave Macmillan, London (1999). https://doi.org/10.1057/9780230372924_8

14. Prolisko E., Shuts V.: Mathematical model of work "INFOBUSOV". In: The VII Ukrainian-Polish Scientific Practical Conference "Electronics and Information Technology (EIT-2015)". Lviv-Chinadi, Ukraine (2015)

15. Prolisko E., Shuts V.: Dynamic model of the INFOBUS transport system. Artificial Intelligence. Intellectual transport systems, pp. 49–54. Publishing House of Brest State Technical University, Brest (2016)

16. Shuts, V., Shviatsova, A., Prolisko, E.: Collection and analysis of data for organization of transportation in the city passenger information and transportation system. Appl. Quest. Math Model. 4(2.1) (2021). https://doi.org/10.32782/KNTU2618-0340/2021.4.2.1.30

17. Shuts, V., Shviatsova, A.: Intelligent system of urban unmanned passenger vehicle transport. In: 16th European Automotive Congress (EAEC 2019) hosted jointly the Academic Automotive Association (Belarus), the European Automobile Engineers Cooperation (EAEC) and the Federation Internationale des Societes d'Ingenieurs des Techniques de l'Automobile (FISITA), vol. 18 (2019)

Using Generative Design Technologies to Create Park Area Layouts for Urban Improvement

Nikolay Rashevskiy[✉] [iD], Danila Parygin[iD], Artem Shcherbakov,
Nikita Shlyannikov, and Vasily Shlyannikov

Volgograd State Technical University, 1 Akademicheskaya Str., 400074 Volgograd, Russia
rashevsky.n@gmail.com, vshlyannikov@bk.ru

Abstract. This paper presents a solution for using generative design techniques with ontology engineering to create park layouts based on normative documentation. Generative design is a methodology based on the use of algorithms and applications to generate iterative and variable design solutions. It allows the analysis and consideration of multiple factors such as topography, climatic conditions, human flows, transport networks and other parameters to develop the best solutions for a specific site. Ontology engineering is concerned with the creation of formal descriptions and models to represent knowledge about the domain. In urban planning, ontology engineering can be used to create a formal model of a city that integrates information about its physical environment, infrastructure, public spaces and transport network. Combining generative design and ontological engineering in urban planning opens up new possibilities for designing innovative and optimised urban environments. Generative algorithms can use ontology-based knowledge models to automatically generate and evaluate different urban design solutions, given parameters and objectives. This makes it possible to explore a large number of options and find optimal solutions taking into account multiple factors. The article analyses the use of generative design and ontology engineering technologies in the field of urban planning. The ontological model based on the normative documentation - SP 475.1325800.2020 "Parks. Rules of urban design and landscaping". A method of creating a park zone layout using generative design with the use of knowledge represented as an ontological model is proposed. An example of the implementation of the proposed method using the cross-platform computer game development environment Unity is given.

Keywords: Generative Design · Data Analysis · Urban Planning · Layout Generation · Ontological Engineering

1 Introduction

In recent years, technological progress has increased dramatically. The automation of professional activities is becoming more and more advanced. It affects many areas of life in modern society. In urban planning and architecture, computer-assisted design technologies are also evolving.

Urban planning plays a crucial role in shaping the living environment and ensuring sustainable and inclusive urban development. With the advent of new technological advances in urban planning, innovative methodologies have emerged to improve the design and decision-making process. Two such approaches are generative design and ontological engineering.

Urban planning involves the thoughtful analysis, design and management of urban spaces, taking into account factors such as population growth, infrastructure, transportation and environmental sustainability. Traditionally, urban planning has been based on a linear approach, but with the development of computational technology, new techniques have emerged that allow for more efficient and effective decision making. Generative design is an approach to computational design that generates multiple alternatives based on predetermined parameters, constraints and objectives. Ontology engineering, on the other hand, aims to create a structured knowledge representation that captures fundamental concepts and relationships between entities in a given domain.

The integration of generative design and ontology engineering holds great promise for urban and park planning practice. Generative design allows the exploration of a large design space, enabling planners to quickly generate and evaluate multiple alternatives. Combined with ontology engineering, which facilitates knowledge representation and data integration, it becomes possible to analyze and optimize park layouts based on a comprehensive understanding of the domain. This integration can lead to improved decision making, resource allocation and stakeholder engagement, ultimately resulting in a more sustainable and inclusive urban environment.

Therefore, this research aims to explore the integration of generative design and ontological engineering in urban planning, and to contribute to a better understanding of its potential implications for sustainable and inclusive urban development. By exploring the theoretical foundations, methodology and practical application of these approaches, this study aims to illuminate the transformative potential of generative design and ontological engineering in the design of parkland.

2   Analysis of Existing Approaches for Creating Infrastructure Facilities

Generative design is a design approach based on a set of computational algorithms that select a set of options for solving a particular problem based on given parameters and select the most optimal results [1].

The generation of a huge set of solutions (samples) is performed by a computer through mathematical algorithms and machine learning. The result of this process is not one or a few suitable solutions, but a set of samples. In this regard, the design turns into the study of cause-and-effect relationships.

Domestic studies of generative design and its technologies, from the point of view of urban planning practice, are not numerous. This direction is only developing, however, the works of a theoretical orientation answer many questions related to the advantages [1] and the possibilities of using generative design [2]. The scientific article by A. A. Laushkina [3] considers the existing methods and algorithms of generative design in urban planning, taking into account changes in the characteristics of the environment. Based on the analysis of existing solutions, various limitations were identified that developers face, the main of which is the need to make changes in the user mode.

Practical research also takes place in the scientific works of domestic scientists. For example, in the project of A. Ya. Pakhtaeva and Yu.V. Rodionova [4] developed a generative design method for landscape design, which forms the terms of reference for developers of artificial intelligence systems. The idea is that based on certain factors that affect generative decisions, the system models regular and natural processes by describing them using a set of rules in a computer-aided design system. The method makes it possible to form a pedestrian-path network of the park based on determining the points of attraction of residents and constructing a predictable projection of the movement of pedestrians, as well as using machine learning to conduct an aesthetic selection of objects. The principles of an innovative approach in the processes of the pre-project stage are disclosed in the article by N. G. Airapetyan and A. A. Zaitsev [5], namely, the analysis of the most efficient use of a land plot for future development using generative design. This approach allows you to get the maximum economic potential of the territories, increase the efficiency of the process of developing a preliminary legal examination at the early stages of the project.

In the work of V.V. Garyaeva and A.N. Garyaeva [6] presents the results of the analysis and practical implementation of approaches to information processing in the automation of building design using generative design technology. The developed method allowed using certain software products to automatically create many solutions for the problem of modeling conceptual development, thereby reducing the time spent by a specialist on the development of project documentation.

Foreign scientists have made a huge contribution to the innovative development of the generative design industry, in terms of its implementation in practical urban planning. The works of the following researchers can be noted: O. Moskowitz, Sheini Barat [7], Yue Sun [8], D. Kumalasari [9], Dongjie Wang [10], Reinhard Koenig [11, 12], Seiki Koma, Yuichiro Yamabe [13].

An article by Reinhard Koenig [12] describes the successful application of the evolutionary optimization algorithm (EMO) to create several planning structures, such as a street network, neighborhoods, land plots, and buildings. The use of the data structure is implemented in the Grasshopper software for Rhino3D as part of a flexible, modular and extensible optimization system that can be used to solve various urban design problems and is able to reconcile potentially conflicting design goals in a semi-automatic manner. Seiki Koma and Yuichiro Yamabe [13] in their experimental study proposed an urban landscape design optimization system using an interactive genetic algorithm (IGA). Using this method, the researchers determined the best way to integrate the opinions of citizens regarding a comfortable urban environment into computer-aided design technology to assess the front of street development.

In addition to scientific research, there are ready-made software solutions:

– Procedural Modelling Pipeline with Geometry Nodes (PMP) - this product is a modification of the free professional 3D modelling software with open source code - Blender. PMP is a 3-dimensional object that changes in real time according to the parameters set on it. With the help of this modification you can create furniture of different size, type and style [14];

- Road Path Creator (RPC) - This product is also a modification of the professional free open source 3D modelling software Blender. RPC turns a bend into a fairly realistic model of any type of road. It also has a large number of parameters, ranging from the smoothing of the curves to the material of the road itself. The modification can create both a regular tarmac road with markings and a dirt road with puddles. RPC also allows you to add additional objects to the roadside, such as stones or lampposts [15];

- Buildify - Another modification for Blender. With this modification you can create urban environments in seconds. For example, if you copy the same object, it will be different every time, which allows you to fill the game world with different buildings of the same type. The building also changes when you change its size or parameters, of which there are many. You can change the presence of split systems, the number of windows and entrances to the building. Buildings can also be created from closed curves. And if you insert the object of one building into another, they will combine to form a completely new building. Buildify modification allows you to generate buildings from a map image. All changes happen in real time [16];

- Generative Design in Revit AutoDesk - Revit offers the ability to define the dimensions of a building, including the footprint and floor plan, at the conceptual design stage using so-called "studies" based on generative design. This optimises the workflow by reducing the need to consider different requirements and conditions, track dependencies and select optimal solutions. "Generative design allows us to identify the interrelationships of all the important aspects of a project at the concept stage and to arrive at an informed optimal solution quite quickly. Autodesk's Revit-based generative design tools are becoming increasingly relevant to problem solving and are proving their usefulness in conceptual design [17].

3 Designing a Program for Generating Area Layout

3.1 The Main Stages in the Development of the Layout for the Park

Preparatory Phase
Information about the site is collected: visual assessment of the work front, geodetic surveys of the site, geological surveys of the soil and so on [18, 19]. The condition of the territory is analyzed. The objectives of the project are defined. The requirements of normative acts that should be taken into account in the design are described. The stage is completed with the creation of the terms of reference.

Development of the Concept and Sketch Design of the Landscape
After discussing the vision for the project, the architect begins concept development. Initial versions of the design are provided by sketches, then the agreed version is documented in the format of color plans and 3D visualizations.

The documentation of the conceptual design contains: a situational plan, functional zoning scheme, landscaping plan, layout plan, pavement plan, small architectural forms placement, landscaping schemes, lighting plan, explanatory note. Often, an estimate is added to the preliminary design.

Preparation of the Detailed Design of the Landscaping Project

At this stage, detailed documentation is developed, details are elaborated in depth, the materials used are specified, and specifications of the equipment to be used are specified. Plans, structural and engineering solutions are drawn up. Approximate rules for the location of various objects. The placement of zones in the park is determined by:

– Their purpose;
– The location of the main entrance;
– The location of the park;
– The topography of the area;
– Presence of water bodies, composition of plantations.

Areas of mass entertainment and physical fitness facilities that attract many visitors are located near the main entrance of the park. The main entrance to the park shall be arranged taking into account the feeder highways and streets. In addition, there should be secondary entrances from adjacent streets and utility entrances. The children's area should be located away from the entertainment area and physical education facilities. The quiet recreation zone should be located in the most picturesque part of the park, among plantings and near water bodies. It should include areas of rugged terrain and, if possible, be adjacent to natural massifs [20].

The main background of the park is green spaces, so all the buildings in the park should be inscribed in the greenery and harmoniously combine with each other, complementing the beauty of each other, creating the impression of a single harmonious ensemble.

The main means of artistic composition of the park are green spaces, which change over time. Therefore, the architectural and planning composition of parks should take into account their development over a number of years [21].

Approximate data on the location, composition and landscaping of multifunctional park zones are given in Table 1.

3.2 Road Generation Algorithm

This algorithm is based on the family of pathfinding algorithms (hereafter referred to as PA), in particular the A* algorithm [22]. The basic concepts for understanding the workings of this algorithm are as follows:

– A graph is a mathematical abstraction of a real system of any kind, whose objects have pairwise relations. A graph as a mathematical object is a set of two sets - the set of objects themselves, called the set of vertices, and the set of their pairwise connections, called the set of edges. An element of the set of edges is a pair of elements of the set of vertices;
– Vertex - in this case the vertices of the graph are called the positions of the pointer that will build the road. A vertex can store the following information: name, address, available neighbours and previous vertex;

Table 1. Location, composition and landscaping of multifunctional park areas.

Types of zones*	Percentage of total park area	Accommodation as part of the park	Indicative composition**
1. Mass events zone	5–15	Near the main entrance	Security station, theatre, dance, cinema and variety theatres, dance halls, amusement centres, rental shops, catering and retail outlets, toilets, fields for festivals, mass games, etc
2. Quiet recreation area	40–75	Placed in the least frequented areas. Must be separated ornamental green plantings from areas mass events, physical training and recreational, cultural and educational events	Placement of structures is not allowed. Recreational areas
3. Cultural and educational events zone	3–8	Allocation in a separate zone Allocation in a separate zone or free placement of objects on the territory capital and non-capital construction	Exhibition halls, catering and retail establishments, reading pavilions, facilities for amateur activities, lecture theatres, toilets
4. Fitness and recreational area	10–20	It is recommended consolidation into single complex	Fitness, recreational and sports facilities: grounds for volleyball, basketball, badminton, table tennis, multifunctional sports grounds, sports grounds for extreme sports, skating rink, recreation grounds, hire shop, catering and catering and retailers, toilets

(continued)

Table 1. (*continued*)

Types of zones*	Percentage of total park area	Accommodation as part of the park	Indicative composition**
5. Recreation area for children	5–10	Detached, a little away from the entrances to the park	Children's playgrounds, recreation grounds, amusement rides
6. Administrative and economic zone	2–7	Separately	Utility grounds, administrative facilities, self-contained exit to adjacent street, car parks car parks for disabled people's vehicles, security point security, ticket office, ticket office, rental play and sports equipment, picnic equipment, information stands, places for cleaning equipment, toilets, areas for dog walking

* Depending on local conditions in the park, one or two zones may prevail while reducing the area of other zones (while maintaining the minimum area of the quiet recreation zone)
** Placement of facilities necessary for servicing recreationists and related to the natural specifics of the park environment with maximum preservation of the natural landscape

– An edge is a path from one vertex to another. Edges can be either one-way or two-way, depending on the context of use. For example, if the vertices are two benches that are in the same plane, then the edge can be two-sided because we can go from one bench to the other without interference. In the case of a one-sided edge, we can give the following example: a vertex (a) is elevated in space above another vertex (b). In this case, we can jump from vertex a to vertex b, but not vice versa;

– Accessible Neighbours (AN) - two or more vertices between which there are edges. An accessible neighbour is the vertex to which there is an edge from the given vertex;

– Pointer is an abstract object that looks through vertices to read their information and build a path. It is used to detect DCs and stores R and E arrays of data. In addition, the pointer stores the previous vertex in the current vertex, i.e. when it arrives at a new vertex, it writes which vertex it came from;

– Explored vertices (explored - E) - vertices that the pointer has already passed through;

– Reachable vertices (R) - vertices that the pointer can reach from E.

PA is based on representing the search environment as a graph. As mentioned above, the vertex of the graph in our case will be the position in the search environment, and the edge will be the transition from one position to another. An example from life can be any intercity flights, where the vertices are cities and the edges are the flights themselves. Stages of the algorithm:

1. The pointer finds vertices adjacent to the given vertex;
2. If we have already been to these vertices, i.e. if they are in E, we simply ignore them;
3. If we have not been to them yet, we add them to R, and also immediately write the current vertex as the previous vertex for all such found vertices;
4. The pointer moves to one of the vertices in R. It chooses it randomly among the available ones. Then the vertex to which the transition was made is removed from R and written to E;
5. If the given vertex is a finite vertex, the algorithm stops and proceeds to construct the path;
6. If there are no such vertices, the algorithm also stops and outputs nothing, i.e. the path simply does not exist;
7. To build a path, the pointer writes the current vertex into the path and moves from the current vertex to the previous vertex. This happens until the pointer reaches the initial vertex, then it inverts the path and we get the path from the initial to the end point.

This is the simplest implementation of PA, but it is not optimal. That is, this search does not promise us the shortest and optimal route from one point to another. Sometimes this can be useful, but first we need to find the shortest routes from one input to another [23].

To improve this algorithm, we don't need to ignore some vertices that are in E. Because we may well have found a more optimal route to that vertex. To find out, we need to add a cost (cost - C) to the edge. And now we add another condition to our algorithm in point 2: "If we have already been to these vertices, i.e. if they are in E, we simply ignore them. Instead, we first check the C of the current edge plus one and the C of the adjacent one, even if it is in E, and if it is smaller, we change the previous vertex for the adjacent one to the current one [24].

It is also worth correcting point 4: "The pointer goes to one of the R vertices. It chooses it randomly from the available ones. Then the vertex to which the transition was made is removed from R and written to E". It is worth choosing not a random one, but one that we can reach faster, i.e. its C is smaller.

This improvement allows the PA to look first at paths with lower costs when building a path, but finding the endpoint is still not optimal and takes quite a long time, so the algorithm still "crawls" in all directions until it finds the endpoint.

To tell our PA which way to go, we no longer need to ignore the fact that we know where the endpoint is, so we can find the distance to it from any vertex. The distance is calculated taking into account that there is nothing between the current vertex and the destination vertex [25]. To find the distance, it is sufficient to use formula (1):

$$|Ax - Bx| + |Ay - By| \tag{1}$$

where A is the current cell, B is the final cell. If it is possible to move diagonally, the following formula (2) is more suitable:

$$\sqrt{(Ax - Bx)^2 + (Ay - By)^2} \tag{2}$$

Now we need to modify point 4 again. Now we need to look from which of the adjacent vertices the distance to the end point will be smaller. Based on all the modifications we get the following:

1. The pointer finds vertices adjacent to the given vertex.
2. If we have already been in these vertices, i.e. if they are in E, we check C of the current edge plus one and C of the adjacent one, if it is less, we change the previous vertex for the adjacent one to the current one.
3. If we have not been in them yet, we add them to R and immediately write the current vertex as the previous vertex for all such found vertices.
4. The pointer moves to one of the R vertices. It chooses the R vertex from which the distance to the final vertex is the smallest. Then the vertex to which the transition was made is removed from R and written to E.
5. If this vertex is the final vertex, the algorithm stops and proceeds to path construction.
6. If there are no such vertices, the algorithm also stops and outputs nothing, i.e. the path simply does not exist.
7. To build a path, the pointer writes the current vertex into the path and moves from the current vertex to the previous vertex. This happens until the pointer reaches the initial vertex, then it inverts the path and we get the path from the initial to the end point.

3.3   Conceptual-Architectural Solution of the Program

The functioning of the designed system and the interaction of its modules are presented in the form of a scheme in the Fig. 1 below.

4   Implementing a Generative Design Program to Create a Park Layout

4.1   Tools Used

For the implementation of this product we have chosen a programming language such as C#. It is object-oriented, which allows you to create classes of different objects to simplify development. It was chosen because development is carried out in the cross-platform computer game development environment Unity, which allows you to create applications that run on more than 25 different platforms, including personal computers, game consoles, mobile devices, Internet applications and others.

Unity is installed through Hub, which allows you to install the "kernels" of the development environment yourself. The version of Hub used is the latest (3.4.x), and the "kernels" are v2021.3.19f1.

The code editor is Microsoft Visual Studio 2022 version 17.5.3 with the following workloads installed:

– Visual Studio's main editor;
– Game development with Unity;
– Developing for the Universal Windows Platform

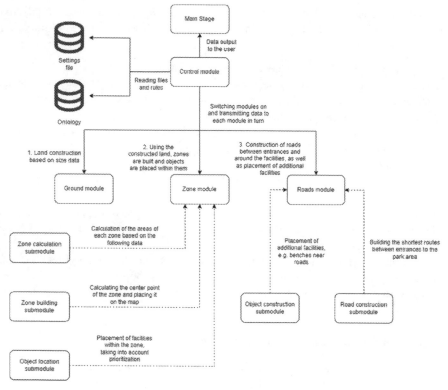

Fig. 1. Interaction of system modules

These tools were chosen to reduce development time, as most of it is already implemented in Unity. As an alternative, it was possible to use the Unreal Engine 4 game engine, which has been free since 2015, and which has also been developed enough that it is now possible to make not only first-person shooters with it.

We could have used any other programming language, but we would have had to implement a lot more algorithms and it would have taken a lot more time and resources.

4.2 Data and State Storage System

As a data storage system, an ontology is used to store all possible objects that can be located in the park, as well as the rules for their location. The ontology should store a set of zones and their location rules (example in Sect. 2), as well as a set of objects that are allowed to be located in these zones (example in Fig. 2, 3). In addition, each object must have rules for its location relative to other objects.

In the future, it is planned to extend the ontology to allow for a better layout. To achieve this, it is possible to store not only the rules of location relative to other objects, but also to take into account the topography or even the neighboring infrastructure.

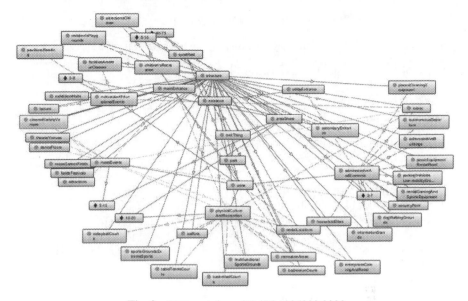

Fig. 2. OWL ontology SP 475.1325800.2020

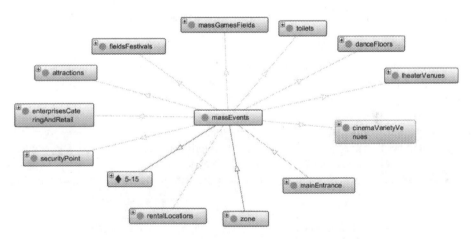

Fig. 3. Detailed fragment OWL ontology SP 475.1325800.2020

In addition to the ontology, there should be a settings file, which is a set of initial parameters from which the layout is generated. This set includes the following parameters:

- Parking area;
- Entry list (coordinates relative to the area);
- Generated zones;
- A set of objects for each zone.

4.3 Development of Special Functions and Algorithms

As mentioned above, the solution architecture consists of several modules:

- Soil construction module;
- zone construction module;
- Road construction module;
- post construction module.

For each of these modules, algorithms have been developed to determine the layout construction behavior. These algorithms take into account the rules defined by the user.

Algorithm of Land Construction

This is the simplest algorithm. It represents uniform filling of a grid of a given area. The following classes have been developed for the operation of this algorithm:

- The Groud class - with this class you can create instances of a soil cell. This object will be able to store the following data:

  - Whether it is available for building;
  - What type of object is above it;
  - What zone it belongs to;
  - And also material - needed to color the zone the object belongs to. In the future it will be used for textures.

- The GroudBuilder class is the main class of this module. It can be used to execute the algorithm for building the ground cells and it also stores the ground mesh. The process of the algorithm is as follows:

  - Getting the dimensionality - length and width of the grid.
  - Creating a virtual grid - a grid of the obtained dimension is created, each cell of which corresponds to an instance of the Ground class.
  - Model building - a ground model of the park is built based on the data stored in the virtual grid.

In the future this algorithm will be extended. It will include the functionality of building the ground from Open Street Maps with machine learning can scale up collaborative map production and map quality to the level needed to enable global and state-of-the-art land mapping, as well as terrain simulation [26].

Algorithm for Building Zones

This algorithm is responsible for calculating the area of each zone, plotting these zones on the ground cells and placing objects within the zone. At this stage, this algorithm is overloaded and should be broken down into several parts. The process of the algorithm is:

1. The algorithm receives a list of zones to generate.

2. The calculation of areas based on the total area takes place. The area of a zone is calculated using the following formula (3):

$$Sz = \frac{p*100}{S},$$ (3)

where, Sz is the area of the zone, p is its percentage of the total area and S is the total built-up area.
3. Based on the generation order (presented in Table 1), the generation of each zone starts, following the rules set by the user. The generation of one zone proceeds as follows:
   a. The center point of the zone is calculated relative to the landmark point. That is, the zone must be within the park boundaries with its entire area (intersection with other zones is allowed). The point of reference can be an obvious object, as in the case of the mass event zone, where the point of reference can be the main entrance to the park, if there is one.
   b. Once the center point is found, the coordinates of the bottom left and top right cells are calculated to construct the zone rectangle. In the future, the algorithm will be redesigned to build polygonal zones.
   c. A rectangular zone is constructed using the coordinates.
   d. Objects are placed in this zone. According to the following principle: highest priority → largest size.
   e. Move to the next zone and start working from point a.

Road Construction Algorithm
The conceptual algorithm was described in Sect. 2. It will now be examined with the existing classes. A virtual network created in the land construction phase and updated in the zone construction phase is used as the graph. This algorithm also takes into account the possibility of building a road in a cell. That is, the algorithm uses the data of each ground cell, namely the buildability and whether the object is above the cell. If both factors allow the road to be built, then the road is built.
    The process of the algorithm is:

1. The start cell is set to one of the park entrances and the end cell is set to any other cell.
2. The algorithm gets a list of available cells to move the cells. The available cells are those that are adjacent to the current cell and on which it is possible to build objects.
3. For all cells found, the current cell is written as the previous cell.
4. Next, the cost of each cell is calculated based on its cost and distance to the endpoint. The distance is calculated using the formula (1). And the cost is calculated using the following formula (4) [27]:

$$D - (Ac + Bc),$$ (4)

where A is the current cell, B is the adjacent free cell, D is the distance from the current cell to the destination cell.

5. The cost of all cells to be calculated is looked up, even if the cell was in the explored cell list.
6. If the cost of the cell under consideration is lower than the others, it becomes the current cell, even if it has already been explored, but then its previous cell is overwritten.
7. If it was an endpoint, the algorithm terminates, otherwise it repeats steps 2–5.
8. As a result, it turns out that from the end cell we have a path from the previous cells to the initial cell, along which the road is built.

4.4 Features of Using Unity

As mentioned above, the Unity game engine is used for implementation. It allows you to create cross-platform games using the C# programming language. It was chosen by me because of its user-friendliness, and also because it is easy to generate 3D terrain, and there is a large number of extensions that will further improve this solution.

5 Testing and Examples of Using the Program for Generating the Territory Layout

5.1 Description of the Developed Program Functionality

The program is a set of algorithms written in the C# programming language, which interact with the Unity game development environment. This system of algorithms provides functionality to generate a layout based on parameters, terrain configuration file and normative rules loaded from ontology. The result of the generation is a park area layout with a specific set of objects, points of interest and roads.

In Unity, each developed module is represented as empty objects in a hierarchy. Attached to each such object are scripts containing the programmatic implementation of the algorithms. It is also possible to set generation parameters through these objects.

5.2   Input and Output Data

As input data, the user sets the parameters within the objects discussed above. The output data is the generated layout inside the Unity interface.

5.3   Demonstration of the Operation of the Proposed Solution

The program operation starts with reading all the entered parameters. Next, the land module starts working, which, based on the scale, builds a plane of land cells (Fig. 4).

Fig. 4. Example of ground module operation

Next, the program calculates each zone and builds them on the generated land, filling them with objects (Fig. 5, 6).

Once the zones are built, the roads module starts and builds roads from entrance to entrance, around the zones and builds additional objects such as benches and garbage cans (Fig. 7).

Fig. 5. Building zones and filling them with objects (initial zones)

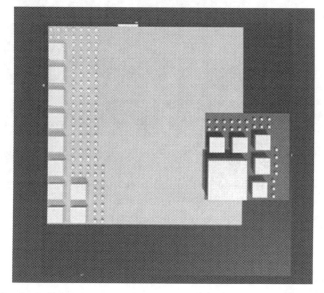

Fig. 6. Building zones and filling them with objects (extended zones)

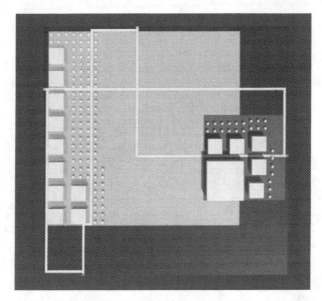

Fig. 7. Building roads around facilities

6 Conclusion

This article provides an overview of existing generative design approaches in urban planning. Generative design and ontological engineering play an increasingly important role in urban planning, as these approaches allow to optimize the process of designing and planning the urban environment, taking into account the growing need for efficient use of resources. We propose a method for designing the layout of a park area based on generative design technologies as well as ontological engineering. This approach will reduce the time for designing new areas and evaluating existing projects.

The application of generative design and ontological engineering in urban planning can lead to significant benefits, such as more efficient use of resources, improved quality of life and comfort of citizens, as well as the formation of a sustainable and inclusive urban environment. They enable a more detailed analysis and optimization of urban systems, taking into account various factors, including economic, environmental and social aspects.

Future research in generative design and ontological engineering in urban planning will contribute to the development of new methods, tools and approaches, as well as to their practical application to create smart and sustainable cities of the future. The use of these approaches will lead to a more efficient development of urban planning projects that combine functionality, environmental sustainability and quality of life for city dwellers. In further research, it is planned to extend the ontological model with new sets of rules, as well as rules for the formation of urban areas, and to implement the proposed approaches and methods in the most popular software products.

Acknowledgments. The reported study was funded by VSTU, project number 45/558-23.

References

1. Slizh, V.D., Salnikov, V.B.: Benefits of generative design. Ural TIM readings. Technologies of information modeling of buildings and territories. In: Materials of the Scientific and Practical All-Russian Conference, 5–6 November 2020, pp. 23–27. LTD Tipografiya Agraf (2020)
2. Smetanina, N.I.: Generative design as a new design and design tool. In: Chihachyova, M.M., Perepich, N.V., Sablina, M.V. Art through the Eyes of the Young: Proceedings of the X International Scientific Conference 2018, pp. 76–77. Federal State Budgetary Educational Institution of Higher Education (2018)
3. Laushkina, A.A., Basov, O.O.: Application of generative design methods using multimodal data in the field of architecture and urban planning. scientific result. Inf. Technol. **3**, 3–10 (2021)
4. Rodionova, U.V., Pahtaeva, A.Y.: Application of artificial intelligence technologies for generative landscape design. In: Materials of the Scientific-Practical Conference with International Participation, 05–06 November 2020, p. 19. Ural State University of Architecture and Art (2020)
5. Ajrapetyan, N.G., Zajcev, A.A.: Increasing the efficiency of land use based on generative design. J. Leg. Econ. Res. **3**, 129–136 (2021)
6. Garyaeva, V.V., Garyaev, A.N.: Information processing in building design automation using generative design technology. Sci. Tech. Bull. Volga Reg. **4**, 61–63 (2022)
7. Moscovitz, O., Barath, S.: A generative design approach to urban sustainability rating systems during early-stage planning (2022). https://doi.org/10.52842/conf.caadria.2022.1.171
8. Sun, Y., Dogan, T.: Generative methods for Urban design and rapid solution space exploration (2022). https://doi.org/10.48550/arXiv.2212.06783
9. Kumalasari, D., Koeva, M., Vahdatikhaki, F., et al.: Generative design for walkable cities: a case study of Sofia. In: The International Archives of the Photogrammetry, Remote Sensing and Spatial Information Sciences, vol. XLVIII-4/W5-2022, pp. 75–82 (2022). https://doi.org/10.5194/isprs-archives-XLVIII-4-W5-2022-75-2022
10. Wang, D., Wu, L., Zhang, D., et al.: Human-instructed deep hierarchical generative learning for automated urban planning (2022). https://doi.org/10.48550/arXiv.2212.00904
11. Miao, Y., Koenig, R., Knecht, K.: The development of optimization methods in generative urban design. A review (2020)
12. Koenig, R., Miao, Y., Aichinger, A., et al.: Integrating urban analysis, generative design, and evolutionary optimization for solving urban design problems. Environ. Plan. B Urban Anal. City Sci. **47**(6), 997–1013 (2020)
13. Koma, S., Yamabe, Y., Tani, A.: Research on urban landscape design using the interactive genetic algorithm and 3D images. Vis. Eng. **5**, 1 (2017)
14. Blender Artists Community. Procedural Modeling Pipeline with Geometry Nodes - a blog. https://blenderartists.org/t/procedural-modeling-pipeline-with-geometry-nodes-a-blog/1324182. Accessed 20 July 2023
15. Blender Market. (n.d.). Road Path Creator. https://blendermarket.com/products/road-path-creator. Accessed 20 July 2023
16. Gumroad. Buildify 1.0. https://paveloliva.gumroad.com/l/buildify. Accessed 20 July 2023
17. Autodesk Community. Webinar 'Generative Design for Revit Conceptual Design'. https://forums.autodesk.com/t5/revit-i-navisworks-russkiy/vebinar-quot-generativnyy-dizayn-dlya-kontseptualnogo/td-p/10047470. Accessed 20 July 2023
18. Bozhuk, V.N.: Internet-journal 'SCIENCE' (2016). http://naukovedenie.ru/PDF/68EVN316.pdf. Accessed 20 July 2023
19. Ivlyakova, A.Y., Chesnokov, N.N., Rudaya, O.A.: Landscape architecture and urban planning (2021). http://opusmgau.ru/index.php/see/article/view/3077/3071. Accessed 25 July 2023

20. Zelenskiy, I., Parygin, D., Savina, O., Finogeev, A., Gurtyakov, A.M.: Effective implementation of integrated area development based on consumer attractiveness assessment, vol. 14, no. 23, p. 16239 (2022). https://doi.org/10.3390/su142316239
21. Parygin, D., Sadovnikova, N., Gamidullaeva, L., Finogeev, A., Rashevskiy, N.M.: Tools and technologies for sustainable territorial development in the context of a quadruple innovation helix, vol. 14, no. 15, pp. 9086–9086 (2022). https://doi.org/10.3390/su14159086
22. Habr.: A* pathfinding algorithm in voxel-based 3d game on Unity (2018). https://habr.com/ru/post/416737/. Accessed 21 July 2023
23. Sadovnikova, N., Savina, O., Danila, P., Alexey, C., Alexey, S.: Application of scenario forecasting methods and fuzzy multi-criteria modeling in substantiation of urban area development strategies, vol. 14, no. 4, p. 241 (2023). https://doi.org/10.3390/info14040241
24. Frieze, A., Tomasz, T.: Shortest paths with a cost constraint: a probabilistic analysis, vol. 302, pp. 46–53 (2021). https://doi.org/10.1016/j.dam.2021.06.001
25. Cui, M., Levinson, D.: Shortest paths, travel costs, and traffic. Environ. Plan. B Urban Anal. City Sci. **48**(4), 828–844 (2020). https://doi.org/10.1177/2399808319897619
26. Estima, J., Painho, M.: Exploratory analysis of OpenStreetMap for land use classification (2013). https://doi.org/10.1145/2534732.2534734
27. Lu, H., Zheng, W., Wang, T.-B., Wang, S.-H.: An effective cost distance calculation based on raster data model improved algorithm. https://doi.org/10.1109/iccsnt.2011.6182416

Spatial Data Analysis for Decision Support in Urban Infrastructure Development Planning

Ivan Danilov[(✉)], Alexey Shuklin[ⓘ], Ilya Zelenskiy[ⓘ], Alexander Gurtyakov[ⓘ], and Mikhail Kulikov

Volgograd State Technical University, 1 Akademicheskaya Str., 400074 Volgograd, Russia
danilov_ivan98@bk.ru

Abstract. Modern cities meet many of the criteria for a comfortable and safe life for their citizens. However, the rapid researches and developments in the fields of information technology and telecommunications stimulates further modernization of urban environment in order to provide maximum possible conveniences to everyone - from a resident to an urban planner and manager. The work of the latter largely determines the comfort and safety of urban residents. In this regard, it is necessary that urban planners and managers can make decisions based on objective factual data, which needs to be easily and quickly obtainable without spending a lot of time on it. For this reason, there is a need to develop IT solutions aimed at the optimization of the work of planners and managers. In order to justify solutions for transforming the urban environment to make it more comfortable, safe and harmonious, sustainable and integrated development, methods for analyzing and assessing the current state and monitoring changes are needed. This paper considers the problem of collecting data on the state of urban infrastructure. The application of spatial data analysis to solve the problems of urban territories management and urban planning are investigated. A method for estimating the area of the city, occupied by the objects of different categories, is presented. Implementation of the proposed approach is shown on the example of calculating the area occupied by industrial objects.

Keywords: Spatial Data Analysis · Geoinformation Systems · City Infrastructure · Urban Planning · Decision Support

1 Introduction

In recent decades, urbanization has become one of the key trends in global development, causing increased interest from economists, geographers, sociologists and representatives of other scientific disciplines. First of all, this is due to the fact that the prevailing proportion of the world's population lives in cities. At the same time, urban areas occupy only 0.5% to 1.5% of the total surface area of the Earth, according to various assessments.

Today the viability of cities depends on many factors. For example, the presence of a variety of economic, social, and cultural activities, which in turn are linked to population density and a well-developed urban infrastructure [1]. In order to improve the quality of

A. G. Kravets et al. (Eds.): CIT&DS 2023, CCIS 1909, pp. 568–578, 2023.
https://doi.org/10.1007/978-3-031-44615-3_40

life of the urban population, as well as to ensure the sustainability and comprehensiveness [2] of the development of cities themselves, the optimization and harmonization of urban space, based on the analysis of data on the territory under study, is required. To solve this problem, spatial data analysis technologies are increasingly used to identify patterns of spatial distribution of urban objects, using the tools of geographic information systems (GIS) [3].

Spatial data analysis can be used to analyze the location of objects, identify areas with specified properties, determine the structural features of urban space, verification of object location compliance with requirements and standards, analysis of the dynamics of spatial development of the territory and much more [4–6]. Such methods are necessary to assess the potential of the territory's development and to form strategies for its development. In addition, spatial information is the basis for creating advanced solutions for various interdisciplinary projects aimed at sustainable development [7].

2 Usage of Spatial Data Analysis Methods in Urban Planning Tasks

Spatial data analysis methods are an important tool for solving urban planning problems. They can be used for land plot analysis, prediction of terrain changes, housing and transport planning, as well as for detailing urban construction projects. That is why many scientists and researchers are interested in the development of this direction.

Spatial data analysis in [5] was used to study the coherence of urban infrastructure development on the example of Vienna. The term Coherence of Territories (CT), introduced by the authors, would be relevant in [6]. "CT is the coherence of the development of providing infrastructure that meets the needs of the population." For our research, the work is interesting in terms of spatial analysis of the availability of urban infrastructure in ultralocal areas of the territory (ULUT), as well as in pedestrian accessibility (PAT). The method of work is as follows: we form a query to a database with a list of tags of all objects, the calculation of PAT of which is currently performed, then we set the point and radius (800m in the work) of pedestrian accessibility, in the resulting area we search for objects from the list. As a result, the authors conclude that for a balanced development of the city it is necessary to have objective analytics, which, in turn, should be obtained by using spatial analysis of data.

In [6] there is an example of Spatial Urban Data System (SUDS). With the help of third-party services with open API, the authors of the article obtained various heterogeneous data combined to provide qualitative analytics about the life levels in UK. The system not only identified unsuitable places to live, but also allowed to identify specific reasons for low interest in this housing (poor transport infrastructure, high rent, lack of jobs nearby, etc.). Such service has the potential for scalability and further integration with other services. The data obtained with the help of such system will be especially valuable for city administration as it will allow developing the city on the basis of analytical socio-economic data. With this system, the development of urban infrastructure will be balanced, and the elimination of negative factors identified by this system will lead to an increase in the attractiveness of previously unsuitable areas of the city (for example, due to low accessibility of transport infrastructure or a large distance from workplaces).

Spatial analysis should not neglect the social factor. In [7], the authors proposed the idea of using social networks to promote urban projects, as well as to identify the reaction of citizens to these projects. The authors developed a program based on the open API of Vkontakte for parsing comments, likes and responses to the post. After that, using a special library, they visualized this data, graphing the dynamics of reaction to the event over time. Thus, according to the Socratic Method, the dialogue between citizens and planners will generate new ideas that meet the needs of citizens. Undoubtedly, the lack of dialogue between authorities and citizens reduces trust between these groups. Proposing a city development project for consideration by citizens, getting a reaction to it, and following the trend of that reaction, a correct and adequate management decision can be made. The pros of such an approach to city development are that the residents participate, the planners receive feedback (positive or negative) on their projects, and the authorities gain the trust of the citizens.

There are many scientific studies devoted to the analysis of urban environment, and development of methods to improve it. For example, Neil Jean in his work [8] proposed a method for analyzing the urban environment based on satellite imagery data to assess the environmental condition of cities. The method involves acquiring high-resolution satellite images, preprocessing them for corrections, classifying land cover types, analyzing vegetation indices, assessing the urban heat island effect, evaluating green space distribution, detecting urban changes, and conducting spatial analysis to understand the overall environmental condition of cities.

Geodata are the basis for the development of spatial management systems and include a wide range of tasks related to land use [9]. This includes tasks such as land parcel identification, zoning, land cover classification, urban planning, infrastructure development, resource management, environmental assessment, and decision-making processes. By utilizing geodata, spatial management systems can effectively analyze and optimize land use, promoting sustainable development and informed decision-making in relation to our built and natural environments.

The article [10] presents an overview of researches of Semantic Web Technologies application in urban planning tasks. These technologies enable the integration of heterogeneous datasets, facilitate interoperability between different systems and applications, support advanced querying and analysis of urban data, and enable the development of smart and interconnected urban planning systems that can improve decision-making and urban development processes.

The research conducted by A.E. Avdyushina [11] explored the possibilities of integrating machine learning methods and GIS technologies. The study focused on utilizing pattern recognition methods to identify urban objects and analyze their boundaries. By applying machine learning algorithms to GIS data, the research aimed to automatically identify and delineate various urban objects, such as buildings, roads, and vegetation, based on their distinct patterns and characteristics. This integration of machine learning and GIS technologies provides a valuable approach for efficiently and accurately analyzing urban landscapes, supporting tasks like urban mapping, infrastructure planning, and land use management.

Spatial analysis was also used in [12]. The study analyzed data from 286 cities in China from 2003 to 2015 to examine the impact of industrial agglomerations and transport infrastructure development on land use efficiency. The results demonstrated that the presence of industrial agglomerations positively influenced land use efficiency, indicating that cities with concentrated industrial activities tend to make more efficient use of their land resources. Additionally, the development of transport infrastructure, such as roads and railways, was found to have a significant positive effect on land use efficiency, suggesting that improved transportation connectivity enhances the overall effectiveness of land utilization in cities. These findings highlight the importance of coordinated industrial and transportation planning in optimizing land use efficiency in urban areas.

Another example of application of spatial analysis to improve safety, comfort and quality of life of citizens, through the rational planning of the urban environment, is presented in [13]. The authors apply spatial analysis to determine the "coverage zones" of hospitals in the large Iranian city of Esfahan. The authors, based on their analysis, conclude that the city hospitals cover about 32% of the area of the city, and provide a visualization of this information.

The application of spatial analysis in planning the development of the urban environment, taking into account the principles of green urban planning is demonstrated in [14]. Applying the ArcGIS software package, the authors managed to allocate green areas for a number of Belarusian cities. In addition, the objects falling within the 15-min walking accessibility zones of residents of these cities were also defined in order to determine the most attractive points of these cities, and the visualization of these data was presented. A similar method was used by the authors of the article [6], but with different data acquisition tools.

Urban greening is a cost-effective and efficient way to mitigate the negative effect of urban heat islands on citizens. An urban heat island is a meteorological phenomenon that consists in temperature increase of urban space relative to the surrounding rural areas [15]. Analyzing the occurrence of such islands in order to predict the zones where the next island is formed is extremely important to mitigate the effect and take preventive measures against this phenomenon in these areas. Such a solution would improve the quality of life of residents in cities where summer temperatures can exceed 30 °C. The work of the authors L. Sanchez and T. Rims [16] applied the method of spatial analysis, as well as GIS-technology to analyze the terrain and predict the appearance of heat islands in Detroit. The work is comprehensive because in addition to the geospatial analysis, it also provides social analysis of population living in these areas. For the purposes of our work, our interest is focused rather on the geoanalytical part of the paper. The authors used ArcMap tool to obtain the thermal relief of the map of Detroit, Buffer tool was used to generate a polygon of walking accessibility of citizens, Landstat8 tool was used to obtain data, from which the thermal island (normalized index of vegetation differentiation) was then calculated. Thus, the authors were able to calculate and visualize heat islands in Detroit.

Despite the existence of literature on similar topics, as well as the expansion of popularity of "smart" cities technologies usage, the problem of spatial data analysis application in planning of urban infrastructure in scientific researches has been touched relatively superficially at the moment. This study aims to close this gap.

3   Area Occupied by Urban Infrastructure Facilities Assessment Method

The territories of urban agglomerations include objects of various categories, defined according to the functional purposes. These include various types of manufacturing objects (factories, enterprises, etc.), places of cultural, entertainment and municipal events, etc.

The method of spatial analysis proposed in this paper includes automated collecting and processing of data on urban infrastructure facilities and the areas occupied by them (in this case, the area of an object means the area of the land plot allocated to it) with subsequent provision of obtained data to the user.

The list of objects categories considered in this article includes, in particular, industrial, tourist, cultural and municipal objects, as well as unused land areas. The collected data may be provided to the user in the following forms:

1. Absolute value. In the form of individual objects area or the sum of all object's areas for a certain category (industrial, municipal, etc.) within an urban agglomeration or a separate part of it.
2. Relative value. As a share of industrial facilities areas of the total urban agglomeration area (or part of it), depending on the end user's needs.

Such information can be useful for decision makers in the framework of urban management tasks.

An example is the choice of the development direction for an urban agglomeration. Deciding on the further development of an unused (or inefficiently used) territory based on the total tourist objects area and having studied the relative indicators, the decision maker may come to the conclusion about the redundancy or, on the contrary, the lack of development of this infrastructure category. Thus, a decision can be made to carry on an additional development of the tourism sector of the city, including creation of new facilities.

Thereby, the need for this method is justified and has prospects for its further practical application.

At the current stage of the study the main urban environment state data source is the Open Street Map (OSM) service [17]. This service is a non-commercial geographic information system (GIS) with a wiki-like function of open editing by community members [17], which ensures prompt data updating, although it may also lead to data inaccuracy. Also, it provides the ability utilize a variety of tools and APIs for spatial analysis and visualization.

At the first stage, we obtain the list of all objects of a certain category.

Then, after collecting information from OSM, the data are filtered by object tag (category) and unnecessary records are removed leaving only the objects necessary for further processing.

On the next stage all objects' tags are checked and, if they match the required ones, the objects' names are saved into the names array. This is necessary for the final data output and for further obtain the coordinates of the objects.

Coordinates are collected on the next stage. The data received is stored in two temporal arrays (an array of longitude and an array of latitude). Based on these data, an array of coordinates is to be formed.

The algorithm of urban objects information collecting and processing is presented in detail in Fig. 1.

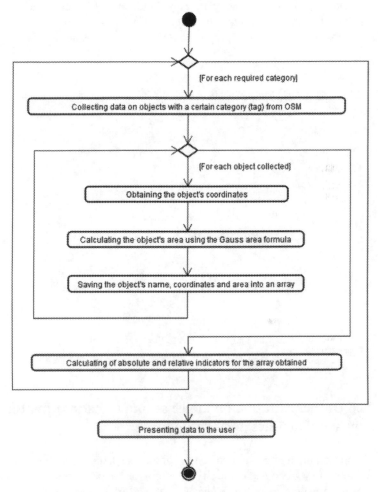

Fig. 1. Data obtaining and processing algorithm.

It includes the following steps:

1. Collecting of a primary data array on objects of the required categories (industrial, tourist, etc.) from OSM. Selection of objects of necessary categories can be carried out using the tag system implemented in OSM;
2. Building a list of objects' names (identifiers) received from OSM;
3. Collecting geographical coordinates of objects (longitude and latitude) based on the previously built names list using OSM;

4. Calculating the area of each object based on previously obtained geographic coordinates using the Gauss area formula, also known as the surveyor's formula [18].

Thus, the area of all objects for each category (tag) will be obtained, after which additional calculations can be carried out in accordance with the end user's needs. For example, calculations of absolute and relative areal indicators for a given urban agglomeration, or part of it. Data can be presented both in the numerical values and in graphical forms, in particular, in the form of graphs and/or charts. An example of a diagram is shown in Fig. 2.

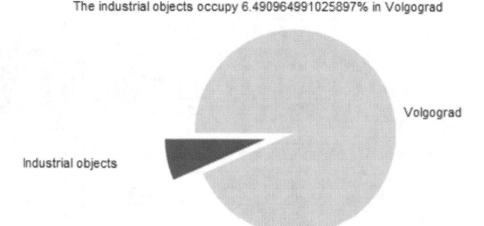

Fig. 2. The ratio of production facilities' areas to the total area of the city of Volgograd.

4   Method Implementation on the Example of Estimating the Area of Industrial Facilities and Warehouses

To test the proposed method, it was decided to conduct a spatial analysis of data on production facilities and warehouses in the city of Volgograd. In particular, it was necessary to obtain the total absolute and relative area of all objects of this category within the city.

The Python programming language was used to implement the method, as it has an extensive ecosystem of geospatial libraries, which made the work much easier and more efficient. To work with geodata, the Osmnx library (OpenStreetMap to NetworkX) [19] was used. It allowed us to get geographic data such as polygons, lines and points by querying OpenStreetMap servers [17].

For the calculation, filters and queries were applied to select only production facilities and warehouses. Filtering was based on attributes to highlight objects with certain characteristics.

The area calculation process can be described by the following sequence of steps:

1. Geo object representation: A geo object, such as a polygon, is represented in a data structure that contains information about its geometry, such as vertex coordinates.
2. Triangulation: If the geo object had a complex shape, it is divided into simpler geometric elements, such as triangles, by triangulation. Triangulation splits a geo object into a set of non-intersecting triangles using its vertices.
3. Calculating the area of triangles: For each triangle in the geo object, the area is calculated using the Gauss formula. The Gauss formula is based on the mathematical theory of vector fields and integrals, and allows you to calculate the area of a closed surface. It is important to note that any other similar methods could be used for the calculation.
4. Getting the total absolute area: The obtained areas of all triangles are summed up to get the total area of the geo object. This is done by using mathematical summation algorithms.
5. Obtaining the relative area: The resulting total absolute area is divided by the total area of the city of Volgograd and as a result the relative area of industrial facilities is calculated.

The results of applying this method can be seen in the form of a graphical visualization in Fig. 2.

The method presented in our work has, as noted earlier, some similarity with the work of Avdyushina A.E. [11]. However, our research took different paths: the ITMO team focused on the visualization of spatial research methods, while our research focused more on the implementation and practical application of spatial analysis methods themselves. However, such data indeed needs high-quality visualization. By training a neural network, we can achieve a reduction in the risk of erroneous recognition of an object or incorrect recognition of its boundaries, which will allow us to use this method to determine objects of certain categories for our spatial analysis method.

5 Conclusions

The proposed method has prospects for development and application. So far, spatial data analysis has only been applied to production facilities and warehouses. It would be justified to further scale the method towards processing other objects categories (social, cultural and entertainment, tourist, etc.), as well as adding these categories to determine the share of land occupied from the total city area of each of these categories. In addition, scaling can be expressed by connecting additional data sources (for example, other GIS).

Also, the proposed method of spatial analysis has the potential for scaling in the form of integration, together with other similar methods of analytics, into one common service that provides decision makers in urban area management with quick and convenient access to the necessary data. The use of the proposed method, with its further development, can contribute to the integrated and sustainable development of urban areas [15], i.e. ultimately achieving the goal of "Sustainable Cities", which occupies the 11th line in the list of UN goals [20, 21].

An example of the concept of such a service is shown in Fig. 3.

This example shows the acquisition of the data described in this paper in the context of a complete program solution. However, this concept extends to other methods that we

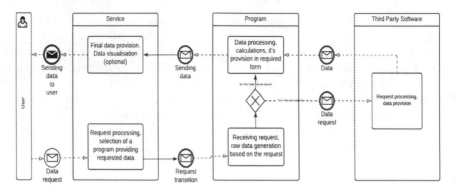

Fig. 3. Service workflow scheme.

talked about earlier (for example, the analysis of urban canyons). As stated above, city planners need different data, which can be obtained in different ways. Making it easy to get this data is only half the solution. Let's say you are a planner. You are faced with the task of developing a city, for which you will need various data, such as, for example, the area of urban agglomeration, population, income data, transport infrastructure data, etc. This heterogeneous data can be obtained using several separate methods (search for information on the Internet, the use of special programs, etc.) or using one service that would reduce the number of your actions to one: enter a request for the information you are interested in.

Such a simple approach will become a big benefit from different points of view. First of all, one of the biggest pros for universal solution is optimization. The optimization process starts with modern digital solutions for information collecting (GIS for example) instead of obtaining this information manually. The next big step in the goal of optimization is developing new ways to obtain information, as well as ways to obtain various information via just a single tool – computer. User would rather use google search to find answer for a particular question than flip through a bunch of pages of various reference books and encyclopedias. The method described above works the same. User would just create a request to get, for example, data about city population and their income. The third big step is to find a way to combine these different methods of obtaining information and also find a way to store all heterogeneous data obtained by these methods together and provide user with simple and easy-to-use service that will fulfill a city planner's needs. You probably would rather use one particular program or service that allows you to obtain all the data you need with various presentation of this data (chart, diagram, raw data, etc.).

The second benefit that an end user will get is relevance. All the data that is being obtained by sensors, satellites and other devices are up-to-date. In fact, it is the most relevant data you can get by a single request. Sensors obtain data right now, not in 5 min, not in 10, not tomorrow. Data collecting and processing takes some time to complete but in terms of days of manual work, it takes from few seconds to few minutes to provide user with relevant and reliable data. Thus a user can save time and be sure that data he uses is reliable and relevant and focus on his main goal – improving citizens' life.

The third benefit is scalability and flexibility of the system proposed. The idea of a combined service for city planners is not new. But our goal in future is to present a system that allows users to propose new methods of obtaining information, picking particular method of obtaining (if it exists), add new methods and data that can be collected and a lot more. Flexibility and user involvement is a key to create a strong service that can satisfy every – even picky – user.

Acknowledgments. The study has been supported by the grant from the Russian Science Foundation (RSF) and the Administration of the Volgograd Oblast (Russia) No. 22-11-20024, https://rscf.ru/en/project/22-11-20024/. The authors express gratitude to colleagues from the Department of Digital Technologies for Urban Studies, Architecture and Civil Engineering, VSTU involved in the development of the project.

References

1. Jacobs, J.: The Death and Life of Great American Cities. Vintage Books, New York (1961)
2. Zelenskiy, I., Parygin, D., Savina, O., Finogeev, A., Gurtyakov, A.: Effective implementation of integrated area development based on consumer attractiveness assessment. Sustainability **14**(23), Article 16239 (2022). https://doi.org/10.3390/su142316239
3. Haining, R.P.: Spatial Data Analysis: Theory and Practice, p. 453. Cambridge University Press, Cambridge (2003)
4. Kumar, S., Jailia, M.: Manisha, smart cities with spatial data infrastructure and big data - a critical review. Int. J. Adv. Stud. Sci. Res. **3**(11) (2018). SSRN: https://ssrn.com/abstract=3319275
5. Zuev, A., Parygin, D., Sadovnikova, N., Aleshkevich, A., Boiko, D.: Analysis methods of spatial structure metrics for assessment of area development effectiveness. In: Alexandrov, D.A., Boukhanovsky, A.V., Chugunov, A.V., Kabanov, Y., Koltsova, O., Musabirov, I. (eds.) Digital Transformation and Global Society. DTGS 2020. CCIS, vol. 1242, pp. 273–288. Springer, Cham (2020). https://doi.org/10.1007/978-3-030-65218-0_21
6. Obinna, C.D.A., et al.: Spatial urban data system: a cloud-enabled big data infrastructure for social and economic urban analytics. Futur. Gener. Comput. Syst. **98**, 456–473 (2019). https://doi.org/10.1016/j.future.2019.03.052
7. Sadovnikova, N., Savina, O., Parygin, D., Churakov, A., Shuklin, A.: Application of scenario forecasting methods and fuzzy multi-criteria modeling in substantiation of urban area development strategies. Information **14**(4), Art. no. 241 (2023). Mode of access: https://www.mdpi.com/2078-2489/14/4/241/pdf, https://doi.org/10.3390/info14040241
8. Jean, N., et al.: Combining satellite imagery and machine learning to predict poverty. Science **353**(6301), 790–794 (2016)
9. Karmanov, A.G., Knyshev, A.I., Eliseeva, V.V.: Geoinformation systems of territorial management, no. 128, pp. 70–78. ITMO University, St. Petersburg (2015)
10. von Richthofen, A., Herthogs, P., Kraft, M., Cairns, S.: Semantic city planning systems (SCPS): a literature review. J. Plan. Lit. **37**(3), 415–432 (2022)
11. Avdyushina, A.E., Danilina, E.Y.: Digital urban studies: a study of urban infrastructure. Results of modern scientific research and development, pp. 10–14 (2021)
12. Zhang, W., et al.: How does industrial agglomeration affect urban land use efficiency? A spatial analysis of Chinese cities. Land Use Policy **119**, 106178 (2022)
13. Soltani, A., et al.: Spatial analysis and urban land use planning with emphasis on hospital site selection, case study: Isfahan city. Bull. Geograp. Socio-econ. Ser. (43), 71–89 (2019)

14. Sysoeva, V.A., Semenuk, A.S.: Method of spatial analysis for urban development planning, taking into account the principles of green urban planning (2023)
15. Santamouris, M.: Cooling the cities—a review of reflective and green roof mitigation technologies to fight heat island and improve comfort in urban environments. Sol. Energy **103**, 682–703 (2014)
16. Sanchez, L., Reames, T.G.: Cooling Detroit: a socio-spatial analysis of equity in green roofs as an urban heat island mitigation strategy. Urban Forestry Urban Green. **44**, 126331 (2019)
17. Open Street Map. www.openstreetmap.org. Accessed 16 June 2023
18. Richard, R., George, M.: Robert Whipple. Geometry for Enjoyment and Challenge. new. McDougal Littell, pp. 717–718 (1991). ISBN 0-86609-965-4
19. Osmnx. https://osmnx.readthedocs.io/. Accessed 13 June 2023
20. Parygin, D., Sadovnikova, N., Gamidullaeva, L., Finogeev, A., Rashevskiy, N.: Tools and technologies for sustainable territorial development in the context of a quadruple innovation helix. Sustainability **14**(15), Art. no. 9086 (2022). Mode of access: https://www.mdpi.com/2071-1050/14/15/9086/pdf. https://doi.org/10.3390/su14159086
21. Sustainable development Goals. https://www.un.org/sustainabledevelopment/ru/sustainable-development-goals/. Accessed 15 May 2023

Author Index

A

Al-Darraji, Hasan Chasib   467
Al-Gunaid, Mohammed A.   171, 323
Andreeva, Yulia   351
Arinkin, Nikita   420
Artyushin, Vladimir O.   323
Asanova, Natalia   351
Astafurova, Olga   337

B

Belov, Sergey V.   323
Berestneva, Olga   206
Bershadsky, Aleksander   527
Birukov, Svyatoslav   49
Bogdanova, Diana   220
Bolshakov, Alexander   288
Bondarev, Alexander   143
Boyko, Grigory   155

C

Chigirinskaya, Nataly   274
Chistyakova, Tamara B.   251, 262

D

Danilov, Ivan   568
Davtian, Aleksandr   206
Deev, Mikhail   377
Demarev, Andrey   513
Demareva, Valeriia   513
Dubinina, Irina   365
Dyatlov, Maksim   500

E

Egunov, Vitaly A.   433
Erdenechimeg, Selenge   450

F

Fantrov, Pavel   337
Fedin, Alexey   155
Filist, Sergei   467

Finogeev, Alexey   377, 390
Fomenkov, Sergey   35
Frolov, Evgeniy   143
Furaev, Dmitry N.   262

G

Gamidullaeva, Leyla   390
Gerget, Olga M.   131
Golodova, Olga   64
Golovanchikov, Alexander   35
Golovnin, Oleg   365
Golovnina, Anastasia   365
Gorbatenko, Dmitry   49
Grushevsky, Alexander   377
Gudkov, Pavel   527
Gureyeva, Anna   420
Guriev, Vladislav   478, 488
Gurtyakov, Alexander   568

I

Isakova, Inna   513
Ivaschenko, Anton   365

K

Kallimulina, Renata   288
Kamardin, Igor   377
Kataev, Alexander   405, 478
Katerinin, Konstantin   500
Khairov, Alexander   405
Khoperskov, Alexander V.   191, 306
Khrapov, Sergei S.   191
Klikunova, Anna Yu.   191
Kolpashchikov, Dmitrii Yu.   131
Kornienko, Ivan G.   251
Korobkin, Dmitriy   35
Kotov, Artemiy   420
Kozhevnikova, Alla   143
Kravets, Alla G.   3, 49, 433
Kravets, Evgeny   433
Kraynev, Dmitriy   143
Kudrin, Rodion   500

A. G. Kravets et al. (Eds.): CIT&DS 2023, CCIS 1909, pp. 579–580, 2023.
https://doi.org/10.1007/978-3-031-44615-3

Kulikov, Mikhail   568
Kuzmin, Alexander   467
Kuzmina, Tatyana   64

L
Lanko, Alexander   98
Leskovets, I.   155
Lomakin, Nikolay   64

M
Maramygin, Maxim   64
Minaeva, Oksana   64
Moffat, David C.   405, 488
Molodtsova, Irina   488

N
Nazarov, Nikolay   513
Niiazgulov, Albert   220
Nikitina, Marina   288
Novozhilova, Inna V.   262

P
Parygin, Danila   206, 549
Pavlenko, Ivan D.   433
Petrenko, M.   155
Petrova, Tatyana   478
Plekhanov, Aleksandr A.   251
Podmarkova, Ekaterina   527
Polianskaya, Liubov   83
Polyakov, Maxim V.   191

R
Radchenko, Viktor P.   306
Rashevskiy, Nikolay   549
Redl, Jozef   155
Rogachev, Alexander   274
Rogachev, Alexey F.   232
Romanov, Vyacheslav   98
Rublev, Alexander   35

S
Sadovnikova, Natalia   206
Salnikova, Natalia   49
Shabalina, Olga   206, 405
Shakhmametova, Gyuzel   220
Shashikhina, Olga E.   251
Shcherbakov, Artem   549
Shcherbakov, Maxim.V.   323
Shklyar, Aleksey   117
Shkolny, Dmitry V.   323
Shlyannikov, Nikita   549
Shlyannikov, Vasily   549
Shuklin, Alexey   568
Shuts, Vasily   538
Shviatsova, Alena   538
Simonov, Alexey B.   232
Sitnikov, Pavel   365
Skorobogatchenko, Dmitry   337
Smolova, Elizaveta   49
Sodnom, Bazarragchaa   450
Sukhbaatar, Gantsetseg   450
Sukhomlinov, Artem   467

T
Tchigirinsky, Julius   274
Tikhonova, Zhanna   143, 274
Todorev, Aleksej   500
Trubitsin, Vladislav   171
Tsyganov, Vladimir   19
Tudevdagva, Uranchimeg   64, 450

V
Vekhter, Evgeniya   117
Volkova, Liliya   83, 98
Voronina, Angelina   478, 488

Z
Zakharova, Alena   117
Zayceva, Irina   513
Zelenskiy, Ilya   568
Zhdanov, Alexey   274
Zhokhov, Vladislav   337
Zhukov, Boris   351
Zinina, Anna   420

Printed in the United States
by Baker & Taylor Publisher Services